The Bruins Book

THE MOST COMPLETE BOSTON BRUINS FACT BOOK EVER PUBLISHED

THE BRUINS BOOK

1997-98

The most complete Boston Bruins fact book ever published

KEVIN VAUTOUR

ECW PRESS

CANADIAN CATALOGUING IN PUBLICATION DATA

Vautour, Kevin
The Boston Bruins book: the most complete
Boston Bruins fact book ever published

ISBN 1-55022-334-8

1. Boston Bruins (Hockey team) – History.   1. Title.
GV848.B68V38 1997 796.962'64'0974461 C97-931339-2

Design and imaging by ECW Type & Art, Oakville, Ontario.
Printed and bound by Webcom, Scarborough, Ontario.

Distributed by General Distribution Services,
30 Lesmill Road, Don Mills, Ontario M3B 2T6.
(416) 445-3333, (800) 387-0172 (Canada), FAX (416) 445-5967.

Distributed to the trade in the United States exclusively
by InBook / Login Publishers Consortium,
1436 West Randolph Street, Chicago, Illinois, U.S.A. 60607.
Customer service: (800) 626-4330, fax (800) 334-3892.

Published by ECW PRESS,
2120 Queen Street East, Suite 200
Toronto, Ontario M4E 1E2.
(416) 694-3348, fax (416) 698-9906

www.ecw.ca/press

PRINTED AND BOUND IN CANADA

TABLE OF CONTENTS

INTRODUCTION

Everett, Massachusetts, 1961, was a quilt work of ethnic enclaves — Blacks and Jews in Everett Springs; English, Irish, and Poles in Woodlawn and North Everett; Italians down the Line and in the Village. West Everett had a good mix of Irish, Italians, English, and French Canadians. The French Canadians were of particular interest to me since my father had emigrated to Everett from West Arichat, Cape Breton, Nova Scotia.

French Canadians had the foresight back at the turn of the century to organize a parish and school, St. Joseph's, to accommodate the French-speaking families that dotted Belmont, Hancock, Bradford, Bucknam, Kinsman, and Andrew Streets.

Their names could have filled the roster of Le Club de Hockey Canadien: Brodeur, Fournier, Comeau, Doucette, LeBlanc, LaPierre, Pineau, Boucher, LeBrun, Marchand, Michaud, Boudreau, Theriault, Dionne, Goyetche.

1961 was John Kennedy's first year as President of the United States. The Red Sox had not won a pennant since 1946. The Patriots were still in their infancy, starting their second season in the American Football League. The Boston Celtics were now perennial champions of the National Basketball Association.

Stories are often told of fathers bringing their children to Fenway Park for the first time and the impression it left on the kids. I went through the same revelation, but it wasn't at "Friendly Fenway."

November 16, 1961, was a day that would change my sport-viewing life forever. It was a cloudy day. The last vestiges of leaves had fallen although the day had a smoky, warm quality to it (smoky warm because folks were still allowed to burn leaves in the gutters outside their homes). During an after school game of touch football at Swan Street Park, my brothers Ron and Don and our neighbor Paul Amici came by and offered me a chance to go with them to see the Boston Bruins that evening. I had never been to the Boston Garden for a hockey game. The circus, rodeo, and ice shows, yes, but a hockey game, no.

Back in those days, the now defunct First National Stores grocery chain would give $1 off coupons to events at Boston Garden for every $10 worth of groceries that my parents bought. With the amount of food that the Vautours consumed each week, I can well imagine that my mother and father had plenty of coupons left over from their treks to the market. With a $1 coupon used to purchase a $1 seat in the "Heavens" — well, you do the math. Bruins games were affordable.

Part of the fun of going to the Garden was the elevated train ride to North Station. We'd head down to the bus stop for the ride to Everett Station. Along the way, the bus would pick up the kids from West Everett and the Line going in to see the B's. Paul and Carl Amici, Johnny Glynn, Norman Brodeur, Al Fournier, Mike Aieisi, Joe Fonzo, Tony Ranieri, Joe Maddox, Paul Delorey, Joe Bucchino, Norm Jordan, Larry Tuck, the *real* Mills brothers (Charlie and Steve), Bobby and Doug MacLeod, Jerry O'Hearn — we'd see them all at Everett Station talking Bruins talk. Along the way, the train would pick up Somerville and Medford fans at Sullivan Station, Townies at Thompson Square, and Chelsea rooters at City Square. The train seemed to be electrified by talk of the B's, Habs, Leafs, Wings, Hawks, or Rangers emanating from the car. The aroma of fresh-baked bread from the Stop and Shop bakery told us that the train had just turned onto Causeway Street and it was time to get off. After alighting from the train and purchasing our tickets in the old east lobby, we had to walk out onto Causeway Street and around the corner onto Haverhill Street for the entrance to the second balcony.

At seven o'clock, the large brown double doors opened. The only instruction I received was "to run as fast as you can" until you get to the top landing, which I followed precisely.

The whole idea was to get into the balcony as early as possible, find an aisle, and sit in the first row of that aisle. The front two rows of the second balcony, reserved for season ticket holders — "The Gallery Gods" — were excellent locations from which to watch the action. The seats seemed to hang over the ice.

The Garden was lit dimly but you could not mistake the markings on the white sheet of ice. The checkered center ice line, end line, goal creases, and face-off circles, all red, were sandwiched between the two blues which seemed to have more of a shade of purple. A large spoked "B," facing the north side of the building, encompassed the center ice circle. This arrangement with the spoked "B" facing the north side of the building lasted until the early 70's. Bruins games began broadcasting on TV38 on a regular basis for the 1967–68 season. Those first few seasons of televised games had the home viewer watching the spoked "B" at center ice from an upside down position.

The rafters had eight flags: the Stars and Stripes of the United States; the Union Jack in the Canadian ensign; and the six National Hockey League teams — the gold-trimmed Boston Bruins banner, the red banners of Detroit, Montreal, and Chicago, with the blue banners of Toronto and New York, all hanging majestically some fifty feet above the ice surface.

Weeknight game time in those days was 8:00 p.m. At 7:30 on this November evening, the Garden lit up, John Kiley played the strains of "Paree" on the organ, and the Bruins trekked onto the ice in their black and gold shirts followed by the white-garbed Montreal Canadiens, entering the rink to the sounds of "Alouette." A tremendous cheer emanated from the crowd as the players pushed themselves through the rink doors and onto the ice. It was entertaining to watch and hear the skates slashing, the pucks being pounded into the vacant nets, the goalies doing their stretching with their large pads and gloves. At 7:45 a loud siren went off signifying the end of the warmups. The players skated furiously in a clockwise circle followed by a counter-clockwise circle, then off to the dressing rooms.

The Zamboni made its appearance from the Garden's west end. It was painted yellow with black trim. The Bruins logo appeared at the front end of the Zamboni. After the new sheet of ice was put down, the referee and linesmen appeared. The linesmen checked the sturdiness of the nets and skated in circles until they were joined by the players. Frank Fallon, the longtime public address announcer, introduced the starting line-up and scratches from the evening's program. The players then lined up for the anthems of both countries: the "Star-Spangled Banner" followed by the Canadian anthem, "O Canada." During the anthems, the Garden was in darkness save for the lights that adorned the players at each blue line and at the goal creases.

An exciting and entertaining game followed. Two goals off the stick of Terry Gray punctuated by a fight with Lou Fontinato of Montreal helped propel the Bruins to a 3–2 win. The last minute of the game had the crowd in a frenzy as the Bruins were about to win one of only 15 victories in that season.

Every game played is a first game for somebody — a player, a coach, an official, a broadcaster, a fan. If it's true that first impressions are lasting, then I was hooked for life. I still remember the first hockey magazine that I ever bought, *Hockey Illustrated*, January 1962 edition, Jacques Plante of Montreal hanging in mid-air, pads stacked; Ted Hampson of the Rangers trapped inside the net. The writers, editors, and announcers — Bob Wilson, Fred Cusick, Johnny Peirson, Bill Harrington, Jim Laing, Don Earle, Ken McKenzie, Ben Olan, D. Leo Monahan, Margaret Scott, Tom Fitzgerald, Fran Rosa, Fred Cedorchuck, Red Burnett, Red Fisher, Stan Fischler, Herb Ralby, Gil Smith; Hockey Pictorial's "Camera in the Corridor"; *Blueline* magazine; *The Hockey News* — all magical and devoured from cover to cover.

American Hockey League news was as important to follow as the big boys. Ahhh, those AHL names: the Quebec Aces, Providence Reds, Buffalo Bisons, Springfield Indians, Pittsburgh Hornets, Hershey Bears, Cleveland Barons, Rochester Americans, Gil Mayer, Fred Glover, Zelio Toppazzini, Obie O'Brien, Andy Branigan, Fred Glover, Bill Needham, Les Duff, Harry Pidhirny, Bo Elik, Bob "Battleship" Kelly . . . the list could continue on and on.

Being a Bruins fan meant that you loved your team through thick and thin. In the early sixties, it was mostly thin with the Bruins unable to develop enough talent to escape the bottom of the six-team league. The opposition became the easy target of ridicule for both dirty and unfair play. But there were certain opposing players that escaped the fans' wrath. Two that come to mind immediately were Bobby Hull of Chicago and Jean Beliveau of Montreal. Many evenings after the Hawks had trounced the Bruins and with fans in a foul mood, Bobby would patiently sign autographs for the kids, and he did it with a smile.

Jean Beliveau was on the same plane as Bobby Hull. Beliveau had caught my eye in that first game I had witnessed. He seemed to be very tall in comparison to the other players but he was very graceful. He appeared to glide along the ice, effortlessly passing to teammates, opposing players bouncing off him when they tried to wrest the puck away from him. I was very enamored with "Le Gros Bill." One day, I decided to write to Jean and ask for an autographed picture. I handwrote a letter to which I taped a dime and a nickel and sent it heading for the Forum on St. Catherine Street West.

A few weeks later, an envelope arrived with a postmark of Montreal, Quebec. Grabbing the package, I could feel the nickel and dime with my fingers. I was disheartened, no photo, no autograph. I figured I could at least spend the fifteen cents down at Bib's Variety store so I opened the envelope. Was I stunned. Not only was the fifteen cents returned to me, but an autographed picture of every Montreal player was included. There was coach Toe Blake, Charlie Hodge, Jean-Guy Talbot, John Ferguson, Henri Richard, Bill Hicke, Jean-Claude Tremblay, Red Berenson, Gump Worsley, Gilles Tremblay, Claude Provost, Ralph Backstrom, Bobby Rousseau, Jacques Laperriere, Brian Watson, "Boom Boom" Geoffrion, and my hero, Jean Beliveau. The pictures still hang on my walls.

These memories started by a lucky break: two brothers and a friend taking me to see the Bruins. I've never quite been able to get the team out of my blood. I've just sat back for the last 36 years and enjoyed the ride.

The Bruins have a rich tradition and history. I hope you enjoy this book. Accuracy is most important. Notification of any errors would be sincerely appreciated. This effort is just a very small contribution to help document the history of the Boston Bruins.

THE BOSTON TRANSIT DEPARTMENT

BOSTON ELEVATED RAILWAY COMPANY
(1918–1949)

METROPOLITAN TRANSIT AUTHORITY (MTA)
(1948–1964)

MASSACHUSETTS BAY TRANSPORTATION AUTHORITY (MBTA)
(1964–PRESENT)

FARE HISTORY

With the opening of the Boston-Madison Square Garden in 1928 and the FleetCenter in 1995, train service to Boston Bruins games has always been an easy connection since both facilities are over the North Station, a major terminal for rapid transit, commuter rail, and streetcar service in and out of Boston. The price (in cents) of a train ride to Bruins games is as follows:

1928 to 1950	.10
1950 to 1955	.15
1955 to 1968	.20
1968 to 1980	.25
1980 to 1981	.50
1981 to 1982	.75
1982 to 1989	.60
1989 to 1991	.75
1991 to present	.85

TRAINING CAMP VENUES

1987–1996	Ristuccia Exposition Center, Wilmington, Mass.
1980–1986	Town Line Twin Rinks, Danvers, Mass.
1973–1979	George R. Wallace Civic Center, Fitchburg, Mass.
1964–1972	London, Ontario
1962–1963	Boston, Massachusetts
1961	Niagara Falls, Ontario
1956–1960	Boston, Massachusetts
1946–1955	Hershey, Pennsylvania
1942–1945	Quebec City, Quebec
1939–1941	Hershey, Pennsylvania
1938	Boston Garden
1937	Hershey, Pennsylvania
1936	Boston Garden
1935	St. John, New Brunswick
1932–1934	Quebec City, Quebec
1931	Boston Arena
1930	Boston Garden
1929	Boston Arena
1928	Providence, Rhode Island
1926–1927	Boston Arena
1925	Boston Arena, Montreal Forum, & Mt. St. Royal, Montreal, Quebec
1924	Boston Arena

FIRST GAME IN
BOSTON BRUINS HISTORY

Saturday, December 1, 1924
Boston Arena
Boston Bruins 2
Montreal Maroons 1

BOSTON BRUINS	MONTREAL MAROONS
Fred Harris	Punch Broadbent
Fern Headley	Fred Lowery
Alf Skinner	Louis Berlinquette
Lloyd Cook	Dutch Cain
Jimmy Herberts	Gerald Munro
Hec Fowler	Clint Benedict
Herb Mitchell	Sammy Rothschild
Werner Schnarr	Charlie Dinsmore
Carson Cooper	Ganton Scott
Bobbie Rowe	Dunc Munro
George Redding	

First period
GOALS: Montreal . . . . Dinsmore (unassisted) 9:00

Second period
GOALS: Boston . . . . Harris (Cooper) 3:30
               Boston . . . . Cooper (unassisted) 7:00

Third period
GOALS: No scoring

GOALTENDERS: Boston . . . . Hec Fowler
               Montreal . . . . Clint Benedict

REFEREE: Mickey Rodden
GOAL JUDGES: Geezil, Beckwith
TIMERS: Carleton, Kanaly, Murphy

HOME OPENERS

The 1997–98 season is the 74th year of Boston Bruins hockey. The Bruins have opened the season 45 times at Boston and 28 times on the road. The following pages are a recap of all 73 opening games. An asterisk next to the home opener indicates that this is also the first game of the season.

BOSTON ARENA

*December 1, 1924 . . . . . . Montreal Maroons . . . . Win 2–1
*November 26, 1925 . . . . . Pittsburgh Pirates . . . . Loss 2–1
*November 16, 1926 . . . . . Montreal Canadiens . . . . . . Win 4–1
*November 15, 1927 . . . . . Chicago Blackhawks . . . . . . Tie 1–1

BOSTON GARDEN

November 20, 1928 . . . . . . Montreal Canadiens . . . . . . Loss 1–0
November 19, 1929 . . . . . . New York Rangers . . . . Win 3–2
*November 11, 1930 . . . . . New York Americans . . . . . . Win 1–0
November 17, 1931 . . . . . . Detroit Falcons . . . . Win 1–0 (OT)
November 15, 1932 . . . . . . Montreal Maroons . . . . Win 3–2
November 14, 1933 . . . . . . Detroit Red Wings . . . . Loss 4–2
November 17, 1934 . . . . . . St. Louis Eagles . . . . Win 1–0
November 19, 1935 . . . . . . New York Americans . . . . . . Win 1–0
November 15, 1936 . . . . . . Montreal Canadiens . . . . . . Win 2–1
November 14, 1937 . . . . . . New York Rangers . . . . Win 3–2
November 15, 1938 . . . . . . Toronto Maple Leafs . . . . . . Tie 1–1
November 14, 1939 . . . . . . Chicago Blackhawks . . . . . . Win 3–1
November 12, 1940 . . . . . . Chicago Blackhawks . . . . . . Loss 6–5
November 16, 1941 . . . . . . New York Rangers . . . . Win 2–1
November 14, 1942 . . . . . . New York Rangers . . . . Win 5–3
November 16, 1943 . . . . . . Montreal Canadiens . . . . . . Tie 2–2
November 14, 1944 . . . . . . Chicago Blackhawks . . . . . . Win 7–5

*October 24, 1945 . . . . Chicago Blackhawks . . . . Loss 5–4
October 20, 1946 . . . . Chicago Blackhawks . . . . . . Tie 2–2
*October 19, 1947 . . . . New York Rangers . . . . Win 3–1
October 20, 1948 . . . . Chicago Blackhawks . . . . . . Win 8–3
October 16, 1949 . . . . New York Rangers . . . . Tie 2–2
October 15, 1950 . . . . Montreal Canadiens . . . . Loss 2–1
October 14, 1951 . . . . Montreal Canadiens . . . . . . Loss 4–3
*October 12, 1952 . . . . Montreal Canadiens . . . . . . Tie 1–1
*October 11, 1953 . . . . Montreal Canadiens . . . . . . Win 4–1
October 11, 1954 . . . . Montreal Canadiens . . . . . . Tie 2–2

October 9, 1955 . . . . Montreal Canadiens . . . . Loss 5–2
*October 11, 1956 . . . . Toronto Maple Leafs . . . . Tie 4–4
*October 12, 1957 . . . . Chicago Blackhawks . . . . Win 3–1
October 11, 1958 . . . . New York Rangers . . . . Tie 4–4
October 10, 1959 . . . . New York Rangers . . . . Win 6–4
October 9, 1960 . . . . Montreal Canadiens . . . . Tie 4–4
*October 11, 1961 . . . . New York Rangers . . . . Loss 6–2
*October 11, 1962 . . . . Montreal Canadiens . . . . Win 5–0
*October 8, 1963 . . . . Montreal Canadiens . . . . Tie 4–4
*October 12, 1964 . . . . New York Rangers . . . . Loss 6–2
*October 24, 1965 . . . . Chicago Blackhawks . . . . Loss 6–2
*October 19, 1966 . . . . Detroit Red Wings . . . . Win 6–2
*October 11, 1967 . . . . Detroit Red Wings . . . . Tie 4–4
*October 11, 1968 . . . . Detroit Red Wings . . . . Win 4–2
*October 12, 1969 . . . . New York Rangers . . . . Win 2–1
*October 11, 1970 . . . . Detroit Red Wings . . . . Win 7–3
*October 10, 1971 . . . . New York Rangers . . . . Loss 4–1

*October 8, 1972 . . . . . . Los Angeles Kings . . . . Loss 4–2
*October 10, 1973 . . . . . . Vancouver Canucks . . . . Win 6–4
 October 13, 1974 . . . . . . Toronto Maple Leafs . . . . . . Tie 2–2
*October 9, 1975 . . . . . . Montreal Canadiens . . . . . Loss 9–4
*October 7, 1976 . . . . . . Minnesota North Stars . . . . . Win 6–2
*October 13, 1977 . . . . . . Atlanta Flames . . . . Tie 2–2
*October 12, 1978 . . . . . . Pittsburgh Penguins . . . . . . Win 8–2
*October 11, 1979 . . . . . . Winnipeg Jets . . . . Win 4–0
*October 9, 1980 . . . . . . New York Rangers . . . . Win 7–2
*October 8, 1981 . . . . . . Quebec Nordiques . . . . . . Loss 7–5
*October 7, 1982 . . . . . . Montreal Canadiens . . . . . . Loss 5–1
*October 6, 1983 . . . . . . Quebec Nordiques . . . . Win 9–3
*October 11, 1984 . . . . . . Pittsburgh Penguins . . . . . . Win 4–3
*October 10, 1985 . . . . . . Toronto Maple Leafs . . . . . . Win 3–1
*October 9, 1986 . . . . . . Calgary Flames . . . . Loss 5–3
*October 8, 1987 . . . . . . Washington Capitals . . . . . Win 4–3
*October 6, 1988 . . . . . . Toronto Maple Leafs . . . . . . Win 2–1
*October 5, 1989 . . . . . . Pittsburgh Penguins . . . . . . Win 5–4
*October 4, 1990 . . . . . . Philadelphia Flyers . . . . . . Win 4–1
*October 3, 1991 . . . . New York Rangers . . . . Win 5–3
*October 8, 1992 . . . . . . Hartford Whalers . . . . Win 3–2 (OT)
 October 7, 1993 . . . . Buffalo Sabres . . . . Loss 5–3
*January 22, 1995 . . . . . . Philadelphia Flyers . . . . . . Win 4–1
Season opening delayed by owners' lockout

FLEETCENTER

*October 7, 1995 . . . . . . New York Islanders . . . . Tie 4–4
*October 5, 1996 . . . . . . New York Rangers . . . . Tie 4–4

Anthem singer Rene Rancourt

HOME OPENER RECAP

Boston Arena: . . . . 2 wins, 1 loss, 1 tie
Boston Garden: . . . . 37 wins, 17 losses, 13 ties
FleetCenter: . . . . 0 wins, 0 losses, 2 ties
At Boston: . . . . 39 wins, 18 losses, 16 ties

EARLIEST HOME OPENING GAME OF THE SEASON

October 3, 1991 vs. New York Rangers

LATEST HOME OPENING GAME OF THE SEASON

January 22, 1995 vs. Philadelphia Flyers

MOST CONSECUTIVE HOME OPENERS AGAINST

Montreal Canadiens   6 — 1950 to 1955

Closing night ceremony at Boston Garden.

HOME OPENER OPPONENTS

MONTREAL CANADIENS

Games played: . . . . 15 (4 wins, 6 losses, 5 ties)
last win October 11, 1962 5–0
last loss October 7, 1982 5–1
last tie October 8, 1963 4–4

NEW YORK RANGERS

Games played: . . . . 15 (9 wins, 3 losses, 3 ties)
last win October 3, 1991 5–3
last loss October 10, 1971 4–1
last tie October 5, 1996 4–4

CHICAGO BLACKHAWKS

Games played: . . . . 9 (4 wins, 3 losses, 2 ties)
last win October 12, 1957 3–1
last loss October 24, 1965 6–2
last tie October 20, 1946 2–2

DETROIT RED WINGS/FALCONS

Games played: . . . . 6 (4 wins, 1 loss, 1 tie)
last win October 11, 1970 7–3
last loss November 14, 1933 4–2
last tie October 11, 1967 4–4

TORONTO MAPLE LEAFS

Games played: . . . . 5 (2 wins, 0 losses, 3 ties)
last win October 6, 1988 2–1
last tie October 13, 1974 2–2

PITTSBURGH PENGUINS

Games played: . . . . 3 (3 wins, 0 losses, 0 ties)
last win October 5, 1989 5–4

PHILADELPHIA FLYERS

Games played: . . . . 2 (2 wins, 0 losses, 0 ties)
Last win January 22, 1995 4–1

CALGARY/ATLANTA FLAMES

Games played: . . . . 2 (0 wins, 1 loss, 1 tie)
last loss October 9, 1986 5–3
last tie October 13, 1977 2–2

QUEBEC NORDIQUES

Games played: . . . . 2 (1 win, 1 loss, 0 ties)
last win October 6, 1983 9–3
last loss October 8, 1981 7–5

LOS ANGELES KINGS

Games played: . . . . 1 (0 wins, 1 loss, 0 ties)
last loss October 8, 1972 4–2

VANCOUVER CANUCKS

Games played: . . . . 1 (1 win, 0 losses, 0 ties)
last win October 10, 1973 6–4

WASHINGTON CAPITALS

Games played: . . . . 1 (1 win, 0 losses, 0 ties)
last win October 8, 1987 4–3

HARTFORD WHALERS

Games played: . . . . 1 (1 win, 0 losses, 0 ties)
last win October 8, 1992 . . . . . . 3–2 (OT)

BUFFALO SABRES

Games played: . . . . 1 (0 wins, 1 loss, 0 ties)
last loss October 7, 1993 5–3

NEW YORK ISLANDERS

Games played: . . . . 1 (0 wins, 0 losses, 1 tie)
last tie game October 7, 1995 4–4

MINNESOTA NORTH STARS

Games played: . . . . 1 (1 win, 0 losses, 0 ties)
last win October 7, 1976 6–2

WINNIPEG JETS

Games played: . . . . 1 (1 win, 0 losses, 0 ties)
last win October 11, 1979 4–0

MONTREAL MAROONS

Games played: . . . . 2 (2 wins, 0 losses, 0 ties)
last win November 15, 1932 3–2

NEW YORK AMERICANS

Games played: . . . . 2 (2 wins, 0 losses, 0 ties)
last win November 19, 1935 1–0

ST. LOUIS EAGLES

Games played: . . . . 1 (1 win, 0 losses, 0 ties)
last win November 17, 1934 1–0

PITTSBURGH PIRATES

Games played: . . . . 1 (0 wins, 1 loss, 0 ties)
last loss November 26, 1925 2–1

OPENING GAMES ON THE ROAD

The Bruins have opened the National Hockey League season 28 times on the road.

November 15, 1928	at Pittsburgh Pirates	Win 1–0
November 14, 1929	at Detroit Cougars	Win 5–2
November 14, 1931	at Montreal Maroons	Loss 4–1
November 10, 1932	at Toronto	Tie 1–1
November 9, 1933	at Toronto	Loss 6–1
November 8, 1934	at Toronto	Loss 5–3
November 16, 1935	at Montreal Maroons	Loss 1–0
November 7, 1936	at Montreal Canadiens	Loss 2–0
November 6, 1937	at Montreal Maroons	Win 1–0
November 3, 1938	at Toronto	Win 3–2
November 4, 1939	at Toronto	Loss 5–0
November 3, 1940	at Montreal	Tie 1–1
November 8, 1941	at Toronto	Loss 2–0
October 31, 1942	at Montreal	Loss 3–2
October 30, 1943	at Montreal	Tie 2–2
October 28, 1944	at Montreal	Loss 3–2
October 19, 1946	at Montreal	Tie 1–1
October 16, 1948	at Toronto	Win 4–1
October 12, 1949	at Detroit	Loss 2–1
October 14, 1950	at Montreal	Tie 1–1
October 11, 1951	at Detroit	Loss 1–0
October 9, 1954	at Montreal	Loss 4–1
October 8, 1955	at Montreal	Loss 2–0
October 9, 1958	at Montreal	Loss 3–2
October 8, 1959	at Montreal	Loss 4–1
October 5, 1960	at New York Rangers	Loss 2–1
October 10, 1974	at Buffalo	Loss 9–5
October 5, 1993	at New York Rangers	Win 4–3

EARLIEST ROAD OPENING GAME OF THE SEASON

October 5, 1960 at New York Rangers
October 5, 1993 at New York Rangers

LATEST ROAD OPENING GAME OF THE SEASON

November 16, 1935 at Montreal Maroons

RECAP OF OPENING GAMES ON THE ROAD

Games played: . . . . 28 (6 wins, 17 losses, 5 ties)

Montreal Canadiens

Games played: . . . . 11 (0 wins, 7 losses, 4 ties)
last loss October 8, 1959 4–1
last tie October 14, 1950 1–1

Toronto Maple Leafs

Games played: . . . . 7 (2 wins, 4 losses, 1 tie)
last win October 16, 1948 4–1
last loss November 8, 1941 2–0
last tie November 10, 1931 1–1

Detroit Red Wings

Games played: . . . . 3 (1 win, 2 losses)
last win November 14, 1929 5–2
last loss October 11, 1951 1–0

New York Rangers

Games played: . . . . 2 (1 win, 1 loss)
last win October 5, 1993 4–3
last loss October 5, 1960 2–1

Buffalo Sabres

Games played: . . . . 1 (0 wins, 1 loss)
last loss October 10, 1974 9–5

Montreal Maroons

Games played: . . . . 3 (1 win, 2 losses)
last win November 6, 1937 4–2
last loss November 16, 1935 1–0

Pittsburgh Pirates

Games played: . . . . 1 (1 win, 0 losses)
last win November 15, 1928 1–0

FIRST AND LAST GAMES
PLAYED AT VARIOUS ARENAS

ALL-TIME RECORDS
THROUGH THE 1996-97 SEASON

BOSTON ARENA
St. Botolph Street
Boston, Massachusetts
1924–25 to 1927–28

FIRST GAME . . . . December 1, 1924 . . . . 2–1 win
at Boston Arena vs. Montreal Maroons

LAST GAME . . . . February 26, 1952 . . . . 4–3 loss
at Boston Arena vs. Detroit Red Wings

BOSTON GARDEN
150 Causeway Street
Boston, Massachusetts
1928–29 to 1994–95

FIRST GAME . . . . November 20, 1928 . . . . 1–0 loss
at Boston Garden vs. Montreal Canadiens

LAST GAME . . . . May 14, 1995 . . . . 3–2 loss
at Boston Garden vs. New Jersey Devils

FLEETCENTER
One FleetCenter
Boston, Massachusetts
1995

FIRST GAME . . . . October 7, 1995 4–4
at FleetCenter vs. New York Islanders

PROVIDENCE CIVIC CENTER
1 LaSalle Square
Providence, Rhode Island

vs. New Jersey Devils . . . . . March 16, 1993 . . . . 3–1 win
(neutral site game)

Forbes Kennedy of the Bruins is surrounded by Bobby Rousseau #15,
Goaltender Charlie Hodge #1, and Jacques Laperriere #2,
in a Bruins–Montreal battle of the mid-1960s.

BOSTON BRUINS VS. ALL OPPONENTS

W	L	T	GF	GA
228	242	6	1405	1422

SERIES	W	L
98	46	52

MIGHTY DUCKS OF ANAHEIM
1993–94 to 1996–97

Arrowhead Pond of Anaheim
2695 Katella Avenue
Anaheim, California
1993–94 to present

FIRST GAME	October 15, 1993	1–1 tie
AT Anaheim		

ALL-TIME RECORD - REGULAR SEASON

W	L	T	P	GF	GA
3	2	1	7	23	16
AT Anaheim					
1	1	1	3	9	6
AT Boston					
2	1	0	4	14	10

ALL-TIME RECORD - PLAYOFFS

W	L	T	GF	GA
0	0	0	0	0

SERIES	W	L
0	0	0

BUFFALO SABRES
1970–71 to 1995–96

Memorial Auditorium
140 Main Street
Buffalo, New York
1970–71 to 1995–96

FIRST GAME	December 3, 1970	4–4 tie
AT Memorial Auditorium		
LAST GAME	March 31, 1996	6–5 win
AT Memorial Auditorium		

Marine Midland Arena
One Seymour Knox Plaza
Buffalo, New York
1996–97 to present

FIRST GAME	November 16, 1996	Postponed*

AT Marine Midland Arena		
	February 23, 1997	5 – 1 loss

* *Jumbotron scoreboard crashed to the ice*

ALL-TIME RECORD – REGULAR SEASON

W	L	T	P	GF	GA
82	71	25	189	634	609
AT Buffalo					
31	44	14	76	275	335
AT Boston					
51	27	11	113	359	274

ALL-TIME RECORD – PLAYOFFS

W	L	T	GF	GA
19	14	0	132	113

SERIES	W	L
6	5	1

CALIFORNIA SEALS
OAKLAND SEALS
CALIFORNIA GOLDEN SEALS
1967–68 to 1975–76

Oakland Alameda County Coliseum Arena
303 Hegenberger Road
Oakland, California

FIRST GAME	December 15, 1967	4–1 loss
AT Oakland		
LAST GAME	March 5, 1976	4–3 loss
AT Oakland		

CLEVELAND BARONS
1976–77 to 1977–78

Richfield Coliseum
2923 Streetsboro Road
Richfield, Ohio

FIRST GAME	December 18, 1976	6–4 loss
AT Cleveland		
LAST GAME	March 21, 1978	5–3 win
AT Cleveland		

ALL-TIME RECORD – REGULAR SEASON

W	L	T	P	GF	GA
44	12	6	94	281	160
AT California/Cleveland					
18	8	5	41	143	97
AT Boston					
26	4	1	53	138	63

ALL-TIME RECORD – PLAYOFFS

W	L	T	GF	GA
0	0	0	0	0
SERIES	W	L		
0	0	0		

CALGARY FLAMES
1980–81 to 1996–97
ATLANTA FLAMES
1972–73 to 1979–80

Stampede Corral
Station M
Calgary, Alberta
1980–81 to 1982–83

FIRST GAME   October 16, 1980   2–1 loss
AT Stampede Corral
LAST GAME   February 11, 1983   6–3 loss
AT Stampede Corral

Olympic Saddledome
Canadian Airlines Saddledome
Station M
Calgary, Alberta
1983–84 to present

FIRST GAME   December 28, 1983   5–3 win
AT Saddledome

The Omni
100 Techwood Drive, N.W.
Atlanta, Georgia
1972–73 to 1979–80

FIRST GAME   November 24, 1972   4–0 win
AT Atlanta
LAST GAME   March 22, 1980 5–2 win
AT Atlanta

ALL-TIME RECORD – REGULAR SEASON

W	L	T	P	GF	GA
46	26	9	101	288	261
AT Calgary/Atlanta					
21	16	3	45	143	150
AT Boston					
25	10	6	56	145	111

ALL-TIME RECORD – PLAYOFFS

W	L	T	GF	GA
0	0	0	0	0
SERIES	W	L		
0	0	0		

CHICAGO BLACKHAWKS
1926–27 to 1996–97

Chicago Coliseum
1926–27 to 1928–29

FIRST GAME   November 20, 1926   5–1 loss
AT Chicago Coliseum
LAST GAME   December 1, 1929   3–1 loss
AT Chicago Coliseum

Chicago Stadium
1800 West Madison Street
Chicago, Illinois
1929–30 to 1993–94

FIRST GAME   January 16, 1930   2–1 loss
AT Chicago Stadium
LAST GAME   February 27, 1994   4–0 win
AT Chicago Stadium

United Center
1901 W. Madison Street
Chicago, Illinois
1994–95 to present

FIRST GAME   February 15, 1996   3–0 loss
AT United Center

During the mid 1950's, attendance at Chicago Stadium dwindled. In order to improve attendance, some of the Blackhawk games were moved to other arenas.

St. Paul, Minn.   February 23, 1955   3–3
St. Louis Arena   October 25, 1955   2–0 loss

ALL-TIME RECORD – REGULAR SEASON

W	L	T	P	GF	GA
252	229	77	581	1756	1690
AT Chicago					
93	143	44	230	748	904
AT Boston					
159	86	33	351	1008	786

ALL-TIME RECORD – PLAYOFFS

W	L	T	GF	GA
16	5	1	97	63
SERIES	W	L		
6	5	1		

COLORADO AVALANCHE
1995–96 to 1996–97

McNichols Sports Arena
1635 Clay Street
Denver, Colorado

FIRST GAME   October 11, 1995   3–1 loss
AT McNichols Arena

QUEBEC NORDIQUES
1979–80 to 1994–95

Le Colisée de Quebec
2205 Avenue du Colisée
Quebec City, Quebec

FIRST GAME   November 20, 1979   5–3 won
AT Le Colisée
LAST GAME   March 22, 1995   6–2 lost
AT Le Colisée

ALL-TIME RECORD – REGULAR SEASON

W	L	T	P	GF	GA
63	39	14	140	483	393

AT Colorado/Quebec

33	20	6	72	256	215

AT Boston

30	19	8	68	227	178

ALL-TIME RECORD – PLAYOFFS

W	L	T	GF	GA
6	5	0	37	36
SERIES	W	L		
2	1	1		

DALLAS STARS
1993–94 to 1996–97

Reunion Arena
211 Cowboys Parkway
Irving, Texas
1993–94 to present

FIRST GAME   February 16, 1994   3–0 win
AT Reunion Arena

MINNESOTA NORTH STARS
1967–68 to 1992–93

Metropolitan Sports Center
7901 Cedar Avenue South
Bloomington, Minnesota
1967–68 to 1992–93

FIRST GAME   December 30, 1967   5–4 loss
at Metropolitan Sports Center
LAST GAME   December 31, 1992   5–3 loss
at Metropolitan Sports Center

ALL-TIME RECORD – REGULAR SEASON

W	L	T	P	GF	GA
69	21	20	158	455	288

AT Dallas/Minnesota

29	15	11	69	207	157

AT Boston

40	6	9	89	248	131

ALL-TIME RECORD – PLAYOFFS

W	L	T	GF	GA
0	3	0	13	20
SERIES	W	L		
1	0	1		

DETROIT RED WINGS
1926–27 to 1996–97

The Detroit Red Wings were originally known as the Cou-
gars. They changed their name to Falcons for the 1929–30
season, and then finally Red Wings for the 1932–33 season.

Border Cities Arena
Windsor, Ontario
1926–27

FIRST GAME   November 18, 1926   2–0 win
AT Windsor
LAST GAME   March 19, 1927   3–1 win
AT Windsor

Detroit Olympia
5920 Grand River at McGraw
Detroit, Michigan
1927–28 to 1979–80

FIRST GAME   December 11, 1927   2–1 win in OT
at Olympia
LAST GAME   December 1, 1979   6–3 loss
at Olympia

Joe Louis Arena
600 Civic Center Drive
Detroit, Michigan
1979–80 to present

FIRST GAME   March 5, 1980   5–3 win
at Joe Louis Arena

ALL-TIME RECORD – REGULAR SEASON

W	L	T	P	GF	GA
227	239	95	549	1694	1685
AT Detroit					
76	152	52	204	702	938
AT Boston					
151	87	43	345	992	747

ALL-TIME RECORD – PLAYOFFS

W	L	T	GF	GA
19	14	0	96	98
SERIES	W	L		
7	4	3		

FLORIDA PANTHERS
1993-94 to 1996–97

Miami Arena
100 Northeast Third Avenue
Miami, Florida

FIRST GAME   December 19, 1993   2–1 win in OT

ALL-TIME RECORD – REGULAR SEASON

W	L	T	P	GF	GA
7	6	2	16	35	36
AT Florida					
4	3	0	8	16	16
AT Boston					
3	3	2	8	19	20

ALL-TIME RECORD – PLAYOFFS

W	L	T	GF	GA
I	4	0	16	22
SERIES	W	L		
I	0	I		

EDMONTON OILERS
1979–80 to 1996–97

Edmonton Coliseum
11230–110 Street
Edmonton, Alberta

FIRST GAME   November 4, 1979   2–1 win

ALL-TIME RECORD – REGULAR SEASON

W	L	T	P	GF	GA
29	15	5	63	196	157
AT Edmonton					
12	9	3	27	86	84
AT Boston					
17	6	2	36	110	73

ALL-TIME RECORD – PLAYOFFS

W	L	T	GF	GA
I	8	0	20	41
SERIES	W	L		
2	0	2		

HAMILTON TIGERS
1924–25

Hamilton Arena
Hamilton Ontario
1924–25

FIRST GAME   December 10, 1924   7–1 loss
LAST GAME   March 7, 1925   2–0 win

ALL-TIME RECORD – REGULAR SEASON

W	L	T	P	GF	GA
I	5	0	2	10	23
AT Hamilton					
I	2	0	2	6	15
AT Boston					
0	3	0	0	4	8

ALL-TIME RECORD – PLAYOFFS

W	L	T	GF	GA
0	0	0	0	0
SERIES	W	L		
0	0	0		

HARTFORD WHALERS
1979–80 to 1996–97

Hartford Civic Center
242 Trumbull Street
Hartford, Connecticut
1979–80 to present

FIRST GAME	January 30, 1980	8–2 loss
LAST GAME	March 12, 1997	6–3 loss

ALL-TIME RECORD – REGULAR SEASON

W	L	T	P	GF	GA
70	41	13	153	469	382
AT Hartford					
27	27	7	61	217	215
AT Boston					
43	14	6	92	252	167

ALL-TIME RECORD – PLAYOFFS

W	L	T		GF	GA
8	5	0		24	17
SERIES	W	L			
2	2	0			

LOS ANGELES KINGS
1967–68 to 1996–97

Sports Arena
3939 South Figueroa Street
Los Angeles, California
1967–68

FIRST AND LAST GAME
December 16, 1967   5–2 win

The Forum
3900 West Manchester Boulevard,
Inglewood, California
1967–68 to present

FIRST GAME   February 18, 1968   6–5 win

ALL-TIME RECORD – REGULAR SEASON

W	L	T	P	GF	GA
72	29	10	153	475	346
AT Los Angeles					
30	19	6	66	208	192
AT Boston					
42	10	4	88	267	154

ALL-TIME RECORD – PLAYOFFS

W	L	T		GF	GA
8	5	0		56	38
SERIES	W	L			
2	2	0			

MONTREAL CANADIENS
1924–25 to 1996–97

Montreal Forum
2313 St. Catherine Street West
Montreal, Quebec
1924–25 to 1995–96

FIRST GAME at Forum	December 25, 1924	5–0 loss
LAST GAME at Forum	January 28, 1996	5–4 loss

Molson Centre
1260 de la Gauchetière Street West,
Montreal, Quebec
1995–96 to present

FIRST GAME
at Molson Centre   April 3, 1996   4–1 win

ALL-TIME RECORD – REGULAR SEASON

W	L	T	P	GF	GA
233	301	99	565	1675	1941
AT Montreal					
88	183	45	221	737	1078
AT Boston					
145	118	54	344	938	863

ALL-TIME RECORD – PLAYOFFS

W	L	T		GF	GA
52	87	0		339	430
SERIES	W	L			
28	7	21			

MONTREAL MAROONS
1924–25 to 1937–38

Montreal Forum
2313 St. Catherine Street West
Montreal, Quebec

FIRST GAME AT Forum	December 24, 1924	6–2 loss

LAST GAME   January 29, 1938   2–2
AT Forum

ALL-TIME RECORD – REGULAR SEASON

W	L	T	P	GF	GA
40	27	7	87	174	158

AT Montreal

17	17	3	37	81	84

AT Boston

23	10	4	50	93	74

ALL-TIME RECORD – PLAYOFFS

W	L	T	GF	GA
4	3	0	17	13

SERIES	W	L
2	1	1

NEW JERSEY DEVILS
1982–83 to 1996–97

The New Jersey Devils were born as the Kansas City Scouts where they played for 2 seasons. They moved to Denver and became the Colorado Rockies and played there for 5 seasons. They moved to the New Jersey Meadowlands in 1982 and became the New Jersey Devils.

*Continental Airlines Arena
(formerly Brendan Byrne Arena)
50 Route 120 North
East Rutherford, New Jersey*

FIRST GAME   October 12, 1982   2–2
AT Continental/Brendan Byrne Arena

KANSAS CITY SCOUTS
1974–75 to 1975–76

*Crosby Kemper Arena
18th & Genessee
Kansas City, Missouri*

FIRST GAME   December 10, 1974   6–2 win
AT Crosby Kemper Arena
LAST GAME   March 18, 1976   5–2 win
AT Crosby Kemper Arena

COLORADO ROCKIES
1976–77 to 1981–82

*McNichols Arena
1635 Clay Street
Denver, Colorado*

FIRST GAME   October 20, 1976   2–1 win
AT McNichols Arena
LAST GAME   October 16, 1981   6–1 win
AT McNichols Arena

ALL-TIME RECORD – REGULAR SEASON

W	L	T	P	GF	GA
49	20	12	110	322	238

AT New Jersey/Kansas City/Colorado

22	9	8	52	138	105

AT Boston

27	11	4	58	184	133

ALL-TIME RECORD – PLAYOFFS

W	L	T	GF	GA
7	11	0	52	55

SERIES	W	L
3	1	2

NEW YORK AMERICANS
BROOKLYN AMERICANS
1925–26 to 1941–42

*Madison Square Garden
307 West 49th Street
New York, New York*

FIRST GAME   January 7, 1926   2–2
AT New York
LAST GAME   February 19, 1942   6–4 loss
AT New York

ALL-TIME RECORD – REGULAR SEASON

W	L	T	P	GF	GA
56	32	10	122	325	216

AT New York

23	20	6	52	162	132

AT Boston

33	12	4	70	163	84

ALL-TIME RECORD – PLAYOFFS

W	L	T	GF	GA
0	0	0	0	0

SERIES	W	L
0	0	0

NEW YORK ISLANDERS
1972–73 to 1996–97

Nassau Veterans Memorial Coliseum
1255 Hempstead Turnpike
Uniondale, Long Island, New York

FIRST GAME   October 14, 1972   7–4
AT Nassau Coliseum

ALL-TIME RECORD – REGULAR SEASON

W	L	T	P	GF	GA
48	29	15	111	335	287
AT New York Islanders					
23	19	5	51	158	157
AT Boston					
25	10	10	60	177	130

ALL-TIME RECORD – PLAYOFFS

W	L	T	GF	GA
3	8	0	35	49
SERIES	W	L		
2	0	2		

NEW YORK RANGERS
1926–27 to 1996–97

Madison Square Garden
307 West 49th Street
New York, New York

FIRST GAME   December 12, 1926   2–1 loss
AT West 49th Street
LAST GAME   January 24, 1968   2–1 loss
AT West 49th Street

Madison Square Garden
4 Pennsylvania Plaza
New York, New York

FIRST GAME   March 13, 1968   2–1 win
AT Pennsylvania Plaza

ALL-TIME RECORD – REGULAR SEASON

W	L	T	P	GF	GA
260	217	95	615	1838	1675
AT New York					
109	125	54	272	809	875
AT Boston					
151	92	41	343	1029	800

ALL-TIME RECORD – PLAYOFFS

W	L	T	GF	GA
22	18	2	114	104
SERIES	W	L		
9	6	3		

OTTAWA SENATORS
1924–25 to 1930–31
& 1932–33 to 1933–34

Ottawa Auditorium
Ottawa, Ontario

FIRST GAME   January 1, 1925   5–2 lost
AT Ottawa
LAST GAME   February 24, 1934   9–4 lost
AT Ottawa

ST. LOUIS EAGLES
1934–35

St. Louis Arena
5700 Oakland Avenue
St. Louis, Missouri

FIRST GAME   November 24, 1934   4–1 win
AT St. Louis
LAST GAME   February 16, 1935   3–0 lost
AT St. Louis

OTTAWA SENATORS
1992–93 to 1996–97

Ottawa Civic Center
301 Moodie Drive
Nepean, Ontario

FIRST GAME   November 23, 1992   3–2 win
AT Civic Center
LAST GAME   November 25, 1995   3–3
AT Civic Center

Ottawa Corel Centre
(Palladium)

FIRST GAME   January 31, 1996   3–1 win
AT Corel Centre

ALL-TIME RECORD – REGULAR SEASON

W	L	T	P	GF	GA
21	4	2	44	114	67
AT Ottawa					
10	1	2	22	49	25
AT Boston					
11	3	0	22	65	42

ALL-TIME RECORD – PLAYOFFS

W	L	T	GF	GA
0	0	0	0	0
SERIES	W	L		
0	0	0		

ALL-TIME RECORD – REGULAR SEASON

W	L	T	P	GF	GA
66	41	14	146	429	384
AT Philadelphia					
26	27	6	58	175	204
AT Boston					
40	14	8	88	254	180

ALL-TIME RECORD – PLAYOFFS

W	L	T	GF	GA
11	9	0	60	57
SERIES	W	L		
4	2	2		

PHOENIX COYOTES
1996–97

The Phoenix Coyotes were originally the Winnipeg Jets and transferred to Phoenix on July 1, 1996.

America West Arena
One Renaissance Square
Phoenix, Arizona

FIRST GAME   February 15, 1997
AT America West Arena

PHILADELPHIA FLYERS
1967–68 to 1996–97

Philadelphia Spectrum
Pattison Place
Philadelphia, Pennsylvania

FIRST GAME   January 4, 1968   3–2 win
AT the Spectrum
LAST GAME   April 7, 1996   4–2 win
AT the Spectrum

CoreStates Center
1 CoreStates Complex
Philadelphia, Pennsylvania

FIRST GAME   December 15, 1996   6–0 loss
AT CoreStates Center

Due to a storm in 1968, the roof of the Philadelphia Spectrum blew off necessitating of Flyer home game being moved to neutral sites. The Bruins played one neutral site game against the Flyers in Toronto.

Maple Leaf Gardens
60 Carlton Street
Toronto, Ontario

March 7, 1968   2–1 win
Neutral site game at Minnesota

Metropolitan Sports Center
7901 Cedar Avenue South
Bloomington, Minnesota

December 31, 1993   4–3 loss

WINNIPEG JETS
1979–80 to 1995–96

Winnipeg Arena
15–1430 Maroons Road
Winnipeg, Manitoba

FIRST GAME   October 26, 1979   3–2 lost
AT Winnipeg Arena
LAST GAME   December 31, 1995   5–3 win
AT Winnipeg Arena

ALL-TIME RECORD – REGULAR SEASON

W	L	T	P	GF	GA
30	14	5	65	207	170
AT Phoenix/Winnipeg					
13	10	2	28	95	91
AT Boston					
17	4	3	37	112	79

ALL-TIME RECORD – PLAYOFFS

W	L	T	GF	GA
0	0	0	0	0
SERIES	W	L		
0	0	0		

PITTSBURGH PIRATES
1925–26 to 1929–30

Duquesne Gardens
Pittsburgh, Pennsylvania

FIRST GAME — December 11, 1925 — 5–3 lost
AT Duquesne Gardens
LAST GAME — February 12, 1930 — 4–3 win
AT Duquesne Gardens

PHILADELPHIA QUAKERS
1930–31

The Philadelphia Quakers were originally the Pittsburgh Pirates and moved to Philadelphia for the 1930–31 season.

Philadelphia Arena
Philadelphia, Pennsylvania

FIRST GAME — December 6, 1930 — 4–3 win
AT Philadelphia Arena
LAST GAME — February 24, 1931 — 5–1 win
AT Philadelphia Arena

ALL-TIME RECORD – REGULAR SEASON

W	L	T	P	GF	GA
23	9	4	50	105	60
AT Philadelphia/Pittsburgh					
9	8	I	19	44	42
AT Boston					
14	I	3	31	61	18

ALL-TIME RECORD – PLAYOFFS

W	L	T	GF	GA
0	0	0	0	0
SERIES	W	L		
0	0	0		

PITTSBURGH PENGUINS
1967–68 to

Pittsburgh Civic Arena
Gate 7
Pittsburgh, Pennsylvania

FIRST GAME — November 22, 1967 — 4–1 loss
AT Pittsburgh
Neutral site game
AT Atlanta Omni
— February 8, 1993 — 4–0 loss
Neutral site game
AT Cleveland Richfield Coliseum
— April 3, 1994 — 6–2 loss

ALL-TIME RECORD – REGULAR SEASON

W	L	T	P	GF	GA
72	39	17	161	538	420
AT Pittsburgh					
27	27	11	65	246	233
AT Boston					
45	12	6	96	292	187

ALL-TIME RECORD – PLAYOFFS

W	L	T	GF	GA
9	10	0	62	67
SERIES	W	L		
4	2	2		

ST. LOUIS BLUES
1967–68 to 1996–97

St. Louis Arena
(known as Checkerdome from 1977–82)
5700 Oakland Avenue
St. Louis, Missouri

FIRST GAME — November 1, 1967 — 5–1 lost
AT the Arena
LAST GAME — February 18, 1994 — 3–1 lost
AT the Arena

Kiel Center
1401 Clark Avenue
St. Louis, Missouri

FIRST GAME — October 17, 1995 — 7–4 win
AT Kiel Center

ALL-TIME RECORD – REGULAR SEASON

W	L	T	P	GF	GA
57	33	17	131	423	314
AT St. Louis					
23	22	9	55	190	171
AT Boston					
34	11	8	76	233	143

ALL-TIME RECORD – PLAYOFFS

W	L	T	GF	GA
8	0	0	48	15
SERIES	W	L		
2	2	0		

SAN JOSE SHARKS
1991–92 to 1996–97

Cow Palace
San Francisco, California

FIRST GAME   October 19, 1991   4–1 win
AT Cow Palace
LAST GAME   October 15, 1992   8–2 win
AT Cow Palace

San Jose Arena
525 West Santa Clara Street
San Jose, California

FIRST GAME   October 16, 1993   1–1 tie
AT San Jose Arena

ALL-TIME RECORD – REGULAR SEASON

W	L	T	P	GF	GA
7	0	3	17	45	28
AT San Jose					
3	0	2	8	24	13
AT Boston					
4	0	I	9	21	15

ALL-TIME RECORD – PLAYOFFS

W	L	T	GF	GA
0	0	0	0	0
SERIES	W	L		
0	0	0		

TAMPA BAY LIGHTNING
1992–93 to 1996–97

Expo Hall
at Florida State Fairgrounds
Tampa, Florida

FIRST GAME   February 14, 1993   3–3

Thunderdome
Tampa, Florida

FIRST GAME   December 18, 1993   5–3 win
AT Thunderdome
LAST GAME   December 8, 1995   3–1 win
AT Thunderdome

Florida Suncoast Dome
401 Channelside Drive
Tampa, Florida

FIRST GAME   February 1, 1997   3–0 win
AT Suncoast Dome

ALL-TIME RECORD – REGULAR SEASON

W	L	T	P	GF	GA
10	4	3	23	59	44
AT Tampa Bay					
4	3	2	10	28	26
AT Boston					
6	I	I	13	31	18

ALL-TIME RECORD – PLAYOFFS

W	L	T	GF	GA
0	0	0	0	0
SERIES	W	L		
0	0	0		

TORONTO MAPLE LEAFS
1924–25 to 1996–97

The Toronto Maple Leafs were originally known as the St. Pats (1924–26). They changed their name to the Maple Leafs for the 1927–28 season.

Arena Gardens
60 Mutual Street
Toronto, Ontario

FIRST GAME   December 3, 1924   5–3 lost
AT Arena Gardens
LAST GAME   February 21, 1931   4–2 lost
AT Arena Gardens

Maple Leaf Gardens
60 Carlton Street
Toronto, Ontario

FIRST GAME   November 28, 1931   6–5 lost
AT Maple Leaf Gardens

ALL-TIME RECORD – REGULAR SEASON

W	L	T	P	GF	GA
237	232	95	569	1660	1715
AT Toronto					
86	148	48	220	734	961
AT Boston					
151	84	47	349	926	754

ALL-TIME RECORD – PLAYOFFS

W	L	T	GF	GA
30	31	I	153	150
SERIES	W	L		
13	5	8		

VANCOUVER CANUCKS
1970–71 to 1996–97

Pacific Coliseum
100 North Renfrew Street
Vancouver, British Columbia

FIRST GAME	October 18, 1970	5–3 win
AT Pacific Coliseum		
LAST GAME	October 19, 1993	5–4 lost
AT Pacific Coliseum		

General Motors Place
800 Griffiths Way
Vancouver, British Columbia

| FIRST GAME | February 17, 1996 | 4–1 win |
| AT General Motors Place | | |

ALL-TIME RECORD – REGULAR SEASON

W	L	T	P	GF	GA
60	19	12	132	397	259
AT Vancouver					
24	14	8	56	196	154
AT Boston					
36	5	4	76	201	105

ALL-TIME RECORD Ä PLAYOFFS

W	L	T	GF	GA
0	0	0	0	0
SERIES	W	L		
0	0	0		

WASHINGTON CAPITALS
1974–75 to 1996–97

Capital Centre–USAir Arena
1 Harry S. Truman Drive
Landover, Maryland

| FIRST GAME | January 7, 1975 | 3–3 |
| AT Washington | | |

ALL-TIME RECORD – REGULAR SEASON

W	L	T	P	GF	GA
45	23	15	105	321	241
AT Washington					
21	10	10	52	155	122
AT Boston					
24	13	5	53	166	119

ALL-TIME RECORD – PLAYOFFS

W	L	T	GF	GA
4	0	0	15	6
SERIES	W	L		
1	1	0		

ALL-TIME YEAR-BY-YEAR STANDINGS

BOSTON ADMITTED TO HOCKEY LEAGUE

MONTREAL, Oct 12—The Boston Hockey Club and a second Montreal club were admitted to the National Hockey League at a meeting of the league directors today, bringing the number of teams to six.

The new Montreal club paid $15,000 for its franchise and the Boston club a like amount for the American franchise, which was taken out by T. J. Duggan two years ago. It was announced.

The other four clubs in the circuit are Ottawa, Toronto, Canadiens of Montreal, Hamilton and a New York city may al...

NEW YORK AND BOSTON IN INTERNATIONAL HOCKEY

MONTREAL, Feb 10—Directors of the International Hockey League decided today to include New York and Boston in their organisation, which will also have teams in Montreal, Ottawa, Toronto and Hamilton.

Hockey Practice at Arena Held Up

Cooling System Goes Bad—Bruins in Montreal for Practice—Game Thursday Will Be Played

BY FRED HOEY

All hockey practice at the Arena has been held up, owing to a defect in the cooling system. Leaks in the pipes running through the ammonia tank were discovered last Friday. New pipes are being installed. Rather than lose any more practice time here, Coach Art Ross last night took his Boston Bruins to Montreal, where they will practice either at the Forum or Mt. St. Royal.

Manager George V. Brown expects to have the ice ready late tonight or tomorrow morning.

BIG OPENING THURSDAY

Hockey of the most sensational character is expected to develop Thursday night at the Arena, when the Boston Bruins and the Hamburg Yellow Jackets open the National Hockey league season.

In addition to the usual league rivalry between these teams there is a very bitter feeling between these outfits over last year's developments when the Yel-

hockey. Any team boasting Sprague Cleghorn and either Lionel Hitchman or Red Stuart in front of the nets, with Dr. Charlie Stewart in the strings, is one that won't be scored on very frequently.

The acquisition of Cleghorn has made the Bruins a sound hockey outfit. His own individual brilliancy is remarkable asset in itself. Add to this the coaching he can impart to his brother Bruins and the locals are pretty well fixed.

Flock of Good Forwards

Coach Ross is still undecided about his attacking forces. He has a raft of good men. Jimmy Herberts, the star of a year ago, has been indisposed for the past few days, but Coach Ross says the big fellow will be ready for the championship game Thanksgiving night. Ross has a lot of faith in Spider Brackenborough, star centre ice man of the Hamilton Tigers, Allan Cup winners two years ago. This little fellow is bound to go big in this city. He is fast and shifty and bounds around the ice like a rubber ball. The harder he's hit, the harder he plays.

Carson Cooper, in excellent condition after his unfortunate run of bad luck last season, is a factor that the Bruins are banking on for scores. Coop packs a shot second only to that propelled by Babe Dye of the St. Pats.

BRUINS LOSE FIRST CLASH

Saskatoon Sheiks, Canadian Hockey Champs, Turn Trick at Arena by Score of 2 to 1

BY FRED HOEY

Before a packed house, professional hockey opened last night at the Boston Arena, when the Saskatoon Sheiks turned back the Boston Bruins, 2 to 1.

Although at times the game appeared to lag, the fans saw some of the finest brand of hockey ever witnessed in this city. The programme is far different than the simon pure. The players are all past masters in the art of stick handling and their passing and shots travel with lightening speed.

Continued on Page 20—First Col.

BRIDE'S VEIL CATCHES FIRE

BIBLE IN MODERN ENGLISH

Scotch Savant Brings Old Testament Up to Date

GARDEN OF EDEN IS REFERRED TO AS PARK

1924–1925
(1st year)

TEAM OWNER:	Charles Adams	PLAYOFFS:	Do not qualify
PRESIDENT:	Charles Adams	STANLEY CUP WINNER:	Victoria Cougars (PCHL)
GM & OWNER:	Art Ross	ALL-STARS:	None
COACH:	Art Ross	TROPHY WINNERS:	None

UNIFORMS

- Home and road uniforms are the same. Jersey is brown with yellow trim. A crouched bear with the word "Bruins" is in the center of the jersey. Jersey shoulders and arms are brown and gold. Pants are brown. Socks are alternating vertical stripes of brown, yellow, and white.

POTPOURRI

- At an NHL Governors meeting held on February 9th, two franchises are granted to Thomas Duggan to be operated in the United States. Mr. Duggan completes the arrangements by having Charles Adams of Boston purchase one of the franchises. Mr. Duggan previously had tried to purchase the Montreal Canadiens in 1921. Although the NHL had granted a franchise to Boston in February, on October 12th, at the Windsor Hotel in Montreal, final arrangements for a team in Boston are completed. On November 1, 1924, the Boston franchise is admitted in to the National Hockey League. Art Ross is the first Governor of the Boston team.
- Bruins win opening game at Boston Arena against the Montreal Maroons, 2–1.
- After opening night win over the Montreal Maroons, the Bruins lose 11 straight games. Bruins also suffer through a 7-game losing streak.
- Do not qualify for playoffs.
- Babe Dye of the Toronto St. Pats scores five goals in one game against the Bruins at Boston on December 22.
- Finish in last place, behind Hamilton, Toronto, Montreal Canadiens, Ottawa, and Montreal Maroons, with 6 wins, 24 losses.

TRANSACTIONS

- Acquisitions from the Pacific Coast Hockey Association and Western Canada Hockey League include Fred Harris, Lloyd Cook, Bobbie Rowe, Bernie Morris, Spunk Sparrow, Alf Skinner, Bobbie Benson, Fern Headley, Norman Fowler, Carson Cooper, Jimmy Herberts, Charles Stewart, George Redding, Norm Shay, and Werner Schnarr.
- Acquire George Carroll from the Montreal Maroons for Alf Skinner.
- Acquire Lionel Hitchman from the Ottawa Senators for cash.
- Obtain Stan Jackson and Bill Stuart from Toronto.

1924-25 STANDINGS

	W	L	T	P	GF	GA
Hamilton	19	10	1	39	90	60
Toronto	19	11	0	38	90	84
Montreal Canadiens	17	11	2	36	93	56
Ottawa	17	12	1	35	83	66
Montreal Maroons	9	19	2	20	45	65
Boston	6	24	0	12	49	119

1924-25 RESULTS

December 1924

	AT	VERSUS	W-L-T	SCR
1	Boston	Montreal Maroons	W	2–1
3	Toronto	St. Pats	L	5–3
8	Boston	Montreal Canadiens	L	4–3
10	Hamilton	Tigers	L	7–1
15	Boston	Ottawa	L	10–2
17	Montreal	Maroons	L	6–2
22	Boston	Toronto	L	10–1
25	Montreal	Canadiens	L	5–0
29	Boston	Hamilton	L	2–1

January 1925

1	Ottawa	Senators	L	5–2
3	Montreal	Maroons	L	4–3
5	Boston	Toronto	L	3–2
10	Montreal	Canadiens	W	3–2 (OT)
12	Boston	Hamilton	L	4–2
17	Ottawa	Senators	L	3–2
20	Boston	Montreal Maroons	L	2–0
24	Toronto	St. Pats	L	4–3
27	Boston	Montreal Canadiens	L	4–0
31	Hamilton	Tigers	L	8–3

February 1925

3	Boston	Ottawa	L	3–1
7	Montreal	Maroons	W	1–0
10	Boston	Toronto	L	5–1

14	Montreal	Canadiens	L	5–1
17	Boston	Hamilton	L	2–1
21	Ottawa	Senators	L	3–0
24	Boston	Montreal Maroons	W	2–1
28	Toronto	St. Pats	L	5–1

March 1925

3	Boston	Montreal Canadiens	W	3–2
7	Hamilton	Tigers		W	2–0
9	Boston	Senators		L	4–1

1924-25 SCORING

	GP	SO	GAA
Charles Stewart	21	2	3.1
Howard Lockhart	2		5.5
Norman Fowler	7		6.1

	G	A	P
Jimmy Herberts	17	5	22
Carson Cooper	5	3	8
Bill Stuart	5	2	7
Stan Jackson	5	0	5
George Redding	3	2	5
Fred Harris	3	1	4
Lionel Hitchman	3	0	3
Herb Mitchell	3	0	0
Lionel Hitchman	3	0	3
Norman Shay	1	1	2
Lloyd Cook	1	0	1
Bobbie Rowe	1	0	1
Bernie Morris	1	0	0
Bobbie Benson	0	1	1
Alf Skinner	0	0	0
Fern Headley	0	0	0
George Carroll	0	0	0
Werner Schnarr	0	0	0
Emory Sparrow	0	0	0
Jack Ingram	0	0	0

NO PLAYOFF SCORING

1925–1926
(2nd year)

TEAM OWNER:	Charles Adams	PLAYOFFS:	Do not qualify
PRESIDENT:	Charles Adams	STANLEY CUP WINNER:	Montreal Maroons
GM & OWNER:	Art Ross	ALL-STARS:	None
COACH:	Art Ross	TROPHY WINNERS:	None

UNIFORMS

- Home and road uniforms are the same. Jersey is brown with yellow trim. A crouched bear with the word "Bruins" is in the center of the jersey. Jersey shoulders and arms are brown and gold. Pants are brown. Socks are alternating vertical stripes of brown, yellow and white.

POTPOURRI

- Finish in fourth place, behind Ottawa, Montreal Maroons, and Pittsburgh.
- Do not qualify for the playoffs.
- League rules stipulate that no team's aggregate players' payroll to exceed $35,000.
- Hamilton club moves to New York and becomes the New York Americans. The Pittsburgh Pirates also enter the league.
- This is the last season that the Stanley Cup is competed for by teams outside the NHL.
- Bruins finish last 17 games at 13 wins, 3 losses, and 1 tie.

TRANSACTIONS

- Acquire Sprague Cleghorn from Montreal Maroons for $5,000.
- First appearances of Hago Harrington, Charlie Cahill, Jerry Geran, and Paul Stevens.

Somerville, Massachusetts, native and the first Bruins Jewish goaltender Maurice Roberts.

1925-26 STANDINGS

	W	L	T	P	GF	GA
Ottawa	24	8	4	52	77	42
Montreal Maroons	20	11	5	45	91	73
Pittsburgh	19	16	1	39	82	70
Boston	17	15	4	38	92	85
New York Americans	12	20	4	28	68	89
Toronto	12	21	3	27	92	114
Montreal Canadiens	11	24	1	23	79	108

1925-26 RESULTS

November 1925

AT		VERSUS	W-L-T	SCR
26	Boston	Pittsburgh	L	2–1
28	Toronto	St. Pats	W	3–2

December 1925

	AT	VERSUS	W-L-T	SCR
1	Boston	Montreal Canadiens	L	3–2
3	Ottawa	Senators	L	2–0
5	Montreal	Maroons	L	4–0

8	Boston	Montreal Maroons	W	3–2
11	Pittsburgh	Pirates	L	5–3
15	Boston	Ottawa	L	2–1
19	Montreal	Canadiens	L	6–5 (OT)
22	Boston	New York Americans	L	3–2
29	Boston	Toronto	W	3–0

January 1926

5	Boston	Pittsburgh	W	3–0
7	New York	Americans	T	2–2
9	Toronto	St. Pats	L	3–2
12	Boston	Montreal Canadiens	L	4–2
15	Pittsburgh	Pirates	L	5–1
19	Boston	Montreal Maroons	T	3–3
23	New York	Americans	T	2–2
26	Boston	Ottawa	L	8–2
30	Montreal	Maroons	W	5–0

February 1926

2	Boston	Toronto	W	3–2
4	Ottawa	Senators	W	3–2
6	Montreal	Canadiens	T	3–3
9	Boston	New York Americans	W	4–0
13	Toronto	St. Pats	W	7–4
16	Boston	Pittsburgh	W	3–2 (OT)
18	New York	Americans	W	7–3
20	Montreal	Canadiens	W	3–1
22	Boston	Toronto	W	2–1 (OT)
27	Ottawa	Senators	L	3–2

March 1926

2	Boston	Montreal	W	4–1
4	Montreal	Maroons	W	3–2
6	Boston	Ottawa	W	1–0
9	Boston	New York Americans	L	1–0
12	Pittsburgh	Pirates	L	2–1 (OT)
16	Boston	Montreal Maroons	W	1–0

1925-26 SCORING

	GP	SO	GAA
Charles Stewart	35	6	2.3
Maurice Roberts	1		5.0

	G	A	P
Carson Cooper	28	3	31
Jimmy Herberts	26	5	31
Lionel Hitchman	7	4	11
Sprague Cleghorn	6	5	11
Hago Harrington	7	2	9
Bill Stuart	6	1	7
George Geran	5	1	6
Stan Jackson	3	3	6
Herb Mitchell	3	0	3
Norman Shay	2	0	2
Charlie Cahill	0	1	1
John Brackenborough	0	0	0
George Redding	0	0	0
Joe Matte	0	0	0
Fred Bergdinon	0	0	0
Paul Stevens	0	0	0
Werner Schnarr	0	0	0
Charles Larose	0	0	0

NO PLAYOFF SCORING

1926–1927

(3rd year)

TEAM OWNER:	Charles Adams		*Stanley Cup finals:*
PRESIDENT:	Charles Adams		Lose to Ottawa Senators
GM & OWNER:	Art Ross		0 wins – 2 losses – 2 ties
COACH:	Art Ross	STANLEY CUP WINNER:	Ottawa Senators
PLAYOFFS:	*Quarter finals:*	ALL-STARS:	None
	Defeat Chicago Blackhawks	TROPHY WINNERS:	None
	1 win – 0 losses – 1 tie		
	Semi-finals:		
	Defeat New York Rangers		
	1 win – 0 losses – 1 tie		

UNIFORMS

- Home and road uniforms are the same. Jersey is brown with yellow trim. A crouched bear with the word "Bruins" is in the center of the jersey. Jersey shoulders and arms are brown and gold. Pants are brown. Socks are alternating vertical stripes of brown, yellow, and white.

POTPOURRI

- Harry Oliver scores 4 goals against Chicago on January 11.
- Frank Fredrickson scores 4 goals against the New York Rangers on January 18.
- Qualify for the playoffs for the first time.
- Defeat Chicago and New York Rangers in the first two rounds.
- Lose in the Stanley Cup finals to Ottawa, 2 games to 0 with 2 games ending in ties.
- All road games against Detroit are played in Windsor, Ontario because the construction of the rink in Detroit is not finished.
- The first playoff game scheduled to be played at Chicago on March 29, is transferred to New York.
- Three new teams enter the league with the addition of the New York Rangers, Chicago Blackhawks, and Detroit Cougars.
- With the NHL now divided into two sections, the Bruins are assigned to the American Division along with the Rangers, Chicago, Pittsburgh, and Detroit.
- Finish in second place in the American Division behind the Rangers.
- After the season, it is announced that bonuses would be awarded as follows:

  Galbraith – $1,600
  Hitchman – $1,400
  Cleghorn, Oliver, Herberts, and Shore – $1,000
  Winkler – $850
  Fredrickson – $750
  Couture – $700
  Stuart and Boucher – $300
  Meeking, and Trainer Murray – $250

- NHL Board of Governors vote to establish uniform starting times for all games. Games would start no earlier than 8:15 p.m. and no later than 8:30 p.m.
- The NHL starts employing official scorers for all games.
- The Toronto St. Pats change their nickname to the Maple Leafs.
- This is the last season in which the Ottawa Senators win the Stanley Cup.
- Bad blood between the Ottawa Senators and Bruins in the finals results in the expelling of Boston defenseman Billy Couture. Lionel Hitchman and Jimmy Herberts are also fined for their actions. Money collected from the fines is donated to Boston and Ottawa charities.
- Of the 220 league games, 84 result in shutouts.

TRANSACTIONS

- Obtain Eddie Shore, Duke Keats, Archie Briden, Hal Winkler, and Harry Oliver from the defunct Pacific Coast Hockey Association.
- Trade Duke Keats to Detroit for Frank Fredrickson.
- Trade Carson Cooper to Canadiens for Billy Boucher.

1926-27 STANDINGS

Canadian Division	W	L	T	P	GF	GA
Ottawa	30	10	4	64	69	64
Montreal Canadiens	28	14	2	58	99	67
Montreal Maroons	20	20	4	44	71	68
New York Americans	17	25	2	36	82	91
Toronto	15	24	5	35	79	94

American Division

New York Rangers	25	13	6	56	95	72
Boston	21	20	3	45	97	89
Chicago	19	22	3	41	115	116
Pittsburgh	15	26	3	33	79	108
Detroit	12	28	4	28	76	105

1926-27 RESULTS

November 1926

	AT	VERSUS	W-L-T	SCR
16	Boston	Montreal Canadiens	W	4–1
18	Windsor, Ontario	Detroit Cougars	W	2–0
20	Chicago	Blackhawks	L	5–1
23	Boston	Montreal Maroons	L	2–1
30	Boston	Ottawa	L	2–1

December 1926

4	Pittsburgh	Pirates	W	4–3 (OT)
7	Boston	New York Rangers	L	1–0
12	New York	Rangers	L	2–1 (OT)
14	Boston	Detroit	W	7–2
16	Montreal	Canadiens	T	2–2
18	Boston	Pittsburgh	W	3–0
21	Boston	Toronto	L	5–3
23	Montreal	Maroons	W	2–1
28	Boston	New York Americans	W	2–1
30	Toronto	Maple Leafs	L	4–1

January 1927

2	New York	Americans	L	3–0
4	Boston	Ottawa	W	2–1 (OT)
8	Boston	Montreal Maroons	L	3–0
11	Boston	Chicago	W	6–3
13	Windsor, Ontario	Detroit Cougars	L	3–2
15	Ottawa	Senators	L	5–4
18	Boston	New York Rangers	W	7–3

20	New York	Rangers	T	2–2
22	Chicago	Blackhawks	T	2–2
25	Boston	Pittsburgh	W	3–1
29	Pittsburgh	Pirates	L	2–0

February 1927

1	Boston	Toronto	W	1–0
5	Toronto	Maple Leafs	L	1–0
8	Boston	Detroit	W	2–0
12	Montreal	Maroons	W	3–2
15	Boston	Chicago	W	3–0
20	New York	Rangers	L	3–1
22	Boston	Detroit	W	3–2
26	Montreal	Canadiens	L	2–0

March 1927

1	New York	Americans	L	3–0
5	Boston	New York Americans	W	5–0
8	Boston	Pittsburgh	W	5–2
12	Boston	Chicago	L	4–0
15	Chicago	Blackhawks	W	2–1 (OT)
17	Ottawa	Senators	L	1–0
19	Windsor, Ontario	Detroit Cougars	W	3–1
22	Boston	Montreal Canadiens	L	1–0
24	Pittsburgh	Pirates	L	4–3
26	New York	Rangers	W	4–3 (OT)

1926-27 SCORING

	GP	SO	GAA	
Hal Winkler	23	4	1.7	
Charles Stewart	21	6	2.3	

	G	A	P	PIM
Harry Oliver	18	6	24	17
Jimmy Herberts	15	7	22	51
Frank Fredrickson	17	7	24	33
Eddie Shore	12	6	18	130

Percy Galbraith	9	8	17	26
Lionel Hitchman	3	6	9	70
Sprague Cleghorn	7	1	8	84
Bill Stuart	3	1	4	20
Billy Couture	1	1	2	25
Billy Boucher	2	0	2	12
Harry Meeking	1	0	1	2
Carson Cooper	0	0	0	14
Caskey	0	0	0	0

1926-27 **PLAYOFF RESULTS**

March 1927

	AT	VERSUS	W-L-T	SCR	
29	New York	Chicago	W	6–1	
31	Boston	Chicago	T	4–4 (OT)	

April 1927

	AT	VERSUS	W-L-T	SCR
2	Boston	New York Rangers	T	0–0 (OT)
4	New York	Rangers	W	3–1
7	Boston	Ottawa	T	0–0 (OT)

	AT	VERSUS	W-L-T	SCR
9	Boston	Ottawa	L	3–1
11	Ottawa	Senators	T	1–1 (OT)
13	Ottawa	Senators	L	3–1

1926–27 playoffs: 2 wins – 2 losses – 4 ties

1926-27 **PLAYOFFS**

vs. Chicago Blackhawks	1 win – 0 losses – 1 tie
at Chicago	no games
at Boston	1 win – 0 losses – 1 tie

vs. New York Rangers	1 win – 0 losses – 1 tie
at New York	1 win – 0 losses – 0 ties
at Boston	0 wins – 0 losses – 1 tie

vs. Ottawa Senators	0 wins – 2 losses – 2 ties
at Ottawa	0 wins – 1 loss – 1 tie
at Boston	0 wins – 1 loss – 1 tie

1926-27 **PLAYOFF SCORING**

	GP	SO	GAA
Hal Winkler	8	13	2.0

	G	A	P	PIM
Harry Oliver	4	1	5	2
Percy Galbraith	3	2	5	4
Frank Fredrickson	2	2	4	18
Jimmy Herberts	3	0	3	8

Eddie Shore	1	1	2	40
Lionel Hitchman	1	0	1	26
Billy Couture	1	0	1	4
Sprague Cleghorn	1	0	1	8
Bill Stuart	0	0	0	4
Harry Meeking	0	0	0	0
Billy Boucher	0	0	0	2

1927–1928
(4th year)

TEAM OWNER:	Charles Adams
PRESIDENT & GOVERNOR:	Charles Adams
GM:	Art Ross
COACH:	Art Ross
PLAYOFFS:	*Semi-finals:*
	Lose to New York Rangers
	0 wins – 1 loss – 1 tie

STANLEY CUP WINNER:	New York Rangers
ALL-STARS:	None
TROPHY WINNERS:	Prince of Wales
	— Boston Bruins

UNIFORMS

- Home and road uniforms are the same. Jersey has white chest with the word "Boston" in brown arched across the top. Brown bear is below "Boston" lettering. "Bruins" is located below brown bear and is white in a brown square. Jersey shoulders and arms are brown and yellow. Pants are brown. Socks are alternating vertical stripes of brown, yellow, and white.

POTPOURRI

- Win the Prince of Wales Trophy for finishing first in the American Division.
- Lose to New York Rangers in the first round of the playoffs.
- The Ross goal, developed by General Manager Art Ross, is adopted as the official net of the NHL.
- The O'Brien Cup is awarded to the first-place finisher in the Canadian Division and the Prince of Wales Cup is awarded to the first-place finisher in the American Division.

TRANSACTIONS

- Acquire Fred Gordon from Detroit.
- Sell Jimmy Herberts to Toronto for a reported $12,500. Sell Duke Keats to Chicago, Carson Cooper to Detroit, and Billy Boucher to the New York Americans.
- Bill Stuart retires and Billy Couture is suspended for fighting in the previous season's playoffs.

1927–1928 souvenir program

1927-28 STANDINGS						
Canadian Division	W	L	T	P	GF	GA
Montreal Canadiens	26	11	7	59	116	48
Montreal Maroons	24	14	6	54	96	77
Ottawa	20	14	10	50	78	57
Toronto	18	18	8	44	89	88
New York Americans	11	27	6	28	63	128

American Division

Boston	20	13	11	51	77	70
New York Rangers	19	16	9	47	94	79
Pittsburgh	19	17	8	46	67	76
Detroit	19	19	6	44	88	79
Chicago	7	34	3	17	68	134

1927-28 RESULTS

November 1927

	AT	VERSUS	W-L-T	SCR
15	Boston	Chicago	T	1–1
19	Boston	Detroit	W	5–2
22	Boston	Toronto	W	1–0
26	Boston	New York Americans	L	4–3 (OT)
27	New York	Rangers	T	1–1
29	Boston	Montreal Maroons	W	4–0

December 1927

1	Pittsburgh	Pirates	T	1–1
3	Ottawa	Senators	L	3–2
6	Boston	Montreal Canadiens	T	1–1
10	Chicago	Blackhawks	W	2–0
11	Detroit	Cougars	W	2–1 (OT)
13	Boston	New York Rangers	L	3–2
17	Montreal	Canadiens	L	5–1
20	Boston	Ottawa	W	1–0
27	Boston	New York Rangers	W	2–0
29	Toronto	Maple Leafs	L	2–1

January 1928

1	New York	Americans	W	3–2
3	Boston	Pittsburgh	T	0–0
7	Montreal	Maroons	L	4–1
10	Boston	Chicago	W	3–1
12	New York	Rangers	T	2–2
14	Ottawa	Senators	W	4–2
17	Boston	Montreal Canadiens	L	3–1
21	Chicago	Blackhawks	T	1–1
22	Detroit	Cougars	L	3–2 (OT)
24	Boston	Pittsburgh	T	0–0
28	Pittsburgh	Pirates	L	1–0
31	Boston	New York Americans	W	2–1

February 1928

7	Boston	Detroit	W	4–2
11	Montreal	Canadiens	T	1–1
14	Boston	Chicago	W	1–0
19	New York	Rangers	W	2–0
21	Boston	Pittsburgh	W	2–0
25	Montreal	Maroons	L	3–1
28	Boston	Montreal Maroons	W	2–1

March 1928

3	Toronto	Maple Leafs	T	0–0
6	Boston	Ottawa	W	1–0
10	Boston	New York Rangers	T	3–3
11	New York	Americans	W	1–0
13	Boston	Detroit	W	3–0
16	Chicago	Blackhawks	W	3–1
17	Pittsburgh	Pirates	L	3–1
20	Boston	Toronto	L	6–2
24	Detroit	Cougars	L	7–2

1927-28 SCORING

	GP	SO	GAA	
Hal Winkler	44	15	1.59	

	G	A	P	PIM
Harry Oliver	13	5	18	20
Eddie Shore	11	6	17	165
Frank Fredrickson	10	4	14	83
Dutch Gainor	8	4	12	35
Percy Galbraith	6	5	11	26
Harry Connor	9	1	10	36
Lionel Hitchman	5	3	8	87
Dit Clapper	4	1	5	20
Fred Gordon	3	2	5	40
Sprague Cleghorn	2	2	4	14
Hago Harrington	1	0	1	7
Martin Lauder	0	0	0	0
Andrew Clark	0	0	0	0

1927-28 PLAYOFF RESULTS

April 1928

	AT	VERSUS	W-L-T	SCR
1	New York	Rangers	T	1–1 (OT)
3	Boston	New York Rangers	L	4–1

1927–28 playoffs: 1 loss – 1 tie

1927-28 PLAYOFFS

vs. New York Rangers	0 wins – 1 loss – 1 tie
at New York	0 wins – 0 losses – 1 tie
at Boston	0 wins – 1 loss

1927-28 PLAYOFF SCORING

	GP	SO	GAA					
Hal Winkler	2	0	2.5	Dit Clapper	0	0	0	2
				Dutch Gainor	0	0	0	6
	G	A	P	PIM	Eddie Shore	0	0	0	8
Harry Oliver	2	0	2	4	Harry Connor	0	0	0	0
Frank Fredrickson	0	1	1	4	Fred Gordon	0	0	0	0
Percy Galbraith	0	1	1	6	Sprague Cleghorn	0	0	0	0
Lionel Hitchman	0	0	0	2	Hugo Harrington	0	0	0	0

1928–1929

(5th year)

TEAM OWNER:	Charles Adams	
PRESIDENT & GOVERNOR:	Charles Adams	
GM:	Art Ross	
COACH:	Cy Denneny	
PLAYOFFS:	*Semi-finals:*	
	Defeat Montreal Canadiens	
	3 wins – 0 losses	

Stanley Cup finals:
Defeat New York Rangers
2 wins – 0 losses

STANLEY CUP WINNER:	Boston Bruins
ALL-STARS:	None
TROPHY WINNERS:	Prince of Wales
	— Boston Bruins

UNIFORMS

- Home and road uniforms are the same. Jersey has white chest with the word Boston in brown arched across the top. Brown bear is below Boston lettering. Bruins is located below brown bear and is white in a brown square. Jersey shoulders and arms are brown and gold. Pants are brown. Socks are alternating vertical stripes of brown, yellow, and white.

POTPOURRI

- Win the first Stanley Cup in franchise history on March 29, 1929, against the Rangers.
- Bill Carson scores the Cup-winning goal.
- Cooney Weiland, Dit Clapper, and Dutch Gainor form "Dynamite Line."

- Have 13-game winning streak.
- Win the Prince of Wales Trophy for the second straight year.
- Tiny Thompson records three shutouts in five playoff games and the team goes undefeated in 5 playoff games.
- Lose to Canadiens, 1–0, in the opening game at Boston Garden, November 20 on a goal by Sylvio Mantha.
- The new Boston Garden is opened on November 20 with a loss to the Montreal Canadiens.
- The first Stanley Cup Final between two American teams takes place on March 28 at Boston Garden between the Rangers and Boston Bruins.
- December 28, 1928, game between Montreal Canadiens and Ottawa Senators is broadcast for the first time on Montreal radio.
- Hal Winkler, who had retired before the 1928–29 season, as an honor, has his name placed on the Stanley Cup as a "sub-goaltender."
- Nine of the ten February games end in shutouts.

TRANSACTIONS

- Tiny Thompson replaces Hal Winkler in goal.
- Mickey Mackay obtained from Pittsburgh for Frank Fredrickson.
- Cooney Weiland is signed.
- Bill Carson is obtained from Toronto.
- George Owen, a player from Harvard, makes his debut on January 8th.

1928-29 STANDINGS

Canadian Division	W	L	T	P	GF	GA
Montreal Canadiens	22	7	15	59	71	43
New York Americans	19	13	12	50	53	53
Toronto	21	18	5	47	85	69
Ottawa	14	17	13	41	54	67
Montreal Maroons	15	20	9	39	67	65
American Division						
Boston	26	13	5	57	89	52
New York Rangers	21	13	10	52	72	65
Detroit	19	16	9	47	72	63
Pittsburgh	9	27	8	26	46	80
Chicago	7	29	8	22	33	85

1928-29 RESULTS

November 1928

	AT	VERSUS	W-L-T	SCR
15	Pittsburgh	Pirates	W	1–0 (OT)
17	Ottawa	Senators	T	2–2
20	Boston	Montreal Canadiens	L	1–0
22	Detroit	Cougars	L	2–0
25	Chicago	Blackhawks	T	1–1
27	Boston	Pittsburgh	W	1–0

December 1928

4	Boston	New York Rangers	W	2–0

8	Boston	Montreal Maroons	W	5–1
9	New York	Americans	L	2–1
11	Boston	New York Americans	L	3–0
15	Toronto	Maple Leafs	L	2–0
18	Boston	Detroit	W	3–1
25	Boston	Chicago	L	2–1
30	New York	Rangers	L	2–0

January 1929

1	Boston	Ottawa	W	3–0
3	Montreal	Maroons	W	1–0

5	Boston	Pittsburgh	W	3–2
8	Boston	Toronto	W	5–2
10	Montreal	Canadiens	W	4–2
12	Boston	Detroit	W	3–2
15	Boston	New York Rangers	W	4–1
17	Detroit	Cougars	T	1–1
20	Chicago	Blackhawks	W	2–0
22	Boston	Montreal Canadiens	T	0–0
27	New York	Rangers	W	2–1
29	Boston	Chicago	W	4–1
31	Toronto	Maple Leafs	W	3–1

February 1929

2	Boston	Toronto	L	3–0
5	Boston	New York Americans	L	1–0
9	Montreal	Maroons	L	1–0

12	Boston	Detroit	W	1–0
14	Pittsburgh	Pirates	L	2–0
16	Chicago	Blackhawks	W	3–0
19	Boston	Pittsburgh	W	1–0
24	New York	Americans	T	2–2
26	Boston	Montreal Maroons	W	1–0
28	Ottawa	Senators	W	4–0

March 1929

2	Montreal	Canadiens	L	3–0
5	Boston	New York Rangers	W	2–1
9	Boston	Ottawa	L	2–1
10	New York	Rangers	W	3–2
12	Boston	Chicago	W	11–1
14	Detroit	Cougars	W	5–1
16	Pittsburgh	Pirates	W	3–1

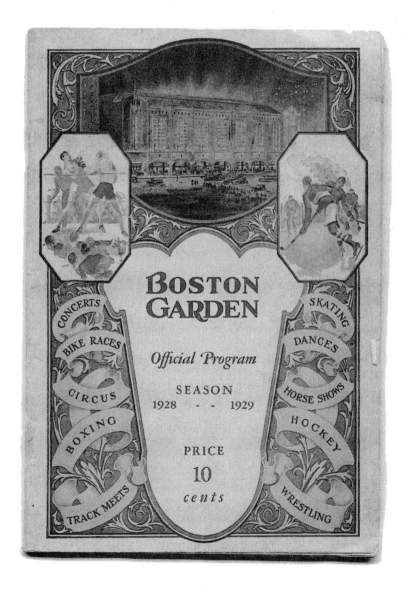

BOSTON GARDEN

Official Program

SEASON
1928 - - 1929

PRICE
10
cents

CONCERTS · BIKE RACES · CIRCUS · BOXING · TRACK MEETS · SKATING · DANCES · HORSE SHOWS · HOCKEY · WRESTLING

1928-29 SCORING

	GP	SO	GAA	
Tiny Thompson	44	12	1.18	
	G	A	P	PIM
Harry Oliver	17	6	23	24
Dutch Gainor	14	5	19	30
Eddie Shore	12	7	19	96
Cooney Weiland	11	7	18	16
Dit Clapper	9	2	11	48
Mickey Mackay	8	2	10	18
George Owen	5	4	9	48

	G	A	P	PIM
Bill Carson	4	2	6	10
Frank Fredrickson	3	1	4	24
Percy Galbraith	2	1	3	44
Cy Denneny	1	2	3	2
Lionel Hitchman	1	0	1	64
Dede Klein	1	0	1	5
Miles Lane	1	0	1	2
Redvers Green	0	0	0	16
Eddie Rodden	0	0	0	10
Eric Pettinger	0	0	0	17

1928-29 PLAYOFF RESULTS

March 1929

	AT	VERSUS	W-L-T	SCR
19	Boston	Montreal Canadiens	W	1–0
21	Boston	Montreal Canadiens	W	1–0
23	Montreal	Canadiens	W	3–2
28	Boston	New York Rangers	W	2–0
29	New York	Rangers	W	2–1

1928–29 Playoffs: 5 wins – 0 losses

1928-29 PLAYOFFS

vs. Montreal Canadiens	3 wins – 0 losses	vs. New York Rangers	2 wins – 0 losses
at Montreal	1 win – 0 losses	at New York	1 win – 0 losses
at Boston	2 wins – 0 losses	at Boston	1 win – 0 losses

BRUINS CLINCH WORLD'S TITLE

Carson's Goal Near End Defeats Rangers 2-1, Giving Team Coveted Stanley Cup

YES MR BRUIN, YOU'RE A BEAR

1928-29 PLAYOFF SCORING

	GP	SO	GAA		Lionel Hitchman	0	1	1	22
Tiny Thompson	5	3	0.60		Mickey Mackay	0	0	0	2
					Percy Galbraith	0	0	0	2
	G	A	P	PIM	Miles Lane	0	0	0	0
Cooney Weiland	2	0	2	2	George Owen	0	0	0	0
Bill Carson	2	0	2	8	Cy Denneny	0	0	0	0
Dutch Gainor	2	0	2	4	Frank Fredrickson	0	0	0	0
Harry Oliver	1	1	2	8	Redvers Green	0	0	0	0
Eddie Shore	1	1	2	28	Eddie Rodden	0	0	0	0
Dit Clapper	1	0	1	0	Dede Klein	0	0	0	0

This "B"-shaped publicity photo taken in the Boston Garden circa 1930

1929–1930
(6th year)

TEAM OWNER:	Charles Adams
PRESIDENT & GOVERNOR:	Charles Adams
GM:	Art Ross
COACH:	Art Ross
PLAYOFFS:	*Semi-finals:*
	Defeat Montreal Maroons
	3 wins – 1 loss – 1 tie

Stanley Cup finals:
Lose to Montreal Canadiens
0 wins – 2 losses

STANLEY CUP WINNER: Montreal Canadiens
ALL-STARS: None
TROPHY WINNERS: Prince of Wales
— Boston Bruins
Art Ross — Cooney Weiland
Vezina — Tiny Thompson

UNIFORMS

- Home and road uniforms are the same. Jersey has white chest with the word "Boston" in brown arched across the top. Brown bear is below "Boston" lettering. "Bruins" is located below brown bear and is white in a brown square. Jersey shoulders and arms are brown and yellow. Pants are brown. Socks are alternating vertical stripes of brown, yellow, and white.

POTPOURRI

- Win 38 of 44 games played. Win 14 consecutive games from December 1 to January 12.
- Tiny Thompson wins Vezina Trophy.
- Cooney Weiland scores 43 goals to lead league in goals and scoring.
- Bruins win Prince of Wales trophy for the third consecutive year, and championship of the NHL for compiling the best record in the league.
- Of the 179 goals that the Bruins scored, 102 are scored by the Weiland, Clapper, Gainor "Dynamite" line.
- Lose to Montreal Canadiens in the Stanley Cup finals, 2 games to 0. It is the first time all season the Bruins lost 2 games in a row. Bruins lose Dutch Gainor for the finals because of injury.
- Eddie Shore, known for his fighting ability, is challenged to a bout with Art Shires, a baseball player. Baseball commissioner Judge Landis intervenes and forbids Shires to fight Shore.
- After a November 23 game against the Montreal Maroons, Eddie Shore is given a check for $500 by Charles Adams — supposed to represent $100 for each scar he received from the rough Montreal players.
- Detroit Cougars change their name to Detroit Falcons.

TRANSACTIONS

- Marty Barry signed.

1929-30 STANDINGS

	W	L	T	P	GF	GA
Canadian Division						
Montreal Maroons	23	16	5	56	141	114
Montreal Canadiens	21	14	9	51	142	114
Ottawa	21	15	8	50	138	118
Toronto	17	21	6	40	116	124
New York Americans	14	25	5	33	113	161
American Division						
Boston	38	5	1	77	179	98
Chicago	21	18	5	47	117	111
New York Rangers	17	17	10	44	136	143
Detroit	14	24	6	34	117	133
Pittsburgh	5	36	3	13	102	185

1929-30 RESULTS

November 1929

	AT	VERSUS	W-L-T	SCR
16	Toronto	Maple Leafs	W	6–5
19	Boston	New York Rangers	W	3–2
23	Montreal	Maroons	W	4–3
26	Boston	Montreal Maroons	L	6–1
30	Pittsburgh	Pirates	W	3–2

December 1929

3	Boston	Montreal Canadiens	W	3–1
7	Boston	Detroit	W	2–1
10	Boston	Pittsburgh	W	5–4
12	Ottawa	Senators	W	3–2
15	New York	Americans	W	8–4
17	Boston	Ottawa	W	6–2
21	Boston	Chicago	W	4–1
25	Boston	Toronto	W	6–2
26	New York	Rangers	W	4–2
28	Montreal	Canadiens	W	3–2

January 1930

1	Boston	New York Americans	W	5–2
4	Montreal	Maroons	W	4–2
7	Boston	New York Rangers	W	3–0
9	Pittsburgh	Pirates	W	4–3
12	New York	Americans	L	3–2

14	Boston	Ottawa	W	5–1
16	Chicago	Blackhawks	L	2–1
19	Detroit	Falcons	W	5–4
21	Boston	Chicago	W	5–1
23	Boston	New York Americans	W	2–1 (OT)
25	Montreal	Canadiens	W	2–1
28	Boston	Pittsburgh	W	6–0

February 1930

2	New York	Rangers	T	3–3
4	Boston	Detroit	W	3–1
11	Boston	Toronto	W	6–5 (OT)
12	Pittsburgh	Pirates	W	4–3
15	Toronto	Maple Leafs	W	5–3 (OT)
16	Detroit	Falcons	W	4–2
18	Boston	Montreal Maroons	W	3–2
23	New York	Rangers	W	3–2
25	Boston	Pittsburgh	W	7–0

March 1930

4	Boston	Montreal Canadiens	W	5–2
11	Boston	Chicago	W	4–3
13	Chicago	Blackhawks	L	3–2 (OT)
15	Boston	Detroit	W	5–2
18	Boston	New York Rangers	W	9–2

1929-30 SCORING

	GP	SO	GAA	
Tiny Thompson	44	3	2.23	

	G	A	P	PIM
Cooney Weiland	43	30	73	27
Dit Clapper	41	20	61	48
Dutch Gainor	18	31	49	39
Marty Barry	18	15	33	34
Eddie Shore	12	19	31	105
Harry Oliver	16	5	21	12
Percy Galbraith	7	9	16	38
George Owen	9	4	13	21
Bill Carson	7	4	11	24
Mickey Mackay	4	5	9	13
Lionel Hitchman	2	7	9	58
Bill Hutton	2	0	2	2
Art Gagne	0	1	1	6
Robert Taylor	0	0	0	6
Miles Lane	0	0	0	0
Harry Connor	0	0	0	0

1929-30 PLAYOFF RESULTS

March 1930

	AT	VERSUS	W-L-T	SCR
22	Montreal	Maroons	W	4–2
25	Boston	Montreal Maroons	L	1–0 (OT)
27	Boston	Montreal Maroons	W	5–1

April 1930

1	Boston	Montreal Canadiens	L	3–0
3	Montreal	Canadiens	L	4–3

1929-30 PLAYOFFS

vs. Montreal Canadiens		vs. Montreal Maroons	
vs. Montreal Canadiens	0 wins – 2 losses	vs. Montreal Maroons	3 wins – 1 loss
at Montreal	0 wins – 1 loss	at Montreal	2 wins – 0 losses
at Boston	0 wins – 1 loss	at Boston	1 win – 1 loss

1929-30 PLAYOFF SCORING

	GP	SO	GAA					
Tiny Thompson	6	0	2.00	George Owen	0	2	2	6
				Bill Carson	1	0	1	6
				Lionel Hitchman	1	0	1	14
	G	A	P	PIM	Eddie Shore	1	0	1	26
Marty Barry	3	3	6	14	Mickey Mackay	0	0	0	4
Cooney Weiland	1	5	6	2	Dutch Gainor	0	0	0	0
Dit Clapper	4	0	4	4	Harry Connor	0	0	0	0
Percy Galbraith	1	3	4	8	Miles Lane	0	0	0	0
Harry Oliver	2	1	3	6					

1930–1931
(7th year)

TEAM OWNER:	Charles Adams	STANLEY CUP WINNER:	Montreal Canadiens
PRESIDENT:	Charles Adams	ALL-STARS:	Eddie Shore (1st team)
GM & OWNER:	Art Ross		Tiny Thompson (2nd team)
COACH:	Art Ross		Dit Clapper (2nd team)
PLAYOFFS:	*Semi-finals:*	TROPHY WINNERS:	Prince of Wales
	Lose to Montreal Canadiens		— Boston Bruins
	2 wins – 3 losses		

UNIFORMS

- Home and road uniforms are the same. Jersey has white chest with the word "Boston" in brown arched across the top. Brown bear is below "Boston" lettering. "Bruins" is located below brown bear and is white in a brown square. Jersey shoulders and arms are brown and yellow. Pants are brown. Socks are alternating vertical stripes of brown, yellow, and white.

POTPOURRI

- Dit Clapper scores 3 goals on Christmas Day.
- Bruins win 4th consecutive Prince of Wales Trophy.
- Nels Stewart of the Montreal Maroons scores 2 goals in 4 seconds against the Bruins on January 3.
- Lose second round of playoffs to the Montreal Canadiens, 3 games to 2.
- Pittsburgh Pirates move to Philadelphia and become known as the Quakers.
- Defeat Philadelphia Quakers on Christmas Day, 8–0, in a game marred by a free-for-all that had to be quelled by the Boston Police.
- In a game on March 10 that ended in a 3–3 tie, Coach Art Ross of Boston and Conn Smythe of Toronto engage in a battle, the result of a long-standing feud.
- NHL makes it mandatory for each player to wear a number, at least 10 inches in height, to be worn on the back of the jersey.

- In the second game of the playoffs against Montreal, Art Ross of the Bruins pulls goaltender Tiny Thompson for an extra attacker. This is the first time that this maneuver had been attempted in a Stanley Cup playoff game.

TRANSACTIONS
- Art Chapman, Red Beattie, Harold Darragh, Jack Pratt, and Bill Hutton are signed.

1930-31 STANDINGS

Canadian Division	W	L	T	P	GF	GA
Montreal Canadiens	26	10	8	60	129	89
Toronto	22	13	9	53	118	99
Montreal Maroons	20	18	6	46	105	106
New York Americans	18	16	10	46	76	74
Ottawa	10	30	4	24	91	142
American Division						
Boston	28	10	6	62	143	90
Chicago	24	17	3	51	108	78
New York Rangers	19	16	9	47	106	87
Detroit	16	21	7	39	102	105
Philadelphia	4	36	4	12	76	184

1930-31 RESULTS

November 1930

	AT	VERSUS	W-L-T	SCR
11	Boston	New York Americans	W	1–0
18	Boston	Montreal Canadiens	W	5–2
20	Chicago	Blackhawks	L	1–0
23	Detroit	Falcons	T	2–2
25	Boston	Chicago	L	4–3 (OT)
27	Boston	Ottawa	W	2–1
29	Montreal	Canadiens	L	3–2

December 1930

2	Boston	Toronto	W	3–2
6	Philadelphia	Quakers	W	4–3
9	Boston	Montreal Maroons	W	2–1
11	New York	Americans	L	2–1
13	Toronto	Maple Leafs	W	7–3
16	Boston	Detroit	W	3–2
18	New York	Rangers	W	4–2
20	Boston	New York Rangers	T	2–2
25	Boston	Philadelphia	W	8–0
30	Boston	Ottawa	W	7–3

January 1931

1	New York	Rangers	W	4–3 (OT)
3	Montreal	Maroons	L	5–3
6	Boston	Chicago	W	5–2
8	Ottawa	Senators	W	3–1
11	Detroit	Falcons	W	4–1
13	Boston	New York Rangers	T	2–2
15	Chicago	Blackhawks	L	2–0
20	Boston	Ottawa	W	4–2
22	New York	Americans	L	2–1
24	Philadelphia	Quakers	W	4–2
27	Boston	Philadelphia	T	3–3
29	New York	Rangers	W	4–3

February 1931

3	Boston	Detroit	W	7–2
7	Montreal	Canadiens	W	2–1
10	Chicago	Blackhawks	W	2–1
14	Montreal	Maroons	W	4–2
17	Boston	New York Americans	W	2–0
19	Boston	Montreal Canadiens	T	1–1
21	Toronto	Maple Leafs	L	4–2
24	Philadelphia	Quakers	W	5–1

March 1931

3	Boston	New York Rangers	W	4–1
7	Boston	Philadelphia	W	7–2
10	Boston	Toronto	T	3–3
12	Chicago	Blackhawks	L	3–2
15	Detroit	Falcons	L	5–2 (OT)
17	Boston	Detroit	W	4–2
21	Boston	Montreal Maroons	W	3–1

1930-31 SCORING

	GP	SO	GAA			G	A	P	PIM
Tiny Thompson	44	3	2.05	Art Chapman	7	7	14	22	
				Dutch Gainor	8	3	11	14	
	G	A	P	PIM	Henry Harris	2	4	6	20
Cooney Weiland	25	13	38	14	Harold Darragh	2	4	6	4
Marty Barry	20	11	31	26	Percy Galbraith	2	3	5	28
Eddie Shore	15	16	31	105	Jack Pratt	2	0	2	36
Dit Clapper	22	8	30	50	Lionel Hitchman	0	2	2	40
Harry Oliver	16	14	30	18	Paul Runge	0	0	0	0
George Owen	12	13	25	33	Ronald Lyons	0	0	0	21
John Beattie	10	11	21	25	Bill Hutton	0	0	0	2

1930-31 PLAYOFF RESULTS

March 1931

	AT	VERSUS	W-L-T	SCR
26	Boston	Montreal Canadiens	L	1–0
28	Montreal	Canadiens	L	4–3 (OT)
30	Montreal	Canadiens	W	3–1

April 1931

1	Montreal	Canadiens	L	3–2 (OT)

1930-31 PLAYOFFS

vs. Montreal Canadiens	2 wins – 3 losses
at Montreal	1 win – 2 losses
at Boston	1 win – 1 loss

1930-31 PLAYOFF SCORING

	GP	SO	GAA			G	A	P	PIM
Tiny Thompson	5	0	2.60	Dutch Gainor	0	1	1	2	
				Art Chapman	0	1	1	7	
				Harold Darragh	0	1	1	2	
	G	A	P	PIM	Harry Oliver	0	0	0	2
Cooney Weiland	6	3	9	2	Percy Galbraith	0	0	0	6
Dit Clapper	2	4	6	4	Ron Lyons	0	0	0	0
George Owen	2	3	5	13	John Beattie	0	0	0	0
Eddie Shore	2	1	3	22	Lionel Hitchman	0	0	0	0
Marty Barry	1	1	2	4					

1931–1932
(8th year)

TEAM OWNER:	Charles Adams	PLAYOFFS:	Out of playoffs
PRESIDENT & GOVERNOR:	Charles Adams	STANLEY CUP WINNER:	Toronto Maple Leafs
GM:	Art Ross	ALL-STARS:	Eddie Shore (1st team)
COACH:	Art Ross	TROPHY WINNERS:	None

UNIFORMS

- Home and road uniforms are the same. Jersey has white chest with the word "Boston" in brown arched across the top. Brown bear is below "Boston" lettering. "Bruins" is located below brown bear and is white in a brown square. Jersey shoulders and arms are brown and yellow. Pants are brown. Socks are alternating vertical stripes of brown, yellow, and white.

POTPOURRI

- In a game played on March 15 at Boston Garden, Toronto goalie Lorne Chabot is handed a 2-minute penalty for tripping. While he is in the box, the Bruins score 3 goals as various Maple Leaf players tended to protect the Toronto net.
- Lose to Rangers on November 19, their first loss to the Rangers since 1928.
- Bruins finish in last place in the American Division.
- Eddie Shore receives a match penalty for striking referee Cooper Smeaton in a game at Chicago on February 2.

- In a game played on December 29 at Boston Garden, referees begin to use signals for infractions.
- Montreal Maroons offer $40,000 for Eddie Shore which the Bruins turn down.
- The American Hockey League is declared an outlaw league by the NHL and their challenge for the Stanley Cup is not considered.
- Philadelphia Quakers cease operations.
- With the December 8 loss to the Americans, the Bruins lose for the first time in a regular season game at Boston since November 25, 1930.

TRANSACTIONS

- Obtain Bill Touhey from Ottawa in the dispersal draft of Ottawa and Pittsburgh players.
- Dutch Gainor traded to the Rangers for Joe Jerwa.
- New additions include Eddie Burke, Frank Jerwa, and Dede Klein.
- Bruins sign Bud Cook, younger brother of Bill and Bun Cook of the Rangers.

1931-32 STANDINGS

Canadian Division	W	L	T	P	GF	GA
Montreal Canadiens	25	16	7	57	128	111
Toronto	23	18	7	53	155	127
Montreal Maroons	19	22	7	45	142	139
New York Americans	16	24	8	40	95	142
American Division						
New York Rangers	23	17	8	54	134	112
Chicago	18	19	11	47	86	101
Detroit	18	20	10	46	95	108
Boston	15	21	12	42	122	117

1931-32 RESULTS

November 1931

	AT	VERSUS	W-L-T	SCR
14	Montreal	Maroons	L	4–1
17	Boston	Detroit	W	1–0 (OT)
19	New York	Rangers	L	2–1
21	Montreal	Canadiens	L	3–0
24	Boston	Montreal Canadiens	W	7–1
26	Boston	Chicago	W	1–0
28	Toronto	Maple Leafs	L	6–5 (OT)

December 1931

1	Boston	Montreal Maroons	W	7–3
8	Boston	New York Americans	L	3–2
10	Detroit	Falcons	T	1–1
13	Chicago	Blackhawks	W	3–0
15	Boston	New York Rangers	T	2–2
22	Boston	Detroit	W	6–2
26	Montreal	Maroons	T	4–4
29	Boston	Chicago	T	3–3
31	Boston	Montreal Canadiens	W	5–0

January 1932

3	New York	Americans	T	0–0
5	Boston	Toronto	T	3–3
7	Detroit	Falcons	T	0–0
10	Chicago	Blackhawks	T	1–1
12	Boston	New York Rangers	L	5–3 (OT)
14	New York	Rangers	L	3–1
16	Montreal	Canadiens	T	2–2
19	Boston	Chicago	L	3–2
23	Boston	Detroit	L	2–0
26	Boston	Montreal Maroons	L	4–3
28	New York	Rangers	W	4–1

February 1932

2	Boston	New York Americans	L	4–3
4	New York	Americans	W	5–0
6	Toronto	Maple Leafs	L	6–0
9	Boston	New York Rangers	W	2–1
11	Boston	Montreal Maroons	L	7–4
14	New York	Americans	W	3–1
16	Boston	Toronto	W	3–0
18	Detroit	Falcons	T	0–0

20	Chicago	Blackhawks	L	2–1		8	Boston	Detroit	W	2–0		
23	Boston	New York Rangers	L	2–0 (OT)		10	Boston	Chicago	L	3–2		
25	New York	Rangers	T	3–3		12	Toronto	Maple Leafs	L	5–3 (OT)		
27	Montreal	Canadiens	L	4–2		15	Boston	Toronto	W	6–2		
						18	Detroit	Falcons	T	1–1		
March 1932						20	Chicago	Blackhawks	L	1–0		
1	Boston	Montreal Canadiens	W	7–6		22	New York	Americans	L	8–6		
5	Montreal	Maroons	L	3–1								

1931-32 SCORING

	GP	SO	GAA					
Tiny Thompson	43	9	2.42		Alex Cook	4	5	9	22
Percy Jackson	3	0	2.33		Carson Cooper	4	4	8	14
Wilf Cude	2	1	3.00		Lionel Hitchman	4	3	7	36

	G	A	P	PIM		Eddie Burke	3	0	3	12
						Percy Galbraith	2	1	3	28
Dit Clapper	17	22	39	21		Irwin Boyd	2	1	3	10
Marty Barry	21	17	38	22		Harry Foster	1	2	3	12
Cooney Weiland	14	12	26	20		Dede Klein	1	0	1	0
Art Chapman	11	14	25	18		Paul Runge	0	1	1	8
George Owen	12	10	22	29		Jack Pratt	0	0	0	6
Eddie Shore	9	13	22	80		Joe Jerwa	0	0	0	0
Harry Oliver	13	7	20	22		John Beattie	0	0	0	0
Frank Jerwa	5	4	9	12		Ron Sutherland	0	0	0	0
George Touhey	5	4	9	12						

NO PLAYOFF SCORING

1932–1933
(9th year)

TEAM OWNER:	Charles Adams	STANLEY CUP WINNER:	New York Rangers
PRESIDENT & GOVERNOR:	Charles Adams	ALL-STARS:	Eddie Shore (1st team)
GOVERNOR:	Robert Duncan	TROPHY WINNERS:	Prince of Wales
GM:	Art Ross		— Boston Bruins
COACH:	Art Ross		Hart — Eddie Shore
PLAYOFFS:	*Semi-finals:*		Vezina — Tiny Thompson
	Lose to Toronto Maple Leafs		
	2 wins – 3 losses		

UNIFORMS
- Use same uniform both home and away. Jersey is white trimmed in brown and gold. Logo on front is a block letter "B" in brown outlined in yellow. Pants are brown. Socks are alternating stripes of white, brown, and yellow.

POTPOURRI
- Win the Prince of Wales Trophy for leading the American Division.
- Eddie Shore wins the Hart trophy for the first time.

- Tiny Thompson wins the Vezina Trophy.
- Lose to Toronto in opening round of the Stanley Cup playoffs.
- By winning game 2 of the playoffs, Toronto wins for the first time in Boston since 1929.
- In a December 18 game at Detroit, the Bruins lose to the Falcons, 2–1, but at the conclusion of the game, a fight between the two teams occurs in the Olympia corridors.
- In a January 24 game at Boston against the Canadiens, Lionel Hitchman coaches the team in the absence of Art Ross. Referee Cooper Smeaton suffers two broken ribs when he is punched by Eddie Shore during Shore's fight with Sylvio Mantha.
- Charles Adams resigns as an NHL Governor on February 11.
- Robert Duncan replaces Adams on the NHL Board of Governors.
- The American Hockey League disbands.
- The Bruins and the Maple Leafs compete in the longest overtime goal in league history with Ken Doraty's goal at 104 minutes and 46 seconds of overtime notching the victory for Toronto.
- In a March 14 game against Chicago at the Boston Garden, Tommy Gorman, the coach of the Blackhawks, becomes embroiled in a fight with Referee Bill Stewart. Upon refusal to leave the bench area, Gorman is ejected and escorted from the rink by the Boston Police with the game being forfeited to Boston.
- Bruins play Ottawa at Boston 4 times while visiting Ottawa only twice. This leads to 25 home games for Boston and 23 road contests for the Bruins.

TRANSACTIONS
- Cooney Weiland and Dutch Gainor are sent to Ottawa.
- Nels Stewart is obtained from the Montreal Maroons.
- Joe Lamb is obtained from the Americans.
- Billy Burch is obtained from the Americans but later sold to Chicago.

1932-33 STANDINGS

Canadian Division	W	L	T	P	GF	GA
Toronto	24	18	6	54	119	111
Montreal Maroons	22	20	6	50	135	119
Montreal Canadiens	18	25	5	41	92	115
New York Americans	15	22	11	41	91	118
Ottawa	11	27	10	32	88	131
American Division						
Boston	25	15	8	58	124	88
Detroit	25	15	8	58	111	93
New York Rangers	23	17	8	54	135	107
Chicago	16	20	12	44	88	101

1932-33 RESULTS

November 1932

	AT	VERSUS	W-L-T	SCR
10	Toronto	Maple Leafs	T	1–1
12	Montreal	Canadiens	W	4–0
15	Boston	Montreal Maroons	W	3–2
17	New York	Americans	L	4–2
22	Boston	Chicago	W	5–1
26	Boston	Ottawa	W	6–4

29	Boston	New York Rangers	L	6–4

December 1932

3	Montreal	Maroons	L	2–0
6	Boston	New York Americans	W	2–0 (OT)
11	New York	Rangers	L	3–1 (OT)
13	Boston	Toronto	W	5–1
15	Chicago	Blackhawks	W	1–0

18	Detroit	Red Wings	L	2–1
20	Boston	Ottawa	W	2–1
22	Boston	Detroit	W	7–0
24	Ottawa	Senators	T	1–1
27	Boston	Montreal Canadiens	W	1–0

January 1933

1	New York	Americans	L	5–4
3	Boston	New York Americans	T	0–0
5	Chicago	Blackhawks	T	0–0
8	Detroit	Red Wings	L	3–1
10	Boston	Ottawa	W	3–2 (OT)
12	New York	Rangers	L	3–1
14	Montreal	Maroons	W	3–2
17	Boston	Montreal Maroons	W	6–2
19	Toronto	Maple Leafs	L	3–0
21	Montreal	Canadiens	L	5–2
24	Boston	Montreal Canadiens	W	3–2
26	Boston	Toronto	W	4–2
31	Boston	Chicago	L	5–1

February 1933

2	Boston	Detroit	T	1–1
4	Ottawa	Senators	L	3–2
7	Boston	New York Rangers	W	2–1
9	Boston	Montreal Maroons	W	1–0
11	Montreal	Maroons	L	1–0
14	Boston	Toronto	W	4–2
16	Chicago	Blackhawks	L	2–1
19	Detroit	Red Wings	L	2–1
21	Boston	Montreal Canadiens	W	10–0
28	Boston	Ottawa	T	0–0

March 1933

5	New York	Rangers	W	2–1
7	Boston	Detroit	W	4–1
9	Boston	New York Americans	W	4–2
11	Toronto	Maple Leafs	W	6–2
14	Boston	Chicago	W	3–2 (OT)
16	New York	Americans	T	1–1
18	Montreal	Canadiens	T	0–0
21	Boston	New York Rangers	W	3–2

1932-33 SCORING

	GP	SO	GAA					
Tiny Thompson	48	11	1.83	Art Chapman		3	6	9	19

	G	A	P	PIM					
Marty Barry	24	13	37	40	Alex Smith	5	4	9	30
Nels Stewart	18	18	36	62	George Owen	6	2	8	10
Eddie Shore	8	27	35	102	Frank Jerwa	3	4	7	23
Dit Clapper	14	14	28	42	Vic Ripley	2	5	7	21
John Beattie	8	12	20	12	Percy Galbraith	1	2	3	28
Joe Lamb	11	8	19	68	Billy Burch	3	1	4	4
Harry Oliver	11	7	18	10	Lionel Hitchman	0	1	1	34
Obs Heximer	7	5	12	12	Earl Roche	0	0	0	0
					Tommy Filmore	0	0	0	0
					Eddie Jerimiah	0	0	0	0

1932-33 PLAYOFF RESULTS

March 1933

	AT	VERSUS	W-L-T	SCR
25	Boston	Toronto	W	2–1 (OT)
28	Boston	Toronto	L	1–0 (OT)
30	Toronto	Maple Leafs	W	2–1 (OT)

April 1933

| 1 | Toronto | Maple Leafs | L | 5–3 |
| 3 | Toronto | Maple Leafs | L | 1–0 (OT) |

1932-33 PLAYOFFS

vs. Toronto Maple Leafs	2 wins – 3 losses
at Toronto	1 win – 2 losses
at Boston	1 win – 1 loss

1932-33 PLAYOFF SCORING

	GP	SO	GAA						
Tiny Thompson	5	0	1.80	Lionel Hitchman	1	0	1	1	
				Eddie Shore	0	1	1	1	
	G	A	P	PIM	Joe Lamb	0	1	1	6
Marty Barry	2	2	4	6	George Owen	0	0	0	6
Nels Stewart	2	0	2	4	Obs Heximer	0	0	0	2
Dit Clapper	1	1	2	2	John Beattie	0	0	0	2
Alex Smith	0	2	2	6	Art Chapman	0	0	0	2
Vic Ripley	1	0	1	0	Percy Galbraith	0	0	0	0
					Harry Oliver	0	0	0	0

1933–1934
(10th year)

TEAM OWNER:	Charles Adams	PLAYOFFS:	Out of playoffs
PRESIDENT & GOVERNOR:	Charles Adams	STANLEY CUP WINNER:	Chicago Blackhawks
GOVERNOR:	Robert Duncan	ALL-STARS:	Eddie Shore (2nd team)
GM:	Art Ross	TROPHY WINNERS:	None
COACH:	Art Ross		

UNIFORMS

- Use same uniform both home and away. Jersey is white trimmed in brown and yellow. Logo on front is a block letter "B" on brown outlined in yellow. Pants are brown. Socks are alternating stripes of white, brown, and yellow.

POTPOURRI

- Eddie Shore holds out for a $7,500.00 contract and misses the first game of the season.
- December 12 game at Boston Garden against Toronto is marred by fisticuffs and the severe injury to Ace Bailey of the Leafs, who suffered a fractured skull when he is hit by a vicious check from Eddie Shore. Shore is suspended for 16 games because of the incident.
- Eddie Shore and Nels Stewart represent the Bruins at the Ace Bailey All-Star game benefit.
- Entire proceeds of the December 19 game between the Bruins and Maroons are donated to the Ace Bailey fund. An All-Star game to benefit Ace Bailey is held in Toronto on February 14, 1934.
- In a March 6 game at Boston, Ace Bailey ceremoniously faces off the opening draw.
- In a January 4 game against Ottawa, all the Boston players wear leather helmets.
- Only 1500 fans attend game at Boston on February 20 due to a snowstorm.
- The salary limit for the 1933–1934 season is set at $65,000.
- Detroit Falcons change name to Red Wings.
- After the February 22 game against Ottawa, Lionel Hitchman retires with his #3 being retired.
- Boston finishes in last place in the American Division.

TRANSACTIONS

- Babe Siebert is obtained from the Rangers for Vic Ripley and Roy Burmeister.
- Art Chapman is traded to Ottawa.
- Obtain George Patterson from the Americans.
- Bob Gracie is bought from Toronto.
- Archie Wilcox signed as a free agent

1933-34 STANDINGS

Canadian Division	W	L	T	P	GF	GA
Toronto	26	13	9	61	174	119
Montreal Canadiens	22	20	6	50	99	101
Montreal Maroons	19	18	11	49	117	122
New York Americans	15	23	10	40	104	132
Ottawa	13	29	6	32	115	143
American Division						
Detroit	24	14	10	58	113	98
Chicago	20	17	11	51	88	83
New York Rangers	21	19	8	50	120	113
Boston	18	25	5	41	111	130

1933-34 RESULTS

November 1933

	AT	VERSUS	W-L-T	SCR
9	Toronto	Maple Leafs	L	6–1
11	Montreal	Maroons	L	3–2
14	Boston	Detroit	L	4–2
18	Montreal	Canadiens	W	2–1
21	Boston	Chicago	W	2–0
23	Detroit	Red Wings	W	6–0
26	Chicago	Blackhawks	L	1–0
28	Boston	Ottawa	W	2–1
30	Ottawa	Senators	L	2–1

December 1933

2	Boston	New York Rangers	L	3–0
5	Boston	Montreal Canadiens	W	5–2
9	Boston	New York Americans	W	4–2
12	Boston	Toronto	L	4–1
14	New York	Americans	W	5–4
17	New York	Rangers	T	2–2
19	Boston	Montreal Maroons	W	1–0 (OT)
23	Boston	Chicago	L	3–1
26	Boston	Toronto	T	2–2
28	Montreal	Canadiens	W	4–3

January 1934

2	Boston	Montreal Maroons	L	1–0
4	Ottawa	Senators	L	9–2
6	Montreal	Maroons	L	4–2
9	Boston	New York Americans	L	2–1
11	Chicago	Blackhawks	T	0–0
14	Detroit	Red Wings	L	2–0
16	Boston	Montreal Canadiens	W	4–0
18	Toronto	Maple Leafs	L	6–2
21	New York	Americans	L	4–2
23	Boston	Detroit	L	3–1

Billy Burch models 1933–34 uniform.

| 28 | New York | Rangers | L | 4–2 |
| 30 | Boston | New York Rangers | W | 2–1 |

February 1934

1	Detroit	Red Wings	T	2–2
4	Chicago	Blackhawks	W	2–1 (OT)
6	Boston	New York Americans	L	1–0
10	Montreal	Maroons	L	1–0
13	Boston	New York Rangers	L	6–4
15	Boston	Montreal Maroons	T	4–4
17	Toronto	Maple Leafs	L	6–4
20	Boston	Detroit	L	4–1

22	Boston	Ottawa	L	3–1 (OT)
24	Ottawa	Senators	L	9–4
27	Boston	Chicago	W	3–1

March 1934

1	Boston	Montreal Canadiens	W	3–1
3	Montreal	Canadiens	L	2–1
6	Boston	Toronto	W	7–2
13	Boston	Ottawa	W	2–1
15	New York	Rangers	W	3–2
18	New York	Americans	W	9–5

1933-34 SCORING

	GP	SO	GAA
Tiny Thompson	48	5	2.70

	G	A	P	PIM
Marty Barry	27	12	39	12
Nels Stewart	22	17	39	68
Joe Lamb	10	15	25	47
Dit Clapper	10	12	22	6
John Beattie	9	13	22	26
Harry Oliver	5	9	14	6
Eddie Shore	2	10	12	57
Babe Siebert	5	6	11	18
Alex Smith	4	6	10	32
Bob Gracie	2	6	8	16
Art Chapman	3	2	5	6
James O'Neill	2	2	4	15
Don Smillie	2	2	4	4
Miles Lane	2	1	3	17
Bert McInenly	2	1	3	4
Vic Ripley	2	1	3	6
Percy Galbraith	1	2	3	5
Lloyd Gross	1	0	1	6
George Patterson	0	1	1	2
Archie Wilcox	0	1	1	2
Lionel Hitchman	0	1	1	4
Robert Davie	0	0	0	6
Joe Jerwa	0	0	0	2
Happy Harnott	0	0	0	2
Tommy Filmore	0	0	0	0
Johnny Sheppard	0	0	0	0

NO PLAYOFF SCORING

1934–1935
(11th year)

TEAM OWNER:	Charles Adams	STANLEY CUP WINNER:	Montreal Maroons
PRESIDENT:	Charles Adams	ALL-STARS:	Eddie Shore (1st team)
GM:	Art Ross		Tiny Thompson (2nd team)
COACH:	Frank Patrick		Dit Clapper (2nd team)
GOVERNORS:	Charles Adams, Art Ross, Robert Duncan, Frank Patrick	TROPHY WINNERS:	Prince of Wales — Boston Bruins
			Hart — Eddie Shore
PLAYOFFS:	*Semi-finals:* Lose to Toronto Maple Leafs 1 win – 3 losses		

UNIFORMS

- Use same uniform both home and away. Jersey is white trimmed in brown and yellow. Logo on front is a block letter "B" on brown outlined in yellow. Pants are brown. Socks are alternating stripes of white, brown, and yellow.

POTPOURRI

- Finish in first place in the American Division.
- Eddie Shore wins the Hart Trophy for the second time.
- Nels Stewart is suspended for one game after a stick-swinging fight with Lloyd Klein of the New York Americans.
- Lose NHL championship to Toronto in the first round of the Stanley Cup playoffs and are eliminated from the playoffs.
- Frank Patrick takes over as coach of the Bruins from Art Ross.
- Team salaries are not to exceed $62,500. Individual player salary is limited to a maximum of $7,000.
- Ottawa Senators are moved to St. Louis and renamed the Eagles.
- The penalty shot is introduced into NHL games.

TRANSACTIONS

- Alex Smith is released to the Americans.
- Obtain Jack Portland from Canadiens.
- Buy Charlie Sands from Toronto.

- Acquire Max Kaminsky from St. Louis for Joe Lamb, who had been on loan to the Canadiens.
- Acquire Paul Haynes from Montreal Maroons, and Johnny Gagnon from the Canadiens.
- Sell Johnny Gagnon back to Canadiens.

1934-35 STANDINGS

Canadian Division	W	L	T	P	GF	GA
Toronto	30	14	4	64	157	111
Montreal Maroons	24	19	5	53	123	92
Montreal Canadiens	19	23	6	44	110	145
New York Americans	12	27	9	33	100	142
St. Louis	11	31	6	28	86	144
American Division						
Boston	26	16	6	58	129	112
Chicago	26	17	5	57	118	88
New York Rangers	22	20	6	50	137	139
Detroit	19	22	7	45	127	114

1934-35 RESULTS

November 1934

	AT	VERSUS	W-L-T	SCR
8	Toronto	Maple Leafs	L	5–3
11	Detroit	Red Wings	W	4–2
17	Boston	St. Louis	W	1–0
20	Boston	Detroit	W	1–0
24	St. Louis	Eagles	W	4–1
25	Chicago	Blackhawks	L	4–0
27	Boston	Chicago	L	3–2

December 1934

1	Montreal	Canadiens	W	2–0
4	Boston	Toronto	L	1–0
8	Boston	Montreal Canadiens	W	4–0
11	Boston	New York Americans	W	4–3
13	New York	Americans	L	4–3 (OT)
16	New York	Rangers	L	2–1
18	Boston	New York Rangers	W	5–3
22	Boston	Detroit	W	4–3
25	Boston	Montreal Maroons	L	5–3
27	Montreal	Maroons	L	1–0
30	New York	Rangers	T	0–0

January 1935

1	Boston	New York Rangers	W	5–2
3	Montreal	Canadiens	W	2–1
5	Boston	Chicago	L	6–0
8	Boston	Toronto	W	3–1
10	St. Louis	Eagles	W	2–1
13	Chicago	Blackhawks	T	1–1
15	Boston	St. Louis	W	5–3
19	Boston	Montreal Canadiens	L	4–1
22	Boston	Montreal Maroons	W	4–3
26	Montreal	Canadiens	L	3–2
27	Detroit	Red Wings	T	2–2
29	Boston	New York Americans	W	4–0

February 1935

2	Montreal	Maroons	L	3–1
5	Boston	Detroit	W	4–2
7	Toronto	Maple Leafs	T	4–4
10	New York	Americans	L	7–5
12	Boston	Toronto	W	6–5 (OT)
16	St. Louis	Eagles	L	3–0
17	Chicago	Blackhawks	W	2–1
19	Boston	Montreal Canadiens	W	3–1
24	New York	Rangers	T	0–0
26	Boston	St. Louis	W	5–0

March 1935

2	Montreal	Maroons	T	2–2
5	Boston	New York Rangers	W	3–1
9	Toronto	Maple Leafs	W	7–4
10	Detroit	Red Wings	W	2–1 (OT)
12	Boston	New York Americans	W	4–1
14	New York	Americans	W	5–4
16	Boston	Chicago	L	5–2
19	Boston	Montreal Maroons	L	4–2

1934-35 SCORING

	GP	SO	GAA						
Tiny Thompson	48	8	2.33	Jack Shill	4	4	8	22
				Paul Haynes	4	3	7	8
				Bert McInenly	2	1	3	24
	G	A	P	PIM	Johnny Gagnon	1	1	2	9
Marty Barry	20	20	40	33	Hap Emms	1	1	2	8
Nels Stewart	21	18	39	45	Jerry Shannon	1	1	2	4
Dit Clapper	21	16	37	21	Jack Portland	1	1	2	2
Eddie Shore	7	26	33	32	Jean Pusie	1	0	1	0
Charlie Sands	15	12	27	0	Art Giroux	1	0	1	0
Max Kaminsky	12	15	27	4	Robert Davie	0	1	1	17
John Beattie	9	18	27	27	Gordon Savage	0	0	0	2
Babe Siebert	6	18	24	80	Joe Jerwa	0	0	0	0
James O'Neill	2	11	13	35	Alex Motter	0	0	0	0

1934-35 PLAYOFF RESULTS

March 1935

	AT	VERSUS	W-L-T	SCR
23	Boston	Toronto	W	1–0 (OT)
26	Boston	Toronto	L	2–0
28	Toronto	Maple Leafs	L	3–0
30	Toronto	Maple Leafs	L	2–1 (OT)

1934-35 PLAYOFFS

vs. Toronto Maple Leafs	1 win – 3 losses
at Toronto	0 wins – 2 losses
at Boston	1 win – 1 loss

1934-35 PLAYOFF SCORING

	GP	SO	GAA						
Tiny Thompson	4	1	1.75	Marty Barry	0	0	0	2
				Bert McInenly	0	0	0	2
				Jerry Shannon	0	0	0	2
	G	A	P	PIM	Charlie Sands	0	0	0	0
Dit Clapper	1	0	1	0	Bob Davie	0	0	0	0
John Beattie	1	0	1	2	Max Kaminsky	0	0	0	0
Eddie Shore	0	1	1	2	Alex Motter	0	0	0	0
Nels Stewart	0	1	1	0	Jack Shill	0	0	0	0
Babe Siebert	0	0	0	6	Paul Haynes	0	0	0	0
James O'Neill	0	0	0	9					

1935–1936
(12th year)

TEAM OWNER:	Charles Adams
PRESIDENT:	Charles Adams
GM:	Art Ross
GOVERNORS:	Charles Adams and Art Ross
COACH:	Frank Patrick
PLAYOFFS:	*Quarter finals:*
	Lose to Toronto Maple Leafs
	1 win – 1 loss
	Lose on total goals (8–6)

STANLEY CUP WINNER:	Detroit Red Wings
ALL-STARS:	Tiny Thompson (1st team)
	Eddie Shore (1st team)
	Babe Siebert (1st team)
TROPHY WINNERS:	Hart — Eddie Shore
	Dufresne — Tiny Thompson

UNIFORMS

- White jersey with brown shoulders. Brown numbers on front and back of jersey trimmed in gold. Large block brown "B" on each arm trimmed in yellow. Brown, yellow brown stripes on arm and base of jersey. Brown pants with yellow stripes along side of pants. Socks have vertical stripes of white, brown, and yellow.

POTPOURRI

- Eddie Shore wins the Hart Trophy for the third time.
- Tiny Thompson the first winner of the Dufresne Trophy for the best Bruins' player of the year.
- Lose first round of playoffs to Toronto in two games.
- Bruins finish in second place, 6 points behind Detroit in the American Division.
- St. Louis Eagles cease operations.
- At the end of the 1935–36 season, it is agreed that the Montreal Canadiens would have first call on the services of players of French-Canadian origin.
- Tiny Thompson becomes the first goaltender to record an assist in a March 17 game against Toronto.

TRANSACTIONS

- Purchase Bill Cowley and Ted Graham from the defunct St. Louis club.
- Nels Stewart and Joe Jerwa are sent to the Americans.
- Roger Jenkins bought from Canadiens.
- Flash Hollett purchased from Toronto.
- Max Kaminsky purchased from St. Louis.
- Woody Dumart and Ray Getliffe join the Bruins.
- Marty Barry traded to Detroit for Cooney Weiland.

1935-36 STANDINGS

Canadian Division	W	L	T	P	GF	GA
Montreal Maroons	22	16	10	54	114	106
Toronto	23	19	6	52	126	106
New York Americans	16	25	7	39	109	122
Montreal Canadiens	11	26	11	33	82	123
American Division						
Detroit	24	16	8	56	124	103
Boston	22	20	6	50	92	83
Chicago	21	19	8	50	93	92
New York Rangers	19	17	12	50	91	96

1935-36 RESULTS

November 1935

	AT	VERSUS	W-L-T	SCR
16	Montreal	Maroons	L	1–0
19	Boston	New York Americans	W	1–0
24	New York	Rangers	L	1–0
26	Boston	Toronto	L	2–1
30	New York	Americans	L	2–1

December 1935

1	Boston	New York Rangers	W	2–0
3	Boston	Chicago	L	3–1
5	Detroit	Red Wings	L	2–1
9	Chicago	Blackhawks	L	1–0
10	Boston	Montreal Maroons	W	2–0
12	Montreal	Canadiens	T	1–1
15	Boston	Montreal Canadiens	W	2–1
17	Boston	Detroit	W	4–1
19	Toronto	Maple Leafs	T	0–0
22	New York	Rangers	L	3–1
25	Boston	New York Rangers	L	3–2
28	Montreal	Maroons	W	6–3
29	Detroit	Red Wings	W	4–3 (OT)

January 1936

1	Boston	Montreal Canadiens	L	2–0
4	Montreal	Canadiens	T	1–1
7	Boston	Chicago	W	2–0
12	New York	Rangers	W	6–3
14	Boston	Toronto	W	4–1

18	Toronto	Maple Leafs	L	5–2
19	Chicago	Blackhawks	L	2–1
21	Boston	Montreal Maroons	W	1–0
26	New York	Americans	W	2–1
28	Boston	Detroit	W	2–0

February 1936

4	Boston	Toronto	L	3–0
6	Montreal	Canadiens	W	4–3
9	New York	Rangers	L	2–0
11	Boston	Boston	W	7–1
13	Detroit	Detroit	L	1–0
16	Chicago	Chicago	L	4–2
18	Boston	Detroit	L	2–1
23	Boston	New York Rangers	L	4–3
25	Boston	New York Americans	W	3–2
27	Montreal	Maroons	W	2–1

March 1936

1	New York	Americans	L	5–2
3	Boston	Montreal Maroons	T	3–3
5	Chicago	Blackhawks	T	2–2
8	Detroit	Red Wings	W	5–2
10	Boston	Detroit	W	1–0
15	Boston	Chicago	W	1–0
17	Boston	Montreal Canadiens	W	1–0
19	Toronto	Maple Leafs	T	2–2
22	Boston	New York Rangers	L	3–1

1935-36 SCORING

	GP	SO	GAA	
Tiny Thompson	48	10	1.73	
			(2 assists)	

	G	A	P	PIM
John Beattie	14	18	32	27
Cooney Weiland	14	13	27	15
Dit Clapper	12	13	25	14
Babe Siebert	12	9	21	66
Bill Cowley	11	10	21	17
Eddie Shore	3	15	18	61
James O'Neill	2	11	13	49
Paul Runge	8	2	10	14
Charlie Sands	6	4	10	8
Roger Jenkins	2	6	8	51
Ted Graham	4	1	5	37

Lorne Duguid	1	4	5	2
Alex Motter	1	4	5	4
Max Kaminsky	1	2	3	20
Bill Hollett	1	2	3	2
Jerry Shannon	0	1	1	6
Robert Davie	0	0	0	2
Ray Getliffe	0	0	0	2
Jack Riley	0	0	0	0
Phil Bessler	0	0	0	0
Red Jackson	0	0	0	0
Robert Blake	0	0	0	0
Eddie Finnigan	0	0	0	0
Bert McInenly	0	0	0	0
Jack Portland	0	0	0	0
Woody Dumart	0	0	0	0
Baines	0	0	0	0

1935-36 PLAYOFF RESULTS

March 1936

	AT	VERSUS	W-L-T	SCR
24	Boston	Toronto	W	3–0
26	Toronto	Maple Leafs	L	8–3

1935-36 PLAYOFFS

vs. Toronto Maple Leafs	1 win – 1 loss
at Toronto	0 wins – 1 loss
at Boston	1 win – 0 losses

Toronto wins series by goals scored, 8–6.

1935-36 PLAYOFF SCORING

	GP	SO	GAA					
Tiny Thompson	2	1	4.00	Dit Clapper	0	1	1	0
				Babe Siebert	0	1	1	0
				Roger Jenkins	0	1	1	2
	G	A	P	PIM	Paul Runge	0	0	0	2
Bill Cowley	2	1	3	2	John Beattie	0	0	0	2
Eddie Shore	1	1	2	12	Ted Graham	0	0	0	0
James O'Neill	1	1	2	4	Charlie Sands	0	0	0	0
Lorne Duguid	1	0	1	2	Alex Motter	0	0	0	0
Cooney Weiland	1	0	1	2	Ray Getliffe	0	0	0	0

1936–1937
(13th year)

TEAM OWNER:	The Adams Family	PLAYOFFS:	*Quarter finals:*
PRESIDENT:	Weston Adams Sr.		Lose to Montreal Maroons
GM:	Art Ross		1 win – 3 losses
GOVERNOR:	Art Ross	STANLEY CUP WINNER:	Detroit Red Wings
COACH:	Art Ross	ALL-STARS:	None
		TROPHY WINNERS:	Dufresne — Eddie Shore

UNIFORMS

- White jersey with brown shoulders. Brown numbers on front and back of jersey trimmed in yellow. Large block brown "B" on each arm trimmed in yellow. Brown, yellow, brown stripes on arm and base of jersey. Brown pants with yellow stripes along side of pants. Socks have vertical stripes of white, brown, and gold.

POTPOURRI

- Art Ross returns as coach of the Bruins.
- Lose the opening round of the playoffs to the Montreal Maroons, 2 games to 1.
- In the opening game in which Boston lost 4–1, Dit Clapper receives a major penalty for punching both referees Dave Trottier and Clarence Campbell.
- Eddie Shore is lost for the season after suffering a cracked vertebra.
- In a January 19 game, Conn Smythe coaches the Leafs in a tuxedo and top hat as a publicity stunt.

- Finish in second place in the American Division, 6 points behind Detroit.
- Russ Blinco of the Montreal Maroons becomes the first player in hockey history to wear eye glasses in a game.

TRANSACTIONS
- Bun Cook purchased from the Rangers.
- Hooley Smith purchased from the Montreal Maroons in exchange for Chuck Shannon.
- Babe Siebert traded to the Canadiens for Leroy Goldsworthy.
- Milt Schmidt makes his first appearance in a Boston uniform.
- Nels Stewart sold to the Americans.
- Ted Graham traded to the Americans for Walter Kalbfleisch.
- Bruins trade Joe Jerwa to the Americans for Allan Shields.
- Bruins sign Sylvio Mantha.
- Bobby Bauer makes his first appearance in a Boston uniform in the last game of the regular season.

1936-37 STANDINGS

Canadian Division	W	L	T	P	GF	GA
Montreal Canadiens	24	18	6	54	115	111
Montreal Maroons	22	17	9	53	126	110
Toronto	22	21	5	49	119	115
New York Americans	15	29	4	34	122	161
American Division						
Detroit	25	14	9	59	128	102
Boston	23	18	7	53	120	110
New York Rangers	19	20	9	47	117	106
Chicago	14	27	7	35	99	131

1936-37 RESULTS

November 1936

	AT	VERSUS	W-L-T	SCR
7	Montreal	Canadiens	L	2–0
15	Boston	Montreal Canadiens	W	2–1
17	Boston	New York Rangers	L	6–1
21	Toronto	Maple Leafs	W	4–3
22	Chicago	Blackhawks	W	2–1
24	Boston	Chicago	T	1–1
26	Boston	Montreal Maroons	W	3–2
28	New York	Rangers	T	2–2

December 1936

5	Montreal	Canadiens	L	4–3
8	Boston	Detroit	L	4–3
13	New York	Americans	W	4–3
15	Boston	New York Americans	W	5–3 (OT)
17	Montreal	Maroons	W	5–0
20	Detroit	Red Wings	L	4–3
22	Boston	Toronto	L	4–2
26	Toronto	Maple Leafs	W	2–1
29	Boston	Montreal Maroons	W	3–0

31	New York	Rangers	T	2–2

January 1937

3	Boston	New York Rangers	W	3–2
5	Boston	Detroit	L	3–2
7	Chicago	Blackhawks	W	2–0
10	Detroit	Red Wings	L	4–2
12	Boston	Chicago	L	4–2
17	New York	Americans	W	3–0
19	Boston	Toronto	L	6–2
21	Montreal	Maroons	W	2–1
24	Boston	New York Americans	T	6–6
26	Boston	New York Rangers	L	3–0
28	New York	Rangers	T	1–1
31	Boston	Detroit	L	2–1

February 1937

2	Boston	Montreal Canadiens	L	1–0
4	Montreal	Canadiens	W	6–2
7	Detroit	Red Wings	L	8–0
9	Boston	Montreal Maroons	L	2–0

13	Toronto	Maple Leafs	W	3–0
14	Chicago	Blackhawks	W	2–1
16	Boston	New York Rangers	W	3–2
18	Montreal	Maroons	W	2–1
21	Boston	Montreal Canadiens	T	2–2
23	Boston	New York Americans	W	5–2
25	New York	Americans	L	3–1

March 1937

2	Boston	Chicago	L	4–2
7	New York	Rangers	W	1–0
9	Boston	Detroit	W	6–1
11	Chicago	Blackhawks	W	6–2
14	Detroit	Red Wings	L	2–1
16	Boston	Toronto	T	1–1
21	Boston	Chicago	W	6–1

1936-37 SCORING

	GP	SO	GAA
Tiny Thompson	48	6	2.29

	G	A	P	PIM
Bill Cowley	13	22	35	4
Ray Getliffe	16	15	31	28
Dit Clapper	17	8	25	25
Charlie Sands	18	5	23	6
Reginald Smith	8	10	18	36
John Beattie	8	7	15	10
Cooney Weiland	6	9	15	6
Leroy Goldsworthy	8	6	14	8
Bill Hollett	3	7	10	22
Milt Schmidt	2	8	10	15
Fred Cook	4	5	9	8
Woody Dumart	4	4	8	2
Joe Jerwa	3	5	8	30
Jack Portland	2	4	6	58
Ted Graham	4	1	5	37
Eddie Shore	3	1	4	12
Nels Stewart	2	2	4	6
Allan Shields	0	4	4	15
James O'Neill	0	2	2	6
Bobby Bauer	1	0	1	0
Lorne Duguid	1	0	1	2
Joe Jerwa	0	1	1	44
Sylvio Mantha	0	0	0	2
Sammy McManus	0	0	0	0
Walter Kalbfleisch	0	0	0	0

1936-37 PLAYOFF RESULTS

March 1937

	AT	VERSUS	W-L-T	SCR
23	Montreal	Maroons	L	4–1
25	Boston	Montreal Maroons	W	4–0
28	Boston	Montreal Maroons	L	4–1

1936-37 PLAYOFFS

vs. Montreal Maroons	1 win – 2 losses
at Montreal	0 wins – 1 loss
at Boston	1 win – 1 loss

1936-37 PLAYOFF SCORING

	GP	SO	GAA
Tiny Thompson	3	1	2.67

	G	A	P	PIM
Ray Getliffe	2	1	3	2
Charlie Sands	1	2	3	0
Bill Cowley	0	3	3	0
Dit Clapper	2	0	2	5
John Beattie	1	0	1	0
Jack Portland	0	0	0	4
Allan Shields	0	0	0	2
Bill Hollett	0	0	0	2
Reginald Smith	0	0	0	0
Cooney Weiland	0	0	0	0
Leroy Goldsworthy	0	0	0	0
Milt Schmidt	0	0	0	0
Woody Dumart	0	0	0	0
Bobby Bauer	0	0	0	0

1937–1938
(14th year)

TEAM OWNER:	The Adams Family	ALL-STARS:	Tiny Thompson (1st team)
PRESIDENT:	Weston Adams		Eddie Shore (1st team)
GM & OWNER:	Art Ross		Bill Cowley (1st team)
COACH:	Art Ross		Art Ross, Coach (2nd team)
PLAYOFFS:	*Semi-finals:*	TROPHY WINNERS:	Prince of Wales
	Lose to Toronto Maple Leafs		— Boston Bruins
	0 wins – 3 losses		Hart — Eddie Shore
STANLEY CUP WINNER:	Chicago Blackhawks		Vezina — Tiny Thompson
			Dufresne — Eddie Shore

UNIFORMS

- White jersey with large black numbers trimmed in gold on front and back of jersey. Gold band trimmed in black on shoulders. Large black trimmed in gold block "B" on arms. Gold and black bands below the "B." Black pants with gold stripes along sides. Alternating gold, black, and white strips on stockings.

POTPOURRI

- Tiny Thompson wins the Vezina Trophy.
- Bruins finish on top of the American Division.
- Eddie Shore wins the Hart Trophy.
- Milt Schmidt breaks his jaw in a game on December 28 against the Rangers and is lost for a month.
- Bruins lose to Toronto, 3 games to 0, in the opening round of the Stanley Cup playoffs.
- The following Bruins participated in the Howie Morenz Memorial Game played in Montreal on November 2: Eddie Shore, Dit Clapper, and Tiny Thompson.
- The icing rule is added to the NHL rule book.
- The Kraut Line of Milt Schmidt, Bobby Bauer, and Woody Dumart makes its debut.
- Tiny Thompson's shutout bid on December 21 against Chicago is spoiled by Tiny's brother, Paul.

TRANSACTIONS

- Art Jackson purchased from Toronto.

1937-38 STANDINGS

Canadian Division	W	L	T	P	GF	GA
Toronto	24	15	9	57	151	127
New York Americans	19	18	11	49	110	111
Montreal Canadiens	18	17	13	49	123	128
Montreal Maroons	12	30	6	30	101	149
American Division						
Boston	30	11	7	67	142	89
New York Rangers	27	15	6	60	149	96
Chicago	14	25	9	37	97	139
Detroit	12	25	11	35	99	133

1937-38 RESULTS

November 1937

	AT	VERSUS	W-L-T	SCR
6	Montreal	Maroons	W	4–2
14	Boston	New York Rangers	W	3–2
16	Boston	Montreal Maroons	W	1–0
18	New York	Americans	W	2–1
20	Toronto	Maple Leafs	W	3–2
21	Chicago	Blackhawks	W	2–1
23	Boston	Montreal Canadiens	T	1–1
28	Boston	New York Americans	T	3–3

December 1937

2	Montreal	Canadiens	L	2–0
5	New York	Rangers	L	4–0
7	Boston	Detroit	L	3–2
14	Boston	Toronto	W	3–1
18	Montreal	Maroons	W	3–1
19	Detroit	Red Wings	W	4–2
21	Boston	Chicago	W	2–1
25	New York	Americans	W	1–0
26	Boston	New York Americans	L	3–1
28	Boston	New York Rangers	W	3–2
31	New York	Rangers	L	5–3

January 1938

2	Detroit	Red Wings	W	4–1
4	Boston	Toronto	W	6–3
8	Montreal	Canadiens	L	6–2
11	Boston	Detroit	W	6–2
16	Boston	Montreal Canadiens	W	1–0
18	Boston	Chicago	W	5–1
22	Toronto	Maple Leafs	W	9–1
23	Chicago	Blackhawks	L	3–2
25	Boston	New York Rangers	L	3–2
29	Montreal	Maroons	T	2–2
30	Detroit	Red Wings	T	2–2

February 1938

1	Boston	Detroit	W	2–0
5	Toronto	Maple Leafs	L	3–1
6	Chicago	Blackhawks	W	7–2
8	Boston	Chicago	W	3–1
13	Boston	Montreal Canadiens	W	1–0 (OT)
15	Boston	Montreal Maroons	W	5–2
17	New York	Rangers	W	3–2 (OT)
20	Boston	New York Rangers	W	3–2
22	Boston	Toronto	W	2–0
24	Montreal	Canadiens	T	1–1

March 1938

1	Boston	Detroit	W	6–1
3	Chicago	Blackhawks	L	3–2
5	Detroit	Red Wings	L	4–3
8	Boston	New York Americans	W	7–0
10	New York	Americans	T	2–2
13	New York	Rangers	W	2–1
15	Boston	Montreal Maroons	T	4–4
20	Boston	Chicago	W	6–1

1937-38 SCORING

	GP	SO	GAA
Tiny Thompson	48	7	1.85

	G	A	P	PIM
Bill Cowley	17	22	39	8
Bobby Bauer	20	14	34	9
Charlie Sands	17	12	29	12
Woody Dumart	13	14	27	6
Milt Schmidt	13	14	27	15
Ray Getliffe	11	13	24	16
Cooney Weiland	11	12	23	16
Leroy Goldsworthy	9	10	19	14
Gordon Pettinger	7	10	17	10
Eddie Shore	3	14	17	42
Dit Clapper	6	9	15	24
Bill Hollett	4	10	14	54
Art Jackson	9	3	12	24
Jack Portland	0	5	5	26
Mel Hill	2	0	2	2
Robert Hamill	0	1	1	2
Jack Crawford	0	0	0	0

1937-38 PLAYOFF RESULTS

March 1938

	AT	VERSUS	W-L-T	SCR
24	Toronto	Maple Leafs	L	1–0 (OT)
26	Toronto	Maple leafs	L	2–1
29	Boston	Toronto	L	3–2

1937-38 PLAYOFFS

vs. Toronto Maple Leafs	0 wins – 3 losses
at Toronto	0 wins – 2 losses
at Boston	0 wins – 1 loss

1937-38 PLAYOFF SCORING

	GP	SO	GAA					
Tiny Thompson	3	0	2.00	Dit Clapper	0	0	0	12
				Leroy Goldsworthy	0	0	0	2
	G	A	P	PIM	Milt Schmidt	0	0	0	0

	G	A	P	PIM					
Bill Cowley	2	0	2	0	Woody Dumart	0	0	0	0
Charlie Sands	1	1	2	0	Bobby Bauer	0	0	0	0
Ray Getliffe	0	1	1	2	Cooney Weiland	0	0	0	0
Bill Hollett	0	1	1	0	Gordon Pettinger	0	0	0	0
Eddie Shore	0	1	1	6	Art Jackson	0	0	0	0
Jack Portland	0	0	0	4	Mel Hill	0	0	0	0

1938–1939
(15th year)

TEAM OWNER:	Adams Family	STANLEY CUP WINNER:	Boston Bruins
PRESIDENT:	Weston Adams Sr.	ALL-STARS:	Frank Brimsek (1st team)
GM:	Art Ross		Eddie Shore (1st team)
GOVERNORS:	Weston Adams & Art Ross		Dit Clapper (1st team)
COACH:	Art Ross		Art Ross, Coach (1st team)
PLAYOFFS:	*Semi-finals:*		Bobby Bauer (2nd team)
	Defeat New York Rangers	TROPHY WINNERS:	Prince of Wales
	4 wins – 3 losses		— Boston Bruins
	Stanley Cup finals:		Vezina — Frank Brimsek
	Defeat Toronto Maple Leafs		Calder — Frank Brimsek
	4 wins – 1 loss		Dufresne — Eddie Shore

UNIFORMS

- White jersey with large black numbers trimmed in gold on front and back of jersey. Gold band trimmed in black on shoulders. Large black trimmed in gold block "B" on arms. Gold and black bands below the "B." Black pants with gold stripes along sides. Alternating gold, black, and white stripes on stockings.

POTPOURRI

- Bruins win second Stanley Cup in their history defeating Toronto, 4 games to 1.
- Roy Conacher scores cup-winning goal.
- Bruins finish on top of the NHL's new single division.
- Finishing atop the league standings allows the Bruins to win their second successive Prince of Wales Trophy.

Ten members of the 1938–39 Bruins posing in a Boston Garden stairwell.
Front, sitting, left to right: Milt Schmidt, Bobby Bauer, Woody Dumart.
Back, standing, left to right: Jack Crawford, Flash Hollett, Art Jackson,
Frank Brimsek, Roy Conacher, Jack Shewchuck, Dit Clapper.

- Frankie Brimsek wins the Calder and Vezina Trophies.
- Mel "Sudden Death" Hill scores 3 overtime goals in the opening round of the playoffs against the New York Rangers.
- The Bruins win the Stanley Cup for the first time at Boston Garden.
- The Bruins sell long-time goaltender, Tiny Thompson.
- With the league now operating as one division, the first-place finisher would receive the Prince of Wales Trophy, and the second-place finisher would receive the O'Brien Trophy.
- The Montreal Maroons suspended operations.
- Because of the great difficulty the Bruins are having signing Eddie Shore, NHL President Frank Calder is brought in to negotiate with Shore. Two weeks after the season started, Shore signed for $7,000, the maximum allowed by the league. Weston Adams and Art Ross are engaged in the final negotiations.
- During the May 13 league meetings, Art Ross, an innovator, submitted for consideration a hockey stick with a metal handle and a replaceable wooden blade.
- The NHL requires the use of the green light showing the expiration of each period.

TRANSACTIONS

- Leroy Goldsworthy sold to the Americans.
- Tiny Thompson is sold to Detroit for $15,000 on November 26, and replaced by Frankie Brimsek.
- Roy Conacher, Jack Shewchuck, Terry Reardon, and Jack Crawford are added to the lineup.

1938-39 STANDINGS

	W	L	T	P	GF	GA
Boston	36	10	2	74	156	76
New York Rangers	26	16	6	58	149	105
Toronto	19	20	9	47	114	107
New York Americans	17	21	10	44	119	157
Detroit	18	24	6	42	107	128
Montreal Canadiens	15	24	9	39	115	146
Chicago	12	28	8	32	91	132

1938-39 RESULTS

November 1938

	AT	VERSUS	W-L-T	SCR
3	Toronto	Maple Leafs	W	3–2
6	Detroit	Red Wings	W	4–1
13	New York	Americans	L	2–1
15	Boston	Toronto	T	1–1
20	Boston	Detroit	W	4–1
22	Boston	New York Rangers	W	4–2
27	Boston	New York Americans	W	8–2

December 1938

1	Montreal	Canadiens	L	2–0
4	Chicago	Blackhawks	W	5–0
6	Boston	Chicago	W	2–0
11	New York	Rangers	W	3–0
13	Boston	Montreal	W	3–2
15	Montreal	Canadiens	W	1–0
18	Detroit	Red Wings	W	2–0
20	Boston	New York Americans	W	3–0
25	Boston	New York Rangers	L	1–0
27	Boston	Toronto	W	8–2
29	New York	Americans	L	4–2
31	New York	Rangers	L	2–1 (OT)

January 1939

1	Boston	Detroit	W	4–1
3	Boston	New York Americans	W	2–1
5	Chicago	Blackhawks	W	2–1
7	Toronto	Maple Leafs	L	2–0

January 1939 (continued)

10	Boston	Chicago	W	3–1
17	Boston	Toronto	W	2–1
19	Montreal	Canadiens	L	1–0
22	Detroit	Red Wings	W	5–0
24	Boston	Montreal	W	6–4
29	New York	Americans	W	3–2
31	Boston	New York Americans	T	2–2

February 1939

2	Toronto	Maple Leafs	W	2–1
5	Chicago	Blackhawks	W	3–0
7	Boston	Toronto	W	2–0
9	New York	Rangers	W	4–2
12	Boston	New York Rangers	L	4–2
14	Boston	Detroit	W	2–1
16	Montreal	Canadiens	W	5–1
19	Detroit	Red Wings	L	4–1
21	Boston	Chicago	W	8–2
25	Toronto	Maple Leafs	L	1–0
26	Chicago	Blackhawks	W	5–1
28	Boston	Montreal	W	6–2

March 1939

5	Boston	New York Rangers	W	5–3 (OT)
7	Boston	Detroit	W	3–0
9	New York	Americans	W	9–6
12	New York	Rangers	W	4–2
14	Boston	Chicago	W	4–2
19	Boston	Montreal	W	7–5 (OT)

1938-39 SCORING

	GP	SO	GAA
Frank Brimsek	44	10	1.58
Tiny Thompson	4	0	1.60

	G	A	P	PIM
Bill Cowley	8	34	42	2
Roy Conacher	26	11	37	12
Milt Schmidt	15	17	32	13
Bobby Bauer	13	18	31	4
Woody Dumart	14	15	29	2
Bill Hollett	10	17	27	25
Dit Clapper	13	13	26	22
Gordon Pettinger	11	14	25	8
Ray Getliffe	10	12	22	11
Mel Hill	10	10	20	16
Eddie Shore	4	14	18	37
Cooney Weiland	7	9	16	9
Charlie Sands	7	5	12	10
Jack Crawford	4	8	12	12
Jack Portland	4	5	9	46
Robert Hamill	0	1	1	0
Jack Shewchuck	0	0	0	2
Pat McReavy	0	0	0	0
Harry Frost	0	0	0	0
Terry Reardon	0	0	0	0

This 1939 photo shows Frank Brimsek follwed by Eddie Shore leading the Bruins onto the Garden Ice. (Note that Brimsek's shoulder colors are solid black, and Shore's shoulder inserts are black and gold.)

1938-39 PLAYOFF RESULTS

March 1939					April 1939				
	AT	VERSUS	W-L-T	SCR	1	New York	Rangers	L	3–1
21	New York	Rangers	W	2–1 (OT)	2	Boston	New York Rangers	W	2–1 (OT)
23	Boston	New York Rangers	W	3–2 (OT)	6	Boston	Toronto	W	2–1
26	Boston	New York Rangers	W	4–1	9	Boston	Toronto	L	3–2 (OT)
28	New York	Rangers	L	2–1	11	Toronto	Maple Leafs	W	3–1
30	Boston	New York Rangers	L	2–1 (OT)	13	Toronto	Maple Leafs	W	2–0
					16	Boston	Toronto	W	3–1

1938-39 PLAYOFFS

vs. New York Rangers	4 wins – 3 losses	vs. Toronto Maple Leafs	4 wins – 1 loss
at New York	1 win – 2 losses	at Toronto	2 wins – 0 losses
at Boston	3 wins – 1 loss	at Boston	2 wins – 1 loss

1938-39 PLAYOFF SCORING

	GP	SO	GAA					
Frank Brimsek	12	1	1.50	Woody Dumart	1	3	4	6
				Bill Hollett	1	3	4	2
	G	A	P	PIM	Jack Crawford	1	1	2	9
					Gordon Pettinger	1	1	2	7
Bill Cowley	3	11	14	2	Ray Getliffe	1	1	2	2
Roy Conacher	6	4	10	12	Dit Clapper	0	1	1	6
Mel Hill	6	3	9	12	Jack Portland	0	0	0	11
Milt Schmidt	3	3	6	2	Cooney Weiland	0	0	0	0
Bobby Bauer	3	2	5	0	Robert Hamill	0	0	0	0
Eddie Shore	0	4	4	19					

1939–1940
(16th year)

TEAM OWNER:	The Adams Family	ALL-STARS:	Dit Clapper (1st team)
PRESIDENT:	Weston Adams Sr.		Milt Schmidt (1st team)
GM:	Art Ross		Frank Brimsek (2nd team)
GOVERNORS:	Weston Adams & Art Ross		Bobby Bauer (2nd team)
COACH:	Cooney Weiland		Woody Dumart (2nd team)
PLAYOFFS:	*Semi-finals:*	TROPHY WINNERS:	Prince of Wales
	Lose to New York Rangers		— Boston Bruins
	2 wins – 4 losses		Art Ross — Milt Schmidt
STANLEY CUP WINNER:	New York Rangers		Lady Byng — Bobby Bauer
			Dufresne —Dit Clapper

UNIFORMS

- White jersey with large gold numbers trimmed in black on front and back of jersey. Gold band trimmed in black on shoulders. Large gold trimmed in black block "B" on arms. Gold and black bands below the "B." Black pants with gold stripes along sides. Alternating gold, black, and white stripes on stockings.

POTPOURRI

- Bruins finish on top of the league standings to win their third straight Prince of Wales Trophy.
- Bobby Bauer wins the Lady Byng Trophy for gentlemanly play.
- Milt Schmidt leads the league in scoring.
- Milt Schmidt, Woody Dumart, Bobby Bauer, and Bill Cowley finish 1 to 4 in league scoring.
- Long time Bruin Eddie Shore is traded.
- Lose opening round of playoffs to Rangers, 4 games to 2.
- Cooney Weiland replaces Art Ross as coach.
- On a December 19 visit by the Toronto Maple Leafs, Conn Smythe, Manager of the Leafs, places an ad in the Boston Globe urging fans to come see Maple Leaf-type hockey.
- The Art Ross puck, with the beveled edges, is adopted as the official puck of the National Hockey League.
- Eddie Shore, after purchasing the Springfield franchise of the International Hockey League, agrees to play in Bruin home games for $200 per game.
- New Canadiens coach and former Bruin Babe Siebert dies in a drowning accident. A benefit game is held at the Montreal Forum on October 29, 1939.
- Red Dutton, Manager of the Americans, declares that the Canadian anthem, "God Save the King," would no longer be played in New York since Montreal and Toronto did not play the "Star Spangled Banner."

TRANSACTIONS

- Eddie Shore traded to the Americans for Eddie Wiseman.
- Ray Getliffe and Charlie Sands traded to the Canadiens for Herb Cain.
- Jack Portland traded to Chicago for Des Smith.

1939-40 STANDINGS

	W	L	T	P	GF	GA
Boston	31	12	5	67	170	98
New York Rangers	27	11	10	64	136	77
Toronto	25	17	6	56	134	110
Chicago	23	19	6	52	112	120
Detroit	16	26	6	38	91	126
New York Americans	15	29	4	34	106	140
Montreal Canadiens	10	33	5	25	90	168

1939-40 RESULTS

November 1939

	AT	VERSUS	W-L-T	SCR
4	Toronto	Maple Leafs	L	5–0
12	Detroit	Red Wings	L	2–1
14	Boston	Chicago	W	3–1
16	Montreal	Canadiens	T	3–3
19	Chicago	Blackhawks	W	2–0
21	Boston	Montreal	L	2–1

| 26 | Boston | New York Rangers | T | 2–2 |
| 28 | Boston | Toronto | W | 6–2 |

December 1939

3	New York	Americans	W	6–2
5	Boston	New York Americans	W	2–1
8	Detroit	Red Wings	W	3–0
10	New York	Rangers	L	3–2

12	Boston	Detroit	W	3–1
14	Toronto	Maple Leafs	T	1–1
17	Chicago	Blackhawks	W	4–2
9	Boston	Toronto	W	3–2 (OT)
21	Montreal	Canadiens	W	3–2
24	New York	Americans	W	3–2
25	Boston	Chicago	W	6–3
29	New York	Rangers	L	4–0
31	Boston	Montreal	W	6–1

January 1940

3	Boston	New York Rangers	L	6–4
7	Boston	New York Americans	W	6–2
9	Boston	Detroit	W	3–1
11	Toronto	Maple Leafs	W	5–2
14	Boston	Montreal	W	4–2
16	Montreal	Canadiens	W	6–1
21	New York	Rangers	L	4–2
23	Boston	Toronto	W	4–1
25	Chicago	Blackhawks	T	2–2
28	Detroit	Red Wings	L	4–2
30	Boston	Chicago	W	5–0

February 1940

4	Boston	New York Americans	W	7–1
6	Boston	New York Rangers	W	6–2
11	New York	Americans	W	4–2
13	Boston	Detroit	W	10–3
20	Boston	Toronto	W	5–0
24	Toronto	Maple Leafs	L	3–1
25	Chicago	Blackhawks	L	3–1
27	Boston	Chicago	W	6–0
29	Montreal	Canadiens	W	4–2

March 1940

3	Detroit	Red Wings	L	6–3
5	Boston	Detroit	W	7–2
7	New York	Americans	W	2–1
9	Boston	New York Americans	L	4–2
12	Boston	New York Rangers	W	2–1
14	New York	Rangers	T	0–0
17	Boston	Montreal	W	7–2

1939-40 SCORING

	GP	SO	GAA
Frank Brimsek	48	6	2.04

	G	A	P	PIM
Milt Schmidt	22	30	52	37
Woody Dumart	22	21	43	16
Bobby Bauer	17	26	43	2
Bill Cowley	13	27	40	24
Herb Cain	21	10	31	30
Roy Conacher	18	12	30	9
Dit Clapper	10	18	28	25
Bill Hollett	10	18	28	18

Art Jackson	7	18	25	6
Mel Hill	9	11	20	19
Robert Hamill	10	8	18	16
Gordon Pettinger	2	6	8	2
Eddie Wiseman	2	6	8	0
Des Smith	2	2	4	43
Jack Shewchuck	2	4	6	55
Jack Crawford	1	4	5	26
Eddie Shore	2	2	4	13
Pat McReavy	0	0	0	2
Jack Portland	0	5	5	16

1939-40 PLAYOFF RESULTS

March 1940

	AT	VERSUS	W–L–T	SCR
19	New York	Rangers	L	4–0
21	Boston	New York Rangers	W	4–2
24	Boston	New York Rangers	W	4–3
26	New York	Rangers	L	1–0
28	Boston	New York Rangers	L	1–0
30	New York	Rangers	L	4–1

1939-40 PLAYOFFS

vs. New York Rangers	2 wins – 4 losses
at New York	0 wins – 3 losses
at Boston	2 wins – 1 loss

1939-40 PLAYOFF SCORING

	GP	SO	GAA					
Frank Brimsek	6	0	2.50	Woody Dumart	1	0	1	0
				Bobby Bauer	1	0	1	2
	G	A	P	PIM	Bill Cowley	0	1	1	7
Herb Cain	1	3	4	2	Terry Reardon	0	1	1	0
Roy Conacher	2	1	3	0	Robert Hamill	0	0	0	5
Eddie Wiseman	2	1	3	2	Jack Crawford	0	0	0	0
Bill Hollett	1	2	3	2	Mel Hill	0	0	0	0
Art Jackson	1	2	3	0	Milt Schmidt	0	0	0	0
Dit Clapper	0	2	2	2	Des Smith	0	0	0	0
					Jack Shewchuck	0	0	0	0

1940–1941
(17th year)

TEAM OWNER:	The Adams Family	
PRESIDENT:	Weston Adams Sr.	
GM:	Art Ross	
GOVERNORS:	Weston Adams & Art Ross	
COACH:	Cooney Weiland	

ALL-STARS: Dit Clapper (1st team)
Bill Cowley (1st team)
Cooney Weiland, Coach (1st team)
Frank Brimsek (2nd team)
Bobby Bauer (2nd team)
Woody Dumart (2nd team)

PLAYOFFS: *Semi-finals:*
Defeat Toronto Maple Leafs
4 wins – 3 losses
Stanley Cup finals:
Defeat Detroit Red Wings
4 wins – 0 losses

STANLEY CUP WINNER: Boston Bruins

TROPHY WINNERS: Prince of Wales
— Boston Bruins
Hart — Bill Cowley
Art Ross — Bill Cowley
Dufresne — Dit Clapper
Lady Byng — Bobby Bauer

UNIFORMS

- White jersey with large gold numbers trimmed in black on front and back of jersey. Gold band trimmed in black on shoulders. Large gold trimmed in black block "B" on arms. Gold and black bands below the "B." Black pants with gold stripes along sides. Alternating gold, black, and white stripes on stockings. Bruins introduce a new jersey for special occasions which is basic gold with black trim on the shoulders. The word "Bruins" is in script across the front of the jersey in black trimmed in white.

POTPOURRI

- Bruins win the third Stanley Cup in franchise history by sweeping Detroit, 4 games to 0. This is the first time a sweep had occurred since the introduction of the seven game format in 1939.
- Bobby Bauer nets the Cup-winning goal.
- Dit Clapper scores 200th goal of career on January 18th.

- Bruins enjoy 23 game unbeaten streak from December 21 until February 25. After losing 1 game, the Bruins finished the season with 6 wins and 2 ties.
- The Bruins lose only 1 game combined in the months of January, February, and March.
- Bruins win the Prince of Wales Trophy for the fourth straight year.
- Bobby Bauer wins the Lady Byng Trophy for the second straight season.
- Bill Cowley wins the scoring title and the Hart Trophy.
- Because of complaints, the Ross puck is not used; the Spalding puck is the official puck of the NHL.
- Bruins defeat Detroit in 4 games to win the Stanley Cup.
- Art Ross offers a trophy to the league to be presented each year to the outstanding player. Later, it is awarded to the leading scorer.
- Because of the unpopularity of the term "Kraut" during the war years, the line of Milt Schmidt, Woody Dumart, and Bobby Bauer is now referred to as the "Kitchener Kids."
- Resurfacing the ice between periods becomes mandatory.

1940-41 STANDINGS

	W	L	T	P	GF	GA
Boston	27	8	13	67	168	102
Toronto	28	14	6	62	145	99
Detroit	21	16	11	53	112	102
New York Rangers	21	19	8	50	143	125
Chicago	16	25	7	39	112	139
Montreal Canadiens	16	26	6	38	121	147
New York Americans	8	29	11	27	99	186

1940-41 RESULTS

November 1940

	AT	VERSUS	W-L-T	SCR
3	Montreal	Canadiens	T	1–1
12	Boston	Chicago	L	6–5
17	Boston	Toronto	L	4–1
19	Boston	Detroit	T	4–4
21	Chicago	Blackhawks	W	2–0
23	New York	Rangers	W	2–1
24	Detroit	Red Wings	T	1–1
26	Boston	Montreal	L	3–2

December 1940

1	New York	Americans	W	10–3
3	Boston	New York Americans	W	6–2
7	Toronto	Maple Leafs	L	3–2
8	Chicago	Blackhawks	L	3–2 (OT)
10	Boston	New York Rangers	W	6–2
17	Boston	Toronto	W	5–2
19	New York	Rangers	L	5–3
21	Montreal	Canadiens	L	3–1
22	Detroit	Red Wings	W	5–3
25	Boston	New York Americans	W	8–1
27	New York	Americans	T	3–3
31	Boston	New York Rangers	T	2–2

January 1941

5	Boston	Chicago	T	2–2
7	Boston	Detroit	T	1–1
11	Montreal	Canadiens	W	2–1

12	Boston	Montreal	W	7–5
16	New York	Rangers	T	2–2
18	Toronto	Maple Leafs	W	1–0
19	Chicago	Blackhawks	T	4–4
21	Boston	New York Rangers	W	4–3 (OT)
26	New York	Americans	W	6–1
28	Boston	Chicago	W	3–2

February 1941

2	Boston	New York Americans	W	4–1
4	Boston	Montreal	W	5–3 (OT)
8	Toronto	Maple Leafs	W	3–2
9	Detroit	Red Wings	T	2–2
11	Boston	Detroit	W	4–0
13	New York	Rangers	W	5–3
15	Montreal	Canadiens	W	5–0
18	Boston	Toronto	T	2–2
23	Boston	New York Americans	W	3–1
25	Boston	New York Rangers	L	2–0

March 1941

1	Toronto	Maple Leafs	T	0–0
2	Chicago	Blackhawks	W	4–3
4	Boston	Chicago	W	3–2
9	Boston	Montreal	W	8–0
11	Boston	Toronto	W	3–2
13	New York	Americans	W	8–3
16	Detroit	Red Wings	T	2–2
18	Boston	Detroit	W	4–1

1940-41 SCORING

	GP	SO	GAA	
Frank Brimsek	48	6	2.12	

	G	A	P	PIM
Bill Cowley	17	45	62	16
Eddie Wiseman	16	24	40	10
Bobby Bauer	17	22	39	2
Roy Conacher	24	14	38	7
Milt Schmidt	13	25	38	23
Woody Dumart	18	15	33	2
Art Jackson	17	15	32	10
Dit Clapper	8	18	26	24
Bill Hollett	9	15	24	23
Herb Cain	8	10	18	6
Des Smith	6	8	14	61
Terry Reardon	6	5	11	19
Jack Crawford	2	8	10	27
Mel Hill	5	4	9	4
Jack Shewchuck	2	2	4	8
Pat McReavy	0	1	1	2
Gordon Bruce	0	1	1	2
Robert Hamill	0	1	1	0

1940-41 PLAYOFF RESULTS

March 1941

	AT	VERSUS	W-L-T	SCR
20	Boston	Toronto	W	3–0
22	Boston	Toronto	L	5–3
25	Toronto	Maple Leafs	L	7–2
27	Toronto	Maple Leafs	W	2–1
29	Boston	Toronto	L	2–1 (OT)

April 1941

1	Toronto	Maple Leafs	W	2–1

3	Boston	Toronto	W	2–1	10	Detroit	Red Wings	W	4–2
6	Boston	Detroit	W	3–2	12	Detroit	Red Wings	W	3–1
8	Boston	Detroit	W	2–1					

1940-41 PLAYOFFS

vs. Detroit Red Wings	4 wins – 0 losses	vs. Toronto Maple Leafs	4 wins – 3 losses
at Detroit	2 wins – 0 losses	at Toronto	2 wins – 1 loss
at Boston	2 wins – 0 losses	at Boston	2 wins – 2 losses

1940-41 PLAYOFF SCORING

	GP	SO	GAA		Dit Clapper	0	5	5	4
Frank Brimsek	11	1	2.09		Bobby Bauer	2	2	4	0
					Pat McReavy	2	2	4	5
	G	A	P	PIM	Art Jackson	1	3	4	16
Milt Schmidt	5	6	11	9	Woody Dumart	1	3	4	9
Eddie Wiseman	6	2	8	0	Mel Hill	1	1	2	0
Bill Hollett	3	4	7	8	Des Smith	0	2	2	12
Terry Reardon	2	4	6	6	Jack Crawford	0	2	2	7
Roy Conacher	1	5	6	4	Bill Cowley	0	0	0	0
Herb Cain	3	2	5	5					

1941–1942
(18th year)

TEAM OWNER:	The Adams Family		*Semi-finals:*
PRESIDENT:	Weston Adams Sr.		Lose to Detroit Red Wings
GM & OWNER:	Art Ross		0 wins – 2 losses
COACH:	Art Ross	STANLEY CUP WINNER:	Toronto Maple Leafs
PLAYOFFS:	*Quarter finals:*	ALL-STARS:	Frank Brimsek (1st team)
	Defeat Chicago Blackhawks	TROPHY WINNERS:	Vezina — Frank Brimsek
	2 wins – 1 loss		Dufresne — Milt Schmidt
			Woody Dumart
			Bobby Bauer

UNIFORMS

- White jersey with large gold numbers trimmed in black on front and back of jersey. Gold band trimmed in black on shoulders. Large gold trimmed in black block "B" on arms. Gold and black bands below the "B." Black pants with gold stripes along sides. Alternating gold, black, and white stripes on stockings.

POTPOURRI

- Frank Brimsek wins the Vezina Trophy.
- Kraut Line makes final appearance before going off to war on February 10. The Kraut Line records 11 points in a 8–1 win over Montreal. The Krauts are carried off the ice by members of the Canadiens.
- Art Ross resigns as a governor for the Boston club and is replaced by R.R. Duncan.
- For the first time since 1937, the Bruins did not win the Prince of Wales Trophy.
- Lose semi-finals to Detroit, 2 games to 0.

- New York Americans change name to Brooklyn Americans.
- November 16 home opener against Rangers has Mayor Maurice Tobin hand out Stanley Cup medals to the Boston players.
- Bruins score 4 goals in overtime at New York against the Americans to win 6–2.
- Bruins finish in third place during the regular season.
- The Rangers and Blackhawks are the last teams to play overtime until 1983–84.

TRANSACTIONS

- Because of the start of World War II, the Bruins lost many players.
- Woody Dumart of the Bruins and Don Metz of Toronto are the first players to be drafted for World War II on January 18.
- Harvey Jackson is purchased from the Americans and Dutch Hiller from Detroit.
- Because of passport problems, Terry Reardon cannot leave Canada, so, the Bruins trade him to Montreal for Paul Gauthier.
- Phil Hergesheimer is purchased from Chicago.

1941-42 STANDINGS

	W	L	T	P	GF	GA
New York Rangers	29	17	2	60	177	143
Toronto	27	18	3	57	158	136
Boston	25	17	6	56	160	118
Chicago	22	23	3	47	145	155
Detroit	19	25	4	42	140	147
Montreal Canadiens	18	27	3	39	134	173
Brooklyn Americans	16	29	3	35	133	175

1941-42 RESULTS

November 1941

	AT	VERSUS	W–L–T	SCR
8	Toronto	Maple Leafs	L	2–0
15	New York	Rangers	W	2–1
16	Boston	New York	W	2–1
18	Boston	Brooklyn	W	7–2
20	Chicago	Blackhawks	L	3–2
23	Detroit	Red Wings	W	4–2
25	Boston	Detroit	W	7–1
27	Brooklyn	Americans	W	6–2 (OT)
29	Montreal	Canadiens	W	3–1
30	Boston	Montreal	W	3–2

December 1941

2	Boston	Toronto	W	3–1 (OT)
7	New York	Rangers	L	5–4
9	Boston	Chicago	T	2–2
14	Chicago	Blackhawks	T	3–3
16	Boston	Montreal	W	4–0
20	Montreal	Canadiens	W	4–2 (OT)
21	Detroit	Red Wings	T	2–2
23	Boston	New York	W	3–2
25	Toronto	Maple Leafs	L	2–0

30	Boston	Toronto	W	4–1

January 1942

1	Boston	Brooklyn	W	5–4
4	Brooklyn	Americans	L	3–2
6	Boston	Chicago	W	3–2
13	Boston	Detroit	W	2–1
18	Chicago	Blackhawks	W	4–3
20	Boston	New York	L	4–2
22	Detroit	Red Wings	L	4–3
24	Montreal	Canadiens	T	2–2
25	Boston	Montreal	W	7–3
27	Boston	Toronto	T	0–0
29	Brooklyn	Americans	L	5–4
31	Toronto	Maple Leafs	W	3–2 (OT)

February 1942

1	Boston	Brooklyn	L	2–1
3	Boston	Chicago	L	5–3
5	New York	Rangers	L	4–1
8	Boston	Detroit	W	3–0
10	Boston	Montreal	W	8–1
15	Chicago	Blackhawks	L	2–0

| 19 | Brooklyn | Americans | L | 6–4 |
| 24 | Boston | New York | L | 4–3 |

March 1942

| 1 | Boston | Detroit | T | 3–3 |
| 3 | Boston | Toronto | W | 5–3 |

7	Montreal	Canadiens	L	4–3 (OT)
8	Detroit	Red Wings	L	3–1
10	Boston	Chicago	W	9–1
12	New York	Rangers	W	2–1
14	Toronto	Maple Leafs	L	6–4
17	Boston	Brooklyn	W	8–3

1941-42 SCORING

	GP	SO	GAA
Frank Brimsek	47	3	2.44
Nick Damore	1	0	3.00

	G	A	P	PIM
Roy Conacher	24	13	37	12
Milt Schmidt	14	21	35	34
Bobby Bauer	13	22	35	11
Eddie Wiseman	12	22	34	8
Bill Hollett	19	14	33	21
Woody Dumart	14	15	29	8
Bill Cowley	4	23	27	6
Art Jackson	6	18	24	25
Jack McGill	8	11	19	2
Herb Cain	8	10	18	2
Wilbur Hiller	7	10	17	19
Dit Clapper	3	12	15	11
Des Smith	7	7	14	50
Harvey Jackson	5	7	12	8
Gordon Bruce	4	8	12	11
Jack Crawford	2	9	11	27
Robert Hamill	6	3	9	2
Lloyd Gronsdal	1	2	3	0
Jack Shewchuck	2	0	2	14
Frank Mario	1	1	2	0
Clare Martin	0	1	1	4
Pat McReavy	0	1	1	0
Cliff Thompson	0	0	0	2
Phil Hergesheimer	0	0	0	2

1941-42 PLAYOFF RESULTS

March 1942

	AT	VERSUS	W-L-T	SCR
22	Chicago	Blackhawks	W	2–1 (OT)
24	Boston	Chicago	L	4–0
26	Boston	Chicago	W	3–2
29	Boston	Detroit	L	6–4
31	Detroit	Red Wings	L	3–1

1941-42 PLAYOFFS

vs. Chicago Blackhawks	2 wins – 1 loss	vs. Detroit Red Wings	0 wins – 2 losses
at Chicago	1 win – 0 losses	at Detroit	0 wins – 1 loss
at Boston	1 win – 1 loss	at Boston	0 wins – 1 loss

1941-42 PLAYOFF SCORING

	GP	SO	GAA
Frank Brimsek	5	0	3.20

	G	A	P	PIM
Jack McGill	4	1	5	6
Gordon Bruce	2	3	5	4
Roy Conacher	2	1	3	0
Des Smith	1	2	3	2
Bill Cowley	0	3	3	5
Herb Cain	1	0	1	0
Eddie Wiseman	0	1	1	0
Jack Shewchuck	0	1	1	7
Wilbur Hiller	0	1	1	0
Jack Crawford	0	1	1	4
Art Jackson	0	1	1	0
Harvey Jackson	0	1	1	0
Clare Martin	0	0	0	0

1942–1943
(19th year)

TEAM OWNER:	The Adams Family	STANLEY CUP WINNER:	Detroit Red Wings
PRESIDENT:	Weston Adams Sr.	ALL-STARS:	Bill Cowley (1st team)
GM:	Art Ross		Frank Brimsek (2nd team)
GOVERNOR:	Robert Duncan		Johnny Crawford (2nd team)
COACH:	Art Ross		Bill Hollett (2nd team)
PLAYOFFS:	*Semi-finals:*		Art Ross, Coach (2nd team)
	Defeat Montreal Canadiens	TROPHY WINNERS:	O'Brien Trophy
	4 wins – 1 loss		— Boston Bruins
	Stanley Cup finals:		Hart — Bill Cowley
	Lose to Detroit Red Wings		Dufresne — Frank Brimsek
	0 wins – 4 losses		

UNIFORMS

- White jersey with large gold numbers trimmed in black on front and back of jersey. Gold band trimmed in black on shoulders. Large gold trimmed in black block "B" on arms. Gold and black bands below the "B." Black pants with gold stripes along sides. Alternating gold, black, and white stripes on stockings.

POTPOURRI

- Finish in second place during the regular season, 4 points behind Detroit.
- Defeat Montreal, 4 games to 1, in semi-finals of the Stanley Cup playoffs.
- On December 26, lose to Detroit at Boston for the first time since 1937.
- Ray Getliffe of Montreal scores 5 goals in one game at Montreal on February 6.
- The Bruins lose to Detroit, 4 games to 0, in the Stanley Cup finals.
- On November 21st, President Calder of the NHL suspends all overtime play in regular season games.
- The Calder Memorial Trophy, awarded to the top rookie, is inaugurated after the death of President Calder on February 4.
- Mervyn "Red" Dutton takes over as President of the NHL.
- The Brooklyn Americans cease operations.
- The Kraut Line, gone off to war, is replaced by the Sprout Line of Bill Shill, Don Gallinger, and Bep Guidolin.
- Bep Guidolin, at 16 years old, becomes the youngest player in NHL history.
- The Bruins play their first afternoon game in history on December 12 against the Montreal Canadiens. A Red Cross fund drive is held between the first and second period of the game.

TRANSACTIONS

- Obtain Buzz Boll and Murph Chamberlain from the defunct Americans.
- Don Gallinger and Bep Guidolin are brought up from junior hockey.
- Dutch Hiller is sold to Montreal.
- Woody Dumart, Bobby Bauer, and Milt Schmidt are inducted into the Canadian Armed Forces.

1942-43 STANDINGS

	W	L	T	P	GF	GA
Detroit	25	14	11	61	169	124
Boston	24	17	9	57	195	176
Toronto	22	19	9	53	198	159
Montreal	19	19	12	50	181	191
Chicago	17	18	15	49	179	180
New York	11	31	8	30	161	253

1942-43 RESULTS

October 1942

	AT	VERSUS	W-L-T	SCR
31	Montreal	Canadiens	L	3-2

November 1942

1	Detroit	Red Wings	L	3-0
5	Chicago	Blackhawks	L	5-1
12	Toronto	Maple Leafs	L	3-1
14	Boston	New York	L	5-3
15	New York	Rangers	W	4-3
17	Boston	Montreal	W	4-1
22	Boston	Toronto	W	7-6
24	Boston	Chicago	T	5-5
28	Montreal	Canadiens	W	6-2
29	New York	Rangers	L	3-2

December 1942

1	Boston	Detroit	W	5-2
6	Boston	New York	W	5-4
8	Boston	Chicago	W	9-6
12	Boston	Montreal	W	3-2
13	Detroit	Red Wings	T	1-1
15	Boston	Detroit	W	3-2
17	New York	Rangers	W	7-3
19	Toronto	Maple Leafs	T	3-3
20	Chicago	Blackhawks	T	4-4
22	Boston	Toronto	T	4-4
26	Toronto	Maple Leafs	L	7-2
27	Montreal	Canadiens	L	4-2
29	Boston	New York	L	5-3

January 1943

1	Boston	Detroit	T	2–2
3	Detroit	Red Wings	W	3–2
9	Montreal	Canadiens	L	7–2
10	Boston	Toronto	W	5–4
12	Boston	Chicago	W	3–0
16	Boston	New York	W	7–5
17	New York	Rangers	W	6–3
19	Boston	Montreal	W	5–2
21	Detroit	Red Wings	L	3–2
24	Chicago	Blackhawks	L	4–3
26	Boston	Detroit	L	5–3
30	Toronto	Maple Leafs	W	5–3
31	New York	Rangers	W	7–2

February 1943

2	Boston	Chicago	L	5–3
6	Montreal	Canadiens	W	8–3
7	Boston	Montreal	W	7–1
9	Boston	Toronto	L	3–1
14	Chicago	Blackhawks	L	3–2
20	Toronto	Maple Leafs	L	4–2
21	Detroit	Red Wings	L	4–0
23	Boston	Boston	L	7–5
28	Chicago	Blackhawks	T	4–4

March 1943

2	Boston	Detroit	W	3–1
9	Boston	Toronto	T	5–5
14	Boston	Montreal	T	4–4
16	Boston	New York	W	11–5

1942-43 SCORING

	GP	SO	GAA
Frank Brimsek	50	1	3.52

	G	A	P	PIM
Bill Cowley	27	45	72	10
Art Jackson	22	31	53	20
Frank Boll	25	27	52	20
Bill Hollett	19	25	44	19
Herb Cain	18	18	36	19
Harvey Jackson	19	15	34	38
Don Gallinger	14	20	34	16
Erwin Chamberlain	9	24	33	67
Dit Clapper	5	18	23	12
Jack Crawford	5	18	23	24
Armand Guidolin	7	15	22	53
John Schmidt	6	7	13	6
Irwin Boyd	6	5	11	6
Jack Shewchuck	2	6	8	50
Ab DeMarco	4	1	5	0
William Shill	4	1	5	4
Oscar Aubuchon	3	0	3	0
Norman Calladine	0	1	1	0
Wilbur Hiller	0	0	0	19

1942-43 PLAYOFF RESULTS

March 1943

	AT	VERSUS	W-L-T	SCR
21	Boston	Montreal	W	5–4 (OT)
23	Boston	Montreal	W	5–3
25	Montreal	Canadiens	W	3–2 (OT)
27	Montreal	Canadiens	L	4–0
30	Boston	Montreal	W	5–4 (OT)

April 1943

1	Detroit	Red Wings	L	6–2
4	Detroit	Red Wings	L	4–3
7	Boston	Detroit	L	4–0
8	Boston	Detroit	L	2–0

1942-43 PLAYOFFS

vs. Detroit Red Wings	0 wins – 4 losses	vs. Montreal Canadiens	4 wins – 1 loss
at Detroit	0 wins – 2 losses	at Montreal	1 win – 1 loss
at Boston	0 wins – 2 losses	at Boston	3 wins – 0 losses

1942-43 PLAYOFF SCORING

	GP	SO	GAA					
Frank Brimsek	9	0	3.67	Armand Guidolin	0	4	4	12
				Ab DeMarco	3	0	3	2
	G	A	P	PIM	Harvey Jackson	1	2	3	10
Art Jackson	6	3	9	7	Jack Crawford	1	1	2	10
Bill Hollett	0	9	9	4	Erwin Chamberlain	1	1	2	12
Bill Cowley	1	7	8	4	Oscar Aubuchon	1	0	1	0
Herb Cain	4	2	6	0	Irwin Boyd	0	1	1	4
Dit Clapper	2	3	5	9	Jack Shewchuck	0	0	0	12
Don Gallinger	3	1	4	10	John Schmidt	0	0	0	0
					Bill Anderson	0	0	0	0

1943–1944
(20th year)

TEAM OWNER:	The Adams Family	ALL-STARS:	Bill Cowley (1st team)
PRESIDENT:	Weston Adams		Dit Clapper (2nd team)
GM & OWNER:	Art Ross		Herb Cain (2nd team)
COACH:	Art Ross	TROPHY WINNERS:	Art Ross — Herb Cain
PLAYOFFS:	Out of playoffs		Dufresne — Bill Cowley
STANLEY CUP WINNER:	Montreal Canadiens		

UNIFORMS

- White jersey with large gold numbers trimmed in black on front and back of jersey. Gold band trimmed in black on shoulders. Large gold trimmed in black block "B" on arms. Gold and black bands below the "B." Black pants with gold stripes along sides. Alternating gold, black, and white stripes on stockings.

POTPOURRI

- Herb Cain registers 80 points to break the record held by Cooney Weiland.
- Finishes out of the playoffs.
- The red line at center ice is adopted as a new rule to help speed up the game. Also, players facing off have to face each other rather than having their backs to the boards.
- Dit Clapper substitutes for Art Ross when Ross is ill during the season.
- In the November 27 game at Toronto, goalie Bert Gardiner takes ill and is replaced by Reverend George Abbott. Despite this divine intervention, the Bruins lost to the Leafs, 7–4.
- In the February 29 game at Boston against Toronto, goalie Bert Gardiner received an assist an a goal by Bill Cowley.
- Detroit's Flash Hollett's 20 goals for a defenseman sets the standard until 1968–69 when Bobby Orr scores 21 goals.
- March 4 game against the Rangers is highlighted by the fact that no penalties are called during the game.

TRANSACTIONS

- Frank Brimsek lost to the Coast Guard for the duration of the war.
- Bert Gardiner obtained from Chicago.
- Trade Flash Hollett to Detroit for Pat Egan.
- Sell Chuck Scherza, Oscar Aubuchon, and Ab Demarco to New York.

1943-44 STANDINGS

	W	L	T	P	GF	GA
Montreal	38	5	7	83	234	109
Detroit	26	18	6	58	214	177
Toronto	23	23	4	50	214	174
Chicago	22	23	5	49	178	187
Boston	19	26	5	43	223	268
New York	6	39	5	17	162	310

1943-44 RESULTS

October 1943

	AT	VERSUS	W-L-T	SCR
30	Montreal	Canadiens	T	2–2

November 1943

6	Toronto	Maple Leafs	W	5–2
7	Detroit	Red Wings	L	6–4
11	Chicago	Blackhawks	L	6–4
13	New York	Rangers	W	6–2
16	Boston	Montreal	T	2–2
18	Chicago	Blackhawks	L	7–3
21	Montreal	Canadiens	L	13–4
23	Boston	Toronto	W	8–5
25	Boston	New York	W	6–2
27	Toronto	Maple Leafs	L	7–4
28	Chicago	Blackhawks	L	5–4
30	Boston	Chicago	W	6–5

December 1943

5	Boston	Montreal	W	5–4
7	Boston	Detroit	T	6–6
11	Boston	New York	W	9–6
12	New York	Rangers	L	6–4
14	Boston	Chicago	W	4–3
19	Montreal	Canadiens	L	3–1
21	Boston	Toronto	W	8–5
26	Detroit	Red Wings	T	4–4
28	Boston	Detroit	W	5–2

January 1944

1	Boston	Toronto	L	5–2
2	New York	Rangers	W	13–3
4	Boston	Chicago	W	6–4
8	Toronto	Maple Leafs	L	12–3
15	Boston	New York	W	7–5
16	New York	Rangers	L	8–6
18	Boston	Toronto	L	7–2
22	Montreal	Canadiens	L	6–2
23	Boston	Montreal	L	4–1
25	Boston	Detroit	L	6–3
29	Detroit	Red Wings	L	6–1

February 1944

1	Boston	Chicago	L	2–0
5	Boston	New York	W	7–2
8	Boston	Montreal	W	3–0
10	Chicago	Blackhawks	W	5–4
13	Boston	Detroit	L	4–1
19	Toronto	Maple Leafs	L	10–4
20	Detroit	Red Wings	L	6–5
26	Montreal	Canadiens	L	10–2
29	Boston	Toronto	L	7–3

March 1944

2	Chicago	Blackhawks	L	4–2
4	Boston	New York	W	10–9
5	New York	Rangers	T	4–4
7	Boston	Detroit	L	8–4
12	Boston	Montreal	W	6–5
14	Boston	Chicago	W	6–4
16	Detroit	Red Wings	L	10–9
18	Toronto	Maple Leafs	L	10–2

1943-44 SCORING

	GP	SO	GAA
Bert Gardiner	41	1	5.17
			(1 assist)
Maurice Courteau	6	0	5.50
George Abbott	1	0	7.0
Jim Franks	1	0	6.0
Benny Grant	1	0	10.0

	G	A	P	PIM
Herb Cain	36	46	82	4
Bill Cowley	30	41	71	12
Art Jackson	21	38	59	8
Frank Boll	19	25	44	2
Norman Calladine	16	27	43	8
Armand Guidolin	17	25	42	58

Harvey Jackson	11	21	32	25	Guy Labrie	2	7	9	2
Dit Clapper	6	25	31	13	Tom Brennan	2	1	3	2
Pat Egan	11	13	24	55	Chuck Scherza	1	1	2	4
Jack Crawford	4	16	20	8	Oscar Aubuchon	1	0	1	0
Don Gallinger	13	5	18	6	Clarence Schmidt	1	0	1	2
Bill Hollett	9	7	16	4	Irwin Boyd	0	1	1	0
Russell Kopak	7	9	16	0	Joe Schmidt	0	0	0	0
Alan Rittinger	3	7	10	0	John Wilkinson	0	0	0	6
Aldo Palazzari	6	3	9	4	Ab DeMarco	0	0	0	0

1944–1945
(21st year)

TEAM OWNER:	The Adams Family	PLAYOFFS:	*Semi-finals:*
PRESIDENT:	Weston Adams Sr.		Lose to Detroit Red Wings
GM & OWNER:	Art Ross		3 wins – 4 losses
COACH:	Art Ross	STANLEY CUP WINNER:	Toronto Maple Leafs
		ALL-STARS:	Bill Cowley (2nd team)
		TROPHY WINNERS:	Dufresne — Jack Crawford

UNIFORMS

- White jersey with large gold numbers trimmed in black on front and back of jersey. Gold band trimmed in black on shoulders. Large gold trimmed in black block "B" on arms. Gold and black bands below the "B." Black pants with gold stripes along sides. Alternating gold, black, and white stripes on stockings.

POTPOURRI

- Bruins make the playoffs finishing in fourth place.
- Finish 44 points behind league-leading Montreal.
- Lose semi-final round to Detroit, 4 games to 3.
- Bruins do not defeat either Montreal or Detroit this season.
- Bruins open with 5 straight games on the road.
- Rocket Richard of Montreal scores 50th goal of the season on the last night at Boston.
- Carl Liscombe scores 4 goals for Detroit in game 7 of the semi-final round of the playoffs to eliminate Boston.
- Conn Smythe of Toronto offers cash for Milt Schmidt but is turned down by Art Ross.
- Dit Clapper becomes the first NHLer to play 18 seasons.
- Bruins score a team record 14 goals in a January 21st game against the Rangers.

TRANSACTIONS

- Harvey Bennett replaces the now retired Bert Gardiner, who retired, in goal.
- Buzz Boll and Harvey Jackson also retired.
- Sell Art Jackson to Toronto.
- Bill Thoms is acquired from Chicago.
- Acquire Bill Jennings from Detroit.
- Paul Bibeault is signed on loan from Montreal.

1944-45 STANDINGS

	W	L	T	P	GF	GA
Montreal	38	8	4	80	228	121
Detroit	31	14	5	67	218	161
Toronto	24	22	4	52	183	161
Boston	19	30	4	36	179	219
Chicago	13	30	7	33	141	194
New York	11	29	10	32	154	247

1944-45 RESULTS

October 1944

	AT	VERSUS	W-L-T	SCR
28	Montreal	Canadiens	L	3–2
29	Detroit	Red Wings	L	7–1

November 1944

4	Toronto	Maple Leafs	L	7–2
5	Chicago	Blackhawks	W	6–3
12	New York	Rangers	T	5–5
14	Boston	Chicago	W	7–5
18	Montreal	Canadiens	L	6–3
19	Detroit	Red Wings	L	4–3
21	Boston	Montreal	L	4–1
23	Boston	Toronto	W	5–1
26	Boston	New York	W	8–4
28	Boston	Detroit	L	6–3
30	Chicago	Blackhawks	W	7–2

December 1944

3	Boston	Toronto	W	5–4
5	Boston	Montreal	L	4–1
9	Toronto	Maple Leafs	W	5–3
10	Detroit	Red Wings	L	7–6
12	Boston	New York	W	7–5
16	Montreal	Canadiens	L	8–5
19	Boston	Detroit	L	6–3
28	Boston	Chicago	W	2–1
31	New York	Rangers	L	3–2

January 1945

2	Boston	Montreal	L	6–3

7	Detroit	Red Wings	L	8–4
10	New York	Rangers	L	5–1
13	Toronto	Maple Leafs	L	2–1
14	Chicago	Blackhawks	L	4–1
16	Boston	Toronto	W	5–3
21	Boston	New York	W	14–3
23	Boston	Detroit	L	5–4
27	Montreal	Canadiens	L	11–3
28	Boston	Montreal	L	4–1
30	Boston	Chicago	L	5–3

February 1945

3	Toronto	Maple Leafs	W	4–2
4	Boston	New York	T	3–3
6	Boston	Toronto	L	5–1
11	Boston	Detroit	L	3–2
13	Boston	Chicago	W	3–2
17	Boston	New York	W	6–1
18	New York	Rangers	L	2–1
21	Chicago	Blackhawks	L	5–0
25	New York	Rangers	T	4–4

March 1945

4	Detroit	Red Wings	L	10–4
6	Boston	Toronto	L	5–2
8	Montreal	Canadiens	L	3–2
10	Toronto	Maple Leafs	L	9–2
11	Boston	Chicago	W	7–2
13	Boston	Detroit	T	2–2
15	Chicago	Blackhawks	W	5–3
18	Boston	Montreal	L	4–2

1944-45 SCORING

	GP	SO	GAA
Harvey Bennett	24	0	4.33
Paul Bibeault	26	0	4.43

	G	A	P	PIM
Bill Cowley	25	40	65	2
Herb Cain	32	13	45	16
Ken Smith	20	14	34	2
Bill Jennings	20	13	33	25
Frank Mario	8	18	26	24
Armand Gaudreault	15	9	24	27
Bill Cupolo	11	13	24	10
Jack Crawford	5	19	24	10
Dit Clapper	8	14	22	16

Pat Egan	7	15	22	76	Norman Calladine	3	1	4	0
Jean Gladu	6	14	20	2	Tom Brennan	0	1	1	0
Gino Rozzini	5	10	15	20	Murray Henderson	0	1	1	4
Art Jackson	5	8	13	10	Marcel Fillion	0	0	0	0
Jack Shewchuck	1	7	8	31	Fern Flaman	0	0	0	0
Jack McGill	4	2	6	0	Pete Leswick	0	0	0	0
Bill Thoms	4	2	6	0					

1944-45 PLAYOFF RESULTS

March 1945

	AT	VERSUS	W-L-T	SCR
20	Detroit	Red Wings	W	4-3
22	Detroit	Red Wings	W	4-2
25	Boston	Detroit	L	3-2
27	Boston	Detroit	L	3-2
29	Detroit	Red Wings	L	3-2

April 1945

1	Boston	Detroit	W	5-3
3	Detroit	Red Wings	L	5-3

1944-45 PLAYOFFS

vs. Detroit Red Wings	3 wins – 4 losses
at Detroit	2 wins – 2 losses
at Boston	1 win – 2 losses

1944-45 PLAYOFF SCORING

	GP	SO	GAA				
Paul Bibeault	7	0	3.14	Jean Gladu	2	2	4	0

	G	A	P	PIM					
					Jean Gladu	2	2	4	0
					Bill Jennings	2	2	4	6
					Bill Cupolo	1	2	3	0
Herb Cain	5	2	7	0	Gino Rozzini	1	2	3	6
Ken Smith	3	4	7	0	Pat Egan	2	0	2	6
Bill Cowley	3	3	6	0	Armand Gaudreault	0	2	2	8
Jack McGill	3	3	6	0	Murray Henderson	0	1	1	2
Jack Crawford	0	5	5	0	Dit Clapper	0	0	0	0
					Bill Thoms	0	0	0	2

1945-1946
(22nd year)

TEAM OWNER:	The Adams Family		*Stanley Cup finals:*
PRESIDENT:	Weston Adams Sr.		Lose to Montreal Canadiens
GM & OWNER:	Art Ross		1 win – 4 losses
COACH:	Dit Clapper	STANLEY CUP WINNER:	Montreal Canadiens
PLAYOFFS:	*Semi-finals:*	ALL-STARS:	Jack Crawford (1st team)
	Defeat Detroit Red Wings		Frank Brimsek (2nd team)
	4 wins – 1 loss	TROPHY WINNERS:	O'Brien Trophy
			— Boston Bruins
			Dufresne — Jack Crawford

UNIFORMS

- White jersey with large gold numbers trimmed in black on front and back of jersey. Gold band trimmed in black on shoulders. Large gold trimmed in black block "B" on arms. Gold and black bands below the "B." Black pants with gold stripes along sides. Alternating gold, black, and white stripes on stockings.

POTPOURRI

- Frank Brimsek and the Kraut Line, Bauer, Dumart, and Schmidt, return from the war.
- Bruins defeat Detroit on New Year's Day for their first victory over the Red Wings since 1943.
- Bruins finish in second place, 5 points behind Montreal.
- Bruins defeat Detroit in first round of the playoffs.
- Bruins lose to Montreal in the Stanley Cup finals.
- Art Ross retires from coaching at age 60 and is replaced by Dit Clapper, making Clapper the Bruins first playing coach.
- Pat Egan, playing robustly for the Bruins defense, becomes known as "Box Car."
- Despite a great blizzard on December 19th, 9,400 fans attend a game against the Rangers won by the Bruins, 8–7, on a goal by Herb Cain with 20 seconds left in the game.
- During a game at Boston on January 12th, a melee erupts and four Blackhawks, Joe Cooper, John Mariucci, Reg Hamilton, and trainer Ed Froelich, are charged with assault and battery. The charges are later dismissed.
- NHL rules that all equipment previously worn outside the uniform, such as elbow pads, must be worn under the uniform.
- Bruins enjoy an uncle–nephew combination in Roy Conacher (uncle) and Murray Henderson (nephew).

TRANSACTIONS

- After Bill Durnan of Montreal is injured, the Bruins are required to return Paul Bibeault to Montreal.
- Mike McMahon is loaned to Boston with an option to purchase his contract.

1945-46 STANDINGS

	W	L	T	P	GF	GA
Montreal	28	17	5	61	172	134
Boston	24	18	8	56	167	156
Chicago	23	20	7	53	200	178
Detroit	20	20	10	50	146	159
Toronto	19	24	7	45	174	185
New York	13	28	9	35	144	191

1945-46 RESULTS

October 1945

	AT	VERSUS	W-L-T	SCR
24	Boston	Chicago	L	5–4
27	Toronto	Maple Leafs	T	1–1
28	Detroit	Red Wings	L	7–0

November 1945

4	Boston	Montreal	W	6–5
7	Toronto	Maple Leafs	W	4–3
10	Montreal	Canadiens	L	5–3
11	New York	Rangers	W	7–1
21	Boston	Montreal	W	3–0
25	Boston	Toronto	W	5–3
28	Boston	New York	W	5–1

December 1945

2	Boston	Detroit	T	2–2
5	Boston	Chicago	W	6–3
9	Chicago	Blackhawks	L	8–3
12	Boston	Detroit	T	2–2
15	Montreal	Canadiens	T	3–3
16	Boston	Toronto	T	3–3

19	Boston	New York	W	8–7
23	Boston	Montreal	L	4–1
29	Toronto	Maple Leafs	W	4–3
30	Detroit	Red Wings	T	3–3

January 1946

1	Boston	Detroit	W	4–0
5	Montreal	Canadiens	L	4–2
6	New York	Rangers	L	4–2
10	Detroit	Red Wings	L	2–1
12	Boston	Detroit	W	4–3
16	Boston	New York	W	3–2
17	New York	Rangers	W	4–2
19	Montreal	Canadiens	L	3–1
20	Boston	Montreal	W	3–0
23	Boston	Toronto	W	7–1
26	Detroit	Red Wings	W	4–2
27	Chicago	Blackhawks	L	4–1
30	Boston	Chicago	W	4–3

February 1946

2	Toronto	Maple Leafs	W	5–3
3	Chicago	Blackhawks	L	3–1
6	Boston	Toronto	T	3–3
10	Boston	Montreal	L	2–0
13	Boston	Detroit	W	3–0
14	New York	Rangers	T	2–2
16	Boston	New York	L	6–2
20	Chicago	Blackhawks	L	4–3
23	Toronto	Maple Leafs	L	7–2
24	Detroit	Red Wings	L	4–3
27	Montreal	Canadiens	W	5–3

March 1946

3	Chicago	Blackhawks	L	5–3
6	Boston	Detroit	W	4–2
10	Boston	Toronto	W	7–3
12	New York	Rangers	W	3–2
13	Boston	New York	L	5–3
17	Boston	Chicago	W	5–3

1945-46 SCORING

	GP	SO	GAA
Paul Bibeault	16	2	2.81
Frank Brimsek	34	2	3.26

	G	A	P	PIM
Don Gallinger	17	23	40	18
Woody Dumart	22	12	34	2
Armand Guidolin	15	17	32	62
Milt Schmidt	13	18	31	21
Herb Cain	17	12	29	4
Bill Shill	15	12	27	12
Bill Cowley	12	12	24	6
Terry Reardon	12	11	23	21
Bobby Bauer	11	10	21	4
Jack McGill	6	14	20	21
Pat Egan	8	10	18	32
Jack Crawford	7	9	16	10
Murray Henderson	4	11	15	30
Ken Smith	2	6	8	0
Jack Church	2	6	8	28
Dit Clapper	2	3	5	0
Roy Conacher	2	1	3	0
Armand Delmonte	0	0	0	0
Fern Flaman	0	0	0	0
Gordon Bruce	0	0	0	0
Mike McMahon	0	0	0	2

1945-46 PLAYOFF RESULTS

March 1946

	AT	VERSUS	W-L-T	SCR
19	Detroit	Red Wings	W	3–1
21	Detroit	Red Wings	L	3–0
24	Boston	Detroit	W	5–2
26	Boston	Detroit	W	4–1
28	Detroit	Red Wings	W	4–3 (OT)
30	Montreal	Canadiens	L	4–3 (OT)

April 1946

2	Montreal	Canadiens	L	3–2
4	Boston	Montreal	L	4–2
7	Boston	Montreal	W	3–2 (OT)
9	Montreal	Canadiens	L	6–3

1945-46 PLAYOFFS

vs. Detroit Red Wings		vs. Montreal Canadiens	
	4 wins – 1 loss		1 win – 4 losses
at Detroit	2 wins – 0 losses	at Montreal	0 wins – 3 losses
at Boston	2 wins – 1 loss	at Boston	1 win – 1 loss

1945-46 PLAYOFF SCORING

	GP	SO	GAA
Frank Brimsek	10	0	2.90

	G	A	P	PIM
Milt Schmidt	3	5	8	2
Armand Guidolin	5	2	7	13
Woody Dumart	4	3	7	0
Bobby Bauer	4	3	7	2
Don Gallinger	2	4	6	2
Terry Reardon	4	0	4	2
Bill Cowley	1	3	4	2
Ken Smith	0	4	4	0
Pat Egan	3	0	3	8
Bill Shill	1	2	3	2
Jack Crawford	1	2	3	4
Murray Henderson	1	1	2	4
Herb Cain	0	2	2	2
Dit Clapper	0	0	0	0
Roy Conacher	0	0	0	0
Jack McGill	0	0	0	0
Jack Church	0	0	0	4

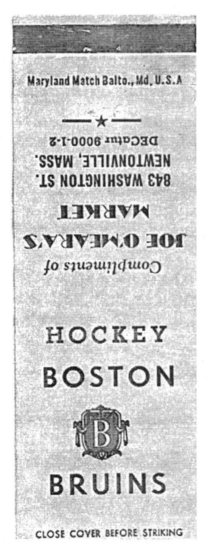

1946–47 Boston Bruins matchbook schedule.

1946–1947

(23rd year)

TEAM OWNER:	The Adams Family	ALL-STARS:	Milt Schmidt (1st team)
PRESIDENT:	Weston Adams Sr.		Frank Brimsek (2nd team)
GM & OWNER:	Art Ross		Bobby Bauer (2nd team)
COACH:	Dit Clapper		Woody Dumart (2nd team)
PLAYOFFS:	*Semi-finals:*	TROPHY WINNERS:	Dufresne — Milt Schmidt
	Lose to Montreal Canadiens		Lady Byng — Bobby Bauer
	1 win – 4 losses	RADIO STATION:	WHDH with Frank Ryan
STANLEY CUP WINNER:	Toronto Maple Leafs		and Leo Egan

UNIFORMS

- White jersey with large gold numbers trimmed in black on front and back of jersey. Gold band trimmed in black on shoulders. Large gold trimmed in black block "B" on arms. Gold and black bands below the "B." Black pants with gold stripes along sides. Alternating gold, black, and white stripes on stockings.

HI-LITES

- Dit Clapper decides to devote full time to coaching.
- Because of injury to Jack Crawford, Dit Clapper returns to man the defense position on November 27 thus becoming the first player to reach 20 seasons of play.
- Joe Carveth scores three goals in a November 13 game against Detroit and March 19 versus Chicago.
- Defeat New York 10–1 on February 12 while celebrating the retirement of Dit Clapper. Mayor Crawford of Kingston, Ontario, presents Clapper with a scroll announcing Clapper's induction into the International Hockey Hall of Fame. Clapper becomes the first living player to enter the Hall of Fame.
- Bruins management also announces it will be retiring jersey #5. In a March 1 game at Montreal, Clapper is presented with a silver tray in recognition of his 20 years in the NHL.
- Bobby Bauer scores three goals in a game March 5 versus Toronto.

- Milt Schmidt wins the Dufrense trophy as the outstanding player in home games.
- Bobby Bauer wins the Lady Byng Trophy.
- Bruins qualify for the playoffs by finishing in third place.
- In a pre-game ceremony before game 4 of the playoffs against Montreal, it is announced by Boston management that Eddie Shore's #2 jersey would be retired. A scroll is also presented to Shore to mark his admittance into the International Hockey Hall of Fame.
- Bruins games are broadcast on radio with Frank Ryan and Leo Egan doing the play by play on WHDH.
- Bruins are shutout in two successive games, February 19 and 20.
- Lose to Montreal, 4 games to 1, in the opening round of the playoffs with Billy Reay of the Canadiens scoring 4 goals in game 4.
- Jack Crawford is the only player in the league to wear a helmet.
- Clarence Campbell replaces Mervyn Dutton as President of the NHL.
- Rules regarding broken stick for netminders is approved allowing goalies to play with a broken stick or to receive a stick from a teammate.
- Regular season is increased from 50 to 60 games.

TRANSACTIONS
- Obtain Don Grosso from Chicago.
- Trade Roy Conacher to Detroit for Joe Carveth.
- Obtain Babe Pratt from Toronto.

1946-47 STANDINGS

	W	L	T	P	GF	GA
Montreal	34	16	10	78	189	138
Toronto	31	19	10	72	209	172
Boston	26	23	11	63	190	175
Detroit	22	27	11	55	190	193
New York	22	32	6	50	167	186
Chicago	19	37	4	42	193	274

1946-47 RESULTS

October 1946
	AT	VERSUS	W-L-T	SCR
19	Montreal	Canadiens	T	1–1
20	Boston	Chicago	T	2–2
23	Boston	Toronto	T	3–3
26	Boston	New York	W	3–1
30	New York	Rangers	T	3–3

November 1946
2	Toronto	Maple Leafs	W	5–0
3	Chicago	Blackhawks	L	5–3
6	Detroit	Red Wings	T	3–3
9	Montreal	Canadiens	L	5–2
10	New York	Rangers	W	4–0
13	Boston	Detroit	W	5–2
17	Boston	Montreal	L	4–1
20	Boston	Toronto	W	4–1
24	Boston	Montreal	L	4–2
27	Boston	New York	W	5–2

December 1946
1	Boston	Detroit	T	3–3
4	Boston	Toronto	T	2–2
7	Toronto	Maple Leafs	L	5–1
8	Boston	New York	L	6–4
11	Boston	Chicago	W	4–1
15	Boston	Detroit	W	3–2
18	Boston	New York	W	3–2
21	Montreal	Canadiens	L	5–1
22	Chicago	Blackhawks	L	5–1
25	Boston	Chicago	L	5–3
28	Toronto	Maple Leafs	L	4–3
29	New York	Rangers	T	2–2

January 1947

1	Boston	New York	W	3–1
4	Montreal	Canadiens	L	4–1
5	Detroit	Red Wings	L	3–1
8	New York	Rangers	W	3–1
11	Toronto	Maple Leafs	L	4–3
12	Detroit	Red Wings	L	5–1
15	Boston	Chicago	W	6–3
18	Boston	Chicago	W	3–1
19	Boston	Toronto	W	3–2
22	Boston	Montreal	L	4–3
25	Montreal	Canadiens	L	4–1
26	Boston	Detroit	W	4–3
29	Boston	Detroit	W	4–1

February 1947

1	Detroit	Red Wings	T	2–2
2	Chicago	Blackhawks	L	3–1
5	Boston	Montreal	L	3–2
8	Toronto	Maple Leafs	L	5–2
9	Chicago	Blackhawks	L	6–4
12	Boston	New York	W	10–1
16	Boston	Montreal	T	2–2
19	New York	Rangers	L	6–0
20	Detroit	Red Wings	L	3–0
23	Chicago	Blackhawks	W	9–4

March 1947

1	Montreal	Canadiens	W	2–1
2	New York	Rangers	W	3–2
5	Boston	Toronto	W	5–4
9	Boston	Detroit	W	6–0
12	Chicago	Blackhawks	W	8–3
13	Detroit	Red Wings	W	3–2
15	Toronto	Maple Leafs	T	5–5
16	Boston	Toronto	W	5–3
19	Boston	Chicago	W	7–3
23	Boston	Montreal	L	3–2

1946-47 SCORING

	GP	SO	GAA	
Frank Brimsek	60	3	2.91	

	G	A	P	PIM
Milt Schmidt	27	35	62	40
Bobby Bauer	30	24	54	4
Woody Dumart	24	28	52	12
Bill Cowley	13	25	38	16
Joe Carveth	21	15	36	18
Don Gallinger	11	19	30	12
Pat Egan	7	18	25	89
Armand Guidolin	10	13	23	73
Ken Smith	14	7	21	4
Terry Reardon	6	14	20	17
Jack Crawford	1	17	18	16
Murray Henderson	5	12	17	63
Jack McGill	5	9	14	19
Mark Marquess	5	4	9	6
Walter Pratt	4	4	8	25
Fern Flaman	1	4	5	41
Eddie Barry	1	3	4	2
Clare Martin	3	0	3	0
Bill Shill	2	0	2	2
Don Grosso	0	2	2	2
Norm McAtee	0	1	1	0
John Peirson	0	0	0	0
Dit Clapper	0	0	0	0

1946-47 PLAYOFF RESULTS

March 1947

	AT	VERSUS	W-L-T	SCR
25	Montreal	Canadiens	L	3–1
27	Montreal	Canadiens	L	2–1
29	Boston	Montreal	W	4–2

April 1947

1	Boston	Montreal	L	5–1
3	Montreal	Canadiens	L	4–3 (OT)

1946-47 PLAYOFFS

vs. Montreal Canadiens	1 win – 4 losses
at Montreal	0 wins – 3 losses
at Boston	1 win – 1 loss

1946-47 PLAYOFF SCORING

	GP	SO	GAA					
Frank Brimsek	5	0	3.20	Pat Egan	0	2	2	6
				Clare Martin	0	1	1	0
				Armand Guidolin	0	1	1	6
	G	A	P	PIM				
Milt Schmidt	3	1	4	4	Pentti Lund	0	0	0	0
Ken Smith	3	0	3	2	Jack Crawford	0	0	0	0
Joe Carveth	2	1	3	0	Mark Marquess	0	0	0	0
Terry Reardon	0	3	3	2	Murray Henderson	0	0	0	4
Bobby Bauer	1	1	2	0	Don Gallinger	0	0	0	7
Woody Dumart	1	1	2	8	Fern Flaman	0	0	0	8
Bill Cowley	0	2	2	0	Jack McGill	0	0	0	11

1947–1948

(24th year)

TEAM OWNER:	The Adams Family	STANLEY CUP WINNER:	Toronto Maple Leafs
PRESIDENT:	Weston Adams Sr.	ALL-STARS:	Frank Brimsek (2nd team)
GM & OWNER:	Art Ross	TROPHY WINNERS:	Dufresne — Frank Brimsek
COACH:	Dit Clapper	RADIO STATION:	WHDH Radio with
PLAYOFFS:	*Semi-finals:*		Frank Ryan and Leo Egan
	Lose to Toronto Maple Leafs		
	1 win – 4 losses		

UNIFORMS
- White jersey with large gold numbers trimmed in black on front and back of jersey. Gold band trimmed in black on shoulders. Large gold trimmed in black block "B" on arms. Gold and black bands below the "B." Black pants with gold stripes along sides. Alternating gold, black, and white stripes on stockings.

POTPOURRI
- In a November 12 game at New York against the Rangers, Bruins score 3 goals in 57 seconds.
- Bruins finish in third place.
- Frank Brimsek appears in all 60 games.
- Johnny Quilty's career is cut short after suffering a compound fracture of the leg at Chicago on January 11.
- Toronto wins at Boston for first time in 3 years.
- Don Gallinger and Billy Taylor are suspended by the NHL for betting on games.
- In a March 30 playoff loss to Toronto, the game is marred by a melee involving both players and fans.
- Bruins lose playoffs to Toronto, 4 games to 1, with Ted Kennedy of Toronto scoring 4 goals in game 2.
- Opening night against the Rangers, October 19, is played in 80-degree temperatures. The game is delayed 40 minutes after the second period so that the players could have their skates sharpened.
- The Art Ross Trophy, awarded annually since 1941 to the outstanding player, would now be awarded to the leading scorer.
- First annual All-Star game for the benefit of the player's fund is held on October 13 in Toronto.
- Montreal Maroons franchise, suspended since 1938, is terminated.

TRANSACTIONS

- Billy Taylor is acquired from Detroit for Bep Guidolin.
- Billy Taylor and Pentti Lund are traded to the Rangers for Grant Warwick.
- Joe Carveth traded to Montreal for Jimmy Peters and John Quilty.
- Pete Babando, Paul Ronty, Ed Harrison, and Eddie Sandford are brought up from the minors.
- Bobby Bauer retires.

1947-48 STANDINGS

	W	L	T	P	GF	GA
Toronto	32	15	13	77	182	143
Detroit	30	18	12	72	187	148
Boston	23	24	13	59	167	168
New York	21	26	13	55	176	201
Montreal	20	29	11	51	147	169
Chicago	20	34	6	46	195	225

1947-48 RESULTS

October 1947

	AT	VERSUS	W-L-T	SCR
19	Boston	New York	W	3–1
22	Boston	Montreal	W	3–1
25	Montreal	Canadiens	L	5–0
26	Boston	Chicago	W	3–2
29	New York	Rangers	W	3–1

November 1947

1	Toronto	Maple Leafs	T	1–1
2	Detroit	Red Wings	L	2–1
5	Chicago	Blackhawks	W	2–1
12	New York	Rangers	W	8–2
15	Montreal	Canadiens	W	9–1
16	Boston	Detroit	L	3–2
19	Boston	Toronto	W	7–2
22	Toronto	Maple Leafs	L	4–3
23	Boston	Montreal	T	2–2
26	Chicago	Blackhawks	L	5–3
27	Detroit	Red Wings	L	4–1
30	Boston	Toronto	T	0–0

December 1947

3	Boston	Chicago	T	4–4
6	Boston	New York	T	5–5
7	Boston	Montreal	W	1–0
10	Chicago	Blackhawks	L	6–5
14	Boston	Toronto	T	1–1
17	New York	Rangers	L	5–2
20	Montreal	Canadiens	W	4–2
21	Boston	Detroit	L	6–5
25	Boston	Chicago	L	6–1
27	Toronto	Maple Leafs	L	2–1

28	Detroit	Red Wings	L	3–0
31	New York	Rangers	L	7–3

January 1948

1	Boston	New York	W	4–1
3	Montreal	Canadiens	T	2–2
10	Detroit	Red Wings	W	4–1
11	Chicago	Blackhawks	L	4–1
14	Boston	Detroit	T	3–3
17	Toronto	Maple Leafs	L	4–1
18	Boston	Montreal	T	1–1
21	Boston	Toronto	W	2–1
25	Boston	New York	W	6–4
28	Boston	Detroit	L	4–2
31	Boston	Chicago	L	7–4

February 1948

1	Boston	Montreal	L	3–0
4	Boston	Toronto	L	4–2
8	Detroit	Red Wings	W	3–1
11	Boston	Chicago	L	3–0
14	Boston	New York	T	4–4
15	Boston	Detroit	W	3–1
18	Chicago	Blackhawks	W	4–2
21	Montreal	Canadiens	W	3–1
22	New York	Rangers	L	4–1
25	Toronto	Maple Leafs	L	4–2
29	Chicago	Blackhawks	L	5–1

March 1948

3	Boston	Chicago	T	4–4
4	Montreal	Canadiens	T	1–1
7	Boston	Toronto	W	3–1

10	Boston	New York	W	6–3		16	New York	Rangers	W	6–2
13	Toronto	Maple Leafs	L	5–2		17	Boston	Detroit	T	0–0
14	Detroit	Red Wings	W	5–1		21	Boston	Montreal	W	4–3

1947-48 SCORING

	GP	SO	GAA		Pat Egan	8	11	19	81
Frank Brimsek	60	3	2.80		Clare Martin	5	13	18	34
					Joe Carveth	8	9	17	0
	G	A	P	PIM	Murray Henderson	6	8	14	50
Woody Dumart	21	16	37	14	Paul Ronty	3	11	14	0
Pete Babando	23	11	34	52	Jack Crawford	3	11	14	10
Don Gallinger	10	21	31	37	Ed Harrison	6	7	13	8
Jimmy Peters	12	15	27	38	Grant Warwick	6	5	11	8
Milt Schmidt	9	17	26	28	Fern Flaman	4	6	10	69
Eddie Sandford	10	15	25	25	John Peirson	4	2	6	0
Ken Smith	11	12	23	14	John Quilty	3	2	5	2
Billy Taylor	4	16	20	25	Arnie Kullman	0	0	0	0
Wally Wilson	11	8	19	18	Ray Manson	0	0	0	0

1947-48 PLAYOFF RESULTS

March 1948	AT	VERSUS	W-L-T	SCR		April 1948				
24	Toronto	Maple Leafs	L	5–4 (OT)		1	Boston	Toronto	W	3–2
27	Toronto	Maple Leafs	L	5–3		3	Toronto	Maple Leafs	L	3–2
30	Boston	Toronto	L	5–1						

1947-48 PLAYOFFS

vs. Toronto Maple Leafs	1 win – 4 losses
at Toronto	0 wins – 3 losses
at Boston	1 win – 1 loss

1947-48 PLAYOFF SCORING

	GP	SO	GAA		Pete Babando	1	1	2	2
Frank Brimsek	5	0	4.00		Eddie Sandford	1	0	1	0
					Ed Harrison	1	0	1	2
	G	A	P	PIM	Murray Henderson	1	0	1	5
Milt Schmidt	2	5	7	2	John Crawford	0	1	1	2
John Peirson	3	2	5	0	Fern Flaman	0	0	0	12
Ken Smith	2	3	5	0	Clare Martin	0	0	0	6
Paul Ronty	0	4	4	0	Woody Dumart	0	0	0	0
Jimmy Peters	1	2	3	2	Pentti Lund	0	0	0	0
Grant Warwick	0	3	3	4	Wally Wilson	0	0	0	0
Pat Egan	1	1	2	2					

DURING the past twenty-four years of National Hockey League competition, the greatest hockey players in the world have appeared on Boston ice. The Bruins are proud that many of the all-time hockey greats have worn Boston uniforms. We of the Bruins deeply appreciate the loyalty of the Boston hockey fans over the years and we pledge our best efforts to keep the Bruins tradition building in the years ahead.

Weston W Adams

President.

1948–1949
(25th year)

TEAM OWNER:	The Adams Family	STANLEY CUP WINNER:	Toronto Maple Leafs
PRESIDENT & GOVERNOR:	Weston Adams	ALL-STARS:	None
GM:	Art Ross	TROPHY WINNERS:	O'Brien Trophy
COACH:	Dit Clapper		— Boston Bruins
PLAYOFFS:	*Semi-finals:*		Dufresne: Pat Egan
	Lose to Toronto Maple Leafs	RADIO STATION:	WHDH with Frank Ryan
	1 win – 4 losses		and Leo Egan

UNIFORMS

- White jersey with spoked "B" appears for the first time. On the vertical spoke to the left and right of the "B" is the numbers 24–49. This represents the 25th anniversary of the Boston Bruins. The "B" in the spoke is rounded as opposed to the block "B" that would appear the next season. Gold band trimmed in black on shoulders. Black pants with gold stripes along sides. Alternating gold, black, and white stripes on stockings.

POTPOURRI

- John Crawford Night is celebrated at Boston Garden on March 16.
- Finish in second place.
- Lose to Toronto in 5 games of the opening round of the playoffs.

- The game against Detroit on November 10 is postponed after 10 minutes because of fog inside the Boston Garden as it had been a warm day. The game is played the next evening.
- In his only Bruins appearance, Les Colvin replaces Frank Brimsek (sent to Minnesota to be with his ill son) on January 22 against Montreal. Bruins sign Jack Gelineau to temporarily replace Brimsek.
- Frank Brimsek's young son passes away.
- NHL players are forbidden to endorse tobacco and alcohol.

TRANSACTIONS
- Signed Ed Kryzanowski, Dave Creighton, and Zelio Toppazzini.
- Les Colvin and Jack Gelineau replace Brimsek in goal during Brimsek's absence.
- Dit Clapper resigns as coach.

1948-49 STANDINGS

	W	L	T	P	GF	GA
Detroit	34	19	7	75	195	145
Boston	29	23	8	66	178	163
Montreal	28	23	9	65	152	126
Toronto	22	25	13	57	147	161
Chicago	21	31	8	50	173	211
New York	18	31	11	47	133	172

1948-49 RESULTS

October 1948

	AT	VERSUS	W-L-T	SCR
16	Toronto	Maple Leafs	W	4–1
20	Boston	Chicago	W	8–3
24	Boston	New York	W	4–1
28	Chicago	Blackhawks	W	5–1
30	Montreal	Canadiens	T	3–3
31	New York	Rangers	L	2–0

November 1948

7	Detroit	Red Wings	L	7–3
11	Boston	Detroit	W	4–1
14	Boston	Montreal	W	3–2
17	Boston	Toronto	W	2–1
20	Toronto	Maple Leafs	T	2–2
21	Boston	New York	L	4–1
24	Detroit	Red Wings	W	5–3
27	Montreal	Canadiens	W	2–0
28	Boston	Toronto	W	6–2

December 1948

1	Boston	Chicago	W	5–1
4	Boston	Detroit	L	3–2
5	Boston	Montreal	W	2–1
7	New York	Rangers	T	2–2
8	Chicago	Blackhawks	L	4–3
11	Toronto	Maple Leafs	L	3–2
12	Boston	Toronto	L	4–3
15	Boston	Montreal	L	4–2

19	Chicago	Blackhawks	L	7–2
22	Boston	Detroit	W	5–2
23	Montreal	Canadiens	L	4–2
25	Boston	Chicago	W	2–1
29	Detroit	Red Wings	L	10–2
31	New York	Rangers	T	2–2

January 1949

1	Boston	New York	W	4–1
5	Toronto	Maple Leafs	L	4–0
6	Detroit	Red Wings	W	3–2
9	Chicago	Blackhawks	L	4–2
12	Boston	Montreal	L	5–3
16	Boston	Chicago	W	3–1
19	New York	Rangers	W	5–2
22	Montreal	Canadiens	L	4–2
23	Boston	Montreal	W	3–0
26	Boston	Toronto	L	3–1
30	Boston	Detroit	L	4–0

February 1949

2	Boston	New York	W	5–3
5	Montreal	Canadiens	W	3–2
6	Boston	Toronto	L	4–2
9	Boston	Chicago	W	5–3
12	Boston	New York	W	4–2
13	Boston	Detroit	T	4–4
16	Chicago	Blackhawks	L	5–1
19	Toronto	Maple Leafs	L	5–2

Sam Bettio wearing his 1948–49 uniform, the first bearing the spoked "B."

21	Detroit	Red Wings	T	2–2
23	New York	Rangers	W	3–2
27	Chicago	Blackhawks	T	2–2

March 1949

| 2 | Boston | Detroit | T | 1–1 |
| 5 | Montreal | Canadiens | L | 4–0 |

6	Boston	Montreal	L	1–0
9	Boston	New York	W	8–1
12	Toronto	Maple Leafs	W	2–1
13	Detroit	Red Wings	W	6–2
15	New York	Rangers	W	4–2
16	Boston	Chicago	L	4–3
20	Boston	Toronto	W	7–2

1948-49 SCORING

	GP	SO	GAA
Frank Brimsek	54	1	2.72
Jack Gelineau	4	0	3.00
Les Colvin	1	0	4.00
Gordon Henry	1	1	0.00

	G	A	P	PIM
Paul Ronty	20	29	49	11
John Peirson	22	21	43	45
Ken Smith	20	20	40	6
Grant Warwick	22	15	37	14
Eddie Sandford	16	20	36	57
Pete Babando	19	14	33	34

Milt Schmidt	10	22	32	25
Jimmy Peters	16	15	31	8
Pat Egan	6	18	24	92
Woody Dumart	11	12	23	6
Fern Flaman	4	12	16	62
Jack Crawford	2	13	15	14
Murray Henderson	2	9	11	28
Ed Harrison	5	5	10	20
Dave Creighton	1	3	4	0
Ed Kryzanowski	1	3	4	10
Zelio Toppazzini	1	1	2	0
Cliff Thompson	0	1	1	0

1948-49 PLAYOFF RESULTS

March 1949

	AT	VERSUS	W-L-T	SCR
22	Toronto	Maple Leafs	L	3–0
24	Toronto	Maple Leafs	L	3–2

26	Boston	Toronto	W	5–4 (OT)
29	Boston	Toronto	L	3–1
30	Toronto	Maple Leafs	L	3–2

1948-49 PLAYOFFS

vs. Toronto Maple Leafs	1 win – 4 losses
at Toronto	1 win – 1 loss
at Boston	0 wins – 3 losses

1948-49 PLAYOFF SCORING

	GP	SO	GAA
Frank Brimsek	5	0	3.20

	G	A	P	PIM
John Peirson	3	1	4	4
Eddie Sandford	1	3	4	2
Woody Dumart	3	0	3	0
Paul Ronty	1	2	3	2
Grant Warwick	2	0	2	0
Ken Smith	0	2	2	4
Milt Schmidt	0	2	2	8

Jimmy Peters	0	1	1	0
Murray Henderson	0	1	1	2
Ed Kryzanowski	0	1	1	2
Fern Flaman	0	1	1	8
Ed Harrison	0	0	0	0
Pat Egan	0	0	0	16
Pete Babando	0	0	0	2
Dave Creighton	0	0	0	0
John Crawford	0	0	0	0
Zellio Toppazzini	0	0	0	0

1949–1950
(26th year)

TEAM OWNER:	The Adams Family	STANLEY CUP WINNER:	Detroit Red Wings
PRESIDENT & GOVERNOR:	Weston Adams Sr.	TROPHY WINNERS:	Calder: Jack Gelineau
GM:	Art Ross		Dufresne: Milt Schmidt
COACH:	George Boucher	RADIO STATION:	WHDH Radio with
PLAYOFFS:	Finish out of the playoffs		Frank Ryan and Leo Egan
ALL-STARS:	None		

UNIFORMS

- Home and road jersey is white with spoked "B." Gold band trimmed in black on shoulders. Black pants with gold stripes along sides. Alternating gold, black, and white stripes on stockings.

POTPOURRI

- Jack Gelineau wins the Calder Trophy as the league's outstanding rookie.
- Center Phil Maloney is runner-up in Calder balloting.
- Bruins longest winning streak this season is 3 games, while longest unbeaten string is 5 games.
- Gerry Couture of Detroit scores 4 goals in a February 11 game. The goals are scored in a 9-minute span of the third period.
- Bruins win only 3 of their final 13 games thus finishing in fifth place, out of the playoffs.
- Bruins record no hat tricks this season.
- A new 70-game schedule is started.
- Viscountess Byng passes away leading the league to authorize a memorial trophy in her name.
- Ken Smith misses first game, December 21, after 237 consecutive games.
- Ice surface is painted white for better television and movie viewing.
- Bruins enjoy two 3-game winning streaks.
- Paul Ronty leads the team with a 7-game scoring streak while Jack Gelineau's longest shutout streak is 117 minutes and 25 seconds.
- Fern Flaman leads the league with 8 major penalties.
- Dick Bittner, Boston Olympics goaltender, records a tie in his only NHL appearance.

TRANSACTIONS

- Frank Brimsek sold to Chicago.
- Bill Quackenbush and Pete Horeck obtained from Detroit for Pete Babando, Jimmy Peters, and Clare Martin.
- Pat Egan is sold to New York.

1949-50 STANDINGS

	W	L	T	P	GF	GA
Detroit	37	19	14	88	229	164
Montreal	29	22	19	77	172	150
Toronto	31	27	12	74	176	173
New York	28	31	11	67	170	189
Boston	22	32	16	60	198	228
Chicago	22	38	10	54	203	244

1949-50 RESULTS

October 1949

	AT	VERSUS	W-L-T	SCR
12	Detroit	Red Wings	L	2–1
16	Boston	New York	T	2–2
19	Boston	Chicago	W	7–4
22	Montreal	Canadiens	W	2–1
23	Boston	Montreal	T	0–0
26	New York	Rangers	L	5–2
29	Toronto	Maple Leafs	L	8–1
30	Chicago	Blackhawks	L	10–4

November 1949

2	Detroit	Red Wings	L	5–3
5	Montreal	Canadiens	T	3–3
9	Boston	Chicago	L	3–1
12	Boston	Detroit	L	7–5
13	Boston	Toronto	W	4–2
16	New York	Rangers	L	2–1
17	Chicago	Blackhawks	L	8–3
20	Boston	Montreal	W	2–1
23	Boston	Toronto	W	3–1
26	Toronto	Maple Leafs	T	3–3
27	Boston	New York	T	1–1
30	Detroit	Red Wings	L	3–0

December 1949

1	Chicago	Blackhawks	L	5–4
3	Boston	Chicago	W	5–3
4	Boston	Montreal	W	4–2
7	Boston	Detroit	L	2–1
8	Montreal	Canadiens	T	2–2
10	Toronto	Maple Leafs	L	2–1
11	Boston	Toronto	W	2–0
14	Boston	Detroit	L	5–2
17	Boston	New York	L	3–1
18	Boston	Montreal	W	3–1
21	Chicago	Blackhawks	W	4–1
24	Toronto	Maple Leafs	W	8–4
25	Boston	Chicago	T	4–4
28	Detroit	Red Wings	T	2–2
31	New York	Rangers	L	4–1

January 1950

1	Boston	New York	W	6–0
5	Montreal	Canadiens	L	5–3
8	Detroit	Red Wings	W	4–3
11	Boston	Detroit	W	2–1
14	Toronto	Maple Leafs	L	4–3
15	Boston	Chicago	L	5–1
18	New York	Rangers	W	4–2
21	Montreal	Canadiens	L	3–1
22	Boston	Montreal	L	5–4
25	Detroit	Red Wings	T	4–4
26	Chicago	Blackhawks	L	5–1
28	Boston	New York	T	2–2
29	Boston	Detroit	W	4–1

February 1950

1	Boston	New York	W	3–2
5	Boston	Toronto	L	2–1
8	Boston	Toronto	L	3–1
11	Boston	Detroit	L	9–4
12	Boston	Montreal	T	3–3
15	New York	Rangers	T	2–2
19	Chicago	Blackhawks	T	4–4
22	Toronto	Maple Leafs	L	3–1
25	Montreal	Canadiens	L	3–2
26	New York	Rangers	L	4–3

March 1950

1	Boston	Toronto	W	5–2
4	Boston	New York	W	5–1
5	Boston	Chicago	W	11–4
8	Boston	Detroit	L	5–3
11	Montreal	Canadiens	L	5–0
12	Boston	Toronto	T	2–2
15	New York	Rangers	W	4–1
18	Detroit	Red Wings	T	1–1
19	Chicago	Blackhawks	W	4–3
22	Boston	Chicago	L	7–5
25	Toronto	Maple Leafs	L	8–0
26	Boston	Montreal	T	3–3

1949-50 SCORING

	GP	SO	GAA
Gordon Henry	2	0	2.50
Dick Bittner	1	0	3.00
Jack Gelineau	67	3	3.28

	G	A	P	PIM
Paul Ronty	23	36	59	8

John Peirson	27	25	52	49
Phil Maloney	15	31	46	6
Milt Schmidt	19	22	41	41
Ken Smith	10	31	41	12
Woody Dumart	14	25	39	14
Dave Creighton	18	13	31	13
Norman Poile	16	14	30	6

Ed Harrison	14	12	26	23	Arnie Kullman	0	1	1	11
Bill Quackenbush	8	17	25	4	John McIntyre	0	1	1	0
Silvio Bettio	9	12	21	32	Gordon Byers	0	1	1	0
Ed Kryzanowski	6	10	16	12	Red Sullivan	0	1	1	0
Murray Henderson	3	8	11	42	Ross Lowe	0	0	0	0
Zellio Toppazzini	5	5	10	18	Norman Corcoran	0	0	0	0
Pete Horeck	5	5	10	22	Bart Bradley	0	0	0	0
Jack Crawford	2	8	10	8					
Fern Flaman	2	5	7	122					
Eddie Sandford	1	4	5	6					
Lorne Ferguson	1	1	2	0					

Penalty minutes: 449 – 6.4 minutes per game

NO PLAYOFF SCORING

1950–1951
(27th year)

TEAM OWNER:	The Adams Family	STANLEY CUP WINNER:	Toronto Maple Leafs
PRESIDENT:	Weston Adams	ALL-STARS:	Bill Quackenbush (1st team)
GM & OWNER:	Art Ross		Milt Schmidt (1st team)
COACH:	Lynn Patrick	TROPHY WINNERS:	Hart — Milt Schmidt
PLAYOFFS:	*Semi-finals:*		Dufresne — Milt Schmidt
	Lose to Toronto Maple Leafs	RADIO STATION:	WHDH with Frank Ryan,
	1 win – 4 losses – 1 tie		Leo Egan and John Brooks

UNIFORMS
- Home and road jersey is white with spoked "B." Gold band trimmed in black on shoulders. Black pants with gold stripes along sides. Alternating gold, black, and white stripes on stockings.

POTPOURRI
- Milt Schmidt wins the Hart Trophy as the league MVP.
- Finish in fourth place.
- Lose semi-finals to Toronto.
- The executors of the Viscountess Lady Byng of Vimy approve of the retirement of the Lady Byng Trophy to be replaced by the Lady Byng Memorial Trophy.
- Discussion of contrasting uniforms is discussed with the home team recommending what uniform the visiting team would wear.
- The Bruins decided that their home uniforms would be white. Chicago, Detroit and Toronto also would wear white-based home uniforms. Montreal would wear red and the Rangers would go with the color blue.
- The March 31 playoff game at Toronto ends in 1–1 tie because of Toronto curfew laws.
- Referees begin wearing numbers on the back of their uniforms.
- Bruins and Rangers play 8 tie games.

TRANSACTIONS
- George Boucher is replaced by Lynn Patrick as coach.
- Fern Flaman, Ken Smith, and Phil Maloney are traded to Toronto for Bill Ezinicki and Vic Lynn.
- Ed Harrison and Zelio Toppazzini are traded to New York for Dunc Fisher.
- Ross Lowe is traded to Montreal for Hal Laycoe.

1950-51 STANDINGS

	W	L	T	P	GF	GA
Detroit	44	13	13	101	236	13
Toronto	41	16	13	95	212	138
Montreal	25	30	15	65	173	184
Boston	22	30	18	62	178	197
New York	20	29	21	61	169	201
Chicago	13	47	10	36	171	280

1950-51 RESULTS

October 1950

	AT	VERSUS	W-L-T	SCR
14	Montreal	Canadiens	T	1–1
15	Boston	Montreal	L	2–1
18	Boston	Toronto	L	2–0
22	Boston	New York	T	0–0
25	New York	New York	T	1–1
28	Toronto	Maple Leafs	L	4–2
29	Detroit	Red Wings	L	2–0

November 1950

2	Chicago	Blackhawks	L	5–2
4	Montreal	Canadiens	W	3–2
5	Detroit	Red Wings	L	4–2
8	Boston	Detroit	T	3–3
11	Boston	Chicago	L	4–2
12	Boston	Toronto	L	7–0
15	New York	Rangers	W	4–3
18	Boston	Detroit	L	2–1
19	Boston	Toronto	W	3–1
23	Chicago	Blackhawks	L	4–1
25	Boston	New York	T	3–3
26	Boston	Montreal	L	3–1
29	Boston	Detroit	W	6–3

December 1950

2	Boston	New York	L	3–2
3	New York	Rangers	W	5–3
6	Boston	Chicago	W	5–4
7	Montreal	Canadiens	W	3–0
9	Toronto	Maple Leafs	L	8–1
10	Boston	Montreal	W	5–2
14	Detroit	Red Wings	L	4–2
16	Boston	Detroit	L	4–1
17	Boston	Toronto	L	4–2
20	New York	Rangers	T	4–4
21	Chicago	Blackhawks	W	3–1
23	Toronto	Maple Leafs	T	2–2
25	Boston	Chicago	W	7–4
27	Boston	Chicago	T	4–4
31	New York	Rangers	L	3–0

January 1951

1	Boston	New York	W	3–2
4	Montreal	Canadiens	W	4–2
7	Detroit	Red Wings	L	3–0
9	Chicago	Blackhawks	W	5–4
13	Montreal	Canadiens	L	4–0
14	Boston	Chicago	W	5–1
17	New York	Rangers	T	3–3
20	Toronto	Maple Leafs	L	2–1
21	Boston	New York	W	5–1
25	Detroit	Red Wings	T	3–3
27	Boston	Detroit	W	3–0
28	Boston	Montreal	T	1–1

February 1951

1	Chicago	Blackhawks	L	5–2
3	Montreal	Canadiens	L	4–1
4	Boston	Toronto	T	3–3
7	Boston	New York	T	2–2
10	Boston	Montreal	W	6–0
11	Boston	Detroit	L	2–1
18	Chicago	Blackhawks	W	7–3
19	Detroit	Red Wings	T	2–2
21	New York	Rangers	T	2–2
24	Toronto	Maple Leafs	L	6–2
25	Chicago	Blackhawks	W	3–2
28	Boston	Detroit	T	1–1

March 1951

3	Boston	New York	T	3–3
4	Boston	Chicago	W	10–2
7	Boston	Montreal	L	3–2
10	Toronto	Maple Leafs	L	5–3
11	Boston	Toronto	W	3–1
15	Detroit	Red Wings	L	4–0
17	Montreal	Canadiens	L	3–1
18	Boston	Montreal	T	2–2
21	Boston	Chicago	W	6–5
24	Toronto	Maple Leafs	L	4–1
25	Boston	Toronto	L	1–0

Max Quackenbush in a 1950–51 uniform. Numbers had not yet appeared on the sleeve at this point.

1950-51 SCORING

	GP	SO	GAA
Jack Gelineau	70	4	2.81

	G	A	P	PIM
Milt Schmidt	22	39	61	33
Woody Dumart	20	21	41	7
John Peirson	19	19	38	43
Bill Ezinicki	16	19	35	119
Lorne Ferguson	16	17	33	31
Paul Ronty	10	22	32	20
Dunc Fisher	9	20	29	20
Bill Quackenbush	5	24	29	12
Eddie Sandford	10	13	23	33
Pete Horeck	10	13	23	57
Vic Lynn	14	6	20	69
Murray Henderson	4	7	11	37

	G	A	P	PIM
Max Quackenbush	4	6	10	26
Dave Creighton	5	4	9	4
Ed Kryzanowski	3	6	9	10
Ross Lowe	5	3	8	40
Ken Smith	1	3	4	11
Phil Maloney	2	0	2	2
Fern Flaman	1	1	2	37
Ed Reigle	0	2	2	25
Hal Laycoe	1	1	2	4
Ed Harrison	1	0	1	0
Zelio Toppazzini	0	1	1	0
Steve Kraftcheck	0	0	0	8
Bob Armstrong	0	0	0	2

Penalty minutes: 654 – 9.3 per game

1950-51 PLAYOFF RESULTS

March 1951

	AT	VERSUS	W-L-T	SCR
28	Toronto	Maple Leafs	W	2–0
31	Toronto	Maple Leafs	T	1–1

April 1951

1	Boston	Toronto	L	3–0
3	Boston	Toronto	L	3–1
7	Toronto	Maple Leafs	L	4–1
8	Boston	Toronto	L	6–0

1950-51 PLAYOFFS

vs. Toronto Maple Leafs	1 win – 4 losses – 1 tie
at Toronto	1 win – 1 loss – 1 tie
at Boston	0 wins – 3 losses

1950-51 PLAYOFF SCORING

	GP	SO	GAA
Jack Gelineau	4	1	1.75
Gordon Henry	2	0	5.00

	G	A	P	PIM
Woody Dumart	1	2	3	0
Johnny Peirson	1	1	2	2
Bill Ezinicki	1	1	2	18
Duncan Fisher	1	0	1	0
Lorne Ferguson	1	0	1	2
Dave Creighton	0	1	1	0
Bill Quackenbush	0	1	1	0
Paul Ronty	0	1	1	2
Ed Sandford	0	1	1	4

	G	A	P	PIM
Hal Laycoe	0	1	1	5
Milt Schmidt	0	1	1	7
Jack McIntyre	0	0	0	0
Ed Kryzanowski	0	0	0	2
Steve Kraftcheck	0	0	0	7
Pete Horeck	0	0	0	13
Vic Lynn	0	0	0	2
Murray Henderson	0	0	0	2
Max Quackenbush	0	0	0	4
Red Sullivan	0	0	0	2

Penalty minutes: 72 – 12 per game

1951–1952
(28th year)

TEAM OWNER:	Boston Garden Arena Corporation	STANLEY CUP WINNER:	Detroit Red Wings
PRESIDENT:	Walter Brown	ALL-STARS:	Jim Henry (2nd team)
GM & OWNER:	Art Ross		Milt Schmidt (2nd team)
COACH:	Lynn Patrick	TROPHY WINNERS:	Dufresne — Jim Henry
PLAYOFFS:	*Semi-finals:*	RADIO STATION:	WHDH Radio with
	Lose to Montreal Canadiens		Frank Ryan and Leo Egan
	3 wins – 4 losses		

UNIFORMS

- Home jersey is white with spoked "B." Gold band trimmed in black on shoulders. Black pants with gold stripes along sides. Alternating gold, black, and white stripes on stockings. Road jersey, introduced for the playoffs, is black with large block letter "B" in gold trimmed in white. Jersey has gold shoulder band. White, gold, white vertical stripes on arms. Pants and socks are same as home.

POTPOURRI

- Woody Dumart scores 200th career goal on February 5 at Boston.
- Finish the season in fourth place.
- 13,121 fans attend November 11 tie game against Toronto.
- Bruins enjoy a 4-game winning streak and a 6-game undefeated streak.
- Lose to Montreal in semi-finals, 4 games to 3.
- Weston Adams resigns as president of the Bruins and is replaced by Walter Brown, General Manager of the Boston Garden. Brown purchases 60% interest in the Bruins.
- February 26 game against Detroit is transferred to Boston Arena because the brine pipes in the Boston Garden collapsed. The game is played before 4,049 fans, the smallest crowd to attend a Bruins game in 24 years.
- Newly acquired Gus Kyle leads the league in penalty minutes with 127. Before joining the Bruins Kyle worked as a Royal Canadian Mounted Policeman but is able to leave the Mounties by getting married. The RCMP had a rule that you had to be on the force at least 7 years before getting married.
- The Bruins record 1 hat trick on the season.
- Weston Adams sells 60% of the Bruins to Walter Brown, who is the operating director of the Boston Garden.
- Bruins and Toronto tie for most ties this season with 16.
- Milt Schmidt scores 200th career goal on March 18 at Boston. In this game, Bobby Bauer comes out of retirement and joins fellow Kraut Liners, Schmidt and Dumart, in a game honoring their contributions to the Boston Bruins and hockey.

TRANSACTIONS

- Jim Henry replaces Jack Gelineau in goal.
- Adam Brown purchased from Chicago for Max Quackenbush.
- Paul Ronty is traded to New York for Pentti Lund and Gus Kyle.
- Acquire Fleming Mackell from Toronto.

1951-52 STANDINGS

	W	L	T	P	GF	GA
Detroit	44	14	12	100	215	133
Montreal	34	26	10	78	195	164
Toronto	29	25	16	74	168	157
Boston	25	29	16	66	162	176
New York	23	34	13	59	192	219
Chicago	17	44	9	43	158	241

1951-52 RESULTS

October 1951

	AT	VERSUS	W-L-T	SCR
11	Detroit	Red Wings	L	1–0
13	Montreal	Canadiens	W	2–1
14	Boston	Montreal	L	4–3
17	Toronto	Maple Leafs	L	4–2
21	Boston	New York	T	1–1
24	New York	Rangers	W	3–1
28	Chicago	Blackhawks	W	2–0

November 1951

	AT	VERSUS	W-L-T	SCR
1	Detroit	Red Wings	W	3–2
4	Chicago	Blackhawks	W	4–2
6	Boston	Detroit	T	0–0
8	Montreal	Canadiens	L	4–2
11	Boston	Toronto	T	1–1
13	Boston	Chicago	L	3–1
17	Toronto	Maple Leafs	T	1–1
18	Boston	Montreal	T	3–3
20	Boston	Detroit	L	2–0
21	New York	Rangers	T	3–3
25	Boston	Toronto	L	4–1
27	Boston	New York	T	1–1
29	Detroit	Red Wings	T	1–1

December 1951

	AT	VERSUS	W-L-T	SCR
2	Boston	Montreal	W	4–1
4	Boston	Chicago	W	3–1
5	New York	Rangers	W	3–2
9	Chicago	Blackhawks	L	4–3
11	Boston	New York	W	4–2
12	New York	Rangers	L	6–3
15	Montreal	Canadiens	L	3–1
16	Boston	Montreal	L	4–2
18	Boston	Detroit	T	5–5
22	Toronto	Maple Leafs	L	3–2
23	Boston	Toronto	W	4–2
25	Boston	Chicago	L	6–2
29	Toronto	Maple Leafs	L	4–0

January 1952

1	Boston	New York	L	4–2
5	Montreal	Canadiens	W	3–2
6	Detroit	Red Wings	L	4–2
8	Chicago	Blackhawks	W	7–2
13	Boston	Chicago	W	5–4
15	Boston	Toronto	L	1–0
17	Detroit	Red Wings	L	5–0
19	Toronto	Maple Leafs	L	6–2
20	Boston	Montreal	W	2–1
22	Boston	New York	T	3–3
26	Montreal	Canadiens	L	5–3
27	Boston	Toronto	L	3–0
29	Boston	Detroit	W	3–1
31	Chicago	Blackhawks	T	0–0

February 1952

2	Toronto	Maple Leafs	T	1–1
3	Boston	Montreal	W	1–0
5	Boston	Chicago	W	5–0
9	Boston	New York	L	4–2
10	Boston	Detroit	L	2–0
13	New York	Rangers	L	6–2
17	Chicago	Blackhawks	W	5–2
18	Detroit	Red Wings	L	4–2
21	Montreal	Canadiens	T	3–3
24	New York	Rangers	L	5–2
26	Boston	Detroit	L	4–3

March 1952

1	Toronto	Maple Leafs	T	1–1
2	Boston	Toronto	T	2–2
4	Boston	New York	W	4–1
6	Detroit	Red Wings	L	2–1
9	Boston	Chicago	T	4–2
11	Boston	Detroit	W	3–2
13	Chicago	Blackhawks	T	3–3
15	Montreal	Canadiens	W	2–0
16	Boston	Montreal	W	2–1
18	Boston	Chicago	W	4–0
19	New York	Rangers	L	6–4
23	Boston	Toronto	W	4–2

1951-52 SCORING

	GP	SO	GAA
Jim Henry	70	7	2.51

	G	A	P	PIM
Milt Schmidt	21	29	50	57
John Peirson	20	30	50	30
Dave Creighton	20	17	37	18
Jack McIntyre	12	19	31	18
Dunc Fisher	15	12	27	2
Eddie Sandford	13	12	25	54
Real Chevrefils	8	17	25	8
Red Sullivan	12	12	24	24
Bill Quackenbush	2	17	19	6
Adam Brown	8	9	17	6
Woody Dumart	5	8	13	0
Gus Kyle	1	12	13	127
Hal Laycoe	5	7	12	61
Bill Ezinicki	5	5	10	47
Fleming Mackell	1	8	9	24
Ed Kryzanowski	5	3	8	33
Lorne Ferguson	3	4	7	14
Leo Labine	2	4	6	9
Murray Henderson	0	6	6	51
Pentti Lund	0	5	5	0
Vic Lynn	2	2	4	4
Ray Barry	1	2	3	6
Bob Bauer	1	1	2	0
Jim Morrison	0	2	2	2

Penalty minutes: 601 – 8.6 per game

1951-52 PLAYOFF RESULTS

March 1952

	AT	VERSUS	W-L-T	SCR
25	Montreal	Canadiens	L	5–1
27	Montreal	Canadiens	L	4–0
30	Boston	Montreal	W	4–1

April 1952

1	Boston	Montreal	W	3–2
3	Montreal	Canadiens	W	1–0
6	Boston	Montreal	L	3–2 (OT)
8	Montreal	Canadiens	L	3–1

1951-52 PLAYOFFS

vs. Montreal Canadiens	3 wins – 4 losses
at Montreal	1 win – 3 losses
at Boston	2 wins – 1 loss

1951-52 PLAYOFF SCORING

	GP	SO	GAA
Jim Henry	7	1	2.57

	G	A	P	PIM
Ed Sandford	2	2	4	0
Fleming Mackell	2	1	3	12
Milt Schmidt	2	1	3	0
Dave Creighton	2	1	3	2
Jack McIntyre	1	2	3	2
Bill Quackenbush	0	3	3	0
Real Chevrefils	1	1	2	6
Hal Laycoe	1	1	2	11
Johnny Peirson	0	2	2	4
Pentti Lund	1	0	1	0
Leo Labine	0	1	1	4
Woody Dumart	0	1	1	0
Duncan Fisher	0	0	0	0
Gus Kyle	0	0	0	4
Bob Armstrong	0	0	0	2
Ed Kryzanowski	0	0	0	0
Red Sullivan	0	0	0	0
Murray Henderson	0	0	0	4

Penalty minutes: 51 – 7.3 per game

1952–1953
(29th year)

TEAM OWNER:	Boston Professional Hockey Association
PRESIDENT:	Walter Brown
GM & OWNER:	Art Ross
COACH:	Lynn Patrick
PLAYOFFS:	*Semi-finals:* Defeat Detroit Red Wings 4 wins – 2 losses

Stanley Cup finals:
Lose to Montreal Canadiens
1 win – 4 losses

STANLEY CUP WINNER: Montreal Canadiens

ALL-STARS: Fleming Mackell (1st team)
Bill Quackenbush (2nd team)

TROPHY WINNERS: Dufresne — Fleming Mackell

RADIO STATION: WHDH with Fred Cusick

UNIFORMS

- Home jersey is white with spoked "B." Gold band trimmed in black on shoulders. Black pants with gold stripes along sides. Alternating gold, black, and white stripes on stockings. Road jersey is black with large block letter "B" in gold trimmed in white. Jersey has gold shoulder band. White, gold, white vertical stripes on arms. Pants and socks are same as home.

POTPOURRI

- Defeat the Rangers on January 24, 9–0, on 3 goals by Jerry Toppazzini.
- Finish in third place during the regular season.
- Defeat Detroit in the semi-final round of the playoffs.
- Lose to Detroit on December 11, 10–1.
- Lose to Detroit 10–2 on March 2, with Ted Lindsay getting 4 goals.
- Lose to Montreal in the Stanley Cup finals as the Canadiens win the Cup for the first time in 7 years.
- Dave Creighton scored 2 goals in a New Year's Day win over Toronto, breaks his leg in the same game.
- Jim Hendy, on behalf of the Cleveland Barons of the American Hockey League, issues a challenge to play for the Stanley Cup. The offer is rejected.
- The first game televised from coast to coast on the CBC occurs on November 1, 1952, between the Bruins and Maple Leafs from Toronto.
- Maine Governor Burton Cross presents the Bruins with a 7-foot bear named "Buster" which serves as the team's mascot.
- During the playoffs against Montreal, an injured Sugar Jim Henry is replaced by Gordon "Red" Henry for two games.
- Bruins play back-to-back consecutive home games against the Rangers on January 24 and 25.
- On a late February road trip, the Bruins play in Chicago 3 times.

TRANSACTIONS

- Obtain Joe Klukay from Toronto.
- Bill Ezinicki is sold to Toronto.
- Ed Kryzanowski and Vic Lynn are lost to Chicago.

1952-53 STANDINGS

	W	L	T	P	GF	GA
Detroit	36	16	18	90	222	133
Montreal	28	23	19	75	155	148
Boston	28	29	13	69	152	172
Chicago	27	28	15	69	169	175
Toronto	27	30	13	67	156	167
New York	17	37	16	50	152	211

1952-53 **RESULTS**

October 1952

	AT	VERSUS	W-L-T	SCR
12	Boston	Montreal	T	1–1
16	Boston	Toronto	W	2–1
18	Montreal	Canadiens	L	2–1
19	Boston	New York	T	2–2
22	New York	Rangers	T	3–3
25	Toronto	Maple Leafs	W	4–0
26	Chicago	Blackhawks	T	1–1
30	Detroit	Red Wings	L	4–1

November 1952

1	Toronto	Maple Leafs	L	3–2
2	Chicago	Blackhawks	L	4–1
6	Boston	Detroit	W	2–0
9	Boston	Chicago	W	4–1
11	Boston	Toronto	W	4–0
13	Detroit	Red Wings	L	3–0
15	Montreal	Canadiens	L	2–0
16	Boston	Detroit	L	5–2
19	Toronto	Maple Leafs	W	2–1
20	Chicago	Blackhawks	L	3–1
23	Boston	Toronto	W	6–5
27	Boston	New York	W	3–1
30	Boston	Montreal	W	3–1

December 1952

4	Boston	Chicago	W	5–1
6	Montreal	Canadiens	W	2–1
7	Detroit	Red Wings	T	1–1
10	New York	Rangers	W	4–1
11	Boston	Detroit	L	10–1
14	Boston	Chicago	T	2–2
17	New York	Rangers	L	5–0
18	Chicago	Blackhawks	T	3–3
20	Montreal	Canadiens	W	6–3
21	Boston	Montreal	L	4–3
25	Boston	New York	L	2–1
27	Toronto	Maple Leafs	L	3–0
28	Detroit	Red Wings	L	7–1

January 1953

1	Boston	Toronto	W	5–1
3	Montreal	Canadiens	W	1–0
4	New York	Rangers	L	5–2
8	Detroit	Red Wings	L	4–0
10	Toronto	Maple Leafs	L	3–1
11	Boston	Chicago	L	4–2
15	Boston	Detroit	L	4–0
18	Boston	Toronto	W	2–1
22	Boston	Chicago	T	3–3
24	Boston	New York	W	9–0
25	Boston	New York	L	2–1
29	Boston	Toronto	T	2–2
31	Montreal	Canadiens	T	0–0

February 1953

1	Boston	Montreal	W	4–3
5	Boston	Chicago	W	4–1
8	Boston	Detroit	L	5–3
12	Boston	Detroit	W	3–1
14	Boston	New York	W	5–4
15	Boston	Montreal	W	1–0
18	New York	Rangers	L	4–2
21	Toronto	Maple Leafs	T	2–2
22	Chicago	Blackhawks	L	2–0
25	New York	Rangers	L	2–1
27	Chicago	Blackhawks	L	3–0

March 1953

1	Chicago	Blackhawks	T	2–2
2	Detroit	Red Wings	L	10–2
5	Boston	Montreal	W	5–0
7	Boston	New York	L	2–1
8	Boston	Chicago	W	2–1
12	Boston	Detroit	T	2–2
14	Toronto	Maple Leafs	W	3–1
15	Boston	Montreal	W	2–1
18	New York	Rangers	W	2–1
19	Detroit	Red Wings	L	6–1
21	Montreal	Canadiens	W	2–1
22	Boston	Toronto	L	3–1

1952-53 **SCORING**

	GP	SO	GAA	
Jim Henry	70	7	2.46	

	G	A	P	PIM
Fleming Mackell	27	17	44	63
Eddie Sandford	14	21	35	44
Milt Schmidt	11	23	34	30
Real Chevrefils	19	14	33	44

John Peirson	14	15	29	32
Joe Klukay	13	16	29	20
Jerry Toppazzini	10	13	23	36
Leo Labine	8	15	23	69
Jack McIntyre	7	15	22	31
Bill Quackenbush	2	16	18	6
Pentti Lund	8	9	17	2
Dave Creighton	8	8	16	14

Woody Dumart	5	9	14	2
Warren Godfrey	1	13	14	40
Hal Laycoe	2	10	12	36
Red Sullivan	3	8	11	8
Bob Armstrong	0	8	8	45
Frank Martin	0	2	2	6
Dunc Fisher	0	1	1	0

Norm Corcoran	0	0	0	0
Willie Marshall	0	0	0	0

Penalty minutes: 528 – 7.5 per game

1952-53 PLAYOFF RESULTS

March 1953

AT		VERSUS	W-L-T	SCR
24	Detroit	Red Wings	L	7–0
26	Detroit	Red Wings	W	5–3
29	Boston	Detroit	W	2–1 (OT)
31	Boston	Detroit	W	6–2

April 1953

2	Detroit	Red Wings	L	6–4
5	Boston	Detroit	W	4–2
9	Montreal	Canadiens	L	4–2
11	Montreal	Canadiens	W	4–1
12	Boston	Montreal	L	3–0
14	Boston	Montreal	L	7–3
16	Montreal	Canadiens	L	1–0

1952-53 PLAYOFFS

vs. Detroit Red Wings	4 wins – 2 losses	vs. Montreal Canadiens	1 win – 4 losses
at Detroit	1 win – 2 losses	at Montreal	1 win – 2 losses
at Boston	3 wins – 0 losses	at Boston	0 wins – 2 losses

1952-53 PLAYOFF SCORING

	GP	SO	GAA
Jim Henry	9	0	2.89
Gordon Henry	3	0	3.67

	G	A	P	PIM
Ed Sandford	8	3	11	11
Dave Creighton	4	5	9	10
Johnny Peirson	3	6	9	2
Fleming Mackell	2	7	9	7
Milt Schmidt	5	1	6	6
Jack McIntyre	4	2	6	2
Bill Quackenbush	0	4	4	4
Leo Labine	2	1	3	19

Joe Klukay	1	2	3	9
Jerry Toppazzini	0	3	3	9
Bob Armstrong	1	1	2	10
Woody Dumart	0	2	2	0
Hal Laycoe	0	2	2	10
Frank Martin	0	1	1	2
Real Chevrefils	0	1	1	6
Warren Godfrey	0	1	1	2
Pentti Lund	0	0	0	0
Red Sullivan	0	0	0	0

Penalty minutes: 109 – 9.9 per game

1953–1954
(30th year)

TEAM OWNER: Boston Professional Hockey Association

PRESIDENT & GOVERNOR: Walter Brown

GENERAL MANAGERS: Art Ross & Lynn Patrick

COACH: Lynn Patrick

PLAYOFFS: *Semi-finals:* Lose to Montreal Canadiens 0 wins – 4 losses

STANLEY CUP WINNER: Detroit Red Wings

ALL-STARS: Ed Sandford (2nd team)

TROPHY WINNERS: Dufresne — Jim Henry

RADIO STATION: WHDH Radio with Fred Cusick

UNIFORMS

- Home jersey is white with spoked "B." Gold band trimmed in black on shoulders. Black pants with gold stripes along sides. Alternating gold, black, and white stripes on stockings. Road jersey is black with large block letter "B" in gold trimmed in white. Jersey has gold shoulder band. White, gold, white vertical stripes on arms. Pants and socks are same as home.

POTPOURRI

- Finish in fourth place.
- Lead league in being shut out only 4 times and in penalty minutes with 685.
- Sugar Jim Henry plays goal in all 70 games.
- In the November 14 game at Toronto, both Bill Quackenbush and Real Chevrefils break legs.
- Lose 4 straight games to Montreal in opening round of the playoffs.
- In game 2, Canadien Dickie Moore scores 2 goals and 4 assists in 1 game, a playoff record that stood until 1983.
- Art Ross announces his retirement and is replaced by Lynn Patrick.
- For the second January in a row, the Rangers play consecutive, back-to-back games to the Boston Garden. The dates are January 23 and 24. Detroit also enjoyed this scheduling in Boston on February 6 and 7.
- The Norris Trophy is presented to the NHL by the family of the late James Norris, owner of the Detroit Red Wings.
- Bruins record 3 consecutive shutouts at home on March 7, 11, and 14.

TRANSACTIONS

- Jack McIntyre is traded to Chicago for Cal Gardner.

1953-54 STANDINGS

	W	L	T	P	GF	GA
Detroit	37	19	14	88	191	132
Montreal	35	24	11	81	195	141
Toronto	32	24	14	78	152	131
Boston	32	28	10	74	177	181
New York	29	31	10	68	161	182
Chicago	12	51	7	31	133	242

1953-54 RESULTS

October 1953

	AT	VERSUS	W-L-T	SCR
11	Boston	Montreal	W	4–1
15	Boston	Toronto	L	4–1
17	Montreal	Canadiens	L	5–2
18	Boston	New York	W	3–2
22	New York	Rangers	L	4–3
24	Toronto	Maple Leafs	W	3–2
25	Chicago	Blackhawks	W	4–3
31	Detroit	Red Wings	W	3–1

November 1953

1	Chicago	Blackhawks	T	0–0
5	Boston	Chicago	W	4–2
7	Montreal	Canadiens	L	5–2
8	Boston	Montreal	W	2–0
11	Boston	Detroit	T	2–2
14	Toronto	Maple Leafs	L	2–0
15	Boston	Toronto	T	1–1
19	Detroit	Red Wings	L	3–2
20	Chicago	Blackhawks	W	2–0
22	Boston	Montreal	T	2–2
25	New York	Rangers	L	5–3
26	Boston	New York	W	5–2
29	Boston	Toronto	W	2–1

December 1953

3	Boston	Chicago	W	3–1
5	Montreal	Canadiens	L	4–2
6	Boston	Montreal	L	7–2
10	Boston	Detroit	W	6–3
12	Detroit	Red Wings	L	7–1
13	Chicago	Blackhawks	T	2–2
16	New York	Rangers	L	4–3
17	Boston	Toronto	W	3–2
19	Montreal	Canadiens	L	7–3
20	Boston	Detroit	L	4–2
25	Boston	Chicago	W	4–1
27	Detroit	Red Wings	L	2–1
29	New York	Rangers	W	6–2

January 1954

1	Boston	New York	L	2–1
2	Montreal	Canadiens	T	1–1
7	Detroit	Red Wings	L	3–1
9	Toronto	Maple Leafs	L	3–2
10	Boston	Chicago	W	5–3
14	Boston	Detroit	L	2–1
16	Montreal	Canadiens	L	2–1
17	Boston	Montreal	W	3–2
20	New York	Rangers	L	8–3
21	Chicago	Blackhawks	W	3–2
23	Boston	New York	L	4–3
24	Boston	New York	W	2–1
28	Boston	Chicago	W	3–2
30	Toronto	Maple Leafs	L	4–2
31	Boston	Toronto	W	2–0

February 1954

4	Detroit	Red Wings	L	5–0
6	Boston	Detroit	L	4–2
7	Boston	Detroit	T	1–1
10	Toronto	Maple Leafs	W	3–2
11	Boston	Toronto	L	3–1
13	Boston	New York	W	1–0
14	Boston	Montreal	W	4–1
17	New York	Rangers	L	2–1
20	Toronto	Maple Leafs	L	3–2
21	Chicago	Blackhawks	W	4–3
24	New York	Rangers	W	5–3

March 1954

4	Boston	Montreal	T	1–1
6	Montreal	Canadiens	T	3–3
7	Boston	Chicago	W	6–0
11	Boston	New York	W	1–0
13	Toronto	Maple Leafs	W	2–1
14	Boston	Toronto	W	3–0
16	Boston	Detroit	W	4–2
18	Detroit	Red Wings	T	3–3
19	Chicago	Blackhawks	L	7–0
21	Boston	Chicago	W	9–5

1953-54 SCORING

	GP	SO	GAA
Jim Henry	70	8	2.58

	G	A	P	PIM
Eddie Sandford	16	31	47	42
Fleming Mackell	15	32	47	60
John Peirson	21	19	40	55
Dave Creighton	20	20	40	27
Joe Klukay	20	17	37	27
Leo Labine	16	19	35	57
Cal Gardner	14	20	34	62
Milt Schmidt	14	18	32	28
Doug Mohns	13	14	27	27
Frank Martin	3	17	20	38
Hal Laycoe	3	16	19	29
Bill Quackenbush	0	17	17	6

Warren Godfrey	5	9	14	71	Real Chevrefils	4	1	5	2
Bob Armstrong	2	10	12	81	Jerry Toppazzini	0	5	5	24
Woody Dumart	4	3	7	6					
Ray Gariepy	1	6	7	39	Penalty minutes: 685 – 9.8 per game				
Gus Bodnar	3	3	6	10					

1953-54 PLAYOFF RESULTS

March 1954

	AT	VERSUS	W-L-T	SCR					
23	Montreal	Canadiens	L	2–0	25	Montreal	Canadiens	L	8–1
					28	Boston	Montreal	L	4–3
					30	Boston	Montreal	L	2–0

1953-54 PLAYOFFS

vs. Montreal Canadiens	0 wins – 4 losses
at Montreal	0 wins – 2 losses
at Boston	0 wins – 2 losses

1953-54 PLAYOFF SCORING

	GP	SO	GAA
Jim Henry	4	0	4.00

	G	A	P	PIM					
Cal Gardner	1	1	2	0	Hal Laycoe	0	0	0	0
Fleming Mackell	1	1	2	8	Bill Quackenbush	0	0	0	0
Doug Mohns	1	0	1	4	Joe Klukay	0	0	0	0
Milt Schmidt	1	0	1	20	Dave Creighton	0	0	0	0
Frank Martin	0	1	1	0	Woody Dumart	0	0	0	0
Bob Armstrong	0	1	1	0	Guyle Fielder	0	0	0	2
Ed Sandford	0	1	1	4	Wayne Brown	0	0	0	2
Leo Labine	0	1	1	28	Johnny Peirson	0	0	0	2
Gus Bodnar	0	0	0	0	Warren Godfrey	0	0	0	4

Penalty minutes: 74 – 18.5 per game

1954–1955
(31st year)

TEAM OWNER:	Boston Professional Hockey Association	STANLEY CUP WINNER:	Detroit Red Wings
		ALL-STARS:	Fernie Flaman (2nd team)
PRESIDENT & GOVERNOR:	Walter Brown	TROPHY WINNERS:	Dufresne — Leo Labine
GM:	Lynn Patrick	RADIO STATION:	WHDH Radio with
COACHES:	Lynn Patrick & Milt Schmidt		Fred Cusick
PLAYOFFS:	*Semi-finals:* Lose to Montreal Canadiens 1 win – 4 losses		

UNIFORMS

- Home jersey is white with spoked "B." Gold band trimmed in black on shoulders. Black pants with gold stripes along sides. Alternating gold, black, and white stripes on stockings. Road jersey is black with large block letter "B" in gold trimmed in white. Jersey has gold shoulder band. White, gold, white vertical stripes on arms. Pants and socks are same as home.

POTPOURRI

- Finish in fourth place during the regular season.
- Doug Mohns scores a goal in the All-Star game on October 2, 1954, in Detroit.
- In a March 13 game at Boston Garden, a fight between Maurice Richard of Montreal and Hal Laycoe of the Bruins ends with Richard striking linesman Cliff Thompson. Richard is suspended for the remaining games of the regular season and the playoffs, precipitating the "Richard Riot" in Montreal.
- Boston loses the semi-final round of the playoffs to Montreal, 4 games to 1.
- Milt Schmidt and Woody Dumart retire.
- Wearing of each player's number is to be painted in white on the outside of each player's hockey boot for identification purposes on television and photographs.
- In a March 10 game at Toronto between the Leafs and Montreal, the Zamboni ice machine makes its first appearance at an NHL arena.
- 4 Bruins, Fern Flaman, Cal Gardner, Hal Laycoe, and Doug Mohns, play in all 70 games.
- Bruins enjoy a 9-game unbeaten streak.
- Largest home crowd of the season on January 16, 1955, against Montreal played before 12,863 fans.

TRANSACTIONS

- Art Ross announces his retirement from the Bruins and is replaced by Lynn Patrick as General Manager.
- Woody Dumart retires.
- Dave Creighton is traded to Toronto for Fernie Flaman.
- Clare Martin is traded to Chicago for Murray Costello.
- Trade Joe Klukay to Toronto for Leo Boivin.
- Milt Schmidt, appointed acting coach while recovering from a knee injury, retires.

1954-55 STANDINGS

	W	L	T	P	GF	GA
Detroit	42	17	11	95	204	134
Montreal	41	18	11	93	228	157
Toronto	24	24	22	70	147	135
Boston	23	26	21	67	169	188
New York	17	35	18	52	150	210
Chicago	13	40	17	43	161	235

1954-55 RESULTS

October 1954

	AT	VERSUS	W-L-T	SCR
9	Montreal	Canadiens	L	4–1
11	Boston	Montreal	T	2–2
14	Boston	New York	W	5–3
17	Boston	Toronto	T	1–1
20	New York	Rangers	L	6–2
21	Detroit	Red Wings	L	5–3
23	Toronto	Maple Leafs	T	3–3
30	Detroit	Red Wings	L	4–0

November 1954

	AT	VERSUS	W-L-T	SCR
4	Boston	Detroit	L	3–2
7	Boston	Montreal	L	4–3
10	Boston	Chicago	W	4–3
13	Montreal	Canadiens	L	2–1

14	Boston	Toronto	L	3–1
17	New York	Rangers	T	2–2
18	Chicago	Blackhawks	W	5–1
20	Toronto	Maple Leafs	W	1–0
21	Boston	Montreal	W	2–0
24	New York	Rangers	L	3–1
25	Boston	New York	T	2–2
28	Boston	Detroit	W	6–2

December 1954

1	Toronto	Maple Leafs	L	6–0
2	Chicago	Blackhawks	W	3–2
4	Boston	New York	W	6–3
5	Boston	Toronto	L	4–2
9	Boston	Chicago	W	2–1
11	Montreal	Canadiens	W	3–0
12	Boston	Montreal	T	2–2
16	Boston	Detroit	L	4–2
18	Detroit	Red Wings	L	4–1
19	Chicago	Blackhawks	L	6–1
25	Boston	Chicago	T	3–3
30	New York	Rangers	L	6–1

January 1955

1	Boston	New York	W	4–0
2	New York	Rangers	T	3–3
5	Toronto	Maple Leafs	W	2–1
6	Detroit	Red Wings	T	3–3
8	Montreal	Canadiens	T	1–1
9	Boston	Toronto	T	1–1
12	Chicago	Blackhawks	T	1–1
13	Detroit	Red Wings	L	4–0
15	Toronto	Maple Leafs	L	4–2
16	Boston	Montreal	W	6–0

20	Boston	Detroit	W	3–2
22	Boston	New York	W	3–1
23	Boston	New York	L	2–0
27	Boston	Chicago	W	5–2
29	Montreal	Canadiens	L	4–0
30	Boston	Toronto	W	3–0

February 1955

2	Chicago	Blackhawks	W	3–2
3	Detroit	Red Wings	T	1–1
5	Boston	Detroit	W	8–4
6	Boston	Detroit	T	2–2
10	Boston	Chicago	W	4–2
12	Boston	New York	T	5–5
13	Boston	Toronto	T	3–3
16	New York	Rangers	T	2–2
17	Chicago	Blackhawks	L	10–2
19	Toronto	Maple Leafs	T	1–1
21	Detroit	Red Wings	T	2–2
23	St. Paul Minn.	Chicago Blackhawks	T	3–3
26	Montreal	Canadiens	L	4–1

March 1955

2	New York	Rangers	W	2–1
3	Boston	Montreal	L	4–1
5	Toronto	Maple Leafs	T	2–2
6	Boston	Toronto	W	3–1
10	Boston	Chicago	L	3–2
12	Montreal	Canadiens	L	2–1
13	Boston	Montreal	W	4–2
16	Boston	Detroit	L	5–4
20	Boston	Chicago	L	4–3

1954-55 SCORING

	GP	SO	GAA
John Henderson	44	5	2.48
Jim Henry	27	1	2.93

	G	A	P	PIM
Leo Labine	24	18	42	75
Don McKenney	22	20	42	34
Real Chevrefils	18	22	40	30
Cal Gardner	16	22	38	40
Fleming Mackell	11	24	35	76
Lorne Ferguson	20	14	34	24
Eddie Sandford	14	20	34	38
Doug Mohns	14	18	32	82

Bill Quackenbush	2	20	22	8
Fernie Flaman	4	14	18	150
Warren Godfrey	1	17	18	58
Leo Boivin	6	11	17	105
Hal Laycoe	4	13	17	34
Murray Costello	4	11	15	25
Milt Schmidt	4	8	12	26
Gus Bodnar	4	4	8	14
Bob Armstrong	1	3	4	38
Floyd Smith	0	1	1	0
Alan Teal	0	0	0	0
Norm Corcoran	0	0	0	2
Joe Klukay	0	0	0	4

3 Goal Games
Leo Labine & Lorne Ferguson

Penalty minutes
863 - 12.3 per game

1954-55 PLAYOFF RESULTS

March 1955

	AT	VERSUS	W-L-T	SCR
22	Montreal	Canadiens	L	2–0
24	Montreal	Canadiens	L	3–1
27	Boston	Montreal	W	4–2
29	Boston	Montreal	L	4–3 (OT)
31	Montreal	Canadiens	L	5–1

1954-55 PLAYOFFS

vs. Montreal Canadiens	1 win – 4 losses
at Montreal	0 wins – 3 losses
at Boston	1 win – 1 loss

1954-55 PLAYOFF SCORING

	GP	SO	GAA
Jim Henry	3	0	2.67
John Henderson	2	0	4.00

	G	A	P	PIM
Bill Quackenbush	0	5	5	0
Real Chevrefils	2	1	3	4
Leo Labine	2	1	3	11
Don McKenney	1	2	3	4
Ed Sandford	1	1	2	6
Lorne Ferguson	1	0	1	2
Fernie Flaman	1	0	1	2
Hal Laycoe	1	0	1	0
Fleming Mackell	0	1	1	0
Gus Bodnar	0	1	1	4
Leo Boivin	0	1	1	4
Warren Godfrey	0	0	0	0
Gordon Wilson	0	0	0	0
Don Cherry	0	0	0	0
Bob Armstrong	0	0	0	2
Murray Costello	0	0	0	2
Cal Gardner	0	0	0	4
Doug Mohns	0	0	0	4
Norm Corcoran	0	0	0	6

1955–1956
(32nd year)

TEAM OWNER:	Boston Professional Hockey Association	STANLEY CUP WINNER:	Montreal Canadiens
		ALL-STARS:	None
PRESIDENT & GOVERNOR:	Walter Brown	TROPHY WINNERS:	Dufresne: Terry Sawchuk
GM:	Lynn Patrick	RADIO STATION:	WHDH Radio with
COACH:	Milt Schmidt		Fred Cusick
PLAYOFFS:	Out of playoffs		

UNIFORMS

- Home jersey is white with spoked "B." Gold shoulder band trimmed in gold with alternating gold and black stripes on the arms. Pants are black with gold striping on the side. Stockings are vertical gold, white, and black stripes. Road jersey is black with gold and white trim. This jersey now has the spoked "B" as opposed to the plain, block "B." The Bruins also add the new gold jersey trimmed in black and white. This jersey features the spoke "B." Pants and socks are the same with all uniforms.

POTPOURRI

- Claude Pronovost, brother of Marcel Pronovost of Detroit, replaces John Henderson in goal for Boston and shuts out Montreal 2–0 in a January 14 game at the Forum.

- Of Montreal's 5 home losses this year, 3 are to the Bruins.
- November 6 game at the Garden draws 13,634 fans, the largest crowd in 2 years.
- Jean Beliveau scores all 4 goals in a November 5 Montreal win at the Forum. Beliveau scored 3 of the goals on the same power play.
- December 15 game at Boston against Chicago is attended by only 5,549 fans.
- Finish in fifth place, out of the playoffs.
- Vic Stasiuk has emergency surgery for a blood clot in his leg.
- October 25 game against Chicago is played at St. Louis before 5,668 fans.
- Officials uniforms are changed from orange and black to black and white vertical stripes. These uniforms are introduced for the first time on December 29.
- Cal Gardner and Bill Quackenbush appear in all 70 games.
- 13,909 attend February 12, 1956, game against Montreal.
- Bruins lead league in being shutout 11 times.
- Bruins score least number of goals in NHL, 147.

TRANSACTIONS

- Milt Schmidt now coaching Bruins on a regular basis.
- Trade Warren Godfrey, Gilles Boisvert, Eddie Sandford, Real Chevrefils, and Norm Corcoran to Detroit for Vic Stasiuk, Marcel Bonin, Lorne Davis, and Terry Sawchuk.
- Obtain Orval Tessier from Montreal.
- Johnny Peirson is coaxed out of retirement.
- Obtain Jerry Toppazzini and Real Chevrefils from Detroit for Lorne Ferguson and Murray Costello.

1955-56 STANDINGS

	W	L	T	P	GF	GA
Montreal	45	15	10	100	222	131
Detroit	30	24	16	76	183	148
New York	32	28	10	74	204	203
Toronto	24	33	13	61	153	181
Boston	23	34	13	59	147	185
Chicago	19	39	12	50	155	216

1955-56 RESULTS

October 1955

	AT	VERSUS	W-L-T	SCR
8	Montreal	Canadiens	L	2–0
9	Boston	Montreal	L	5–2
12	Boston	Toronto	W	2–0
15	Toronto	Maple Leafs	T	2–2
16	Boston	New York	W	4–1
20	Montreal	Canadiens	W	3–2
22	Detroit	Red Wings	T	0–0
25	St. Louis	Chicago Blackhawks	L	2–0
29	New York	Rangers	W	1–0

November 1955

3	Boston	Chicago	T	3–3
5	Montreal	Canadiens	L	4–2

6	Boston	Montreal	T	3–3
10	Boston	New York	W	5–1
12	Toronto	Maple Leafs	W	3–2
13	Boston	Detroit	T	0–0
18	Chicago	Blackhawks	L	6–1
19	Toronto	Maple Leafs	L	3–2
20	Boston	Toronto	T	1–1
23	New York	Rangers	L	4–0
24	Boston	New York	L	5–0
26	Montreal	Canadiens	L	3–1
27	Boston	Chicago	L	6–0

December 1955

1	Boston	Montreal	L	2–1
3	Boston	Detroit	L	5–0

Terry Sawchuk

4	Boston	Toronto	W	5-0
8	Detroit	Red Wings	T	2-2
9	Chicago	Blackhawks	T	1-1
11	Boston	Montreal	L	4-2
15	Boston	Chicago	W	4-1
17	Toronto	Maple Leafs	L	5-1
18	Chicago	Blackhawks	L	7-1
21	New York	Rangers	T	3-3
22	Boston	Detroit	L	3-2
25	Boston	Chicago	L	4-2
29	Detroit	Red Wings	L	4-3
31	New York	Rangers	L	6-2

January 1956

1	Boston	New York	L	4-2
7	Toronto	Maple Leafs	L	6-2
8	Detroit	Red Wings	L	4-3
12	Boston	Chicago	L	5-0
14	Montreal	Canadiens	W	2-0
15	Boston	Toronto	L	4-1
19	Detroit	Red Wings	L	4-2
20	Chicago	Blackhawks	W	3-0
22	Boston	New York	W	3-1
26	Boston	Montreal	W	5-1
28	Montreal	Canadiens	L	6-1
29	Boston	Toronto	W	3-1

February 1956

2	Boston	Chicago	T	2-2
4	Boston	New York	W	7-1
5	Boston	Detroit	W	3-1
8	New York	Rangers	T	3-3
9	Boston	Toronto	T	1-1
11	Boston	Detroit	W	3-2
12	Boston	Montreal	L	7-1
15	Toronto	Maple Leafs	L	1-0
17	Chicago	Blackhawks	W	4-2
19	New York	Rangers	W	3-0
21	Detroit	Red Wings	L	4-1
25	Toronto	Maple Leafs	W	3-1
26	Chicago	Blackhawks	L	4-1
29	New York	Rangers	L	4-2

March 1956

1	Boston	Detroit	L	2-0
3	Boston	New York	W	5-2
4	Boston	Toronto	T	2-2
8	Detroit	Red Wings	L	4-2
10	Montreal	Canadiens	W	4-0
11	Boston	Montreal	W	3-1
13	Boston	Detroit	W	4-0
18	Boston	Chicago	L	3-2

1955-56 SCORING

	GP	SO	GAA
Terry Sawchuk	68	9	2.66
John Henderson	1	0	4.00
Claude Pronovost	1	1	0.00

	G	A	P	PIM
Vic Stasiuk	19	18	37	118
Cal Gardner	15	21	36	57
Leo Labine	16	18	34	104
Don McKenney	10	24	34	20
John Peirson	11	14	25	10
Bill Quackenbush	3	22	25	4
Fernie Flaman	4	17	21	70
Leo Boivin	4	16	20	80
Real Chevrefils	11	8	19	20
Doug Mohns	10	8	18	48

Marcel Bonin	9	9	18	49
Fleming Mackell	7	9	16	59
Jerry Toppazzini	7	7	14	22
Lorne Ferguson	7	5	12	18
Bob Armstrong	0	12	12	122
Hal Laycoe	5	5	10	16
Murray Costello	4	6	10	19
Orval Tessier	2	3	5	6
Ed Panagabko	0	3	3	38
Lionel Heinrich	1	1	2	33
Lorne Davis	0	1	1	0
Obie O'Brien	0	0	0	0
Al Nicholson	0	0	0	4

NO PLAYOFF SCORING

3-Goal Game
Leo Labine

Penalty minutes
929 – 13.3 per game

1956–1957
(33rd year)

TEAM OWNER:	Boston Professional Hockey Association	STANLEY CUP WINNER:	Montreal Canadiens
PRESIDENT & GOVERNOR:	Walter Brown	ALL-STARS:	Fernie Flaman (2nd team) Real Chevrefils (2nd team)
GM:	Lynn Patrick	TROPHY WINNERS:	Calder — Larry Regan
COACH:	Milt Schmidt		Dufresne — Jerry Toppazzini
PLAYOFFS:	*Semi-finals:* Defeat Detroit Red Wings 4 wins – 1 loss *Stanley Cup finals:* Lose to Montreal Canadiens 1 win – 4 losses	RADIO STATION:	WHDH Radio with Fred Cusick

UNIFORMS

- Home jersey is white with spoked "B." Gold shoulder band trimmed in gold with alternating gold and black stripes on the arms. Pants are black with gold striping on the side. Stockings are vertical gold, white, and black stripes. Road jersey is black with gold and white trim. This jersey now has the spoked "B" as opposed to the plain, block "B." The Bruins also add the new gold jersey trimmed in black and white. This jersey features the spoke "B." Pants and socks are the same with all uniforms.

POTPOURRI

- Bruins enjoy 9-game winning streak.
- Fleming Mackell scores 3 goals in a December 30 game over Detroit.
- Don Simmons defeats Montreal in his inaugural game on January 27th.
- Larry Regan wins the Calder Trophy as rookie of the year.
- Bruins defeat Detroit, 4 games to 1, in the Stanley Cup semi-finals.
- Finish in 3rd place.
- Terry Sawchuk is hospitalized in mid-December with mononucleosis.
- Terry Sawchuk misses practice on January 16. He claims his nerves are gone and leaves the team. Ironically, on the day he leaves Boston, Sawchuk is named to the All-Star team for the first half of the season.
- Lose Stanley Cup finals to Montreal, 4 games to 1.
- Rocket Richard scores 4 goals in game 1 of the Stanley Cup finals.
- In a January 5 afternoon game between the Rangers and Chicago at New York, the CBS television network broadcasts the game for the first time. January 26 game against the Rangers at Boston is broadcast nationally with Fred Cusick doing the play-by-play.
- Referees and linesmen start to use hand signals to indicate calls and infractions.
- Bruins play consecutive home games against Detroit on March 7 and March 9.
- In a rule change, a penalized player is allowed to return to the ice if his team is scored upon.

TRANSACTIONS

- Allan Stanley is purchased from Chicago and Jack Bionda from Toronto.
- Real Chevrefils is purchased from Detroit.
- Norm DeFelice is brought up to replace the ill Terry Sawchuk in goal.
- Bruins acquire Don Simmons from the Springfield Indians.
- Hal Laycoe and Bill Quackenbush retire.

1956-57 STANDINGS

	W	L	T	P	GF	GA
Detroit	38	20	12	88	198	157
Montreal	35	23	12	82	210	155
Boston	34	24	12	80	195	174
New York	26	30	14	66	184	227
Toronto	21	34	15	57	174	192
Chicago	16	39	15	47	169	225

1956-57 RESULTS

October 1956

11	Boston	Toronto	T	4-4
13	Montreal	Canadiens	L	3-0
14	Boston	Montreal	W	3-1
17	New York	Rangers	L	2-0
20	Toronto	Maple Leafs	T	2-2
21	Detroit	Red Wings	T	3-3
27	Montreal	Canadiens	W	1-0
30	Chicago	Blackhawks	L	4-0

November 1956

1	Boston	Chicago	W	5-2
4	Boston	New York	W	4-1
7	New York	Rangers	W	4-2
8	Boston	Detroit	W	3-1
10	Montreal	Canadiens	W	3-1
11	Boston	Montreal	W	3-2
15	Chicago	Blackhawks	W	5-3
17	New York	Rangers	T	4-4
18	Boston	Toronto	W	4-3
22	Boston	New York	L	4-3
24	Toronto	Maple Leafs	W	3-2
25	Boston	Toronto	W	3-1
28	New York	Rangers	L	2-1
29	Chicago	Blackhawks	W	2-0

December 1956

2	Boston	Chicago	W	3-2
6	Detroit	Red Wings	L	3-2
8	Boston	Detroit	W	5-3
9	Boston	Montreal	T	1-1
13	Boston	Chicago	W	3-2
15	Montreal	Canadiens	L	6-4
16	Boston	Toronto	W	4-2
20	Boston	Detroit	T	1-1
22	Toronto	Maple Leafs	W	3-2
23	Chicago	Blackhawks	L	4-1
25	Boston	Chicago	L	4-2
27	Boston	Detroit	L	5-3
30	Detroit	Red Wings	W	4-2

January 1957

1	Boston	New York	W	5-3
5	Toronto	Maple Leafs	L	3-2
6	Chicago	Blackhawks	T	4-4
10	Detroit	Red Wings	W	2-1
12	Montreal	Canadiens	L	4-1
13	Boston	Montreal	L	3-1
17	Boston	Detroit	T	2-2
19	Toronto	Maple Leafs	L	4-1
20	Boston	Toronto	L	3-2
26	Boston	New York	L	5-3
27	Boston	Montreal	W	5-2
31	Boston	Chicago	W	2-0

February 1957

2	Montreal	Canadiens	W	2-1
3	Boston	New York	W	4-1
6	New York	Rangers	L	3-2
7	Detroit	Red Wings	W	1-0
9	Boston	Montreal	T	2-2
10	Boston	Toronto	W	5-1
13	Toronto	Maple Leafs	T	2-2
16	Chicago	Blackhawks	L	6-5
17	Detroit	Red Wings	L	6-2
20	New York	Rangers	L	5-2
23	Toronto	Maple Leafs	W	5-2
24	Chicago	Blackhawks	L	4-3
28	Boston	Chicago	W	4-0

March 1957

2	Boston	New York	L	3-2
3	Boston	Montreal	W	5-2
7	Boston	Detroit	L	4-2
9	Boston	Detroit	W	4-2
10	Boston	Toronto	T	3-3
13	New York	Rangers	W	2-1
16	Montreal	Canadiens	T	2-2
17	Boston	Chicago	W	6-2
21	Detroit	Red Wings	W	2-0
23	Boston	New York	L	4-2

1956-57 **SCORING**

	GP	SO	GAA
Terry Sawchuk	34	2	2.38
Don Simmons	26	4	2.42
Norm Defelice	10	0	3.00

	G	A	P	PIM
Don McKenney	21	39	60	31
Real Chevrefils	31	17	48	38
Leo Labine	18	29	47	128
Vic Stasiuk	24	16	40	69
Doug Mohns	6	34	40	89
Fleming Mackell	22	17	39	73
John Peirson	13	26	39	41
Jerry Toppazzini	15	23	38	26
Larry Regan	14	19	33	29
Cal Gardner	12	20	32	66
Allan Stanley	6	25	31	45
Fernie Flaman	6	25	31	108
Bob Armstrong	1	15	16	79
Leo Boivin	2	8	10	55
Jack Bionda	2	3	5	43
Jack Caffery	2	2	4	20
Bob Beckett	0	3	3	2
Al Nicholson	0	1	1	0
Floyd Smith	0	0	0	6
Dick Cherry	0	0	0	4
Floyd Hillman	0	0	0	10
George Ranieri	0	0	0	0
Ed Panagabko	0	0	0	0

Penalty minutes: 952 – 13.6 per game

1956-57 **PLAYOFF RESULTS**

March 1957

	AT	VERSUS	W-L-T	SCR
26	Detroit	Red Wings	W	3–1
28	Detroit	Red Wings	L	7–2
31	Boston	Detroit	W	4–3

April 1957

2	Boston	Detroit	W	2–0
4	Detroit	Red Wings	W	4–3
6	Montreal	Canadiens	L	5–1
9	Montreal	Canadiens	L	1–0
11	Boston	Montreal	L	4–2
14	Boston	Montreal	W	2–0
16	Montreal	Canadiens	L	5–1

1956-57 **PLAYOFFS**

vs. Detroit Red Wings	4 wins – 1 loss
at Detroit	2 wins – 1 loss
at Boston	2 wins – 0 losses

vs. Montreal Canadiens	1 win – 4 losses
at Montreal	0 wins – 3 losses
at Boston	1 win – 1 loss

1956-57 **PLAYOFF SCORING**

	GP	SO	GAA
Don Simmons	10	2	2.90

	G	A	P	PIM
Fleming Mackell	5	3	8	4
Don McKenney	1	5	6	4
Doug Mohns	2	3	5	2
Leo Labine	2	3	5	12
Leo Boivin	2	3	5	14
Vic Stasiuk	2	1	3	2
Cal Gardner	2	1	3	2
Real Chevrefils	2	1	3	4
John Peirson	0	3	3	12
Bob Armstrong	0	3	3	10
Fernie Flaman	0	3	3	19
Larry Regan	0	2	2	10
Carl Boone	1	0	1	12
Jack Caffery	1	0	1	4
Jerry Toppazzini	0	1	1	2
Jack Bionda	0	1	1	14

Penalty minutes: 127 – 12.7 per game

1957–1958
(34th year)

TEAM OWNER:	Boston Professional Hockey Association	*Stanley Cup finals:*	Lose to Montreal Canadiens
PRESIDENT & GOVERNOR:	Walter Brown		2 wins – 4 losses
GM:	Lynn Patrick	STANLEY CUP WINNER:	Montreal Canadiens
COACH:	Milt Schmidt	ALL-STARS:	Fernie Flaman (2nd team)
PLAYOFFS:	*Semi-finals:*	TROPHY WINNERS:	Dufresne — Jerry Toppazzini
	Defeat New York Rangers 4 wins – 2 losses	RADIO STATION:	WHDH with Fred Cusick

UNIFORMS

- Home jersey is gold with a black shoulder band. Pants are black with gold striping on the side. Stockings are vertical gold, white, and black stripes. Road jersey is white with a gold shoulder band trimmed in black.

POTPOURRI

- In the January 18 game at Montreal, Willie O'Ree, called up from the Quebec Aces, becomes the first black man to play in the NHL. He plays on a line with Jerry Toppazzini and Don McKenney.
- Johnny Bucyk scores 3 goals in a 7–4 win over the Rangers at New York in a nationally televised game played on January 4.
- Finish in fourth place in the regular season.
- Bruins defeat the Rangers in semi-finals, 4 games to 2. Jerry Toppazzini scores 3 goals in game 6.
- Fleming Mackell's 14 assists in the playoffs breaks record for playoff assists held by Elmer Lach.
- Fleming Mackell, Don McKenney, Vic Stasiuk, and Larry Hillman play complete 70-game schedule.
- Jerry Toppazzini scores 7 short-handed goals.
- Doug Mohns suffers a double fracture of the jaw in a December 8 game at Chicago.
- Real Chevrefils is demoted to Springfield after breaking training rules.
- Bruins lose Stanley Cup finals to Montreal, 4 games to 2.
- A $3-million lawsuit is filed in New York by the NHL Players Association when the NHL declines to negotiate the players' demands for pension and television benefits.
- In the December 29 game at Detroit, Don Simmons is injured with a separated shoulder. Since there is no replacement on the Boston bench, Detroit assistant trainer Ross "Lefty" Wilson plays goal for the Bruins. He gives up 1 goal in a 2–2 tie. In addition to Wilson and Simmons, the Bruins employ Harry Lumley, Al Millar, and Claude Evans in goal.
- In a March 12 game at Boston, Jacques Plante of Montreal suffers an injury and is replaced in goal by Bruin practice goaltender Don Aiken who surrenders 6 of the 7 Bruins goals.
- After the first two games of the semi-finals at New York, the remaining games of the playoffs are played at Boston Garden because of the circus at Madison Square Garden.
- For the benefit of television, the center red line is changed from a solid to a checkered pattern.
- The modern one-piece Stanley Cup is introduced.

TRANSACTIONS

- Obtain Harry Lumley to share goaltending with Don Simmons.
- Obtain Bronco Horvath from Montreal and Norm Johnson from New York in the intra-league draft.
- Trade Terry Sawchuk to Detroit for Johnny Bucyk and Larry Hillman.
- Marcel Bonin is traded to Montreal.

1957-58 STANDINGS

	W	L	T	P	GF	GA
Montreal	43	17	10	96	250	158
New York	32	25	13	77	195	188
Detroit	29	29	12	70	176	207
Boston	27	28	15	69	199	194
Chicago	24	39	7	55	163	202
Toronto	21	38	11	53	192	226

1957-58 RESULTS

October 1957

	AT	VERSUS	W-L-T	SCR
12	Boston	Chicago	W	3–1
13	Boston	New York	W	3–1
16	New York	Rangers	W	6–2
17	Detroit	Red Wings	W	5–1
19	Toronto	Maple Leafs	L	7–0
22	Chicago	Blackhawks	L	2–1
24	Detroit	Red Wings	L	4–3
26	Montreal	Canadiens	L	4–3
31	Boston	New York	L	3–0

November 1957

	AT	VERSUS	W-L-T	SCR
2	New York	Rangers	L	5–0
3	Boston	Detroit	W	4–0
7	Boston	Toronto	L	5–3
9	Montreal	Canadiens	L	4–2
10	Boston	Detroit	W	4–2
14	Boston	Chicago	W	5–2
16	Toronto	Maple Leafs	W	4–2
17	Boston	Toronto	T	2–2
23	Boston	Montreal	L	4–2
24	Chicago	Blackhawks	T	2–2
27	New York	Rangers	W	5–2
28	Boston	New York	W	1–0
30	Toronto	Maple Leafs	L	3–2

December 1957

	AT	VERSUS	W-L-T	SCR
1	Boston	Montreal	L	4–1
5	Boston	Detroit	W	7–2
7	Boston	Chicago	T	2–2
8	Chicago	Blackhawks	W	3–0
12	Detroit	Red Wings	L	3–2
14	Montreal	Canadiens	T	1–1
15	Boston	Toronto	L	3–1
19	Boston	New York	T	3–3
21	Toronto	Maple Leafs	T	3–3
22	Boston	Montreal	L	4–1
25	Boston	Detroit	W	4–1
28	Chicago	Blackhawks	T	0–0
29	Detroit	Red Wings	T	2–2

January 1958

	AT	VERSUS	W-L-T	SCR
1	Boston	Montreal	L	4–3
4	New York	Rangers	W	7–4
5	Chicago	Blackhawks	L	4–3
9	Detroit	Red Wings	L	6–1
11	Toronto	Maple Leafs	T	2–2
12	Boston	Toronto	L	5–3
16	Boston	New York	L	3–2
18	Montreal	Canadiens	W	3–0
19	Boston	Montreal	L	6–2
23	Boston	Chicago	W	4–3
25	Boston	Detroit	W	5–3
26	Boston	Toronto	T	3–3
29	New York	Rangers	T	1–1

February 1958

	AT	VERSUS	W-L-T	SCR
1	Montreal	Canadiens	L	3–1
2	Boston	New York	W	4–3
6	Boston	Chicago	L	4–1
8	Toronto	Maple Leafs	W	7–3
9	Boston	Toronto	L	2–0
13	Boston	Detroit	W	5–0
15	Boston	Montreal	T	2–2
16	New York	Rangers	L	3–2
20	Montreal	Canadiens	L	4–0
22	Detroit	Red Wings	L	6–1
23	Chicago	Blackhawks	W	2–0

March 1958

	AT	VERSUS	W-L-T	SCR
1	Chicago	Blackhawks	W	3–2
4	Detroit	Red Wings	W	2–1
6	Boston	Chicago	T	4–4
8	Toronto	Maple Leafs	T	3–3
9	Boston	Toronto	W	7–0
13	Boston	Montreal	W	7–3
15	Boston	New York	L	4–0
16	Boston	Detroit	L	6–3
19	New York	Rangers	T	1–1
22	Montreal	Canadiens	W	8–5
23	Chicago	Blackhawks	W	7–5

1957-58 SCORING

	GP	SO	GAA
Ross Wilson	1	0	1.15
Don Simmons	38	5	2.45
Harry Lumley	25	3	2.84
Claude Evans	1	0	4.00
Al Millar	6	0	4.17

	G	A	P	PIM
Bronco Horvath	30	36	66	71
Fleming Mackell	20	40	60	72
Don McKenney	28	30	58	22
Vic Stasiuk	21	35	56	55
Johnny Bucyk	21	31	52	57
Jerry Toppazzini	25	24	49	51
Larry Regan	11	28	39	22
Allan Stanley	6	25	31	37
Larry Hillman	3	19	22	60
Leo Labine	7	14	21	60
Doug Mohns	5	16	21	28
Real Chevrefils	9	9	18	21
Fernie Flaman	0	15	15	71
Carl Boone	5	3	8	28
Norm Johnson	2	3	5	8
Jack Bionda	1	4	5	50
Bob Armstrong	1	4	5	66
John Peirson	2	2	4	10
Leo Boivin	0	4	4	54
Jack Caffery	1	0	1	2
Gerry Ehman	1	0	1	2
Willie O'Ree	0	0	0	0
Harry Pidhirny	0	0	0	0
Bob Beckett	0	0	0	2

3-goal game

Johnny Bucyk

Penalty minutes: 851 – 12.1 per game

1957-58 PLAYOFF RESULTS

March 1958

	AT	VERSUS		W-L-T	SCR
25	New York	Rangers		L	5–3
27	New York	Rangers		W	4–3
29	Boston	New York		W	5–0

April 1958

1	Boston	New York		L	5–2
3	Boston	New York		W	6–1
5	Boston	New York		W	8–2
8	Montreal	Canadiens		L	2–1
10	Montreal	Canadiens		W	5–2
13	Boston	Montreal		L	3–0
15	Boston	Montreal		W	3–1
17	Montreal	Canadiens		L	3–2
20	Boston	Montreal		L	5–3

1957-58 PLAYOFFS

vs. New York Rangers	4 wins – 2 losses	vs. Montreal Canadiens	2 wins – 4 losses
at New York	1 win – 1 loss	at Montreal	1 win – 2 losses
at Boston	3 wins – 1 loss	at Boston	1 win – 2 losses

1957-58 PLAYOFF SCORING

	GP	SO	GAA
Don Simmons	11	1	2.45
Harry Lumley	1	0	5.00

	G	A	P	PIM
Fleming Mackell	5	14	19	12
Don McKenney	9	8	17	0
Doug Mohns	3	10	13	18
Jerry Toppazzini	9	3	12	2
Larry Regan	3	8	11	6
Bronco Horvath	5	3	8	8
Vic Stasiuk	0	5	5	13
Norm Johnson	4	0	4	6
Fernie Flaman	2	2	4	10
Allan Stanley	1	3	4	6
Johnny Bucyk	0	4	4	16
Leo Boivin	0	3	3	21
Carl Boone	1	1	2	13
Larry Hillman	0	2	2	6
Leo Labine	0	2	2	10
John Peirson	0	1	1	0
Real Chevrefils	0	0	0	0

1958–1959
(35th year)

TEAM OWNER:	Boston Professional Hockey Association	PLAYOFFS:	*Semi-finals:* Lose to Toronto Maple Leafs 3 wins – 4 losses
PRESIDENT & GOVERNOR:	Walter Brown	STANLEY CUP WINNER:	Montreal Canadiens
GM:	Lynn Patrick	ALL-STARS:	None
COACH:	Milt Schmidt	TROPHY WINNERS:	Dufresne — Vic Stasiuk
		RADIO:	WHDH with Fred Cusick

UNIFORMS

- Home jersey is gold with a black shoulder band. Pants are black with gold striping on the side. Stockings are vertical gold, white, and black stripes. Road jersey is white with a gold shoulder band trimmed in black. For the first time, uniforms also feature numbers on the sleeves of the jersey. The Bruins also introduce gold pants that are worn on occasion during the regular season.

POTPOURRI

- In the February 8th game against the Rangers, Bronco Horvath scores a hat trick while wearing a mask to protect a broken jaw. Two of the 3 goals are short-handed.
- Bruins finish in second place.
- In the October 18 game against Toronto, Doug Mohns and Bronco Horvath have their jaws broken.
- Lose semi-finals to Toronto, 4 games to 3. This marked the last playoff appearance for the Bruins until March, 1968.
- For the first time in their history, the Bruins travel by charter airplane for the 1959 playoffs.
- During the off season, the Bruins and Rangers travel to Europe on an exhibition tour. During the tour, an experimental orange puck is used. This puck is never adopted.
- Bruins Director of player personnel, Punch Imlach, is named general manager of the Toronto Maple Leafs.
- Don McKenney, Vic Stasiuk, Johnny Bucyk, Jerry Toppazzini, Leo LaBine, Jim Morrison, Leo Boivin, and Fernie Flaman play in all 70 games.
- Bruins receive 10 major penalties, least in the league for the season.

TRANSACTIONS

- Trade Allan Stanley to Toronto for Jim Morrison.
- Obtain Earl Reibel from Chicago, Jean-Guy Gendron and Gord Redahl from New York in the intra-league draft.
- Bruins place Real Chevrefils, Norm Johnson, Earl Reibel, and Larry Regan on waivers with Reibel being claimed by New York and Johnson being claimed by Chicago.
- Claim Jean-Guy Gendron from the New York Rangers.

1958-59 STANDINGS

	W	L	T	P	GF	GA
Montreal	39	18	13	91	258	158
Boston	32	29	9	73	205	215
Chicago	28	29	13	69	197	208
Toronto	27	32	11	65	189	201
New York	26	32	12	58	201	217
Detroit	25	37	8	58	167	218

1958-59 RESULTS

October 1958

	AT	VERSUS	W-L-T	SCR
9	Montreal	Canadiens	L	3–2
11	Boston	New York	T	4–4
12	Boston	Montreal	W	4–2
15	New York	Rangers	T	4–4
18	Toronto	Maple Leafs	L	3–2
19	Chicago	Blackawks	W	4–1
23	Detroit	Red Wings	L	3–1
25	Montreal	Canadiens	W	5–2
29	New York	Rangers	T	2–2
30	Chicago	Blackhawks	W	5–2

November 1958

1	Boston	Detroit	W	3–1
2	Boston	Toronto	W	2–0
8	Toronto	Maple Leafs	L	5–3
9	Boston	New York	L	5–1
11	Chicago	Blackhawks	W	8–4
13	Boston	Detroit	L	3–1
15	New York	Rangers	L	4–2
16	Boston	Toronto	T	4–4
18	Detroit	Red Wings	L	6–0

19	Chicago	Blackhawks	L	3–2
22	Boston	Detroit	W	2–1
23	Boston	Montreal	W	2–0
27	Boston	New York	W	3–1
29	New York	Rangers	W	3–1
30	Boston	Toronto	L	2–1

December 1958

4	Detroit	Red Wings	L	4–0
6	Toronto	Maple Leafs	L	4–1
7	Boston	Montreal	L	4–1
13	Boston	Chicago	W	4–2
14	Boston	Toronto	W	6–3
17	Chicago	Blackhawks	L	5–2
20	Toronto	Maple Leafs	T	2–2
21	Boston	Montreal	L	5–0
25	Boston	Chicago	W	4–2
27	Montreal	Canadiens	L	6–1
28	Detroit	Red Wings	L	5–3
31	New York	Rangers	L	4–3

January 1959

1	Boston	New York	L	5–2

3	Detroit	Red Wings	W	8–2
4	Chicago	Blackhawks	L	5–3
8	Boston	Chicago	L	4–2
10	Toronto	Maple Leafs	L	4–1
11	Boston	Montreal	T	3–3
15	Boston	Detroit	W	3–0
17	Montreal	Canadiens	T	3–3
18	Boston	Toronto	W	4–3
24	Toronto	Maple Leafs	W	3–1
25	Boston	New York	L	8–3
31	Boston	Detroit	W	5–4

February 1959

1	Boston	Toronto	W	6–4
5	Boston	Chicago	L	2–1
7	Montreal	Canadiens	W	3–2
8	Boston	New York	W	4–1
11	New York	Rangers	W	5–3

12	Boston	Chicago	W	5–4
14	Boston	Montreal	L	2–1
15	Chicago	Blackhawks	T	3–3
21	Montreal	Canadiens	L	6–0
22	Detroit	Red Wings	W	4–1
28	Chicago	Blackhawks	L	5–2

March 1959

3	Detroit	Red Wings	T	2–2
5	Boston	Detroit	W	3–0
7	Toronto	Maple Leafs	L	4–1
8	Boston	Toronto	W	4–3
12	Boston	New York	W	5–4
14	Boston	Detroit	W	4–2
15	Boston	Montreal	W	5–3
18	New York	Rangers	W	5–3
21	Montreal	Canadiens	W	4–3
22	Boston	Chicago	L	4–1

1958-59 SCORING

	GP	SO	GAA
Don Simmons	58	3	3.17
Harry Lumley	11	1	2.45
Don Keenan	1	0	4.00

	G	A	P	PIM
Don McKenney	32	30	62	20
Vic Stasiuk	27	33	60	63
Johnny Bucyk	24	36	60	36
Jerry Toppazzini	21	23	44	61
Fleming Mackell	17	23	40	28
Bronco Horvath	19	20	39	58
Leo Labine	9	23	32	74
Doug Mohns	6	24	30	40
Jim Morrison	8	17	25	42
Jean-Guy Gendron	15	9	24	57
Leo Boivin	5	16	21	94
Fernie Flaman	0	21	21	101
Larry Leach	4	12	16	26
Earl Reibel	6	8	14	16
Larry Hillman	3	10	13	19
Larry Regan	5	6	11	10
Bob Armstrong	1	9	10	50
Real Chevrefils	1	5	6	8
Norm Johnson	2	3	5	8
Jack Bionda	0	1	1	2
Gordon Redahl	0	1	1	2
Dan Poliziani	0	0	0	0
Ken Yackel	0	0	0	2

3-goal games

   Vic Stasiuk (2)
   Johnny Bucyk
   Don McKenney
   Jean-Guy Gendron
   Bronco Horvath

Penalty minutes: 838 – 11.9 per game

1958-59 PLAYOFF RESULTS

March 1959

	AT	VERSUS	W-L-T	SCR
24	Boston	Toronto	W	5–1
26	Boston	Toronto	W	4–2
28	Toronto	Maple Leafs	L	3–2 (OT)
31	Toronto	Maple Leafs	L	3–2 (OT)

April 1959

2	Boston	Toronto	L	4–1
4	Toronto	Maple Leafs	W	5–4
7	Boston	Toronto	L	3–2

1958-59 PLAYOFFS

vs. Toronto Maple Leafs	3 wins – 4 losses
at Toronto	2 wins – 2 losses
at Boston	1 win – 2 losses

1958-59 PLAYOFF SCORING

	GP	SO	GAA					
Harry Lumley	7	0	2.86	Larry Leach	1	1	2	8
				Doug Mohns	0	2	2	12
	G	A	P	PIM	Bob Armstrong	0	2	2	4

	G	A	P	PIM
Fleming Mackell	2	6	8	8
Don McKenney	2	5	7	0
Jerry Toppazzini	4	2	6	0
Vic Stasiuk	4	2	6	11
Johnny Bucyk	2	4	6	6
Jim Morrison	0	6	6	16
Bronco Horvath	2	3	5	0
Leo Labine	2	1	3	12
Leo Boivin	1	2	3	4

Larry Leach	1	1	2	8
Doug Mohns	0	2	2	12
Bob Armstrong	0	2	2	4
Jean-Guy Gendron	1	0	1	18
Larry Hillman	0	1	1	0
Jack Bionda	0	0	0	0
Ken Yackel	0	0	0	2
Dan Poliziani	0	0	0	0
Earl Reibel	0	0	0	0
Fern Flaman	0	0	0	8

Penalty minutes: 113 – 16.1 per game

1959–1960
(36th year)

TEAM OWNER:	Boston Professional Hockey Association	PLAYOFFS:	Out of playoffs
		STANLEY CUP WINNER:	Montreal Canadiens
PRESIDENT & GOVERNOR:	Walter Brown	ALL-STARS:	Bronco Horvath (2nd team)
GM:	Lynn Patrick	TROPHY WINNERS:	Dufresne — Bronco Horvath
COACH:	Milt Schmidt	RADIO:	WHDH with Fred Cusick

UNIFORMS

- Home jersey is gold with black shoulder inserts with white trim. Road jersey is white with gold shoulder inserts. Pants are black with gold and white trim. Socks are gold, black, and white alternating vertical stripes.

POTPOURRI

- Fern Flaman scores first goal in 145 games on October 11.
- The January 31 game at Boston is Fern Flaman night as Vic Stasiuk scores 3 goals in a 6–5 win over Montreal.
- Don McKenney wins the Lady Byng Memorial Trophy.
- Bronco Horvath scores at least 1 point in each of 22 consecutive games.
- The Bruins play in first year of 8-year playoff drought. They finish 4–9–3 down the stretch to wind up 3 points out of a playoff spot.
- Bobby Hull of Chicago noses out Bronco Horvath by 1 point to win the scoring championship.

- Bruins lose all 7 games in Montreal.
- In the November 1 game at New York between the Rangers and Canadiens, Jacques Plante begins wearing a mask after a facial injury.
- In the November 8 game at Chicago, Larry Leach fails in his bid to score on a penalty shot. There is some confusion over this penalty shot: Al Arbour of Chicago threw his stick trying to stop Bronco Horvath who had broken in clear on Glenn Hall. The referee, Dalton McArthur, awarded a penalty shot and said Chicago could choose the Boston player to take the shot. The Bruins then produced a rule book saying that the captain of the non-offending team (the Bruins) can pick the shooter.
- In a January 10 game against Toronto at Boston, Don Simmons wears a face mask for the first time, becoming the second goaltender, and first Bruin, to do so.
- Bobby Hull of the Chicago Blackhawks scores his first career hat trick against the Bruins on December 27 at Chicago Stadium.

TRANSACTIONS

- Obtain Aut Erickson from Chicago, Charlie Burns from Detroit, and Bruce Gamble from New York in the intra-league draft.
- Obtain Nick Mickoski from Detroit for Jim Morrison.

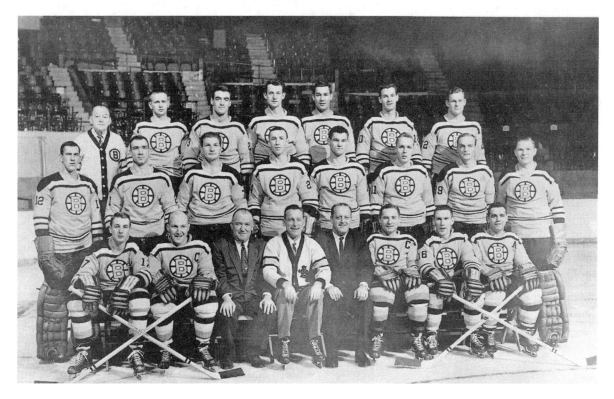

1959-60 STANDINGS

	W	L	T	P	GF	GA
Montreal	40	18	12	92	255	187
Toronto	35	26	9	79	199	195
Chicago	28	29	13	69	191	180
Detroit	26	29	15	67	186	197
Boston	28	34	8	64	220	241
New York	17	38	15	49	187	247

1959-60 RESULTS

October 1959

	AT	VERSUS	W-L-T	SCR
8	Montreal	Canadiens	L	4–1
10	Boston	New York	W	6–4
11	Boston	Montreal	W	8–4
14	New York	Rangers	W	4–3
17	Toronto	Maple Leafs	L	3–0
18	Chicago	Blackhawks	T	2–2
22	Detroit	Red Wings	L	4–1
24	Montreal	Canadiens	L	5–1
29	Boston	Detroit	W	2–1
31	Toronto	Maple Leafs	L	4–3

November 1959

1	Boston	Toronto	W	6–3
3	Chicago	Blackhawks	W	6–3
5	Detroit	Red Wings	W	8–3
8	Boston	Chicago	W	5–3
11	New York	Rangers	L	6–3
12	Boston	Detroit	L	6–5
14	Montreal	Canadiens	L	8–1
15	Boston	Montreal	L	4–1
21	Boston	Detroit	T	3–3
22	Boston	Toronto	L	2–1
25	New York	Rangers	T	3–3
26	Boston	New York	W	4–3
28	Toronto	Maple Leafs	T	2–2
29	Boston	Montreal	L	4–2

December 1959

2	Chicago	Blackhawks	T	2–2
5	Detroit	Red Wings	L	4–3
6	Boston	Chicago	L	6–3
10	Boston	Toronto	W	6–3
12	Boston	New York	L	4–3
13	New York	Rangers	L	4–3
16	Chicago	Blackhawks	L	4–0
20	Boston	Detroit	L	4–2
25	Boston	Chicago	W	5–1
27	Chicago	Blackhawks	L	6–1
29	New York	Rangers	W	4–3

January 1960

1	Boston	New York	W	7–3
2	Montreal	Canadiens	L	6–5
3	Detroit	Red Wings	L	4–3
7	Boston	Chicago	W	5–1
9	Toronto	Maple Leafs	W	3–2
10	Boston	Toronto	W	4–0
14	Boston	New York	W	6–0
16	Montreal	Canadiens	L	8–2
17	Boston	Montreal	L	3–1
20	Chicago	Blackhawks	L	3–1
21	Detroit	Red Wings	L	5–2
23	Toronto	Maple Leafs	T	3–3
24	Boston	Toronto	W	6–2
30	Boston	Detroit	W	3–2
31	Boston	Montreal	W	6–5

February 1960

4	Boston	Chicago	L	7–2
6	Montreal	Canadiens	L	5–3
7	Boston	Toronto	W	3–0
11	Boston	Detroit	W	3–2
13	Boston	Montreal	W	7–6
14	Boston	New York	W	3–0
17	Toronto	Maple Leafs	L	3–1
20	Detroit	Red Wings	L	4–1
21	New York	Rangers	L	7–2
27	Chicago	Blackhawks	W	3–1

March 1960

1	Detroit	Red Wings	L	3–2
3	Boston	Chicago	L	2–0
5	Toronto	Maple Leafs	L	5–2
6	Boston	Toronto	L	3–1
10	Boston	New York	T	3–3
12	Boston	Detroit	W	5–1
13	Boston	Montreal	W	3–2
16	New York	Rangers	W	3–2
19	Montreal	Canadiens	L	5–1
20	Boston	Chicago	T	5–5

1959-60 SCORING

	GP	SO	GAA				
Don Simmons	28	2	3.36	Vic Stasiuk	29	39	68	121
Harry Lumley	42	2	3.50	Johnny Bucyk	16	36	52	26
				Doug Mohns	20	25	45	62
	G	A	P	PIM	Jerry Toppazzini	12	33	45	26
					Leo Labine	16	28	44	58
Bronco Horvath	39	41	80	60	Jean-Guy Gendron	24	11	35	64
Don McKenney	20	49	69	28	Charlie Burns	10	17	27	46

Leo Boivin	4	21	25	65	Nick Mickoski	1	0	1	2
Fleming Mackell	7	15	22	19	Larry Hillman	0	1	1	2
Fernie Flaman	2	18	20	112	Don Ward	0	1	1	16
Larry Leach	7	12	19	47	Gordon Turlik	0	0	0	2
Bob Armstrong	5	14	19	96	Pierre Gagne	0	0	0	0
Dick Meissner	5	6	11	22	Dale Rolfe	0	0	0	0
Autrey Erickson	1	6	7	29	Stan Baliuk	0	0	0	2
Dallas Smith	1	1	2	0					
Lorne Davis	1	1	2	10	NO PLAYOFF SCORING				

1960–1961

(37th year)

TEAM OWNER:	Boston Professional Hockey Association	PLAYOFFS:	Out of playoffs
PRESIDENT & GOVERNOR:	Walter Brown	STANLEY CUP WINNER:	Chicago Blackhawks
		ALL-STARS:	None
GM:	Lynn Patrick	TROPHY WINNERS:	Dufresne — Leo Boivin
COACH:	Milt Schmidt	RADIO:	WHDH with John Peirson

UNIFORMS

- Home jersey is gold with black shoulder inserts with white trim. Road jersey is white with gold shoulder inserts. Pants are black with gold and white trim. Socks are gold, black, and white alternating vertical stripes.

POTPOURRI

- In a December 8 game against Chicago, Charlie Burns scores 2 short-handed goals.
- Willie O'Ree scores first career goal in January 1 game against Montreal.
- October 23 game against Chicago ends in melee as a fan hits Glenn Hall with a light bulb.
- Bruins fail to qualify for the playoffs.
- Former coach George Boucher passes away on October 18.
- Bruins win 2 games and lose 25 games on the road.
- Bruins fail to win any games at Montreal, Chicago, and New York.
- The February 4 game against the Rangers at Boston is delayed 2 hours due to the Rangers arriving late because of a snow storm.
- In the October 29 game against Detroit, Bruins Milt Schmidt becomes the first coach to remove the goalie for an extra attacker on a delayed penalty.
- In the November 10 game against Detroit, Jerry Toppazzini becomes the last regular position player to tend goal as he replaces an injured Don Simmons in the last minute of the game.
- Bruins lead the league in losses with 42 and goals against with 254. They also tie with Detroit in being shut out 5 times.
- Bruins only record 1 shutout win this season.

TRANSACTIONS

- Lose Larry Hillman to Toronto and Floyd Smith to New York in the draft.
- Bruins call up Bruce Gamble to replace Don Simmons, and Willie O'Ree to bolster the forward lines.
- Trade Jean-Guy Gendron to Montreal for Andre Pronovost.
- Trade Leo Labine and Vic Stasiuk to Detroit for Murray Oliver, Gary Aldcorn, and Tom McCarthy.

- Draft Ted Green and Tom Thurlby from Montreal, and Jimmy Bartlett from New York in the intra-league draft.
- Fleming Mackell retires to become the playing coach of the Quebec Aces.

1960-61 STANDINGS

	W	L	T	P	GF	GA
Montreal	41	19	10	92	254	188
Toronto	39	19	12	90	234	176
Chicago	29	24	17	75	198	180
Detroit	25	29	16	66	195	215
New York	22	38	10	54	204	248
Boston	15	42	13	43	176	254

1960-61 RESULTS

October 1960

	AT	VERSUS	W-L-T	SCR
5	New York	Rangers	L	2-1
8	Montreal	Canadiens	T	1-1
9	Boston	Montreal	T	4-4
11	Boston	Detroit	T	3-3
15	Toronto	Maple Leafs	T	1-1
16	Chicago	Blackhawks	L	5-2
20	Detroit	Red Wings	L	5-0
23	Boston	Chicago	T	2-2
27	Boston	New York	W	6-4
29	Montreal	Canadiens	L	3-2
30	Boston	Montreal	W	5-3

November 1960

2	Toronto	Maple Leafs	T	2-2
3	Detroit	Red Wings	L	8-5
6	Boston	Chicago	W	4-0
10	Boston	Detroit	L	4-1
13	Boston	Toronto	L	4-2
16	New York	Rangers	L	4-3
17	Chicago	Blackhawks	L	4-2
19	Boston	Detroit	W	6-4
20	Boston	Toronto	L	3-2
23	New York	Rangers	L	6-3
24	Boston	New York	L	5-3
27	Boston	Montreal	L	3-0
30	Chicago	Blackhawks	T	2-2

December 1960

1	Detroit	Red Wings	W	3-2
3	Montreal	Canadiens	L	3-1
4	Boston	Toronto	L	5-2
8	Boston	Chicago	W	5-1
10	Boston	New York	L	3-0
11	New York	Rangers	T	2-2
17	Toronto	Maple Leafs	T	3-3

18	Boston	Montreal	L	4-2
22	Boston	Chicago	W	4-2
25	Boston	Toronto	L	4-1
28	Chicago	Blackhawks	L	4-3
31	Montreal	Canadiens	L	3-1

January 1961

1	Boston	Montreal	W	3-2
5	Boston	Chicago	L	4-3
7	Toronto	Maple Leafs	L	4-1
8	Detroit	Red Wings	L	5-3
12	Boston	New York	T	4-4
14	Montreal	Canadiens	L	4-0
15	Boston	Toronto	L	6-4
19	Boston	Detroit	W	4-2
21	Toronto	Maple Leafs	W	3-1
22	Chicago	Blackhawks	L	8-3
25	New York	Rangers	L	2-1
26	Boston	Toronto	W	5-4
29	Boston	Detroit	L	3-1

February 1961

2	Boston	Chicago	T	2-2
4	Boston	New York	L	2-1
5	New York	Rangers	L	5-2
9	Boston	Montreal	L	5-1
11	Toronto	Maple Leafs	L	6-3
12	Boston	New York	W	8-3
16	Montreal	Canadiens	L	9-1
18	Detroit	Red Wings	L	5-1
19	Chicago	Blackhawks	T	2-2
23	Detroit	Red Wings	T	3-3
26	Chicago	Blackhawks	L	3-1

March 1961

1	New York	Rangers	L	3-1
2	Boston	Detroit	W	4-2

5	Boston	Montreal	L	2–1		12	Boston	Toronto	L	5–0
7	Detroit	Red Wings	L	3–1		15	Boston	New York	W	6–2
9	Boston	Detroit	L	5–2		18	Toronto	Maple Leafs	L	6–2
11	Montreal	Canadiens	L	7–5		19	Boston	Chicago	W	4–3

1960-61 SCORING

	GP	SO	GAA
Don Simmons	18	1	3.28
Bruce Gamble	52	0	3.75

	G	A	P	PIM
Jerry Toppazzini	15	35	50	35
Don McKenney	26	23	49	22
Charlie Burns	15	26	41	16
Johnny Bucyk	19	20	39	48
Doug Mohns	12	21	33	63
Bronco Horvath	15	15	30	15
Vic Stasiuk	5	25	30	16
Jim Bartlett	15	9	24	95
Leo Boivin	6	17	23	50
Andre Pronovost	11	11	22	30
Leo Labine	7	12	19	34
Murray Oliver	6	10	16	8
Willie O'Ree	4	10	14	26

Fernie Flaman	2	9	11	59
Bob Armstrong	0	10	10	72
Dallas Smith	1	9	10	79
Gerry Ouellette	5	4	9	0
Tom McCarthy	4	5	9	0
Autrey Erickson	2	6	8	65
Jean-Guy Gendron	1	7	8	25
Orval Tessier	3	4	7	0
Gary Aldcorn	2	3	5	12
Dick Meissner	0	1	1	2
Art Chisholm	0	0	0	0
Bill Carter	0	0	0	2
Ted Green	0	0	0	2

Penalty minutes: 810 – 11.5 per game

NO PLAYOFF SCORING

1961–1962
(38th year)

TEAM OWNER:	Boston Professional Hockey Association	STANLEY CUP WINNER:	Toronto Maple Leafs
		ALL-STARS:	None
PRESIDENT & GOVERNOR:	Walter Brown	TROPHY WINNERS:	Dufresne — Doug Mohns
GM:	Lynn Patrick	RADIO:	WHDH Radio with
COACH:	Phil Watson		Johnny Pierson
PLAYOFFS:	Out of playoffs		

UNIFORMS
- Home jersey is gold with black shoulder inserts with white trim. Road jersey is white with gold shoulder inserts. Pants are black with gold and white trim. Socks are gold, black, and white alternating vertical stripes.

POTPOURRI
- Don Head records first shutout in Bruins first victory of season.
- In the November 16 win over Montreal at Boston Garden, Terry Gray scores 2 goals and a fighting decision over Lou Fontinato. Don Head plays in goal for Boston.
- Bruins open the season with an 8-game winless streak.
- Bruins fail to make the playoffs for the third straight season.
- Attract only 5,642 fans for a March 8 game against Detroit.
- In the November 1 game at Montreal won by Boston 5–2, goalie Don Head has a fight with Marcel Bonin of the Canadiens.

- Murray Oliver scores the only hat trick of the season.
- 14-year-old Bobby Orr signs a player development contract with the Bruins.
- Hockey Hall of Fame opens in Toronto.
- Charlie Burns, Don McKenney, Murray Oliver, Cliff Pennington, Andre Pronovost, and Jerry Toppazzini play in all 70 games.
- Bruins suffer through a 20-game winless streak.

TRANSACTIONS

- Phil Watson replaces Milt Schmidt as coach.
- Don Simmons is traded to Toronto for Ed Chadwick.
- Obtain Orland Kurtenbach from New York, plus Earl Balfour and Pat Stapleton from Chicago in the intra-league draft.
- Cliff Pennington is drafted from Montreal.
- Bronco Horvath and Autrey Erickson are sold to Chicago in the intra-league draft.
- Bob Armstrong is traded to Montreal for Wayne Connelly.

1961-62 STANDINGS

	W	L	T	P	GF	GA
Montreal	42	14	14	98	259	166
Toronto	37	22	11	85	232	180
Chicago	31	26	13	75	217	186
New York	26	32	12	64	195	207
Detroit	23	33	14	60	184	219
Boston	15	47	8	38	177	306

1961-62 RESULTS

October 1962

	AT	VERSUS	W-L-T	SCR
11	Boston	New York	L	6-2
12	New York	Rangers	L	6-3
14	Toronto	Maple Leafs	L	3-2
15	Boston	Montreal	T	5-5
17	Chicago	Blackhawks	L	5-3
19	Detroit	Red Wings	L	7-3
21	Montreal	Canadiens	L	6-2
22	Boston	Toronto	L	9-1
26	Boston	Detroit	W	4-0
29	Boston	Chicago	T	2-2

November 1961

2	Montreal	Canadiens	W	5-2
5	Boston	Chicago	L	4-3
8	New York	Rangers	T	4-4
9	Detroit	Red Wings	L	2-1
12	Boston	Toronto	W	4-3
16	Boston	Montreal	W	3-2
19	Boston	Detroit	L	6-2
23	Boston	New York	L	4-3
25	Montreal	Canadiens	L	5-0
26	Boston	Toronto	L	4-1

29	Chicago	Blackhawks	L	7-4
30	Detroit	Red Wings	L	3-1

December 1961

2	Boston	New York	W	3-1
3	New York	Rangers	L	3-1
7	Boston	Chicago	L	5-2
9	Toronto	Maple Leafs	L	9-2
10	Boston	Montreal	L	4-3
13	Chicago	Blackhawks	T	2-2
14	Detroit	Red Wings	L	5-0
16	Montreal	Canadiens	L	8-4
17	Boston	Toronto	L	4-1
21	Boston	Detroit	W	4-2
23	Toronto	Maple Leafs	W	7-4
25	Boston	Montreal	L	5-2
31	New York	Rangers	W	7-4

January 1962

1	Boston	New York	L	4-2
6	Detroit	Red Wings	L	6-2
7	Chicago	Blackhawks	W	2-0
10	Toronto	Maple Leafs	L	7-5
11	Boston	Chicago	L	6-0

13	Montreal	Canadiens	L	5–3
14	Boston	Montreal	L	4–1
18	Boston	Detroit	W	5–3
20	Toronto	Maple Leafs	W	5–4
21	Boston	Toronto	L	5–1
27	Boston	Chicago	W	5–3
28	Boston	Montreal	L	5–1
31	New York	Rangers	L	5–0

February 1962

1	Boston	New York	L	5–3
3	Chicago	Blackhawks	L	6–3
4	Detroit	Red Wings	L	6–0
7	Toronto	Maple Leafs	T	2–2
8	Boston	Chicago	L	6–2
10	Boston	Detroit	T	2–2
11	Boston	New York	L	5–3

15	Montreal	Canadiens	L	9–1
18	Chicago	Blackhawks	L	6–0
21	New York	Rangers	L	4–2
24	Toronto	Maple Leafs	L	7–2
25	Chicago	Blackhawks	L	8–0
28	New York	Rangers	T	2–2

March 1962

1	Boston	Chicago	L	5–4
4	Boston	Toronto	L	5–1
8	Boston	Detroit	L	3–0
10	Montreal	Canadiens	L	5–2
11	Boston	Detroit	T	2–2
15	Detroit	Red Wings	W	4–0
18	Boston	Montreal	W	6–2
22	Boston	New York	L	4–3
25	Boston	Toronto	W	5–4

1961-62 SCORING

	GP	SO	GAA
Bruce Gamble	28	1	4.39
Don Head	38	2	4.24
Ed Chadwick	4	0	5.50

	G	A	P	PIM
Johnny Bucyk	20	40	60	32
Don McKenney	22	33	55	10
Jerry Toppazzini	19	31	50	26
Murray Oliver	17	29	46	20
Doug Mohns	16	29	45	74
Cliff Pennington	9	32	41	2
Charlie Burns	11	17	28	43
Andre Pronovost	15	8	23	74
Leo Boivin	5	18	23	70
Wayne Connelly	8	12	20	34
Terry Gray	8	7	15	15
Tommy Williams	6	6	12	2
Ted Green	3	8	11	116
Eddie Westfall	2	9	11	53
Bob Beckett	7	2	9	14
Larry Leach	2	5	7	18
Pat Stapleton	2	5	7	42
Dick Meissner	3	3	6	13
Bob Armstrong	2	1	3	20
Orland Kurtenbach	0	0	0	6
Dallas Smith	0	0	0	10

3-goal game
  Murray Oliver
Penalty minutes: 712 – 10.1 per game

NO PLAYOFF SCORING

1962–1963
(39th year)

TEAM OWNER:	Boston Professional Hockey Association	PLAYOFFS:	Out of playoffs
		STANLEY CUP WINNER:	Toronto Maple Leafs
PRESIDENT & GOVERNOR:	Walter Brown	ALL-STARS:	None
GM:	Lynn Patrick	TROPHY WINNERS:	Dufresne — Johnny Bucyk
COACHES	Phil Watson & Milt Schmidt	RADIO:	WHDH Radio with
ATTENDANCE:	338,304		Bill Harrington
	9,665 per game		

UNIFORMS

- Home jersey is gold with black shoulder inserts with white trim. Road jersey is white with gold shoulder inserts. Pants are black with gold and white trim. Socks are gold, black, and white alternating vertical stripes.

POTPOURRI

- Bruins win opener, 5–0, over Montreal behind a Bob Perreault shutout.
- Bruins fail to qualify for the playoffs for the fourth straight year.
- Bruins surrender a league high of 281 goals against.
- Chicago Blackhawks offer Toronto $1,000,000 for Frank Mahovlich. The offer is turned down.
- "BOW" line of Bucyk, Oliver, and Williams is lone bright spot for the Bruins.
- Ted Green appears in all 70 games.
- Bruins suffer through a 10-game winless streak.
- Although the Bruins record no hat tricks, the following players have 2 goals games: Johnny Bucyk, Murray Oliver, Tommy Williams, Jean-Guy Gendron, Charlie Burns, and Jerry Toppazzini.
- Bruins are shut out a league-leading 5 times.

TRANSACTIONS

- Obtain Warren Godfrey from Detroit, plus Jean-Guy Gendron and Irv Spencer from New York in the intra-league draft.
- Andre Pronovost is traded to Detroit for Forbes Kennedy.
- Milt Schmidt replaces Phil Watson as coach of the Bruins.
- Don McKenney is traded to New York for Dean Prentice.

1962-63 STANDINGS

	W	L	T	P	GF	GA
Toronto	35	23	12	82	221	180
Chicago	32	21	17	81	194	178
Montreal	28	19	23	79	225	183
Detroit	32	25	13	77	200	194
New York	22	36	12	56	211	233
Boston	14	39	17	45	198	281

1962-63 RESULTS

October 1962

	AT	VERSUS	W-L-T	SCR
11	Boston	Montreal	W	5–0
13	Toronto	Maple Leafs	T	2–2
14	Boston	Chicago	T	2–2
18	Detroit	Red Wings	L	5–3
20	Montreal	Canadiens	L	7–3
21	Boston	Toronto	L	6–4
25	Boston	Detroit	T	3–3

November 1962

	AT	VERSUS	W-L-T	SCR
1	Boston	Chicago	L	4–2
4	Boston	New York	L	4–3
7	Chicago	Blackhawks	T	3–3
10	Boston	Detroit	T	3–3
11	Boston	Montreal	L	4–2
14	New York	Rangers	L	6–2
18	Boston	Detroit	L	3–1
21	New York	Rangers	L	4–2
22	Boston	New York	L	7–1
24	Montreal	Canadiens	T	5–5
25	Boston	Toronto	W	5–2
29	Boston	Chicago	L	5–0

December 1962

	AT	VERSUS	W-L-T	SCR
1	Toronto	Maple Leafs	L	8–2
2	Boston	Montreal	L	3–0
5	Chicago	Blackhawks	L	5–4
6	Detroit	Red Wings	L	5–3
8	Boston	New York	T	3–3
9	New York	Rangers	W	4–2
13	Montreal	Canadiens	T	1–1

15	Toronto	Maple Leafs	L	8–2
16	Boston	Montreal	L	5–2
19	Chicago	Blackhawks	L	3–2
20	Detroit	Red Wings	W	5–3
23	Boston	Toronto	L	5–4
25	Boston	New York	W	6–2
27	New York	Rangers	L	9–3
30	Chicago	Blackhawks	L	4–2

January 1963

1	Boston	Toronto	W	3–0
3	Montreal	Canadiens	L	4–1
5	Toronto	Maple Leafs	L	4–2
6	Detroit	Red Wings	T	5–5
10	Boston	Chicago	W	5–4
12	Montreal	Canadiens	L	7–2
13	Boston	Toronto	T	2–2
16	Chicago	Blackhawks	W	5–4
17	Detroit	Red Wings	L	5–3
19	Boston	New York	L	5–3
20	Boston	Montreal	T	3–3
24	Boston	Toronto	L	6–3
26	Toronto	Maple Leafs	W	5–2
27	Boston	Detroit	L	5–3
31	Boston	Chicago	L	9–2

February 1963

2	Boston	Detroit	T	4–4
3	New York	Rangers	W	6–4
7	Detroit	Red Wings	T	3–3
10	Boston	Montreal	T	5–5
12	Boston	New York	W	6–3
14	Montreal	Canadiens	W	2–1
16	Detroit	Red Wings	L	3–1
17	Chicago	Blackhawks	L	3–1
20	New York	Rangers	T	3–3
23	Toronto	Maple Leafs	W	4–2
24	Chicago	Blackhawks	L	4–3
28	Boston	Detroit	W	5–3

March 1963

3	Boston	Toronto	L	6–3
6	Toronto	Maple Leafs	L	4–0
7	Montreal	Canadiens	L	8–0
10	Boston	Detroit	L	4–3
14	Boston	Chicago	L	2–0
17	Boston	Montreal	T	2–2
20	New York	Rangers	L	5–1
21	Boston	New York	T	2–2
24	Boston	Chicago	L	4–3

1962-63 SCORING

	GP	SO	GAA
Eddie Johnston	49	1	4.00
Bob Perreault	22	1	3.86

	G	A	P	PIM
Johnny Bucyk	27	39	66	36
Murray Oliver	22	40	62	38
Tommy Williams	23	20	43	11
Jean-Guy Gendron	21	22	43	42
Jerry Toppazzini	17	18	35	6
Don McKenney	14	19	33	2
Forbes Kennedy	12	18	30	46
Doug Mohns	7	23	30	63
Leo Boivin	2	24	26	48
Charlie Burns	12	10	22	13
Bob Leiter	9	13	22	34
Irving Spencer	5	17	22	34
Cliff Pennington	7	10	17	4
Wayne Hicks	7	9	16	14
Dean Prentice	6	9	15	4
Eddie Westfall	1	11	12	34
Ted Green	1	11	12	117
Warren Godfrey	2	9	11	56
Wayne Connelly	2	6	8	2
Don Blackburn	0	5	5	4
Pat Stapleton	0	3	3	8
Andre Pronovost	0	2	2	4
Matt Ravlich	1	0	1	0
Jeannot Gilbert	0	0	0	4

Penalty minutes: 636 – 9.1 minutes per game

1963–1964
(40th year)

TEAM OWNER:	Boston Professional Hockey Association	PLAYOFFS:	Out of playoffs
PRESIDENT & GOVERNOR:	Walter Brown	STANLEY CUP WINNER:	Toronto Maple Leafs
GM:	Lynn Patrick	ALL-STARS:	None
COACH:	Milt Schmidt	TROPHY WINNERS:	Dufresne — Ed Johnston
ATTENDANCE:	368,002 10,514 per game	RADIO:	WHDH Radio with Bill Harrington

UNIFORMS

- Introduce new black home jersey, but it is only worn occasionally. Black pants and alternating gold, black, and white vertical striped socks remain the same. White jersey with gold inserts continue to be worn at home on the road.

POTPOURRI

- Andy Hebenton plays in his 581st consecutive on December 4 at Chicago to break the record held by John Wilson.
- Bruins win at Toronto on January 18, 11–0, as Andy Hebenton and Dean Prentice score 3 goals each.
- One week later, January 25, in a game at Montreal, Bruins shut out Habs 6–0 as Andy Hebenton and Gary Dornhoefer score 2 goals apiece.
- The next night, Bruins shut out Toronto, 2–0. Eddie Johnston records both shutouts.
- Eddie Johnston becomes the last goalie to play in every minute of all of his teams games. The following Bruins also played in all 70 games: Murray Oliver, Dean Prentice, Orland Kurtenbach, Forbes Kennedy, Tom Johnson, Doug Mohns, Andy Hebenton, and Ted Green.
- The November 30 game at Montreal ends in a scoreless draw.
- In the January 7 loss to Detroit, only 7,000 are in attendance as the crowd chants "We shall overcome."
- For the fifth straight year, the Bruins fail to qualify for the playoffs.
- Bruins suffer 11-game winless streak (0–10–1).
- Bruins fail to win at Detroit.
- Forbes Kennedy misses on a penalty shot attempt against Glenn Hall of Chicago in a game played at Boston, December 22.
- Tommy Williams misses a penalty shot attempt against Johnny Bower of the Maple Leafs in a game at Toronto, December 28.
- Leo Boivin scores on a penalty shot against Charlie Hodge of the Canadiens, January 4 at Montreal.
- Don McKenney of Toronto is unsuccessful in a penalty shot attempt against Eddie Johnston on March 4 at Toronto.
- Ron Andrews replaces Ken McKenzie, publisher of The Hockey News and Hockey Pictorial, as Publicity Director of the NHL.
- In the February 9 game at Boston Garden, Billy Hicke of Montreal and Leo Boivin of the Bruins stage a fight that continues into the penalty box and involves 4 Boston policemen.
- November 24 game against Detroit is postponed to January 7, 1964, due to President Kennedy's assassination.
- Red Kelly of the Toronto Maple Leafs defeats Alan Eagleson, Bobby Orr's future agent, as a candidate for the Canadian House of Commons.
- NHL holds its first amateur draft.

TRANSACTIONS

- Warren Godfrey and Irving Spencer sold to Detroit.
- Wayne Hicks sold to Montreal.

- Tom Johnson is drafted from Montreal.
- Obtain Andy Hebenton and Wayne Rivers from New York in the intra-league draft.
- Dick Meissner is sold to New York.
- Bruins trade Terry Gray, Dale Rolfe, Bruce Gamble, and Randy Miller to Springfield of the American Hockey League for Bob McCord.
- Draft Wayne Rivers from Detroit.

AMATEUR DRAFT SELECTIONS

- Orest Romashyma, Terrance Lane, Roger Bamburak, and Jim Blair.

1963-64 STANDINGS

	W	L	T	P	GF	GA
Montreal	36	21	13	85	209	167
Chicago	36	22	12	84	218	169
Toronto	33	25	12	78	192	172
Detroit	30	29	11	71	191	204
New York	22	38	10	54	186	242
Boston	18	40	12	48	170	212

1963-64 RESULTS

October 1963

	AT	VERSUS	W-L-T	SCR
8	Boston	Montreal	T	4–4
12	Toronto	Maple Leafs	L	5–1
13	Detroit	Red Wings	L	3–0
16	Chicago	Blackhawks	L	5–2
19	Montreal	Canadiens	L	2–0
20	New York	Rangers	L	5–1
24	Boston	New York	L	2–0
27	Boston	Toronto	W	2–0
30	New York	Rangers	L	4–3

November 1963

3	Boston	Detroit	W	4–1
7	Boston	Toronto	L	4–3
10	Boston	Chicago	W	4–2
13	Chicago	Blackhawks	L	6–4
16	Boston	Detroit	T	1–1
17	Boston	Montreal	L	3–2
20	New York	Rangers	T	1–1
23	Toronto	Maple Leafs	L	4–1
28	Boston	New York	W	5–3
30	Montreal	Canadiens	T	0–0

December 1963

1	Boston	Montreal	L	3–1
4	Chicago	Blackhawks	T	2–2
5	Detroit	Red Wings	L	4–2
7	Boston	New York	W	8–6
8	New York	Rangers	T	2–2
12	Boston	Chicago	W	2–1

14	Montreal	Canadiens	L	3–1
15	Boston	Toronto	T	4–4
18	Chicago	Blackhawks	W	2–1
19	Detroit	Red Wings	L	3–0
22	Boston	Chicago	L	4–1
25	Boston	Toronto	L	5–1
28	Toronto	Maple Leafs	L	2–0
29	Detroit	Red Wings	L	2–1

January 1964

1	Boston	Montreal	T	3–3
4	Montreal	Canadiens	L	5–1
5	Chicago	Blackhawks	L	5–3
7	Boston	Detroit	L	5–0
9	Boston	New York	L	5–3
11	Toronto	Maple Leafs	L	3–1
12	Boston	Toronto	W	6–3
16	Boston	Detroit	W	5–1
18	Toronto	Maple Leafs	W	11–0
19	Boston	Montreal	T	1–1
22	New York	Rangers	L	6–4
23	Boston	Chicago	L	3–1
25	Montreal	Canadiens	W	6–0
26	Boston	Toronto	W	2–0
30	Boston	New York	T	3–1

February 1964

1	Toronto	Maple Leafs	L	5–1
2	Boston	Chicago	L	5–2
5	New York	Rangers	W	3–2
6	Boston	New York	W	4–0

8	Boston	Detroit	L	3–2	
9	Boston	Montreal	T	4–4	
13	Detroit	Red Wings	L	4–1	
16	Chicago	Blackhawks	L	5–3	
20	Montreal	Canadiens	L	3–2	
22	Detroit	Red Wings	L	3–2	
23	Chicago	Blackhawks	L	2–0	
27	Boston	New York	L	4–2	
29	Boston	Detroit	W	2–1	

March 1964

1	Boston	Toronto	W	5–3
4	Toronto	Maple Leafs	T	4–4
5	Boston	Boston	T	4–4
8	Boston	Boston	L	5–3
11	New York	Rangers	W	5–3
12	Detroit	Red Wings	L	2–1
15	Boston	Montreal	W	3–1
21	Montreal	Canadiens	L	5–1
22	Boston	Chicago	L	4–3

1963-64 SCORING

	GP	SO	GAA
Eddie Johnston	70	6	3.01

	G	A	P	PIM
Murray Oliver	24	44	68	41
Johnny Bucyk	18	36	54	36
Dean Prentice	23	16	39	37
Orland Kurtenbach	12	25	37	91
Doug Mohns	9	17	26	95
Forbes Kennedy	8	17	25	95
Tom Johnson	4	21	25	33
Leo Boivin	10	14	24	42
Andy Hebenton	12	11	23	8
Tommy Williams	8	15	23	8
Gary Dornhoefer	12	10	22	20
Bob Leiter	6	13	19	43
Jean-Guy Gendron	5	13	18	43
Ted Green	4	10	14	145
Jerry Toppazzini	7	4	11	15
Bob McCord	1	9	10	49
Wayne Rivers	2	7	9	6
Eddie Westfall	1	5	6	35
Wayne Connelly	2	3	5	12
Ron Schock	1	2	3	0
Don Awrey	1	0	1	4
Bob Beckett	0	1	1	0
Ted Irvine	0	0	0	0
Skip Krake	0	0	0	0

3-goal games
    Andy Hebenton & Dean Prentice

Number of power play advantages	220
Power play goals	28
% successful	12%
Murray Oliver	5
Dean Prentice	5
Tommy Williams	3
Doug Mohns	3
Gary Dornhoefer	3
Orland Kurtenbach	2
Andy Hebenton	1
Bob McCord	1
Bob Leiter	1
Leo Boivin	1
Johnny Bucyk	1
Ted Green	1
Jerry Toppazzini	1
Short-handed goals against	4
Penalty minutes 858 – 12.3 per game	
Times short-handed	242
Power play goals against	45
Penalty kill success	82%
Short-handed goals	3
Leo Boivin	1
Jerry Toppazzini	1
Dean Prentice	1

NO PLAYOFF SCORING

1964–1965
(41st year)

TEAM OWNER:	Boston Professional Hockey Association	PLAYOFFS:	Out of playoffs
		STANLEY CUP WINNER:	Montreal Canadiens
PRESIDENT & GOVERNOR:	Weston Adams	ALL-STARS:	None
GM:	Lynn Patrick	TROPHY WINNERS:	Dufresne — Ted Green
COACH:	Milt Schmidt	RADIO:	WHDH Radio with
ATTENDANCE:	389,886		Bill Harrington
	11,139 per game		

UNIFORMS

- Home and road uniform are the same. White jersey trimmed in gold and black with the spoked "B" on the uniform front. Black pants and socks with gold, black, and white vertical stripes.

POTPOURRI

- Ted Green plays in all 70 games.
- Eddie Johnston records 3 shutouts.
- Johnny Bucyk scores on a penalty shot against Terry Sawchuk at Toronto.
- Dean Prentice scores on a penalty shot against Denis DeJordy at Chicago.
- Murray Oliver has the lone hat trick for the season.
- Reggie Fleming scores 2 short-handed goals in an October 22nd game against Toronto.
- Bruins open season with a 9 game winless streak.
- In the January 7 game at Boston Garden, Gordie Howe slams rookie Billy Knibbs into the board injuring Knibbs. Howe needs a police escort to the dressing room.
- Murray Oliver scores 3 goals in the January 14 game won by the Bruins over the Rangers 5–2.
- February 4 game against Detroit at Boston is marred by a stick-swinging duel between Reggie Fleming and Bill Gadsby.
- The February 21 loss at Chicago is marred again by a bench-clearing brawl. In a February 28 win at Chicago, Tom Johnson's leg muscle is severed by a skate. This proves to be Johnson's last game.
- Bruins fail to qualify for the playoffs for the sixth consecutive season and the fifth straight season with less than 50 points.
- Walter Brown, past President of the Bruins, passes away.
- Art Ross, former General Manager of the Bruins and inventor of the Ross puck, goal nets, tendon guards, and numerous rules, passes away.
- Bruins score only 89 goals at home.
- Bruins are shut out 6 times.
- Because of illness of Eddie Johnston, the Bruins bring up Jack Norris for a January 30 game at Toronto. Norris' goal equipment is stolen from the Royal York Hotel so he is unable to play. In the Bruins 6–1 loss, Johnston breaks his hand. Norris, who eventually plays for the Bruins, wears number 17, the only goalie in NHL history to wear that number.
- NHL linesman George Hayes is suspended for refusing to take an eye test.
- January 10 game against Montreal at Boston is postponed to February 11. Since Montreal is also playing at Boston on February 13, this constitutes the first back-to-back home games against the same teams since Detroit visited Boston on February 7 and 9, 1957.
- Ian "Scotty" Morrison becomes referee-in-chief of the NHL.
- Conn Smythe Trophy is first awarded to the most valuable player in the Stanley Cup playoffs.
- NHL passes a rule that every team must have a goaltender on the bench and ready to play in an emergency for the 1965 playoffs. This rule is extended to the regular season starting in 1965–1966.

- Bruins play a record 17 games in the month of January.
- In another scheduling quirk, the Bruins play 3 games on consecutive nights, December 25, 26, and 27. This is then followed by games being played on 3 consecutive nights the following week, January 1, 2, and 3. This is the first and second time in regular season history that the Bruins are scheduled on 3 consecutive nights and the only time in history that this scheduling fluke has taken place.

TRANSACTIONS
- Bruins trade Doug Mohns to Chicago for Reggie Fleming, and Ab McDonald.
- Trade Jerry Toppazzini and Matt Ravlich to Chicago for Murray Balfour and Mike Draper.
- Obtain Bob Woytowich from New York in the intra-league draft. Lose George Gardner to Detroit and Jim Mikol to New York in the intra-league draft.
- After selecting Ken Dryden in the amateur draft, the Bruins trade his rights to Montreal for Guy Allen and Paul Reid, 2 players who never played in Boston.

AMATEUR DRAFT SELECTIONS:
- Alec Campbell, Jim Booth, Ken Dryden, and Allistair Blair.

1964-65 STANDINGS

	W	L	T	P	GF	GA
Detroit	40	23	7	87	224	175
Montreal	36	23	11	83	211	185
Chicago	34	28	8	76	224	176
Toronto	30	26	14	74	204	173
New York	20	38	12	52	179	246
Boston	21	43	6	48	166	253

1964-65 RESULTS

October 1964

	AT	VERSUS	W-L-T	SCR
12	Boston	New York	L	6-2
14	Chicago	Blackhawks	L	3-0
17	Toronto	Maple Leafs	L	7-2
18	Boston	Montreal	L	3-1
22	Boston	Toronto	T	2-2
25	Boston	Detroit	L	4-0
28	New York	Rangers	L	3-1
29	Detroit	Red Wings	L	2-0
31	Montreal	Canadiens	L	6-2

November 1964

	AT	VERSUS	W-L-T	SCR
1	Boston	Chicago	W	5-2
8	Boston	Chicago	W	3-2
10	Boston	Detroit	T	3-3
11	New York	Rangers	L	4-2
14	Toronto	Maple Leafs	W	3-1
15	Boston	Montreal	T	2-2
21	Boston	Detroit	L	3-1
22	Boston	Toronto	L	3-1
26	Boston	New York	W	6-1
28	Montreal	Canadiens	L	2-1
29	Chicago	Blackhawks	W	4-3

December 1964

	AT	VERSUS	W-L-T	SCR
3	Detroit	Red Wings	L	4-2
5	Boston	New York	T	3-3
10	Boston	Chicago	L	5-1
12	Toronto	Maple Leafs	L	6-3
13	Boston	Montreal	L	5-4
16	Chicago	Blackhawks	L	7-5
17	Detroit	Red Wings	W	5-3
20	Boston	Chicago	L	3-2
25	Boston	New York	L	3-0
26	New York	Rangers	W	2-0
27	Chicago	Blackhawks	L	6-2

January 1965

	AT	VERSUS	W-L-T	SCR
1	Boston	Toronto	W	3-0
2	Montreal	Canadiens	L	3-1
3	Detroit	Red Wings	L	8-1
6	New York	Rangers	L	5-2
7	Boston	Detroit	W	5-2
9	Toronto	Maple Leafs	L	2-1
14	Boston	New York	W	5-2
16	Montreal	Canadiens	L	3-2
17	Boston	Toronto	L	3-1
20	Chicago	Blackhawks	L	7-1
21	Detroit	Red Wings	L	3-0

23	Montreal	Canadiens	L	5–1
24	Boston	Montreal	W	3–0
27	New York	Rangers	L	5–2
28	Boston	Chicago	L	6–2
30	Toronto	Maple Leafs	L	6–1
31	Boston	Toronto	L	4–2

February 1965

4	Boston	Detroit	W	3–1
6	Boston	New York	W	3–2
7	New York	Rangers	L	8–3
11	Boston	Montreal	L	7–1
13	Boston	Montreal	W	5–4
14	Boston	Toronto	T	2–2
20	Montreal	Canadiens	L	6–2
21	Chicago	Blackhawks	L	7–0

24	Toronto	Maple Leafs	W	3–1
27	Detroit	Red Wings	L	4–1
28	Chicago	Blackhawks	W	5–4

March 1965

3	New York	Rangers	W	6–1
4	Boston	New York	L	4–3
6	Boston	Detroit	L	4–3
7	Boston	Toronto	T	3–3
13	Toronto	Maple Leafs	W	2–0
14	Boston	Detroit	L	5–2
17	Boston	Chicago	W	2–1
18	Detroit	Red Wings	L	10–3
21	Boston	Montreal	L	5–2
27	Montreal	Canadiens	W	6–2
28	Boston	Chicago	W	3–1

1964-65 SCORING

	GP	SO	GAA
Eddie Johnston	47	3	3.47
Jack Norris	23	1	3.70

	G	A	P	PIM
Johnny Bucyk	26	29	55	24
Murray Oliver	20	23	43	30
Reggie Fleming	18	23	41	136
Ted Green	8	27	35	156
Tommy Williams	13	21	34	28
Eddie Westfall	12	15	27	65
Orland Kurtenbach	6	20	26	86
Dean Prentice	14	9	23	12
Wayne Rivers	6	17	23	72
Ab McDonald	9	9	18	6
Billy Knibbs	7	10	17	4
Wayne Maxner	7	6	13	42
Leo Boivin	3	10	13	68
Bob Woytowich	2	10	12	16
Ron Schock	4	7	11	14
Forbes Kennedy	6	4	10	41
Tom Johnson	0	9	9	30
Bob McCord	0	6	6	26
Don Awrey	2	3	5	41
Bob Leiter	3	1	4	6
Murray Balfour	0	2	2	26
Jeannot Gilbert	0	1	1	0
Joe Watson	0	1	1	0
Gary Dornhoefer	0	1	1	13
Wayne Cashman	0	0	0	0
Bill Goldsworthy	0	0	0	0

3-goal game
   Murray Oliver

Number of power play advantages	254
Power play goals	25
% successful	10.1%
Johnny Bucyk	7
Murray Oliver	6
Dean Prentice	3
Tommy Williams	2
Ab McDonald	2
Ted Green	2
Wayne Maxner	1
Reg Fleming	1
Ron Schock	1

Short-handed goals against	10
Penalty minutes: 946 – 13.5 per game	
Times short-handed	293
Power play goals against	52
Penalty kill success 82 %	
Short-handed goals – 10	
Forbes Kennedy	4
Reg Fleming	2
Ed Westfall	2
Orland Kurtenbach	1
Dean Prentice	1

NO PLAYOFF SCORING

Late 1960s photo of Boston Garden showing the first and second balconies on the right. Four of the original six team flags can be seen: the New York Rangers, Toronto Maple Leafs, Chicago Blackhawks, and Montreal Canadiens. Even after expansion, only the "Original Six" banners were raised.

1965–1966
(42nd year)

TEAM OWNER:	Boston Professional Hockey Association	PLAYOFFS:	Out of playoffs
PRESIDENT & GOVERNOR:	Weston Adams	STANLEY CUP WINNER:	Montreal Canadiens
GM:	Hap Emms	ALL-STARS:	None
COACH:	Milt Schmidt	TROPHY WINNERS:	Dufresne — Johnny Bucyk
ATTENDANCE:	421,771	RADIO:	WHDH Radio with Fred Cusick and Don Gillis
	12,050 per game		
	13 sellouts	TV:	Beacon Sports Network with Fred Cusick and Don Gillis

UNIFORMS

- Home and road uniform are the same. White jersey trimmed in gold and black with the spoked "B" on the uniform front. Black pants and socks with gold, black, and white vertical stripes.

POTPOURRI

- Pit Martin scores four goals in a 5–3 win over Chicago on January 27.
- Martin also records a hat trick on February 16 against Detroit.
- Boston finishes out of the cellar for the first time since 1960.
- Don Awrey, Murray Oliver, Ron Stewart, and Tommy Williams play in all 70 Bruins' games.
- Milt Schmidt collapses during a November 27 game in Toronto.
- Murray Balfour, who is diagnosed with cancer in March, passes away following surgery in July.
- Following a head injury to Bruin Bob Dillabough, Milt Schmidt expresses an opinion that all players should wear helmets.
- In the January 30 game against Montreal, no penalties are called.
- In the February 9 announcement by the NHL, the league would expand to 12 teams for the 1967–1968 season. It is also announced that NHL clubs would no longer sponsor junior teams after the 1968–1969 season. A universal draft would replace the junior sponsorships.
- Bruins finish with the exact same 21–43–6 record they had in 1964–1965.
- Bobby Ring replaces Eddie Johnston after Johnston is injured in an October 30 game against New York.
- There are no penalty shots called during the 1965–66 season.

TRANSACTIONS

- Obtain Junior Langlois, Parker MacDonald, Bob Dillabough, and Ron Harris from Detroit for Ab McDonald, Bob McCord, and Ken Stephenson.
- Trade Reggie Fleming to New York for John McKenzie.
- Obtain Ron Stewart from Toronto for Orland Kurtenbach, Andy Hebenton, and Pat Stapleton.
- Trade Leo Boivin and Dean Prentice to Detroit for Gary Doak, Ron Murphy, and Bill Lesuk.
- Draft Gerry Cheevers from Toronto and Paul Popiel from Chicago.
- Trade Parker MacDonald to Detroit for Pit Martin.

AMATEUR DRAFT SELECTIONS

- Joe Bailey and Jim Ramsay

1965-66 STANDINGS

	W	L	T	P	GF	GA
Montreal	41	21	8	90	239	173
Chicago	37	25	8	82	240	187
Toronto	34	25	11	79	208	187
Detroit	31	27	12	74	221	194
Boston	21	43	6	48	174	275
New York	18	41	11	47	195	261

1965-66 RESULTS

October 1965

	AT	VERSUS	W-L-T	SCR
24	Boston	Chicago	L	6–2
27	Boston	Toronto	L	2–1
30	Boston	New York	L	8–2

November 1965

3	Chicago	Blackhawks	T	3–2
4	Detroit	Red Wings	L	8–1
6	Montreal	Canadiens	W	3–1
7	Boston	Montreal	L	5–2
10	New York	Rangers	T	2–2
14	Boston	Toronto	W	2–0
20	Boston	Detroit	L	4–2
21	Boston	Montreal	W	3–2
24	New York	Rangers	L	4–1
25	Boston	New York	W	6–2
27	Toronto	Maple Leafs	W	2–1
28	Boston	Detroit	L	5–3

December 1965

1	Chicago	Blackhawks	L	4–2
2	Detroit	Red Wings	L	10–2
4	Boston	Chicago	L	10–1
5	Boston	Montreal	T	4–4
8	Montreal	Canadiens	L	8–3
11	Toronto	Maple Leafs	L	8–3
12	Boston	Detroit	L	5–3
15	Chicago	Blackhawks	L	8–4
16	Detroit	Red Wings	L	2–0
18	Montreal	Canadiens	L	2–1
19	Boston	Toronto	L	3–1
25	Boston	New York	W	4–2
26	New York	Rangers	L	6–4
28	Boston	Detroit	L	1–0

January 1966

1	Toronto	Maple Leafs	L	6–3
2	Chicago	Blackhawks	L	3–1
6	Detroit	Red Wings	L	5–3
8	Montreal	Canadiens	L	6–0
9	New York	Rangers	W	3–1
13	Boston	Chicago	T	1–1
15	Toronto	Maple Leafs	L	6–1
16	Boston	Montreal	L	3–1
20	Boston	Chicago	W	4–3
22	Boston	New York	W	5–3
23	Boston	Toronto	W	2–1
27	Boston	Chicago	W	5–3
29	Toronto	Maple Leafs	L	6–3
30	Boston	Montreal	L	3–1

February 1966

3	Boston	Detroit	L	4–2
5	Boston	New York	W	5–3
6	Detroit	Red Wings	T	3–3
10	Boston	Montreal	W	2–0
12	New York	Rangers	L	9–2
13	Boston	Toronto	T	4–4
16	Boston	Detroit	W	5–4
19	Detroit	Red Wings	W	5–1
20	Chicago	Blackhawks	L	5–1
23	Montreal	Canadiens	L	3–2
26	Toronto	Maple Leafs	L	3–2
27	Chicago	Blackhawks	L	7–1

March 1966

2	New York	Rangers	L	5–3
3	Boston	New York	L	5–4
6	Boston	Toronto	L	5–3
9	Montreal	Canadiens	W	3–1
12	Toronto	Maple Leafs	L	6–0
13	Boston	Detroit	L	8–4
16	New York	Rangers	W	3–1
17	Detroit	Red Wings	L	4–2
20	Boston	New York	W	4–3
24	Boston	Chicago	W	3–1
26	Montreal	Canadiens	L	5–2
27	Boston	Montreal	L	3–1
29	Chicago	Blackhawks	L	4–2
31	Boston	Toronto	W	3–1

April 1966

3	Boston	Chicago	W	4–2

1965-66 SCORING

	GP	SO	GAA
Bernie Parent	39	1	3.66
Eddie Johnston	33	1	3.72
Gerry Cheevers	7	0	5.67
Bobby Ring	1	0	7.06

	G	A	P	PIM
Murray Oliver	18	42	60	30
Johnny Bucyk	27	30	57	12
Tommy Williams	16	22	38	31
Ron Stewart	20	16	36	17
Eddie Westfall	9	21	30	42
Dean Prentice	7	22	29	24
Pit Martin	16	11	27	10
John McKenzie	13	9	22	36
Bob Dillabough	7	13	20	18
Gilles Marotte	3	17	20	52
Bob Woytowich	2	17	19	75
Ted Green	5	13	18	113
Junior Langlois	4	10	14	54
Parker MacDonald	6	4	10	6
Reggie Fleming	4	6	10	42
Forbes Kennedy	4	6	10	55
Gary Doak	0	8	8	28
Don Awrey	4	3	7	74
Leo Boivin	0	5	5	34
Bill Goldsworthy	3	1	4	6
Ron Schock	2	2	4	6
Wayne Maxner	1	3	4	6
Bob Leiter	2	1	3	2
Barry Ashbee	0	3	3	14
Wayne Rivers	1	1	2	2
Paul Popiel	0	1	1	2
Gary Dornhoefer	0	1	1	2
Ron Murphy	0	1	1	0
Don Marcotte	0	0	0	0
Murray Davison	0	0	0	0
Derek Sanderson	0	0	0	0

John Arbour	o	o	o	o		Jean Paul Parise	o	o	o	o
Skip Krake	o	o	o	o		Terry Crisp	o	o	o	o
Dallas Smith	o	o	o	2						

Number of power play advantages	255		Short-handed goals against	6
Power play goals	30		Penalty minutes: 787 – 11.2 per game	
% successful	8.5%		Times short-handed	252
Murray Oliver	5		Power play goals against	53
Ron Stewart	4		Penalty kill success	79%
Johnny Bucyk	3		Short-hand goals	3
Dean Prentice	3		Ed Westfall	1
Pit Martin	2		Parker MacDonald	1
John McKenzie	2		Forbes Kennedy	1
Ed Westfall	2			
Ted Green	2			
Don Awrey	2			
Gilles Marotte	2			
Tom Williams	1			
Parker MacDonald	1			
Ron Schock	1			

NO PLAYOFF SCORING

Parker MacDonald of the Bruins and Roger Crozier of the Red Wings put the squeeze on Detroit defenseman Marcel Provonost in a mid-1960s game at Boston.

Al "Junior" Langois, the last Bruin to wear #4 before Bobby Orr, is sandwiched between Claude Provost and Red Berenson of the Montreal Canadiens.

1966–1967
(43rd year)

TEAM OWNER:	Boston Professional Hockey Association
PRESIDENT & GOVERNOR:	Weston Adams
GM:	Hap Emms
COACH:	Harry Sinden
ATTENDANCE:	457,172 / 13,062 per game / 18 sellouts
PLAYOFFS:	Out of playoffs

STANLEY CUP WINNER:	Toronto Maple Leafs
ALL-STARS:	Bobby Orr (2nd team)
TROPHY WINNERS:	Calder — Bobby Orr / Dufresne — Bobby Orr / Lester Patrick — Charles Adams
RADIO & TV:	WHDH Radio with Fred Cusick & Jim Laing

UNIFORMS

- Home and road uniform are the same. White jersey trimmed in gold and black with the spoked "B" on the uniform front. Black pants and socks with gold, black, and white vertical stripes.

POTPOURRI

- Bobby Orr makes his debut with the Bruins and scores his first career goal in the October 24 loss to Montreal at Boston. Gump Worsley is the Montreal netminder.
- Bobby Orr wins the Calder Trophy as rookie of the year.
- Johnny Bucyk scores 200th career goal.
- Bruins suffer 10-game losing streak.
- Bruins lose Ted Green for the season with a knee operation.
- Bruins record only 1 shutout all season.
- Bruins fail to beat Chicago at Boston Garden all season.
- In a 10–2 loss to Chicago at Boston on December 8, Doug Mohns of the Blackhawks scores a goal at 19:59 of the third period. Vern Buffey, the referee, disallowed the goal but is later overruled by Brian O'Neill giving Mohns his third goal of the game.
- For the first time, the All-Star game is played at mid-season.
- A December 28 meeting between Bruins player and Alan Eagleson to discuss salaries and benefits becomes the first meeting of the NHL Players' Association.
- The NHL signs a contract with CBS to provide "Game of the Week action."

TRANSACTIONS

- Harry Sinden replaces Milt Schmidt as coach of the Bruins.
- Bobby Orr is promoted from Oshawa of the Ontario Hockey Association.
- Bruins purchase Wayne Connelly from San Francisco of the Western Hockey League.

AMATEUR DRAFT SELECTIONS

- Barry Gibbs, Rick Smith, Garnet Bailey, Tom Webster.

1966-67 STANDINGS

	W	L	T	P	GF	GA
Chicago	41	17	12	94	264	170
Montreal	32	25	13	77	202	188
Toronto	32	27	11	75	204	211
New York	30	28	12	72	188	189
Detroit	27	39	4	58	212	241
Boston	17	43	10	44	182	253

1966-67 **RESULTS**

October 1966

	AT	VERSUS	W–L–T	SCR
19	Boston	Detroit	W	6–2
22	Montreal	Canadiens	L	3–1
23	Boston	Montreal	L	3–2
29	Toronto	Maple Leafs	T	3–3
30	Detroit	Red Wings	L	8–1

November 1966

1	Chicago	Blackhawks	W	3–2
3	Boston	New York	L	7–1
6	Boston	Chicago	L	4–2
9	New York	Rangers	T	3–3
10	Boston	Toronto	W	4–0
13	Boston	Montreal	W	2–1
19	Boston	New York	T	3–3
20	Boston	Detroit	W	5–2
23	New York	Rangers	L	5–4
24	Boston	Detroit	W	8–3
26	Toronto	Maple Leafs	L	4–2
27	Boston	Chicago	L	5–4

December 1966

1	Detroit	Red Wings	L	4–1
3	Boston	New York	T	2–2
4	Boston	Toronto	L	8–3
7	New York	Rangers	L	4–2
8	Boston	Chicago	L	10–2
11	Chicago	Blackhawks	T	2–2
14	Toronto	Maple Leafs	L	2–1
15	Detroit	Red Wings	L	4–0
18	Boston	Montreal	W	3–1
21	New York	Rangers	L	5–1
24	Toronto	Maple Leafs	L	3–0
25	Boston	Toronto	L	4–2
27	Boston	Detroit	T	4–4
28	Montreal	Canadiens	T	1–1
31	Detroit	Red Wings	L	3–1

January 1967

1	Chicago	Blackhawks	L	3–2
7	Toronto	Maple Leafs	L	5–2
8	Detroit	Red Wings	W	3–1
12	Boston	New York	L	3–0
14	Montreal	Canadiens	W	5–4
15	Boston	Montreal	L	3–1
19	Boston	Chicago	L	4–2
21	Boston	New York	W	6–2
22	Boston	Toronto	W	3–1
25	New York	Rangers	L	2–1
26	Montreal	Canadiens	W	4–1
29	Boston	Montreal	L	3–2

Such a familiar face!

February 1967

1	Chicago	Blackhawks	L	6–1
2	Detroit	Red Wings	L	4–3
4	Boston	New York	L	4–3
5	Boston	Chicago	L	5–0
8	New York	Rangers	W	2–1
11	Boston	Montreal	L	4–3
12	Boston	Toronto	L	2–1
14	Boston	Detroit	W	6–3
16	Montreal	Canadiens	W	5–1
18	Toronto	Maple Leafs	L	5–3
23	Montreal	Canadiens	T	2–2
25	Chicago	Blackhawks	L	6–3
26	Detroit	Red Wings	T	3–3

March 1967

2	Boston	Chicago	L	5–2
4	Boston	New York	T	4–4
5	Boston	Detroit	L	5–3
8	Chicago	Blackhawks	L	3–1
12	Boston	Detroit	W	7–3
15	Montreal	Canadiens	L	11–2
18	Detroit	Red Wings	W	5–3
19	New York	Rangers	L	3–1
23	Boston	Toronto	L	5–3
25	Toronto	Maple Leafs	L	4–3
26	Boston	Montreal	L	6–3
30	Boston	Chicago	L	3–1

April 1967

2	Boston	Toronto	L	5–2

1966-67 SCORING

	GP	SO	GAA
Bernie Parent	18	0	3.65
Eddie Johnston	34	0	3.74
	(1 assist)		
Gerry Cheevers	22	1	3.27

	G	A	P	PIM
Johnny Bucyk	18	30	48	12
Pit Martin	20	22	42	40
Bobby Orr	13	28	41	102
John McKenzie	17	19	36	98
Eddie Westfall	12	24	36	26
Murray Oliver	9	26	35	16
Wayne Connelly	13	17	30	12
Ron Schock	10	20	30	8
Ron Murphy	11	16	27	6
Ron Stewart	14	10	24	31
Tommy Williams	8	13	21	2
Bob Dillabough	6	12	18	14
Ted Green	6	10	16	67
Gilles Marotte	7	8	15	112
Joe Watson	2	13	15	38
Bob Woytowich	2	7	9	43
Skip Krake	6	2	8	4
Bill Goldsworthy	3	5	5	21
Jean Paul Parise	2	2	4	10
Wayne Rivers	2	1	3	6
Don Awrey	1	0	1	6
Ross Lonsberry	0	1	1	2
Gary Doak	0	1	1	50
Dallas Smith	0	1	1	24
Barry Wilkins	0	0	0	0
Nick Beverley	0	0	0	0
Derek Sanderson	0	0	0	0
Ron Buchanan	0	0	0	0
Ted Hodgson	0	0	0	0
Glen Sather	0	0	0	0

Number of power play advantages 250
Power play goals 34
% successful 13%
- Ron Stewart 5
- Ted Green 5
- Pit Martin 4
- Johnny Bucyk 4
- John McKenzie 3
- Bobby Orr 3
- Tommy William 2
- Skip Krake 2
- Wayne Connelly 1
- Ed Westfall 1
- Ron Schock 1
- Murray Oliver 1
- Gilles Marotte 1
- Joe Watson 1

Short-handed goals against 9
Penalty minutes: 764 – 10.9 per game
Times short-handed 240
Power play goals against 53
Penalty kill success 78%
Short-hand goals 4
- John McKenzie 1
- Bobby Orr 1
- Gilles Marotte 1
- Bob Dillabough 1

NO PLAYOFF SCORING

1967–1968
(44th year)

TEAM OWNER:	Boston Professional Hockey Association	ALL-STARS:	Bobby Orr (1st team)
			Phil Esposito (2nd team)
PRESIDENT & GOVERNOR:	Weston Adams Sr.		Johnny Bucyk (2nd team)
GM:	Milt Schmidt	TROPHY WINNERS:	Calder — Derek Sanderson
COACH:	Harry Sinden		Norris — Bobby Orr
ATTENDANCE:	511,812		Dufresne — Phil Esposito
	13,832 per game		Lester Patrick —
PLAYOFFS:	*Quarter finals:*		Walter Brown
	Lose to Montreal Canadiens	RADIO BROADCASTER:	WHDH Radio with
	0 wins – 4 losses		Bob Wilson
STANLEY CUP WINNER:	Montreal Canadiens	TV BROADCASTER:	WSBK TV38 with Don Earle

UNIFORMS

- Bruins introduce new uniforms. Home jersey is black with gold shoulder inserts, black pants, white socks with one gold band surrounded by two black bands at the calf. Logo is the spoked "B." Road jersey is white with gold shoulder inserts. Pants and socks are the same as the home uniform.

POTPOURRI

- Phil Esposito scores 4 goals in a game against Montreal.
- Gerry Cheevers wears a mask for the first time. Cheevers also stops Bob Pulford of Toronto on a penalty shot.
- Derek Sanderson wins Calder Trophy.
- Bobby Orr wins Norris Trophy.
- Bruins finish third in the Eastern Division and qualify for the playoffs for the first time in 8 seasons.
- Bruins lose in first round of playoffs in 4 straight games to Montreal.
- Bobby Orr suffers broken collar bone and misses 6 games.
- The Bruins start to use the east-end entrance to the rink as opposed to the familiar center-ice entrance to enter and exit the rink.
- NHL expands to 12 teams, the first change in the composition of the league in 25 years. The new teams are: California Seals, Los Angeles Kings, Minnesota North Stars, Philadelphia Flyers, Pittsburgh Penguins, and St. Louis Blues.
- NHL schedule increased to 74 games.
- Bobby Orr plays in his first NHL All-Star game and wears number 5.
- The NHL has its first on-ice fatality as Bill Masterton of the Minnesota North Stars dies after being checked and hitting his head on the ice.
- NHL signs a deal with CBS television network to televise a "Game of the Week." The first nationally televised match is a game between Philadelphia and Los Angeles. That game is played at Los Angeles and is the first game ever played at the Los Angeles Forum.

TRANSACTIONS

- Bruins trade Murray Oliver to Toronto for Eddie Shack.
- Bruins trade Gilles Marotte, Pit Martin, and Jack Norris to Chicago for Phil Esposito, Ken Hodge, and Fred Stanfield.
- Bruins claim Jean Gauthier from Philadelphia after the Flyers claim Ron Buchanan from Boston.
- The expansion draft is held in Montreal on June 6, 1967. The Bruins protected list of players are as follows: Gerry Cheevers, Johnny Bucyk, Ted Green, Ed Westfall, Tom Williams, John McKenzie, Don Awrey, Ken Hodge, Phil Esposito, Eddie Shack, Fred Stanfield, and Gary Doak.
- Players added as fill (protected players after the Bruins lost a player) are as follows: Dallas Smith,

Skip Krake, Ron Buchanan, Wayne Cashman, Jean Pronovost, Bob Heaney, Ted Hodgson, Ron Murphy, John Arbour, Glen Sather, David Woodley, Brian Bradley, Ted Snell, Wayne Maxner, and Bob Leiter.

- Players lost in the expansion draft are as follows: Jean-Paul Parise (California Seals), Ron Harris (California Seals), Paul Popiel (Los Angeles Kings), Ted Irvine (Los Angeles Kings), Bob Woytowich (Minnesota North Stars), Wayne Connelly (Minnesota North Stars), Bill Goldsworthy (Minnesota North Stars), Doug Favell (Philadelphia Flyers), Bernie Parent (Philadelphia Flyers), Joe Watson (Philadelphia Flyers), Dick Cherry (Philadelphia Flyers), Gary Dornhoefer (Philadelphia Flyers), Forbes Kennedy (Philadelphia Flyers), Keith Wright (Philadelphia Flyers), Bob Dillabough (Pittsburgh Penguins), Jeannot Gilbert (Pittsburgh Penguins), Ron Schock (St. Louis Blues), Terry Crisp (St. Louis Blues), Wayne Rivers (St. Louis Blues), and Ron Stewart (St. Louis Blues).

1967-68 STANDINGS

Eastern Division	W	L	T	P	GF	GA
Montreal	42	22	10	94	236	167
New York	39	23	12	90	226	183
Boston	37	27	10	84	259	216
Chicago	32	26	16	80	212	222
Toronto	33	31	19	76	209	176
Detroit	27	35	12	66	245	257
Western Division						
Philadelphia	31	32	11	73	173	179
Los Angeles	31	33	10	72	200	224
St. Louis	27	31	16	70	177	191
Minnesota	27	32	15	69	191	226
Pittsburgh	27	34	13	67	195	216
Oakland	15	42	17	47	153	219

1967-68 RESULTS

October 1967

	AT	VERSUS	W-L-T	SCR
11	Boston	Detroit	T	4–4
15	Boston	Montreal	W	6–2
18	Chicago	Blackhawks	W	7–1
19	Detroit	Red Wings	W	6–3
21	Montreal	Canadiens	L	4–2
26	Boston	Los Angeles	W	2–0
29	Boston	Pittsburgh	W	4–2

November 1967

1	St. Louis	Blues	L	5–1
5	Boston	Toronto	T	2–2
8	New York	Rangers	W	6–3
11	Boston	Oakland	W	2–1
12	Boston	Philadelphia	L	4–2
15	Toronto	Maple Leafs	L	4–2
18	Boston	New York	W	3–1
19	Boston	Toronto	W	6–2
22	Pittsburgh	Penguins	L	4–1
23	Boston	New York	W	4–2
25	Montreal	Canadiens	W	3–1
26	Boston	Detroit	W	7–5

29	Boston	Minnesota	W	5–1

December 1967

2	Boston	Chicago	T	4–4
3	Boston	Montreal	W	5–3
7	Boston	New York	W	3–1
9	Toronto	Maple Leafs	T	3–3
10	Boston	Los Angeles	L	3–1
13	Boston	Montreal	L	6–2
15	Oakland	Seals	L	4–1
16	Los Angeles	Kings	W	5–2
20	Chicago	Blackhawks	L	6–3
23	New York	Rangers	W	4–0
25	Boston	Oakland	W	6–3
27	Boston	Chicago	W	7–2
30	Minnesota	North Stars	L	5–4
31	Detroit	Red Wings	L	6–4

January 1968

3	New York	Rangers	T	5–5
4	Philadelphia	Flyers	W	3–2
6	Toronto	Maple Leafs	T	3–3
7	Chicago	Blackhawks	L	4–2

BOSTON BRUINS

1967 - 1968

OFFICIAL GUIDE $1

97 CENTS
+ 3¢ Sales Tax

11	Boston	Detroit	W	5–4
13	Montreal	Canadiens	L	5–1
14	Boston	Minnesota	W	9–2
18	Boston	Toronto	L	4–2

20	Boston	Philadelphia	W	4–2
21	Boston	Chicago	W	6–0
24	New York	Rangers	L	2–1
25	Boston	Montreal	L	2–0
27	Montreal	Canadiens	L	5–2
28	Boston	Pittsburgh	L	1–0

February 1968

1	Boston	Chicago	T	4–4
3	Boston	New York	T	3–3
4	Boston	Detroit	W	5–4
7	St. Louis	Blues	W	6–4
10	Detroit	Red Wings	T	1–1
11	Boston	St. Louis	T	3–3
14	Chicago	Blackhawks	L	3–1
17	Oakland	Seals	L	3–1
18	Los Angeles	Kings	W	6–5
21	Minnesota	North Stars	L	5–3
22	Detroit	Red Wings	W	3–2
24	Toronto	Maple Leafs	L	1–0
27	Pittsburgh	Penguins	W	5–3
29	Boston	Toronto	W	4–1

March 1968

3	Boston	St. Louis	W	9–3
6	Chicago	Blackhawks	W	5–3
7	Toronto	Philadelphia	W	2–1
10	Boston	Detroit	L	7–5
13	New York	Rangers	W	2–1
16	Toronto	Maple Leafs	L	3–0
17	Boston	Montreal	W	3–1
21	Boston	Chicago	W	8–0
24	Detroit	Red Wings	L	5–3
28	Boston	New York	L	5–4
30	Montreal	Canadiens	W	2–1
31	Boston	Toronto	L	4–1

1967-68 SCORING

	GP	SO	GAA	
Eddie Johnston	28	0	2.87	
Gerry Cheevers	47	3	2.83	
Andre Gill	5	1	2.89	

	G	A	P	PIM
Phil Esposito	35	49	84	21
Johnny Bucyk	30	39	69	8
John McKenzie	28	38	68	107
Fred Stanfield	20	44	64	10
Ken Hodge	25	31	56	31
Tommy Williams	18	32	50	14
Derek Sanderson	24	25	49	98
Ted Green	7	36	43	133
Eddie Shack	23	19	42	107
Eddie Westfall	14	22	36	38
Bobby Orr	11	20	31	63
Glen Sather	8	20	28	34
Dallas Smith	4	23	37	65
Don Awrey	3	12	15	150
Skip Krake	5	7	12	13
Gary Doak	2	9	11	100
Ross Lonsberry	2	2	4	12
Wayne Cashman	0	4	4	2
John Arbour	0	1	1	11
Ron Murphy	0	1	1	4
Barry Gibbs	0	0	0	2

Number of power play advantages	240
Power play goals	45
% successful	19%
Phil Esposito	9
John Mckenzie	7
Johnny Bucyk	6
Ken Hodge	5
Derek Sanderson	4
Eddie Shack	4
Fred Stanfield	3
Ted Green	3
Bobby Orr	3
Ed Westfall	1
Short-handed goals against	4
Penalty minutes	1043 / 14.1 per game
Times short-handed	304
Power play goals against	50
Penalty kill success	82.6%
Short-hand goals	10
Skip Krake	3
Glen Sather	2
Ed Westfall	2
Phil Esposito	1
Johnny Bucyk	1
Derek Sanderson	1

1967-68 PLAYOFF RESULTS

April 1968

	AT	VERSUS	W-L-T	SCR
4	Montreal	Canadiens	L	2–1
6	Montreal	Canadiens	L	5–2
9	Boston	Montreal	L	5–2
11	Boston	Montreal	L	3–2

1967-68 PLAYOFFS

vs. Montreal Canadiens	0 wins – 4 losses
at Montreal	0 wins – 2 losses
at Boston	0 wins – 2 losses

1967-68 PLAYOFF SCORING

	GP	SO	GAA				
Gerry Cheevers	4	0	3.75				

	G	A	P	PIM
Ken Hodge	3	0	3	2
Phil Esposito	0	3	3	0
Eddie Westfall	2	0	2	2
John McKenzie	1	1	2	8
Ted Green	1	1	2	11
Johnny Bucyk	0	2	2	0
Bobby Orr	0	2	2	2
Dallas Smith	0	2	2	0
Derek Sanderson	0	2	2	9
Tommy Williams	1	0	1	2
Eddie Shack	0	1	1	6
Fred Stanfield	0	1	1	0
Don Awrey	0	1	1	4
Wayne Cashman	0	0	0	0

Glen Sather	0	0	0	0	Gary Doak	0	0	0	4
Skip Krake	0	0	0	2	Ron Murphy	0	0	0	0

Power play goals		1	Short-handed goals	0
Ted Green			Short-handed goals against	0
Power play goals against		3	Penalty minutes: 52 – 13 per game	

1968–1969
(45th year)

TEAM OWNER:	Boston Professional Hockey Association	**STANLEY CUP WINNERS:**	Montreal Canadiens
PRESIDENT & GOVERNOR:	Weston Adams Sr.	**ALL-STARS:**	Bobby Orr (1st team)
GM:	Milt Schmidt		Phil Esposito (1st team)
COACH:	Harry Sinden		Ted Green (2nd team)
ATTENDANCE:	563,654	**TROPHY WINNERS:**	Hart — Phil Esposito
	14,833 per game		Ross — Phil Esposito
	38 sellouts		Norris — Bobby Orr
PLAYOFFS:	*Quarter finals:*		Dufresne — Phil Esposito
	Defeat Toronto Maple Leafs		7th Player — Eddie Westfall
	4 wins – 0 losses	**RADIO BROADCASTER:**	WHDH: Bob Wilson
	Semi-finals:	**TV BROADCASTER:**	WSBK TV38: Don Earle
	Lose to Montreal Canadiens		
	2 wins – 4 losses		

UNIFORMS

- Home jersey is black with gold shoulder inserts, black pants, white socks with one gold band surrounded by two black bands at the calf. Logo is the spoked "B." Road jersey is white with gold shoulder inserts. Pants and socks are the same as the home uniform.

POTPOURRI

- The magic number of 13,909, established after the 1942 Coconut Grove fire, is broken as 14,642 fans attend an October 27 game against the Montreal Canadiens.
- Bruins finish in second place in the Eastern Division with the fewest losses in the league.
- Bruins have 18-game unbeaten streak, 13 wins and 5 ties.
- Bruins also enjoy 13-game road undefeated streak.
- Bruins qualify for the playoffs for the second straight year.
- Bruins win opening round of playoffs against Toronto, 4 games to 0 for first playoff series win since 1958.
- Phil Esposito wins Hart Trophy as most valuable player and Ross Trophy as leading scorer. Esposito also becomes the first player in NHL history to score 100 points, finishing with 49 goals and 77 assists for 126 points.
- Bobby Orr wins Norris Trophy for second straight season.
- Bobby Orr sets the record for points and goals in a season by a defenseman.
- Bruins lose Eastern Division final to Montreal, 4 games to 2, losing 3 games in overtime.

This late 1960s photo features players in the Bruins dressing room receiving a greeting card from U.S. servicemen in South Vietnam. Left to right in the back are Fred Stanfield, Don Awrey, Ken Hodge, Ron Murphy, John McKenzie, John Forristal. Middle row, left to right are Wayne Cashman, Bobby Orr, Glen Sather, Johnny Bucyk, and Dan Canney. In the foreground is Eddie Westfall and Phil Esposito.

- Eddie Johnston suffers head injury in pre-game warmup in Detroit on October 31.
- Bobby Orr suffers knee injury and misses 9 games.
- NHL schedule increased to 76 games.
- Bobby Orr plays in his second All-Star game and wears number 2.

TRANSACTIONS
- Bruins trade Skip Krake to Los Angeles for the Kings first draft choice in 1970.
- Bruins sell Jean Pronovost and John Arbour to Pittsburgh.
- Bruins acquire Jean Gauthier from Philadelphia in the intra-league draft.

1968-69 STANDINGS

Eastern Division	W	L	T	P	GF	GA
Montreal	46	19	11	103	271	202
Boston	42	18	16	100	303	221
New York	41	26	9	91	231	196
Toronto	35	26	15	85	234	217
Detroit	33	31	12	78	239	221
Chicago	34	33	9	77	280	246

Western Division

St. Louis	37	25	14	88	204	157
California	29	36	11	69	219	251
Philadelphia	20	35	21	61	174	225
Los Angeles	24	42	10	58	185	260
Pittsburgh	20	45	11	51	189	252
Minnesota	18	43	15	51	189	270

1968-69 RESULTS

October 1968

	AT	VERSUS	W-L-T	SCR
11	Boston	Detroit	W	4–2
13	Boston	Philadelphia	W	3–2
16	Oakland	Seals	W	2–1
17	Los Angeles	Kings	L	2–1
19	Pittsburgh	Penguins	W	5–1
24	Boston	St. Louis	L	2–1
26	Toronto	Maple Leafs	L	2–0
27	Boston	Montreal	W	4–2
30	Minnesota	North Stars	W	4–2
31	Detroit	Red Wings	L	7–5

November 1968

3	Boston	Chicago	W	5–3
6	Boston	Philadelphia	W	7–1
10	Boston	St. Louis	T	1–1
13	Toronto	Maple Leafs	T	1–1
14	Philadelphia	Flyers	L	4–2
17	Boston	Oakland	W	6–3
21	Boston	Los Angeles	W	4–1
23	Boston	New York	W	5–1
24	Boston	Toronto	W	7–4
27	St. Louis	Blues	T	4–4
30	Boston	New York	L	4–1

December 1968

1	Boston	Minnesota	W	4–0
5	Boston	Montreal	T	2–2
7	Boston	Detroit	W	4–1
8	Chicago	Blackhawks	L	7–4
11	New York	Rangers	T	2–2
14	Boston	Chicago	W	10–5
15	Boston	Pittsburgh	W	5–3
19	Boston	Los Angeles	W	6–4
21	Montreal	Canadiens	T	0–0
22	Boston	Montreal	W	7–5
25	Boston	Oakland	L	3–1
28	St. Louis	Blues	W	6–2
29	Detroit	Red Wings	T	3–3

January 1969

2	New York	Rangers	W	4–2
4	Minnesota	North Stars	T	2–2

9	Boston	Toronto	W	3–2
11	Montreal	Canadiens	W	6–3
12	Boston	Pittsburgh	W	8–4
15	Toronto	Maple Leafs	T	5–5
16	Boston	Minnesota	W	5–1
18	Philadelphia	Flyers	W	5–3
19	Boston	Toronto	W	5–3
23	Detroit	Red Wings	T	2–2
25	Boston	St. Louis	W	4–0
26	Boston	Minnesota	W	4–3
29	Oakland	Seals	T	3–3
30	Los Angeles	Kings	W	7–5

February 1969

2	Boston	Detroit	W	4–2
5	Chicago	Blackhawks	W	7–2
6	St. Louis	Blues	L	3–1
8	Boston	Philadelphia	W	6–5
9	Boston	Oakland	T	3–3
11	Boston	Chicago	W	7–3
15	Montreal	Canadiens	L	3–1
16	Chicago	Blackhawks	L	5–1
19	Pittsburgh	Penguins	L	3–0
23	New York	Rangers	L	9–0
26	Los Angeles	Kings	W	4–2
27	Oakland	Seals	W	9–0

March 1969

1	Boston	New York	W	8–5
2	Boston	Pittsburgh	W	4–0
5	Boston	Detroit	T	2–2
8	Detroit	Red Wings	L	7–4
9	Boston	Los Angeles	W	7–2
11	Minnesota	North Stars	T	3–2
13	Philadelphia	Flyers	L	2–1
15	Toronto	Maple Leafs	L	7–4
16	Boston	Toronto	W	11–3
19	Pittsburgh	Penguins	W	3–2
20	Boston	Chicago	T	5–5
22	Chicago	Blackhawks	W	5–3
23	New York	Rangers	L	4–2
27	Boston	New York	T	3–3
29	Montreal	Canadiens	L	5–3
30	Boston	Montreal	W	6–3

1968-69 SCORING

	GP	SO	GAA
Eddie Johnston	24	2	3.08
Gerry Cheevers	52	3	2.80
Joe Junkin	1	0	0.00

	G	A	P	PIM
Phil Esposito	49	77	126	79
Ken Hodge	45	45	90	75
Johnny Bucyk	24	42	66	18
Bobby Orr	21	43	64	133
John McKenzie	29	27	56	99
Fred Stanfield	25	29	54	22
Ron Murphy	16	38	54	26
Derek Sanderson	26	22	48	146
Ted Green	8	38	46	99
Eddie Westfall	18	24	42	22
Wayne Cashman	8	23	31	49
Dallas Smith	4	24	28	74
Eddie Shack	11	11	22	74
Glen Sather	4	11	15	67
Don Awrey	0	13	13	149
Tommy Williams	4	7	11	19
Garnet Bailey	3	3	6	10
Gary Doak	3	3	6	37
Rick Smith	0	5	5	29
Jim Lorentz	1	3	4	6
Jim Harrison	1	2	3	21
Tom Webster	0	2	2	9
Jean Gauthier	0	2	2	8
Barry Wilkins	1	0	1	0
Grant Erickson	1	0	1	0
Don Marcotte	1	0	1	2
Paul Hurley	0	1	1	0
Bill Lesuk	0	1	1	0
Bobby Leiter	0	0	0	0
Steve Atkinson	0	0	0	0
Ross Lonsberry	0	0	0	2
Barry Gibbs	0	0	0	2

Number of power play advantages	266
Power play goals	60
% successful	22.6%
Johnny Bucyk	11
Phil Esposito	10
Ken Hodge	9
John McKenzie	8
Fred Stanfield	6
Ron Murphy	5
Bobby Orr	4
Ted Green	3
Derek Sanderson	1
Ed Westfall	1
Wayne Cashman	1
Eddie Shack	1
Short-handed goals against	4
Penalty minutes 1,297: 17.1 per game	
Times short-handed	351
Power play goals against	54
Penalty kill success	84.6%
Short-hand goals	13
Eddie Westfall	4
Derek Sanderson	3
Phil Esposito	2
Ken Hodge	1
John McKenzie	1
Dallas Smith	1
Glen Sather	1

1968-69 PLAYOFF RESULTS

April 1969

	AT	VERSUS	W-L-T	SCR
2	Boston	Toronto	W	10–0
3	Boston	Toronto	W	7–0
5	Toronto	Maple Leafs	W	4–3
6	Toronto	Maple Leafs	W	3–2
10	Montreal	Canadiens	L	3–2 (OT)
13	Montreal	Canadiens	L	4–3
17	Boston	Montreal	W	5–0
20	Boston	Montreal	W	3–2
22	Montreal	Canadiens	L	4–2
24	Boston	Montreal	L	2–1 (OT)

1968-69 PLAYOFFS

vs. Montreal Canadiens	2 wins – 4 losses	vs. Toronto Maple Leafs	4 wins – 0 losses
at Montreal	0 wins – 3 losses	at Toronto	2 wins – 0 losses
at Boston	2 wins – 1 loss	at Boston	2 wins – 0 losses

1968-69 PLAYOFF SCORING

	GP	SO	GAA
Gerry Cheevers	9	3	1.68
Eddie Johnston	1	0	3.70

	G	A	P	PIM
Phil Esposito	8	10	18	8
Ken Hodge	5	7	12	4
Johnny Bucyk	5	6	11	0
Derek Sanderson	8	2	10	36
Eddie Westfall	3	7	10	11
Ted Green	2	7	9	18
Ron Murphy	4	4	8	12
Bobby Orr	1	7	8	10
John McKenzie	2	2	4	17
Fred Stanfield	2	2	4	0
Dallas Smith	0	3	3	16
Eddie Shack	0	2	2	23
Wayne Cashman	0	1	1	0
Don Awrey	0	1	1	28
Garnet Bailey	0	0	0	2
Bill Lesuk	0	0	0	0
Tom Webster	0	0	0	0
Rick Smith	0	0	0	6
Glen Sather	0	0	0	18

Penalty minutes: 209 – 20.9 per game

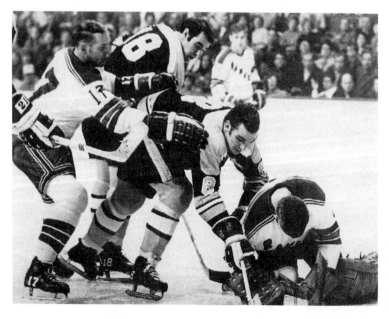

Scramble around the crease depicts Dave Balon #17 of New York, Eddie Westfall #18, Ken Hodge #8 of Boston, and Ed Giacomin, Rangers goaltender, in this late 1960s contest

1969–1970
(46th year)

TEAM OWNER:	Boston Professional Hockey Association	STANLEY CUP WINNERS:	Boston Bruins
GOVERNOR:	Weston Adams, Jr.	ALL-STARS:	Bobby Orr (1st team)
GM:	Milt Schmidt		Phil Esposito (1st team)
COACH:	Harry Sinden		John McKenzie (2nd team)
ATTENDANCE:	563,654	TROPHY WINNERS:	Hart — Bobby Orr

TEAM OWNER: Boston Professional Hockey Association

GOVERNOR: Weston Adams, Jr.

GM: Milt Schmidt

COACH: Harry Sinden

ATTENDANCE: 563,654
14,833 per game
38 sellouts

PLAYOFFS: *Quarter finals:*
Defeat New York Rangers
4 wins – 2 losses
Semi-finals:
Defeat Chicago Blackhawks
4 wins – 0 losses
Stanley Cup finals:
Defeat St. Louis Blues
4 wins – 0 losses

STANLEY CUP WINNERS: Boston Bruins

ALL-STARS: Bobby Orr (1st team)
Phil Esposito (1st team)
John McKenzie (2nd team)

TROPHY WINNERS: Hart — Bobby Orr
Ross — Bobby Orr
Norris — Bobby Orr
Conn Smythe — Bobby Orr
Lester Patrick — Eddie Shore
Dufresne — Bobby Orr
7th Player — John McKenzie

RADIO BROADCASTER: WBZ – Fred Cusick

TV BROADCASTER: WSBK TV38 – Don Earle

UNIFORMS

- Home jersey is black with gold shoulder inserts, black pants, gold socks with one white band surrounded by two black bands at the calf. Logo is the spoked "B." Road jersey is white with gold shoulder inserts. Socks are white with one gold band surrounded by two black bands at the calf. Pants are black with white trim on side.

POTPOURRI

- Bruins win Stanley Cup for the first time since 1941 on a goal by Bobby Orr at 40 seconds of the first overtime period against the St. Louis Blues.
- Bruins win 10 straight playoff games to win Stanley Cup.
- Bruins qualify for the playoffs for the third consecutive year.
- Bruins enjoy 17-game home undefeated streak.
- Bobby Orr wins Conn Smythe Trophy as most valuable player in the playoffs, Hart Trophy as most valuable player, Ross Trophy as the leading scorer, and third consecutive Norris Trophy as the league's best defenseman.
- Phil Esposito sets Stanley Cup record for goals (13) and assists (14).
- In a pre-season game at Ottawa against the St. Louis Blues, Ted Green is involved in a stick-swinging incident with Wayne Maki of the Blues. Green receives a head injury and is out for the season.
- NHL schedule increased to 76 games. Bruins sell out all 38 home games.
- In June of 1969, the NHL holds its first universal amateur draft.
- First-ever playoffs without a Canadian entry.

TRANSACTIONS

- Bruins trade Tommy Williams and Barry Gibbs to Minnesota for Don Tannahill and Fred O'Donnell.
- Trade Eddie Shack and Ross Lonsberry to Los Angeles for Ken Turlik and 2 unnamed players.
- Bruins lose Glen Sather in intra-league draft to Pittsburgh. Bruins claim Billy Speer from Penguins.
- Minnesota drafts Grant Erickson from Boston in intra-league draft.
- Bruins choose Don Tannahill as their #1 draft pick.

1969-70 STANDINGS

EAST DIVISION	W	L	T	P	GF	GA
Chicago	45	22	9	99	250	170
Boston	40	17	19	99	277	216
Detroit	40	21	15	95	246	199
New York	38	22	16	92	246	189
Montreal	38	22	16	92	244	201
Toronto	29	34	13	71	222	242
WEST DIVISION						
St. Louis	37	27	12	86	224	179
Pittsburgh	26	38	12	64	182	238
Minnesota	19	35	22	60	224	257
Oakland	22	40	14	58	169	243
Philadelphia	17	35	24	58	197	225
Los Angeles	14	52	10	38	168	290

1969-70 RESULTS

October 1969

	AT	VERSUS	W-L-T	SCR
12	Boston	New York	W	2-1
15	Boston	Oakland	W	6-0
18	Pittsburgh	Penguins	T	3-3
19	Boston	Pittsburgh	W	4-0
22	Minnesota	North Stars	W	3-2
24	Oakland	Seals	W	4-2
25	Los Angeles	Kings	W	3-2
29	Toronto	Maple Leafs	L	4-2

November 1969

1	Montreal	Canadiens	L	9-2
2	Boston	Toronto	T	4-4
5	Boston	St. Louis	T	4-4
8	Detroit	Red Wings	L	3-2
10	Boston	Oakland	W	8-3
13	Boston	Detroit	W	3-1
15	Boston	New York	L	6-5
16	Boston	Los Angeles	W	7-4
21	Chicago	Blackhawks	T	2-2
23	Boston	Montreal	T	2-2
26	New York	Rangers	L	3-0
27	Boston	Philadelphia	W	6-4
29	Montreal	Canadiens	T	2-2
30	Boston	Toronto	W	4-1

December 1969

4	Detroit	Red Wings	T	4-4
6	Boston	Chicago	W	6-1
7	Boston	Minnesota	T	2-2
10	New York	Rangers	L	5-2
11	Boston	New York	W	2-1
13	Philadelphia	Flyers	W	5-3
14	Boston	Pittsburgh	W	2-1

18	St. Louis	Blues	T	3-3
20	Pittsburgh	Penguins	W	6-4
21	Boston	Montreal	L	5-2
25	Boston	Los Angeles	W	7-1
28	Philadelphia	Flyers	W	5-4
31	Detroit	Red Wings	L	5-1

January 1970

3	Los Angeles	Kings	W	6-2
7	Oakland	Seals	W	6-1
10	Toronto	Maple Leafs	L	4-3
11	Boston	Oakland	W	6-3
15	Boston	Los Angeles	W	6-3
17	Boston	Chicago	L	1-0
18	Boston	Montreal	W	6-3
22	Boston	Philadelphia	T	3-3
24	New York	Rangers	L	8-1
25	Boston	Pittsburgh	W	3-1
29	Boston	Minnesota	W	6-5
31	Montreal	Canadiens	T	3-3

February 1970

1	Boston	Toronto	W	7-6
4	Chicago	Blackhawks	L	8-4
5	Boston	Philadelphia	W	5-1
7	Boston	Detroit	T	2-2
8	Boston	St. Louis	W	7-1
11	St. Louis	Blues	W	3-2
14	Pittsburgh	Penguins	W	3-0
17	Oakland	Seals	T	3-3
18	Los Angeles	Kings	T	5-5
21	Minnesota	North Stars	W	4-2
22	Chicago	Blackhawks	L	6-3
26	Boston	New York	W	5-3
28	Boston	Chicago	W	3-0

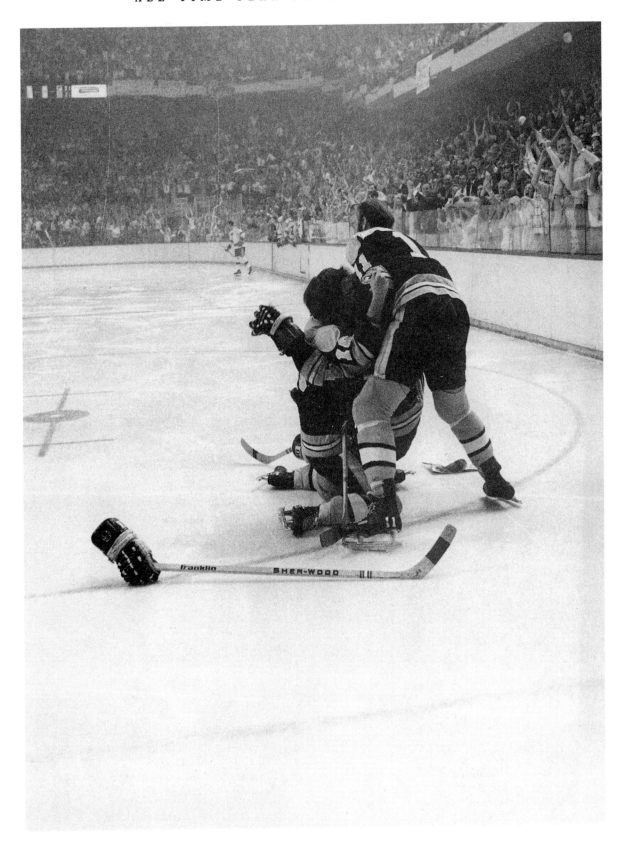

March 1970

1	Boston	St. Louis	W	3–1
4	St. Louis	Blues	L	3–1
7	Philadelphia	Flyers	T	5–5
8	Boston	Montreal	W	2–0
11	Chicago	Blackhawks	T	0–0
14	Toronto	Maple Leafs	L	2–1
15	Boston	Detroit	T	5–5
19	Boston	Chicago	W	3–1
21	Minnesota	North Stars	L	5–4
22	Boston	Minnesota	W	5–0
25	New York	Rangers	W	3–1
28	Boston	Detroit	T	5–5
29	Detroit	Red Wings	T	2–2

April 1970

1	Montreal	Canadiens	L	6–3
4	Toronto	Maple Leafs	W	4–2
5	Boston	Toronto	W	3–1

1969-70 SCORING

	W	L	T	S	GAA	PIM
Eddie Johnston	16	9	11	3	2.98	0
						2 assists
Gerry Cheevers	24	8	8	4	2.72	4

	G	A	P	PIM
Bobby Orr	33	87	120	125
Phil Esposito	43	56	99	50
John McKenzie	29	41	70	114
Johnny Bucyk	31	38	70	13
Fred Stanfield	23	35	58	14
Ken Hodge	25	29	54	87
Derek Sanderson	18	23	41	118
Eddie Westfall	14	22	36	28
Wayne Cashman	9	26	35	79
Wayne Carleton	6	19	25	23
Dallas Smith	7	17	24	119
Jim Lorentz	7	16	23	30
Garnet Bailey	11	11	22	82
Don Awrey	3	10	13	120
Don Marcotte	9	3	12	14
Rick Smith	2	8	10	65
Gary Doak	1	7	8	63
Ron Murphy	2	5	7	8
Jim Harrison	3	1	4	16
Billy Speer	1	3	4	4
Tom Webster	0	1	1	2
Frank Spring	0	0	0	0
Nick Beverley	0	0	0	2
Bill Lesuk	0	0	0	0
Barry Wilkins	0	0	0	2

Number of power play advantages	279
Power play goals	81
% successful	29%
Phil Esposito	18
Johnny Bucyk	14
Fred Stanfield	13
Bobby Orr	11
John McKenzie	9
Ken Hodge	6
Derek Sanderson	5
Jim Lorentz	2
Garnet Bailey	2
Dallas Smith	1

Short-handed goals against	4
Penalty minutes: 1,184	15.7 per game
Times short-handed	360
Power play goals against	80
Penalty kill success	77.8%
Short-hand goals	13
Derek Sanderson	5
Bobby Orr	4
Phil Esposito	1
John McKenzie	1
Dallas Smith	1
Jim Harrison	1

1969-70 PLAYOFF RESULTS

April 1970

	AT	VERSUS	W-L-T	SCR
8	Boston	New York	W	8–2
9	Boston	New York	W	5–3
11	New York	Rangers	L	4–3
12	New York	Rangers	L	4–2
14	Boston	New York	W	3–2
16	New York	Rangers	W	4–1
19	Chicago	Blackhawks	W	6–3
21	Chicago	Blackhawks	W	4–1
23	Boston	Chicago	W	5–2
26	Boston	Chicago	W	5–4

May 1970

3	St. Louis	Blues		W	6–1		7	Boston	St. Louis	W	4–1
5	St. Louis	Blues		W	6–2		10	Boston	St. Louis	W	4–3 (OT)

1969-70 PLAYOFFS

vs. New York Rangers	4 wins – 2 losses
at New York	1 win – 2 losses
at Boston	3 wins – 0 losses
vs. Chicago Blackhawks	4 wins – 0 losses
at Chicago	2 wins – 0 losses
at Boston	2 wins – 0 losses

vs. St. Louis Blues	4 wins – 0 losses
at St. Louis	2 wins – 0 losses
at Boston	2 wins – 0 losses

1969-70 PLAYOFF SCORING

	W	L	SO	GAA	PIM
Gerry Cheevers	12	1	0	2.23	2
					1 assist
Eddie Johnston	0	1	0	4.00	2

	G	A	P	PIM
Phil Esposito	13	14	27	16
Bobby Orr	9	11	20	14
Johnny Bucyk	11	8	19	2
John McKenzie	5	12	17	35
Fred Stanfield	4	12	16	6
Ken Hodge	3	10	13	17
Wayne Cashman	5	4	9	50

	G	A	P	PIM
Derek Sanderson	5	4	9	72
Eddie Westfall	3	5	8	4
Wayne Carleton	2	4	6	14
Don Awrey	0	5	5	32
Rick Smith	1	3	4	17
Dallas Smith	0	3	3	19
Don Marcotte	2	0	2	11
Bill Speer	1	0	1	4
Jim Lorentz	1	0	1	4
Dan Schock	0	0	0	0
Bill Lesuk	0	0	0	0
Gary Doak	0	0	0	9

Power play goals for	14
Power play goals against	14
Short-handed goals for	5

Short-handed goals against	0
Penalty minutes:	326 – 23.3 per game

1970–1971
(47th year)

TEAM OWNER:	Boston Professional Hockey Association
GOVERNOR:	Weston Adams, Jr.
GM:	Milt Schmidt
COACH:	Tom Johnson
ATTENDANCE:	584,748 14,993 per game 39 sellouts

PLAYOFFS:	*Quarter finals:* Lose to Montreal Canadiens 3 wins – 4 losses
STANLEY CUP WINNERS:	Montreal Canadiens
ALL-STARS:	Bobby Orr (1st team) Phil Esposito (1st team) Ken Hodge (1st team) Johnny Bucyk (1st team)

| TROPHY WINNERS: | Prince of Wales —
Boston Bruins
Hart — Bobby Orr
Ross — Phil Esposito
Norris — Bobby Orr
Lady Byng — Johnny Bucyk
Dufresne — Phil Esposito
7th Player — Fred Stanfield | RADIO BROADCASTER:
TV BROADCASTER: | WBZ – Fred Cusick
WSBK TV38 – Don Earle,
John Peirson |

UNIFORMS

- Home jersey is white with gold shoulder inserts. Socks are white with one gold band surrounded by two black bands at the calf. Road jersey is black with gold shoulder inserts, black pants, gold socks with one white band surrounded by two black bands at the calf. Logo is the spoked "B." Pants are black with white trim on side.
- NHL uniform regulations stipulate that home teams wear white and road teams colored uniforms. Bruins change home uniform from base color black with gold and white trim to base color white, with black and gold trim. Road uniform is now the former home uniform.

POTPOURRI

- Bruins enjoy 13-game winning streak.
- Bruins finish in first place with 121 points.
- Bobby Orr wins second straight Hart Trophy and fourth straight Norris Trophy.
- Phil Esposito wins Ross Trophy as leading scorer.
- Johnny Bucyk wins Lady Byng Trophy for gentlemanly play.
- Bruins set 37 individual and team NHL records.
- Eddie Johnston records 12 consecutive victories in the Bruins goal.
- Ted Green returns to action after missing the 1969–70 season with a head injury.
- Eddie Westfall scores 7 short-handed goals as the Bruins team scores 25 short-handed goals.
- Bruins lose in first round of the playoffs to Montreal, 4 games to 3.
- NHL admits Buffalo Sabres and Vancouver Canucks into the league. Both teams assigned to the Eastern Division.
- Schedule increased to 78 games.
- Bruins score 399 goals on 3,167 shots, 12.6 in accuracy.
- Derek Sanderson is the only player in the NHL to wear a moustache.
- Bruins sell out all 39 home games.
- Phil Esposito scores 50th goal on his birthday.
- Bobby Orr is named Sportsman of the Year by *Sports Illustrated* magazine.
- Bruins score fastest 3 goals in history in a February 25 game against Vancouver. The 3 goals are scored 20 seconds apart by Johnny Bucyk, Eddie Westfall, and Ted Green.

TRANSACTIONS

- Bruins lose Bill Lesuk to the Philadelphia Flyers in the intra-league draft.
- Bruins claim Dick Cherry from Philadelphia as a fill-in for Bill Lesuk.
- Bruins lose Tom Webster to Buffalo, Gary Doak and Barry Wilkins to Vancouver in the expansion draft. Bruins fill in Danny Schock and Garnet Bailey for losing Tom Webster and Gary Doak.
- In a deal involving the Toronto Maple Leafs, Philadelphia Flyers, and Boston Bruins, the Bruins trade Rick MacLeish and Danny Schock to Philadelphia. Philadelphia trades Bernie Parent to Toronto. Toronto trades Mike Walton to the Bruins.
- Select Reggie Leach as their #1 draft pick.

1970-71 STANDINGS

Eastern Division	W	L	T	P	GF	GA
Boston	57	14	7	121	399	207
New York	49	18	11	109	259	177
Montreal	42	23	13	97	291	216
Toronto	37	33	8	82	248	211
Buffalo	24	39	15	63	217	291
Vancouver	24	46	8	56	229	296
Detroit	22	45	11	55	209	308
Western Division						
Chicago	49	20	9	107	227	184
St. Louis	34	25	19	87	223	208
Philadelphia	28	33	17	73	207	225
Minnesota	28	34	16	72	191	223
Los Angeles	25	40	13	63	239	303
Pittsburgh	21	37	20	62	221	240
California	20	53	5	45	199	320

1970-71 RESULTS

October 1970

	AT	VERSUS	W-L-T	SCR
11	Boston	Detroit	W	7–3
14	Los Angeles	Kings	W	8–5
16	California	Golden Seals	W	5–1
18	Vancouver	Canucks	W	5–3
22	Boston	Chicago	T	3–3
25	Boston	Philadelphia	W	4–3
29	Detroit	Red Wings	L	5–3
31	Boston	New York	W	6–0

November 1970

1	Boston	Minnesota	W	5–0
5	Boston	St. Louis	L	2–0
7	Pittsburgh	Penguins	T	2–2
8	Boston	Montreal	W	6–1
10	Boston	Vancouver	W	6–3
14	Toronto	Maple Leafs	L	3–2
15	Boston	California	L	2–1
18	Minnesota	North Stars	W	8–4
21	Philadelphia	Flyers	W	5–2
22	Boston	Pittsburgh	W	4–2
24	St. Louis	Blues	T	5–5
26	Boston	Chicago	W	3–2
28	New York	Rangers	T	3–3
29	Boston	Toronto	W	4–2

December 1970

2	Chicago	Blackhawks	L	4–3
3	Buffalo	Sabres	T	4–4
5	Montreal	Canadiens	W	4–2
6	Boston	Pittsburgh	W	6–3
10	Boston	Buffalo	W	8–2
12	Philadelphia	Flyers	W	1–0
13	Boston	Detroit	W	6–2
16	Boston	Los Angeles	W	6–4
19	St. Louis	Blues	W	7–1
20	Boston	Minnesota	W	7–2
23	Detroit	Red Wings	W	2–1
25	Boston	Pittsburgh	W	8–4
26	Pittsburgh	Penguins	L	4–2
30	Minnesota	North Stars	W	6–2

January 1971

1	Buffalo	Sabres	W	9–4
3	Philadelphia	Flyers	W	5–1
7	Boston	Vancouver	W	6–4
9	Chicago	Blackhawks	L	4–3
10	Boston	California	W	7–4
14	Boston	Los Angeles	W	9–5
16	Montreal	Canadiens	L	4–2
17	Boston	Toronto	W	9–1
23	Boston	Chicago	W	6–2
24	Boston	Montreal	W	4–2
27	New York	Rangers	T	2–2
28	Boston	Philadelphia	W	6–2
31	Boston	St. Louis	W	6–0

February 1971

3	Boston	Los Angeles	W	7–3
6	Boston	Buffalo	W	4–3
7	Boston	Minnesota	T	4–4
9	Boston	New York	W	6–3
11	St. Louis	Blues	W	5–3
14	Toronto	Maple Leafs	W	5–1
16	Vancouver	Canucks	L	5–4

19	California	Seals	W	5–0		16	Detroit	Red Wings	W	11–4
20	Los Angeles	Kings	L	5–4		18	Boston	Detroit	W	7–3
23	Buffalo	Sabres	W	6–3		20	Boston	Philadelphia	W	5–3
25	Boston	Vancouver	W	8–3		21	Boston	Buffalo	L	7–5
28	Boston	Toronto	W	4–3		24	Chicago	Blackhawks	L	2–1
						27	Boston	New York	L	6–3
						28	New York	Rangers	L	2–1
						31	Montreal	Canadiens	W	6–3

March 1971

2	Minnesota	North Stars	W	6–0
4	Boston	California	W	7–0
6	Pittsburgh	Penguins	W	6–3
7	Boston	St. Louis	W	4–1
10	California	Seals	W	8–1
11	Los Angeles	Kings	W	7–2
13	Vancouver	Canucks	W	6–3

April 1971

| 3 | Toronto | Maple Leafs | W | 8–3 |
| 4 | Boston | Montreal | W | 7–2 |

1970-71 SCORING

	W	L	T	S	GAA	PIM
Eddie Johnston	30	6	2	4	2.52	6
						1 assist
Gerry Cheevers	27	8	5	3	2.72	4

	G	A	P	PIM
Phil Esposito	76	76	152	71
Bobby Orr	37	102	139	91
Johnny Bucyk	51	65	116	8
Ken Hodge	43	62	105	113
Wayne Cashman	21	58	79	100
John McKenzie	31	46	77	120
Fred Stanfield	24	52	76	12

Derek Sanderson	29	34	63	130
Eddie Westfall	25	34	59	48
Wayne Carleton	22	24	46	44
Dallas Smith	7	38	45	68
Ted Green	5	37	42	60
Don Marcotte	15	13	28	30
Don Awrey	4	21	25	141
Rick Smith	4	19	23	44
Mike Walton	3	5	8	10
Reggie Leach	2	4	6	0
Garnet Bailey	0	6	6	44
Billy Speer	0	0	0	4
Ivan Boldirev	0	0	0	0

Number of power play advantages	289
Power play goals	80
% successful	27.7%
Phil Esposito	25
Johnny Bucyk	22
John McKenzie	11
Fred Stanfield	8
Bobby Orr	5
Ken Hodge	4
Wayne Cashman	4
Derek Sanderson	1
Short-handed goals against	4

Penalty minutes: 1,146 – 14.7 per game	
Times short-handed	336
Power play goals against	53
Penalty kill success	84.2%
Short-hand goals	25
Ed Westfall	7
Derek Sanderson	6
Don Marcotte	6
Bobby Orr	3
Dallas Smith	2
Phil Esposito	1

1970-71 PLAYOFF RESULTS

April 1971

	AT	VERSUS	W-L-T	SCR
7	Boston	Montreal	W	3–1
8	Boston	Montreal	L	7–5
10	Montreal	Canadiens	L	3–1

11	Montreal	Canadiens	W	5–2
13	Boston	Montreal	W	7–3
15	Montreal	Canadiens	L	8–3
18	Boston	Montreal	L	4–2

1970-71 PLAYOFFS

vs. Montreal Canadiens	3 wins – 4 losses
at Montreal	1 wins – 2 losses
at Boston	2 wins – 2 losses

1970-71 PLAYOFF SCORING

	W	L	SO	GAA	PIM
Gerry Cheevers	3	3	0	3.50	4
Eddie Johnston	0	1	0	7.00	0

	G	A	P	PIM
Bobby Orr	5	7	12	10
Phil Esposito	3	7	10	6
Fred Stanfield	3	4	7	0
Johnny Bucyk	2	5	7	0
Ken Hodge	2	5	7	6
Wayne Cashman	3	2	5	15
John McKenzie	2	3	5	22
Derek Sanderson	2	1	3	13
Eddie Westfall	1	2	3	2
Dallas Smith	0	3	3	26
Mike Walton	2	0	2	19
Ted Green	1	0	1	25
Garnet Bailey	0	0	0	10
Reggie Leach	0	0	0	0
Wayne Carleton	0	0	0	0
Rick Smith	0	0	0	0
Don Marcotte	0	0	0	0
Don Awrey	0	0	0	17

Power play goals for	6
Power play goals against	5
Short-handed goals for	2
Short-handed goals against	0
Penalty minutes:	171 – 24.4 per game

1971–1972
(48th year)

TEAM OWNER:	Boston Professional Hockey Association
GOVERNOR:	Weston Adams, Jr.
GM:	Milt Schmidt
COACH:	Tom Johnson
ATTENDANCE:	584,805 14,995 per game 39 sellouts
PLAYOFFS:	*Quarter finals:* Defeat Toronto Maple Leafs 4 wins – 1 loss *Semi-finals:* Defeat St. Louis Blues 4 wins – 0 losses *Stanley Cup finals:* Defeat New York Rangers 4 wins – 2 losses

STANLEY CUP WINNERS:	Boston Bruins
ALL-STARS:	Bobby Orr (1st team) Phil Esposito (1st team)
TROPHY WINNERS:	Prince of Wales — Boston Bruins Hart — Bobby Orr Ross — Phil Esposito Norris — Bobby Orr Conn Smythe — Bobby Orr Lester Patrick — Cooney Weiland Dufresne — Bobby Orr 7th Player — Derek Sanderson
RADIO BROADCASTER:	WBZ – Bob Wilson
TV BROADCASTER:	WSBK TV38 – Fred Cusick, John Peirson

UNIFORMS

- Home jersey is white with gold shoulder inserts. Socks are white with one gold band surrounded by two black bands at the calf. Road jersey is black with gold shoulder inserts, black pants, gold socks with one white band surrounded by two black bands at the calf. Logo is the spoked "B."
- Pants are black with white trim on side.

POTPOURRI

- Bruins win their fifth Stanley Cup by defeating the Rangers in 6 games.
- Bobby Orr wins third consecutive Hart Trophy, fifth consecutive Norris Trophy, and the Conn Smythe Trophy for the second time in his career.
- Phil Esposito wins his second consecutive Ross Trophy.
- Bruins enjoy a 9-game winning streak from February 15 through March 4.
- Derek Sanderson scores 7 short-handed goals.
- Bobby Orr undergoes knee surgery in June, 1972.
- Bobby Orr becomes the first player to win the Conn Smythe Trophy for a second time.
- Bobby Orr becomes the fourth player to score the Stanley Cup winning goal for a second time. The other players to accomplish this feat are Toe Blake, Henri Richard, and Jean Beliveau.
- Eddie Johnston collects 4 assists in a year to break the assist record of 3 in a season by a goaltender. Johnston's record is also attained by Al Smith of Detroit who also collected 4 assists.
- During the 1971–72 season, only 3 non-Canadian born players are in the NHL: Bobby Sheehan and Larry Pleau of the Canadiens are from Massachusetts and Ken Hodge of the Bruins is from England.
- For the second time in his career, Phil Esposito scores his 50th goal on his birthday.
- Bobby Orr becomes hockey's first million-dollar player.

TRANSACTIONS

- Bruins lose Wayne Carleton and Stan Gilbertson to California and Frank Spring to Philadelphia in the intra-league draft. Bruins claim Garry Peters from Philadelphia for losing Frank Spring in the intra-league draft. Bruins claim Ron Jones as their #1 pick in the amateur draft.
- Bruins trade Rick Smith, Bob Stewart, and Reggie Leach to California for Carol Vadnais and Don O'Donoghue.
- Trade Ivan Boldirev to California for Chris Oddleifson and Richie Leduc.
- Bruins purchase Matt Ravlich from Los Angeles.
- Bruins obtain Doug Roberts from the California Seals.

1971-72 **STANDINGS**

Eastern Division	W	L	T	P	GF	GA
Boston	54	13	11	119	330	204
New York	48	17	13	109	317	192
Montreal	46	16	16	108	307	205
Toronto	33	31	14	80	209	208
Detroit	33	35	10	76	261	262
Buffalo	16	43	19	51	203	289
Vancouver	20	50	8	48	203	287
Western Division						
Chicago	46	17	15	107	256	166
Minnesota	37	29	12	86	212	191
St. Louis	28	39	11	67	208	247
Philadelphia	26	38	14	66	220	258
Pittsburgh	26	38	14	66	200	236
California	21	39	18	60	216	288
Los Angeles	20	49	9	49	206	305

Wayne Cashman, Phil Esposito, and Ken Hodge

1971-72 RESULTS

October 1971

	AT	VERSUS	W-L-T	SCR
10	Boston	New York	L	4–1
13	New York	Rangers	W	6–1
14	Boston	Buffalo	W	6–2
17	Boston	Toronto	T	2–2
20	Boston	Detroit	W	4–3
22	California	Seals	W	5–1
24	Vancouver	Canucks	W	4–3
27	Montreal	Canadiens	L	5–2
28	Boston	California	L	2–0
31	Boston	Minnesota	W	5–2

November 1971

4	Boston	St. Louis	W	6–1
6	Detroit	Red Wings	W	2–1
7	Boston	Montreal	L	3–2
10	Chicago	Blackhawks	L	3–1
11	Boston	California	W	5–2
14	Boston	Los Angeles	W	11–2
18	Boston	Vancouver	W	5–0
20	Boston	Chicago	W	2–1
21	Boston	St. Louis	W	6–2
24	Philadelphia	Flyers	W	2–1
25	Boston	Philadelphia	W	4–2
27	St. Louis	Blues	T	6–6

December 1971

4	Toronto	Maple Leafs	W	5–3
5	Boston	Pittsburgh	W	5–3
8	Los Angeles	Kings	W	5–3
11	Vancouver	Canucks	W	6–2
12	California	Seals	L	4–2
16	Boston	New York	W	8–1
18	Pittsburgh	Penguins	W	4–3
19	Boston	Pittsburgh	T	2–2
23	Buffalo	Sabres	T	4–4
25	Boston	Philadelphia	W	5–1
26	Boston	Toronto	W	3–1
29	Chicago	Blackhawks	W	5–1
30	Minnesota	North Stars	T	2–2

January 1972

2	New York	Rangers	W	4–1
5	Toronto	Maple Leafs	W	2–0
6	Buffalo	Sabres	W	5–2
8	St. Louis	Blues	L	5–3
12	Pittsburgh	Penguins	T	2–2
13	Boston	Los Angeles	T	1–1
15	Boston	Chicago	W	4–2
16	Boston	Detroit	W	9–2
18	St. Louis	Blues	W	2–0
22	Montreal	Canadiens	W	8–5

23	Boston	Buffalo	T	3–3
27	Boston	Philadelphia	W	4–2
29	Philadelphia	Flyers	W	4–2
30	Boston	St. Louis	W	5–2

February 1972

2	New York	Rangers	W	2–0
3	Boston	Minnesota	W	6–1
5	Boston	Detroit	W	3–2
6	Buffalo	Sabres	L	8–2
10	Boston	Vancouver	W	9–1
12	Boston	Buffalo	W	5–1
13	Boston	Montreal	T	2–2
15	Boston	California	W	6–3
17	Philadelphia	Flyers	W	4–1
19	Minnesota	North Stars	W	6–4
20	Chicago	Blackhawks	W	3–1
22	Vancouver	Canucks	W	4–3
23	California	Seals	W	8–6
26	Los Angeles	Kings	W	5–4

March 1972

2	Boston	Vancouver	W	7–3
4	Detroit	Red Wings	W	5–3
5	Boston	Los Angeles	L	2–0
8	Minnesota	North Stars	W	5–4
11	Pittsburgh	Penguins	L	6–4
12	Boston	Pittsburgh	T	4–4
16	Los Angeles	Kings	W	8–3
19	Boston	Minnesota	W	7–3
23	Boston	New York	W	4–1
25	Boston	Chicago	T	5–5
26	Boston	Montreal	W	5–4
28	Detroit	Red Wings	L	6–3
29	Toronto	Maple Leafs	L	4–1

April 1972

1	Montreal	Canadiens	L	6–2
2	Toronto	Maple Leafs	W	6–4

1971-72 **SCORING**

	W	L	T	S	GAA	PIM
Eddie Johnston	27	8	3	2	2.70	0
					4 assists	
Gerry Cheevers	27	5	8	2	2.50	25
					2 assists	

	G	A	P	PIM
Phil Esposito	66	67	133	76
Bobby Orr	37	80	117	106
Johnny Bucyk	32	51	83	4
Fred Stanfield	23	56	79	12
John McKenzie	22	47	69	126
Derek Sanderson	25	33	58	108
Mike Walton	28	28	56	45
Ken Hodge	16	40	56	81
Wayne Cashman	23	29	52	103
Eddie Westfall	18	26	44	19
Dallas Smith	8	22	30	132
Garnet Bailey	9	13	22	64
Reggie Leach	7	13	20	12
Ted Green	1	16	17	21
Rick Smith	2	12	14	46
Don Marcotte	6	4	10	12
Carol Vadnais	4	6	10	37
Don Awrey	1	8	9	52
Ivan Boldirev	0	2	2	6
Terry O'Reilly	1	0	1	0
Doug Roberts	1	0	1	0
Matt Ravlich	0	1	1	2
Nick Beverley	0	0	0	0
Ron Jones	0	0	0	0
Garry Peters	0	0	0	2
Bob Stewart	0	0	0	15

Number of power play advantages	256
Power play goals	74
% successful	28.9%
Phil Esposito	28
Johnny Bucyk	13
Bobby Orr	11
John McKenzie	10
Mike Walton	6
Fred Stanfield	5
Wayne Cashman	1
Short-handed goals against	2
Penalty minutes: 1,106 – 14.2 per game	

Times short-handed	290
Power play goals against	51
Penalty kill success	82.4%
Short-hand goals	18
Derek Sanderson	7
Bobby Orr	4
Phil Esposito	2
Ed Westfall	2
Fred Stanfield	1
Ken Hodge	1
Dallas Smith	1

1971-72 PLAYOFF RESULTS

April 1972

	AT	VERSUS	W-L-T	SCR
5	Boston	Toronto	W	5–0
6	Boston	Toronto	L	4–3
8	Toronto	Maple Leafs	W	2–0
9	Toronto	Maple Leafs	W	5–4
11	Boston	Toronto	W	3–2
18	Boston	St. Louis	W	6–1
20	Boston	St. Louis	W	10–2
23	St. Louis	Blues	W	7–2
25	St. Louis	Blues	W	5–3
30	Boston	New York	W	6–5

May 1972

2	Boston	New York	W	2–1
4	New York	Rangers	L	5–2
7	New York	Rangers	W	3–2
9	Boston	New York	L	3–2
11	New York	Rangers	W	3–0

1971-72 PLAYOFFS

vs. Toronto Maple Leafs	4 wins – 1 loss
at Toronto	2 wins – 0 losses
at Boston	2 wins – 1 loss
vs. St. Louis Blues	4 wins – 0 losses
at St. Louis	2 wins – 0 losses
at Boston	2 wins – 0 losses
vs. New York Rangers	4 wins – 2 losses
at New York	2 wins – 1 loss
at Boston	2 wins – 1 loss

1971-72 PLAYOFF SCORING

	W	L	SO	GAA	PIM
Gerry Cheevers	6	2	2	2.61	0
Eddie Johnston	6	1	1	1.86	0

	G	A	P	PIM
Phil Esposito	9	15	24	24
Bobby Orr	5	19	24	19
Johnny Bucyk	9	11	20	6
Ken Hodge	9	8	17	62
John McKenzie	5	12	17	37
Fred Stanfield	7	9	16	0
Mike Walton	6	6	12	13
Wayne Cashman	4	7	11	42
Eddie Westfall	4	3	7	10
Garnet Bailey	2	4	6	16
Dallas Smith	0	4	4	22
Don Awrey	0	4	4	45
Don Marcotte	3	0	3	6
Derek Sanderson	1	1	2	44
Carol Vadnais	0	2	2	43
Garry Peters	0	0	0	0
Chris Hayes	0	0	0	0
Ted Green	0	0	0	0

Power play goals for	18
Power play goals against	11
Short-handed goals for	5
Short-handed goals against	1
Penalty minutes:	389 – 25.9 per game

1972–1973
(49th year)

TEAM OWNER:	Boston Professional Hockey Association	STANLEY CUP WINNER:	Montreal Canadiens
GOVERNOR:	Weston Adams, Jr.	ALL-STARS:	Bobby Orr (1st team)
GM:	Harry Sinden		Phil Esposito (1st team)
COACHES	Tom Johnson & Bep Guidolin	TROPHY WINNERS:	Ross — Phil Esposito
			Norris — Bobby Orr
ATTENDANCE:	585,117		Dufresne — Phil Esposito
	15,003 per game		7th Player — Dallas Smith
	39 sellouts	RADIO BROADCASTER:	WBZ – Bob Wilson, Ron Cantera
PLAYOFFS:	*Quarter finals:* Lose to New York Rangers 1 win – 4 losses	TV BROADCASTER:	WSBK TV38 – Fred Cusick, John Peirson

UNIFORMS

- Home jersey is white with gold shoulder inserts. Socks are white with one gold band surrounded by two black bands at the calf. Road jersey is black with gold shoulder inserts, black pants, gold socks, with one white band surrounded by two black bands at the calf. Logo is the spoked "B."
- Pants are black with white trim on side.

POTPOURRI

- Bobby Orr wins sixth straight Norris Trophy.
- Phil Esposito wins third straight Ross Trophy.
- Bruins finish in second place in the Eastern Division.
- Bruins enjoy a 10-game winning streak.
- Lose first round of playoffs to Rangers, 4 games to 1.
- Atlanta Flames and Islanders join the National Hockey League.
- With the formation of the World Hockey Association, many players are lost to the new league.
- The NHL (Team Canada) plays an 8-game exhibition series against the Soviet national team which Team Canada wins 4 games to 3, with 1 game ending in a tie.
- Derek Sanderson returns from the World Hockey Association.

TRANSACTIONS

- Harry Sinden returns to the Bruins to become the Managing Director.
- Bruins draft Mike Bloom #1.
- Bruins lose Don Tannahill to the Vancouver Canucks in the intra-league draft.
- Bruins lose Dan Bouchard to the Atlanta Flames, Eddie Westfall and Garry Peters to the Islanders in the expansion draft.
- Obtain Gary Doak from Detroit for Garnet Bailey.
- Obtain Jacques Plante from Toronto for Boston's first-round pick and a player to be named later. On May 22, 1973, the Bruins send Eddie Johnston to Toronto to complete the trade.

1972-73 STANDINGS

Eastern Division	W	L	T	P	GF	GA
Montreal	52	10	16	120	329	184
Boston	51	22	5	107	330	235
New York Rangers	47	23	8	102	297	208
Buffalo	37	27	14	88	257	219

Detroit	37	29	12	86	265	243
Toronto	27	41	10	64	247	279
Vancouver	22	47	9	53	233	339
New York Islanders	12	60	6	30	170	347
Western Division						
Chicago	42	27	9	93	284	225
Philadelphia	37	30	11	85	296	256
Minnesota	37	30	11	85	254	230
St. Louis	32	34	12	76	233	251
Pittsburgh	32	37	9	73	257	265
Los Angeles	31	36	11	73	232	245
Atlanta	25	38	15	65	191	239
California	16	46	16	48	213	323

1972-73 RESULTS

	AT	VERSUS	W-L-T	SCR
8	Boston	Los Angeles	L	4–2
11	Detroit	Red Wings	L	4–3
14	New York	Islanders	W	7–4
15	Boston	Pittsburgh	W	8–4
18	New York	Rangers	L	7–1
21	Pittsburgh	Penguins	W	4–2
22	Boston	Vancouver	L	5–4
25	Buffalo	Sabres	T	2–2
26	Boston	Chicago	L	6–3
28	Toronto	Maple Leafs	W	3–2
29	Boston	New York Islanders	W	9–1

November 1972

2	Los Angeles	Kings	L	5–2
3	California	Seals	T	6–6
5	Vancouver	Canucks	W	4–2
9	Boston	Detroit	W	8–3
12	Boston	Montreal	L	5–3
16	Boston	St. Louis	W	4–0
18	New York	Islanders	W	7–3
19	Boston	Toronto	W	6–5
23	Boston	California	W	4–2
24	Atlanta	Flames	W	4–0
29	Montreal	Canadiens	T	3–3
30	Boston	Buffalo	W	5–4

December 1972

3	Boston	New York Islanders	W	5–1
7	Boston	St. Louis	W	5–0
9	Philadelphia	Flyers	W	4–3
10	Boston	California	W	8–4
13	Buffalo	Sabres	L	7–3
14	Boston	New York Rangers	W	4–2
17	Philadelphia	Flyers	W	5–3
19	Pittsburgh	Penguins	W	3–2
21	Boston	Detroit	W	8–1
23	Boston	Atlanta	W	3–1
27	Atlanta	Flames	W	3–1
29	Minnesota	North Stars	W	2–0

January 1973

1	Vancouver	Canucks	W	8–2
4	St. Louis	Blues	L	4–2
7	Chicago	Blackhawks	L	5–4
11	Boston	Minnesota	T	1–1
13	Toronto	Maple Leafs	W	4–1
14	Boston	Buffalo	W	6–0
18	Boston	New York Islanders	L	9–7
20	Pittsburgh	Penguins	L	3–0
21	Boston	California	W	5–2
24	New York	Rangers	L	4–2
25	Boston	Detroit	L	4–2
27	Boston	Chicago	L	4–2
28	Boston	Los Angeles	W	6–5

February 1973

1	Boston	Toronto	W	5–2
3	Boston	New York Rangers	L	7–3
4	Boston	Philadelphia	T	2–2
7	Minnesota	North Stars	W	3–2
10	Boston	Pittsburgh	W	6–3
11	Boston	Los Angeles	W	2–0
13	Boston	Vancouver	W	7–3
15	Philadelphia	Flyers	W	3–1
17	Minnesota	North Stars	L	5–2
18	Chicago	Blackhawks	W	4–1
20	Vancouver	Canucks	W	7–6
21	California	Seals	W	6–2
24	Los Angeles	Kings	W	7–5

March 1973

1	Boston	St. Louis	L	4–3
3	Montreal	Canadiens	L	5–1
4	Boston	Chicago	W	4–0
7	St. Louis	Blues	L	5–2

9	Atlanta	Flames	W	3–2
11	Boston	Montreal	W	5–3
13	New York	Islanders	W	3–0
15	Buffalo	Sabres	W	4–1
16	Detroit	Red Wings	W	5–4
18	Boston	Atlanta	W	7–1
22	Boston	Minnesota	W	5–3

24	Boston	New York Rangers	W	3–0
25	Boston	Buffalo	W	6–1
28	New York	Rangers	L	6–3
31	Toronto	Maple Leafs	L	7–3

April 1973

1	Boston	Montreal	L	5–3

1972-73 SCORING

	W	L	T	S	GAA	PIM
Eddie Johnston	24	17	1	5	3.27	2
						1 assist
Ross Brooks	11	1	3	1	2.64	0
						1 assist
John Adams	9	3	1	1	3.00	0
Jacques Plante	7	1	0	2	2.00	2
						2 assists

	G	A	P	PIM
Phil Esposito	55	75	130	87
Bobby Orr	29	72	101	99
Johnny Bucyk	40	53	93	12
Ken Hodge	37	44	81	58
Fred Stanfield	20	58	78	10
Wayne Cashman	29	39	68	100
Don Marcotte	24	31	55	49

Greg Sheppard	24	26	50	18
Mike Walton	25	22	47	37
Carol Vadnais	7	24	31	127
Dallas Smith	4	27	31	72
Terry O'Reilly	5	22	27	109
Garnet Bailey	8	13	21	89
Don Awrey	2	17	19	90
Derek Sanderson	5	10	15	38
Fred O'Donnell	10	4	14	55
Doug Roberts	4	7	11	7
Nick Beverley	1	10	11	26
Richie Leduc	1	1	2	2
Matt Ravlich	0	1	1	0
Gary Doak	0	0	0	2
Chris Oddleifson	0	0	0	0
Ron Jones	0	0	0	2

Number of power play advantages	241
Power play goals	67
% successful	27.8%
Phil Esposito	19
Ken Hodge	16
Johnny Bucyk	10
Bobby Orr	7
Fred Stanfield	7
Wayne Cashman	6
Don Marcotte	1
Carol Vadnais	1
Short-handed goals against	5

Penalty minutes:	1,097 – 14.0
Times short-handed	275
Power play goals against	43
Penalty kill success	84.4%
Short-hand goals	15
Phil Esposito	5
Garnet Bailey	3
Don Marcotte	2
Greg Sheppard	2
Derek Sanderson	2
Bobby Orr	1

1972-73 PLAYOFF RESULTS

April 1973

	AT	VERSUS	W-L-T	SCR
4	Boston	New York Rangers	L	6–2
5	Boston	New York Rangers	L	4–2

7	New York	Rangers	W	4–2
8	New York	Rangers	L	4–0
10	Boston	New York Rangers	L	6–3

1972-73 PLAYOFFS

vs. New York Rangers	1 win – 4 losses
at New York	1 win – 1 loss
at Boston	0 wins – 3 losses

1972-73 PLAYOFF SCORING

	W	L	SO	GAA	PIM
Eddie Johnston	1	2	0	3.38	0
Jacques Plante	0	2	0	5.00	0
Ross Brooks	0	0	0	9.00	0

	G	A	P	PIM
Greg Sheppard	2	1	3	0
Derek Sanderson	1	2	3	13
Johnny Bucyk	0	3	3	0
Doug Roberts	2	0	2	6
Wayne Cashman	1	1	2	4
Don Marcotte	1	1	2	0
Bobby Orr	1	1	2	7
Fred Stanfield	1	1	2	0
Mike Walton	1	1	2	2
Dallas Smith	0	2	2	2
Ken Hodge	1	0	1	7
Phil Esposito	0	1	1	2
Fred O'Donnell	0	1	1	5
Gary Doak	0	0	0	2
Don Awrey	0	0	0	6
Nick Beverley	0	0	0	0
Terry O'Reilly	0	0	0	2
Carol Vadnais	0	0	0	8

Power play goals for	1
Power play goals against	4
Short-handed goals for	1
Short-handed goals against	0
Penalty minutes:	66 – 13.2 per game

1973–1974
(50th year)

TEAM OWNER:	Storer Broadcasting Company
GOVERNOR:	Weston Adams, Jr.
GM:	Harry Sinden
COACH:	Bep Guidolin
ATTENDANCE:	578,874 14,842 per game
PLAYOFFS:	*Quarter finals:* Defeat Toronto Maple Leafs 4 wins – 0 losses *Semi-finals:* Defeat Chicago Blackhawks 4 wins – 2 losses *Stanley Cup finals:* Lose to Philadelphia Flyers 2 wins – 4 losses
STANLEY CUP WINNER:	Philadelphia Flyers
ALL-STARS:	Bobby Orr (1st team) Phil Esposito (1st team) Ken Hodge (1st team) Wayne Cashman (2nd team)
TROPHY WINNERS:	Prince of Wales — Boston Bruins Hart — Phil Esposito Ross — Phil Esposito Norris — Bobby Orr Lady Byng — Johnny Bucyk Lester Patrick — Weston Adams, Sr. Dufresne — Phil Esposito & Bobby Orr 7th Player — Carol Vadnais & Don Marcotte Three Star — Bobby Orr
RADIO BROADCASTER:	WBZ – Bob Wilson, Ron Cantera
TV BROADCASTER:	WSBK TV38 – Fred Cusick, John Peirson

UNIFORMS

- Home jersey is white with gold shoulder inserts. Socks are white with one gold band surrounded by two black bands at the calf. Road jersey is black with gold shoulder inserts, black pants, gold socks with one white band surrounded by two black bands at the calf. Logo is the spoked "B." Pants are black with white trim on side. Tie string is removed from uniform shirt.
- Bruins wear 50th-anniversary patch on both shoulders. Patch is a stand-up bear with the words "50th Anniversary" superimposed on the bear with the words "Boston" printed bottom to top sideways at the rear of the bear and "Bruins" printed top to bottom at the front of the bear.

POTPOURRI

- In the final year of the East-West format, the Bruins finish on top of the East Division with 113 points and finish with the best record in the NHL.
- Phil Esposito wins his fourth consecutive Ross Trophy as the league's leading scorer and his second career Hart Trophy as the league MVP.
- Bobby Orr wins his seventh straight Norris Trophy as best defenseman.
- Johnny Bucyk wins his second career Lady Byng Trophy.
- Bruins enjoy 16-game (14 wins – 2 ties) undefeated streak.
- Chris Oddleifson and Johnny Bucyk both enjoy 4 goal games.
- Bobby Orr has a 7-point (3 goals – 4 assists) game against the Rangers.
- Ross Brooks records 14 consecutive victories and winds up 16–3–0 on the season.
- Bruins lose in the Stanley Cup finals to the Philadelphia Flyers, 4 games to 2. Philadelphia becomes the first expansion team to win the Stanley Cup.
- Gilles Gilbert, in 3 appearances against the St. Louis Blues, shuts out the Blues all 3 times.
- For the third time in his career, Phil Esposito scores his 50th goal on his birthday.
- In August, 1973, the Boston Garden-Arena Corp. merged with the Storer Broadcasting Corporation.

TRANSACTIONS

- Bruins obtain Bobby Schmautz from Vancouver for Fred O'Donnell and Chris Oddleifson.
- Obtain Darryl Edestrand from Pittsburgh for Nick Beverley.
- Bruins lose Bob Gryp, Mike Bloom, and Ron Anderson in the 1974 expansion draft to stock the new Washington Capitals and Kansas City Scouts.
- Trade Fred Stanfield to Minnesota for Gilles Gilbert.
- Eddie Johnston is sold to Toronto to complete the Jacques Plante deal.
- Sell Doug Roberts to Detroit.
- Select Andre Savard #1 in the draft.

1973-74 STANDINGS

Eastern Division	W	L	T	P	GF	GA
Boston	52	17	9	113	349	221
Montreal	45	24	9	99	293	240
New York Rangers	40	24	14	94	300	251
Toronto	35	27	16	86	274	230
Buffalo	32	34	12	76	242	250
Detroit	29	39	10	68	255	319
Vancouver	24	43	11	59	224	296
New York Islanders	19	41	18	56	182	247
Western Division						
Philadelphia	50	16	12	112	273	164
Chicago	41	14	23	105	272	164
Los Angeles	33	33	12	78	233	231

Atlanta	30	34	14	74	214	238
Pittsburgh	28	41	9	65	242	273
St. Louis	26	40	12	64	206	248
Minnesota	23	38	17	63	235	275
California	13	55	10	36	195	342

1973-74 RESULTS

October 1973

	AT	VERSUS	W-L-T	SCR
10	Boston	Vancouver	W	6–4
13	Detroit	Red Wings	W	9–4
14	Boston	New York Islanders	W	3–2
17	Atlanta	Flames	L	4–3
21	Boston	Pittsburgh	W	8–2
23	St. Louis	Blues	L	3–2
25	Boston	Buffalo	W	9–4
27	Toronto	Maple Leafs	W	3–2
28	Boston	Minnesota	T	3–3
31	Minnesota	North Stars	W	5–0

November 1973

3	New York	Islanders	L	6–4
4	Boston	California	W	4–1
7	New York	Rangers	L	7–3
8	Boston	Montreal	W	2–1
11	Boston	Vancouver	W	4–2
14	Montreal	Canadiens	W	4–3
15	Boston	New York Rangers	W	10–2
17	Boston	Detroit	W	8–0
18	Boston	Atlanta	W	5–2
22	Boston	Philadelphia	W	4–2
25	Boston	Los Angeles	W	3–1
28	Chicago	Blackhawks	T	3–3

December 1973

2	Boston	New York Islanders	W	5–3
8	Boston	Buffalo	W	5–2
9	Philadelphia	Flyers	T	3–3
13	Boston	Minnesota	W	4–2
15	Boston	Vancouver	W	7–2
16	Boston	California	W	5–3
20	Boston	Pittsburgh	W	6–5
22	Detroit	Red Wings	L	4–2
23	Boston	Toronto	W	4–3
29	Los Angeles	Kings	L	4–1
30	California	Seals	W	8–1

January 1974

1	Vancouver	Canucks	T	2–2
4	New York	Rangers	W	4–2
5	New York	Islanders	W	6–2
10	Boston	Chicago	T	2–2
12	Boston	Montreal	L	7–3
13	Pittsburgh	Penguins	W	5–3
16	Chicago	Blackhawks	T	5–5
19	Montreal	Canadiens	W	8–0
20	Boston	Los Angeles	W	5–2
22	St. Louis	Blues	W	1–0
24	Boston	Chicago	L	2–1
26	New York	Islanders	W	4–0
27	Philadelphia	Flyers	W	5–3
31	Atlanta	Flames	W	4–2

February 1974

2	Toronto	Maple Leafs	L	6–2
3	Boston	Pittsburgh	W	5–4
7	Boston	St. Louis	W	5–3
9	Boston	Philadelphia	W	5–3
10	Boston	Minnesota	W	4–0
13	California	Seals	W	9–6
15	Vancouver	Canucks	W	4–2
16	Los Angeles	Kings	W	5–2
20	Minnesota	North Stars	T	5–5
23	Pittsburgh	Penguins	W	6–2
24	Buffalo	Sabres	L	3–2
28	Boston	Detroit	W	8–1

March 1974

2	Detroit	Red Wings	T	4–4
3	Boston	Toronto	L	6–4
5	Atlanta	Flames	L	4–1
6	St. Louis	Blues	W	8–0
9	Los Angeles	Kings	T	4–4
10	California	Seals	L	6–2
12	Boston	Buffalo	W	4–0
14	Buffalo	Sabres	W	4–3
16	Toronto	Maple Leafs	W	5–2
17	Boston	New York Rangers	W	5–2
21	Boston	St. Louis	W	7–0
23	Boston	Atlanta	L	4–3
24	Boston	Montreal	W	6–3
27	New York	Rangers	W	3–2
30	Philadelphia	Flyers	L	5–3
31	Boston	Detroit	W	6–1

April 1974

3	Chicago	Blackhawks	L	6–2
6	Montreal	Canadiens	L	6–2
7	Toronto	Maple Leafs	W	6–4

1973-74 SCORING

	W	L	T	S	GAA	PIM
Ross Brooks	16	3	0	3	2.36	2
Gilles Gilbert	34	12	8	6	2.95	9
						1 assist
Ken Broderick	2	2	1	0	3.20	0
						1 assist

	G	A	P	PIM
Phil Esposito	68	77	145	58
Bobby Orr	32	90	122	82
Ken Hodge	50	55	105	43
Wayne Cashman	30	59	89	111
Johnny Bucyk	31	44	75	8
Carol Vadnais	16	43	59	123
Don Marcotte	24	26	50	18
Greg Sheppard	16	31	47	21
Terry O'Reilly	11	24	35	94

Andre Savard	16	14	30	39
Dallas Smith	6	21	27	64
Dave Forbes	10	16	26	41
Chris Oddleifson	10	11	21	25
Derek Sanderson	8	12	20	48
Bobby Schmautz	7	13	20	31
Fred O'Donnell	5	7	12	43
Al Sims	3	9	12	22
Darryl Edestrand	3	8	11	20
Richie Leduc	3	3	6	12
Gary Doak	0	4	4	44
Doug Roberts	0	1	1	2
Nick Beverley	0	1	1	0
Bob Gryp	0	0	0	0
Doug Gibson	0	0	0	0
Dave Hynes	0	0	0	0
Al Simmons	0	0	0	0

Number of power play advantages	225
Power play goals	65
% successful	28.9%
Ken Hodge	15
Phil Esposito	14
Johnny Bucyk	12
Bobby Orr	11
Carol Vadnais	6
Wayne Cashman	5
Bobby Schmautz	1
Darryl Edestrand	1

Short-handed goals against	2
Penalty minutes: 968 – 12.4 per game	
Times short-handed	258
Power play goals against	48
Penalty kill success	81.4%
Short-hand goals	12
Phil Esposito	4
Don Marcotte	3
Greg Sheppard	3
Wayne Cashman	2

1973-74 PLAYOFF RESULTS

April 1974

	AT	VERSUS	W-L-T	SCR
10	Boston	Toronto	W	1–0
11	Boston	Toronto	W	6–3
13	Toronto	Maple Leafs	W	6–3
14	Toronto	Maple Leafs	W	4–3
18	Boston	Chicago	L	4–2
21	Boston	Chicago	W	8–6
23	Chicago	Blackhawks	L	4–3 (OT)
25	Chicago	Blackhawks	W	5–2
28	Boston	Chicago	W	6–2
30	Chicago	Blackhawks	W	4–2

May 1974

7	Boston	Philadelphia	W	3–2
9	Boston	Philadelphia	L	3–2 (OT)
12	Philadelphia	Flyers	L	4–1
14	Philadelphia	Flyers	L	4–2
16	Boston	Philadelphia	W	5–1
19	Philadelphia	Flyers	L	1–0

1973-74 PLAYOFFS

vs. Toronto Maple Leafs	4 wins – 0 losses
at Toronto	2 wins – 0 losses
at Boston	2 wins – 0 losses
vs. Chicago Blackhawks	4 wins – 2 losses
at Chicago	2 wins – 1 loss

at Boston	2 wins – 1 loss
vs. Philadelphia Flyers	2 wins – 4 losses
at Philadelphia	0 wins – 3 losses
at Boston	2 wins – 1 loss

1973-74 **PLAYOFF SCORING**

	W	L	SO	GAA	PIM
Gilles Gilbert	10	6	1	2.64	8
				3 assists	

	G	A	P	PIM
Greg Sheppard	11	8	19	4
Johnny Bucyk	8	10	18	4
Bobby Orr	4	14	18	28
Ken Hodge	6	10	16	16
Phil Esposito	9	5	14	25
Wayne Cashman	5	9	14	46
Carol Vadnais	1	12	13	42

	G	A	P	PIM
Bobby Schmautz	3	6	9	44
Dallas Smith	1	7	8	20
Terry O'Reilly	2	5	7	38
Don Marcotte	4	2	6	8
Andre Savard	3	2	5	24
Darryl Edestrand	1	2	3	15
Dave Forbes	0	2	2	6
Doug Gibson	0	0	0	0
Al Simmons	0	0	0	0
Richie Leduc	0	0	0	9
Al Sims	0	0	0	12

Power play goals for	12
Power play goals against	12
Short-handed goals for	2

Short-handed goals against	0
Penalty minutes:	349 – 21.8 per game

GOLDILOCKS

1974–1975
(51st year)

TEAM OWNER:	Storer Broadcasting Company	ALL-STARS:	Bobby Orr (1st team) Phil Esposito (2nd team)
GOVERNOR:	Weston Adams, Jr.	TROPHY WINNERS:	Ross — Bobby Orr
GM:	Harry Sinden		Norris — Bobby Orr
COACH:	Don Cherry		Dufresne — Bobby Orr
ATTENDANCE:	585,514		7th Player — Terry O'Reilly
	14,637 per game		Three Star — Phil Esposito
PLAYOFFS:	*Preliminary round:*	RADIO BROADCASTER:	WBZ – Bob Wilson
	Lose to Chicago Blackhawks	TV BROADCASTER:	WSBK TV38 – Fred Cusick,
	1 win – 2 losses		John Peirson
STANLEY CUP WINNER:	Philadelphia Flyers		

UNIFORMS

- Home jersey is white with gold and black trim. Gold shoulder inserts are removed. Socks are white with one gold band surrounded by two black bands at the calf. Road jersey is black with gold and white trim. Gold shoulder inserts are removed. Gold socks with one white band surrounded by two black bands at the calf. Logo is the spoked "B." Pants are black with white trim on side.

POTPOURRI

- Bobby Orr wins the Art Ross Trophy as leading scorer.
- Bobby Orr wins eighth consecutive Norris Trophy as league's best defenseman.
- Bruins finish in second place in the new Adams Division in the Prince of Wales Conference.
- Phil Esposito enjoys a 4-goal game in a February 8 game at Detroit.
- Greg Sheppard scores 7 short-handed goals.
- Bruins lose the preliminary round of the Stanley Cup playoffs to the Chicago Blackhawks, 2 games to 1.
- Washington Capitals and Kansas City Scouts are admitted to the NHL. The schedule is increased to 80 games.
- Bruins record 18 sellouts of 15,003, attracting 585,514 fans for an average of 14,638 fans per game.

TRANSACTIONS

- Select Don Larway #1 in the draft.
- Obtain Hank Nowak and Earl Anderson from Detroit for a draft choice.
- Derek Sanderson traded to the Rangers for Walt McKechnie.

1974-75 **STANDINGS**

PRINCE OF WALES CONFERENCE

Adams Division	W	L	T	P	GF	GA
Buffalo	49	16	15	113	354	240
Boston	40	26	14	94	345	245
Toronto	31	33	16	78	280	309
California	19	48	13	51	212	316
Norris Division						
Montreal	47	14	19	113	374	225
Los Angeles	42	17	21	105	269	185
Pittsburgh	37	28	15	89	326	289
Detroit	23	45	12	58	259	335
Washington	8	67	5	21	181	446

CLARENCE CAMPBELL CONFERENCE
Patrick Division

Philadelphia	51	18	11	113	293	181
New York Rangers	37	29	14	88	319	276
New York Islanders	33	25	22	88	264	221
Atlanta	34	31	15	83	243	233

Smythe Division

Vancouver	38	32	10	86	271	254
St. Louis	35	31	14	84	269	267
Chicago	37	35	8	82	268	241
Minnesota	23	50	7	53	221	241
Kansas City	15	54	11	41	184	328

1974-75 RESULTS

October 1974

	AT	VERSUS	W-L-T	SCR
10	Buffalo	Sabres	L	9–5
13	Boston	Toronto	T	2–2
16	Chicago	Blackhawks	L	4–0
17	Philadelphia	Flyers	W	4–1
20	Boston	California	W	5–0
23	Pittsburgh	Penguins	T	5–5
24	Boston	St. Louis	T	4–4
27	Boston	Kansas City	W	8–2
30	Minnesota	North Stars	T	3–3

November 1974

2	New York	Islanders	L	3–2
3	Boston	Minnesota	W	10–1
5	Boston	Buffalo	T	2–2
7	Boston	Washington	W	10–4
10	Boston	Atlanta	W	4–3
12	St. Louis	Blues	L	4–3
14	Boston	Montreal	L	4–1
16	Boston	Buffalo	W	7–5
17	Detroit	Red Wings	W	5–2
21	Boston	California	W	4–2
23	New York	Rangers	W	5–2
24	Boston	Vancouver	W	7–4
27	California	Seals	W	3–1
30	Los Angeles	Kings	L	2–0

December 1974

4	Montreal	Canadiens	T	4–4
5	Boston	Detroit	L	6–4
8	Boston	Pittsburgh	W	3–2
10	Kansas City	Scouts	W	6–2
12	Boston	Los Angeles	W	8–1
14	Boston	Washington	W	12–1
15	Boston	New York Islanders	W	5–2
17	Boston	Atlanta	W	5–3
19	Boston	New York Rangers	W	11–3
21	Toronto	Maple Leafs	L	8–4

22	Boston	Detroit	W	5–4
27	California	Seals	L	5–2
28	Vancouver	Canucks	L	6–4

January 1975

2	Los Angeles	Kings	W	5–2
4	Minnesota	North Stars	W	8–0
7	Washington	Capitals	T	3–3
9	Boston	Vancouver	W	5–1
11	Boston	Chicago	W	5–1
15	Montreal	Canadiens	L	5–3
16	Boston	Los Angeles	L	4–1
18	Pittsburgh	Penguins	T	4–4
19	Boston	Toronto	W	6–3
23	Boston	Kansas City	L	3–2
26	Boston	Philadelphia	T	2–2
27	Kansas City	Scouts	T	3–3
30	Boston	California	W	6–0

February 1975

1	Toronto	Maple Leafs	L	3–2
2	Boston	Philadelphia	W	5–1
5	Atlanta	Flames	T	3–3
6	Boston	Minnesota	W	3–2
8	Detroit	Red Wings	W	8–5
9	Boston	New York Islanders	W	5–1
12	Chicago	Blackhawks	L	8–3
13	Buffalo	Sabres	L	3–1
16	Philadelphia	Flyers	L	4–3
18	Vancouver	Canucks	W	3–1
21	California	Seals	L	6–4
22	Los Angeles	Kings	L	6–0
25	Boston	Pittsburgh	W	6–4
27	Boston	Detroit	W	9–4

March 1975

2	Boston	Chicago	W	6–2
4	Washington	Capitals	W	8–0
7	Atlanta	Flames	W	4–2

9	Boston	Atlanta	W	5–2
11	Boston	New York Rangers	W	6–3
12	Pittsburgh	Penguins	L	5–3
15	New York	Islanders	L	3–1
16	Boston	St. Louis	W	7–2
19	Montreal	Canadiens	L	2–1
22	Boston	Washington	W	8–2
23	New York	Rangers	L	7–5

26	St. Louis	Blues	L	3–1
29	Toronto	Maple Leafs	T	1–1
30	Boston	Montreal	T	2–2

April 1975

1	Boston	Buffalo	L	3–1
3	Buffalo	Sabres	L	4–2
6	Boston	Toronto	T	4–4

1974-75 SCORING

	W	L	T	S	GAA	PIM
Ross Brooks	10	3	3	0	2.98	0
Gilles Gilbert	23	17	11	3	3.13	10
						1 assist
Ken Broderick	7	6	0	1	2.39	2

	G	A	P	PIM
Bobby Orr	46	89	135	101
Phil Esposito	61	66	127	62
Johnny Bucyk	29	52	81	10
Greg Sheppard	30	48	78	19
Carol Vadnais	18	56	74	129
Ken Hodge	23	43	66	90
Don Marcotte	31	33	64	76
Bobby Schmautz	21	30	51	63
Andre Savard	19	25	44	45

Terry O'Reilly	15	20	35	146
Wayne Cashman	11	22	33	24
Dave Forbes	18	12	30	80
Dallas Smith	3	20	23	84
Al Sims	4	8	12	73
Hank Nowak	4	7	11	26
Darryl Edestrand	1	9	10	56
Walt McKechnie	3	3	6	8
Earl Anderson	2	4	6	4
Dave Hynes	4	0	4	2
Rod Graham	2	1	3	7
Steve Langdon	0	1	1	0
Gordie Clark	0	0	0	0
Jack Rathwell	0	0	0	0
Craig Sarner	0	0	0	0
Gary Doak	0	0	0	30

Number of power play advantages	299
Power play goals	86
% successful	28.8%
Phil Esposito	27
Bobby Orr	16
Ken Hodge	16
Johnny Bucyk	9
Carol Vadnais	6
Greg Sheppard	5
Terry O'Reilly	2
Wayne Cashman	2
Walt McKechnie	1
Don Marcotte	1
Bobby Schmautz	1

Short-handed goals against	10
Penalty minutes:	1,153 – 14.4 per game
Times short-handed	316
Power play goals against	59
Penalty kill success	81.3%
Short-handed goals	14
Greg Sheppard	7
Phil Esposito	4
Bobby Orr	2
Walt McKechnie	1

1974-75 PLAYOFF RESULTS

April 1975

	AT	VERSUS	W-L-T	SCR
8	Boston	Chicago	W	8–2
10	Chicago	Blackhawks	L	4–3 (OT)
11	Boston	Chicago	L	6–4

1974-75 PLAYOFFS

vs. Chicago Blackhawks	1 win – 2 losses
at Chicago	0 wins – 1 loss
at Boston	1 win – 1 loss

1974-75 PLAYOFF SCORING

	W	L	SO	GAA	PIM
Gilles Gilbert	1	2	0	3.83	0

	G	A	P	PIM
Carol Vadnais	1	5	6	0
Bobby Orr	1	5	6	2
Bobby Schmautz	1	5	6	6
Phil Esposito	4	1	5	0
Greg Sheppard	3	1	4	5
Andre Savard	1	1	2	2
Ken Hodge	1	1	2	0
Wayne Cashman	0	2	2	0
Dallas Smith	0	2	2	4
Johnny Bucyk	1	0	1	0
Don Marcotte	1	0	1	0
Hank Nowak	1	0	1	0
Darryl Edestrand	0	1	1	7
Earl Anderson	0	1	1	0
Gary Doak	0	0	0	4
Terry O'Reilly	0	0	0	17
Dave Forbes	0	0	0	0

Power play goals for	2
Power play goals against	4
Short-handed goals for	1
Short-handed goals against	0
Penalty minutes:	47 – 15.6 per game

1975–1976
(52nd year)

TEAM OWNER:	Sportsystems of Buffalo
PRESIDENT & GOVERNOR:	Paul Mooney
GM:	Harry Sinden
COACH:	Don Cherry
ATTENDANCE:	570,287
	14,257 per game
PLAYOFFS:	*Quarter finals:*
	Defeat Los Angeles Kings
	4 wins – 3 losses
	Semi-finals:
	Lose to Philadelphia Flyers
	1 win – 4 losses

STANLEY CUP WINNER:	Montreal Canadiens
ALL-STARS:	Brad Park (1st team)
TROPHY WINNERS:	Lady Byng — Jean Ratelle
	Adams — Don Cherry
	Dufresne — Greg Sheppard
	7th Player — Greg Sheppard
	Three Star — Jean Ratelle
RADIO BROADCASTER:	WBZ – Bob Wilson
TV BROADCASTER:	WSBK TV38 – Fred Cusick,
	John Peirson

UNIFORMS

- Home jersey is white with gold and black trim. Socks are white with one gold band surrounded by two black bands at the calf. Road jersey is black with gold and white trim. Gold socks with one white band surrounded by two black bands at the calf. Logo is the spoked "B."
- Pants are black with white trim on side.

- Bruins uniforms have Massachusetts bi-centennial patch on both shoulders.

POTPOURRI
- Don Cherry wins coach of the year award.
- Bruins win the Adams Division with 113 points.
- Bruins defeat Los Angeles, 4 games to 3 in the quarter-final series.
- Bruins enjoy a 20-game home undefeated streak.
- After one of the biggest trades in NHL history, the Bruins only lose 10 of their final 68 games.
- Johnny Bucyk scores his 500th career goal.
- Bobby Orr, limited to only 10 games, plays his last game for the Bruins as he is forced to have 2 knee operations.
- Bruins lose to Philadelphia, 4 games to 1 in the semi-finals.
- Darryl Sittler scores 6 goals against Boston at Toronto on February 7.
- In a playoff loss to Philadelphia on May 6, Reggie Leach scores 5 goals.
- Bobby Schmautz misses a penalty shot on November 2 at Boston against Gary Simmons of the California Seals.
- In a January 10 game at Boston, Wayne King of the California Seals is unsuccessful in a penalty shot attempt against Gilles Gilbert.
- Sportsystems of Buffalo, New York, purchase the Boston Garden and Boston Bruins from Storer Broadcasting for $10,000,000.

TRANSACTIONS
- Bruins obtain Brad Park, Jean Ratelle, and Joe Zanussi for Phil Esposito and Carol Vadnais.
- Bruins make Doug Halward their #1 pick in the 1975 amateur draft.

1975-76 STANDINGS

PRINCE OF WALES CONFERENCE

Adams Division	W	L	T	P	GF	GA
Boston	48	15	17	113	313	237
Buffalo	46	21	13	105	339	240
Toronto	34	31	15	83	294	276
California	27	42	11	65	250	278
Norris Division						
Montreal	58	11	11	127	337	174
Los Angeles	38	33	9	85	263	265
Pittsburgh	35	33	12	82	339	303
Detroit	26	44	10	62	226	300
Washington	11	59	10	32	224	394

CLARENCE CAMPBELL CONFERENCE

Patrick Division	W	L	T	P	GF	GA
Philadelphia	51	13	16	118	348	209
New York Islanders	42	21	17	101	297	190
Atlanta	35	33	12	82	262	237
New York Rangers	29	42	9	67	262	333
Smythe Division						
Chicago	32	30	18	82	254	261
Vancouver	33	32	15	81	271	272
St. Louis	29	37	14	72	249	290
Minnesota	20	53	7	47	195	303
Kansas City	12	56	12	36	190	351

BRUINS PLAY TEN PRE-SEASON GAMES

Bruins and the Philadelphia Flyers, Stanley Cup finalists, will square off Friday night, Sept. 20, at the Spectrum, in the first of 10 pre-season games for Boston.

Montreal Canadiens will be the opposition in four pre-season games, including two at Boston Garden. The first home game is slated for Thurs. night, Sept. 26, the second on Sun. night, Sept. 29th.

The third and final home pre-season game will be Mon. night, Oct. 7, against New York Rangers.

Bruins will make two other New England appearances: Fri. night, Sept. 27 with Rangers at Providence Civic Ctr. and Tues. night, Oct. 1, against Chicago at Springfield Civic Ctr., in the second game of a doubleheader — Rochester Americans and Springfield Kings meet in the preliminary.

BRUINS PRE-SEASON SCHEDULE
(All Starting Times are Boston Time)

Fri., Sept. 20—Bruins vs. Philadelphia, at Spectrum	8:05 p.m.
Sat., Sept. 21—Bruins vs. Montreal, at The Forum	8:05 p.m.
Mon., Sept. 23—Bruins vs. N.Y. Rangers, at Madison Sq. Garden	7:35 p.m.
Thurs., Sept. 26—Bruins vs. Montreal, at Boston Garden	7:35 p.m.
Fri., Sept. 27—Bruins vs. N.Y. Rangers, at Prov. Civic Ctr.	7:30 p.m.
Sun., Sept. 29—Bruins vs. Montreal, at Boston Garden	7:35 p.m.
Tues., Oct. 1—Bruins vs. Chicago, at Springfield Civic Ctr.	9:00 p.m.
Rochester Americans vs. Springfield Kings	7:00 p.m.
Thurs., Oct. 3—Bruins vs. Montreal, at Moncton, N.B.	7:05 p.m.
Sat., Oct. 5—Bruins vs. Chicago, at Chicago Stadium	8:30 p.m.
Mon., Oct. 7—Bruins vs. N.Y. Rangers, at Boston Garden	7:35 p.m.

READY TO START—Bruins Managing Director Harry Sinden, Coach Don Cherry and Tom Johnson, Asst. to Managing Director

Boston Bruins Hockey Bulletin

BOSTON GARDEN

NORTH STATION, BOSTON, MASS. 02114

ADDRESS CORRECTION REQUESTED

1975-76 RESULTS

October 1975

	AT	VERSUS	W-L-T	SCR
9	Boston	Montreal	L	9–4
12	Boston	New York Islanders	T	3–3
16	Detroit	Red Wings	T	2–2
18	New York	Islanders	W	5–2
19	Boston	Toronto	W	3–0
23	Boston	Kansas City	L	3–2
25	Montreal	Canadiens	L	6–2
26	Boston	Detroit	W	7–3
30	Boston	St. Louis	W	3–2

November 1975

1	Philadelphia	Flyers	L	8–1
2	Boston	California	W	5–0
5	Buffalo	Sabres	L	4–0
8	Vancouver	Canucks	L	4–2
9	California	Seals	W	6–3
13	Boston	Minnesota	W	6–0
15	Atlanta	Flames	W	5–3
16	Boston	Kansas City	W	4–2
19	Detroit	Red Wings	T	3–3
20	Boston	New York Islanders	T	2–2
23	Boston	Toronto	T	3–3
25	Boston	Los Angeles	W	4–2
26	New York	Rangers	W	6–4
29	Chicago	Blackhawks	T	4–4
30	Boston	Pittsburgh	W	4–2

December 1975

4	Boston	Washington	W	3–2
6	Toronto	Maple Leafs	W	4–2
7	Boston	Montreal	T	2–2
11	Boston	New York Rangers	L	5–1
13	Pittsburgh	Penguins	T	4–4
14	Boston	Vancouver	W	3–2
17	Washington	Capitals	W	3–2
20	Boston	Buffalo	W	5–3
21	Boston	Atlanta	L	2–1
23	Boston	Los Angeles	L	4–3
26	Buffalo	Sabres	W	6–3
28	Philadelphia	Flyers	W	4–2
31	Minnesota	North Stars	W	6–1

January 1976

2	Vancouver	Canucks	T	4–4
3	Los Angeles	Kings	W	3–0
10	Boston	California	W	3–2
11	Washington	Capitals	W	7–4
13	Boston	Pittsburgh	W	6–2
15	Boston	Los Angeles	W	4–0
17	St. Louis	Blues	L	7–5
22	Boston	Buffalo	W	5–3
24	Detroit	Red Wings	W	6–1
25	Boston	Philadelphia	W	5–3
29	Boston	Chicago	W	5–3
30	Atlanta	Flames	W	4–2

February 1976

1	Boston	Atlanta	W	5–3
5	Boston	Pittsburgh	W	5–1
7	Toronto	Maple Leafs	L	11–4
8	Boston	Detroit	W	7–0
11	Minnesota	North Stars	W	5–2
13	California	Seals	W	6–5
15	Chicago	Blackhawks	W	4–1
18	Kansas City	Scouts	T	3–3
21	New York	Islanders	W	2–1
22	New York	Rangers	W	5–2
26	Boston	St. Louis	W	4–2
27	Washington	Capitals	T	3–3
29	Boston	Vancouver	W	5–3

March 1976

3	Los Angeles	Kings	W	5–3
5	California	Seals	L	4–3
7	Boston	Washington	W	4–3
9	Atlanta	Flames	L	9–0
11	Boston	Toronto	W	6–2
13	Montreal	Canadiens	L	4–2
14	Boston	California	W	4–2
16	St. Louis	Blues	T	3–3
18	Kansas City	Scouts	W	5–2
20	Boston	New York Rangers	W	8–1
24	Pittsburgh	Penguins	T	5–5
25	Boston	Chicago	W	4–2
27	Boston	Philadelphia	T	4–4
28	Boston	Montreal	T	2–2
30	Boston	Buffalo	T	4–4

April 1976

1	Buffalo	Sabres	L	7–2
3	Toronto	Maple Leafs	W	4–2
4	Boston	Minnesota	T	2–2

1975-76 SCORING

	W	L	T	S	GAA	PIM
Gilles Gilbert	33	8	10	3	2.90	18
Gerry Cheevers	8	2	5	1	2.73	2
Dave Reece	7	5	2	2	3.32	0

	G	A	P	PIM
Jean Ratelle	31	59	90	16
Johnny Bucyk	36	47	83	20
Greg Sheppard	31	43	74	28
Wayne Cashman	28	43	71	87
Bobby Schmautz	28	34	62	116
Ken Hodge	25	36	61	42
Brad Park	16	37	53	95
Terry O'Reilly	23	27	50	150
Andre Savard	17	23	40	60
Don Marcotte	16	20	36	24
Dallas Smith	7	25	32	103
Dave Forbes	16	13	29	52
Doug Gibson	7	18	25	0
Darryl Edestrand	4	17	21	103

	G	A	P	PIM
Bobby Orr	5	13	18	22
Phil Esposito	6	10	16	8
Hank Nowak	7	3	10	41
Joe Zanussi	1	7	8	30
Al Sims	4	3	7	43
Carol Vadnais	2	5	7	17
Gary Doak	1	6	7	60
Doug Halward	1	5	6	6
Barry Smith	1	0	1	2
Kent Ruhnke	0	1	1	0
Earl Anderson	0	1	1	2
Gordie Clark	0	1	1	0
Al Simmons	0	1	1	21
Paul O'Neil	0	0	0	0
Rick Adduono	0	0	0	0
Stan Jonathan	0	0	0	0
Ray Maluta	0	0	0	2
Mike Milbury	0	0	0	9
Steve Langdon	0	0	0	2

Number of power play advantages	289
Power play goals	77
% successful	26.6%
Jean Ratelle	15
Johnny Bucyk	13
Wayne Cashman	9
Ken Hodge	8
Bobby Schmautz	7
Brad Park	7
Greg Sheppard	5
Bobby Orr	3
Phil Esposito	3
Terry O'Reilly	2
Don Marcotte	1
Doug Gibson	1

Darryl Edestrand	1
Carol Vadnais	1
Doug Halward	1
Short-handed goals against	6
Penalty minutes: 1,195 – 14.9 per game	
Times short-handed	345
Power play goals against	56
Penalty kill success	83.8%
Short-handed goals	9
Dave Forbes	4
Greg Sheppard	2
Jean Ratelle	1
Brad Park	1
Bobby Orr	1

1975-76 PLAYOFF RESULTS

April 1976

	AT	VERSUS	W-L-T	SCR
11	Boston	Los Angeles	W	4–0
13	Boston	Los Angeles	L	3–2 (OT)
15	Los Angeles	Kings	L	6–4
17	Los Angeles	Kings	W	3–0
20	Boston	Los Angeles	W	7–1
22	Los Angeles	Kings	L	4–3

	AT	VERSUS	W-L-T	SCR
25	Boston	Los Angeles	W	3–0
27	Philadelphia	Flyers	W	4–2
29	Philadelphia	Flyers	2–1 (OT)	

May 1976

	AT	VERSUS	W-L-T	SCR
2	Boston	Philadelphia	L	5–2
4	Boston	Philadelphia	L	4–2
6	Philadelphia	Flyers	L	6–3

1975-76 PLAYOFFS

vs. Los Angeles Kings	4 wins – 3 losses	vs. Philadelphia Flyers	1 win – 4 losses
at Los Angeles	1 win – 2 losses	at Philadelphia	1 win – 2 losses
at Boston	3 wins – 1 loss	at Boston	0 wins – 2 losses

1975-76 PLAYOFF SCORING

	W	L	SO	GAA	PIM
Gilles Gilbert	3	3	2	3.17	2
Gerry Cheevers	2	4	1	2.14	0

	G	A	P	PIM
Jean Ratelle	8	8	16	4
Greg Sheppard	5	6	11	6
Brad Park	3	8	11	14
Ken Hodge	4	6	10	4
Bobby Schmautz	2	8	10	13
Johnny Bucyk	2	7	9	0
Don Marcotte	4	2	6	8
Wayne Cashman	1	5	6	16
Andre Savard	1	4	5	9
Terry O'Reilly	3	1	4	25
Dallas Smith	2	2	4	19
Darryl Edestrand	1	3	4	23
Dave Forbes	1	1	2	5
Gary Doak	1	0	1	22
Joe Zanussi	0	1	1	2
Doug Halward	0	0	0	0
Gordie Clark	0	0	0	0
Ray Maluta	0	0	0	0
Steve Langdon	0	0	0	0
Hank Nowak	0	0	0	8
Mike Milbury	0	0	0	29

Power play goals for	14
Power play goals against	6
Short-handed goals for	2
Short-handed goals against	0
Penalty minutes: 209 – 17.4 per game	

1976–1977
(53rd year)

TEAM OWNER:	Sportsystems of Buffalo	*Stanley Cup finals:*	
PRESIDENT & GOVERNOR:	Paul Mooney		Lose to Montreal Canadiens
GM:	Harry Sinden		0 wins – 4 losses
COACH:	Don Cherry	STANLEY CUP WINNER:	Montreal Canadiens
ATTENDANCE:	469,823	ALL-STARS:	None
	11,745 per game	TROPHY WINNERS:	Lester Patrick —
PLAYOFFS:	*Quarter finals:*		Johnny Bucyk
	Defeat Los Angeles Kings		Dufresne — Jean Ratelle
	4 wins – 2 losses		7th Player — Gary Doak
	Semi-finals:		Three Star — Jean Ratelle
	Defeat Philadelphia	RADIO BROADCASTER:	WBZ – Bob Wilson
	Flyers	TV BROADCASTER:	WSBK TV38 – Fred Cusick,
	4 wins – 0 losses		John Peirson

UNIFORMS

- Home jersey is white with gold and black trim. Socks are white with one gold band surrounded by two black bands at the calf. Road jersey is black with gold and white trim. Gold socks with one white band surrounded by two black bands at the calf. Logo is the spoked "B." Pants are black with white trim on side. Bearhead appears for the first time on both shoulders on both home and road uniforms.

POTPOURRI

- Finish in first place in the Adams Division.
- Johnny Bucyk is a co-winner of the Lester Patrick Trophy.
- Bruins defeat Los Angeles, 4 games to 2, in the quarter-final series of the Stanley Cup playoffs.
- Bruins defeat Philadelphia, 4 games to 0, in the semi-finals of the Stanley Cup playoffs.
- Jean Ratelle plays in his 1000th career game.
- Bruins lose to Montreal, 4 games to 0, in the Stanley Cup finals.
- In June of 1976, Bobby Orr signs as a free agent with the Chicago Blackhawks.
- Gilles Gilbert stops Bill Lochead on a penalty shot attempt.
- California Seals transfer to Cleveland and become the Cleveland Barons.
- Kansas City Scouts transfer to Denver and become the Colorado Rockies.
- Mike Milbury, with 166 penalty minutes, breaks the record held by Eddie Shore.

TRANSACTIONS

- Bruins make Clayton Pachal their #1 pick in the 1976 universal draft.
- Obtain Rick Smith from St. Louis for Joe Zanussi.
- Trade Andre Savard to Buffalo for Peter McNab.
- Trade Ken Hodge to the Rangers for Rick Middleton.

1976-77 **STANDINGS**

PRINCE OF WALES CONFERENCE

Adams Division

	W	L	T	P	GF	GA
Boston	49	23	8	106	312	240
Buffalo	48	24	8	104	301	220
Toronto	33	32	15	81	301	285
Cleveland	25	42	13	63	240	292

Norris Division

	W	L	T	P	GF	GA
Montreal	60	8	12	132	387	171
Los Angeles	34	31	15	83	271	241
Pittsburgh	34	33	13	81	240	252
Washington	24	42	14	62	221	307
Detroit	16	55	9	41	183	309

CLARENCE CAMPBELL CONFERENCE

Patrick Division

	W	L	T	P	GF	GA
Philadelphia	48	16	16	112	323	213
New York Islanders	47	21	12	106	288	193
Atlanta	34	34	12	80	264	265
New York Rangers	29	37	14	72	272	310

Smythe Division

	W	L	T	P	GF	GA
St. Louis	32	39	9	73	239	276
Minnesota	23	39	18	64	240	310
Chicago	26	43	11	63	240	298
Vancouver	25	42	13	63	235	294
Colorado	20	46	14	54	226	307

1976-77 **RESULTS**

October 1976

	AT	VERSUS	W-L-T	SCR
7	Boston	Minnesota	W	6–2
9	Toronto	Maple Leafs	L	7–5
10	Boston	Cleveland	W	4–3
13	New York	Rangers	W	5–1
15	Boston	Toronto	W	5–3
17	Boston	Montreal	W	5–3
19	St. Louis	Blues	L	6–5
20	Colorado	Rockies	W	2–1
23	Los Angeles	Kings	W	4–2
26	New York	Rangers	W	4–3
30	Montreal	Canadiens	W	4–3
31	Buffalo	Sabres	L	4–1

November 1976

4	Boston	Chicago	W	7–5
7	Boston	Vancouver	W	3–1
10	Detroit	Red Wings	W	6–4
11	Boston	New York Islanders	T	2–2
14	Boston	Colorado	W	5–3
18	Boston	Washington	W	3–2
19	Washington	Capitals	W	4–1
21	Boston	Detroit	W	4–2
24	Pittsburgh	Penguins	W	4–0
25	Boston	Vancouver	W	4–2
27	Toronto	Maple Leafs	L	4–2
30	Boston	Buffalo	L	6–2

December 1976

1	Chicago	Blackhawks	W	5–3
3	Atlanta	Flames	L	3–1
5	Boston	Washington	T	5–5
9	Boston	Philadelphia	L	3–1
11	Philadelphia	Flyers	L	4–3
12	Boston	Detroit	L	5–3
16	Boston	St. Louis	W	5–2
18	Cleveland	Barons	L	6–4
19	Boston	Pittsburgh	W	6–3
21	New York	Islanders	L	3–0
23	Boston	New York Rangers	T	3–3
26	Boston	Cleveland	W	6–3
29	Vancouver	Canucks	W	8–1

January 1977

1	Los Angeles	Kings	L	5–2
5	Cleveland	Barons	W	3–2
8	Minnesota	North Stars	L	3–1
9	Chicago	Blackhawks	W	4–2
11	Washington	Capitals	W	3–2
13	Boston	Los Angeles	W	4–3
15	Boston	Minnesota	T	3–3
17	Boston	Montreal	W	7–3
20	Boston	New York Islanders	L	4–3
21	Cleveland	Barons	W	5–2
23	Boston	Atlanta	W	3–0
27	Boston	Colorado	L	6–4
29	Boston	Toronto	T	3–3
30	Pittsburgh	Penguins	L	5–2

February 1977

1	St. Louis	Blues	T	3–3
3	Boston	St. Louis	W	5–4
4	Atlanta	Flames	L	6–3
6	Boston	Washington	W	5–2
10	Buffalo	Sabres	L	4–3
12	Montreal	Canadiens	L	8–3
13	Boston	Cleveland	W	4–2
16	Vancouver	Canucks	W	7–3
19	Los Angeles	Kings	L	2–0
23	Minnesota	North Stars	L	2–1
25	Colorado	Rockies	W	5–2
27	Pittsburgh	Penguins	T	2–2

March 1977

1	Boston	Detroit	W	8–3
3	New York	Rangers	W	4–1
5	Boston	Buffalo	W	3–1
6	Boston	Chicago	W	6–2
8	Boston	Atlanta	W	3–2
10	Boston	New York Rangers	W	10–3
12	Philadelphia	Flyers	W	3–1
13	Boston	Los Angeles	T	2–2
17	Boston	Buffalo	W	4–2
21	Boston	Montreal	L	5–1
23	Detroit	Red Wings	W	6–0
24	Boston	Philadelphia	L	6–2
26	Toronto	Maple Leafs	W	7–5
27	Boston	Pittsburgh	W	3–0
30	Buffalo	Sabres	W	4–3

April 1977

2	New York	Islanders	W	5–3
3	Boston	Toronto	W	7–4

1976-77 SCORING

	W	L	T	S	GAA	PIM
Gilles Gilbert	18	13	3	1	2.85	15
						1 assist
Gerry Cheevers	30	10	5	3	3.04	46
						4 assists
Jim Pettie	1	0	0	0	3.00	

	G	A	P	PIM
Jean Ratelle	33	61	94	22
Peter McNab	38	48	86	11
Greg Sheppard	31	36	67	20
Brad Park	12	55	67	67
Terry O'Reilly	14	41	55	147
Bobby Schmautz	23	29	52	62
Wayne Cashman	15	37	52	76
Don Marcotte	27	18	45	20
Johnny Bucyk	20	23	43	12
Rick Middleton	20	22	42	2
Stan Jonathan	17	13	30	69
Matti Hagman	11	17	28	0
Mike Milbury	6	18	24	166
Rick Smith	6	16	22	30
Dallas Smith	2	20	22	40
Earl Anderson	10	11	21	4
Dave Forbes	9	11	20	47
Gary Doak	3	13	16	107
Hank Nowak	7	5	12	14
John Wensink	4	6	10	32
Ray Maluta	2	3	5	4
Doug Halward	2	2	4	6
Darryl Edestrand	0	3	3	16
Joe Zanussi	0	1	1	8
Clayton Pachal	0	0	0	12
Al Sims	0	0	0	0

Number of power play advantages	217
Power play goals	46
% successful	21.2%
Jean Ratelle	8
Greg Sheppard	8
Peter McNab	6
Johnny Bucyk	6
Brad Park	4
Bobby Schmautz	4
Wayne Cashman	3
Don Marcotte	3
Terry O'Reilly	1
Stan Jonathan	1
Matti Hagman	1
Earl Anderson	1

Short-handed goals against	10
Penalty minutes:	1,065 – 13.3 per game
Times short-handed	272
Power play goals against	42
Penalty kill success	84.9%
Short-handed goals	7
Dave Forbes	2
Jean Ratelle	1
Greg Sheppard	1
Brad Park	1
Terry O'Reilly	1
Don Marcotte	1

1976-77 PLAYOFF RESULTS

April 1977

	AT	VERSUS	W-L-T	SCR
11	Boston	Los Angeles	W	8–3
13	Boston	Los Angeles	W	6–2
15	Los Angeles	Kings	W	7–6
17	Los Angeles	Kings	L	7–4
19	Boston	Los Angeles	L	3–1
21	Los Angeles	Kings	W	4–3
24	Philadelphia	Flyers	W	4–3 (OT)
26	Philadelphia	Flyers	W	5–4 (OT)
28	Boston	Philadelphia	W	2–1

May 1977

1	Boston	Philadelphia	W	3–0
7	Montreal	Canadiens	L	7–3
10	Montreal	Canadiens	L	3–0
12	Boston	Montreal	L	4–2
14	Boston	Montreal	L	2–1 (OT)

1976-77 PLAYOFFS

vs. Los Angeles Kings	4 wins – 2 losses	vs. Montreal Canadiens	0 wins – 4 losses
at Los Angeles	2 wins – 1 loss	at Montreal	0 wins – 2 losses
at Boston	2 wins – 1 loss	at Boston	0 wins – 2 losses
vs. Philadelphia Flyers	4 wins – 0 losses		
at Philadelphia	2 wins – 0 losses		
at Boston	2 wins – 0 losses		

1976-77 PLAYOFF SCORING

	W	L	SO	GAA	PIM
Gilles Gilbert	0	0	0	9.00	0
Gerry Cheevers	8	6	1	3.08	4

	G	A	P	PIM
Jean Ratelle	5	12	17	4
Bobby Schmautz	11	1	12	10
Greg Sheppard	5	7	12	8
Brad Park	2	10	12	4
Don Marcotte	5	6	11	10
Terry O'Reilly	5	6	11	28
Rick Middleton	5	4	9	0
Wayne Cashman	1	8	9	18
Rick Smith	0	9	9	14
Peter McNab	5	3	8	2
Stan Jonathan	4	2	6	24
Mike Milbury	2	2	4	47
John Wensink	0	3	3	8
Gary Doak	0	2	2	26
Matti Hagman	0	1	1	0
Dave Forbes	0	1	1	2

Al Sims	0	0	0	0
Earl Anderson	0	0	0	0
Darryl Edestrand	0	0	0	2
Johnny Bucyk	0	0	0	0
Doug Halward	0	0	0	4

Number of power play advantages	52
Power play goals	8
% successful	15.4%
Bobby Schmautz	4
Peter McNab	2
Jean Ratelle	1
Greg Sheppard	1
Short-handed goals against	0
Penalty minutes: 217 – 15.5 per game	
Times short-handed	57
Power play goals against	16
Penalty kill success	69.4%
Short-handed goals	2
Greg Sheppard	1
Don Marcotte	1

1977–1978
(54th year)

TEAM OWNER:	Sportsystems of Buffalo	*Stanley Cup finals:*	
PRESIDENT & GOVERNOR:	Paul Mooney	Lose to Montreal Canadiens	
GM:	Harry Sinden	2 wins – 4 losses	
COACH:	Don Cherry	STANLEY CUP WINNER:	Montreal Canadiens
ATTENDANCE:	494,744	ALL-STARS:	Brad Park (1st team)
	12,368 per game	TROPHY WINNERS:	Dufresne — Terry O'Reilly
PLAYOFFS:	*Quarter finals:*		& Brad Park
	Defeat Chicago Blackhawks		7th Player — Stan Jonathan
	4 wins – 0 losses		Three Star — Terry O'Reilly
	Semi-finals:	RADIO BROADCASTER:	WBZ – Bob Wilson
	Defeat Philadelphia Flyers	TV BROADCASTER:	WSBK TV38 – Fred Cusick,
	4 wins – 1 loss		John Peirson

UNIFORMS

- Home jersey is white with gold and black trim. Socks are white with one gold band surrounded by two black bands at the calf. Road jersey is black with gold and white trim. Gold socks with one white band surrounded by two black bands at the calf. Logo is the spoked "B." Pants are black with white trim on side.
- Bearhead appears on both shoulders on both home and road uniforms.
- Players names to be worn on the back of all uniforms becomes mandatory.

POTPOURRI

- Bruins finish in first place in the Adams Division with 113 points.
- Bruins defeat Chicago, 4 games to 0, in the quarter-final series for the Stanley Cup.
- Bruins defeat Philadelphia, 4 games to 1, in the semi-final series.
- Wayne Cashman has 4-goal game against the Rangers on April 2.
- Gilles Gilbert has a 196-minute 13-second shutout string.
- Bruins lose to Montreal, 4 games to 2, in the Stanley Cup finals.
- Bruins have an 11-game home winning streak.
- Bruins play penalty-free game on February 21 against Colorado.
- Clarence Campbell retires as President of the National Hockey League and is replaced by John Ziegler.
- Bruins have no penalty shots taken against them nor do they take any this season.
- Bruins enjoy a shutout streak of 223 minutes and 45 seconds from 1:34 of the third period on November 19 against Toronto until 5:19 of the first period November 26 against the Rangers. The streak includes shutouts against Chicago, Buffalo, and Washington.
- Dennis O'Brien becomes the first player in NHL history to play for 4 teams in 1 season. He played with Minnesota, Cleveland, Colorado, and the Bruins.
- Terry O'Reilly becomes the only player in league history to earn 200 or more penalty minutes and finish in the top 10 in scoring.

TRANSACTIONS

- Bruins make Dwight Foster their #1 pick in the 1977 entry draft.
- Claim Dennis O'Brien on waivers from the Cleveland Barons.
- Sign goaltender Ron Grahame as a free agent.

1977-78 STANDINGS

PRINCE OF WALES CONFERENCE

Adams Division	W	L	T	P	GF	GA
Boston	51	18	11	113	333	218
Buffalo	44	19	17	105	288	215
Toronto	41	29	10	92	271	237
Cleveland	22	45	13	57	230	325
Norris Division						
Montreal	59	10	11	129	359	183
Detroit	32	34	14	78	252	266
Los Angeles	31	34	15	77	243	245
Pittsburgh	25	37	18	68	254	321
Washington	17	49	14	48	195	321

CLARENCE CAMPBELL CONFERENCE

Patrick Division	W	L	T	P	GF	GA
New York Islanders	48	17	15	111	334	210
Philadelphia	45	20	15	105	296	200

Atlanta	34	27	19	87	274	252
New York Rangers	30	37	13	73	279	280
Smythe Division						
Chicago	32	29	19	83	230	220
Colorado	19	40	21	59	257	305
Vancouver	20	43	17	57	239	320
St. Louis	20	47	13	53	195	304
Minnesota	18	53	9	45	218	325

1977-78 **RESULTS**

October 1977

	AT	VERSUS	W-L-T	SCR
13	Boston	Atlanta	T	2–2
15	New York	Islanders	L	3–1
16	Boston	Montreal	L	2–0
19	St. Louis	Blues	W	7–3
22	Los Angeles	Kings	W	4–3
23	Vancouver	Canucks	T	3–3
25	Colorado	Rockies	T	4–4
26	Minnesota	North Stars	L	3–0
29	Pittsburgh	Penguins	W	5–3

November 1977

3	Boston	Buffalo	L	4–1
5	Montreal	Canadiens	L	5–2
6	Boston	New York Islanders	W	5–3
10	Boston	Los Angeles	W	5–2
12	Atlanta	Flames	W	6–3
13	Boston	Cleveland	W	3–1
17	Boston	Vancouver	T	4–4
19	Toronto	Maple Leafs	W	3–1
20	Boston	Chicago	W	1–0
23	Buffalo	Sabres	W	2–0
24	Boston	Washington	W	6–0
26	Boston	New York Rangers	W	3–2
27	Boston	St. Louis	W	4–1

December 1977

1	Boston	Minnesota	W	4–2
3	Cleveland	Barons	T	4–4
4	Boston	Toronto	W	3–1
8	Boston	Detroit	W	6–4
10	Boston	Pittsburgh	W	6–2
11	New York	Rangers	W	8–2
15	Philadelphia	Flyers	L	6–4
17	New York	Islanders	L	4–1
18	Boston	Cleveland	W	2–1
21	Boston	Colorado	W	6–3
23	Boston	Philadelphia	W	6–1
27	Washington	Capitals	W	6–3
28	Cleveland	Barons	T	5–5
31	Detroit	Red Wings	W	7–0

January 1978

4	Chicago	Blackhawks	W	3–0
7	Minnesota	North Stars	W	3–1
8	Buffalo	Sabres	L	5–3
10	Boston	New York Rangers	L	3–2
12	Boston	Los Angeles	W	6–1
14	Montreal	Canadiens	L	5–3
19	Boston	Washington	W	4–1
21	Boston	Detroit	W	7–1
22	Boston	Cleveland	L	3–2
26	Boston	Colorado	W	4–3
27	Washington	Capitals	W	5–2
29	Boston	Pittsburgh	W	8–2

February 1978

1	St. Louis	Blues	W	5–3
2	Buffalo	Sabres	L	3–1
4	Pittsburgh	Penguins	W	8–1
5	Boston	Toronto	T	3–3
9	Detroit	Red Wings	W	5–3
15	Toronto	Maple Leafs	W	4–2
18	Chicago	Blackhawks	L	4–2
21	Colorado	Rockies	W	3–2
22	Vancouver	Canucks	W	6–4
25	Los Angeles	Kings	W	4–2
28	Boston	Philadelphia	T	4–4

March 1977

2	Boston	Atlanta	W	4–3
4	Boston	Buffalo	W	7–3
5	Boston	Vancouver	W	6–3
7	Boston	St. Louis	W	7–2
9	Detroit	Red Wings	T	2–2
11	Philadelphia	Flyers	L	6–2
12	Boston	Los Angeles	W	9–3
16	Boston	Minnesota	W	7–2
18	New York	Rangers	W	6–3
19	Boston	Toronto	W	6–4
21	Cleveland	Barons	W	5–3
23	Boston	Chicago	W	7–0
25	Atlanta	Flames	L	6–3
26	Boston	Montreal	T	2–2
28	Washington	Capitals	T	4–4

30	Boston	Pittsburgh	W	6–3

April 1978				
1	Montreal	Canadiens	L	7–1

2	Boston	New York Rangers	W	8–3
6	Boston	Buffalo	L	5–2
8	Toronto	Maple Leafs	W	3–1
9	Boston	New York Islanders	L	5–2

1977-78 SCORING

	W	L	T	S	GAA	PIM
Gilles Gilbert	15	6	2	2	2.53	8
					1 assist	
Gerry Cheevers	10	15	2	1	2.65	14
					1 assist	
Jim Pettie	0	1	0	0	6.00	6
Ron Grahame	26	6	7	3	2.76	0
					1 assist	

	G	A	P	PIM
Terry O'Reilly	29	61	90	211
Jean Ratelle	25	59	84	10
Peter McNab	41	39	80	4
Brad Park	22	57	79	79
Wayne Cashman	24	38	62	69
Rick Middleton	25	35	60	8
Greg Sheppard	23	36	59	24
Bobby Schmautz	27	27	54	87

	G	A	P	PIM
Don Marcotte	20	34	54	16
Stan Jonathan	27	25	52	116
Bobby Miller	20	20	40	41
Mike Milbury	8	30	38	151
John Wensink	16	20	36	181
Rick Smith	7	29	36	69
Johnny Bucyk	5	13	18	4
Gary Doak	4	13	17	50
Al Sims	2	8	10	6
Matti Hagman	4	1	5	2
Dennis O'Brien	2	3	5	29
Mike Forbes	0	4	4	15
Dwight Foster	2	1	3	6
Doug Halward	0	2	2	2
Darryl Edestrand	0	0	0	0
Steve Langdon	0	0	0	0
Sean Shanahan	0	0	0	7
Clayton Pachal	0	0	0	14

Number of power play advantages	242
Power play goals	49
% successful	20.2%
Brad Park	9
Peter McNab	5
Terry O'Reilly	5
Greg Sheppard	5
Johnny Bucyk	5
Bobby Schmautz	4
Don Marcotte	4
Jean Ratelle	3
Matti Hagman	3
Rick Middleton	2
Wayne Cashman	1

Bobby Miller	1
John Wensink	1
Gary Doak	1
Short-handed goals against	2
Penalty minutes: 1,237 – 15.5 per game	
Times short-handed	296
Power play goals against	53
Penalty kill success	82.1%
Short-handed goals	7
Bobby Schmautz	3
Don Marcotte	2
Greg Sheppard	1
Bobby Miller	1

1977-78 PLAYOFF RESULTS

April 1978	AT	VERSUS	W-L-T	SCR
17	Boston	Chicago	W	6–1
19	Boston	Chicago	W	4–3 (OT)
21	Chicago	Blackhawks	W	4–3 (OT)
23	Chicago	Blackhawks	W	5–2

May 1978				
2	Boston	Philadelphia	W	3–2 (OT)
4	Boston	Philadelphia	W	7–5

7	Philadelphia	Flyers	L	3–1
9	Philadelphia	Flyers	W	4–2
11	Boston	Philadelphia	W	6–3
13	Montreal	Canadiens	L	4–1
16	Montreal	Canadiens	L	3–2 (OT)
18	Boston	Montreal	W	4–0
21	Boston	Montreal	W	4–3 (OT)
23	Montreal	Canadiens	L	4–1
25	Boston	Montreal	L	4–1

1977-78 PLAYOFFS

vs. Chicago Blackhawks	4 wins – 0 losses	vs. Montreal Canadiens	2 wins – 4 losses
at Chicago	2 wins – 0 losses	at Montreal	0 wins – 3 losses
at Boston	2 wins – 0 losses	at Boston	2 wins – 1 loss
vs. Philadelphia Flyers	4 wins – 1 loss		
at Philadelphia	1 win – 1 loss		
at Boston	3 wins – 0 losses		

1977-78 PLAYOFF SCORING

	W	L	SO	GAA	PIM
Gerry Cheevers	8	4	0	2.87	6
Ron Grahame	2	1	0	2.08	0

	G	A	P	PIM
Brad Park	9	11	20	14
Peter McNab	8	11	19	2
Bobby Schmautz	7	8	15	11
Terry O'Reilly	5	10	15	40
Greg Sheppard	2	10	12	6
Wayne Cashman	4	6	10	13
Jean Ratelle	3	7	10	0
Don Marcotte	5	4	9	8
Mike Milbury	1	8	9	27
Rick Middleton	5	2	7	0
Rick Smith	1	5	6	18
John Wensink	2	2	4	54
Bobby Miller	0	3	3	15
Gary Doak	1	0	1	4
Dennis O'Brien	0	1	1	28
Stan Jonathan	0	1	1	36
Al Sims	0	0	0	0

Bench minors	4	Short-handed goals against	0
Number of power play advantages	42	Penalty minutes:	286 – 19.0 per game
Power play goals	11	Time short-handed	54
% successful	26.2%	Power play goals against	11
Brad Park	4	Penalty kill success	79.6%
Wayne Cashman	3	No short-handed goals for	
Bobby Schmautz	2		
Terry O'Reilly	1		
Don Marcotte	1		

1978–1979
(55th year)

TEAM OWNER:	Sportsystems of Buffalo	*Semi-finals:*	
PRESIDENT & GOVERNOR:	Paul Mooney	Lose to Montreal Canadiens	
GM:	Harry Sinden	3 wins – 4 losses	
COACH:	Don Cherry	STANLEY CUP WINNER:	Montreal Canadiens
ATTENDANCE:	519,444	ALL-STARS:	None
	12,986 per game	TROPHY WINNERS:	Dufresne — Rick Middleton
PLAYOFFS:	*Quarter finals:*		7th Player — Rick Middleton
	Defeat Pittsburgh Penguins		Three Star — Rick Middleton
	4 wins – 0 losses	RADIO BROADCASTER:	WITS – Bob Wilson
		TV BROADCASTER:	WSBK TV38 – Fred Cusick, Johnny Bucyk

UNIFORMS

- Home jersey is white with gold and black trim. Socks are white with one gold band surrounded by two black bands at the calf. Road jersey is black with gold and white trim. Gold socks with one white band surrounded by two black bands at the calf. Logo is the spoked "B." Pants are black with white trim on side.
- Bearhead appears on both shoulders on both home and road uniforms.

POTPOURRI

- Bruins do not get shut out the entire season.
- In the November 19 game against St. Louis, the Blues only manage 12 shots.
- In the February 14 game against the Rangers at New York, the Bruins fail to get a shot on goal in the first period.
- May 10 playoff game at Montreal is won by the Canadiens in overtime after tieing the Bruins in the third period on a too-many-men-on-the-ice penalty.
- Cleveland Barons merge with the Minnesota North Stars and stay the Minnesota North Stars.
- For the first time since 1941–42, there will be an odd number of teams (17) in the NHL. Therefore, for the first time in 37 years, there will not be a night in the regular season in which all teams play.
- The Bruins are involved in 2 penalty shots this season. Lanny McDonald scores on a penalty shot for the Toronto Maple Leafs while Rick Middleton nets a penalty shot goal against the Colorado Rockies.
- Bruins place 5 players in the top 17 leaders in shooting accuracy in the NHL. The five players are Rick Middleton, 25%, Terry O'Reilly, 22%, John Wensink, 21%, Wayne Cashman, 20%, and Al Secord, 20%.
- The NHL and WHA announce that the WHA would cease operation after the 1979 playoffs with four WHA clubs. The Edmonton Oilers, Hartford Whalers, Quebec Nordiques, and Winnipeg Jets join the NHL.
- Bobby Orr's number is retired before the January 9 exhibition game between the Bruins and the Soviet Wings.

TRANSACTIONS

- Bruins claim Al Secord #1 in the 1978 amateur draft.
- In a three-way deal between Atlanta, Pittsburgh, and the Bruins, Greg Sheppard winds up in Pittsburgh and Dick Redmond is traded to Boston from Atlanta. The Penguins send Jean Pronovost to Atlanta to complete the deal.
- Sign Mike Walton as a free agent.

1978-79 STANDINGS

PRINCE OF WALES CONFERENCE

Adams Division	W	L	T	P	GF	GA
Boston	43	23	14	100	316	270
Buffalo	36	28	16	88	280	263
Toronto	34	33	13	81	267	252
Minnesota	28	40	12	68	257	289
Norris Division						
Montreal	52	17	11	115	337	204
Pittsburgh	36	31	13	85	281	279
Los Angeles	34	34	12	80	292	286
Washington	24	41	15	63	273	338
Detroit	23	41	16	62	252	295

CLARENCE CAMPBELL CONFERENCE
Patrick Division

New York Islanders	51	15	14	116	358	214
Philadelphia	40	25	15	95	281	248
New York Rangers	40	29	11	91	316	292
Atlanta	41	31	8	90	327	280

Smythe Division

Chicago	29	36	15	73	244	277
Vancouver	25	42	13	63	217	291
St. Louis	18	50	12	48	249	348
Colorado	15	53	12	42	210	331

1978-79 RESULTS

October 1978

	AT	VERSUS	W-L-T	SCR
12	Boston	Pittsburgh	W	8-2
14	Pittsburgh	Penguins	T	4-4
15	Boston	Toronto	W	4-2
18	Los Angeles	Kings	W	3-2
20	Vancouver	Canucks	W	5-1
22	Chicago	Blackhawks	L	6-5
24	St. Louis	Blues	W	7-2
25	Minnesota	North Stars	T	2-2
28	Toronto	Maple Leafs	W	5-3

November 1978

2	Boston	New York Islanders	W	4-1
4	Boston	Philadelphia	L	7-3
5	Boston	Montreal	T	1-1
9	Boston	Washington	W	6-2
11	Detroit	Red Wings	L	7-1
12	Buffalo	Sabres	T	4-4
16	Boston	Toronto	L	6-4
17	Atlanta	Flames	W	6-2
19	Boston	St. Louis	W	5-2
23	Boston	Buffalo	W	5-2
25	Washington	Capitals	T	5-5
26	Boston	Atlanta	W	4-2
30	Buffalo	Sabres	W	4-3

December 1978

2	Boston	Philadelphia	W	5-3
3	New York	Rangers	W	3-2
5	Toronto	Maple Leafs	W	5-1
7	Boston	Detroit	W	6-5
9	Philadelphia	Flyers	L	9-2
10	Boston	Minnesota	T	4-4
12	Boston	Vancouver	W	7-3
14	Boston	Washington	W	5-2
16	Boston	New York Rangers	W	4-1
17	New York	Rangers	W	4-1
21	Boston	Colorado	W	4-2
23	Boston	Buffalo	W	6-4

27	Toronto	Maple Leafs	T	1-1
30	Montreal	Canadiens	L	6-1
31	Buffalo	Sabres	W	7-3

January 1979

3	Chicago	Blackhawks	W	6-3
5	Colorado	Rockies	W	5-3
6	Minnesota	North Stars	W	5-2
11	Boston	Minnesota	W	6-4
13	Pittsburgh	Penguins	L	5-3
14	Boston	Los Angeles	L	6-3
16	St. Louis	Blues	L	5-2
18	Boston	St. Louis	W	4-0
20	Boston	Buffalo	L	2-1
22	Boston	Atlanta	W	3-1
25	Boston	New York Islanders	L	4-2
27	Montreal	Canadiens	L	3-1
28	Boston	Los Angeles	L	5-3
31	Chicago	Blackhawks	T	2-2

February 1979

1	Boston	Chicago	W	6-1
3	New York	Islanders	T	4-4
4	Boston	Vancouver	W	6-1
14	New York	Rangers	L	5-1
15	Philadelphia	Flyers	L	5-3
17	Minnesota	North Stars	T	3-3
20	Colorado	Rockies	W	5-3
21	Los Angeles	Kings	L	3-1
24	Vancouver	Canucks	W	4-3
27	Boston	Colorado	L	4-2

March 1979

1	Boston	Philadelphia	T	4-4
3	Boston	Minnesota	W	5-0
4	Detroit	Red Wings	W	6-4
8	Atlanta	Flames	L	7-5
10	Minnesota	North Stars	W	4-3
11	Boston	New York Islanders	T	4-4
13	New York	Islanders	L	7-2

15	Boston	New York Rangers	L	7–4
17	Boston	Chicago	W	4–2
19	Boston	Toronto	W	4–3
22	Boston	Pittsburgh	L	3–1
24	Boston	Detroit	W	5–2
28	Buffalo	Sabres	L	9–2
29	Boston	Minnesota	W	7–4

| 31 | Washington | Capitals | W | 4–1 |

April 1979

1	Boston	Montreal	T	3–3
4	Toronto	Maple Leafs	T	3–3
5	Boston	Buffalo	L	9–3
8	Boston	Toronto	W	6–3

1978-79 SCORING

	W	L	T	S	GAA	PIM
Gilles Gilbert	12	8	2	0	3.54	16
Gerry Cheevers	23	9	10	1	3.16	23
						2 assists
Jim Pettie	8	6	2	1	3.59	17

	G	A	P	PIM
Rick Middleton	38	48	86	7
Peter McNab	35	45	80	10
Terry O'Reilly	26	51	77	205
Jean Ratelle	27	45	72	12
Wayne Cashman	27	40	67	63
Bobby Miller	15	33	48	30
Don Marcotte	20	27	47	10
John Wensink	28	18	46	106
Bobby Schmautz	20	22	42	77

	G	A	P	PIM
Brad Park	7	32	39	10
Mike Milbury	1	34	35	149
Dick Redmond	7	26	33	21
Al Sims	9	20	29	28
Rick Smith	7	18	25	46
Dwight Foster	11	13	24	14
Al Secord	16	7	23	125
Gary Doak	6	11	17	28
Stan Jonathan	6	9	15	96
Dennis O'Brien	2	8	10	107
Mike Walton	4	2	6	0
Bill Bennett	1	4	5	2
Tom Songin	3	1	4	0
Graeme Nicolson	0	0	0	0
Ab DeMarco	0	0	0	0

Number of power play advantages	249
Power play goals	59
% successful	23.7%
Rick Middleton	12
Jean Ratelle	11
Wayne Cashman	10
Bobby Schmautz	6
Peter McNab	4
Dick Redmond	4
Terry O'Reilly	3
Brad Park	3
Don Marcotte	2
Dwight Foster	2
Gary Doak	1
Tom Songin	1

Short-handed goals against	9
Penalty minutes: 1,222 – 15.3 per game	
Times short-handed	285
Power play goals against	72
Penalty kill success	74.7%
Short-hand goals	6
Don Marcotte	4
Rick Middleton	1
Bobby Schmautz	1

1978-79 PLAYOFF RESULTS

April 1979

	AT	VERSUS	W-L-T	SCR
16	Boston	Pittsburgh	W	6–2
18	Boston	Pittsburgh	W	4–3
21	Pittsburgh	Penguins	W	2–1
22	Pittsburgh	Penguins	W	4–1
26	Montreal	Canadiens	L	4–2
28	Montreal	Canadiens	L	5–2

May 1979

1	Boston	Montreal	W	2–1
3	Boston	Montreal	W	4–3 (OT)
5	Montreal	Canadiens	L	5–1
8	Boston	Montreal	W	5–2
10	Montreal	Canadiens	L	5–4 (OT)

1978-79 PLAYOFFS

vs. Pittsburgh Penguins	4 wins – 0 losses	vs. Montreal Canadiens	3 wins – 4 losses
at Pittsburgh	2 wins – 0 losses	at Montreal	0 wins – 4 losses
at Boston	2 wins – 0 losses	at Boston	3 wins – 0 losses

1978-79 PLAYOFF SCORING

	W	L	SO	GAA	PIM
Gerry Cheevers	4	2	0	2.50	0
Gilles Gilbert	3	2	0	3.06	0

	G	A	P	PIM
Jean Ratelle	7	6	13	2
Rick Middleton	4	8	12	0
Wayne Cashman	4	5	9	8
Peter McNab	5	3	8	0
Don Marcotte	5	3	8	10
Mike Milbury	1	7	8	7
Terry O'Reilly	0	6	6	25
Stan Jonathan	4	1	5	12
Brad Park	1	4	5	8
Bobby Schmautz	2	2	4	6
Dwight Foster	1	3	4	0
Dick Redmond	1	3	4	2
Rick Smith	0	4	4	12
Bobby Miller	1	1	2	8
Gary Doak	0	2	2	4
Al Sims	0	2	2	0
John Wensink	0	1	1	19
Al Secord	0	0	0	4

Bench minors	4	Short-handed goals against	0
Number of power play advantages	25	Penalty minutes:	131 – 11.9 per game
Power play goals	6	Times short-handed	32
% successful	24%	Power play goals against	8
Jean Ratelle	2	Penalty kill success	5%
Rick Middleton	2	Short-handed goals	1
Wayne Cashman	1	Dick Redmond	1
Bobby Schmautz	1		

1979–1980
(56th year)

TEAM OWNER:	Sportsystems of Buffalo	STANLEY CUP WINNER:	New York Islanders
PRESIDENT & GOVERNOR:	Paul Mooney	ALL-STARS:	Ray Bourque (1st team)
GM:	Harry Sinden	TROPHY WINNERS:	Calder — Ray Bourque
COACHES:	Fred Creighton		Dufresne —Ray Bourque
	& Harry Sinden		7th Player — Ray Bourque
ATTENDANCE:	494,633		Three Star —
	12,365 per game		Rick Middleton
PLAYOFFS:	*Preliminary round:*	RADIO BROADCASTER:	WITS – Bob Wilson
	Defeat Pittsburgh Penguins	TV BROADCASTER:	WSBK TV38 – Fred Cusick,
	3 wins – 2 losses		John Peirson
	Quarter finals:		
	Lose to New York Islanders		
	1 win – 4 losses		

UNIFORMS

- Home jersey is white with gold and black trim. Socks are white with one gold band surrounded by two black bands at the calf. Road jersey is black with gold and white trim. Gold socks with one white band surrounded by two black bands at the calf. Logo is the spoked "B." Pants are black with white trim on side. Bearhead appears on both shoulders on both home and road uniforms.

POTPOURRI

- Bruins enjoy a 9-game winning streak from November 4 to November 22.
- Gilles Gilbert enjoys the longest winning streak by a goalie for the season when he wins 8 in a row.
- In the January 17 game, the Bruins hold the Edmonton Oilers to 12 shots.
- Ray Bourque, with 65 points, establishes the NHL record for most points by a rookie defenseman.
- Wayne Cashman plays his 800th career game.
- Bruins retire Johnny Bucyk's number 9 on March 13.
- Ray Bourque becomes the first non-goaltender to win the Calder Trophy and to be named to the first All-Star team in the same season.
- NHL expands to 21 teams with the addition of the Edmonton Oilers, Hartford Whalers, Quebec Nordiques, and Winnipeg Jets from the WHA.
- Bruins lead league with 94 major penalties.
- In the preliminary series against Pittsburgh, the final 3 games are played on 3 consecutive days.
- Terry O'Reilly breaks his own team mark for penalty minutes in a season with 265 minutes.
- The NHL adopts a balanced, 80-game schedule with each team playing its 20 other opponents 4 times each, 2 at home and 2 away.
- Players signing contracts after June 1, 1979, are required to wear protective head gear.

TRANSACTIONS

- Obtain Bobby Lalonde from Atlanta for future considerations.
- Bruins select Ray Bourque #1 in the 1979 Amateur Draft.
- Trade Bobby Schmautz to Edmonton for Dan Newman.
- The expansion draft for the four WHA teams entering the NHL is held on June 13, 1979, in Montreal. The Bruins lost the following players: Mike Forbes (claimed by the Edmonton Oilers), Al Sims (claimed by the Hartford Whalers), Bill Bennett (claimed by the Hartford Whalers), and Dave Parro (claimed by the Quebec Nordiques).

1979-80 STANDINGS

PRINCE OF WALES CONFERENCE

Adams Division

	W	L	T	P	GF	GA
Buffalo	47	17	16	110	318	201
Boston	46	21	13	105	310	234
Minnesota	36	28	16	88	311	253
Toronto	35	40	5	75	304	327
Quebec	25	44	11	61	248	313

Norris Division

	W	L	T	P	GF	GA
Montreal	47	20	13	107	328	240
Los Angeles	30	36	14	74	290	313
Pittsburgh	30	37	13	73	251	303
Hartford	27	34	19	73	303	312
Detroit	26	43	11	63	268	306

CLARENCE CAMPBELL CONFERENCE

Patrick Division

	W	L	T	P	GF	GA
Philadelphia	48	12	20	116	327	254
New York Islanders	39	28	13	91	281	247
New York Rangers	38	32	10	86	308	284
Atlanta	35	32	13	83	282	269
Washington	27	40	13	67	261	293

Smythe Division

	W	L	T	P	GF	GA
Chicago	34	27	19	87	241	250
St. Louis	34	34	12	80	266	278
Vancouver	27	37	16	70	256	281
Edmonton	28	39	13	69	301	322
Winnipeg	20	49	11	51	214	314
Colorado	19	48	13	51	234	308

1979-80 RESULTS

October 1979

	AT	VERSUS	W-L-T	SCR
11	Boston	Winnipeg	W	4–0
12	Washington	Capitals	W	5–2
14	Boston	Pittsburgh	L	4–1
18	Boston	New York Islanders	W	3–2
20	Boston	Los Angeles	W	5–4
23	St. Louis	Blues	T	5–5
26	Winnipeg	Jets	L	3–2
28	Chicago	Blackhawks	W	4–1
30	Los Angeles	Kings	T	4–4

November 1979

2	Vancouver	Canucks	W	3–3
4	Edmonton	Oilers	W	2–1
8	Boston	Edmonton	W	4–2
10	Pittsburgh	Penguins	W	6–1
11	Boston	Atlanta	W	6–3
15	Boston	Washington	W	3–2
17	Toronto	Maple Leafs	W	2–0
18	Boston	Hartford	W	5–4
20	Quebec	Nordiques	W	5–3
22	Boston	Quebec	W	7–4
24	Montreal	Canadiens	L	3–1
25	Boston	Montreal	W	4–2
27	Boston	Buffalo	L	5–2

December 1979

1	Detroit	Red Wings	L	6–3
2	Boston	Colorado	L	5–3
4	Philadelphia	Flyers	T	2–2
6	New York	Islanders	L	4–3
9	Vancouver	Canucks	W	5–3
13	Boston	Detroit	T	6–6
15	Boston	Chicago	L	2–1
16	Buffalo	Sabres	W	5–1
20	Boston	Toronto	W	10–0
22	Boston	Philadelphia	L	5–2
23	New York	Rangers	W	4–3
26	Atlanta	Flames	W	5–3

30	Chicago	Blackhawks	L	5–3

January 1980

2	Minnesota	North Stars	L	2–1
4	Winnipeg	Jets	W	2–1
8	Colorado	Rockies	T	2–2
10	Boston	St. Louis	L	7–4
12	Boston	Atlanta	W	5–3
13	Boston	Colorado	W	6–2
16	Quebec	Nordiques	W	3–1
17	Boston	Edmonton	W	7–1
19	Boston	New York Rangers	W	6–3
21	Boston	Minnesota	W	3–0
24	Boston	Buffalo	W	4–3
26	Pittsburgh	Penguins	W	6–4
27	Boston	Pittsburgh	L	5–3
30	Hartford	Whalers	L	8–2
31	Boston	New York Islanders	W	4–2

February 1980

2	Boston	Quebec	W	7–2
3	Philadelphia	Flyers	T	3–3
7	Boston	Toronto	W	8–6
9	Boston	Chicago	W	5–2
10	Boston	Montreal	L	3–2
14	Buffalo	Sabres	T	3–3
16	Colorado	Rockies	W	5–3

20	Los Angeles	Kings	L	3–0
23	Vancouver	Canucks	T	4–4
24	Edmonton	Oilers	W	4–2
27	Hartford	Whalers	W	6–3
28	Boston	New York Rangers	L	5–2

March 1980

1	Boston	Los Angeles	W	4–0
2	New York	Rangers	L	2–1
5	Detroit	Red Wings	W	5–3
8	New York	Islanders	W	5–3
9	Boston	Hartford	T	1–1
12	Washington	Capitals	L	6–4
13	Boston	Detroit	W	4–2
15	Boston	Vancouver	T	2–2
16	Boston	Washington	T	3–3
18	St. Louis	Blues	T	3–3
19	Minnesota	North Stars	L	7–4
22	Atlanta	Flames	W	5–2
23	Boston	Philadelphia	W	7–2
27	Boston	St. Louis	W	7–1
30	Boston	Winnipeg	W	3–1

April 1980

2	Toronto	Maple Leafs	W	5–2
5	Montreal	Canadiens	L	6–1
6	Boston	Minnesota	W	4–2

1979-80 SCORING

	W	L	T	S	GAA	PIM
Gilles Gilbert	20	9	3	1	2.73	10
						1 assist
Gerry Cheevers	24	11	7	4	2.81	62
Marco Baron	0	0	0	0	3.00	
Yves Belanger	2	0	3	0	3.48	
Jim Stewart	0	1	0	0	15.00	

	G	A	P	PIM
Rick Middleton	40	52	92	24
Peter McNab	40	38	78	10
Jean Ratelle	28	45	73	8
Ray Bourque	17	48	65	73
Terry O'Reilly	19	42	61	265
Dick Redmond	14	33	47	39
Bobby Miller	16	25	41	53
Stan Jonathan	21	19	40	208

Al Secord	23	16	39	170
Dwight Foster	10	28	38	42
Bobby Lalonde	10	25	35	28
Wayne Cashman	11	21	32	19
Craig MacTavish	11	17	28	8
Rick Smith	8	18	26	62
Mike Milbury	10	13	23	59
Brad Park	5	16	21	27
John Wensink	9	11	20	110
Brad McCrimmon	5	11	16	94
Don Marcotte	4	11	15	0
Bobby Schmautz	8	6	14	8
Gary Doak	0	5	5	45
Tom Songin	1	3	4	16
Dennis O'Brien	0	0	0	2
Doug Morrison	0	0	0	0

Number of power play advantages	246	
Power play goals	60	
% successful	24.4%	
Jean Ratelle	14	
Peter McNab	11	

Rick Middleton	9
Dick Redmond	6
Bobby Schmautz	4
Ray Bourque	3
Terry O'Reilly	3

Wayne Cashman	3	Short-handed goals		8
Brad Park	2	Ray Bourque		2
Al Secord	1	Bobby Lalonde		2
Dwight Foster	1	Bob Miller		1
Bobby Lalonde	1	Dwight Foster		1
Mike Milbury	1	Wayne Cashman		1
Brad McCrimmon	1	Don Marcotte		1

Short-handed goals against	4
Penalty minutes: 1,460 – 18.3 per game	
Times short-handed	312
Power play goal against	53
Penalty kill success	83%

1979-80 PLAYOFF RESULTS

April 1980

	AT	VERSUS	W-L-T	SCR						
8	Boston	Pittsburgh	L	4–2	14	Boston	Pittsburgh	W	6–2	
10	Boston	Pittsburgh	W	4–1	16	Boston	New York Islanders	L	2–1	(OT)
12	Pittsburgh	Penguins	L	4–1	17	Boston	New York Islanders	L	5–4	(OT)
13	Pittsburgh	Penguins	W	8–3	19	New York	Islanders	L	5–3	
					21	New York	Islanders	W	4–3	
					22	Boston	New York Islanders	L	4–2	

1979-80 PLAYOFFS

vs. Pittsburgh Penguins	3 wins – 2 losses	vs. New York Islanders	1 win – 4 losses
at Pittsburgh	1 win – 1 loss	at New York	1 win – 1 loss
at Boston	2 wins – 1 loss	at Boston	0 wins – 3 losses

1979-80 PLAYOFF SCORING

	W	L	SO	GAA	PIM
Gerry Cheevers	4	6	0	3.10	0

	G	A	P	PIM
Peter McNab	8	6	14	2
Ray Bourque	2	9	11	27
Brad Park	3	6	9	4
Terry O'Reilly	3	6	9	69
Dwight Foster	3	5	8	2
Rick Middleton	4	2	6	5
Wayne Cashman	3	3	6	32
Bobby Miller	3	2	5	4
Craig MacTavish	2	3	5	7
Don Marcotte	2	3	5	4
Al Secord	0	3	3	65
Dick Redmond	0	3	3	9
Rick Smith	1	1	2	2
Brad McCrimmon	1	1	2	28
Mike Milbury	0	2	2	50
Bobby Lalonde	0	1	1	2
Jean Ratelle	0	0	0	0
John Wensink	0	0	0	5
Gary Doak	0	0	0	0
Stan Jonathan	0	0	0	29

Number of power play advantages	37
Power play goals	6
% successful	16.2%
Peter McNab	3
Terry O'Reilly	2
Wayne Cashman	1
Short-handed goals against	1

Penalty minutes: 346 – 34.6 per game	
Times short-handed	33
Power play goals against	8
Penalty kill success	75.8%
Short-handed goals	2
Dwight Foster	1
Bob Miller	1

1980–1981
(57th year)

TEAM OWNER:	Sportsystems of Buffalo	STANLEY CUP WINNER:	New York Islanders
PRESIDENT & GOVERNOR:	Paul Mooney	ALL-STARS:	Ray Bourque (2nd team)
GM:	Harry Sinden	TROPHY WINNERS:	Dufresne — Rick Middleton
COACH:	Gerry Cheevers		7th Player — Steve Kasper
ATTENDANCE:	446,903		Three Star —
	11,172 per game		Rick Middleton
PLAYOFFS:	*Preliminary round:*	RADIO BROADCASTER:	WITS – Bob Wilson,
	Lose to Minnesota		Johnny Bucyk
	North Stars	TV BROADCASTER:	WSBK TV38 – Fred Cusick,
	0 wins – 3 losses		John Peirson

UNIFORMS

- Home jersey is white with gold and black trim. Socks are white with one gold band surrounded by two black bands at the calf. Road jersey is black with gold and white trim. Gold socks with one white band surrounded by two black bands at the calf. Logo is the spoked "B." Pants are black with white trim on side. Bearhead appears on both shoulders on both home and road uniforms.

POTPOURRI

- Goalie Jim Craig goes through a 7-game unbeaten streak (4-0-3).
- Steve Kasper scores Bruins 11,000th goal on November 22.
- Bobby Lalonde scores 2 short-handed goals in the same period of a Stanley Cup game.
- Rick Middleton scores 2 short-handed goals (1:16 apart) in the February 26 game against Minnesota. The Bruins score 3 short-handed goals in this game. Bruins and Minnesota amass 406 minutes in penalties in this game. 332 of these penalty minutes are called in the first period.
- Brad Park plays in his 800th career game.
- Rogie Vachon notches his 50th career shutout.
- In the December 14th game against Los Angeles, Doug Morrison scores a pure hat trick.
- Jean Ratelle of the Bruins, Phil Esposito of the Rangers, Gordie Howe and Bobby Hull of the Whalers, and Stan Mikita of the Blackhawks retire after the 1980–81 season. This leaves Dave Keon as the lone survivor of the 6-team era.
- Gerry Cheevers becomes only the fourth goaltender in NHL history to become a coach; the others are Hugh Lehman of the Blackhawks, Emile Francis of the Rangers, and Eddie Johnston of the Penguins.
- Keith Crowder set a team mark for most penalty minutes in 1 game with 43.
- Peter McNab takes the first-ever Bruins penalty shot in a playoff game.
- Because of his trade from Chicago to Boston, Mike O'Connell plays in 82 games of an 80-game season.
- Bruins are not involved in any penalty shot situations this season.
- Bruins are not shut out at home or on the road.
- Bruins lead the league with 102 major penalties.
- Atlanta Flames are sold to Nelson Skalbania, a Vancouver businessman, and shifted to Calgary.

TRANSACTIONS

- Obtain Mike O'Connell from Chicago for Al Secord.
- Obtain Mike Gillis from Colorado for Bobby Miller.
- Select Barry Pederson as the #1 pick in the 1980 NHL draft.
- Obtain Jim Craig from Calgary for Boston's second and third round picks in the 1981 draft.

- Trade Gilles Gilbert to Detroit for Rogie Vachon.
- Gerry Cheevers retires and becomes the Bruins' head coach.

1980-81 STANDINGS

PRINCE OF WALES CONFERENCE

Adams Division

	W	L	T	P	GF	GA
Buffalo	39	20	21	99	327	250
Boston	37	30	13	87	316	272
Minnesota	35	28	17	87	291	263
Quebec	30	32	18	78	314	318
Toronto	28	37	15	71	322	367

Norris Division

	W	L	T	P	GF	GA
Montreal	45	22	13	103	332	232
Los Angeles	43	24	13	99	337	290
Pittsburgh	30	37	13	73	302	345
Hartford	21	41	18	60	292	372
Detroit	19	43	18	56	252	339

CLARENCE CAMPBELL CONFERENCE

Patrick Division

	W	L	T	P	GF	GA
New York Islanders	48	18	14	110	355	260
Philadelphia	41	24	15	97	313	249
Calgary	39	27	14	92	329	298
New York Rangers	30	36	14	74	312	317
Washington	26	36	18	70	286	317

Smythe Division

	W	L	T	P	GF	GA
St. Louis	45	18	17	107	352	281
Chicago	31	33	16	78	304	315
Vancouver	28	32	20	76	289	301
Edmonton	29	35	16	74	328	327
Colorado	22	45	13	57	258	344
Winnipeg	9	57	14	32	246	400

1980-81 RESULTS

October 1980

	AT	VERSUS	W-L-T	SCR
9	Boston	New York Rangers	W	7-2
11	New York	Rangers	L	5-2
12	Boston	Montreal	W	3-2
15	Minnesota	North Stars	L	3-2
16	Calgary	Flames	L	2-1
18	St. Louis	Blues	L	3-2
22	Los Angeles	Kings	L	4-0
24	Vancouver	Canucks	L	3-2
26	Winnipeg	Jets	T	7-7
30	Boston	Calgary	L	3-1

November 1980

	AT	VERSUS	W-L-T	SCR
2	Philadelphia	Flyers	L	4-2
6	Boston	New York Islanders	L	4-2
9	Boston	Pittsburgh	W	7-4
11	Detroit	Red Wings	T	4-4
13	Boston	Winnipeg	T	5-5
15	Pittsburgh	Penguins	W	7-4
16	Boston	Philadelphia	W	1-0
20	Boston	Colorado	W	4-2
22	Washington	Capitals	T	2-2
23	Boston	Toronto	T	5-5
26	New York	Rangers	L	6-4
27	Boston	Pittsburgh	T	3-3
29	Boston	Edmonton	W	6-3

December 1980

	AT	VERSUS	W-L-T	SCR
2	Boston	Detroit	W	5-3
6	Montreal	Canadiens	L	4-1
7	Boston	Washington	W	7-3
10	Quebec	Nordiques	W	6-4
11	Boston	Quebec	L	5-3

13	Boston	Vancouver	L	2–1
14	Boston	Los Angeles	W	7–1
17	Hartford	Whalers	L	5–4
18	Boston	St. Louis	L	7–3
20	Boston	Hartford	T	4–4
27	Toronto	Maple Leafs	W	6–3
28	Buffalo	Sabres	L	5–2
31	Chicago	Blackhawks	W	4–2

January 1981

2	Edmonton	Oilers	L	7–5
3	Colorado	Rockies	L	4–1
5	Winnipeg	Jets	W	4–1
8	Boston	Detroit	W	7–4
10	New York	Islanders	W	3–2
12	Boston	Minnesota	W	4–3
13	Detroit	Red Wings	T	3–3
15	Chicago	Blackhawks	L	3–2
17	Boston	Philadelphia	W	6–4
19	Boston	Buffalo	W	5–1
22	Boston	St. Louis	W	7–3
24	Boston	Los Angeles	L	6–4
26	Boston	Colorado	W	5–3
29	Boston	Winnipeg	W	7–6

February 1981

1	Boston	New York Islanders	W	6–3
4	Hartford	Whalers	T	3–3
5	Boston	New York Rangers	W	6–3
7	Montreal	Canadiens	L	6–2

8	Boston	Quebec	L	4–3
12	Colorado	Rockies	T	3–3
14	Los Angeles	Kings	W	5–4
18	Vancouver	Canucks	W	7–5
20	Edmonton	Oilers	W	5–1
21	Calgary	Flames	L	7–2
25	Quebec	Nordiques	L	5–3
26	Boston	Minnesota	W	5–1

March 1981

1	Boston	Buffalo	W	6–4
3	St. Louis	Blues	L	4–2
4	Minnesota	North Stars	T	3–3
7	Boston	Chicago	W	7–1
8	Boston	Vancouver	W	4–1
11	Toronto	Maple Leafs	T	4–4
13	Washington	Capitals	W	7–1
15	Boston	Hartford	W	4–2
18	New York	Rangers	L	3–2
19	Philadelphia	Flyers	L	5–3
21	Boston	Calgary	W	4–3
23	Boston	Edmonton	W	7–2
26	Boston	Toronto	L	3–2
28	Boston	Chicago	W	5–2
30	Buffalo	Sabres	T	2–2

April 1981

2	Boston	Washington	L	3–2
4	Pittsburgh	Penguins	W	5–2
5	Boston	Montreal	L	4–2

1980-81 SCORING

	W	L	T	S	GAA	PIM
Marco Baron	3	4	1	0	2.84	7
Rogie Vachon	25	19	6	1	3.34	6
						1 assist
Jim Craig	9	7	6	0	3.68	11
						1 assist

	G	A	P	PIM
Rick Middleton	44	59	103	16
Peter McNab	37	46	83	24
Brad Park	14	52	66	111
Wayne Cashman	25	35	60	80
Ray Bourque	27	29	56	96
Steve Kasper	21	35	56	94
Dwight Foster	24	28	52	62
Terry O'Reilly	8	35	43	223
Stan Jonathan	14	24	38	192

Jean Ratelle	11	26	37	16
Dick Redmond	15	20	35	60
Don Marcotte	20	13	33	32
Mike O'Connell	10	22	32	42
Brad McCrimmon	11	18	29	148
Keith Crowder	13	12	25	172
Mike Milbury	0	18	18	222
Bobby Lalonde	4	12	16	31
Doug Morrison	7	3	10	13
Bobby Miller	4	4	8	19
Craig MacTavish	3	5	8	13
Mike Gillis	2	4	6	15
Barry Pederson	1	4	5	6
Larry Melnyk	0	4	4	39
Al Secord	0	3	3	42
Tom Songin	1	1	2	6
Gary Doak	0	0	0	12

Number of power play advantages	342
Power play goals	87
% successful	25.4%
Rick Middleton	16
Peter McNab	16
Brad Park	10
Ray Bourque	9
Wayne Cashman	7
Dick Redmond	6
Steve Kasper	5
Jean Ratelle	4
Don Marcotte	4
Dwight Foster	3
Mike O'Connell	2
Doug Morrison	2
Brad McCrimmon	1

Keith Crowder	1
Barry Pederson	1
Short-handed goals against	8
Penalty minutes:	1,836 – 23.0
Times short-handed	358
Power play goals against	82
Penalty kill success	77.1%
Short-handed goals	13
Rick Middleton	4
Dwight Foster	3
Dick Redmond	2
Ray Bourque	1
Mike O'Connell	1
Don Marcotte	1
Bobby Lalonde	1

1980-81 PLAYOFF RESULTS

April 1981

AT		VERSUS	W-L-T	SCR
8	Boston	Minnesota	L	5–4 (OT)
9	Boston	Minnesota	L	9–6
11	Minnesota	North Stars	L	6–3

1980-81 PLAYOFFS

vs. Minnesota North Stars	0 wins – 3 losses
at Minnesota	0 wins – 1 loss
at Boston	0 wins – 2 losses

1980-81 PLAYOFF SCORING

	W	L	SO	GAA	PIM
Rogie Vachon	0	3	0	5.85	0
Marco Baron	0	0	0	9.00	0

	G	A	P	PIM
Don Marcotte	2	2	4	6
Brad Park	1	3	4	11
Mike O'Connell	1	3	4	2
Peter McNab	3	0	3	0
Bobby Lalonde	2	1	3	2
Terry O'Reilly	1	2	3	12
Keith Crowder	2	0	2	9
Dwight Foster	1	1	2	0
Mike Milbury	0	1	1	10
Ray Bourque	0	1	1	2
Dick Redmond	0	1	1	2
Brad McCrimmon	0	1	1	2
Steve Kasper	0	1	1	0
Wayne Cashman	0	1	1	0
Rick Middleton	0	1	1	0
Mike Gillis	0	0	0	0
Jean Ratelle	0	0	0	0
Stan Jonathan	0	0	0	30

Number of power play advantages	8
Power play goals	2
% successful	25%
Brad Park	1
Peter McNab	1
Short-handed goals against	1
Penalty minutes:	90 – 30 per game

Times short-handed	19
Power play goals against	5
Penalty kill success	73.7%
Short-handed goals	3
Bobby Lalonde	2
Mike O'Connell	1

1981–1982
(58th year)

TEAM OWNER:	Sportsystem of Buffalo	TROPHY WINNERS:	Lady Byng — Rick Middleton
PRESIDENT & GOVERNOR:	Paul Mooney		Selke Trophy — Steve Kasper
GM:	Harry Sinden		Dufresne — Rick Middleton
COACH:	Gerry Cheevers		7th Player — Barry Pederson
ATTENDANCE:	480,989 12,024 per game		Three Star — Rick Middleton
PLAYOFFS:	*Division semi-finals:* Defeat Buffalo Sabres 3 wins – 1 loss *Division finals:* Lose finals to Quebec Nordiques 3 wins – 4 losses	RADIO BROADCASTER:	WITS – Bob Wilson, Johnny Bucyk
STANLEY CUP WINNER:	New York Islanders	TV BROADCASTER:	WSBK TV38 – Fred Cusick, John Peirson
ALL-STARS:	Ray Bourque (1st team) Rick Middleton (2nd team)		

UNIFORMS

- Home jersey is white with gold and black trim. Socks are white with one gold band surrounded by two black bands at the calf. Road jersey is black with gold and white trim. Gold socks with one white band surrounded by two black bands at the calf. Logo is the spoked "B." Pants are black. Bearhead appears on both shoulders on both home and road uniforms.

POTPOURRI

- Don Marcotte plays his 800th career game.
- Wayne Cashman plays his 900th career game.
- Rick Middleton becomes the first Bruin since Phil Esposito to score 50 goals in a season.
- Mike Moffat becomes the first rookie since Ross Brooks to start a playoff game.
- Terry O'Reilly plays his 700th career game.
- Barry Pederson breaks the goal scoring record for rookies with 44.
- Mike O'Connell, Peter McNab, and Barry Pederson play in all 80 games.
- Ray Bourque breaks his wrist in the playoff round against Quebec and is out of the series.
- Bruin goalie Marco Baron is the only Bruin goalie to be trilingual (English, French, Italian).
- Wayne Cashman becomes the last Bruin left from the 1972 Stanley Cup winners.
- Keith and Bruce Crowder become the first Bruin brothers since Bill and Max Quackenbush in 1950–51.
- Barry Pederson becomes the only Bruin to score a point against every opponent.
- NHL approves the use of aluminum-shaft sticks.
- Bobby Carpenter, drafted by the Washington Capitals, becomes the first American to be taken in the first round of the draft. Grant Fuhr, drafted by the Edmonton Oilers, becomes the first black to be taken in the first round of the draft.
- The NHL realigns with the Bruins being joined in the Adams Division by the Montreal Canadiens, Quebec Nordiques, Hartford Whalers, and Buffalo Sabres.
- The Islanders, by winning 15 straight games, break the record for consecutive wins held by the 1929–30 Bruins.

TRANSACTIONS

- Select Normand Leveille as the #1 pick in the 1981 NHL draft. At 18, Normand is the youngest player ever drafted by the Bruins.

- Jean Ratelle announces his retirement.
- Bruins trade Dwight Foster to Colorado for the Rockies second-round pick and the exchange of first-round picks.

1981-82 STANDINGS

PRINCE OF WALES CONFERENCE

Adams Division

	W	L	T	P	GF	GA
Montreal	46	17	17	109	360	223
Boston	43	27	10	96	323	285
Buffalo	39	26	15	93	307	273
Quebec	33	31	16	82	356	345
Hartford	21	41	18	60	264	351

Patrick Division

	W	L	T	P	GF	GA
New York Islanders	54	16	10	118	385	250
New York Rangers	39	27	14	92	316	306
Philadelphia	38	31	11	87	325	313
Pittsburgh	31	36	13	75	310	337
Washington	26	41	13	65	319	338

CLARENCE CAMPBELL CONFERENCE

Norris Division

	W	L	T	P	GF	GA
Minnesota	37	23	20	94	346	288
Winnipeg	33	33	14	80	319	332
St. Louis	32	40	8	72	315	349
Chicago	30	38	12	72	332	363
Toronto	20	44	16	56	298	380
Detroit	21	47	12	54	270	351

Smythe Division

	W	L	T	P	GF	GA
Edmonton	48	17	15	111	417	295
Vancouver	30	33	17	77	290	286
Calgary	29	34	17	75	334	345
Los Angeles	24	41	15	63	314	369
Colorado	18	49	13	49	241	362

1981-82 RESULTS

October 1981

	AT	VERSUS	W-L-T	SCR
8	Boston	Quebec	L	7–5
10	Hartford	Whalers	T	1–1
11	Boston	Capitals	W	6–3
14	Chicago	Blackhawks	W	8–5
16	Colorado	Rockies	W	6–1
17	Los Angeles	Kings	W	5–4
20	St. Louis	Blues	W	4–3
22	Detroit	Red Wings	T	2–2
24	Montreal	Canadiens	L	7–0
29	Boston	Montreal	T	5–5
31	Boston	New York Rangers	W	7–3

November 1981

	AT	VERSUS	W-L-T	SCR
1	Boston	Hartford	W	4–1
5	Boston	Vancouver	W	2–1
7	Quebec	Nordiques	W	10–1
8	Boston	Minnesota	L	4–1
12	Boston	Edmonton	W	5–2
14	Boston	Pittsburgh	T	3–3
15	Buffalo	Sabres	L	3–1
19	Boston	Hartford	W	6–1
21	Toronto	Maple Leafs	W	5–3
22	Boston	Quebec	L	6–1
24	New York	Islanders	L	3–1
26	Boston	Philadelphia	L	3–1
28	Boston	New York Islanders	W	5–4

December 1981

	AT	VERSUS	W-L-T	SCR
3	Boston	Buffalo	W	6–3
5	Quebec	Nordiques	W	5–3

9	New York	Rangers	W	4–3
10	Boston	St. Louis	L	3–2
13	Boston	Colorado	W	5–1
17	Boston	Montreal	L	5–1
19	Montreal	Canadiens	L	5–2
20	Boston	Los Angeles	W	6–4
23	Washington	Capitals	W	7–4
26	Hartford	Whalers	W	9–6
29	Vancouver	Canucks	W	5–3
30	Calgary	Flames	W	4–2

January 1982

2	Edmonton	Oilers	T	4–4
3	Winnipeg	Jets	W	8–5
5	Montreal	Canadiens	L	3–1
7	Boston	Winnipeg	W	8–6
9	Quebec	Nordiques	L	6–1
11	Boston	Toronto	W	5–2
14	Boston	New York Islanders	W	5–4
16	Boston	Hartford	T	3–3
17	Philadelphia	Flyers	L	7–3
20	Pittsburgh	Penguins	L	5–4
21	Boston	Toronto	W	4–2
23	Boston	Washington	W	3–1
25	Boston	Calgary	T	3–3
28	Boston	Montreal	L	6–3
30	Hartford	Whalers	L	3–2
31	Boston	Colorado	W	4–2

February 1982

3	Buffalo	Sabres	W	5–2

4	Boston	Buffalo	W	5–2
6	Boston	Chicago	L	4–3
11	Minnesota	North Stars	W	4–2
13	Calgary	Flames	L	6–3
14	Edmonton	Oilers	T	2–2
17	Vancouver	Canucks	L	6–3
20	Detroit	Red Wings	W	7–5
21	Philadelphia	Flyers	W	1–0
24	Hartford	Whalers	L	4–3
27	Boston	New York Rangers	L	6–4

March 1982

2	St. Louis	Blues	T	2–2
3	Pittsburgh	Penguins	W	3–2
6	Boston	Los Angeles	W	4–0
7	Chicago	Blackhawks	L	5–1
9	Montreal	Canadiens	L	4–2
11	Boston	Winnipeg	W	7–4
13	Boston	Detroit	W	5–3
14	Boston	Montreal	L	5–2
16	Buffalo	Sabres	T	3–3
20	Boston	Buffalo	W	6–4
22	Boston	Quebec	W	5–4
25	Boston	Buffalo	W	5–1
27	Boston	Minnesota	L	6–5
28	Buffalo	Sabres	L	9–5

April 1982

1	Boston	Quebec	L	8–5
3	Quebec	Nordiques	W	5–4
4	Boston	Hartford	W	7–2

1981-82 SCORING

	W	L	T	S	GAA	PIM
Marco Baron	22	16	4	1	3.44	35
						2 assists
Rogie Vachon	19	11	6	1	3.66	0
						1 assist
Mike Moffat	2	0	0	0	3.00	0

	G	A	P	PIM
Rick Middleton	51	43	94	12
Barry Pederson	44	48	92	53
Peter McNab	36	40	76	19
Ray Bourque	17	49	66	51
Brad Park	14	42	56	82
Terry O'Reilly	22	30	52	213
Steve Kasper	20	31	51	72
Keith Crowder	23	21	44	101
Wayne Cashman	12	31	43	59
Mike O'Connell	5	35	40	75
Tom Fergus	15	24	39	12
Don Marcotte	13	21	34	14
Normand Leveille	14	19	33	49
Bruce Crowder	16	11	27	31
Stan Jonathan	6	17	23	57
Mike Gillis	9	8	17	54
Mike Milbury	2	10	12	71
Brad McCrimmon	1	8	9	83
Randy Hillier	0	8	8	29
Larry Melnyk	0	8	8	84
Mike Krushelynski	3	3	6	2
Craig MacTavish	0	1	1	0
Dave Barr	0	0	0	0
Dick Redmond	0	0	0	4
Doug Morrison	0	0	0	0

Number of power play advantages	289
Power play goals	65
% successful	22.5%
Rick Middleton	19
Barry Pederson	13
Peter McNab	11

Brad Park	8
Ray Bourque	4
Wayne Cashman	3
Tom Fergus	2
Steve Kasper	1
Mike O'Connell	1
Normand Leveille	1
Bruce Crowder	1
Stan Jonathan	1
Short-handed goals against	7
Penalty minutes:	1,266 – 15.8 per game

Times short-handed	291
Power play goals against	54
Penalty kill success	81.4
Short-handed goals	11
Barry Pederson	4
Steve Kasper	3
Rick Middleton	1
Peter McNab	1
Terry O'Reilly	1
Mike Krushelynski	1

1981-82 PLAYOFF RESULTS

April 1982

	AT	VERSUS	W-L-T	SCR						
7	Boston	Buffalo	W	3–1		16	Boston	Quebec	W	8–4
8	Boston	Buffalo	W	7–3		18	Quebec	Nordiques	L	3–2 (OT)
10	Buffalo	Sabres	L	5–2		19	Quebec	Nordiques	L	7–2
11	Buffalo	Sabres	W	5–2		21	Boston	Quebec	L	4–3
15	Boston	Quebec	W	4–3		23	Quebec	Nordiques	W	6–5 (OT)
						25	Boston	Quebec	L	2–1

1981-82 PLAYOFFS

vs. Buffalo Sabres	3 wins – 1 loss	vs. Quebec Nordiques	3 wins – 4 losses
at Buffalo	1 win – 1 loss	at Quebec	1 win – 2 losses
at Boston	2 wins – 0 losses	at Boston	2 wins – 2 losses

1981-82 PLAYOFF SCORING

	W	L	SO	GAA	PIM
Rogie Vachon	0	0	0	3.00	0
Mike Moffat	6	5	0	3.44	8

	G	A	P	PIM
Barry Pederson	7	11	18	2
Rick Middleton	6	9	15	0
Peter McNab	6	8	14	6
Terry O'Reilly	5	4	9	56
Steve Kasper	3	6	9	22
Bruce Crowder	5	3	8	9
Ray Bourque	1	5	6	16
Brad Park	1	4	5	4
Mike O'Connell	2	2	4	20
Keith Crowder	2	2	4	14
Mike Milbury	0	4	4	6
Don Marcotte	0	4	4	10
Tom Fergus	3	0	3	0
Mike Gillis	1	2	3	6
Larry Melnyk	0	3	3	40
Wayne Cashman	0	2	2	6
Dave Barr	1	0	1	0
Randy Hillier	0	1	1	16
Mike Krushelnyski	0	0	0	2
Dick Redmond	0	0	0	0
Brad McCrimmon	0	0	0	2
Stan Jonathan	0	0	0	6

Number of power play advantages	40
Power play goals	9
% successful	22.5%
Tom Fergus	2
Rick Middleton	2
Peter McNab	2
Barry Pederson	1
Steve Kasper	1

Bruce Crowder	1
Short-handed goals against	1
Penalty minutes:	251 – 22.8 per game
Times short-handed	42
Power play goals against	14
Penalty kill success	66.6%
Short-handed goals for	0

1982–1983
(59th year)

TEAM OWNER:	Sportsystems of Buffalo	STANLEY CUP WINNER:	New York Islanders
PRESIDENT & GOVERNOR:	Paul Mooney	ALL-STARS:	Pete Peeters (1st team)
GM:	Harry Sinden		Ray Bourque (2nd team)
COACH:	Gerry Cheevers	TROPHY WINNERS:	Vezina — Peter Peeters
ATTENDANCE:	530,870		Dufresne — Pete Peeters
	13,271 per game		7th Player — Pete Peeters
PLAYOFFS:	*Division semi-finals:*		Three Star —
	Defeat Quebec Nordiques		Rick Middleton
	3 wins – 1 loss	RADIO BROADCASTER:	WITS – Bob Wilson,
	Division finals:		Johnny Bucyk
	Defeat Buffalo Sabres	TV BROADCASTER:	WSBK TV38 – Fred Cusick,
	4 wins – 3 losses		John Peirson
	Conference finals:		
	Lose to New York Islanders		
	2 wins – 4 losses		

UNIFORMS

- Home jersey is white with gold and black trim. Socks are white with one gold band surrounded by two black bands at the calf. Road jersey is black with gold and white trim. Gold socks with one white band surrounded by two black bands at the calf. Logo is the spoked "B." Pants are black. Bearhead appears on both shoulders on both home and road uniforms.

POTPOURRI

- Bruins finish first overall in the NHL with 110 points.
- Bruins enjoy 17-game undefeated streak (15–0–2).
- Bruins lead the league in shutouts with 8.
- Bruins are not shut out all season.
- Pete Peeters enjoys a 9-game winning streak. Peeters also goes 31 games without a loss (26 wins and 5 ties).
- Bruce Crowder, Tom Fergus, Rick Middleton, and Mike O'Connell play in all 80 regular season games.
- The Bruins score over 300 goals for the 13th consecutive season.
- Lose conference finals to the New York Islanders.
- Ray Bourque misses first 13 games of the season with a broken sinus bone.
- In the October 23 game at Vancouver, Normand Leveille suffers a cerebral hemorrhage. Normand, the youngest player ever drafted by the Bruins, never plays another game in the NHL.
- Colorado Rockies move from Denver to New Jersey and become the New Jersey Devils.
- Barry Pederson's hat trick at Montreal on December 4 is the first for a Bruin at Montreal since Vic Stasiuk did it in 1959.

TRANSACTIONS

- Select Gord Kluzak #1 in the 1982 NHL draft.
- Obtain Dave Donnelly and Brad Palmer from Minnesota as part of an agreement for the Bruins not to select Brian Bellows with their #1 draft pick. Bruins select Gord Kluzak as their #1 draft pick.
- Trade Brad McCrimmon to Philadelphia for Pete Peeters.

1982-83 STANDINGS

PRINCE OF WALES CONFERENCE

Adams Division	W	L	T	P	GF	GA
Boston	50	20	10	110	327	228
Montreal	42	24	14	98	350	286
Buffalo	38	29	13	89	318	285
Quebec	34	34	12	80	343	336
Hartford	19	54	7	45	261	403
Patrick Division						
Philadelphia	49	23	8	106	326	240
New York Islanders	42	26	12	96	302	226
Washington	39	25	16	94	306	283
New York Rangers	35	35	10	80	306	287
New Jersey	17	49	14	48	230	338
Pittsburgh	18	53	9	45	257	394

CLARENCE CAMPBELL CONFERENCE

Norris Division	W	L	T	P	GF	GA
Chicago	47	23	10	104	338	268
Minnesota	40	24	16	96	321	290
Toronto	28	40	12	68	293	330
St. Louis	25	40	15	65	285	316
Detroit	21	44	15	57	263	344
Smythe Division						
Edmonton	47	21	12	106	424	315
Calgary	32	34	14	78	321	317
Vancouver	30	35	15	75	303	309
Winnipeg	33	39	8	74	311	333
Los Angeles	27	41	12	66	308	365

1982-83 RESULTS

October 1982

	AT	VERSUS	W-L-T	SCR
7	Boston	Montreal	L	5–1
9	Hartford	Whalers	W	5–4
10	Boston	Pittsburgh	W	4–3
12	New Jersey	Devils	T	2–2
14	Boston	Vancouver	W	2–1
16	Boston	Edmonton	T	6–6
19	Calgary	Flames	W	3–1
21	Edmonton	Oilers	W	5–3
23	Vancouver	Canucks	L	3–2
24	Los Angeles	Kings	L	5–4
27	Toronto	Maple Leafs	L	4–1
30	Montreal	Canadiens	T	4–4

November 1982

3	Buffalo	Sabres	W	3–2
4	Boston	Hartford	L	5–2
7	Boston	Detroit	W	7–0
11	Boston	Quebec	L	3–2
13	Boston	Buffalo	W	3–2
14	Boston	St. Louis	W	7–3
16	Quebec	Nordiques	W	7–4
18	New York	Islanders	W	3–1
20	Pittsburgh	Penguins	L	4–3
21	Boston	Calgary	W	2–1
24	Philadelphia	Flyers	T	4–4
25	Boston	New York Islanders	T	1–1
27	Boston	Hartford	W	8–0

December 1982

2	Boston	Quebec	T	3–3
4	Montreal	Canadiens	W	6–4
5	Boston	Philadelphia	W	6–4
7	Quebec	Nordiques	L	10–5
9	Boston	Montreal	W	8–5
11	Boston	Chicago	W	4–2
12	Washington	Capitals	L	4–3
16	Boston	Buffalo	W	8–1
18	Boston	Los Angeles	W	4–0

23	Hartford	Whalers	W	5-1
26	Boston	New Jersey	W	5-2
28	St. Louis	Blues	W	3-0
31	Minnesota	North Stars	W	5-3

January 1983

2	Winnipeg	Jets	L	6-4
5	Chicago	Blackhawks	W	4-1
7	New Jersey	Devils	T	2-2
8	Montreal	Canadiens	W	2-1
12	Toronto	Maple Leafs	W	6-4
13	Boston	Quebec	W	2-0
15	Boston	New York Rangers	W	2-0
17	Boston	Minnesota	W	4-3
20	Boston	Buffalo	W	4-0
22	Detroit	Red Wings	W	3-1
25	New York	Rangers	W	3-1
29	Boston	Detroit	W	7-3
31	Boston	Winnipeg	T	2-2

February 1983

3	Boston	Quebec	W	5-3
5	Boston	Hartford	W	7-4
6	Buffalo	Sabres	W	5-1
10	Boston	Pittsburgh	W	7-3
13	Boston	Vancouver	W	3-1
16	Buffalo	Sabres	L	3-1

18	Winnipeg	Jets	L	6-5
19	Minnesota	North Stars	W	6-2
22	Los Angeles	Kings	L	5-3
25	Buffalo	Sabres	L	7-6
27	Hartford	Whalers	W	4-3
28	Boston	Toronto	W	6-3

March 1983

3	Boston	Buffalo	L	3-2
5	Boston	Chicago	W	6-3
6	Boston	Edmonton	W	5-2
8	Quebec	Nordiques	W	11-5
10	Boston	Montreal	L	3-1
12	Boston	Philadelphia	W	5-2
13	Washington	Capitals	L	6-4
17	Boston	Washington	L	2-1
19	Boston	Calgary	T	2-2
20	New York	Rangers	W	4-0
22	New York	Islanders	W	3-1
24	Boston	St. Louis	W	7-6
26	Boston	Hartford	W	7-4
27	Hartford	Whalers	L	5-1
29	Quebec	Nordiques	W	4-3

April 1983

2	Montreal	Canadiens	L	2-1
3	Boston	Montreal	T	4-4

1982-83 SCORING

	W	L	T	S	GAA	PIM
Marco Baron	6	3	0	0	3.84	4
Mike Moffat	4	6	1	0	4.37	2
Pete Peeters	40	11	9	8	2.36	33
						2 assists

	G	A	P	PIM
Barry Pederson	46	61	107	47
Rick Middleton	49	47	96	8
Keith Crowder	35	39	74	105
Peter McNab	22	52	74	23
Ray Bourque	22	51	73	20
Mike Krushelynski	23	42	65	43
Tom Fergus	28	35	63	39
Mike O'Connell	14	39	53	42
Bruce Crowder	21	19	40	58

	G	A	P	PIM
Brad Park	10	26	36	82
Craig MacTavish	10	20	30	18
Luc Dufour	14	11	25	107
Mike Milbury	9	15	24	216
Terry O'Reilly	6	14	20	40
Brad Palmer	6	11	17	18
Wayne Cashman	4	11	15	20
Marty Howe	1	11	12	24
Randy Hillier	0	10	10	99
Normand Leveille	3	6	9	0
Steve Kasper	2	6	8	24
Gord Kluzak	1	6	7	105
Dave Barr	1	1	2	7
Mike Gillis	0	1	1	0
Larry Melnyk	0	0	0	0
Scott McLellan	0	0	0	0

Number of power play advantages	302
Power play goals	68
% successful	22.2%
Barry Pederson	15
Keith Crowder	10
Ray Bourque	7

Mike O'Connell	7
Rick Middleton	6
Peter McNab	5
Brad Park	5
Mike Krushelnyski	4
Tom Fergus	4

Normand Leveille	2	Penalty kill success		80.7%
Bruce Crowder	1	Short-handed goals		8
Mike Milbury	1	Rick Middleton		3
Wayne Cashman	1	Mike Krushelnyski		2
Short-handed goals against	6	Barry Pederson		1
Penalty minutes: 1,202 – 15.0 per game		Mike O'Connell		1
Times short-handed	275	Terry O'Reilly		1
Power play goals against	53			

1982-83 PLAYOFF RESULTS

April 1983

	AT	VERSUS	W-L-T	SCR
5	Boston	Quebec	W	4–3 (OT)
7	Boston	Quebec	W	4–2
9	Quebec	Nordiques	L	2–1
10	Quebec	Nordiques	W	2–1
14	Boston	Buffalo	L	7–4
15	Boston	Buffalo	W	5–3
17	Buffalo	Sabres	L	4–3
18	Buffalo	Sabres	W	6–2
20	Boston	Buffalo	W	9–0
22	Buffalo	Sabres	L	5–3
24	Boston	Buffalo	W	3–2 (OT)
26	Boston	New York Islanders	L	5–2
28	Boston	New York Islanders	W	4–1
30	New York	Islanders	L	7–3

May 1983

3	New York	Islanders	L	8–3
5	Boston	New York Islanders	W	5–1
7	New York	Islanders	L	8–4

1982-83 PLAYOFFS

vs. Quebec Nordiques	3 wins – 1 loss	vs. New York Islanders	2 wins – 4 losses
at Quebec	1 win – 1 loss	at New York	0 wins – 3 losses
at Boston	2 wins – 0 losses	at Boston	2 wins – 1 loss
vs. Buffalo Sabres	4 wins – 3 losses		
at Buffalo	1 win – 2 losses		
at Boston	3 wins – 1 loss		

1982-83 PLAYOFF SCORING

	W	L	SO	GAA	PIM
Pete Peeters	9	8	1	3.57	8

	G	A	P	PIM
Rick Middleton	11	22	33	6
Barry Pederson	14	18	32	21
Ray Bourque	8	15	23	10
Mike Krushelnyski	8	6	14	12
Brad Park	3	9	12	18
Peter McNab	3	5	8	4
Mike O'Connell	3	5	8	12
Keith Crowder	1	6	7	54
Gord Kluzak	1	4	5	54

Bruce Crowder	3	1	4	32
Craig MacTavish	3	1	4	18
Tom Fergus	2	2	4	15
Mike Gillis	1	3	4	2
Steve Kasper	2	1	3	10
Brad Palmer	1	0	1	0
Luc Dufour	1	0	1	30
Wayne Cashman	0	1	1	0
Marty Howe	0	1	1	9
Randy Hillier	0	0	0	4
Dave Barr	0	0	0	2
Larry Melnyk	0	0	0	9

Number of power play advantages	77	Rick Middleton	4
Power play goals	13	Ray Bourque	2
% successful	16.9%	Mike Krushelnyski	2

Mike O'Connell	2	Penalty kill success	87.5%
Barry Pederson	1	Short-handed goals	4
Brad Park	1	Rick Middleton	1
Keith Crowder	1	Barry Pederson	1
Short-handed goals against	0	Steve Kasper	1
Penalty minutes: 330 = 19.4 per game		Brad Palmer	1
Times short-handed	67	Penalty minutes: 322 – 18.9 per game	
Power play goals against	3		

1983–1984
(60th year)

TEAM OWNER:	Sportsystems of Buffalo	STANLEY CUP WINNER:	Edmonton Oilers
PRESIDENT & GOVERNOR:	Paul Mooney	ALL-STARS:	Ray Bourque (1st team)
GM:	Harry Sinden	TROPHY WINNERS:	Lester Patrick — Art Ross
COACH:	Gerry Cheevers		Dufresne — Rick Middleton
ATTENDANCE:	543,534		7th Player — Mike O'Connell
	13,588 per game		Three Star — Rick Middleton
PLAYOFFS:	*Division semi-finals:*	RADIO BROADCASTER:	WPLM – Bob Wilson,
	Lose to Montreal Canadiens		Johnny Bucyk
	0 wins – 3 losses	TV BROADCASTER:	WSBK TV38 – Fred Cusick,
			John Peirson

UNIFORMS

- Home jersey is white with gold and black trim. Socks are white with one gold band surrounded by two black bands at the calf. Road jersey is black with gold and white trim. Gold socks with one white band surrounded by two black bands at the calf. Logo is the spoked "B." Pants are black. Bearhead appears on both shoulders on both home and road uniforms.

POTPOURRI

- Bruins finish tied with the second-best record in the league.
- Ray Bourque becomes the sixth defenseman in history to score 30 goals in a season.
- Doug Keans has a 10-game winning streak and back-to-back shutouts.
- Rick Middleton ties Bruins' record for most points by a right winger with 105.
- Rick Middleton becomes the first Bruin to score an overtime goal in the regular season since 1942.
- Barry Pederson becomes the first Bruin since 1978 to score 4 goals in a game.
- Bruins have 5 players compete in the NHL All-Star game at the Meadowlands in New Jersey. They are Ray Bourque, Mike O'Connell, Pete Peeters, Rick Middleton, and Barry Pederson.
- Barry Pederson, Rick Middleton, and Gord Kluzak play in all 80 games.
- Bruins enjoy three 5-game winning streaks.
- Bruins only manage to score 2 goals in a 3-game playoff sweep at the hands of Montreal who play rookie Steve Penney in goal.
- NHL reinstates overtime for the first time since the 1941–42 season.
- In 3 playoff games against Montreal, the Bruins only score 2 goals. Tom Fergus scores both goals.
- Pete Peeters ejected from a March 4 game in Hartford even though he is the back-up goalie.
- The Bruins end the season on the road for the first time since 1944.
- The Bruins are not involved in any penalty shot situations.

- The St. Louis Blues, owned by the Ralston Purina Company, refuse to participate in the 1983 amateur draft because of financial losses.
- Prior to the February 11 game against Edmonton, Normand Leveille makes his first Boston Garden appearance since his cerebral hemorrhage.
- Bruins are 1-0-6 in overtime games.

TRANSACTIONS

- Trade Peter McNab to Vancouver for Jim Nill.
- Obtain John Blum from Edmonton for Larry Melnyk.
- Select Nevin Markwart #1 in the 1983 NHL entry draft.
- Bruins sign Guy Lapointe as a free agent.
- Sign Jim Schoenfeld as a free agent.
- Sign Doug Keans as a free agent.
- Trade Dave Barr to the Rangers for Dave Silk.

1983-84 STANDINGS

PRINCE OF WALES CONFERENCE

Adams Division

	W	L	T	P	GF	GA
Boston	49	25	6	104	336	261
Buffalo	48	25	7	103	315	257
Quebec	42	28	10	94	360	278
Montreal	35	40	5	75	286	295
Hartford	28	42	10	66	288	320

Patrick Division

	W	L	T	P	GF	GA
New York Islanders	50	26	4	104	357	269
Washington	48	27	5	101	308	226
Philadelphia	44	26	10	98	350	290
New York Rangers	42	29	9	93	314	304
New Jersey	17	56	7	41	231	350
Pittsburgh	16	58	6	38	254	390

CLARENCE CAMPBELL CONFERENCE

Norris Division

	W	L	T	P	GF	GA
Minnesota	39	31	10	88	345	344
St. Louis	32	41	7	71	293	316
Detroit	31	42	7	69	298	323
Chicago	30	42	8	68	277	311
Toronto	26	45	9	61	303	387

Smythe Division

	W	L	T	P	GF	GA
Edmonton	57	18	5	119	446	314
Calgary	34	32	14	82	311	314
Vancouver	32	39	9	73	306	328
Winnipeg	31	38	11	73	340	374
Los Angeles	23	44	13	59	309	376

1983-84 RESULTS

October 1983

	AT	VERSUS	W-L-T	SCR
6	Boston	Quebec	W	9-3
8	Hartford	Whalers	L	4-3
9	Boston	Hartford	W	4-1
13	Boston	Montreal	W	4-2
15	Boston	Buffalo	W	5-3
18	Quebec	Nordiques	L	5-3

20	Philadelphia	Flyers	T	3–3
22	Pittsburgh	Penguins	W	6–1
25	Chicago	Blackhawks	L	5–1
27	Minnesota	North Stars	W	8–1
29	St. Louis	Blues	W	3–2

November 1983

3	Boston	St. Louis	W	9–5
5	Montreal	Canadiens	W	10–4
6	Boston	Los Angeles	W	7–3
9	Buffalo	Sabres	L	3–1
12	Quebec	Nordiques	W	6–4
13	Boston	Washington	W	4–2
17	Boston	Toronto	W	4–1
19	Boston	New York Rangers	T	6–6
22	Montreal	Canadiens	L	4–2
24	Boston	Quebec	L	6–3
26	Boston	New Jersey	W	6–2

December 1983

1	Boston	Vancouver	W	7–1
3	Boston	Minnesota	L	6–2
5	Washington	Capitals	W	4–1
6	Pittsburgh	Penguins	W	5–3
8	Boston	Montreal	W	6–2
10	Boston	Buffalo	L	4–2
11	Boston	Winnipeg	W	4–2
15	Boston	Hartford	W	4–2
17	Boston	Chicago	L	5–2
18	Chicago	Blackhawks	W	5–1
20	Hartford	Whalers	W	7–2
22	Boston	Minnesota	L	4–2
26	Buffalo	Sabres	W	2–1
28	Calgary	Flames	W	5–3
30	Edmonton	Oilers	L	2–0
31	Vancouver	Canucks	T	5–5

January 1984

3	New York	Islanders	W	4–2
5	Boston	Quebec	L	8–3
7	Boston	New York Rangers	W	5–2
11	Detroit	Red Wings	W	7–2
12	St. Louis	Blues	W	6–2

14	Boston	Pittsburgh	W	7–3
16	Boston	New York Islanders	W	2–0
17	Quebec	Nordiques	L	7–3
19	Boston	Quebec	W	4–3
21	Hartford	Whalers	W	2–0
23	Boston	Buffalo	L	5–3
28	Boston	Winnipeg	W	5–2
29	Boston	Montreal	L	7–2

February 1984

2	Boston	Buffalo	W	5–3
4	Boston	Philadelphia	W	8–5
5	Boston	Detroit	L	6–5
8	Toronto	Maple Leafs	L	6–4
9	Boston	Toronto	L	6–3
11	Boston	Edmonton	W	4–1
15	Buffalo	Sabres	L	7–4
17	Edmonton	Oilers	L	5–2
18	Calgary	Flames	T	5–5
21	Vancouver	Canucks	W	5–2
22	Los Angeles	Kings	W	6–3
25	Winnipeg	Jets	L	5–2
27	Buffalo	Sabres	W	3–1

March 1984

1	Boston	Los Angeles	W	4–3 (OT)
3	Boston	Hartford	T	3–3
4	Hartford	Whalers	L	6–4
8	Boston	Calgary	W	3–2
10	Montreal	Canadiens	W	4–2
11	Boston	Washington	L	2–1
14	Detroit	Red Wings	W	4–2
15	Philadelphia	Flyers	L	6–3
17	Boston	New Jersey	L	5–3
20	New York	Rangers	W	6–4
22	Boston	New York Islanders	T	3–3
24	Montreal	Canadiens	W	5–2
27	Quebec	Nordiques	W	6–4
29	Boston	Hartford	W	4–3
31	Boston	Montreal	W	2–1

April 1984

1	New Jersey	Devils	W	3–1

1983-84 SCORING

	W	L	T	S	GAA	PIM
Doug Keans	19	8	3	2	3.10	2
Mike Moffat	1	1	1	0	4.84	0
Pete Peeters	29	16	2	0	3.16	36

	G	A	P	PIM
Barry Pederson	39	77	116	64
Rick Middleton	47	58	105	14

Ray Bourque	31	65	96	57
Tom Fergus	25	36	61	12
Mike O'Connell	18	42	60	42
Keith Crowder	24	28	52	128
Mike Krushelynski	25	20	45	55
Craig MacTavish	20	23	43	35
Gord Kluzak	10	27	37	135
Nevin Markwart	14	16	30	121

Peter McNab	14	16	30	10	Dave Donnelly	3	4	7	2
Dave Silk	13	17	30	64	Lyndon Byers	2	4	6	32
Terry O'Reilly	12	18	30	124	Jim Nill	3	2	5	81
Bruce Crowder	6	14	20	44	Doug Kostynski	3	1	4	2
Mike Milbury	2	17	19	159	Greg Johnston	2	1	3	2
Guy Lapointe	2	16	18	34	John Blum	1	1	2	30
Mike Gillis	6	11	17	35	Brian Curran	1	1	2	57
Randy Hillier	3	12	15	125	Jim Schoenfeld	0	2	2	20
Steve Kasper	3	11	14	19	Dave Reid	1	0	1	2
Luc Dufour	6	4	10	47	Geoff Courtnall	0	0	0	0

Number of power play advantages	342	Short-handed goals against	7
Power play goals	82	Penalty minutes: 1,606 – 20.1 per game	
% successful	24%	Times short-handed	336
Rick Middleton	16	Power play goals against	70
Ray Bourque	12	Penalty kill success	83.3%
Barry Pederson	10	Short-handed goals	10
Mike O'Connell	9	Rick Middleton	4
Craig MacTavish	7	Barry Pederson	3
Tom Fergus	6	Mike Krushelnyski	2
Gord Kluzak	5	Ray Bourque	1
Dave Silk	5		
Keith Crowder	4		
Mike Krushelnyski	3		
Terry O'Reilly	2		
Peter McNab	2		
Guy Lapointe	1		

1983-84 PLAYOFF RESULTS

April 1984

	AT	VERSUS	W-L-T	SCR
4	Boston	Montreal	L	2–1
5	Boston	Montreal	L	3–1
7	Montreal	Canadiens	L	5–0

1983-84 PLAYOFFS

vs. Montreal Canadiens	0 wins – 3 losses
at Montreal	0 wins – 1 loss
at Boston	0 wins – 2 losses

1983-84 PLAYOFF SCORING

	W	L	SO	GAA	PIM					
Pete Peeters	0	3	0	3.33	2	Craig MacTavish	0	0	0	0
						Mike Krushelnyski	0	0	0	0
		G	A	P	PIM	John Blum	0	0	0	4
Tom Fergus		2	0	2	9	Bruce Crowder	0	0	0	0
Ray Bourque		0	2	2	0	Keith Crowder	0	0	0	7
Barry Pederson		0	1	1	2	Brian Curran	0	0	0	7
						Dave Donnelly	0	0	0	0

Mike Gillis	o	o	o	2	Jim Nill	o	o	o	4
Steve Kasper	o	o	o	7	Mike O'Connell	o	o	o	o
Gord Kluzak	o	o	o	o	Terry O'Reilly	o	o	o	14
Rick Middleton	o	o	o	o	Dave Silk	o	o	o	7
Mike Milbury	o	o	o	12					

Number of power play advantages	13	Times short-handed	12
Power play goals	1	Power play goals against	2
% successful	7.7%	Penalty kill success	3.3%
Tom Fergus	1	Short-handed goals	0
Penalty minutes:	77 – 25.7 per game		

1984–1985
(61st year)

TEAM OWNER:	Sportsystems of Buffalo	STANLEY CUP WINNER:	Edmonton Oilers
PRESIDENT & GOVERNOR:	Paul Mooney	ALL-STARS:	Ray Bourque (1st team)
GM:	Harry Sinden	TROPHY WINNERS:	Dufresne — Ray Bourque
COACH:	Gerry Cheevers & Harry Sinden		7th Player — Keith Crowder
			Three Star — Ray Bourque
ATTENDANCE:	530,297 13,257 per game	RADIO BROADCASTER:	WPLM – Bob Wilson, Johnny Bucyk
PLAYOFFS:	*Division semi-finals:* Lose to Montreal Canadiens 2 wins – 3 losses	TV BROADCASTER:	WSBK TV38 & NESN – Fred Cusick, John Peirson

UNIFORMS

- Home jersey is white with gold and black trim. Socks are white with one gold band surrounded by two black bands at the calf. Road jersey is black with gold and white trim. Gold socks with one white band surrounded by two black bands at the calf. Logo is the spoked "B." Pants are black. Bearhead appears on both shoulders on both home and road uniforms.

POTPOURRI

- Bruins score over 300 goals for the 15th consecutive season.
- Bruins score 17 short-handed goals.
- Bruins have 8 short-handed goals scored against them.
- Bruins lose in playoffs to Montreal, 3 games to 2.
- Steve Kasper's hat trick on November 25 against Montreal is the only 3-goal game of the season for Boston.
- Bruins score 8 goals on 3 different occasions.
- Bruins are not involved in any penalty shot situations this season.
- Bruins are 4–4–10 in overtime games.
- NHL adopt Mag-nets goal posts to help prevent injuries.
- Mario Lemieux of the Pittsburgh Penguins scores his first NHL goal on his first shot on opening night, October 11. Pete Peeters of the Bruins is the goaltender for Boston on Lemieux's goal.

TRANSACTIONS

- Obtain Charlie Simmer from the Los Angeles Kings for Boston's 1985 first-round pick.
- Obtain Butch Goring on waivers from the Islanders.

- Trade Luc Dufour to Quebec for Louis Sleigher.
- Trade Jim Nill to Winnipeg for Morris Lukowich.
- Select Dave Pasin #1 in the 1984 NHL entry draft.
- Trade Mike Krushelnyski to Edmonton for Ken Linseman.

1984-85 STANDINGS

PRINCE OF WALES CONFERENCE

Adams Division

	W	L	T	P	GF	GA
Montreal	41	27	12	94	309	262
Quebec	41	30	9	91	323	275
Buffalo	38	28	14	90	290	237
Boston	36	34	10	82	303	287
Hartford	30	41	9	69	268	318

Patrick Division

	W	L	T	P	GF	GA
Philadelphia	53	20	7	113	348	241
Washington	46	25	9	101	322	240
New York Islanders	40	34	6	86	345	312
New York Rangers	26	44	10	62	295	345
New Jersey	22	48	10	54	264	346
Pittsburgh	24	51	5	53	276	385

CLARENCE CAMPBELL CONFERENCE

Norris Division

	W	L	T	P	GF	GA
St. Louis	37	31	12	86	299	288
Chicago	38	25	7	83	309	299
Detroit	27	41	12	66	313	357
Minnesota	25	43	12	62	268	321
Toronto	20	52	8	48	253	358

Smythe Division

	W	L	T	P	GF	GA
Edmonton	49	20	11	109	401	298
Winnipeg	43	27	10	96	358	332
Calgary	41	27	12	94	363	302
Los Angeles	34	32	14	82	339	326
Vancouver	25	49	9	59	284	401

1984-85 RESULTS

October 1984

	AT	VERSUS	W-L-T	SCR
11	Boston	Pittsburgh	W	4-3
13	Hartford	Whalers	L	3-2 (OT)
14	Boston	Hartford	W	4-2
16	Edmonton	Oilers	L	7-2
19	Calgary	Flames	L	8-2
21	Winnipeg	Jets	L	3-2
24	St. Louis	Blues	W	4-1
27	New York	Islanders	W	8-3
28	New York	Rangers	W	6-4

November 1984

	AT	VERSUS	W-L-T	SCR
1	Boston	Quebec	W	7-1
3	Montreal	Canadiens	L	3-1
4	Boston	New York Islanders	W	6-2
8	Boston	Detroit	W	5-2
10	Detroit	Red Wings	W	4-2
11	Boston	St. Louis	T	1-1
14	Buffalo	Sabres	L	4-2
15	Boston	New Jersey	W	5-3
17	Boston	Philadelphia	L	5-3
21	Philadelphia	Flyers	L	4-3
24	Boston	Chicago	L	2-1
25	Boston	Montreal	W	7-4
29	Boston	Edmonton	L	4-2

December 1984

1	Boston	Washington	L	5–4 (OT)
3	Quebec	Nordiques	T	3–3
5	Buffalo	Sabres	T	3–3
6	Boston	Montreal	L	3–1
8	Boston	Buffalo	L	3–1
12	New York	Rangers	T	3–3
13	Boston	Quebec	T	5–5
15	Boston	Vancouver	W	2–1 (OT)
18	Montreal	Canadiens	W	6–4
19	Hartford	Whalers	L	6–5
22	Toronto	Maple Leafs	L	6–4
23	Boston	Minnesota	W	4–3
27	Los Angeles	Kings	T	6–6
29	Minnesota	North Stars	W	5–3
30	Winnipeg	Jets	W	5–3

January 1985

1	Washington	Capitals	L	5–1
5	Boston	New York Rangers	T	3–3
7	Boston	Los Angeles	W	5–4 (OT)
9	Toronto	Maple Leafs	W	5–3
10	Boston	Buffalo	L	3–0
12	Boston	Detroit	W	4–3
15	New Jersey	Devils	W	3–2
17	Boston	Calgary	L	4–3
19	Quebec	Nordiques	L	4–3
21	Boston	Montreal	W	3–1
24	Boston	Buffalo	W	5–2
26	Boston	Hartford	L	3–2
27	Hartford	Whalers	W	8–4
30	Buffalo	Sabres	L	6–2
31	Boston	Quebec	W	6–5

February 1985

2	Boston	Winnipeg	L	4–3
7	Boston	Hartford	W	7–5
9	Boston	Chicago	L	6–5
10	Chicago	Blackhawks	L	4–3
14	Los Angeles	Kings	T	3–3
16	Vancouver	Canucks	L	3–2 (OT)
20	Minnesota	North Stars	W	3–2
23	New York	Islanders	L	7–1
28	Boston	Philadelphia	W	6–1

March 1985

2	Boston	Vancouver	W	5–0
5	Quebec	Nordiques	L	6–4
7	Boston	Hartford	W	4–0
9	Boston	Pittsburgh	L	6–5 (OT)
10	Washington	Capitals	W	3–2
13	Pittsburgh	Penguins	W	7–3
14	New Jersey	Devils	W	7–4
16	Boston	Calgary	L	5–3
18	Boston	Quebec	L	8–4
21	Boston	St. Louis	T	1–1
23	Hartford	Whalers	L	5–2
25	Buffalo	Sabres	W	4–3 (OT)
26	Montreal	Canadiens	L	5–3
28	Boston	Edmonton	W	6–3
30	Boston	Montreal	L	7–3

April 1985

2	Quebec	Nordiques	L	6–4
4	Boston	Buffalo	W	5–3
6	Montreal	Canadiens	T	4–4
7	Boston	Toronto	W	5–1

1984-85 SCORING

	W	L	T	S	GAA	PIM
Doug Keans	16	6	3	1	3.29	6
Pete Peeters	19	26	4	1	3.47	20
Don Sylvestri	0	0	2	0	3.53	2
Cleon Daskalakis	1	2	1	0	4.98	0

	G	A	P	PIM
Ray Bourque	20	66	86	53
Rick Middleton	30	46	76	6
Ken Linseman	25	49	74	126
Tom Fergus	30	43	74	75
Keith Crowder	32	38	70	142
Charlie Simmer	33	30	63	35
Mike O'Connell	15	40	55	64
Butch Goring	13	21	34	6
Steve Kasper	16	24	40	33
Louis Sleigher	12	19	31	45
Terry O'Reilly	13	17	30	168
Geoff Courtnall	12	16	28	82
Dave Reid	14	13	27	27
Mats Thelin	5	13	18	78
John Blum	3	13	16	263
Mike Milbury	3	13	16	152
Dave Donnelly	6	8	14	46
Morris Lukowich	5	8	13	21
Barry Pederson	4	8	12	10
Lyndon Byers	3	8	11	41
Frank Simonetti	1	5	6	26
Nevin Markwart	0	4	4	36
Brian Curran	0	1	1	158
Doug Morrison	0	0	0	2
Greg Johnston	0	0	0	0
Doug Kostynski	0	0	0	2

Number of power play advantages	323	Times short-handed		337
Power play goals	69	Power play goals against		67
% successful	21.4%	Penalty kill success		80.1%
Keith Crowder	14	Short-handed goals		17
Charlie Simmer	12	Steve Kasper		5
Rick Middleton	12	Rick Middleton		3
Ray Bourque	10	Butch Goring		2
Mike O'Connell	8	Barry Pederson		2
Ken Linseman	5	Ray Bourque		1
Tom Fergus	4	Ken Linseman		1
Butch Goring	2	Terry O'Reilly		1
Dave Reid	2	Mike Milbury		1
Short-handed goals against	8	Dave Donnelly		1
Penalty minutes:	1825 – 22.8 per game			

1984-85 PLAYOFF RESULTS

April 1985

	AT	VERSUS		W-L-T	SCR
10	Montreal	Canadiens		W	5–3
11	Montreal	Canadiens		L	5–3

	AT	VERSUS		W-L-T	SCR
13	Boston	Montreal		L	4–2
14	Boston	Montreal		W	7–6
16	Montreal	Canadiens		L	1–0

1984-85 PLAYOFFS

vs. Montreal Canadiens	2 wins – 3 losses
at Montreal	1 win – 2 losses
at Boston	1 win – 1 loss

1984-85 PLAYOFF SCORING

	W	L	SO	GAA	PIM
Pete Peeters	0	1	0	4.00	0
Doug Keans	2	2	0	3.75	0

	G	A	P	PIM
Ken Linseman	4	6	10	8
Mike O'Connell	1	5	6	0
Keith Crowder	3	2	5	19
Charlie Simmer	2	2	4	2
Rick Middleton	3	0	3	0
Terry O'Reilly	1	2	3	9
Ray Bourque	0	3	3	4
Butch Goring	1	1	2	0

	G	A	P	PIM
Geoff Courtnall	0	2	2	7
Steve Kasper	1	0	1	9
Dave Reid	1	0	1	0
Frank Simonetti	0	1	1	2
Dave Donnelly	0	0	0	0
Morris Lukowich	0	0	0	0
Nevin Markwart	0	0	0	0
John Blum	0	0	0	13
Tom Fergus	0	0	0	4
Mike Milbury	0	0	0	10
Louis Sleigher	0	0	0	4
Mats Thelin	0	0	0	6

Number of power play advantages	15	Times short-handed	21
Power play goals	1	Power play goals against	5
% successful	6.7%	Penalty kill success	76.2%
Mike O'Connell	1	Short-handed goals	0
Short-handed goals against	0		
Penalty minutes:	97 – 19.4 per game		

1985–1986
(62nd year)

TEAM OWNER:	Sportsystems of Buffalo	ALL-STARS:	Ray Bourque (2nd team)
PRESIDENT & GOVERNOR:	Paul Mooney	TROPHY WINNERS:	Masterton — Charlie Simmer
GM:	Harry Sinden		Dufresne — Ray Bourque
COACH:	Butch Goring		7th Player — Randy Burridge
ATTENDANCE:	497,277		Three Star — Ray Bourque
	12,431 per game	RADIO BROADCASTER:	WPLM – Bob Wilson,
PLAYOFFS:	*Division semi-finals:*		Johnny Bucyk
	Lose to Montreal Canadiens	TV BROADCASTER:	WSBK TV38 & NESN –
	0 wins – 3 losses		Fred Cusick, Dave Shea
STANLEY CUP WINNER:	Montreal Canadiens		

UNIFORMS

- Home jersey is white with gold and black trim. Socks are white with one gold band surrounded by two black bands at the calf. Road jersey is black with gold and white trim. Gold socks with one white band surrounded by two black bands at the calf. Logo is the spoked "B." Pants are black. Bearhead appears on both shoulders on both home and road uniforms.

POTPOURRI

- Steve Kasper plays in all 80 games.
- Ken Linseman plays in his 500th career game.
- Rick Middleton collects his 400th career goal.
- Charlie Simmer scores his 300th career goal.
- Bruins score 7 short-handed goals.
- Bruins lose division semi-finals in 3 straight to Montreal.
- Rick Middleton's season ends after 49 games because of a concussion.
- Bruins surrender 5 short-handed goals.
- Bruins have 4 former WHA Birmingham Bulls in their line-up: Keith Crowder, Ken Linseman, Louis Sleigher, and Pat Riggin.
- Assistant coach Mike Milbury suspends his coaching duties and returns as a player because of the number of injuries to the teams defensemen. Milbury plays in 22 games.
- Bruins are awarded 2 penalty shots in a season for the first time since 1966–67.
- Bruins are 2–3–12 in overtime games.
- NHL rules committee votes to allow substitutions in the event of coincidental minor penalties.

TRANSACTIONS

- Trade Tom Fergus to Toronto for Bill Derlago.
- Trade Pete Peeters to Washington for Pat Riggin.
- Trade Bill Derlago to Winnipeg for Wade Campbell.
- Trade Mike O'Connell to Detroit for Reed Larson.
- Trade Dave Donnelly to Detroit for Dwight Foster.
- Select Alain Cote, their first pick in the second round of the 1985 NHL draft. The Bruins do not have a #1 pick in the amateur draft.
- Terry O'Reilly retires.

1985-86 STANDINGS

PRINCE OF WALES CONFERENCE

Adams Division	W	L	T	P	GF	GA
Quebec	43	31	6	92	330	289
Montreal	40	33	7	87	330	280
Boston	37	31	12	86	311	288
Hartford	40	36	4	84	332	302
Buffalo	37	37	6	80	296	291

Patrick Division						
Philadelphia	53	23	4	110	335	241
Washington	50	23	7	107	315	272
New York Islanders	39	29	12	90	327	284
New York Rangers	36	38	6	78	280	276
Pittsburgh	34	38	8	76	313	305
New Jersey	28	49	3	59	300	374

CLARENCE CAMPBELL CONFERENCE

Norris Division						
Chicago	39	33	8	86	351	349
Minnesota	38	33	9	85	327	305
St. Louis	37	34	9	83	302	291
Toronto	25	48	7	57	311	386
Detroit	17	57	6	40	266	415

Smythe Division						
Edmonton	56	17	7	119	426	310
Calgary	40	31	9	89	354	315
Winnipeg	26	47	7	59	295	372
Vancouver	23	44	13	59	282	333
Los Angeles	23	49	8	54	284	389

1985-86 RESULTS

October 1985

	AT	VERSUS	W-L-T	SCR
10	Boston	Toronto	W	3–1
12	Detroit	Red Wings	W	9–2
13	Boston	Montreal	W	7–2
16	Vancouver	Canucks	T	3–3
18	Edmonton	Oilers	L	3–2
19	Calgary	Flames	W	6–3
22	Los Angeles	Kings	W	5–2
27	New York	Rangers	L	2–1
29	New Jersey	Devils	W	6–4
31	Boston	Los Angeles	W	7–4

November 1985

2	Boston	Chicago	W	5–4
5	Quebec	Nordiques	L	7–5
7	Boston	Hartford	W	2–1
9	Philadelphia	Flyers	L	5–3
10	Boston	Minnesota	W	2–1
13	Buffalo	Sabres	L	6–4
14	Toronto	Maple Leafs	T	6–6
16	Boston	Washington	T	2–2
18	Montreal	Canadiens	L	6–2
21	Boston	New York Islanders	T	4–4
23	Boston	Philadelphia	W	5–4
28	Boston	Quebec	L	3–0
30	Quebec	Nordiques	L	2–0

December 1985

1	Boston	New Jersey	W	4–2
5	Boston	Montreal	W	8–6
7	Hartford	Whalers	L	7–2
8	Boston	Buffalo	T	3–3
10	Philadelphia	Flyers	L	7–4
12	Boston	Quebec	T	1–1
14	Boston	New York Rangers	W	4–2
19	Boston	Hartford	W	2–1
21	Boston	Minnesota	W	5–2
22	Buffalo	Sabres	L	5–3
26	Pittsburgh	Penguins	L	4–3

28	St. Louis	Blues	W	5–1
29	Chicago	Blackhawks	L	4–3
31	Buffalo	Sabres	T	6–6

January 1986

2	New York	Islanders	L	7–5
4	Boston	Buffalo	W	4–0
8	Montreal	Canadiens	L	5–3
9	Boston	St. Louis	L	7–2
11	Boston	Winnipeg	W	8–4
13	Boston	Edmonton	L	5–3
16	Boston	Calgary	W	3–2
19	Winnipeg	Jets	W	2–1
22	Detroit	Red Wings	L	6–5 (OT)
23	Boston	Winnipeg	W	7–5
25	Boston	Detroit	W	6–3
27	Boston	Hartford	W	6–3
29	Hartford	Whalers	W	5–4 (OT)

February 1986

1	Montreal	Canadiens	L	2–1
2	Boston	Pittsburgh	W	3–2
6	Boston	Buffalo	L	8–6
8	Boston	New York Rangers	L	3–2
9	Boston	Quebec	L	4–3 (OT)
11	Chicago	Blackhawks	L	5–4
15	St. Louis	Blues	L	5–1

16	Minnesota	North Stars	W	5–3
18	Calgary	Flames	L	7–4
22	Edmonton	Oilers	W	6–5 (OT)
23	Vancouver	Canucks	W	6–1
25	Quebec	Nordiques	W	7–4
27	Boston	Washington	L	2–1

March 1986

1	Boston	New Jersey	W	8–3
2	Hartford	Whalers	L	4–1
6	Boston	Quebec	L	5–4 (OT)
8	Montreal	Canadiens	L	8–3
12	Pittsburgh	Penguins	W	5–2
13	Boston	Montreal	W	3–2
15	Boston	Vancouver	T	1–1
20	Boston	Los Angeles	W	6–3
22	Boston	New York Islanders	T	3–3
23	Hartford	Whalers	T	5–5
25	Washington	Capitals	L	6–3
27	Boston	Montreal	T	3–3
29	Boston	Buffalo	W	2–1
30	Buffalo	Sabres	W	5–3

April 1986

3	Boston	Toronto	W	4–2
5	Quebec	Nordiques	T	2–2
6	Boston	Hartford	L	4–3

1985-86 SCORING

	W	L	T	S	GAA	PIM
Bill Ranford	3	1	0	0	2.50	0
Pat Riggin	17	11	8	1	3.35	4
Doug Keans	14	13	3	0	3.65	12
						1 assist
Pete Peeters	3	4	1	0	3.84	4
Cleon Daskalakis	0	2	0	0	5.00	

	G	A	P	PIM
Keith Crowder	38	46	84	177
Ken Linseman	23	58	81	97
Barry Pederson	29	47	76	60
Ray Bourque	19	57	76	68
Charlie Simmer	36	24	60	42
Rick Middleton	14	30	44	10
Randy Burridge	17	25	42	28
Steve Kasper	17	23	40	73
Gord Kluzak	8	31	39	155
Geoff Courtnall	21	16	37	61
Dave Pasin	18	19	37	50
Kraig Nienhuis	16	14	30	37
Mike O'Connell	8	21	29	47
Michael Thelven	6	20	26	48
Nevin Markwart	7	15	22	207
Bill Derlago	5	16	21	15
Dave Reid	10	10	20	10
John Blum	1	7	8	80
Reed Larson	3	4	7	8
Brian Curran	2	5	7	192
Mike Milbury	2	5	7	102
Louis Sleigher	4	2	6	20
Alain Cote	0	6	6	14
Mats Thelin	2	3	5	29
Morris Lukowich	1	4	5	10
Jay Miller	3	0	3	178
Lyndon Byers	0	2	2	9
Greg Johnston	0	2	2	0
Frank Simonetti	1	0	1	14
Wade Campbell	0	0	0	15
John Carter	0	0	0	0
Dave Donnelly	0	0	0	17
Dwight Foster	0	0	0	4

Number of power play advantages	412
Power play goals	95
% successful	23.1%
Keith Crowder	20
Charlie Simmer	14
Barry Pederson	12
Ray Bourque	11
Ken Linseman	8
Rick Middleton	4
Dave Pasin	4
Dave Reid	4
Mike O'Connell	4
Gord Kluzak	3
Kraig Nienhuis	3
Geoff Courtnall	2
Reed Larson	1

Randy Burridge	1
Steve Kasper	1
Michael Thelven	1
Mats Thelin	1
Bill Derlago	1
Short-handed goals against	5
Penalty minutes: 1,919 – 24.0 per game	
Times short-handed	402
Power play goals against	97
Penalty kill success	75.9%
Short-handed goals	7
Steve Kasper	3
Rick Middleton	2
Bill Derlago	1
Mike O'Connell	1

1985-86 PLAYOFF RESULTS

April 1986

	AT	VERSUS		W-L-T	SCR
9	Montreal	Canadiens		L	3–1
10	Montreal	Canadiens		L	3–2
12	Boston	Montreal		L	4–3

1985-86 PLAYOFFS

vs. Montreal Canadiens	0 wins – 3 losses
at Montreal	0 wins – 2 losses
at Boston	0 wins – 1 loss

1985-86 PLAYOFF SCORING

	W	L	SO	GAA	PIM
Pat Riggin	0	1	0	3.00	2
Bill Ranford	0	2	0	3.50	0

	G	A	P	PIM
Randy Burridge	0	4	4	12
Keith Crowder	2	0	2	21
Gord Kluzak	1	1	2	16
Dwight Foster	0	2	2	2
Steve Kasper	1	0	1	4
Reed Larson	1	0	1	6
Barry Pederson	1	0	1	0
Ken Linseman	0	1	1	17
Dave Pasin	0	1	1	0
Mike Milbury	0	0	0	17
Louis Sleigher	0	0	0	14
Brian Curran	0	0	0	4
Jay Miller	0	0	0	17
Kraig Nienhuis	0	0	0	14
John Blum	0	0	0	6
Ray Bourque	0	0	0	0
Geoff Courtnall	0	0	0	2
Charlie Simmer	0	0	0	4
Frank Simonetti	0	0	0	0
Michael Thelven	0	0	0	0

Number of power play advantages	16
Power play goals	2
% successful	12.5%
Gord Kluzak	1
Reed Larson	1
Short-handed goals against	1

Penalty minutes: 158 – 52.6 per game	
Times short-handed	20
Power play goals against	3
Penalty kill success	85.0%
Short-handed goals	1
Steve Kasper	1

1986–1987
(63rd year)

TEAM OWNER:	Sportsystems of Buffalo	ALL-STARS:	Ray Bourque (1st team)
PRESIDENT & GOVERNOR:	Paul Mooney	TROPHY WINNERS:	Norris — Ray Bourque
GM:	Harry Sinden		Dufresne — Ray Bourque
COACH:	Butch Goring & Terry O'Reilly		7th Player — Cam Neely
ATTENDANCE:	485,159		Three Star — Ray Bourque
	12,128 per game	RADIO BROADCASTER:	WPLM – Bob Wilson,
PLAYOFFS:	*Division semi-finals:*		Johnny Bucyk
	Lose to Montreal Canadiens	TV BROADCASTER:	WSBK TV38 & NESN –
	0 wins – 3 losses		Fred Cusick, Dave Shea
STANLEY CUP WINNER:	Edmonton Oilers		

UNIFORMS

- Home jersey is white with gold and black trim. Socks are white with one gold band surrounded by two black bands at the calf. Road jersey is black with gold and white trim. Gold socks with one white band surrounded by two black bands at the calf. Logo is the spoked "B." Pants are black. Bearhead appears on both shoulders on both home and road uniforms.

POTPOURRI

- On top of being named the Norris Trophy winner and being on the first All-Star team, Ray Bourque collects his 600th career point.
- Reed Larson scores his 200th career goal.
- Charlie Simmer plays in all 80 games.
- Charlie Simmer scores 13,000th goal in team history.
- Bruins qualify for the playoffs for the 20th straight season.
- For the second time in his career, Gord Kluzak misses the entire season because of knee surgery.
- Louis Sleigher also misses the entire season due to a groin injury.
- Bruins are swept by Montreal in the division semi-finals.
- Bob Sweeney's first NHL goal is scored against his high school teammate, Tom Barrasso of the Buffalo Sabres.
- Cam Neely scores his first career hat trick.
- Bruins are not involved in any penalty shot situations.
- Bruins are 2–3–7 in overtime games.

TRANSACTIONS

- Obtain Pat Boutillier from the New York Islanders as compensation for the Islanders signing Brian Curran.
- Trade Pat Boutillier to Minnesota for Minnesota's fourth pick in the 1987 draft.
- Trade John Blum to Washington for the Capitals seventh pick in 1988 draft.
- Pick Craig Janney #1 in the 1986 NHL draft.
- Obtain Tom McCarthy from Minnesota for a 1987 draft pick.
- Obtain Cam Neely and a 1987 #1 draft pick from Vancouver for Barry Pederson.
- Sign free agent Thomas Gradin from Vancouver.
- Trade Pat Riggin to Pittsburgh for Roberto Romano.
- Bruins fire Butch Goring and replace him with Terry O'Reilly.

1986-87 STANDINGS

PRINCE OF WALES CONFERENCE

Adams Division

	W	L	T	P	GF	GA
Hartford	43	30	7	93	287	270
Montreal	41	29	10	92	277	241
Boston	39	34	7	85	301	276
Quebec	31	39	10	72	267	276
Buffalo	28	44	8	64	280	308

Patrick Division

	W	L	T	P	GF	GA
Philadelphia	46	26	8	100	310	245
Washington	38	32	10	86	285	278
New York Islanders	35	33	12	82	279	281
New York Rangers	34	38	8	76	307	323
Pittsburgh	30	38	12	72	297	290
New Jersey	29	45	6	64	293	368

CLARENCE CAMPBELL CONFERENCE

Norris Division

	W	L	T	P	GF	GA
St. Louis	32	33	15	79	281	293
Detroit	34	36	10	78	260	274
Chicago	29	37	14	72	290	310
Toronto	32	42	6	70	286	319
Minnesota	30	40	10	70	296	314

Smythe Division

	W	L	T	P	GF	GA
Edmonton	50	24	6	106	372	284
Calgary	46	31	3	95	318	289
Winnipeg	40	32	8	88	279	271
Los Angeles	31	41	8	70	318	341
Vancouver	29	43	8	66	282	314

1986-87 RESULTS

October 1986

	AT	VERSUS	W-L-T	SCR
9	Boston	Calgary	L	5–3
11	New Jersey	Devils	L	5–4
12	Boston	Hartford	W	7–2
14	Winnipeg	Jets	W	2–1
16	Minnesota	North Stars	W	5–3
18	Los Angeles	Kings	W	4–1
22	Vancouver	Canucks	L	5–1
24	Edmonton	Oilers	L	6–2
26	Calgary	Flames	W	6–0
30	Boston	Montreal	T	3–3

November 1986

	AT	VERSUS	W-L-T	SCR
1	Philadelphia	Flyers	L	4–2
2	Boston	Buffalo	L	7–1
5	Buffalo	Sabres	L	8–3
8	Quebec	Nordiques	W	5–1
12	Pittsburgh	Penguins	L	2–1
13	Boston	Edmonton	W	4–3 (OT)
15	Boston	New Jersey	T	5–5
17	Montreal	Canadiens	L	3–2 (OT)
19	Buffalo	Sabres	T	4–4
20	Boston	Montreal	L	3–1
22	Boston	St. Louis	W	6–5
24	Toronto	Maple Leafs	W	3–2
26	Washington	Capitals	T	2–2
28	Buffalo	Sabres	L	4–3
29	Boston	Buffalo	W	6–2

December 1986

	AT	VERSUS	W-L-T	SCR
4	Boston	Quebec	W	6–2
6	Boston	Philadelphia	W	3–2
7	Boston	New York Islanders	W	5–0
11	Boston	Vancouver	W	3–1
13	Montreal	Canadiens	W	4–2
14	Quebec	Nordiques	W	6–2
18	Boston	Hartford	L	6–5
20	Boston	Chicago	L	6–2
23	Hartford	Whalers	L	2–0

| 27 | Los Angeles | Kings | L | 2–1 (OT) |
| 30 | St. Louis | Blues | L | 4–3 |

January 1987

2	New Jersey	Devils	W	7–2
3	New York	Islanders	W	5–4
5	Boston	Montreal	L	2–1
8	Boston	Detroit	T	4–4
10	Boston	Philadelphia	L	5–4
12	Boston	New York Rangers	W	4–1
14	Hartford	Whalers	L	2–0
15	Boston	Hartford	W	6–4
17	Boston	Pittsburgh	W	4–2
20	Quebec	Nordiques	W	5–3
22	Boston	Montreal	W	7–3
24	Boston	Calgary	W	5–3
26	Boston	Buffalo	W	6–2
29	Boston	Hartford	L	6–3
31	Boston	Winnipeg	W	6–3

February 1987

1	New York	Rangers	L	5–4
5	Boston	Pittsburgh	W	6–5
7	Boston	Toronto	W	8–5
8	Boston	Quebec	L	2–1
14	Toronto	Maple Leafs	L	5–4
16	Montreal	Canadiens	L	7–3

18	Buffalo	Sabres	L	4–3
20	Winnipeg	Jets	L	6–2
21	Minnesota	North Stars	W	1–0
25	Hartford	Whalers	L	6–4
26	Boston	Quebec	W	6–2
28	Boston	Buffalo	W	5–1

March 1987

2	Boston	Detroit	L	4–3
3	New York	Islanders	T	4–4
5	Hartford	Whalers	L	10–2
7	Boston	Washington	W	3–2 (OT)
11	New York	Rangers	L	3–2
12	Boston	St. Louis	W	6–4
14	Boston	Chicago	T	4–4
17	Detroit	Red Wings	L	3–1
19	Boston	Minnesota	W	6–2
21	Boston	Los Angeles	W	8–6
22	Washington	Capitals	L	4–3
26	Boston	Edmonton	W	4–1
28	Boston	Vancouver	W	2–1
29	Chicago	Blackhawks	W	8–6
31	Quebec	Nordiques	W	4–3

April 1987

| 4 | Montreal | Canadiens | L | 3–1 |
| 5 | Boston | Quebec | L | 6–4 |

1986-87 SCORING

	W	L	T	S	GAA	PIM
Bill Ranford	16	20	2	3	3.33	8
						1 assist
Doug Keans	18	8	4	0	3.34	24
						2 assists
Pat Riggin	3	5	1	0	3.39	0
Cleon Daskalakis	2	0	0	0	4.43	0
Roberto Romano	0	1	0	0	6.00	0

	G	A	P	PIM
Ray Bourque	23	72	95	36
Cam Neely	36	36	72	143
Charlie Simmer	29	40	69	59
Rick Middleton	31	37	68	6
Tom McCarthy	30	29	59	31
Keith Crowder	22	30	52	106
Steve Kasper	20	30	50	51
Ken Linseman	15	34	49	126
Thomas Gradin	12	31	43	18
Geoff Courtnall	13	23	36	117
Reed Larson	12	24	36	95
Greg Johnston	12	15	27	79
Mike Milbury	6	16	22	96
Michael Thelven	5	15	20	18
Nevin Markwart	10	9	19	225
Paul Boutilier	5	9	14	84
Dwight Foster	4	12	16	37
Allan Pederson	1	11	12	71
Kraig Nienhuis	4	2	6	2
Dave Reid	3	3	6	0
Bob Sweeney	2	4	6	21
Lyndon Byers	2	3	5	53
Randy Burridge	1	4	5	16
Jay Miller	1	4	5	208
Mats Thelin	1	3	4	69
Wade Campbell	0	3	3	24
Frank Simonetti	1	0	1	17
John Carter	0	1	1	0
Alain Cote	0	0	0	0

Number of power play advantages	334
Power play goals	65
% successful	19.5%
Charlie Simmer	11
Reed Larson	9
Cam Neely	7
Tom McCarthy	7
Ray Bourque	6
Keith Crowder	4

Steve Kasper	4	
Rick Middleton	4	
Ken Linseman	3	
Michael Thelven	3	
Thomas Gradin	2	
Geoff Courtnall	2	
Kraig Nienhuis	2	
Paul Boutilier	1	
Short-handed goals against	5	
Penalty minutes: 1870 – 23.4 per game		
Times short-handed	325	

Power play goals against	60
Penalty kill success	81.5%
Short-handed goals	13
Rick Middleton	4
Thomas Gradin	3
Steve Kasper	2
Ray Bourque	1
Mike Milbury	1
Dwight Foster	1
Paul Boutilier	1

1986-87 PLAYOFF RESULTS

April 1987

	AT	VERSUS	W-L-T	SCR
8	Montreal	Canadiens	L	6–2
9	Montreal	Canadiens	L	4–3
11	Boston	Montreal	L	5–4
12	Boston	Montreal	L	4–2

1986-87 PLAYOFFS

vs. Montreal Canadiens	0 wins – 4 losses
at Montreal	0 wins – 2 losses
at Boston	0 wins – 2 losses

1986-87 PLAYOFF SCORING

	W	L	SO	GAA	PIM
Bill Ranford	0	2	0	3.90	0
Doug Keans	0	2	0	5.50	4

	G	A	P	PIM
Cam Neely	5	1	6	8
Rick Middleton	2	2	4	0
Thomas Gradin	0	4	4	0
Ray Bourque	1	2	3	0
Ken Linseman	1	1	2	22
Tom McCarthy	1	1	2	4
Steve Kasper	0	2	2	0
Reed Larson	0	2	2	2
Randy Burridge	1	0	1	2
Keith Crowder	0	1	1	4
Lyndon Byers	0	0	0	0
Geoff Courtnall	0	0	0	0
Charlie Simmer	0	0	0	2
Dave Reid	0	0	0	0
Dwight Foster	0	0	0	0
Bob Sweeney	0	0	0	0
Wade Campbell	0	0	0	11
Greg Johnston	0	0	0	0
Nevin Markwart	0	0	0	9
Mike Milbury	0	0	0	4
Allan Pederson	0	0	0	4
Frank Simonetti	0	0	0	6

Number of power play advantages	19
Power play goals	5
% successful	26.3%
Cam Neely	3
Rick Middleton	1
Tom McCarthy	1
Short-handed goals against	1
Penalty minutes: 82 – 20.5 per game	
Times short-handed	18
Power play goals against	4
Penalty kill success	77.8%
Short-handed goals	1
Rick Middleton	1

1987–1988
(64th year)

TEAM OWNER:	Delaware North
PRESIDENT & GOVERNOR:	William Hassett, Jr.
GM:	Harry Sinden
COACH:	Terry O'Reilly
ATTENDANCE:	548,301
	13,707 per game

PLAYOFFS:
Division semi-finals:
Defeat Buffalo Sabres
4 wins – 2 losses
Division finals:
Defeat Montreal Canadiens
4 wins – 1 loss
Conference finals:
Defeat New Jersey Devils
4 wins – 3 losses
Stanley Cup finals:
Lose to Edmonton Oilers
0 wins – 4 losses – 1 game
suspended (blackout)

STANLEY CUP WINNER:	Edmonton Oilers
ALL-STARS:	Ray Bourque (1st team)
	Cam Neely (2nd team)
TROPHY WINNERS:	Norris — Ray Bourque
	Lester Patrick — Fred Cusick
	Durfesne — Cam Neely
	7th Player — Glen Wesley
	Three Star — Cam Neely
RADIO BROADCASTER:	WPLM – Bob Wilson, Johnny Bucyk
TV BROADCASTER:	WSBK TV38 & NESN – Fred Cusick, Derek Sanderson, Dave Shea

UNIFORMS

- Home jersey is white with gold and black trim. Socks are white with one gold band surrounded by two black bands at the calf. Road jersey is black with gold and white trim. Gold socks with one white band surrounded by two black bands at the calf. Logo is the spoked "B." Pants are black. Bearhead appears on both shoulders on both home and road uniforms.

POTPOURRI

- Bruins score 14 short-handed goals.
- Bruins score 7 hat tricks on the season.
- Bruins enjoy a 7-game winning streak.
- Ray Bourque plays in his 600th career game.
- Keith Crowder plays in his 500th career game.
- Steve Kasper plays in his 500th career game.
- Gord Kluzak returns after missing the entire 1986–87 campaign.
- Cam Neely becomes the first Bruin to score over 40 goals since 1983–84.
- Bob Sweeney is the only Bruin to play in all 80 games.
- Bruins qualify for the playoffs for the 21st straight season, tying the record with Montreal.
- Bruins eliminate Montreal in the playoffs for the first time in 45 years.
- Bruins have 10 short-handed goals scored against them.
- Bruins lose Stanley Cup final round to Edmonton in 5 games. Game 4 of the series ends in a tie because of a power failure.
- Nevin Markwart limited to 25 games due to injuries.
- Bruins are 4–4–6 in overtime games.
- On Phil Esposito Night, December 3, Ray Bourque changes his number from 7 to 77.
- Jay Miller establishes new single-season penalty-minute record with 302 minutes.
- Despite playing 78 games, Allan Pederson fails to score a goal.
- Glen Wesley is chosen for the All-Rookie team.
- In the suspended playoff game against Edmonton, Glen Wesley has both a power-play goal and a short-handed goal.

- In a playoff game against New Jersey, substitute officials replace the regular officials who refuse to take the ice after Jim Schoenfeld, coach of the Devils, gets a temporary restraining order allowing him to coach the game. This incident grew out of the infamous "donut insult" between Schoenfeld and referee Don Koharski.

TRANSACTIONS

- Have 2 picks in the first round of the 1987 NHL draft. Choose Glen Wesley first and Stephane Quintal second in the first round of the entry draft.
- Bruins choose Willi Plett in the 1987 waiver draft.
- Obtain Mike Stevens from Vancouver for cash.
- Trade Alan May to Edmonton for Moe Lemay.
- Trade Geoff Courtnall and Bill Ranford to Edmonton for Andy Moog.
- Obtain Steve Tsujiura from New Jersey for Boston's 10th-round pick in the 1988 draft.

1987-88 STANDINGS

PRINCE OF WALES CONFERENCE

Adams Division	W	L	T	P	GF	GA
Montreal	45	22	13	103	298	238
Boston	44	30	6	94	300	251
Buffalo	37	32	11	85	283	305
Hartford	35	38	7	77	249	267
Quebec	32	43	5	69	271	306
Patrick Division						
New York Islanders	39	31	10	88	308	267
Philadelphia	38	33	9	85	281	249
Washington	38	33	9	85	292	292
New Jersey	38	36	6	82	295	296
New York Rangers	36	34	10	82	300	283
Pittsburgh	36	35	9	81	319	316

CLARENCE CAMPBELL CONFERENCE

Norris Division	W	L	T	P	GF	GA
Detroit	41	28	11	93	322	269
St. Louis	34	38	8	76	278	294
Chicago	30	41	9	69	284	328
Toronto	21	49	10	52	273	345
Minnesota	19	48	13	51	242	349
Smythe Division						
Calgary	48	23	9	105	397	305
Edmonton	44	25	11	99	363	288
Winnipeg	33	36	11	77	292	310
Los Angeles	30	42	8	68	318	359
Vancouver	25	46	9	59	272	320

1987-88 RESULTS

October 1987

	AT	VERSUS	W-L-T	SCR
8	Boston	Washington	W	4–3
10	Quebec	Nordiques	L	6–5 (OT)
11	Boston	Hartford	W	5–2
15	Los Angeles	Kings	W	3–2
17	Edmonton	Oilers	L	4–3
18	Calgary	Flames	W	6–5 (OT)
21	Vancouver	Canucks	W	5–4
24	St. Louis	Blues	L	4–0

| 29 | Boston | Quebec | L | 4–2 |
| 31 | Montreal | Canadiens | T | 3–3 |

November 1987

1	Boston	New York Islanders	L	6–5 (OT)
4	Hartford	Whalers	T	2–2
5	Boston	Toronto	L	7–6
7	Boston	Pittsburgh	W	4–1
9	Quebec	Nordiques	L	6–4
11	Toronto	Maple Leafs	W	3–2
12	Boston	Montreal	W	3–2
14	Boston	Hartford	W	4–1
17	Calgary	Flames	W	6–3
18	Winnipeg	Jets	W	4–3
21	Minnesota	North Stars	W	7–5
22	Detroit	Red Wings	W	1–0
25	Washington	Capitals	L	4–1
26	Boston	Winnipeg	W	5–3
28	Boston	Detroit	L	3–2 (OT)
30	Montreal	Canadiens	L	6–4

December 1987

2	Hartford	Whalers	W	5–3
3	Boston	New York Rangers	W	4–3
5	Boston	Chicago	W	7–3
8	Philadelphia	Flyers	L	5–2
10	Boston	Los Angeles	W	4–3
12	Boston	Buffalo	T	3–3
17	Boston	Vancouver	W	3–2 (OT)
19	Boston	St. Louis	L	7–5
20	Chicago	Blackhawks	W	4–2
22	Boston	Buffalo	W	9–0
26	New York	Islanders	L	2–1
27	New York	Rangers	L	4–1
30	Pittsburgh	Penguins	T	4–4
31	Buffalo	Sabres	W	2–0

January 1988

2	Boston	Quebec	W	5–1
4	Boston	Edmonton	T	2–2
7	Pittsburgh	Penguins	W	3–2
9	St. Louis	Blues	W	2–1 (OT)

11	Boston	Hartford	L	4–3
13	Montreal	Canadiens	L	5–4
14	Boston	Montreal	W	3–2
16	Boston	Buffalo	W	5–1
20	Buffalo	Sabres	L	5–3
21	Boston	Minnesota	W	6–1
23	Boston	Philadelphia	L	6–4
28	Boston	Quebec	W	3–0
30	Boston	New York Rangers	L	4–2

February 1988

1	Chicago	Blackhawks	W	5–3
4	Boston	Montreal	W	7–3
6	Quebec	Nordiques	W	3–2
7	Boston	New Jersey	W	6–3
12	Edmonton	Oilers	W	7–4
13	Vancouver	Canucks	L	6–5
17	Montreal	Canadiens	L	3–2
21	New Jersey	Devils	W	4–1
23	Hartford	Whalers	L	3–2
25	Boston	Hartford	W	5–2
27	Boston	Minnesota	W	7–4

March 1988

3	Boston	Toronto	W	5–3
5	Boston	New Jersey	L	7–6 (OT)
6	Buffalo	Sabres	L	3–0
8	Detroit	Red Wings	L	2–0
10	Boston	Los Angeles	T	3–3
12	Quebec	Nordiques	W	4–3
13	Boston	Washington	L	3–0
17	Boston	Calgary	L	7–5
19	Boston	Buffalo	L	4–3
20	Buffalo	Sabres	W	6–2
22	Philadelphia	Flyers	W	3–0
24	Boston	Winnipeg	W	4–3 (OT)
26	Boston	Quebec	W	6–2
31	Boston	Montreal	L	3–1

April 1988

| 12 | Hartford | Whalers | L | 4–2 |
| 3 | Boston | New York Islanders | W | 3–2 |

1987-88 SCORING

	W	L	T	S	GAA	PIM
Doug Keans	16	11	0	1	3.25	2
						2 assists
Rejean Lemelin	24	17	6	3	2.93	2
Andy Moog	4	2	0	1	2.83	0

	G	A	P	PIM
Ray Bourque	17	64	81	72
Ken Linseman	29	45	74	167
Steve Kasper	26	44	70	35
Cam Neely	42	27	69	175
Geoff Courtnall	32	26	58	108
Randy Burridge	27	28	55	105
Bob Sweeney	22	23	45	73
Keith Crowder	17	26	43	173
Glen Wesley	7	30	37	69
Gord Kluzak	6	31	37	135
Reed Larson	10	24	34	93

Rick Middleton	13	19	32	11	Bruce Shoebottom	0	1	1	0
Michael Thelven	6	25	31	57	John Carter	0	1	1	2
Lyndon Byers	10	14	24	236	Wade Campbell	0	1	1	21
Jay Miller	7	12	19	304	Mike Stevens	0	1	1	9
Billy O'Dwyer	7	10	17	83	John Blum	0	1	1	70
Craig Janney	7	9	16	0	Greg Hawgood	0	0	0	0
Nevin Markwart	1	12	13	85	Kraig Nienhuis	0	0	0	0
Bobby Joyce	7	5	12	10	Alain Cote	0	0	0	0
Tom McCarthy	2	5	7	6	Paul Beraldo	0	0	0	0
Allan Pederson	0	6	6	90	Alan May	0	0	0	15
Frank Simonetti	2	3	5	19	Dave Reid	0	0	0	0
Willi Plett	2	3	5	170	Moe Lemay	0	0	0	0
Tom Lehman	1	3	4	6	Taylor Hall	0	0	0	4

Number of power play advantages	446		Short-handed goals against	10
Power play goals	74		Penalty minutes:	2,443 – 30.5 per game
% successful	16.6%		Times short-handed	425
Cam Neely	11		Power play goals against	70
Steve Kasper	9		Penalty kill success	83.5%
Geoff Courtnall	8		Short-handed goals	14
Ray Bourque	7		Steve Kasper	3
Ken Linseman	7		Randy Burridge	3
Bob Sweeney	6		Rick Middleton	3
Keith Crowder	6		Glen Wesley	2
Randy Burridge	5		Ray Bourque	1
Reed Larson	5		Gord Kluzak	1
Rick Middleton	2		Reed Larson	1
Bobby Joyce	2			
Glen Wesley	1			
Michael Thelven	1			
Billy O'Dwyer	1			
Craig Janney	1			
Tom McCarthy	1			
Willi Plett	1			

1987-88 PLAYOFF RESULTS

April 1988

	AT	VERSUS	W-L-T	SCR
6	Boston	Buffalo	W	7–3
7	Boston	Buffalo	W	4–1
9	Buffalo	Sabres	L	6–2
10	Buffalo	Sabres	L	6–5 (OT)
12	Boston	Buffalo	W	5–4
14	Buffalo	Sabres	W	5–2
18	Montreal	Canadiens	L	5–2
20	Montreal	Canadiens	W	4–3
22	Boston	Montreal	W	3–1
24	Boston	Montreal	W	2–0
26	Montreal	Canadiens	W	4–1

May 1988

2	Boston	New Jersey	W	5–3
4	Boston	New Jersey	L	3–2 (OT)
6	New Jersey	Devils	W	6–1
8	New Jersey	Devils	L	3–1
10	Boston	New Jersey	W	7–1
12	New Jersey	Devils	L	6–3
14	Boston	New Jersey	W	6–2
18	Edmonton	Oilers	L	2–1
20	Edmonton	Oilers	L	4–2
22	Boston	Edmonton	L	6–3
24	Boston	Edmonton	sp.	3–3*
26	Edmonton	Oilers	L	6–3

*game suspended because of a blackout at Boston Garden.

1987-88 PLAYOFFS

vs. Buffalo Sabres	4 wins – 2 losses		vs. New Jersey Devils	4 wins – 3 losses
at Buffalo	1 win – 2 losses		at New Jersey	1 win – 2 losses
at Boston	3 wins – 0 losses		at Boston	3 wins – 1 loss
vs. Montreal Canadiens	4 wins – 1 loss		vs. Edmonton Oilers	0 wins – 4 losses
at Montreal	2 wins – 1 loss			– 1 suspended
at Boston	2 wins – 0 losses		at Edmonton	0 wins – 3 losses
			at Boston	0 wins – 1 loss
				– 1 suspended

1987-88 PLAYOFF SCORING

	W	L	SO	GAA	PIM
Rejean Lemelin	11	6	1	2.63	2
					1 assist
Andy Moog	1	4	0	4.24	0

	G	A	P	PIM
Ken Linseman	11	14	25	56
Ray Bourque	3	18	21	26
Cam Neely	9	8	17	51
Craig Janney	6	10	16	11
Bobby Joyce	8	6	14	18
Bob Sweeney	6	8	14	66
Glen Wesley	6	8	14	22
Steve Kasper	7	6	13	10
Gord Kluzak	4	8	12	59
Keith Crowder	3	9	12	44
Randy Burridge	2	10	12	16
Rick Middleton	5	5	10	4
Tom McCarthy	3	4	7	18
Moe Lemay	4	2	6	32
Michael Thelvin	3	3	6	26
Willi Plett	2	4	6	74
Lyndon Byers	1	2	3	62
Greg Hawgood	1	0	1	0
Bruce Shoebottom	1	0	1	42
John Blum	0	1	1	0
Greg Johnston	0	1	1	2
Reed Larson	0	1	1	6
Nevin Markwart	0	0	0	2
Billy O'Dwyer	0	0	0	0
Jay Miller	0	0	0	124
Allen Pederson	0	0	0	34

Number of power play advantages	131
Power play goals	20
% successful	15.3%
Ken Linseman	4
Craig Janney	4
Glen Wesley	4
Bobby Joyce	3
Cam Neely	2
Bob Sweeney	1
Keith Crowder	1
Michael Thelven	1
Short-handed goals against	1

Penalty minutes:	813 – 36.3 per game
Times short-handed	125
Power play goals against	24
Penalty kill success	80.8%
Short-handed goals	6
Ken Linseman	1
Bob Sweeney	1
Glen Wesley	1
Steve Kasper	1
Gord Kluzak	1
Rick Middleton	1

1988–1989
(65th year)

TEAM OWNER:	Delaware North	STANLEY CUP WINNER:	Calgary Flames
PRESIDENT & GOVERNOR:	William Hassett, Jr.	ALL-STARS:	Ray Bourque (2nd team)
GM:	Harry Sinden	TROPHY WINNERS:	Dufresne — Randy Burridge
COACH:	Terry O'Reilly		7th Player — Randy Burridge
ATTENDANCE:	563,730		Three Star — Cam Neely
	14,093 per game	RADIO BROADCASTER:	WPLM – Bob Wilson,
PLAYOFFS:	*Division semi-finals:*		Johnny Bucyk
	Defeat Buffalo Sabres	TV BROADCASTER:	WSBK TV38 & NESN – Fred
	4 wins – 1 loss		Cusick, Derek Sanderson,
	Division finals:		Dave Shea
	Lose to Montreal Canadiens		
	1 win – 4 losses		

UNIFORMS

- Home jersey is white with gold and black trim. Socks are white with one gold band surrounded by two black bands at the calf. Road jersey is black with gold and white trim. Gold socks with one white band surrounded by two black bands at the calf. Logo is the spoked "B." Pants are black. Bearhead appears on both shoulders on both home and road uniforms.

POTPOURRI

- The Bruins have a phenomenal 29–1–0 record when leading into the third period.
- Bruins qualify for the playoffs for the 22nd consecutive season. This is also the 22nd consecutive season that the Bruins have had a winning record.
- Ray Bourque scores his 200th goal, 700th point, and plays in the 700th game of his career.
- Randy Burridge plays in his 200th NHL game.
- Garry Galley plays in his 300th NHL game.
- Reggie Lemelin plays in his 400th NHL game.
- Ken Linseman records his second career hat trick.
- Ken Linseman plays in his 700th NHL game.
- Cam Neely, leading the team in scoring, plays in his 400th career game. It is also his third consecutive 30+ goal season. Neely also records his fifth career hat trick.
- Glen Welsey becomes the first defenseman since Bobby Orr in 1973 to enjoy a 6-point game (1 goal and 5 assists).
- For only the fourth time in team history, the Bruins boast back-to-back 20+ road win seasons.
- Bruins score 10 short-handed goals.
- Ray Bourque's penalty shot against the New York Rangers is unsuccessful.
- Because of injuries, Gord Kluzak is limited to 3 games.
- Bruins are eliminated by Montreal in the playoffs.
- Ray Bourque, player of the week for February 13 to 19, is the only NHL defenseman to be named player of the week in 1988–89 season. Bourque had 4 goals and 5 assists.
- Randy Burridge is the only Bruin to play in all 80 games.

TRANSACTIONS

- Select Rob Cimetta #1 in the 1988 NHL entry draft.
- Obtain Andy Brickley in the 1988 waiver draft.
- Trade Dave Pasin to Los Angeles for Paul Guay.
- Trade Jean-Marc Lanthier to New Jersey for Dan Dorion.

- Jay Miller traded to Los Angeles for future considerations.
- Steve Kasper traded to Los Angeles for Bobby Carpenter.
- Obtain Ron Flockhart from St. Louis for future considerations.
- Obtain Frank Caprice from Vancouver for Boston's 12th-round pick in the 1989 draft.
- Trade Tommy Lehman to Edmonton for Edmonton's 3rd choice in the 1989 draft.
- Trade Moe Lemay to Winnipeg for Ray Neufeld.

1988-89 STANDINGS

PRINCE OF WALES CONFERENCE

Adams Division	W	L	T	P	GF	GA
Montreal	53	18	9	115	315	218
Boston	37	29	14	88	289	256
Buffalo	38	35	7	83	291	299
Hartford	37	38	5	79	299	290
Quebec	27	46	7	61	269	342
Patrick Division						
Washington	41	29	10	92	305	259
Pittsburgh	40	33	7	87	347	349
New York Rangers	37	35	8	82	310	307
Philadelphia	36	36	8	80	307	285
New Jersey	27	41	12	66	281	325
New York Islanders	28	47	5	61	265	325

CAMPBELL CONFERENCE

Norris Division	W	L	T	P	GF	GA
Detroit	34	34	12	80	313	316
St. Louis	33	35	12	78	275	285
Minnesota	27	37	16	70	258	278
Chicago	27	41	12	66	297	335
Toronto	28	46	6	62	259	342
Smythe Division						
Calgary	54	17	9	117	354	226
Los Angeles	42	31	7	91	376	335
Edmonton	38	34	8	84	325	306
Vancouver	33	39	8	74	251	253
Winnipeg	26	42	12	64	300	355

1988-89 RESULTS

October 1988

	AT	VERSUS	W-L-T	SCR
6	Boston	Toronto	W	2–1
8	Hartford	Whalers	W	6–2
9	Boston	Hartford	W	3–1
12	Los Angeles	Kings	L	6–2
15	Minnesota	North Stars	L	5–1
16	Chicago	Blackhawks	W	10–3
19	Winnipeg	Jets	W	5–2
22	St. Louis	Blues	W	5–2
25	Boston	Montreal	T	1–1
27	Boston	Quebec	W	6–2
29	Boston	Buffalo	T	3–3
30	Buffalo	Sabres	T	3–3

November 1988

	AT	VERSUS	W-L-T	SCR
2	Toronto	Maple Leafs	W	7–2
3	Boston	Hartford	L	5–3
6	Boston	Vancouver	W	4–2
11	New York	Rangers	T	4–4
12	Boston	Calgary	L	2–1
15	Quebec	Nordiques	T	5–5
17	Boston	Montreal	L	5–2
18	Detroit	Red Wings	L	5–2

20	Boston	Detroit	L	5–4 (OT)
23	Montreal	Canadiens	L	2–0
24	Boston	Philadelphia	W	2–1 (OT)
26	Boston	Chicago	W	8–2
29	Philadelphia	Flyers	L	5–1

December 1988

1	Boston	Minnesota	L	4–1
3	Washington	Capitals	T	1–1
4	Boston	Pittsburgh	T	3–3
6	New York	Islanders	W	4–3
8	Boston	Buffalo	L	4–2
10	Boston	New York Rangers	T	1–1
12	Montreal	Canadiens	L	3–1
15	Boston	Edmonton	W	4–3 (OT)
17	Boston	Quebec	T	2–2
18	Quebec	Nordiques	L	4–2
21	Hartford	Whalers	W	4–3
22	Boston	Montreal	L	4–2
26	Buffalo	Sabres	L	2–1
29	New Jersey	Devils	W	6–2

January 1989

2	Boston	St. Louis	W	8–7
5	Boston	New York Islanders	L	5–3
7	Montreal	Canadiens	L	3–1
8	Quebec	Nordiques	W	4–2
12	Boston	Montreal	L	5–3
14	Boston	Detroit	T	5–5
15	Washington	Capitals	W	4–3
19	Boston	Calgary	L	7–2
21	Boston	Buffalo	L	6–5 (OT)
22	Buffalo	Sabres	L	6–4
25	Toronto	Maple Leafs	W	2–1 (OT)
26	Boston	St. Louis	W	4–2

| 28 | Boston | Winnipeg | L | 4–3 |

February 1988

1	Minnesota	North Stars	T	4–4
3	Winnipeg	Jets	W	4–2
5	Boston	Pittsburgh	L	5–2
9	Boston	Los Angeles	W	4–1
11	Boston	Edmonton	W	5–2
14	Vancouver	Canucks	L	5–2
15	Los Angeles	Kings	W	7–3
18	Calgary	Flames	W	4–3
19	Edmonton	Oilers	W	4–2
25	Hartford	Whalers	W	9–1
28	New Jersey	Devils	T	3–3

March 1989

2	Boston	Quebec	W	5–2
4	Boston	Vancouver	W	6–4
5	New York	Rangers	W	5–0
7	New York	Islanders	W	2–1
9	Boston	Washington	L	7–2
11	Boston	Buffalo	T	6–6
12	Buffalo	Sabres	L	3–2
14	Pittsburgh	Penguins	W	8–2
16	Boston	Quebec	T	2–2
18	Boston	Philadelphia	W	6–3
19	Boston	Hartford	L	3–2
22	Hartford	Whalers	L	4–2
23	Boston	New Jersey	W	5–3
25	Boston	Chicago	W	6–3
27	Montreal	Canadiens	L	5–2

April 1989

| 1 | Quebec | Nordiques | W | 5–4 |
| 2 | Boston | Hartford | W | 3–2 |

1988-89 SCORING

	W	L	T	S	GAA	PIM
Rejean Lemelin	19	15	6	0	3.01	6
					1 assist	
Andy Moog	18	14	8	1	3.22	6
					1 assist	

	G	A	P	PIM
Cam Neely	37	38	75	190
Ken Linseman	27	45	72	164
Craig Janney	16	46	62	12
Randy Burridge	31	30	61	39
Ray Bourque	18	43	61	52
Glen Wesley	19	35	54	61
Bobby Joyce	18	31	49	46
Greg Hawgood	16	24	40	84
Andy Brickley	13	22	35	20

Keith Crowder	15	18	33	147
Garry Galley	8	21	29	80
Bob Sweeney	14	14	28	99
Steve Kasper	10	16	26	49
John Carter	12	10	22	24
Greg Johnston	11	10	21	32
Michael Thelven	3	18	21	71
Bobby Carpenter	5	9	14	10
Don Sweeney	3	5	8	20
Tom Lehman	4	2	6	10
Jay Miller	2	4	6	168
Allan Pederson	0	6	6	69
Alain Cote	2	3	5	51
Bruce Shoebottom	1	3	4	44
Lyndon Byers	0	4	4	218
Ray Neufeld	1	3	4	28

Billy O'Dwyer	1	2	3	8	Dale Dunbar	0	0	0	0
Rob Cimetta	2	0	2	0	Ron Flockhart	0	0	0	0
Paul Guay	0	2	2	0	Paul Beraldo	0	0	0	4
Gord Kluzak	0	1	1	2	Carl Mokosak	0	0	0	31
Ray Podloski	0	1	1	22	Moe Lemay	0	0	0	23
Stephane Quintal	0	1	1	29					

Number of power play advantages	429	Michael Thelven		1
Power play goals	85	Tom Lehmann		1
% successful	19.8%	Short-handed goals against		4
Cam Neely	18	Penalty minutes: 1,929 – 24.1 per game		
Ken Linseman	13	Times short-handed		374
Glen Wesley	8	Power play goals against		67
Bobby Joyce	7	Penalty kill success		82.1 %
Randy Burridge	6	Short-handed goals		10
Ray Bourque	6	Randy Burridge		2
Greg Hawgood	5	Ken Linseman		1
Keith Crowder	5	Glen Wesley		1
John Carter	4	Garry Galley		1
Craig Janney	2	Bob Sweeney		1
Andy Brickley	2	John Carter		1
Garry Galley	2	Greg Johnston		1
Bob Sweeney	2	Michael Thelven		1
Steve Kasper	2	Tom Lehmann		1
Bobby Carpenter	1			

1988-89 PLAYOFF RESULTS

April 1989

	AT	VERSUS	W-L-T	SCR					W	
5	Boston	Buffalo	L	6–0	11	Boston	Buffalo		W	4–1
6	Boston	Buffalo	W	5–3	17	Montreal	Canadiens		L	3–2
8	Buffalo	Sabres	W	4–2	19	Montreal	Canadiens		L	3–2 (OT)
9	Buffalo	Sabres	W	3–2	21	Boston	Montreal		L	5–4
					23	Boston	Montreal		W	3–2
					25	Montreal	Canadiens		L	3–2

1988-89 PLAYOFFS

vs. Buffalo Sabres	4 wins – 1 loss	vs. Montreal Canadiens	1 win – 4 losses
at Buffalo	2 wins – 0 losses	at Montreal	0 wins – 3 losses
at Boston	2 wins – 1 loss	at Boston	1 win – 1 loss

1988-89 PLAYOFF SCORING

	W	L	SO	GAA	PIM					
Rejean Lemelin	1	3	0	3.81	2	Michael Thelvin	1	7	8	8
Andy Moog	4	2	0	2.34	0	Bobby Joyce	5	2	7	2
				1 assist		Randy Burridge	5	2	7	8
						Bob Sweeney	2	4	6	19
						Ray Neufeld	2	3	5	9
	G	A	P	PIM		Ray Bourque	0	4	4	6
Craig Janney	4	9	13	21		John Carter	1	2	3	6
Cam Neely	7	2	9	8		Bobby Carpenter	1	1	2	4

Andy Brickley	0	2	2	0	Garry Galley	0	1	1	33
Keith Crowder	0	2	2	37	Rob Cimetta	0	0	0	15
Greg Hawgood	0	2	2	2	Carl Mokosak	0	0	0	0
Bruce Shoebottom	0	2	2	35	Lyndon Byers	0	0	0	0
Glen Wesley	0	2	2	4	Allen Pederson	0	0	0	2
Greg Johnston	1	0	1	6					

Number of power play advantages	47	Penalty minutes:	229 – 22.9 per game	
Power play goals	6	Times short-handed		44
% successful	12.8%	Power play goals against		7
Cam Neely	4	Penalty kill success		84.1%
Randy Burridge	1	Short-handed goals		2
Bob Carpenter	1	Greg Johnston		1
Short-handed goals against	2	Randy Burridge		1

1989–1990
(66th year)

OWNER & GOVERNOR:	Jeremy Jacobs	STANLEY CUP WINNER:	Edmonton Oilers
GM:	Harry Sinden	ALL-STARS:	Ray Bourque (1st team)
COACH:	Mike Milbury		Cam Neely (2nd team)
ATTENDANCE:	572,571	TROPHY WINNERS:	Norris — Ray Bourque
	14,314 per game		Jennings —Andy Moog
PLAYOFFS:	*Division semi-finals:*		& Reggie Lemelin
	Defeat Hartford Whalers		Masterton — Gord Kluzak
	4 wins – 3 losses		Dufresne — Ray Bourque
	Division finals:		7th Player — John Carter
	Defeat Montreal Canadiens		Three Star — Cam Neely
	4 wins – 1 loss	RADIO BROADCASTER:	WPLM – Bob Wilson,
	Conference finals:		Johnny Bucyk
	Defeat Washington Capitals	TV BROADCASTER:	WSBK TV38 & NESN – Fred
	4 wins – 0 losses		Cusick, Derek Sanderson,
	Stanley Cup finals:		Dave Shea
	Lose to Edmonton Oilers		
	1 win – 4 losses		

UNIFORMS
- Home jersey is white with gold and black trim. Socks are white with one gold band surrounded by two black bands at the calf. Road jersey is black with gold and white trim. Gold socks with one white band surrounded by two black bands at the calf. Logo is the spoked "B." Pants are black. Bearhead appears on both shoulders on both home and road uniforms.

POTPOURRI
- Cam Neely has both an 8-game and a 6-game consecutive goal-scoring streak.
- In the November 16 game against Montreal in which the Bruins are trailing 2–0, the Bruins strike for 3 goals in the final 2 minutes to eke out a 3–2 win.
- Reggie Lemelin wins "Player of the Week" award for the week of January 1 to 7, 1990.
- Andy Moog sets a new Bruins playoff record as he plays 1,196 minutes.

- Bruins come back from a 3-goal deficit against Hartford in game 4 of the Adams Division semi-finals to win 6–5.
- Glen Wesley plays in his 200th career game.
- Bruins score 5 short-handed goals.
- Bruins qualify for the playoffs for the 23rd straight season.
- Bruins are the only club to reach 100 points.
- Lose in the Stanley Cup finals to the Edmonton Oilers.
- Because of injury, Michael Thelven plays in only 6 games, Gord Kluzak and Nevin Markwart play in only 8 games.
- Bruins surrender 3 short-handed goals.
- Allan Pederson snaps a 238 game goalless streak on February 6 against Detroit.
- Mike Milbury becomes the second Bruins coach to lead the team to the Stanley Cup Finals in his rookie season as coach. The other coach is Dit Clapper.
- Game 1 of the finals against Edmonton turns out to be the longest final game in Stanley Cup history. Petr Klima scores the overtime goal at 15 minutes and 13 seconds of the second overtime period.
- All three games against Philadelphia end in 2–1 Bruin wins.

TRANSACTIONS
- Select Shayne Stevenson #1 in the 1989 NHL entry draft.
- Alain Côté traded to Washington for Bobby Gould.
- Trade Bob Joyce to Washington for Dave Christian.
- Trade Ken Linseman to Philadelphia for Dave Poulin.
- Obtain Brian Propp from Philadelphia for Boston's 2nd choice in the 1990 draft.
- Jeff Sirkka traded to Hartford for Steve Dykstra.
- Trade Greg Johnston to the Rangers for Chris Nilan.
- Bruins sign free agent Brian Lawton.

1989-90 STANDINGS

PRINCE OF WALES CONFERENCE

Adams Division	W	L	T	P	GF	GA
Boston	46	25	9	101	289	232
Buffalo	45	27	8	98	286	248
Montreal	41	28	11	93	288	234
Hartford	38	33	9	85	275	268
Quebec	12	61	7	31	240	407
Patrick Division						
New York Rangers	36	31	13	85	279	287
New Jersey	37	34	9	83	295	288
Washington	36	38	6	78	284	275
New York Islanders	31	38	11	73	281	288
Pittsburgh	32	40	8	72	318	359
Philadelphia	30	39	11	71	290	297

CLARENCE CAMPBELL

Norris Division						
Chicago	41	33	6	88	316	294
St. Louis	37	34	9	83	295	279
Toronto	38	38	4	80	337	358
Minnesota	36	40	4	76	284	291
Detroit	28	38	14	70	288	323

Smythe Division

Calgary	42	23	15	99	348	265
Edmonton	38	28	14	90	315	283
Winnipeg	37	32	11	85	298	290
Los Angeles	34	39	7	75	338	337
Vancouver	25	41	14	64	245	306

1989-90 RESULTS

October 1989

	AT	VERSUS	W-L-T	SCR
5	Boston	Pittsburgh	W	5–4
7	Quebec	Nordiques	L	4–1
9	Boston	Montreal	W	2–0
11	Montreal	Canadiens	L	4–2
13	Edmonton	Oilers	T	3–3
15	Vancouver	Canucks	L	7–6
17	Los Angeles	Kings	W	3–2
20	Edmonton	Oilers	W	3–0
21	Calgary	Flames	L	5–2
26	Boston	Quebec	W	4–2
28	Boston	Hartford	L	1–0
29	Buffalo	Sabres	L	4–3

November 1989

2	Boston	Los Angeles	W	5–4 (OT)
4	Boston	Buffalo	T	3–3
9	Boston	Edmonton	W	6–2
10	Washington	Capitals	W	5–3
15	Hartford	Whalers	W	5–2
16	Boston	Montreal	W	3–2
18	Boston	New Jersey	W	6–4
21	Detroit	Red Wings	W	2–1 (OT)
23	Boston	Toronto	W	6–0
25	Montreal	Canadiens	L	5–3
28	St. Louis	Blues	W	5–1
30	Boston	Buffalo	W	5–1

December 1989

2	Boston	St. Louis	L	2–1
3	Philadelphia	Flyers	W	2–1
5	Quebec	Nordiques	T	3–3
7	Boston	Hartford	L	4–3
9	Boston	Washington	L	7–3
12	Pittsburgh	Penguins	L	7–5
13	Buffalo	Sabres	W	4–2
16	Boston	Buffalo	L	3–1
17	New Jersey	Devils	L	3–1
20	Hartford	Whalers	L	4–3
21	Boston	Minnesota	W	4–2
23	Boston	Detroit	W	6–5
26	Boston	Toronto	W	6–4
29	Buffalo	Sabres	W	4–3 (OT)
30	Toronto	Maple Leafs	L	7–6 (OT)

January 1990

2	Pittsburgh	Penguins	W	5–2
4	Boston	Winnipeg	W	4–2
6	Boston	Washington	W	5–3
7	Buffalo	Sabres	W	2–1
11	Boston	Quebec	W	4–2
13	Boston	New York Rangers	L	2–1
15	Boston	Hartford	W	4–1
17	Hartford	Whalers	T	5–5
18	Boston	Calgary	T	2–2
23	Quebec	Nordiques	W	9–2
25	Boston	New York Islanders	W	5–2
27	Boston	Philadelphia	W	2–1
29	Montreal	Canadiens	W	2–1

February 1990

1	Boston	Montreal	L	4–2
3	Boston	New York Rangers	L	2–1
4	Quebec	Nordiques	W	3–2
6	Detroit	Red Wings	W	2–0
8	Boston	Quebec	W	5–1
10	Boston	New York Islanders	L	4–3 (OT)
11	Boston	Vancouver	L	4–2
14	Winnipeg	Jets	L	3–2
18	Vancouver	Canucks	W	7–2
20	Calgary	Flames	W	5–3
22	Chicago	Blackhawks	W	6–3
24	Minnesota	North Stars	W	3–2
26	New York	Rangers	L	6–1

March 1990

1	Boston	Montreal	W	5–3
3	Boston	Chicago	W	4–3
4	Chicago	Blackhawks	W	4–1
6	Philadelphia	Flyers	W	2–1
8	Boston	Buffalo	L	10–4
10	New York	Islanders	T	3–3
11	Hartford	Whalers	W	4–3
15	Boston	Winnipeg	T	3–3
17	Boston	Los Angeles	L	5–4
22	Boston	Quebec	W	7–3
24	Boston	Minnesota	L	7–6
27	St. Louis	Blues	W	3–0
29	Boston	Hartford	W	3–2
31	Montreal	Canadiens	T	2–2

April 1990

| 1 | Boston | New Jersey | T | 3–3 |

1989-90 SCORING

	W	L	T	S	GAA	PIM
Rejean Lemelin	22	15	2	2	2.81	32
Andy Moog	24	10	7	3	2.89	18
					3 assists	

	G	A	P	PIM
Cam Neely	55	37	92	117
Ray Bourque	19	65	84	50
Craig Janney	24	38	62	4
Bobby Carpenter	25	31	56	97
Bob Sweeney	22	24	46	93
Andy Brickley	12	28	40	8
John Carter	17	22	39	26
Greg Hawgood	11	27	38	76
Glen Wesley	9	27	36	48
Garry Galley	8	27	35	75
Randy Burridge	17	15	32	47
Dave Christian	12	17	29	8
Bobby Gould	8	17	25	92
Dave Poulin	6	19	25	12
Ken Linseman	6	16	22	66
Jim Weimer	5	14	19	63
Rob Cimetta	8	9	17	33
Brian Propp	3	9	12	10
Peter Douris	5	6	11	15
Lyndon Byers	4	4	8	159
Don Sweeney	3	5	8	58
Mike Millar	1	4	5	0
Jarmo Kekalainen	2	2	4	8
Stephane Quintal	2	2	4	22
Nevin Markwart	1	2	3	15
Allan Pederson	1	2	3	71
Bobby Joyce	1	2	3	22
Wes Walz	1	1	2	0
Greg Johnston	1	1	2	6
Michael Thelven	0	2	2	23
Gord Kluzak	0	2	2	11
Bob Beers	0	1	1	6
Billy O'Dwyer	0	1	1	2
Brian Lawton	0	0	0	14
Ray Neufeld	0	0	0	0
John Blum	0	0	0	0
Ron Hoover	0	0	0	0
Bruce Shoebottom	0	0	0	4
Graeme Townshend	0	0	0	7
Lou Crawford	0	0	0	20

Number of power play advantages	352
Power play goals	83
% successful	23.6%
Cam Neely	25
Craig Janney	11
Ray Bourque	8
Randy Burridge	7
Andy Brickley	6
Bob Carpenter	5
Bob Sweeney	5
Glen Wesley	5
Dave Christian	2
John Carter	2
Greg Hawgood	2
Garry Galley	1
Peter Douris	1
Nevin Markwart	1
Wes Walz	1
Ken Linseman	1
Short-handed goals against	3
Penalty minutes: 1,458 – 18.2 per game	
Times short-handed	316
Power play goals against	53
Penalty kill success	83.2%
Short-handed goals	5
Bob Sweeney	2
Dave Poulin	1
Brian Propp	1
John Carter	1

1989-90 PLAYOFF RESULTS

April 1990

	AT	VERSUS	W-L-T	SCR						
5	Boston	Hartford	L	4–3		13	Boston	Hartford	W	3–2
7	Boston	Hartford	W	3–1		15	Hartford	Whalers	L	3–2 (OT)
9	Hartford	Whalers	L	5–3		17	Boston	Hartford	W	3–1
11	Hartford	Whalers	W	6–5		19	Boston	Montreal	W	1–0
						21	Boston	Montreal	W	5–4 (OT)
						23	Montreal	Canadiens	W	6–3

25	Montreal	Canadiens	L	4–1	
27	Boston	Montreal	W	3–1	

May 1990

3	Boston	Washington	W	5–3	
5	Boston	Washington	W	3–0	
7	Washington	Capitals	W	4–1	

9	Washington	Capitals	W	3–2	
15	Boston	Edmonton	L	3–2 (OT)
18	Boston	Edmonton	L	7–2	
20	Edmonton	Oilers	W	2–1	
22	Edmonton	Oilers	L	5–1	
24	Boston	Edmonton	L	4–1	

1989-90 PLAYOFFS

vs. Hartford Whalers	4 wins – 3 losses
at Hartford	1 win – 2 losses
at Boston	3 wins – 1 loss
vs. Montreal Canadiens	4 wins – 1 loss
at Montreal	1 win – 1 loss
at Boston	3 wins – 0 losses

vs. Washington Capitals	4 wins – 0 losses
at Washington	2 wins – 0 losses
at Boston	2 wins – 0 losses
vs. Edmonton Oilers	1 win – 4 losses
at Edmonton	1 win – 1 loss
at Boston	0 wins – 3 losses

1989-90 PLAYOFF SCORING

	W	L	SO	GAA	PIM
Rejean Lemelin	0	1	0	5.78	0
Andy Moog	13	7	2	2.21	6

	G	A	P	PIM
Cam Neely	12	16	28	51
Craig Janney	3	19	22	2
Ray Bourque	5	12	17	16
Randy Burridge	4	11	15	14
Dave Poulin	8	5	13	8
Brian Propp	4	9	13	2
Bobby Carpenter	4	6	10	39
John Carter	6	3	9	45
Glen Wesley	2	6	8	36
Garry Galley	3	3	6	34
Don Sweeney	1	5	6	18
Dave Christian	4	1	5	4
Greg Hawgood	1	3	4	12
John Byce	2	0	2	2
Bob Beers	1	1	2	18
Bob Sweeney	0	2	2	30
Greg Johnston	1	0	1	4
Lyndon Byers	1	0	1	12
Peter Douris	0	1	1	5
Jim Weimer	0	1	1	4
Lou Crawford	0	0	0	0
Billy O'Dwyer	0	0	0	2
Andy Brickley	0	0	0	0
Bobby Gould	0	0	0	4
Allen Pederson	0	0	0	41

Number of power play advantages	93
Power play goals	15
% successful	16.1%
Cam Neely	4
Dave Poulin	2
Bob Carpenter	2
Craig Janney	1
Ray Bourque	1
Brian Propp	1
Garry Galley	1
Don Sweeney	1
Dave Christian	1
Greg Hawgood	1

Short-handed goals against	1
Penalty minutes:	421 – 20.0
Times short-handed	88
Power play goals against	9
Penalty kill success	89.8%
Short-handed goals	3
Cam Neely	1
Randy Burridge	1
John Carter	1

1990–1991
(67th year)

OWNER & GOVERNOR:	Jeremy Jacobs	STANLEY CUP WINNER:	Pittsburgh Penguins
GM:	Harry Sinden	ALL-STARS:	Ray Bourque (1st team)
COACH:	Mike Milbury		Cam Neely (2nd team)
ATTENDANCE:	573,607	TROPHY WINNERS:	Norris — Ray Bourque
	14,340 per game		Dufresne — Cam Neely
PLAYOFFS:	*Division semi-finals:*		7th Player — Ken Hodge
	Defeat Hartford Whalers		Three Star — Cam Neely
	4 wins – 2 losses	RADIO BROADCASTER:	WEEI – Bob Wilson,
	Division finals:		Johnny Bucyk
	Defeat Montreal Canadiens	TV BROADCASTER:	WSBK TV38 & NESN – Fred
	4 wins – 3 losses		Cusick, Derek Sanderson,
	Conference finals:		Dave Shea
	Lose to Pittsburgh Penguins		
	2 wins – 4 losses		

UNIFORMS

- Home jersey is white with gold and black trim. Socks are white with one gold band surrounded by two black bands at the calf. Road jersey is black with gold and white trim. Gold socks with one white band surrounded by two black bands at the calf. Logo is the spoked "B." Pants are black. Bearhead appears on both shoulders on both home and road uniforms.

POTPOURRI

- Cam Neely scores a goal in 8 consecutive games.
- In the October 6 game against Quebec, Dave Poulin and Craig Janney score short-handed goals.
- Bruins score 11 short-handed goals.
- The Bruins are awarded 2 penalty shots this season and score on 1, by Bob Sweeney against Hartford. This is the first successful penalty shot scored for Boston since 1979.
- For the fourth time in his career, Ray Bourque leads the team in scoring.
- Ray Bourque plays in his 800th career game.
- Garry Galley plays in 400th career game.
- Glen Wesley and Bob Sweeney play in all 80 games for the Bruins.
- Bruins qualify for the playoffs for the 24th straight season.
- Bruins have 8 short-handed goals scored against them.
- The Bruins have 1 penalty shot called against them. Wayne Presley of Chicago scores against Reggie Lemelin.
- Bruins lose conference championship to the Pittsburgh Penguins.
- Bobby Carpenter is limited to 29 regular season and 1 playoff game due to a serious knee injury.
- Vladimir Ruzicka becomes the first Czechoslovakian to play for the Bruins.
- Ron Tugnutt of Quebec records a 73-save performance in a March 21, 3–3 tie.
- After the 1991 playoffs, the Minnesota North Stars and the expansion San Jose Sharks agree to a "cross-pollination" draft in which the Sharks would be allowed to secure the rights to a number of Minnesota players, then both teams would participate in an expansion draft in which each NHL team would lose 1 player.
- After the Pittsburgh Penguins won the Stanley Cup, the top band of the Cup, containing winners of the Cup from 1928 to 1940 are removed and retired to the Hockey Hall of Fame so that new names could be added.

TRANSACTIONS

- Select Bryan Smolinski #1 in the 1990 NHL draft.
- Lose Allan Pederson to Minnesota in the 1991 expansion draft.
- Obtain Ken Hammond from Toronto for cash.
- Trade Greg Hawgood to Edmonton for Vladimir Ruzicka.
- Trade Rob Cimetta to Toronto for Steve Bancroft.
- Obtain Petri Skriko from Vancouver for Boston's second draft choice in the 1992 draft.
- Trade Randy Burridge to Washington for Steve Leach.

1990-91 STANDINGS

PRINCE OF WALES CONFERENCE

Adams Division

	W	L	T	P	GF	GA
Boston	44	24	12	100	299	264
Montreal	39	30	11	89	273	249
Buffalo	31	30	19	81	292	278
Hartford	31	38	11	73	238	276
Quebec	16	50	14	46	236	354

Patrick Division

	W	L	T	P	GF	GA
Pittsburgh	41	33	6	88	342	305
New York Rangers	36	31	13	85	297	265
Washington	37	36	7	81	258	258
New Jersey	32	33	15	79	272	264
Philadelphia	33	37	10	76	252	267
New York Islanders	25	45	10	60	223	290

CLARENCE CAMPBELL CONFERENCE

Norris Division

	W	L	T	P	GF	GA
Chicago	49	23	8	106	284	211
St. Louis	47	22	11	105	310	250
Detroit	34	38	8	76	273	298
Minnesota	27	39	14	68	256	266
Toronto	23	46	11	57	241	318

Smythe Division

	W	L	T	P	GF	GA
Los Angeles	46	24	10	102	340	254
Calgary	46	26	8	100	344	263
Edmonton	37	37	6	80	272	272
Vancouver	28	43	9	65	243	315
Winnipeg	26	43	11	63	260	288

1990-91 RESULTS

October 1991

	AT	VERSUS	W-L-T	SCR
4	Boston	Philadelphia	W	4-1
6	Boston	Quebec	W	7-1
7	Quebec	Nordiques	W	5-2
10	Winnipeg	Jets	W	4-2
11	Minnesota	North Stars	T	3-3
13	Los Angeles	Kings	L	7-1
17	Vancouver	Canucks	L	3-1
19	Edmonton	Oilers	L	8-1
20	Calgary	Flames	L	8-1
25	Boston	Vancouver	W	4-2
27	Boston	Chicago	W	5-4
31	Buffalo	Sabres	T	3-3

November 1990

	AT	VERSUS	W-L-T	SCR
1	Boston	St. Louis	W	3-2 (OT)
3	Boston	Buffalo	L	4-1

5	New York	Rangers	W	3–2 (OT)
7	Montreal	Canadiens	W	2–0
10	Boston	Pittsburgh	T	3–3
11	Washington	Capitals	W	5–3
14	Hartford	Whalers	L	3–1
15	Boston	Quebec	W	6–0
17	Boston	Montreal	T	1–1
19	Toronto	Maple Leafs	W	5–2
23	Boston	Hartford	L	4–3
24	Hartford	Whalers	W	4–3
29	Boston	Edmonton	W	4–2

December 1990

1	Boston	New York Rangers	L	5–4
4	Detroit	Red Wings	W	5–4 (OT)
6	Boston	Montreal	L	6–4
8	Montreal	Canadiens	L	7–1
9	Buffalo	Sabres	W	3–2
12	Hartford	Whalers	W	5–1
13	Boston	Hartford	W	8–2
15	Boston	New Jersey	T	1–1
18	New Jersey	Devils	L	8–3
20	Boston	Buffalo	W	4–1
22	Boston	Minnesota	W	6–2
23	New York	Rangers	T	5–5
26	Buffalo	Sabres	T	3–3
28	Winnipeg	Jets	L	6–0
29	Minnesota	North Stars	T	4–4

January 1991

3	Boston	Vancouver	W	8–3
5	Boston	Washington	L	5–3
7	Boston	Winnipeg	W	5–3
8	Quebec	Nordiques	L	4–2
10	Boston	Quebec	W	5–3
12	Boston	Philadelphia	L	3–1
14	Boston	Detroit	W	6–1

15	New York	Islanders	W	5–4
17	Boston	Los Angeles	W	5–3
22	Buffalo	Sabres	L	6–4
24	Boston	Hartford	W	3–0
26	Boston	Calgary	W	5–2
27	Montreal	Canadiens	W	3–1
31	Boston	Montreal	W	5–2

February 1991

2	Pittsburgh	Penguins	L	6–2
3	Boston	Pittsburgh	W	6–3
5	Boston	Edmonton	W	6–5 (OT)
7	Boston	Calgary	L	4–1
9	Boston	Chicago	W	5–3
10	Quebec	Nordiques	W	7–4
13	Montreal	Canadiens	W	7–4
16	Los Angeles	Kings	W	5–4 (OT)
21	Chicago	Blackhawks	L	4–1
23	St. Louis	Blues	L	9–2
28	Boston	New York Islanders	W	5–0

March 1991

2	Boston	Buffalo	L	7–4
3	New Jersey	Devils	W	3–1
5	Toronto	Maple Leafs	L	6–3
7	Boston	St. Louis	T	5–5
9	Boston	Toronto	W	2–0
14	Boston	Montreal	W	3–2
16	Boston	Detroit	L	5–3
17	Philadelphia	Flyers	W	3–1
19	Hartford	Whalers	T	1–1
21	Boston	Quebec	T	3–3
23	Boston	Buffalo	W	6–3
24	Washington	Capitals	T	3–3
26	Quebec	Nordiques	W	7–4
30	New York	Islanders	L	5–3
31	Boston	Hartford	W	7–3

1990-91 SCORING

	W	L	T	S	GAA	PIM
Rejean Lemelin	17	10	3	1	3.64	10
Andy Moog	25	13	9	4	2.87	20
					2 assists	
Matt Delguidice	0	0	0	0	0.00	0
Norm Foster	2	1	0	0	4.57	0

	G	A	P	PIM
Ray Bourque	21	73	94	75
Craig Janney	26	66	92	8
Cam Neely	51	40	91	98
Ken Hodge	30	29	59	20
Dave Christian	32	21	53	41
Bob Sweeney	15	33	48	115
Glen Wesley	11	32	43	78
Randy Burridge	15	13	28	40
Garry Galley	6	21	27	84
Jim Weimer	4	19	23	62
Don Sweeney	8	13	21	67
Dave Poulin	8	12	20	25
Petri Skriko	5	14	19	9
Jeff Lazaro	5	13	18	67
Bobby Carpenter	8	8	16	22
Vladimir Ruzicka	8	8	16	19
Wes Walz	8	8	16	32
Chris Nilan	6	9	15	277
John Carter	4	7	11	68
Andy Brickley	2	9	11	8

Stephane Quintal	2	6	8	89	Ralph Barahona	2	1	3	0
Allan Pederson	2	6	8	107	Jarmo Kekalainen	2	1	3	6
Peter Douris	5	2	7	9	Ken Hammond	1	0	1	2
Graeme Townshend	2	5	7	12	Bob Beers	0	1	1	10
Nevin Markwart	3	3	6	36	Bruce Shoebottom	0	0	0	5
Ron Hoover	4	0	4	31	Gord Kluzak	0	0	0	0
Lyndon Byers	2	2	4	82	Shayne Stevenson	0	0	0	26
John Byce	1	3	4	6					

Number of power play advantages	351	Short-handed goals against	8
Power play goals	74	Penalty minutes: 1,694 – 21.2 per game	
% successful	21.1%	Times short-handed	368
Cam Neely	18	Power play goals against	64
Ken Hodge	12	Penalty kill success	82.6%
Craig Janney	9	Short-handed goals	11
Dave Christian	9	Ken Hodge	2
Ray Bourque	7	Dave Poulin	2
Glen Wesley	5	Craig Janney	1
Vladimir Ruzicka	4	Cam Neely	1
Bob Carpenter	2	Bob Sweeney	1
Randy Burridge	1	Glen Wesley	1
Petri Skriko	1	Don Sweeney	1
Garry Galley	1	Jeff Lazaro	1
Jeff Lazaro	1	John Carter	1
Wes Walz	1		
John Carter	1		
Stephane Quintal	1		
Peter Douris	1		

1990-91 PLAYOFF RESULTS

April 1991

	AT	VERSUS	W-L-T	SCR
3	Boston	Hartford	L	5–2
5	Boston	Hartford	W	4–3
7	Hartford	Whalers	W	6–3
9	Hartford	Whalers	L	4–3
11	Boston	Hartford	W	6–1
13	Hartford	Whalers	W	3–1
17	Boston	Montreal	W	2–1
19	Boston	Montreal	L	4–3 (OT)
21	Montreal	Canadiens	W	3–2
23	Montreal	Canadiens	L	6–2
25	Boston	Montreal	W	4–1
27	Montreal	Canadiens	L	3–2 (OT)
29	Boston	Montreal	W	2–1

May 1991

1	Boston	Pittsburgh	W	6–3
3	Boston	Pittsburgh	W	5–4 (OT)
5	Pittsburgh	Penguins	L	4–1
7	Pittsburgh	Penguins	L	4–1
9	Boston	Pittsburgh	L	7–2
11	Pittsburgh	Penguins	L	5–3

1990-91 PLAYOFFS

vs. Hartford Whalers	4 wins – 2 losses
at Hartford	2 wins – 1 loss
at Boston	2 wins – 1 loss
vs. Montreal Canadiens	4 wins – 3 losses
at Montreal	1 win – 2 losses
at Boston	3 wins – 1 loss

vs. Pittsburgh Penguins	2 wins – 4 losses
at Pittsburgh	0 wins – 3 losses
at Boston	2 wins – 1 loss

1990-91 PLAYOFF SCORING

	W	L	SO	GAA	PIM				
Rejean Lemelin	0	0	0	0.00	0				
Andy Moog	10	9	0	3.18	4				

	G	A	P	PIM			G	A	P	PIM
Ray Bourque	7	18	25	12	Jeff Lazaro	3	2	5	30
Craig Janney	4	18	22	11	Jim Weimer	1	3	4	14
Cam Neely	16	4	20	36	Don Sweeney	3	0	3	25
Vladimir Ruzicka	2	11	13	0	Randy Burridge	0	3	3	39
Dave Christian	8	4	12	4	Chris Nilan	0	2	2	62
Glen Wesley	2	9	11	19	Nevin Markwart	1	0	1	22
Ken Hodge	4	6	10	6	Bobby Carpenter	0	1	1	2
Dave Poulin	0	9	9	20	Stephane Quintal	0	1	1	7
Petri Skriko	4	4	8	4	Peter Douris	0	1	1	6
Bob Sweeney	4	2	6	45	Lyndon Byers	0	0	0	10
Garry Galley	1	5	6	17	Chris Winnes	0	0	0	0
					Wes Walz	0	0	0	0
					Bob Beers	0	0	0	4
					Ken Hammond	0	0	0	10
					Ron Hoover	0	0	0	18
					Allen Pederson	0	0	0	10

Number of power play advantages	100	Short-handed goals against		3
Power play goals	24	Penalty minutes:	439 – 23.1 per game	
% successful	24%	Times short-handed		92
Cam Neely	9	Power play goals against		17
Craig Janney	4	Penalty kill success		81.5%
Ray Bourque	3	Short-handed goals		0
Petri Skriko	3			
Glen Wesley	2			
Vladimir Ruzicka	1			
Ken Hodge	1			
Jim Wiemer	1			

1991–1992
(68th year)

OWNER & GOVERNOR:	Jeremy Jacobs	STANLEY CUP WINNER:	Pittsburgh Penguins
GM:	Harry Sinden	ALL-STARS:	Ray Bourque (1st team)
COACH:	Rick Bowness	TROPHY WINNERS:	Dufresne —
ATTENDANCE:	570,957		Vladimir Ruzicka
	14,273 per game		7th Player —
PLAYOFFS:	*Division semi-finals:*		Vladimir Ruzicka
	Defeat Buffalo Sabres		Three Star — Andy Moog
	4 wins – 3 losses		King Clancy — Andy Moog
	Division finals:	RADIO BROADCASTER:	WEEI – Bob Wilson,
	Defeat Montreal Canadiens		Johnny Bucyk
	4 wins – 0 losses	TV BROADCASTER:	WSBK TV38 & NESN – Fred
	Conference finals:		Cusick, Derek Sanderson,
	Lose to Pittsburgh Penguins		Dave Shea
	0 wins – 4 losses		

Bob Sweeney, unidentified player, Ken Hodge Jr., Petri Skriko,
Rick Bowness behind bench, all wearing classic uniforms.

UNIFORMS

- Home jersey is white with gold and black trim. Socks are white with one gold band surrounded by two black bands at the calf. Road jersey is black with gold and white trim. Gold socks with one white band surrounded by two black bands at the calf. Logo is the spoked "B." Pants are black. Bearhead appears on both shoulders on both home and road uniforms.
- Because of the 75th anniversary of the NHL, the Bruins wear a special classic jersey that will be worn on opening night and at other occasions during the season. The jersey is white, trimmed in black and gold, with a large capital "B" for a front crest.
- After the mid-point of the season, the teams will reverse their uniforms for home and away games. The home teams will wear the basic colored uniforms, and the road team will wear basic white.
- All 1991–92 uniforms will have the 75th anniversary patch.

POTPOURRI

- The season opener on October 3 is the earliest regular season game played by the Bruins.
- The season is suspended from April 1 to April 12, 1992, due to the players strike.
- Bruins qualify for the playoffs for the 25th straight season.
- Bruins score 7 short-handed goals.
- Ray Bourque wins the King Clancy Trophy for leadership and community contributions.
- Ray Bourque becomes the third defenseman to reach the 1,000th-point plateau.

- Glen Featherstone plays in only 7 games because of injury.
- Despite playing in only 9 games because of injury, Cam Neely scores 9 goals.
- For the second season in a row, the Bruins lose the conference championship to Pittsburgh.
- Bruins have 14 short-handed goals scored against.
- The San Jose Sharks become the 22nd team to enter the NHL.
- The NHL celebrates its 75th anniversary.
- Video replays are used to help in goal vs. no-goal situations.
- This is the first season since 1966–67 that the Bruins have scored fewer goals than they have allowed.

TRANSACTIONS

- Select Glen Murray #1 in the 1991 NHL entry draft.
- Jeff Lazaro is lost to Ottawa and Shayne Stevenson is lost to Tampa Bay in the 1992 expansion draft.
- Obtain Jim Vesey from Winnipeg for future considerations.
- Norm Foster traded to Edmonton for future considerations.
- Obtain Alan Stewart from New Jersey for future considerations.
- Obtain Barry Pederson from Hartford for future considerations.
- Obtain Scott Arniel from Winnipeg for future considerations.
- Garry Galley and Wes Walz traded to Philadelphia for Gord Murphy and Brian Dobbin.
- Steve Bancroft traded to Chicago for future draft choices.
- Obtain Daniel Berthiaume from Los Angeles for future considerations.
- Trade Craig Janney and Stephane Quintal to St. Louis for Adam Oates.
- Trade John Byce and Dennis Smith to Washington for Brent Hughes.
- Bob Beers traded to Tampa Bay for Stephane Richer.
- Trade Petri Skriko to Winnipeg for Brent Ashton.
- Sign free agent Glen Featherstone.

1991-92 STANDINGS

PRINCE OF WALES CONFERENCE
Adams Division

	W	L	T	P	GF	GA
Montreal	41	28	11	93	267	207
Boston	36	32	12	84	270	275
Buffalo	31	37	12	74	289	299
Hartford	26	41	13	65	247	283
Quebec	20	48	12	52	255	318

Patrick Division

	W	L	T	P	GF	GA
New York Rangers	50	25	5	105	321	246
Washington	45	27	8	98	330	275
Pittsburgh	39	32	9	87	343	308
New Jersey	38	31	11	87	289	259
New York Islanders	34	35	11	79	291	299
Philadelphia	32	37	11	75	252	273

CLARENCE CAMPBELL CONFERENCE
Norris Division

	W	L	T	P	GF	GA
Detroit	43	25	12	98	320	256
Chicago	36	29	15	87	257	236
St. Louis	36	33	11	83	279	266
Minnesota	32	42	6	70	246	270
Toronto	30	43	7	67	234	294

Smythe Division

Vancouver	42	26	12	96	285	250
Los Angeles	35	31	14	84	287	296
Edmonton	36	34	19	82	295	297
Winnipeg	33	32	15	81	251	244
Calgary	31	37	12	74	296	305
San Jose	17	58	5	39	219	359

1991-92 RESULTS

October 1991

	AT	VERSUS	W-L-T	SCR
3	Boston	New York Rangers	W	5–3
5	Boston	New York Islanders	L	4–3
7	New York	Rangers	L	2–1 (OT)
9	Buffalo	Sabres	T	4–4
12	Boston	Montreal	L	6–0
17	Vancouver	Canucks	T	3–3
19	San Jose	Sharks	W	4–1
24	St. Louis	Blues	L	6–5
26	Minnesota	North Stars	L	4–0
27	Chicago	Blackhawks	W	6–3
31	Boston	Los Angeles	L	4–2

November 1991

2	Boston	Detroit	W	4–1
4	New York	Islanders	L	6–4
5	Pittsburgh	Penguins	T	5–5
7	Boston	Calgary	T	4–4
9	Boston	New Jersey	W	4–0
14	Boston	Quebec	W	5–2
16	Hartford	Whalers	W	5–4 (OT)
20	Buffalo	Sabres	L	3–1
22	Washington	Capitals	L	6–3
23	Boston	Buffalo	W	7–4
25	Montreal	Canadiens	L	4–3
27	New York	Islanders	W	3–2
29	Boston	Montreal	W	5–4 (OT)

December 1991

1	Boston	Hartford	W	5–4
5	Boston	Quebec	T	2–2
7	Boston	Philadelphia	L	5–3
8	New York	Rangers	L	4–0
10	Quebec	Nordiques	L	5–2
12	Boston	Montreal	W	5–2
14	Boston	Toronto	W	4–3
19	Boston	Pittsburgh	L	6–4
21	Boston	Edmonton	W	6–3
22	Montreal	Canadiens	L	3–2
26	Boston	Hartford	W	3–2
27	Buffalo	Sabres	L	8–1
29	Winnipeg	Jets	W	6–3
31	Detroit	Red Wings	W	5–3

January 1992

2	Boston	Winnipeg	L	3–1
4	Boston	Buffalo	W	4–2
8	Montreal	Canadiens	L	3–2
9	Boston	Quebec	W	5–4
11	Boston	Philadelphia	W	5–1
15	Hartford	Whalers	W	4–3
16	Boston	Hartford	W	4–3 (OT)
22	Toronto	Maple Leafs	W	5–2
23	Boston	Montreal	L	3–1
25	Hartford	Whalers	T	4–4
27	Boston	Minnesota	W	3–2
28	Quebec	Nordiques	W	4–2
30	Boston	Calgary	W	3–1

February 1992

1	Boston	Buffalo	T	2–2
4	Winnipeg	Jets	T	3–3
6	Philadelphia	Flyers	L	5–1
8	Boston	New Jersey	L	6–4
9	Boston	Pittsburgh	W	6–3
13	St. Louis	Blues	L	4–0
17	Los Angeles	Kings	L	6–3
19	Calgary	Flames	L	6–4
21	Edmonton	Oilers	W	5–3
23	Vancouver	Canucks	L	2–1 (OT)
27	Boston	Toronto	W	4–2
29	Boston	Washington	T	5–5

March 1992

1	Washington	Capitals	W	4–1
3	Hartford	Whalers	L	4–0
5	Boston	Vancouver	T	2–2
7	Boston	Chicago	L	2–1
8	Chicago	Blackhawks	L	4–0
11	Buffalo	Sabres	L	6–3
14	Quebec	Nordiques	W	5–4 (OT)
15	Boston	Los Angeles	W	5–1
19	Boston	St. Louis	L	4–1
21	Boston	Edmonton	L	4–3
23	Boston	San Jose	W	7–6
26	New Jersey	Devils	L	4–2
28	Boston	Buffalo	W	4–3 (OT)
31	Quebec	Nordiques	W	5–4 (OT)

April 1992

12	Boston	Quebec		T	1–1		
13	Boston	Hartford		W	6–3		
15	Montreal	Canadiens		T	4–4		

1991-92 **SCORING**

	W	L	T	S	GAA	PIM
Rejean Lemelin	5	1	0	0	3.39	2
					1 assist	
Andy Moog	28	22	9	1	3.23	52
					3 assists	
Matt Delguidice	2	5	1	0	3.96	0
Daniel Berthiaume	1	4	2	0	3.16	0

	G	A	P	PIM
Ray Bourque	21	60	81	56
Vladimir Ruzicka	39	36	75	48
Steve Leach	31	29	60	147
Craig Janney	12	39	51	20
Bobby Carpenter	25	23	48	46
Glen Wesley	9	37	46	54
Brent Ashton	17	22	39	47
Adam Oates	10	20	30	10
Andy Brickley	10	17	27	2
Peter Douris	10	13	23	10
Bob Sweeney	6	14	20	103
Joe Juneau	5	14	19	4
Ken Hodge	6	11	17	10
Dave Reid	7	7	14	27
Stephane Quintal	4	10	14	77
Don Sweeney	3	11	14	74
Garry Galley	2	12	14	83
Cam Neely	9	3	12	16
Chris Nilan	5	5	10	186
Barry Pederson	3	6	9	8
Jeff Lazaro	3	6	9	31
Gord Murphy	3	6	9	51
Nevin Markwart	3	6	9	44
Jim Wiemer	1	8	9	84
Scott Arniel	5	3	8	20
Dave Poulin	4	4	8	18
Steve Heinze	3	4	7	6
Gord Hynes	0	5	5	6
Bob Beers	0	5	5	29
Glenn Murray	3	1	4	0
Chris Winnes	1	3	4	6
Lou Crawford	2	1	3	9
Ted Donato	1	2	3	8
Wes Walz	0	3	3	12
Brent Hughes	1	1	2	38
Lyndon Byers	1	1	2	129
John Byce	1	0	1	0
Josef Stumpel	1	0	1	0
Brian Dobbin	1	0	1	22
Glen Featherstone	1	0	1	20
Petri Skriko	1	0	1	6
Ralph Barahona	0	1	1	0
Shayne Stevenson	0	1	1	2
Clark Donatelli	0	1	1	22
Dave Thomlinson	0	1	1	17
Matt Hervey	0	1	1	55
Jack Capuano	0	0	0	0
Petr Prajsler	0	0	0	2
Matt Glennon	0	0	0	2
Jim Vesey	0	0	0	0
Alan Stewart	0	0	0	17

Number of power play advantages	406		
Power play goals	77		
% successful	19%		
Vladimir Ruzicka	18		
Steve Leach	12		
Ray Bourque	7		
Bobby Carpenter	6		
Brent Ashton	6		
Andy Brickley	5		
Glen Wesley	4		
Adam Oates	3		
Ken Hodge	3		
Craig Janney	3		
Dave Reid	2		
Joe Juneau	2		
Barry Pederson	1		
Cam Neely	1		
Glen Murray		1	
John Byce		1	
Garry Galley		1	
Short-handed goals against	14		
Penalty minutes:	1,752 – 21.9 per game		
Times short-handed	363		
Power play goals against	72		
Penalty kill success	80.2%		
Short-handed goals for	7		
Ray Bourque		1	
Bob Carpenter		1	
Brent Ashton		1	
Bob Sweeney		1	
Ken Hodge		1	
Dave Reid		1	
Dave Poulin		1	

1991-92 PLAYOFF RESULTS

April 1992	AT	VERSUS		W-L-T	SCR
19	Boston	Buffalo		L	3–2
21	Boston	Buffalo		W	3–2 (OT)
23	Buffalo	Sabres		W	3–2
25	Buffalo	Sabres		W	5–4 (OT)
27	Boston	Buffalo		L	2–0
29	Buffalo	Sabres		L	9–3

May 1992				
1	Boston	Buffalo	W	3–2
3	Montreal	Canadiens	W	6–4
5	Montreal	Canadiens	W	3–2 (OT)
7	Boston	Montreal	W	3–2
9	Boston	Montreal	W	2–0
17	Pittsburgh	Penguins	L	4–3 (OT)
19	Pittsburgh	Penguins	L	5–2
21	Boston	Pittsburgh	L	5–1
23	Boston	Pittsburgh	L	5–1

1991-92 PLAYOFFS

vs. Buffalo Sabres	4 wins – 3 losses
at Buffalo	2 wins – 1 loss
at Boston	2 wins – 2 losses
vs. Montreal Canadiens	4 wins – 0 losses
at Montreal	2 wins – 0 losses
at Boston	2 wins – 0 losses

vs. Pittsburgh Penguins	0 wins – 4 losses
at Pittsburgh	0 wins – 2 losses
at Boston	0 wins – 2 losses

1991-92 PLAYOFF SCORING

	W	L	SO	GAA	PIM
Rejean Lemelin	0	0	0	3.33	0
					1 assist
Andy Moog	8	7	1	3.19	17

	G	A	P	PIM
Adam Oates	5	14	19	4
Joe Juneau	4	8	12	21
Ray Bourque	3	6	9	12
Ted Donato	3	4	7	4
Dave Reid	2	5	7	4
Glenn Murray	4	2	6	10
Dave Poulin	3	3	6	22
Glen Wesley	2	4	6	16
Peter Douris	2	3	5	0
Vladimir Ruzicka	2	3	5	2
Steve Leach	4	0	4	10
Jim Weimer	1	3	4	14
Gord Hynes	1	2	3	6
Steve Heinze	0	3	3	17
Brent Hughes	2	0	2	20
Bob Sweeney	1	0	1	25
Gord Murphy	1	0	1	12
Bob Carpenter	0	1	1	6
Jeff Lazaro	0	1	1	2
Bob Beers	0	0	0	0
Clark Donatelli	0	0	0	0
Lyndon Byers	0	0	0	12
Matt Hervey	0	0	0	6
Don Sweeney	0	0	0	10

Number of power play advantages	61
Power play goals	11
% successful	18%
Adam Oates	3
Joe Juneau	2
Ray Bourque	2
Vladimir Ruzicka	2
Glen Murray	1
Dave Poulin	1

Penalty minutes:	254 – 16.9 per game	
Times short-handed		77
Power play goals against		15
Penalty kill success		80.5%
Short-handed goals		1
Bob Sweeney		1

1992–1993
(69th year)

OWNER & GOVERNOR:	Jeremy Jacobs	ALL-STARS:	Ray Bourque (1st team)
GM:	Harry Sinden	TROPHY WINNERS:	Dufresne — Adam Oates
COACH:	Brian Sutter		7th Player — Don Sweeney
ATTENDANCE:	583,562		Three Star — Adam Oates
	14,233 per game	RADIO BROADCASTER:	WEEI – Bob Wilson,
PLAYOFFS:	*Division semi-finals:*		Johnny Bucyk
	Lose to Buffalo Sabres	TV BROADCASTER:	WSBK TV38 & NESN – Fred
	0 wins – 4 losses		Cusick, Derek Sanderson,
STANLEY CUP WINNER:	Montreal Canadiens		Dave Shea

UNIFORMS

- Home jersey is white with gold and black trim. Socks are white with one gold band surrounded by two black bands at the calf. Road jersey is black with gold and white trim. Gold socks with one white band surrounded by two black bands at the calf. Logo is the spoked "B." Pants are black. Bearhead appears on both shoulders on both home and road uniforms. 100th Stanley Cup Anniversary patch worn on all uniforms.

POTPOURRI

- Bruins qualify for the playoffs for the 26th straight season.
- Ray Bourque plays in 1,000th career game in a neutral site tilt against Pittsburgh in Atlanta, Georgia.
- Joe Juneau establishes a Bruins rookie record by scoring in 14 consecutive games.
- Cam Neely plays in only 13 games because of injury.
- Adam Oates plays his 500th career game, and also scores a point in 21 straight games.
- Gord Roberts becomes the first U.S. born player to appear in 1000 games.
- Ray Bourque becomes the career assists leader for the Bruins.
- Bruins tie a team record by winning eight straight road contests.
- Bruins also enjoy an 8-game winning streak.
- Bruins score 19 short-handed goals.
- Bruins lose division semi-finals to Buffalo, 4 games to 0.
- Bruins have 8 short-handed goals scored against them.
- The NHL celebrates the 100th anniversary of the Stanley Cup.
- Tampa Bay Lightning and Ottawa Senators become 23rd and 24th teams in the NHL.
- Bruins draft 5 players from the former Soviet Union. This is the first time that the Bruins have selected players from the former Soviet Union.
- Gil Stein is named President, replacing John Zeigler.

TRANSACTIONS

- Select Dmitri Kvartalnov #1 in the 1992 NHL entry draft.
- Lose Tim Sweeney to Anaheim and Stephane Richer to Florida in the 1993 expansion draft.
- Obtain David Shaw from Minnesota for future considerations.
- Matt Hervey and Ken Hodge traded to Tampa Bay for Darin Kimble.
- Trade Daniel Berthiaume to Winnipeg for Doug Evans.
- Doug Evans lost to Philadelphia in the 1992 waiver draft.
- Trade Brent Ashton to Calgary for C.J. Young.
- Obtain Daniel Marois from New York Islanders for future considerations.
- Sign Gord Roberts as a free agent.

- Trade Gord Murphy to Dallas for future considerations.
- Trade Andy Moog to Dallas for Jon Casey.

1992-93 STANDINGS

PRINCE OF WALES CONFERENCE

Adams Division

	W	L	T	P	GF	GA
Boston	51	26	7	109	332	268
Quebec	47	27	10	104	351	300
Montreal	48	30	6	102	326	280
Buffalo	38	36	10	86	335	297
Hartford	26	52	6	58	284	369
Ottawa	10	70	4	24	202	395

Patrick Division

	W	L	T	P	GF	GA
Pittsburgh	56	21	7	119	367	268
Washington	43	34	7	93	325	286
New York Islanders	40	37	7	87	335	297
New Jersey	40	37	7	87	308	299
Philadelphia	36	37	11	83	319	319
New York Rangers	34	39	11	79	304	308

CLARENCE CAMPBELL CONFERENCE

Norris Division

	W	L	T	P	GF	GA
Chicago	47	25	12	106	279	230
Detroit	47	28	9	103	369	280
Toronto	44	29	11	99	288	241
St. Louis	37	36	11	85	282	278
Minnesota	36	38	10	82	272	293
Tampa Bay	23	54	7	53	245	332

Smythe Division

	W	L	T	P	GF	GA
Vancouver	46	29	9	101	346	278
Calgary	43	30	11	97	322	282
Los Angeles	39	35	10	88	338	340
Winnipeg	40	37	7	87	322	320
Edmonton	26	50	8	60	242	337
San Jose	11	71	2	24	218	414

1992-93 RESULTS

October 1992

	AT	VERSUS	W-L-T	SCR
8	Boston	Hartford	W	3–2 (OT)
10	Boston	New York Islanders	T	3–3
12	Boston	Ottawa	W	6–3
15	San Jose	Sharks	W	8–2
17	Los Angeles	Kings	L	8–6
22	Calgary	Flames	W	4–2
23	Edmonton	Oilers	W	6–3
25	Vancouver	Canucks	W	5–3
29	Boston	Los Angeles	W	8–3
31	Boston	Chicago	L	3–2

November 1992

	AT	VERSUS	W-L-T	SCR
5	Boston	Quebec	W	6–4
7	Boston	New York Rangers	T	2–2
11	Buffalo	Sabres	L	7–2
12	Boston	Calgary	W	5–3
14	Boston	Toronto	L	4–1
16	Montreal	Canadiens	L	6–3
19	Boston	New York Islanders	W	5–2
21	Boston	Philadelphia	W	4–3
23	Ottawa	Senators	W	3–2
25	Washington	Capitals	L	6–2
27	Boston	Hartford	W	5–4 (OT)
28	Hartford	Whalers	L	4–3 (OT)
30	Quebec	Nordiques	W	4–3

December 1992

3	Boston	Montreal	W	4–3	
5	New Jersey	Devils	W	4–2	
6	Philadelphia	Flyers	W	7–1	
9	Buffalo	Sabres	L	5–2	
10	Boston	Ottawa	W	4–2	
12	Montreal	Canadiens	L	5–1	
15	Boston	Buffalo	L	3–2	
18	Detroit	Red Wings	L	6–1	
19	Boston	Washington	W	4–3	
22	Boston	Tampa Bay	W	5–3	
26	Hartford	Whalers	W	9–4	
27	New York	Rangers	L	6–5	
29	Winnipeg	Jets	L	5–4	
31	Minnesota	North Stars	L	5–3	

January 1993

2	Boston	Hartford	W	3–2 (OT)	
5	Pittsburgh	Penguins	L	6–2	
7	Boston	Quebec	L	3–2 (OT)	
9	Boston	New Jersey	L	6–2	
12	Boston	Buffalo	W	5–2	
14	Boston	Pittsburgh	W	7–0	
16	Boston	Philadelphia	L	5–4	
18	Boston	San Jose	W	4–3	
19	New York	Islanders	T	2–2	
21	Philadelphia	Flyers	W	5–4	
23	Boston	New Jersey	W	7–5	
25	Montreal	Canadiens	L	3–2 (OT)	
26	Quebec	Nordiques	T	4–4	
28	Boston	Winnipeg	W	6–2	
30	New York	Islanders	W	6–5	

February 1993

2	Boston	Edmonton	L	4–3	
3	Quebec	Nordiques	W	4–1	
8	Atlanta	Pittsburgh	L	4–0	
9	St. Louis	Blues	W	6–1	
11	Chicago	Blackhawks	L	6–3	
14	Tampa Bay	Lightning	T	3–3	
17	Montreal	Canadiens	W	5–2	
20	Toronto	Maple Leafs	T	4–4	
25	Boston	Minnesota	T	3–3	
27	Boston	Washington	W	5–4 (OT)	

March 1993

1	Boston	Montreal	L	5–2	
4	Boston	Vancouver	W	4–3	
6	Boston	St. Louis	W	4–3 (OT)	
9	Pittsburgh	Penguins	L	3–2	
11	Boston	Montreal	W	5–2	
13	Boston	Ottawa	W	6–3	
15	New York	Rangers	W	3–1	
16	Providence, RI	New Jersey	W	3–1	
18	Ottawa	Senators	W	4–1	
20	Boston	Detroit	L	7–4	
22	Boston	Hartford	W	5–4	
24	Buffalo	Sabres	W	2–0	
25	Boston	Montreal	W	2–0	
27	Boston	Pittsburgh	L	5–3	
30	Hartford	Whalers	W	3–1	

April 1993

3	Boston	Buffalo	W	3–2	
4	Buffalo	Sabres	W	3–0	
6	Quebec	Nordiques	W	7–1	
8	Boston	Quebec	W	6–2	
10	Montreal	Canadiens	W	5–1	
11	Boston	Ottawa	W	4–2	
14	Ottawa	Senators	W	4–2	

1992-93 SCORING

	W	L	T	S	GAA	PIM
Rejean Lemelin	5	4	0	0	3.43	4
Andy Moog	37	14	3	3	3.16	14
						1 assist
Mike Bales	0	0	0	0	2.40	0
John Blue	0	8	4	1	2.90	6
						2 assists

	G	A	P	PIM
Adam Oates	45	97	142	32
Joe Juneau	32	70	102	33
Ray Bourque	19	63	82	40
Dmitri Kvartalnov	30	42	72	16
Steve Leach	26	25	51	126
Dave Poulin	16	33	49	62
Vladimir Ruzicka	19	22	41	38
Dave Reid	20	16	36	10
Ted Donato	15	20	35	61
Don Sweeney	7	27	34	68
Glen Wesley	8	25	33	47
Steve Heinze	18	13	31	24
David Shaw	10	14	24	108
Cam Neely	11	7	18	25
Gord Murphy	5	12	17	62
Gordie Roberts	5	12	17	105
Grigori Panteleev	8	6	14	12
Darin Kimble	7	3	10	177
Glen Featherstone	5	5	10	102
C.J. Young	4	5	9	12
Brent Hughes	5	4	9	191

Peter Douris	4	4	8	4	Josef Stumpel	1	3	4	4
Tim Sweeney	1	7	8	6	Darren Banks	2	1	3	64
Glenn Murray	3	4	7	8	Sergei Zholtok	0	1	1	0
Jim Wiemer	1	6	7	48	Chris Winnes	0	1	1	0
Stephane Richer	1	4	5	18	Bill Huard	0	0	0	0
Brent Ashton	2	2	4	11	Dennis Chervyakov	0	0	0	2
Andy McKim	1	3	4	0	Dominic Lavoie	0	0	0	2
Bryan Smolinski	1	3	4	0					

Number of power play advantages	435	Short-handed goals against	8
Power play goals	91	Penalty minutes: 1,552 – 18.5 per game	
% successful	20.9%	Times short-handed	413
Adam Oates	24	Power play goals against	70
Dmitri Kvartalnov	11	Penalty kill success	83.1%
Joe Juneau	9	Short-handed goals	19
Steve Leach	9	Dave Pouin	5
Ray Bourque	8	Dave Reid	5
Vladimir Ruzicka	7	Ted Donato	2
Cam Neely	6	Steve Heinze	2
Glen Wesley	4	Adam Oates	1
Ted Donato	3	Don Sweeney	1
Gord Murphy	3	Glen Wesley	1
Grigori Panteleev	2	David Shaw	1
Glen Murray	2	Peter Douris	1
Dave Reid	1		
Dave Shaw	1		
Glen Featherstone	1		

1992-93 PLAYOFF RESULTS

April 1993

	AT	VERSUS		W-L-T	SCR
18	Boston	Buffalo		L	5–4 (OT)
20	Boston	Buffalo		L	4–0
22	Buffalo	Sabres		L	4–3 (OT)
24	Buffalo	Sabres		L	6–5 (OT)

1992-93 PLAYOFFS

vs. Buffalo Sabres	0 wins – 4 losses
at Buffalo	0 wins – 2 losses
at Boston	0 wins – 2 losses

1992-93 PLAYOFF SCORING

	W	L	SO	GAA	PIM
John Blue	0	1	0	3.13	0
Andy Moog	0	3	0	5.22	0

	G	A	P	PIM
Adam Oates	0	9	9	4
Joe Juneau	2	4	6	6
Cam Neely	4	1	5	4
Steve Leach	1	1	2	2
Dave Poulin	1	1	2	10
Steve Heinze	1	1	2	2
Ray Bourque	1	0	1	2
Peter Douris	1	0	1	0
Bryan Smolinski	1	0	1	2
David Shaw	0	1	1	6
Ted Donato	0	1	1	0
Brent Hughes	0	0	0	2
Jim Wiemer	0	0	0	4

Tim Sweeney	o	o	o	o
Stephane Richer	o	o	o	o
Darin Kimble	o	o	o	2
Gordie Roberts	o	o	o	6

Don Sweeney	o	o	o	4
Glen Wesley	o	o	o	o
Dmitri Kvartalnov	o	o	o	o

Number of power play advantages	22
Power play goals	4
% successful	18.2%
Joe Juneau	2
Cam Neely	1
Ray Bourque	1
Short-handed goals against	1

Penalty minutes:	56 – 14.0 per game
Times short-handed	19
Power play goals against	5
Penalty kill success	73.7%
Short-handed goals	1
Dave Poulin	1

1993–1994
(70th year)

OWNER & GOVERNOR:	Jeremy Jacobs
GM:	Harry Sinden
COACH:	Brian Sutter
ATTENDANCE:	576,996
	14,073 per game
PLAYOFFS:	*Conference quarter finals:*
	Defeat Montreal Canadiens
	4 wins – 3 losses
	Conference semi-finals:
	Lose to New Jersey Devils
	2 wins – 4 losses
STANLEY CUP WINNER:	New York Rangers

ALL-STARS:	Ray Bourque (1st team)
	Cam Neely (2nd team)
TROPHY WINNERS:	Norris — Ray Bourque
	Masterton — Cam Neely
	Dufresne — Ray Bourque
	7th Player — Cam Neely
	Three Star — Cam Neely
RADIO BROADCASTER:	WEEI – Bob Wilson,
	Johnny Bucyk
TV BROADCASTER:	WSBK TV38 & NESN – Fred
	Cusick, Derek Sanderson,
	Dave Shea

UNIFORMS

- Home jersey is white with gold and black trim. Socks are white with one gold band surrounded by two black bands at the calf. Road jersey is black with gold and white trim. Gold socks with one white band surrounded by two black bands at the calf. Logo is the spoked "B." Pants are black. Bearhead appears on both shoulders on both home and road uniforms.

POTPOURRI

- Bruins qualify for the playoffs for the 27th consecutive season.
- Despite playing in only 49 games, Cam Neely leads the league in game-winning goals with 13. Cam Neely scores 50 goals in only 44 games.
- Bryan Smolinski leads all rookies with 3 short-handed goals.
- Bruins score 17 short-handed goals.
- Ray Bourque plays in his 1,100th career game and scores his 1,100th career point.
- Opposing teams score 9 short-handed goals.
- The NHL adds two new teams, the Mighty Ducks of Anaheim and the Florida Panthers.
- The Minnesota North Stars move to Dallas and become the Dallas Stars.
- The Prince of Wales and Campbell Conferences are replaced by Eastern and Western Conferences.
- The Adams, Patrick, Norris, and Smythe Divisions are replaced by Northeast and Atlantic in the

Eastern Conference, and Central and Pacific in the Western Conference. Winnipeg is moved to the Central Division, Tampa Bay is moved to the Atlantic Division, and Pittsburgh is moved to the Northeast Division.

- On a team-by-team average for the previous 5 seasons, the Bruins lead the league with an average of 98.2 points.
- Gary Bettman replaces Gil Stein as President and the title of the office is changed to Commissioner.

TRANSACTIONS

- Select Kevyn Adams #1 in the 1993 NHL entry draft.
- Paul Stanton obtained from the Pittsburgh Penguins for a future draft choice.
- Jon Morris purchased from San Jose for cash.
- Sell Mark Krys to Buffalo for cash.
- Trade Joe Juneau to Washington for Al Iafrate.
- Dave Capuano purchased from San Jose for cash.
- Gord Murphy traded to Dallas for future considerations.
- Andy Moog traded to Dallas for Jon Casey.

1993-94 STANDINGS

EASTERN CONFERENCE

Northeast Division	W	L	T	P	GF	GA
Pittsburgh	44	27	13	101	299	285
Boston	42	29	13	97	289	252
Montreal	41	29	14	96	283	248
Buffalo	43	32	9	95	282	218
Quebec	34	42	8	76	277	292
Hartford	27	48	9	63	227	288
Ottawa	14	61	9	37	201	397
Atlantic Division						
New York Rangers	52	24	8	112	299	231
New Jersey	47	25	12	106	306	220
Washington	39	35	10	88	277	263
New York Islanders	36	36	12	84	282	264
Florida	33	34	17	83	233	233
Philadelphia	35	39	10	80	294	314
Tampa Bay	30	43	11	71	224	251

WESTERN CONFERENCE

Central Division	W	L	T	P	GF	GA
Detroit	46	30	8	100	356	275
Toronto	43	29	12	98	280	243
Dallas	42	29	13	97	286	265
St. Louis	40	33	11	91	270	283
Chicago	39	36	9	87	254	240
Winnipeg	24	51	9	57	245	344
Pacific Division						
Calgary	42	29	13	97	302	256
Vancouver	41	40	3	85	279	276
San Jose	33	35	16	82	252	265
Anaheim	33	46	5	71	229	251
Los Angeles	27	45	12	66	294	322
Edmonton	25	45	14	64	261	305

1993-94 RESULTS

October 1993

	AT	VERSUS	W-L-T	SCR
5	New York	Rangers	W	4–3
7	Boston	Buffalo	L	5–3
9	Boston	Quebec	W	7–3
11	Boston	Montreal	T	1–1
15	Anaheim	Mighty Ducks	T	1–1
16	San Jose	Sharks	T	1–1
19	Vancouver	Canucks	L	5–4
22	Edmonton	Oilers	W	3–1
23	Calgary	Flames	T	3–3
28	Boston	Ottawa	W	6–2
30	Boston	St. Louis	L	2–1

November 1993

2	Detroit	Red Wings	L	6–1
4	Boston	Calgary	W	6–3
6	Boston	Tampa Bay	T	1–1
7	Buffalo	Sabres	W	4–3
11	Boston	Edmonton	W	5–1
13	New York	Islanders	W	5–2
17	Hartford	Whalers	W	4–2
18	Boston	San Jose	W	3–1
20	Boston	Philadelphia	T	5–5
24	Pittsburgh	Penguins	L	7–3
26	Boston	Florida	W	3–2
27	Toronto	Maple Leafs	L	4–2
30	Quebec	Nordiques	W	5–2

December 1993

2	Boston	New York Islanders	W	7–3
4	Boston	Montreal	L	8–1
5	Buffalo	Sabres	L	3–1
9	Boston	Vancouver	L	3–2
11	Boston	Chicago	L	5–4
12	Boston	Hartford	T	2–2
15	New Jersey	Devils	W	5–4
18	Tampa Bay	Lightning	W	5–3
19	Florida	Panthers	W	2–1 (OT)
23	Boston	Pittsburgh	L	4–3
27	Ottawa	Senators	W	5–3
31	Minnesota	Philadelphia	L	4–3

January 1994

2	Boston	Washington	W	8–2
6	Boston	Winnipeg	W	5–4
8	Boston	Florida	T	2–2
10	Boston	Toronto	L	3–0
11	Pittsburgh	Penguins	L	5–4 (OT)
13	Philadelphia	Flyers	L	6–2
15	Boston	Detroit	L	3–2
17	Boston	Hartford	W	5–3
19	Montreal	Canadiens	T	3–3
24	Hartford	Whalers	W	2–1
25	Washington	Capitals	W	3–1
28	New York	Islanders	W	3–0
29	Boston	New York Islanders	W	2–1
31	Boston	Quebec	W	4–3

February 1994

3	Boston	New York Rangers	L	3–0
5	Boston	Philadelphia	W	4–0
6	Florida	Panthers	L	3–0
8	Quebec	Nordiques	W	6–1
10	Boston	Buffalo	T	3–3
12	Boston	New Jersey	W	5–3
14	Los Angeles	Kings	W	3–2 (OT)
16	Dallas	Stars	W	3–0
18	St. Louis	Blues	L	3–1
20	Tampa Bay	Lightning	T	2–2
23	New York	Rangers	W	6–3
25	Winnipeg	Jets	W	7–6
27	Chicago	Blackhawks	W	4–0

March 1994

3	Boston	Los Angeles	W	6–4
5	Boston	Ottawa	W	6–1
7	Boston	Washington	W	6–3
8	Pittsburgh	Penguins	L	7–3
10	Boston	New York Rangers	T	2–2
12	New Jersey	Devils	L	2–1
14	Montreal	Canadiens	L	5–4
17	Boston	Pittsburgh	L	4–2
19	Boston	New Jersey	L	8–6
22	Quebec	Nordiques	L	5–3
24	Boston	Anaheim	W	5–3
26	Boston	Montreal	W	6–3
27	Washington	Capitals	W	6–4
31	Boston	Dallas	T	2–2

April 1994

1	Buffalo	Sabres	L	5–0
3	Cleveland	Pittsburgh	L	6–2
7	Boston	Ottawa	W	5–4
9	Boston	Tampa Bay	L	3–0
10	Philadelphia	Flyers	W	4–3
13	Ottawa	Senators	W	8–0
14	Boston	Hartford	L	3–2

1993-94 SCORING

	W	L	T	S	GAA	PIM
John Blue	5	8	3	0	2.99	7
Jon Casey	30	15	9	4	2.88	14
					2 assists	
Vincent Riendeau	7	6	1	0	3.07	0
					1 assist	

	G	A	P	PIM
Adam Oates	32	80	112	45
Ray Bourque	20	71	91	58
Cam Neely	50	24	74	54
Joe Juneau	14	58	72	35
Glen Wesley	14	44	58	64
Ted Donato	22	32	54	59
Bryan Smolinski	31	20	51	82
Glenn Murray	18	13	31	48
Brent Hughes	13	11	24	143
Josef Stumpel	8	15	23	14
Dave Reid	6	17	23	25
Steve Heinze	10	11	21	32
Don Sweeney	6	15	21	50
Dmitri Kvartalnov	12	7	19	10
Steve Leach	5	10	15	74
Al Iafrate	5	8	13	20
Daniel Marois	7	3	10	18
Paul Stanton	3	7	10	54
David Shaw	1	9	10	85
Cam Stewart	3	6	9	66
Glen Featherstone	1	8	9	152
Gordie Roberts	1	6	7	40
Fred Knipscheer	3	2	5	14
Marius Czerkawski	2	1	3	0
Sergei Zholtok	2	1	3	2
Darren Banks	0	1	1	9
John Gruden	0	1	1	2
Andy McKim	0	1	1	4
Jamie Huscroft	0	1	1	144
Mikhail Tatarinov	0	0	0	2
Jon Morris	0	0	0	0
Jim Wiemer	0	0	0	2
Grigori Panteleev	0	0	0	0

Number of power play advantages	387
Power play goals	84
% successful	21.7%
Cam Neely	20
Adam Oates	16
Ray Bourque	10
Ted Donato	9
Glen Wesley	6
Bryan Smolinski	4
Joe Juneau	4
Dmitri Kvartalnov	4
Daniel Marois	3
Al Iafrate	2
Brent Hughes	1
Don Sweeney	1
Steve Leach	1
Paul Stanton	1
Mariusz Czerkawski	1
Sergei Zholtok	1
Short-handed goals against	9
Penalty minutes: 1,442 – 17.2 per game	
Times short-handed	378
Power play goals against	58
Penalty kill success	84.7%
Short-handed goals	17
Ray Bourque	3
Bryan Smolinski	3
Adam Oates	2
Ted Donato	2
Dave Reid	2
Steve Heinze	2
Don Sweeney	2
Glen Wesley	1

1993-94 PLAYOFF RESULTS

April 1994

	AT	VERSUS	W-L-T	SCR
16	Boston	Montreal	W	3–2
18	Boston	Montreal	L	3–2
21	Montreal	Canadiens	W	6–3
23	Montreal	Canadiens	L	5–2
25	Boston	Montreal	L	2–1 (OT)
27	Montreal	Canadiens	W	3–2
29	Boston	Montreal	W	5–3

May 1994

1	New Jersey	Devils	W	2–1
3	New Jersey	Devils	W	6–5 (OT)
5	Boston	New Jersey	L	4–2
7	Boston	New Jersey	L	5–4 (OT)
9	New Jersey	Devils	L	2–0
11	Boston	New Jersey	L	5–3

1993-94 PLAYOFFS

vs. Montreal Canadiens	4 wins – 3 losses	vs. New Jersey Devils	2 wins – 4 losses
at Montreal	2 wins – 1 loss	at New Jersey	2 wins – 1 loss
at Boston	2 wins – 2 losses	at Boston	0 wins – 3 losses

1993-94 PLAYOFF SCORING

	W	L	SO	GAA	PIM
Jon Casey	5	6	0	2.92	0
Vincent Riendeau	1	1	0	4.00	0

	G	A	P	PIM
Adam Oates	3	9	12	8
Ray Bourque	2	8	10	0
Bryan Smolinski	5	4	9	4
Glenn Murray	4	5	9	14
Josef Stumpel	1	7	8	4
Ted Donato	4	2	6	10
Glen Wesley	3	3	6	12
Marius Czerkawski	3	3	6	4
Steve Heinze	2	3	5	7
Al Iafrate	3	1	4	6
Don Sweeney	2	1	3	4
Fred Knipscheer	2	1	3	6
Brent Hughes	2	1	3	27
Dave Reid	2	1	3	2
David Shaw	1	2	3	16
Cam Stewart	0	3	3	7
Steve Leach	0	1	1	2
Daniel Marois	0	1	1	16

	G	A	P	PIM
Gordie Roberts	0	1	1	8
Glen Featherstone	0	0	0	0
Jamie Huscroft	0	0	0	9

Number of power play advantages	54
Power play goals	10
% successful	18.5%
Adam Oates	2
Bryan Smolinski	2
Ted Donato	2
Ray Bourque	1
Glen Wesley	1
Mariusz Czerkawski	1
Al Iafrate	1
Short-handed goals against	0
Penalty minutes: 168 – 12.9 per game	
Times short-handed	51
Power play goals against	11
Penalty kill success	78.4%
Short-handed goals	0

1994–1995
(71st year)

OWNER & GOVERNOR:	Jeremy Jacobs	ALL-STARS:	Ray Bourque (2nd team)
GM:	Harry Sinden	TROPHY WINNERS:	Dufresne — Cam Neely
COACH:	Brian Sutter		7th Player — Blaine Lacher
ATTENDANCE:	343,218		Three Star — Cam Neely
	14,300 per game	RADIO BROADCASTER:	WBNW – Bob Wilson,
PLAYOFFS:	*Conference quarter-finals:*		Johnny Bucyk
	Lose to New Jersey Devils	TV BROADCASTER:	WSBK TV38 & NESN – Fred
	1 win – 4 losses		Cusick, Derek Sanderson,
STANLEY CUP WINNER:	New Jersey Devils		Dave Shea

UNIFORMS

- Home jersey is white with gold and black trim. Socks are white with one gold band surrounded by two black bands at the calf. Road jersey is black with gold and white trim. Gold socks with one white band surrounded by two black bands at the calf. Logo is the spoked "B." Pants are black. Bearhead appears on both shoulders on both home and road uniforms.

POTPOURRI

- Bruins qualify for the playoffs for the 28th consecutive season.
- Cam Neely leads the league with 16 power play goals.
- Bruins score only 3 short-handed goals although they lead the league in penalty killing.
- Ray Bourque, by being named to the second All-Star team, is the only player in NHL history to be named to the first or second team each year in the league.
- Adam Oates scores his 200th career goal.
- Bruins surrender 4 short-handed goals.
- Al Iafrate misses the entire season due to injury.
- NHL lockout lasts from October 1, 1994, to January 19, 1995. 468 games are cancelled. All teams play a 48-game schedule. No inter-conference games are played. This is the first time since 1941–42 that the Bruins played only 48 games.
- Bruins are not involved in any penalty shot situations this season.

TRANSACTIONS

- Select Evgeny Ryabchikov #1 in the NHL entry draft.
- Glen Featherstone traded to New York Rangers for Daniel Lacroix.
- Obtain Craig Billington from the Ottawa Senators for future considerations.

1994-95 STANDINGS

EASTERN CONFERENCE

Northeast Division

	W	L	T	P	GF	GA
Quebec	30	13	5	65	185	134
Pittsburgh	29	16	3	61	181	158
Boston	27	18	3	57	150	127
Buffalo	22	19	7	51	130	119
Hartford	19	24	5	43	127	141
Montreal	18	23	7	43	125	148
Ottawa	9	34	5	23	117	174

Atlantic Division

	W	L	T	P	GF	GA
Philadelphia	28	16	4	60	150	132
New Jersey	22	18	8	52	136	121
Washington	22	18	8	52	136	120
New York Rangers	22	23	3	47	139	134
Florida	20	22	6	46	115	127
Tampa Bay	17	28	3	37	120	144
New York Islanders	15	28	5	35	126	158

WESTERN CONFERENCE

Central Division

	W	L	T	P	GF	GA
Detroit	33	11	4	70	180	117
St. Louis	28	15	5	61	178	135
Chicago	24	19	5	53	156	115
Toronto	21	19	8	50	135	146
Dallas	17	23	8	42	136	135
Winnipeg	16	25	7	39	157	177

Pacific Division

Calgary	24	17	7	55	163	135
Vancouver	18	18	12	48	153	148
San Jose	19	25	4	42	129	161
Los Angeles	16	23	9	41	142	174
Edmonton	17	27	4	38	136	183
Anaheim	16	27	5	37	125	164

1994-95 RESULTS

January 1995

	AT	VERSUS	W-L-T	SCR
22	Boston	Philadelphia	W	4–1
23	New York	Rangers	W	2–1
26	Boston	New Jersey	W	1–0 (OT)
28	Philadelphia	Flyers	L	2–1
30	Boston	Florida	L	2–1

February 1995

2	Boston	Ottawa	W	6–4
4	Boston	Hartford	W	5–4
7	Boston	Montreal	W	7–4
9	Boston	Quebec	L	4–3
11	Boston	Washington	T	1–1
12	Buffalo	Sabres	W	2–1
14	Pittsburgh	Penguins	L	5–3
17	Florida	Panthers	W	5–4
18	Tampa Bay	Lightning	L	3–1
22	Hartford	Whalers	L	3–2 (OT)
23	New Jersey	Devils	W	3–2
25	Quebec	Nordiques	T	1–1
27	Ottawa	Senators	W	2–0

March 1995

2	Boston	New Jersey	W	7–2
4	Boston	Pittsburgh	L	4–3 (OT)
5	Hartford	Whalers	W	5–2
7	Boston	Washington	L	3–1
9	Philadelphia	Flyers	L	3–2

11	Boston	Florida	L	2–0
16	Boston	Montreal	W	6–0
18	Boston	New York Islanders	W	4–3
19	New Jersey	Devils	L	4–3 (OT)
22	Quebec	Nordiques	L	6–2
24	Tampa Bay	Lightning	W	4–3 (OT)
28	Boston	Philadelphia	W	5–1
30	New York	Islanders	W	3–2

April 1995

1	Boston	New York Rangers	L	3–2
2	Washington	Capitals	L	2–1
6	Boston	Buffalo	T	1–1
8	Boston	Tampa Bay	W	5–1
9	Buffalo	Sabres	W	6–5
12	Boston	Quebec	L	4–0
14	New York	Rangers	L	5–3
15	Montreal	Canadiens	W	3–2
19	Boston	Buffalo	W	4–1
20	Ottawa	Senators	W	6–5
23	Boston	New York Rangers	W	5–4
24	New York	Islanders	L	5–3
26	Boston	Hartford	W	1–0
28	Pittsburgh	Penguins	L	4–1
30	Boston	Pittsburgh	W	5–2

May 1995

1	Boston	Ottawa	W	5–4
3	Montreal	Canadiens	W	4–2

1994-95 SCORING

	W	L	T	S	GAA	PIM
Vincent Riendeau	3	6	1	0	2.87	2
Blaine Lacher	19	11	2	4	2.41	4
						1 assist
Craig Billington	5	1	0	0	3.06	2

	G	A	P	PIM
Adam Oates	12	41	53	8
Ray Bourque	12	31	43	20
Cam Neely	27	14	41	72
Bryan Smolinski	18	13	31	31
Marius Czerkawski	12	14	26	31
Mats Naslund	8	14	22	4
Don Sweeney	3	19	22	24
Ted Donato	10	10	20	10
Josef Stumpel	5	13	18	8
Steve Heinze	7	9	16	23
Alexei Kasatonov	2	14	16	33
Brent Hughes	6	6	12	139
Steve Leach	5	6	11	68
Jon Rohloff	3	8	11	39
Dave Reid	5	5	10	10

Sandy Moger	2	6	8	6
Glenn Murray	5	2	7	46
David Shaw	3	4	7	36
Jamie Huscroft	0	6	6	103
John Gruden	0	6	6	22
Fred Knipscheer	3	1	4	2
Miko Makela	1	2	3	0

Daniel Lacroix	1	0	1	38
Brett Harkins	0	1	1	0
Marc Potvin	0	1	1	4
Jeff Serowik	0	0	0	0
Grigori Panteleev	0	0	0	0
Cam Stewart	0	0	0	2

Number of power play advantages	211
Power play goals	46
% successful	21.8%
Cam Neely	16
Ray Bourque	9
Bryan Smolinski	6
Adam Oates	4
Mats Naslund	2
Sandy Moger	2
David Shaw	1
Mikko Makela	1
Mariusz Czerkawski	1
Don Sweeney	1
Ted Donato	1
Josef Stumpel	1
Steve Leach	1

Short-handed goals against	4
Penalty minutes: 793 – 16.5 per game	
Times short-handed	183
Power play goals against	24
Penalty kill success	86.9%
Short-handed goals	3
Adam Oates	1
Steve Heinze	1
Alexei Kasatonov	1

1994-95 PLAYOFF RESULTS

May 1995

	AT	VERSUS	W-L-T	SCR
7	Boston	New Jersey	L	5–0
8	Boston	New Jersey	L	3–0
10	New Jersey	Devils	W	3–2
12	New Jersey	Devils	L	1–0 (OT)
14	Boston	New Jersey	L	3–2

1994-95 PLAYOFFS

vs. New Jersey Devils	1 win – 4 losses
at New Jersey	1 win – 1 loss
at Boston	0 wins – 3 losses

1994-95 PLAYOFF SCORING

	W	L	SO	GAA	PIM
Craig Billington	0	0	0	2.40	0
Blaine Lacher	1	4	0	2.54	0

	G	A	P	PIM
Ray Bourque	0	3	3	0
Cam Neely	2	0	2	2
Mats Naslund	1	0	1	0
Adam Oates	1	0	1	2
Marius Czerkawski	1	0	1	0
Bryan Smolinski	0	1	1	4
David Shaw	0	1	1	4
Glenn Murray	0	0	0	2
Guy Larose	0	0	0	0
Fred Knipscheer	0	0	0	0
Brent Hughes	0	0	0	4
Jamie Huscroft	0	0	0	11
Alexei Kasatonov	0	0	0	2
Dave Reid	0	0	0	0
Don Sweeney	0	0	0	4
Ted Donato	0	0	0	4
Steve Heinze	0	0	0	0
Jon Rohloff	0	0	0	6
Josef Stumpel	0	0	0	0

Number of power play advantages	20	Penalty minutes:	45 – 9.0 per game
Power play goals	2	Times short-handed	17
% successful	10%	Power play goals against	5
Cam Neely	1	Penalty kill success	70.6%
Adam Oates	1	Short-handed goals	0
Short-handed goals against	1		

1995–1996
(72nd year)

OWNER & GOVERNOR:	Jeremy Jacobs	TROPHY WINNERS:	Dufresne — Ray Bourque
GM:	Harry Sinden		7th Player — Kyle McLaren
COACH:	Steve Kasper		Three Star — Adam Oates
ATTENDANCE:	716,443	RADIO BROADCASTER:	WBZ – Bob Neumeier,
	17,474 per game		Barry Pederson
PLAYOFFS:	*Conference quarter-finals:*	TV BROADCASTER:	UPN38 – Fred Cusick,
	Lose to Florida Panthers		Derek Sanderson
	1 win – 4 losses		NESN – Dale Arnold,
STANLEY CUP WINNER:	Colorado Avalanche		Gord Kluzak
ALL-STARS:	Ray Bourque (1st team)		

UNIFORMS

- Introduce newly designed uniforms. "Home" uniform is white, trimmed in black and gold. Black arm stripes travel from shoulder to elbow, interrupted by two gold stripes sandwiched around a white stripe. A newly designed bearhead appears on both shoulders. The spiked "B" logo is slightly redesigned to emphasize the spokes. Socks are white with a black stripe surrounded by two gold stripes. Pants at home and away are black. Road uniform has a black body with gold and white stripes. Gold arm stripes travel from shoulder to elbow interrupted by two white stripes sandwiched around a gold stripe. Socks are gold with a black stripe surrounded by two white stripes. Alternate jersey is based in gold, trimmed in black and white with black jagged stripes resembling claw marks. The bear on the shoulder of the home and road uniform will form the logo on the alternate jersey with the block letters "Bruins" on both shoulders.

POTPOURRI

- The final game ever at Boston Garden is played in two 25-minute periods against the Montreal Canadiens. Don Sweeney scores the final Garden goal. The new FleetCenter is opened with the first game against the New York Islanders on October 7. Sandy Moger scores the first-ever goal at the FleetCenter. In the same game, Cam Neely scores 3 goals. This is the second opening game in a row that Neely scores 3 goals.
- Adam Oates enjoys a 4-goal game in December against Florida.
- Defenseman Al Iafrate misses the entire season with an injury. An arbitrator rules that the Bruins must pay his salary.
- Bruins allow 3 final-minute goals in 1-goal loss at Dallas for a score of 6–5.
- Benching of Cam Neely and Kevin Stevens in game at Toronto causes major uproar among Bruins fans.
- Ray Bourque is named Most Valuable Player in NHL All-Star game played at FleetCenter. New FoxTrax puck is introduced and will be used in other league games this season.
- Dave Reid scores 6 short-handed goals.
- Ray Bourque is the second leading scorer among defensemen with 82 points and the second leading shot taker in the league with 390 shots.

- In the only penalty shot for the Bruins, Rick Tocchet is foiled by Geoff Sarjeant of the San Jose Sharks. In the 2 penalty shots against the Bruins, Blaine Lacher stops Steve Yzerman of the Red Wings and Bill Ranford stops Randy Burridge of the Sabres.
- Bruins drop from #1 in the league in penalty killing to #20.
- Six of Sandy Moger's 15 goals turn out to be game winners.

TRANSACTIONS
- Select Kyle McLaren #1 in the entry draft.
- Trade Bryan Smolinski and Glen Murray to Pittsburgh for Kevin Stevens.
- Trade Fred Knipscheer to the Blues for Rick Zombo.
- Lose Brent Hughes to the Sabres in the waiver draft.
- Obtain Dean Chynoweth from the Islanders.
- Trade Mariusz Czerkawski and Sean Brown to Edmonton for Bill Ranford.
- Trade Kevin Stevens to Los Angeles for Rick Tocchet.
- Trade Steve Leach to St. Louis for Kevin Sawyer and Steve Staois.
- Sign Ron Sutter as a free agent.

1995-96 STANDINGS

EASTERN CONFERENCE

Northeast Division

	W	L	T	P	GF	GA
Pittsburgh	49	29	4	102	362	284
Boston	40	31	11	91	282	269
Montreal	40	32	10	90	265	248
Hartford	34	39	9	77	237	259
Buffalo	33	42	7	73	247	262
Ottawa	18	59	5	41	191	291

Atlantic Division

	W	L	T	P	GF	GA
Philadelphia	45	24	13	103	282	208
New York Rangers	41	27	14	96	272	237
Florida	41	31	10	92	254	234
Washington	39	32	11	89	234	204
Tampa Bay	38	32	12	88	238	248
New Jersey	37	33	12	86	215	202
New York Islanders	22	50	10	54	229	315

WESTERN CONFERENCE

Central Division

	W	L	T	P	GF	GA
Detroit	62	13	7	131	325	181
Chicago	40	28	14	94	273	220
Toronto	34	36	12	80	247	252
St. Louis	32	34	16	80	219	248
Winnipeg	36	40	6	78	275	291
Dallas	26	42	14	66	227	280

Pacific Division

	W	L	T	P	GF	GA
Colorado	47	25	10	104	326	240
Calgary	34	37	11	79	241	240
Vancouver	32	35	15	79	278	278
Anaheim	35	39	8	78	234	247
Edmonton	30	44	8	68	240	304
Los Angeles	24	40	18	66	256	302
San Jose	20	55	7	47	252	357

1995-96 **RESULTS**

October 1995

	AT	VERSUS	W-L-T	SCR	
7	Boston	New York Islanders	T	4–4	
9	Boston	Buffalo	W	5–3	
11	Colorado	Avalanche	L	3–1	
12	San Jose	Sharks	T	6–6	
14	Dallas	Stars	L	6–5	
17	St. Louis	Blues	W	7–4	
21	Detroit	Red Wings	L	4–2	
26	Boston	Washington	L	4–2	
28	Boston	Hartford	W	3–0	
31	Boston	Montreal	L	3–1	

November 1995

2	Boston	Detroit	L	6–5	(OT)
4	Montreal	Canadiens	L	4–1	
7	Washington	Capitals	W	4–3	
9	Boston	Ottawa	W	4–3	
11	Boston	Toronto	L	3–1	
14	Tampa Bay	Lightning	L	5–3	
16	Boston	New Jersey	T	2–2	
18	Boston	St. Louis	W	5–2	
21	Boston	Winnipeg	W	5–4	
24	Boston	Los Angeles	W	2–1	
25	Ottawa	Senators	T	3–3	
30	Boston	Pittsburgh	L	9–6	

December 1995

2	Boston	Buffalo	W	6–4	
3	Philadelphia	Flyers	L	6–1	
5	Boston	Dallas	W	6–4	
8	Tampa Bay	Lightning	L	3–1	
9	Florida	Panthers	L	3–1	
13	New York	Rangers	L	4–2	
14	Boston	Florida	W	6–4	
16	Boston	Calgary	W	6–3	
22	Buffalo	Sabres	W	3–2	(OT)
23	Boston	Tampa Bay	W	7–5	
26	New York	Islanders	T	3–3	
31	Winnipeg	Jets	W	5–3	

January 1996

2	Boston	Chicago	L	5–2	
3	Toronto	Maple Leafs	T	4–4	
6	Boston	Hartford	W	5–2	
9	Boston	Colorado	L	3–0	
11	Boston	Anaheim	W	7–2	
13	Boston	New Jersey	W	3–2	
15	Boston	Vancouver	L	6–0	
16	New Jersey	Devils	W	4–2	
22	Pittsburgh	Penguins	L	7–6	(OT)
25	Boston	Tampa Bay	W	4–3	
27	Boston	New York Rangers	L	5–3	
28	Montreal	Canadiens	L	5–4	
31	Ottawa	Senators	W	3–1	

February 1996

1	Boston	Florida	T	2–2	
3	Boston	Buffalo	W	4–2	
6	Pittsburgh	Penguins	L	6–5	
7	Buffalo	Sabres	L	2–1	(OT)
10	Boston	Philadelphia	L	6–2	
14	Hartford	Whalers	W	3–0	
15	Chicago	Blackhawks	L	3–0	
17	Vancouver	Canucks	W	4–1	
19	Los Angeles	Kings	T	3–3	
21	Anaheim	Mighty Ducks	L	4–3	(OT)
23	Edmonton	Oilers	W	7–4	
24	Calgary	Flames	W	2–1	
27	Boston	Edmonton	L	4–3	(OT)
28	New York	Rangers	W	3–1	

March 1996

2	Boston	Washington	L	2–0	
5	New York	Islanders	L	5–3	
7	Boston	New York Islanders	W	4–3	
9	Boston	Philadelphia	W	3–2	
10	Florida	Panthers	W	4–1	
14	Boston	Pittsburgh	W	4–2	
15	Washington	Capitals	W	5–2	
18	Boston	San Jose	T	3–3	
20	New Jersey	Devils	W	2–1	
21	Boston	Ottawa	W	3–1	
23	Boston	New York Rangers	L	5–4	
27	Hartford	Whalers	W	6–5	(OT)
28	Boston	Montreal	L	4–3	(OT)
31	Buffalo	Sabres	W	6–5	

April 1996

1	Ottawa	Senators	T	1–1	
3	Montreal	Canadiens	W	4–1	
4	Boston	Montreal	T	3–3	
7	Philadelphia	Flyers	W	4–2	
11	Boston	Hartford	W	3–2	
13	Hartford	Whalers	L	2–0	
14	Boston	Pittsburgh	W	6–5	

Cam Neely in new third jersey.

1995-96 SCORING

	W	L	T	S	GAA	PIM
Blaine Lacher	3	5	2	0	3.93	4
Craig Billington	10	13	3	1	3.43	2
Bill Ranford	21	12	4	1	2.83	0
Rob Tallas	1	0	0	0	3.00	0
Scott Bailey	5	1	2	0	3.26	0

	G	A	P	PIM
Adam Oates	25	67	92	18
Ray Bourque	20	62	82	58
Josef Stumpel	18	36	54	14
Sean McEachern	24	29	53	34
Ted Donato	23	26	49	46
Cam Neely	26	20	46	31
Todd Elik	13	33	46	40
Dave Reid	23	21	44	4
Sandy Moger	15	14	29	65
Steve Heinze	16	12	28	43
Don Sweeney	4	24	28	42
Rick Tocchet	16	8	24	64
Kevin Stevens	10	13	23	49
Steve Leach	9	13	22	86
Kyle McLaren	5	12	17	73
Tim Sweeney	8	8	16	14
Joe Mullen	8	7	15	0
Rick Zombo	4	10	14	53
Jon Rohloff	1	12	13	59
Ron Sutter	5	7	12	24
Marius Czerkawski	5	6	11	10
Dean Chynoweth	2	5	7	88
Clayton Beddoes	1	6	7	44
Phil Von Stefenelli	0	4	4	16
Alexei Kasatonov	1	0	1	12
Ryan Hughes	0	0	0	0
Andre Roy	0	0	0	0
Cam Stewart	0	0	0	0
Mark Cornforth	0	0	0	4
Davis Payne	0	0	0	7
Kevin Sawyer	0	0	0	5
Steve Staios	0	0	0	4
John Gruden	0	0	0	4
Marc Potvin	0	0	0	12

Number of power play advantages	363
Power play goals	68
% successful	18.7%
Ray Bourque	9
Adam Oates	7
Ted Donato	7
Cam Neely	7
Todd Elik	6
Rick Tocchet	6
Josef Stumpel	5
Sandy Moger	4
Joe Mullen	4
Kevin Stevens	3
Shawn McEachern	3
Don Sweeney	2
Dave Reid	1

Jon Rohloff	1
Mariusz Czerkawski	1
Tim Sweeney	1
Steve Leach	1
Short-handed goals against	7
Penalty minutes: 1,039 – 12.7 per game	
Times short-handed	341
Power play goals against	67
Penalty kill success	80.4%
Short-handed goals	13
Dave Reid	6
Ray Bourque	2
Shawn McEachern	2
Steve Heinze	1
Ron Sutter	1
Adam Oates	1

1995-96 PLAYOFF RESULTS

April 1996

	AT	VERSUS	W-L-T	SCR
17	Florida	Panthers	L	6–3
22	Florida	Panthers	L	6–2
24	Boston	Florida	L	4–2
25	Boston	Florida	W	6–2
27	Florida	Panthers	L	4–3

1995-96 PLAYOFFS

vs. Florida Panthers	1 win – 4 losses
at Florida	0 wins – 3 losses
at Boston	1 win – 1 loss

1995-96 PLAYOFF SCORING

	W	L	SO	GAA	PIM
Bill Ranford	1	3	0	4.02	0
Craig Billington	0	1	0	6.00	2

	G	A	P	PIM
Adam Oates	1	6	7	2
Ray Bourque	1	6	7	2
Rick Tocchet	4	0	4	21
Sandy Moger	2	2	4	12
Sean McEachern	2	1	3	8
Ted Donato	1	2	3	2
Jon Rohloff	1	2	3	2
Josef Stumpel	1	2	3	0
Steve Heinze	1	1	2	4
Todd Elik	0	2	2	16
Dave Reid	0	2	2	2
Don Sweeney	0	2	2	6
Cam Stewart	1	0	1	2
John Gruden	0	1	1	0
Marc Potvin	0	1	1	18
Tim Sweeney	0	0	0	2
Steve Staios	0	0	0	0
Dean Chynoweth	0	0	0	24
Ron Sutter	0	0	0	8
Kyle McLaren	0	0	0	14

Number of power play advantages	27	Short-handed goals against	0
Power play goals	7	Penalty minutes:	147 – 29.4 per game
% successful	25.9%	Times short-handed	30
Rick Tocchet	3	Power play goals against	5
Ray Bourque	1	Penalty kill success	83.35
Sandy Moger	1	Short-handed goals	2
Ted Donato	1	Adam Oates	1
Jon Rohloff	1	Steve Heinze	1

1996–1997
(73rd year)

OWNER & GOVERNOR:	Jeremy Jacobs	RADIO BROADCASTERS:	WBZ – Bob Neumeier, Andy Brickley
GM:	Harry Sinden		
COACH:	Steve Kasper	TV BROADCASTERS:	UPN38 – Fred Cusick, Derek Sanderson
PLAYOFFS:	Out of playoffs		NESN – Dale Arnold, Gord Kluzak
STANLEY CUP WINNER:	Detroit Red Wings		
TROPHY WINNERS:	Dufresne — Jozef Stumpel		
	7th Player — Ted Donato		
	Three Star — Ray Bourque		

UNIFORMS

- Home uniform is white, trimmed in black and gold. Black arm stripes travel from shoulder to elbow, interrupted by two gold stripes sandwiched around a white stripe. A newly designed bearhead appears on both shoulders. The spiked "B" logo is slightly redesigned to emphasize the spokes. Socks are white with a black stripe surrounded by two gold stripes. Pants at home and away are black. Road uniform has a black body with gold and white stripes. Gold arm stripes travel from shoulder to elbow interrupted by two white stripes sandwiched around a gold stripe. Socks are gold with a black stripe surrounded by two white stripes. Alternate jersey is based in gold, trimmed in black and white with black jagged stripes resembling claw marks. The bear on the shoulder of the home and road uniform will form the logo on the alternate jersey with the block letters "Bruins" on both shoulders.

POTPOURRI

- Bruins forward Sheldon Kennedy admits that he had been sexually abused by his junior hockey coach at Swift Current, Graham James. James is sentenced to three-and-a-half years in prison.
- On March 17, 1968, the Bruins clinched a playoff spot for the first time in 8 seasons. On April 2, 1997, the Bruins are eliminated from the playoffs, thus ending a string of 29 consecutive seasons in the Stanley Cup playoffs.
- Ray Bourque becomes the Bruins all-time leading point scorer. Bourque also recorded his 1,000th assist on March 27, thus becoming the fifth player in NHL history to record 1,000 assists and the first to do it with 1 team.
- Adam Oates enjoys a 20-game point-scoring streak.
- Bruins suffer a 10-game winless streak from February 4 to February 24, losing 8 and tieing 2.
- Bruins lose the season series with Ottawa for the first time since Ottawa rejoined the NHL.
- The Bruins finish below .500 at home for the first time since 1966–67.
- They also finish below .500 for the season for the first time since 1966–67.
- Bruins win in Pittsburgh for the first time since 1990.
- Bruins play their first game at new rinks in Philadelphia, Buffalo, and Tampa Bay. The Bruins also play their first game in Phoenix, Arizona, against the Coyotes, the transplanted Winnipeg Jets.
- For only the second time in Bruins history, and for the first time since 1961–62, the Bruins allow 300 goals in a season.
- Bruins fire coach Steve Kasper. Kasper coached for 2 seasons.
- Longtime Bruins play-by-play announcer Fred Cusick retires. Cusick had been announcing Bruins games for 45 years.

TRANSACTIONS

- Select Jonathan Aitken #1 in the entry draft.
- Sign free agent Sheldon Kennedy.
- Trade Sean McEachern to Ottawa for Trent McCleary.
- Trade Al Iafrate to San Jose for Jeff Odgers.
- Trade their 1998 first-round pick to Colorado for Landon Wilson and Anders Myrvold.
- Trade Adam Oates, Rick Tocchet, and Bill Ranford to Washington for Jim Carey, Jason Allison, and Anson Carter, plus a 1997 third-round draft pick and a conditional 1998 second-round draft pick.
- Steve Staios picked up on waivers by Vancouver.

1996-97 STANDINGS

EASTERN CONFERENCE

Northeast Division	W	L	T	P	GF	GA
Buffalo	40	30	12	92	237	208
Pittsburgh	38	36	8	84	285	280
Ottawa	31	36	15	77	226	234

Montreal	31	36	15	77	249	276
Hartford	32	39	11	75	226	256
Boston	26	47	9	61	234	300

Atlantic Division

New Jersey	45	23	14	104	231	182
Philadelphia	45	24	13	103	274	217
Florida	35	28	19	89	221	201
New York Rangers	38	34	10	86	258	231
Washington	33	40	9	75	214	231
Tampa Bay	32	40	10	74	217	247
New York Islanders	29	41	12	70	240	250

WESTERN CONFERENCE

Central Division

Dallas	48	26	8	104	252	198
Detroit	38	26	18	94	253	197
Phoenix	38	37	7	83	240	243
St. Louis	36	35	11	83	236	239
Chicago	34	35	13	81	223	210
Toronto	30	44	8	68	230	273

Pacific Division

Colorado	49	24	9	107	277	205
Anaheim	36	33	13	85	245	233
Edmonton	36	37	9	81	252	247
Vancouver	35	40	7	77	257	273
Calgary	32	41	9	73	214	239
Los Angeles	28	43	11	67	214	268
San Jose	27	47	8	62	211	278

1996-97 RESULTS

October 1996

	AT	VERSUS	W-L-T	SCR
5	Boston	New York Rangers	T	4–4
7	Boston	Phoenix	L	5–2
12	San Jose	Sharks	W	5–3
14	Vancouver	Canucks	W	5–4 (OT)
17	Los Angeles	Kings	L	4–2
20	Anaheim	Mighty Ducks	W	5–1
24	Boston	Toronto	L	2–1
26	Boston	Detroit	L	2–1
29	Boston	New Jersey	W	5–2
31	Boston	Hartford	T	4–4

November 1996

2	Boston	New York Rangers	L	5–2
4	Boston	Los Angeles	T	4–4
6	Hartford	Whalers	L	5–1
7	Boston	Edmonton	L	6–0
9	Ottawa	Senators	W	4–3
14	Boston	Pittsburgh	W	2–1 (OT)
16	Buffalo	Sabres		
	postponed to 3/17/97			
18	Boston	San Jose	W	4–2
19	Washington	Capitals	T	2–2
21	Boston	Montreal	L	6–2
23	Boston	Buffalo	L	3–2 (OT)
26	Boston	Philadelphia	W	2–0
29	Boston	Vancouver	W	7–3
30	Pittsburgh	Penguins	L	6–2

December 1996

4	Montreal	Canadiens	W	4–3
5	Boston	Hartford	L	4–2
7	Boston	Calgary	T	1–1
9	Boston	Anaheim	L	5–2
12	Boston	New Jersey	L	7–4
14	Boston	Buffalo	L	4–0
15	Philadelphia	Flyers	L	6–0
17	Pittsburgh	Penguins	W	6–4
19	Boston	Tampa Bay	W	3–0
21	Boston	Washington	W	4–3
23	Boston	Chicago	T	3–3
27	Dallas	Stars	L	6–4
29	St. Louis	Blues	L	4–2

January 1997

1	Ottawa	Senators	L	3–2
2	Hartford	Whalers	W	5–4
4	Boston	Dallas	W	3–2
7	Philadelphia	Flyers	L	7–3
9	Boston	Montreal	W	5–4
11	Montreal	Canadiens	L	6–3
13	Boston	Ottawa	L	4–3
14	New Jersey	Devils	L	4–2
20	Boston	Washington	L	3–2
22	Ottawa	Senators	W	4–1
23	Boston	Florida	L	4–1
25	Boston	Colorado	W	4–1
30	Florida	Panthers	L	3–1

February 1997

1	Tampa Bay	Lightning	W	3–0
2	New York	Rangers	W	3–2
4	Boston	Ottawa	L	4–3
6	Boston	Hartford	L	5–3
8	Boston	St. Louis	T	3–3
11	Calgary	Flames	L	5–1
12	Edmonton	Oilers	L	4–3
15	Phoenix	Coyotes	L	5–4 (OT)
18	Colorado	Avalanche	L	4–3 (OT)
20	Chicago	Blackhawks	L	5–3
23	Buffalo	Sabres	L	5–1

24	Washington	Capitals	T	3–3
27	Boston	Tampa Bay	W	6–2

March 1997

1	Boston	Philadelphia	T	5–5
3	Toronto	Maple Leafs	L	4–2
6	New York	Islanders	L	5–2
8	Tampa Bay	Lightning	W	6–4
9	Florida	Panthers	W	3–1
12	Hartford	Whalers	L	6–3
13	Boston	Montreal	L	3–0
15	Boston	New York Islanders	W	5–2
17	Buffalo	Sabres*	L	5–1
19	Detroit	Red Wings	L	4–1
22	Boston	Ottawa	L	5–4
24	Montreal	Canadiens	L	3–1
27	Boston	New York Islanders	L	6–3
29	New York	Islanders	L	8–2

Makeup of 11/16/96

April 1997

3	New York	Rangers	L	5–4
5	Boston	Florida	W	4–2
8	Pittsburgh	Penguins	L	3–1
10	Boston	Buffalo	L	5–1
11	New Jersey	Devils	L	2–0
13	Boston	Pittsburgh	W	7–3

1996-97 SCORING

	W	L	T	S	GAA	PIM
Bill Ranford	12	16	8	2	3.49	0
Tim Cheveldae	0	1	1	0	3.23	0
Scott Bailey	1	5	0	0	3.65	0
Rob Tallas	8	12	1	1	3.33	0
Jim Carey	5	13	0	0	3.82	2
Paxton Schafer	0	0	0	0	4.68	0

	G	A	P	PIM
Josef Stumpel	21	55	76	14
Adam Oates	18	52	70	10
Ted Donato	25	26	51	37
Ray Bourque	19	31	50	18
Rick Tocchet	16	14	30	67
Rob Dimaio	13	15	28	82
Don Sweeney	3	23	26	39
Steve Heinze	17	8	25	27
Jean-Yves Roy	10	15	25	22
Tim Sweeney	10	11	21	14
Landon Wilson	8	12	20	72
Sheldon Kennedy	8	10	18	30
Barry Richter	5	13	18	32
Brett Harkins	4	14	18	8
Todd Elik	4	12	16	16

	G	A	P	PIM
Jeff Odgers	7	8	15	197
Troy Mallette	6	8	14	155
Kyle McLaren	5	9	14	54
Sandy Moger	10	3	13	45
Anson Carter	8	5	13	2
Jason Allison	3	9	12	9
Steve Staios	3	8	11	71
Mattias Timander	1	8	9	14
Jon Rohloff	3	5	8	31
Trent McCleary	3	5	8	33
Bob Beers	3	4	7	8
Clayton Beddoes	1	2	3	13
Dean Chynoweth	0	3	3	171
Anders Myrvold	0	2	2	4
Andre Roy	0	2	2	12
Yevgeny Shaldybin	1	0	1	0
Davis Payne	0	1	1	7
Cam Stewart	0	1	1	4
Dean Malkoc	0	0	0	68
Randy Robitaille	0	0	0	0
Kevin Sawyer	0	0	0	0
P.C. Drouin	0	0	0	0
Tim Cheveldae	0	0	0	0
Paxton Schafer	0	0	0	0

Scott Bailey	0	0	0	0	Jim Carey	0	0	0	2
Rob Tallas	0	0	0	0	Bill Ranford	0	0	0	0

Number of power play advantages	310	Short-handed goals against	6
Power play goals	46	Penalty minutes	1373
% successful	14.8%	Times short-handed	308
Ray Bourque	8	Power play goals against	56
Ted Donato	6	Penalty kill success	81.8%
Jozef Stumpel	6	Short-handed goals	15
Steve Heinze	4	Sheldon Kennedy	4
Brett Harkins	3	Rob DiMaio	3
Sandy Moger	3	Ted Donato	2
Rick Tocchet	3	Steve Heinze	2
Adam Oates	2	Adam Oates	2
Jean-Yves Roy	2	Ray Bourque	1
Tim Sweeney	2	Anson Carter	1
Jason Allison	1		
Bob Beers	1		
Anson Carter	1		
Todd Elik	1		
Jeff Odgers	1		
Barry Richter	1		
Jon Rohloff	1		

BOSTON BRUINS LEADERS
REGULAR SEASON

SEASONS

Johnny Bucyk	21
Dit Clapper	20
Ray Bourque	18
Wayne Cashman	16
Milt Schmidt	16
Woody Dumart	15
Eddie Shore	14
Gary Doak	13
Don Marcotte	13
Dallas Smith	12
Fernie Flaman	12
Rick Middleton	12

GAMES

Johnny Bucyk	1436
Ray Bourque	1290
Wayne Cashman	1027
Rick Middleton	881
Don Marcotte	868
Dallas Smith	861
Dit Clapper	830
Milt Schmidt	776
Woody Dumart	771
Mike Milbury	754
Eddie Westfall	727
Leo Boivin	717

GOALS

Johnny Bucyk	545
Phil Esposito	459
Rick Middleton	402
Ray Bourque	362
Cam Neely	344
Ken Hodge	289
Wayne Cashman	277
Bobby Orr	264
Peter McNab	263
Don Marcotte	230
Milt Schmidt	229
Dit Clapper	228
Keith Crowder	219
Woody Dumart	211
Terry O'Reilly	204

ASSISTS

Ray Bourque	1001
Johnny Bucyk	794
Bobby Orr	624
Phil Esposito	553
Wayne Cashman	516
Rick Middleton	496
Terry O'Reilly	402
Ken Hodge	385
Adam Oates	357
Bill Cowley	346
Milt Schmidt	346
Peter McNab	324
Brad Park	317
Jean Ratelle	295
Fred Stanfield	274

PENALTY MINUTES

Terry O'Reilly	2095
Mike Milbury	1552
Keith Crowder	1261
Wayne Cashman	1041
Eddie Shore	1038
Ted Green	1029
Fernie Flaman	1002
Lyndon Byers	959
Dallas Smith	934
Bobby Orr	924

SHUTOUTS

Tiny Thompson	74
Frank Brimsek	35
Ed Johnston	27
Gerry Cheevers	26
Jim Henry	24
Hal Winkler	19
Gilles Gilbert	16
Don Simmons	15
Andy Moog	13
Terry Sawchuk	11

BOSTON BRUINS ALL-TIME POINTS
REGULAR SEASON

	GP	G	A	P
Ray Bourque	1290	362	1001	1363
Johnny Bucyk	1436	545	794	1339
Phil Esposito	625	459	553	1012
Rick Middleton	881	402	496	898
Bobby Orr	631	264	624	888
Wayne Cashman	1027	277	516	793
Ken Hodge Sr.	652	289	385	674
Terry O'Reilly	891	204	402	606
Cam Neely	525	344	246	590
Peter McNab	595	263	324	587
Milt Schmidt	778	229	346	575
Bill Cowley	508	190	346	536
Adam Oates	368	142	357	499
Don Marcotte	868	230	254	484
Keith Crowder	607	219	258	477
Dit Clapper	833	228	246	474
Don McKenney	592	195	267	462
Jean Ratelle	419	155	295	450
Woody Dumart	771	211	218	429
Barry Pederson	379	166	251	417
Brad Park	501	100	317	417
Fred Stanfield	448	135	274	409
John McKenzie	453	169	227	396
Greg Sheppard	416	155	220	375
Ken Linseman	389	125	247	372
Jerry Toppazzini	659	148	216	364
Steve Kasper	564	135	220	355
Doug Mohns	710	118	229	347
Ed Westfall	734	126	213	339
Murray Oliver	426	116	214	330
John Peirson	545	153	173	326
Fleming Mackell	513	127	185	312
Glen Wesley	537	77	230	307
Leo LaBine	571	123	180	303
Dallas Smith	861	54	248	302
Bob Schmautz	354	134	161	295
Derek Sanderson	391	135	159	294
Vic Stasiuk	378	125	166	291
Craig Janney	262	85	198	283
Eddie Shore	543	103	176	279
Mike O'Connell	424	70	198	268
Bobby Bauer	328	123	137	260
Herb Cain	314	140	119	259
Ted Green	620	48	206	254
Mike Milbury	754	49	189	238
Ralph Weiland	266	131	105	236
Tom Fergus	289	98	138	236
Tom Williams	390	96	136	232
Ed Sandford	439	94	136	230
Randy Burridge	359	108	115	223
Marty Barry	279	130	88	218
Art Jackson	305	87	131	218
Bronco Horvath	227	103	112	215
Ted Donato	372	96	116	212
Leo Boivin	717	47	164	211
Bill Hollett	357	84	115	199
Stan Jonathan	391	91	107	198
Real Chevrefils	349	101	93	194
Bob Sweeney	382	81	112	193
Charlie Simmer	198	98	94	192
Joe Juneau	161	51	141	192
Don Sweeney	611	40	142	182
Dave Reid	387	89	92	181
Carol Vadnais	263	47	134	181
John Crawford	539	38	140	178
Fernie Flaman	682	30	147	177
Jozef Stumpel	274	54	122	176
Ken Smith	331	80	91	171
Harry Oliver	355	109	59	168
Rick Smith	512	36	125	161
Geoff Courtnall	259	78	81	159
Steve Leach	293	76	83	159
Bill Quackenbush	461	22	133	155
Paul Ronty	224	56	98	154
Don Gallinger	222	65	88	153
Roy Conacher	166	94	51	145
Cal Gardner	280	57	83	140
Dave Creighton	295	72	65	137
Red Beattie	288	58	79	137
Bob Miller	263	55	82	137
Bob Carpenter	187	63	71	134
Dwight Foster	252	51	82	133
Vladimir Ruzicka	166	66	66	132
Pat Egan	294	47	85	132

Steve Heinze	306	71	57	128	Lyndon Byers	261	24	42	66
Jean-Guy Gendron	260	66	62	128	Al Secord	166	39	26	65
Gord Kluzak	209	25	98	123	Eddie Shack	120	34	30	64
Armand Guidolin	195	49	70	119	Bobby Joyce	115	26	38	64
Nels Stewart	152	63	55	118	Wayne Connelly	169	25	38	63
Charlie Burns	262	48	70	118	Orland Kurtenbach	142	18	45	63
Mike Walton	168	60	57	117	Todd Elik	90	17	45	62
Mike Krushelynski	162	51	65	116	Allan Stanley	129	12	50	62
Dick Redmond	235	36	79	115	Ron Stewart	126	34	26	60
Andre Savard	228	52	62	114	Percy Galbraith	345	29	31	60
Andy Brickley	177	37	76	113	Jack McGill	97	23	36	59
John Wensink	248	57	55	112	Jimmy Peters	97	28	30	58
Craig MacTavish	217	44	66	110	Cliff Pennington	97	16	42	58
Don Awrey	543	21	87	108	Jim Wiemer	201	11	47	58
Dean Prentice	170	50	56	106	Duncan Fisher	129	24	33	57
Nevin Markwart	299	39	67	106	Warren Godfrey	258	9	28	57
Garry Galley	257	24	82	106	Hal Laycoe	258	17	39	56
Dave Forbes	284	53	52	105	Rick Tocchet	67	32	22	54
Dave Poulin	165	34	68	102	Greg Johnston	183	26	28	54
Charlie Sands	215	64	38	101	Terry Reardon	147	24	30	54
Gary Doak	609	20	80	100	Jack McIntyre	123	19	35	54
Michael Thelven	207	20	80	100	Brad McCrimmon	228	17	37	54
Bob Armstrong	542	13	86	99	Joe Carveth	73	29	24	53
Frank Boll	82	44	52	96	Art Chapman	159	24	29	53
Norman Gainor	155	48	43	91	Shawn McEachern	82	24	29	53
Dmitri Kvartalnov	112	42	49	91	Lionel Hitchman	377	26	26	52
Ron Murphy	133	29	61	90	Mel Hill	130	26	25	51
Lorne Ferguson	201	47	41	88	Reggie Fleming	101	22	29	51
Bruce Crowder	217	43	44	87	Bobby Lalonde	133	14	37	51
Bryan Smolinski	136	50	36	86	Sandy Moger	132	27	23	50
Murray Henderson	405	24	62	86	Ed Harrison	190	26	24	50
Larry Regan	164	30	53	83	Gordon Pettinger	104	20	30	50
Dave Christian	128	44	38	82	Glen Murray	148	29	20	49
Eddie Wiseman	110	30	52	82	Peter Douris	148	24	25	49
Harvey Jackson	113	35	43	78	Grant Warwick	76	28	20	48
Greg Hawgood	134	27	51	78	Bobby Leiter	135	20	28	48
George Owen	192	44	33	77	Norm Calladine	63	19	29	48
Ray Getliffe	128	37	40	77	Ron Schock	128	17	31	48
Garnet Bailey	232	31	46	77	Phil Maloney	83	17	31	48
Reed Larson	141	25	52	77	Andre Pronovost	138	26	21	47
Ken Hodge Jr.	112	36	40	76	Brent Hughes	191	25	22	47
Jimmy Herberts	101	58	17	75	Albert Siebert	107	18	28	46
Forbes Kennedy	221	30	45	75	Bill Ezinicki	81	21	24	45
John Carter	185	33	41	74	Tim Sweeney	91	19	26	45
Wayne Carleton	111	28	43	71	Darryl Edestrand	215	8	37	45
Al Sims	311	22	48	70	Joe Lamb	90	21	23	44
Hubert Martin	111	36	33	69	Brent Ashton	87	19	24	43
Pete Babando	118	42	25	67	Thomas Gradin	64	12	31	43
Joe Klukay	150	33	33	66	Dave Silk	64	20	22	42
Tom J. McCarthy	75	32	34	66	Normand Leveille	75	17	25	42

Larry Leach	126	13	29	42	Reggie Leach	79	9	17	26
Mike Gillis	125	17	24	41	Gord Murphy	91	8	18	26
David Shaw	176	14	27	41	Chris Nilan	80	11	14	25
Bob Woytowich	153	6	34	40	Jean-Yves Roy	52	10	15	25
Mariusz Czerkawski	84	19	21	40	Bob Gould	77	8	17	25
Carson Cooper	58	33	6	39	Doug Gibson	52	7	18	25
Frank Frederickson	84	27	12	39	Jimmy Bartlett	63	15	9	24
Bob Dillabough	113	13	25	38	Armand Gaudreault	44	15	9	24
Dave Pasin	71	18	19	37	Gary Dornhoefer	62	12	12	24
Louis Sleigher	83	16	21	37	Bill Cupolo	47	11	13	24
Ed Kryzanowski	234	15	22	37	Vic Lynn	68	16	8	24
Wayne Rivers	80	11	26	37	Gord Roberts	124	6	18	24
Kraig Nienhuis	88	20	16	36	Sprague Cleghorn	109	15	8	23
George Sullivan	102	15	21	36	Andy Hebenton	70	12	11	23
Larry Hillman	127	6	30	36	Kevin Stevens	41	10	13	23
Luc Dufour	114	20	15	35	Clare Martin	78	8	14	22
Glen Sather	146	12	23	35	Pentti Lund	77	8	14	22
Gilles Marotte	118	10	25	35	Mats Naslund	34	8	14	22
Allen Pedersen	333	4	31	35	Irvin Spencer	69	5	17	22
Bill Shill	79	21	13	34	Frank Martin	82	3	19	22
Butch Goring	39	13	21	34	Chris Oddleifson	55	10	11	21
Tom Johnson	121	4	30	34	Wes Walz	73	9	12	21
Bill Jennings	39	20	13	33	Dave Donnelly	62	9	12	21
Hank Nowak	111	18	15	33	Sam Bettio	44	9	12	21
Roy Goldsworthy	92	17	16	33	Billy O'Dwyer	102	8	13	21
Pete Horeck	100	15	18	33	Bill Derlago	39	5	16	21
Matti Hagman	90	15	18	33	Phil Krake	87	11	9	20
Jay Miller	216	13	20	33	Landon Wilson	40	8	12	20
Murph Chamberblain	45	9	24	33	Glen Featherstone	99	7	13	20
Randy Hillier	164	3	30	33	Paul Gladu	40	6	14	20
Irwin Boyd	55	16	16	32	Petri Skriko	37	6	14	20
Des Smith	114	15	17	32	Billy Taylor	39	4	16	20
Jon Rohloff	149	7	25	32	Mickey MacKay	70	12	7	19
James O'Neil	141	6	26	32	Wally Wilson	53	11	8	19
Robert Hamill	58	16	14	30	Rob Cimetta	54	10	9	19
Norman Poile	39	16	14	30	Alex Smith	63	9	10	19
Max Kaminsky	75	13	17	30	Brett Harkins	47	4	15	19
Rob DiMaio	72	13	15	28	Billy Stuart	100	14	4	18
Earl Anderson	64	12	16	28	Marcel Bonin	67	9	9	18
Jack Shewchuck	187	9	19	28	Alvin McDonald	60	9	9	18
Frank Mario	53	9	19	28	Dick Meissner	135	8	10	18
Murray Costello	95	10	17	27	Sheldon Kennedy	56	8	10	18
Mats Thelin	163	8	19	27	Reginald Smith	43	8	10	18
Stephane Quintal	157	8	19	27	Morris Lukowich	36	6	12	18
Jim Morrison	84	8	19	27	Barry Richter	50	5	13	18
Jim Lorentz	79	8	19	27	Guy Lapointe	25	2	16	18
Jeff Lazaro	76	8	19	27	Bill Carson	63	11	6	17
Jack Portland	187	7	20	27	Wayne Maxner	62	8	9	17
John Blum	169	5	22	27	Adam Brown	33	8	9	17
Fred O'Donnell	115	15	11	26	Billy Knibbs	53	7	10	17

Ray Bourque and John Bucyk

Wilbert Hiller	43	7	10	17	Leland Harrington	48	8	2	10
Brad Palmer	73	6	11	17	Darin Kimble	55	7	3	10
Kyle McLaren	132	10	21	31	Doug Morrison	23	7	3	10
Alexei Kasatonov	63	3	14	17	Daniel Marois	22	7	3	10
Frank Jerwa	75	7	9	16	Parker MacDonald	29	6	4	10
Wayne Hicks	65	7	9	16	Tom Songin	43	5	5	10
Russ Kopak	24	7	9	16	Fred Harris	40	5	5	10
Joe Watson	73	2	14	16	Tommy Lehmann	35	5	5	10
Bob McCord	108	1	15	16	Max Quackenbush	47	4	6	10
Terry Gray	42	8	7	15	Vic Ripley	37	4	6	10
Joe Mullen	37	8	7	15	Brian Curran	115	3	7	10
Jeff Odgers	80	7	8	15	Paul Stanton	71	3	7	10
Gino Rozzini	31	5	10	15	Alan Rittinger	19	3	7	10
Dennis O'Brien	83	4	11	15	Cam Stewart	83	3	7	10
Jim Nill	76	4	11	15	Dean Chynoweth	94	2	8	10
Aut Erickson	126	3	12	15	Pat Stapleton	90	2	8	10
Grigori Panteleev	50	8	6	14	Clayton Beddoes	60	2	8	10
Gus Bodnar	82	7	7	14	Ed Johnston	443	0	10	10
Troy Mallette	68	6	8	14	Andy Moog	261	0	10	10
Earl Reibel	63	6	8	14	Fred Knipscheer	27	6	3	9
Paul Boutilier	52	5	9	14	Al Pallazzari	23	6	3	9
Rick Zombo	67	4	10	14	Gerry Ouellette	39	5	4	9
Al Langlois	65	4	10	14	Mark Marquess	27	5	4	9
Willie O'Ree	45	4	10	14	Bill Touhey	26	5	4	9
Bob Beers	77	3	11	14	Fred Cook	40	4	5	9
Anson Carter	19	8	5	13	Tom McCarthy	24	4	5	9
Bob Beckett	66	7	6	13	C.J. Young	15	4	5	9
John Schmidt	45	6	7	13	Guy Labrie	15	2	7	9
Zelio Toppazzini	45	6	7	13	Joe Zanussi	68	1	8	9
Frank Simonetti	115	5	8	13	Mattias Timander	41	1	8	9
Doug Roberts	55	5	8	13	Gerry Cheevers	416	0	9	9
Al Iafrate	12	5	8	13	Ross Lowe	43	5	3	8
Gordie Bruce	28	4	9	13	Carl Boone	34	5	3	8
Gus Kyle	69	1	12	13	Scott Arniel	29	5	3	8
Orville Heximer	48	7	5	12	Jack Shill	45	4	4	8
Bill Goldsworthy	33	6	6	12	Richie Leduc	33	4	4	8
Orval Tessier	57	5	7	12	Walter Pratt	31	4	4	8
Ron Sutter	18	5	7	12	Alex Cook	28	4	4	8
Doug Halward	65	3	9	12	Trent McCleary	59	3	5	8
Jason Allison	19	3	9	12	Joe Jerwa	35	3	5	8
Brian Propp	14	3	9	12	Jack Church	43	2	6	8
Marty Howe	78	1	11	12	Roger Jenkins	42	2	6	8
Larry Melnyk	75	0	12	12	Bob Gracie	24	2	6	8
Stan Jackson	52	8	3	11	Jim Harrison	39	4	3	7
Paul Runge	49	8	3	11	Paul Haynes	37	4	3	7
Jack Bionda	80	3	8	11	Jarmo Kekalainen	27	4	3	7
Steve Staios	66	3	8	11	Graeme Townshend	22	2	5	7
Alain Cote	68	2	9	11	Ray Gariepy	35	1	6	7
Nick Beverley	42	1	10	11	Jamie Huscroft	70	0	7	7
Harry Connor	55	9	1	10	John Gruden	59	0	7	7

Herb Mitchell	53	6	0	6	Eddie Burke	16	3	0	3
George Geran	33	5	1	6	Bert McInenly	43	2	1	3
Bill Thoms	17	4	2	6	Normie Shay	31	2	1	3
Walt McKechnie	53	3	3	6	Lou Crawford	26	2	1	3
Lorne Duguid	30	2	4	6	Rod Graham	14	2	1	3
Hal Darragh	25	2	4	6	Gerry Shannon	42	1	2	3
Ted Graham	48	4	1	5	Harry Foster	34	1	2	3
Ab DeMarco Sr.	6	4	1	5	Matt Ravlich	32	1	2	3
Jack Caffery	54	3	2	5	Lorne Davis	25	1	2	3
Fred Gordon	41	3	2	5	Cy Denneny	23	1	2	3
George Redding	35	3	2	5	Ray Barry	18	1	2	3
John Quilty	6	3	2	5	Mikko Makela	11	1	2	3
Ray Maluta	25	2	3	5	Lloyd Gronsdahl	10	1	2	3
Willi Plett	65	2	3	5	Bill Ranford	82	0	3	3
Gary Aldcorn	21	2	3	5	Ed Panagabko	29	0	3	3
John Byce	21	2	3	5	Barry Ashbee	14	0	3	3
Norm Johnson	15	2	3	5	Jack Pratt	37	2	0	2
Andrew McKim	36	1	4	5	Bill Hutton	25	2	0	2
Bruce Shoebottom	35	1	4	5	Jim Klein	20	2	0	2
Chris Winnes	29	1	4	5	Billy Boucher	14	2	0	2
Alex Motter	28	1	4	5	Bernie Morris	6	2	0	2
Stephane Richer	21	1	4	5	Billy Couture	41	1	1	2
Mike Millar	15	1	4	5	Lionel Heinrich	35	1	1	2
Bill Bennett	7	1	4	5	Johnny Gagnon	24	1	1	2
Gilles Gilbert	277	0	5	5	Dave Barr	12	1	1	2
Doug Keans	154	0	5	5	Leighton Emms	11	1	1	2
Gord Hynes	15	0	5	5	Charlie Scherza	10	1	1	2
Don Blackburn	6	0	5	5	Reggie Lemelin	183	0	2	2
Dave Hynes	22	4	0	4	Rogie Vachon	91	0	2	2
Ron Hoover	17	4	0	4	Marco Baron	64	0	2	2
Oscar Aubuchon	14	4	0	4	Jon Casey	57	0	2	2
Myles Lane	36	3	1	4	John Blue	41	0	2	2
Billy Burch	23	3	1	4	Jim Schoenfeld	39	0	2	2
Doug Kostynski	15	3	1	4	Don Grosso	33	0	2	2
Ross Lonsberry	33	2	2	4	Pat McCreavy	21	0	2	2
Sergei Zholtok	25	2	2	4	Ed Reigle	17	0	2	2
Tom Brennan	22	2	2	4	Murray Balfour	15	0	2	2
Jean-Paul Parise	21	2	2	4	Ivan Boldirev	13	0	2	2
Darren Banks	20	2	2	4	Andre Roy	13	0	2	2
Don Smillie	12	2	2	4	Jean Gauthier	11	0	2	2
Ralph Barahona	6	2	2	4	Anders Myrvold	9	0	2	2
Bill Speer	28	1	3	4	Jacques Plante	8	0	2	2
Eddie Barry	19	1	3	4	Paul Guay	5	0	2	2
Ray Neufeld	15	1	3	4	Daniel Lacroix	23	1	0	1
Pete Peeters	171	0	4	4	Harry Meeking	23	1	0	1
Mike Forbes	32	0	4	4	Barry Smith	19	1	0	1
Wade Campbell	28	0	4	4	Nick Mickoski	18	1	0	1
Phil Von Stefenelli	27	0	4	4	Art Giroux	10	1	0	1
Alan Shields	18	0	4	4	Barry Wilkins	8	1	0	1
Tom Webster	11	0	4	4	Brian Dobbin	7	1	0	1

Clarence Schmidt	7	I	O	I	Jim Henry	236	O	O	O
Lloyd Gross	6	I	O	I	Don Simmons	168	O	O	O
Lloyd Cook	4	I	O	I	Jack Gelineau	141	O	O	O
Jean Pusie	4	I	O	I	Terry Sawchuk	102	O	O	O
Bobby Rowe	4	I	O	I	Bruce Gamble	80	O	O	O
Yevgeny Shaldybin	3	I	O	I	Harry Lumley	78	O	O	O
Grant Erickson	2	I	O	I	Charles Stewart	77	O	O	O
Gerry Ehman	I	I	O	I	Hal Winkler	67	O	O	O
Ken Hammond	I	I	O	I	Bernie Parent	57	O	O	O
Ross Brooks	54	O	I	I	Pat Riggin	49	O	O	O
Bob Davie	41	O	I	I	John Henderson	45	O	O	O
Bert Gardiner	41	O	I	I	Paul Bibeault	42	O	O	O
Ron Grahame	40	O	I	I	Don Head	38	O	O	O
Blaine Lacher	35	O	I	I	Craig Billington	35	O	O	O
Marc Potvin	33	O	I	I	Dean Malkoc	33	O	O	O
Charles Cahill	32	O	I	I	Rob Tallas	29	O	O	O
Don Ward	31	O	I	I	Redvers Green	25	O	O	O
Vincent Riendeau	20	O	I	I	Werner Schnarr	25	O	O	O
Floyd Smith	26	O	I	I	Harvey Bennett	24	O	O	O
Davis Payne	24	O	I	I	Barry Gibbs	24	O	O	O
Jim Craig	23	O	I	I	Jack Norris	23	O	O	O
Ken Broderick	20	O	I	I	Steve Kraftcheck	22	O	O	O
Al Nicholson	19	O	I	I	Bob Perreault	22	O	O	O
Shayne Stevenson	19	O	I	I	Jim Pettie	21	O	O	O
George Redahl	18	O	I	I	Ken Broderick	20	O	O	O
Matt Hervey	16	O	I	I	Eddie Rodden	20	O	O	O
Archie Wilcox	16	O	I	I	Scott Bailey	19	O	O	O
Arnie Kullman	13	O	I	I	Jim Carey	19	O	O	O
Norm McAtee	13	O	I	I	Mike Moffat	19	O	O	O
Cliff Thompson	13	O	I	I	Eric Pettinger	17	O	O	O
Dave Thomlinson	12	O	I	I	Paul Stevens	17	O	O	O
Fern Headley	11	O	I	I	John Adams	14	O	O	O
Clark Donatelli	10	O	I	I	Moe Lemay	14	O	O	O
George Patterson	10	O	I	I	Peaches Lyons	14	O	O	O
Al Simmons	10	O	I	I	Dave Reece	14	O	O	O
Bobby Benson	8	O	I	I	Cleon Daskalakis	12	O	O	O
Gordie Clark	8	O	I	I	George Carroll	11	O	O	O
Bill Lesuk	8	O	I	I	Matt DelGiudice	11	O	O	O
Ray Podloski	8	O	I	I	Clayton Pachal	11	O	O	O
Steve Langdon	7	O	I	I	Paul Beraldo	10	O	O	O
Mike Stevens	7	O	I	I	Norm Defelice	10	O	O	O
John Arbour	6	O	I	I	Jeannot Gilbert	9	O	O	O
Art Gagne	6	O	I	I	Alfie Skinner	9	O	O	O
Bill Burega	4	O	I	I	Jack Wilkinson	9	O	O	O
Paul Popiel	3	O	I	I	Scott Bailey	8	O	O	O
Kent Ruhnke	2	O	I	I	Yves Belanger	8	O	O	O
Gordon Byers	I	O	I	I	Daniel Berthiaume	8	O	O	O
Paul Hurley	I	O	I	I	Phil Bessler	8	O	O	O
Cecil Thompson	468	O	O	O	Billy Carter	8	O	O	O
Frank Brimsek	444	O	O	O	Ron Jones	8	O	O	O

Brian Lawton	8	o	o	o	Ryan Hughes	3	o	o	o
Jack Riley	8	o	o	o	Martin Lauder	3	o	o	o
Gordon Savage	8	o	o	o	Joe Matte	3	o	o	o
Bob Stewart	8	o	o	o	Alan May	3	o	o	o
Bobby Taylor	8	o	o	o	Petr Prajsler	3	o	o	o
Stan Baluik	7	o	o	o	Earl Roche	3	o	o	o
Mickey Blake	7	o	o	o	Dale Rolfe	3	o	o	o
John Brackenborough	7	o	o	o	Paxton Schafer	3	o	o	o
Norm Fowler	7	o	o	o	Don Sylvestri	3	o	o	o
Taylor Hall	7	o	o	o	Fred Bergdinon	2	o	o	o
Carl Mokosak	7	o	o	o	Jack Capuano	2	o	o	o
Craig Sarner	7	o	o	o	Denis Chervyakov	2	o	o	o
Burr Williams	7	o	o	o	Tim Cheveldae	2	o	o	o
Dick Cherry	6	o	o	o	Wilf Cude	2	o	o	o
Mark Cornforth	6	o	o	o	Pierre Gagne	2	o	o	o
Maurice Courteau	6	o	o	o	Bill Huard	2	o	o	o
Walter Harnott	6	o	o	o	Dominic Lavoie	2	o	o	o
Floyd Hillman	6	o	o	o	Pete Leswick	2	o	o	o
Ed Jeremiah	6	o	o	o	Howard Lockhart	2	o	o	o
Charles Larose	6	o	o	o	Scott McLellan	2	o	o	o
Al Millar	6	o	o	o	Mike McMahon	2	o	o	o
Danny Schock	6	o	o	o	Ellard O'Brien	2	o	o	o
Sean Shanahan	6	o	o	o	Garry Peters	2	o	o	o
Emory Sparrow	6	o	o	o	Harry Pidhirny	2	o	o	o
Ken Yackel	6	o	o	o	George Ranieri	2	o	o	o
Andrew Clark	5	o	o	o	Maurice Roberts	2	o	o	o
Andre Gill	5	o	o	o	Joseph Schmidt	2	o	o	o
Ed Chadwick	4	o	o	o	Ron Sutherland	2	o	o	o
Norm Corcoran	4	o	o	o	Mikhail Tatarinov	2	o	o	o
Ron Flockhart	4	o	o	o	Gordon Turlik	2	o	o	o
Ted Hodgson	4	o	o	o	Gordie Wilson	2	o	o	o
Percy Jackson	4	o	o	o	George Abbott	1	o	o	o
Sylvio Mantha	4	o	o	o	Rick Adduono	1	o	o	o
Jon Morris	4	o	o	o	Steve Atkinson	1	o	o	o
Kevin Sawyer	4	o	o	o	Mike Bales	1	o	o	o
John Shephard	4	o	o	o	Dick Bittner	1	o	o	o
Al Stewart	4	o	o	o	Bart Bradley	1	o	o	o
Jim Vesey	4	o	o	o	Les Colvin	1	o	o	o
Ron Buchanan	3	o	o	o	Nick Damore	1	o	o	o
Art Chisholm	3	o	o	o	Murray Davison	1	o	o	o
Terry Crisp	3	o	o	o	Armand Delmonte	1	o	o	o
Ab DeMarco Jr.	3	o	o	o	Dale Dunbar	1	o	o	o
P.C. Drouin	3	o	o	o	Claude Evans	1	o	o	o
Tom Filmore	3	o	o	o	Marcel Filion	1	o	o	o
Eddie Finnigan	3	o	o	o	Jim Franks	1	o	o	o
Norm Foster	3	o	o	o	Benny Grant	1	o	o	o
Harry Frost	3	o	o	o	Bob Gryp	1	o	o	o
Matt Glennon	3	o	o	o	Jack Ingram	1	o	o	o
Gordon Henry	3	o	o	o	Ted Irvine	1	o	o	o
Phil Hergesheimer	3	o	o	o	Joe Junkin	1	o	o	o

Walt Kalbfleish	I	0	0	0	Bobby Ring	I	0	0	0
Don Keenan	I	0	0	0	Randy Robitaille	I	0	0	0
Ray Manson	I	0	0	0	Roberto Romano	I	0	0	0
Sammy McManus	I	0	0	0	Jeff Serowik	I	0	0	0
Graeme Nicolson	I	0	0	0	Frank Spring	I	0	0	0
Paul O'Neil	I	0	0	0	Jim Stewart	I	0	0	0
Dan Poliziani	I	0	0	0	Allen Teal	I	0	0	0
Claude Pronovost	I	0	0	0	Ross Wilson	I	0	0	0
Jack Rathwell	I	0	0	0					

Ray Bourque

BOSTON BRUINS LEADERS
PLAYOFFS

GAMES

Ray Bourque	162
Wayne Cashman	145
Don Marcotte	132
Rick Middleton	111
Johnny Bucyk	109
Terry O'Reilly	108
Glen Wesley	105
Brad Park	91
Gerry Cheevers	88
Woody Dumart	88
Dit Clapper	86
Ken Hodge Sr.	86
Mike Milbury	86
Cam Neely	86
Milt Schmidt	86
Jean Ratelle	23

GOALS

Cam Neely	55
Phil Esposito	46
Rick Middleton	45
Johnny Bucyk	40
Peter McNab	38
Ray Bourque	34
Ken Hodge	34
Don Marcotte	34
Wayne Cashman	31
Greg Sheppard	28
Bobby Orr	26
Bobby Schmautz	26
Terry O'Reilly	25
Milt Schmidt	24
Brad Park	23

ASSISTS

Ray Bourque	112
Bobby Orr	66
Johnny Bucyk	60
Wayne Cashman	57
Phil Esposito	56
Craig Janney	56
Rick Middleton	55
Brad Park	55
Ken Hodge Sr.	47
Terry O'Reilly	42
Peter McNab	37
Adam Oates	37
Bill Cowley	34
Jean Ratelle	33
Cam Neely	32

PENALTY MINUTES

Terry O'Reilly	335
Wayne Cashman	250
Mike Milbury	219
Keith Crowder	209
Derek Sanderson	187
Eddie Shore	185
Cam Neely	160
Jay Miller	141
Stan Jonathan	137
Ray Bourque	135
Don Awrey	132
Gord Kluzak	129
Dallas Smith	128
John McKenzie	119
Ken Hodge Sr.	118

SHUTOUTS

Gerry Cheevers	7	Jack Gelineau	1
Tiny Thompson	6	Eddie Johnston	1
Don Simmons	3	Gilles Gilbert	1
Frank Brimsek	2	Reggie Lemelin	1
Andy Moog	2	Jim Henry	1
Hal Winkler	2	Pete Peeters	1

BOSTON BRUINS ALL-TIME POINTS
PLAYOFFS

	GP	G	A	P
Ray Bourque	162	34	112	146
Phil Esposito	71	46	56	102
Rick Middleton	111	45	55	100
Johnny Bucyk	109	40	60	100
Bobby Orr	74	26	66	92
Wayne Cashman	145	31	57	88
Cam Neely	86	55	32	87
Ken Hodge Sr.	86	34	47	81
Brad Park	91	23	55	78
Peter McNab	79	38	36	74
Craig Janney	69	17	56	73
Terry O'Reilly	108	25	42	67
Greg Sheppard	65	28	33	61
Don Marcotte	132	34	27	61
Jean Ratelle	58	23	33	56
Bob Schmautz	70	26	30	56
Barry Pederson	34	22	30	52
Fleming Mackell	53	17	33	50
Milt Schmidt	86	24	25	49
Adam Oates	42	11	37	48
Glen Wesley	105	15	32	47
Fred Stanfield	55	17	29	46
Bill Cowley	64	13	33	46
John McKenzie	50	15	30	45
Randy Burridge	78	12	30	42
Ken Linseman	35	16	22	38
Keith Crowder	78	13	22	35
Don McKenney	34	13	20	33
Dallas Smith	85	3	28	31
Steve Kasper	63	14	16	30
Aubrey Clapper	86	13	17	30
Ed Westfall	50	13	17	30
Dave Poulin	53	12	18	30
Derek Sanderson	50	17	12	29
Bob Sweeney	87	13	16	29
Mike Milbury	86	4	24	28
Woody Dumart	88	12	15	27
John Peirson	48	9	17	26
Herb Cain	45	14	11	25
Bill Hollett	48	5	20	25
Rick Smith	75	3	22	25
Ed Sandford	42	13	11	24
Roy Conacher	37	11	11	22
Mike O'Connell	38	7	15	22
Jerry Toppazzini	40	13	9	22
Bobby Joyce	32	13	8	21
Ken Smith	30	8	13	21
Doug Mohns	35	6	15	21
Carol Vadnais	39	2	19	21
Bobby Bauer	48	11	8	19
Gord Kluzak	46	6	13	19
Ralph Weiland	36	10	8	18
Leo LaBine	49	8	10	18
Joe Juneau	19	6	12	18
Vladimir Ruzicka	30	4	14	18
Dave Christian	40	12	5	17
Ted Donato	42	8	9	17
Art Jackson	33	8	9	17
Eddie Shore	52	6	11	17
John Crawford	66	4	13	17
Mike Walton	25	9	7	16
Dwight Foster	29	5	11	16
Glen Murray	30	8	7	15
Mike Krushelynski	20	8	6	14
Don Sweeney	81	6	8	14
Vic Stasiuk	29	6	8	14
Terry Reardon	27	6	8	14
Bob Carpenter	38	5	9	14
Michael Thelven	34	4	10	14
Harry Oliver	30	9	4	13
Bronco Horvath	19	7	6	13
Dave Creighton	30	6	7	13
Dave Reid	45	5	8	13
Al Iafrate	12	5	8	13
Garry Galley	46	4	9	13
Brian Propp	20	4	9	13
Larry Regan	20	3	10	13
Bill Quackenbush	33	0	13	13
Stan Jonathan	63	8	4	12
Bruce Crowder	31	8	4	12
Eddie Wiseman	22	8	4	12
John Carter	31	7	5	12
Marty Barry	20	6	6	12
Andre Savard	31	5	7	12
Armand Guidolin	22	5	7	12
Steve Heinze	34	4	8	12

Ted Green	31	4	8	12	Dave Forbes	45	1	4	5
Leo Boivin	34	3	9	12	Des Smith	22	1	4	5
Don Awrey	54	0	11	11	David Shaw	2	1	4	5
Jack McGill	27	7	4	11	Norm Johnson	12	4	0	4
Mel Hill	24	7	4	11	Rick Tocchet	5	4	0	4
Bryan Smolinski	22	6	5	11	Lionel Hitchman	31	3	1	4
Percy Galbraith	31	4	7	11	Lyndon Byers	37	2	2	4
Jozef Stumpel	23	2	9	11	Charlie Simmer	9	2	2	4
Don Gallinger	23	5	5	10	Paul Gladu	7	2	2	4
Bob Miller	34	4	6	10	Bill Jennings	7	2	2	4
Ken Hodge Jr.	15	4	6	10	Bobby Lalonde	7	2	2	4
Tom Fergus	29	7	2	9	Sandy Moger	5	2	2	4
Pat Egan	32	6	3	9	Reed Larson	15	1	3	4
Real Chevrefils	30	5	4	9	Harvey Jackson	14	1	3	4
Craig MacTavish	28	5	4	9	Cam Stewart	13	1	3	4
Jack McIntyre	19	5	4	9	Allan Stanley	12	1	3	4
Tom J. McCarthy	17	4	5	9	Jimmy Peters	9	1	3	4
Fernie Flaman	48	3	6	9	Gilles Gilbert	31	0	0	4
Jim Wiemer	40	2	7	9	Thomas Gradin	4	0	4	4
Petri Skriko	18	4	4	8	Bill Carson	11	3	0	3
Ron Murphy	14	4	4	8	Ab DeMarco Sr.	9	3	0	3
Peter Douris	26	3	5	8	Jimmy Herberts	8	3	0	3
John Wensink	40	2	6	8	Carl Boone	22	2	1	3
Darryl Edestrand	24	2	6	8	Greg Johnston	22	2	1	3
Bob Armstrong	42	1	7	8	Norman Gainor	18	2	1	3
Dick Redmond	26	1	7	8	Fred Knipscheer	16	2	1	3
Paul Ronty	16	1	7	8	Nels Stewart	9	2	1	3
Steve Leach	24	5	2	7	Joe Carveth	5	2	1	3
Mariusz Czerkawski	18	4	3	7	Joe Klukay	15	1	2	3
Greg Hawgood	28	2	5	7	Brad McCrimmon	15	1	2	3
Mike Gillis	27	2	5	7	Bruce Shoebottom	14	1	2	3
George Owen	21	2	5	7	Gord Hynes	12	1	2	3
Frank Frederickson	10	2	5	7	Jon Rohloff	10	1	2	3
Moe Lemay	15	4	2	6	Bill Cupolo	7	1	2	3
Jeff Lazaro	28	3	3	6	Bill Shill	7	1	2	3
Pat McCreavy	20	3	3	6	Gino Rozzini	6	1	2	3
Ray Getliffe	19	3	3	6	Shawn McEachern	5	1	2	3
Gary Doak	66	2	4	6	Larry Melnyk	22	0	3	3
Hal Laycoe	31	2	4	6	Larry Hillman	18	0	3	3
Wayne Carleton	18	2	4	6	Al Secord	14	0	3	3
Willi Plett	17	2	4	6	Eddie Shack	13	0	3	3
Garnet Bailey	15	2	4	6	Red Beattie	16	2	0	2
Jim Morrison	6	0	6	6	Lorne Ferguson	10	2	0	2
Brent Hughes	29	4	1	5	John Byce	8	2	0	2
Cal Gardner	19	3	2	5	Doug Roberts	5	2	0	2
Murray Henderson	41	2	3	5	Bob Beers	21	1	1	2
Charlie Sands	24	2	3	5	Gordon Pettinger	15	1	1	2
Ray Neufeld	10	2	3	5	Pete Babando	9	1	1	2
Grant Warwick	10	2	3	5	Larry Leach	7	1	1	2
Gordie Bruce	7	2	3	5	Murph Chamberlain	6	1	1	2

Bill Ezinicki	6	1	1	2	Earl Anderson	5	0	1	1
Butch Goring	5	1	1	2	Irwin Boyd	5	0	1	1
James O'Neil	5	1	1	2	Hal Darragh	5	0	1	1
Al Sims	37	0	2	2	Wilbert Hiller	5	0	1	1
Andy Moog	70	0	2	2	Joe Lamb	5	0	1	1
Chris Nilan	19	0	2	2	Fred O'Donnell	5	0	1	1
Andy Brickley	12	0	2	2	Marc Potvin	5	0	1	1
Geoff Courtnall	9	0	2	2	Joe Zanussi	4	0	1	1
Armand Gaudreault	7	0	2	2	John Gruden	3	0	1	1
Alex Smith	5	0	2	2	Dave Pasin	3	0	1	1
Todd Elik	4	0	2	2	Stephane Quintal	3	0	1	1
Nevin Markwart	19	1	0	1	Roger Jenkins	2	0	1	1
Luc Dufour	17	1	0	1	Allen Pedersen	64	0	0	0
Dave Barr	15	1	0	1	Jack Portland	18	0	0	0
Gord Murphy	15	1	0	1	Bob Gould	17	0	0	0
Hank Nowak	13	1	0	1	Jay Miller	14	0	0	0
Jim Lorentz	11	1	0	1	Dennis O'Brien	14	0	0	0
Jack Caffery	10	1	0	1	Glen Sather	13	0	0	0
Ed Harrison	9	1	0	1	George Sullivan	12	0	0	0
Duncan Fisher	8	1	0	1	Myles Lane	10	0	0	0
Bill Speer	8	1	0	1	Billy O'Dwyer	10	0	0	0
Billy Couture	7	1	0	1	Jack Church	9	0	0	0
Jean-Guy Gendron	7	1	0	1	Jamie Huscroft	9	0	0	0
Pentti Lund	7	1	0	1	Mickey MacKay	9	0	0	0
Brad Palmer	7	1	0	1	Billy Boucher	8	0	0	0
Oscar Aubuchon	6	1	0	1	Harry Connor	8	0	0	0
Mats Naslund	5	1	0	1	Ken Hammond	8	0	0	0
Vic Ripley	5	1	0	1	Ron Hoover	8	0	0	0
Tom Williams	4	1	0	1	Harry Meeking	8	0	0	0
Gerry Cheevers	88	0	1	1	Billy Stuart	8	0	0	0
Reggie Lemelin	28	0	1	1	Doug Halward	7	0	0	0
Jack Shewchuck	20	0	1	1	Roy Goldsworthy	6	0	0	0
Warren Godfrey	18	0	1	1	Steve Kraftcheck	6	0	0	0
Ed Kryzanowski	18	0	1	1	Alex Motter	6	0	0	0
Robert Hamill	16	0	1	1	Max Quackenbush	6	0	0	0
Gord Roberts	16	0	1	1	Louis Sleigher	6	0	0	0
Clare Martin	15	0	1	1	Brian Curran	5	0	0	0
John Blum	14	0	1	1	Matt Hervey	5	0	0	0
Marty Howe	12	0	1	1	Orville Heximer	5	0	0	0
Frank Simonetti	12	0	1	1	Alexei Kasatonov	5	0	0	0
Jack Bionda	11	0	1	1	Richie Leduc	5	0	0	0
Randy Hillier	11	0	1	1	Vic Lynn	5	0	0	0
Daniel Marois	11	0	1	1	Peaches Lyons	5	0	0	0
Mike Moffat	11	0	1	1	Kyle McLaren	5	0	0	0
Art Chapman	10	0	1	1	John Schmidt	5	0	0	0
Sprague Cleghorn	10	0	1	1	Ron Sutter	5	0	0	0
Frank Martin	10	0	1	1	Mats Thelin	5	0	0	0
Matti Hagman	8	0	1	1	Nick Beverley	4	0	0	0
Gus Bodnar	6	0	1	1	Wayne Brown	4	0	0	0
Albert Siebert	6	0	1	1	Wade Campbell	4	0	0	0

Dean Chynoweth	4	o	o	o	Ted Graham	2	o	o	o
Norm Corcoran	4	o	o	o	Leland Harrington	2	o	o	o
Dave Donnelly	4	o	o	o	Fred Harris	2	o	o	o
Paul Haynes	4	o	o	o	Gus Kyle	2	o	o	o
Pete Horeck	4	o	o	o	Ray Maluta	2	o	o	o
Max Kaminsky	4	o	o	o	Kraig Nienhuis	2	o	o	o
Darin Kimble	4	o	o	o	Paul Runge	2	o	o	o
Phil Krake	4	o	o	o	Zelio Toppazzini	2	o	o	o
Dmitri Kvartalnov	4	o	o	o	Wes Walz	2	o	o	o
Steve Langdon	4	o	o	o	Ken Yackel	2	o	o	o
Guy Larose	4	o	o	o	Gordie Wilson	2	o	o	o
Mark Marquess	4	o	o	o	Bill Anderson	1	o	o	o
Bert McInenly	4	o	o	o	Don Cherry	1	o	o	o
Jack Pratt	4	o	o	o	Rob Cimetta	1	o	o	o
Jean Pusie	4	o	o	o	Gordie Clark	1	o	o	o
Earl Reibel	4	o	o	o	Murray Costello	1	o	o	o
Gerry Shannon	4	o	o	o	Lou Crawford	1	o	o	o
Jack Shill	4	o	o	o	Glen Featherstone	1	o	o	o
Tim Sweeney	4	o	o	o	Harry Frost	1	o	o	o
Reggie Leach	3	o	o	o	Doug Gibson	1	o	o	o
Bill Lesuk	3	o	o	o	Fred Gordon	1	o	o	o
Jim Nill	3	o	o	o	Chris Hayes	1	o	o	o
Dan Poliziani	3	o	o	o	Morris Lukowich	1	o	o	o
Stephane Richer	3	o	o	o	Carl Mokosak	1	o	o	o
Alan Shields	3	o	o	o	Garry Peters	1	o	o	o
Dave Silk	3	o	o	o	Danny Schock	1	o	o	o
Reginald Smith	3	o	o	o	Al Simmons	1	o	o	o
Steve Staios	3	o	o	o	Bill Thoms	1	o	o	o
Cy Denneny	2	o	o	o	Tom Webster	1	o	o	o
Clark Donatelli	2	o	o	o	Wally Wilson	1	o	o	o
Guyle Fielder	2	o	o	o	Chris Winnes	1	o	o	o

BOSTON BRUINS ALL-TIME RECORDS

MOST CONSECUTIVE YEARS IN PLAYOFFS

29   (1967–68 to 1995–96)
9   (1934–35 to 1942–43)

MOST WINS IN A SEASON

57   (1970–71, 78 games)

MOST LOSSES IN A SEASON

47   (1961–62, 70 games)

MOST TIES IN A SEASON

21   (1954–55, 70 games)

MOST POINTS IN A SEASON

121   (1970–71, 78 games)

MOST WINS AT HOME IN A SEASON

33   (1970–71 & 1973–74, 39 games)

MOST LOSSES AT HOME IN A SEASON

22   (1961–62, 35 games)

MOST CONSECUTIVE YEARS OUT OF THE PLAYOFFS

8   (1959–60 to 1966–67)
2   (1924–25 to 1925–26)

FEWEST WINS IN A SEASON

14   (1962–63, 70 games)
6   (1924–25, 30 games)

FEWEST LOSSES IN A SEASON

5   (1929–30, 44 games)
13   (1971–72, 78 games)

FEWEST TIES IN A SEASON

5   (1972–73, 78 games)
5   (1943–44, 50 games)
5   (1939–40, 48 games)
5   (1933–34, 48 games)
1   (1929–30, 44 games)
0   (1924–25, 30 games)

FEWEST POINTS IN A SEASON

38   (1961–62, 70 games)
12   (1924–25, 30 games)

FEWEST WINS AT HOME IN A SEASON

3   (1924–25, 15 games)
7   (1962–63, 35 games)
9   (1961–62, 35 games)
9   (1936–37, 24 games)

FEWEST LOSSES AT HOME IN A SEASON

1   (1929–30, 24 games)
1   (1930–31, 23 games)
2   (1932–33, 25 games)
2   (1938–39, 24 games)
3   (1937–38, 24 games)
3   (1939–40, 24 games)

MOST TIES AT HOME
IN A SEASON

10	(1947–48, 30 games)
10	(1950–51, 35 games)
10	(1962–63, 35 games)

FEWEST TIES AT HOME
IN A SEASON

0	(1924–25, 15 games)
0	(1926–27, 21 games)
0	(1929–30, 24 games)
0	(1934–35, 24 games)

MOST WINS ON THE ROAD
IN A SEASON

26   (1971–72, 39 games)

FEWEST WINS ON THE ROAD
IN A SEASON

2   (1960–61, 35 games)

MOST LOSSES ON THE ROAD
IN A SEASON

26	(1964–65, 35 games)
26	(1965–66, 35 games)

FEWEST LOSSES ON THE ROAD
IN A SEASON

4	(1929–30, 20 games)
4	(1940–41, 24 games)

MOST TIES ON THE ROAD
IN A SEASON

12   (1954–55, 35 games)

FEWEST TIES ON THE ROAD
IN A SEASON

0	(1924–25, 15 games)
0	(1938–39, 24 games)
0	(1964–65, 35 games)

MOST GOALS IN A SEASON

399   (1970–71, 78 games)

FEWEST GOALS IN A SEASON

49	(1924–25, 30 games)
77	(1927–28, 44 games)
92	(1935–36, 48 games)
147	(1955–56, 70 games)

MOST GOALS AGAINST
IN A SEASON

306   (1961–62, 70 games)

FEWEST GOALS AGAINST
IN A SEASON

52	(1928–29, 44 games)
76	(1938–39, 48 games)
172	(1952–53, 70 games)

MOST CONSECUTIVE WINS

14   (December 3, 1929 to January 9, 1930)

MOST CONSECUTIVE HOME WINS

20   (December 3, 1929 to March 18, 1930)

MOST CONSECUTIVE ROAD WINS

8   (February 17 to March 8, 1972
& March 15 to April 14, 1993)

MOST CONSECUTIVE TIES

4	(January 3 to January 10, 1932)
4	(December 27, 1940 to January 7, 1941)
4	(January 6, 1955 to January 12, 1955)
4	(October 8, 1960 to October 15, 1960)

MOST CONSECUTIVE GAMES WITHOUT A TIE

42	(December 1, 1924 to January 5, 1926)
38	(February 26, 1929 to January 28, 1930)
32	(January 2, 1986 to March 15, 1986)

LONGEST UNDEFEATED STREAK

23	(December 22, 1940 to February 23, 1941 / 15 wins-8 ties)

LONGEST HOME UNDEFEATED STREAK

27	(November 22, 1970 to March 20, 1971 / 26 wins-1 tie)

LONGEST ROAD UNDEFEATED STREAK

15	(December 22, 1940 to March 16, 1941 / 9 wins-6 ties)

LONGEST LOSING STREAK

11	(December 3, 1924 to January 5, 1925)

LONGEST HOME LOSING STREAK

11	(December 8, 1924 to February 17, 1925)

LONGEST ROAD LOSING STREAK

14	(December 27, 1964 to February 21, 1965)

LONGEST WINLESS STREAK

20	(January 28 1962 to March 11, 1962 / 16 losses-4 ties)

LONGEST WINLESS STREAK AT HOME

11	(December 8, 1924 to February 17, 1925 / 11 losses)

LONGEST WINLESS STREAK ON THE ROAD

18	(January 22, 1961 to October 21, 1961 / 16 losses-2 ties)
18	(February 24, 1963 to December 14, 1964 / 14 losses - 4 ties)

MOST CONSECUTIVE GAMES TIED

4	(January 3, 5, 7, 10, 1932)
4	(December 27, 31, 1940 / January 5, 7, 1941)
4	(January 6, 8, 9, 12, 1955)
4	(October 8, 9, 11, 15, 1960)

MOST CONSECUTIVE SHUTOUTS AGAINST OPPONENTS

3	(February 14, 19, 21, 1928)
3	(March 10, 15, 17, 1936)
3	(December 4, 6, 11, 1938)
3	(December 15, 18, 20, 1938)
3	(November 20, 23, 24, 1977)

MOST CONSECUTIVE GAMES BEING SHUT OUT

3	(February 2, 5, 9, 1929)

MOST GAMES ON CONSECUTIVE NIGHTS

3	(April 12, 13, 14, 1980 vs. Pittsburgh — playoff games)

MOST CONSECUTIVE HOME GAMES AGAINST THE SAME OPPONENT — REGULAR SEASON

2	(January 15 & 18, 1947 vs. Chicago)
	(January 26 & 29, 1947 vs. Detroit)
	(February 5 & 8, 1950 vs. Toronto)
	(December 25 & 27, 1950 vs. Chicago)
	(January 24 & 25, 1953 vs. New York)
	(February 8 & 12, 1953 vs. Detroit)
	(January 23 & 24, 1954 vs. New York)
	(February 6 & 7, 1954 vs. Detroit)
	(January 22 & 23, 1955 vs. New York)
	(February 5 & 6, 1955 vs. Detroit)
	(March 7 & 9, 1957 vs. Detroit)
	(November 1 & 8, 1964 vs. Chicago)
	(February 11 & 13, 1965 vs. Montreal)

MOST CONSECUTIVE ROAD GAMES AGAINST THE SAME OPPONENT — REGULAR SEASON

2	(February 23 & March 1, 1958 at Chicago)

MOST SHOTS ON GOAL — ONE GAME

83	(March 4, 1941 at Boston 3 vs. Chicago 2)
73	(March 21, 1991 at Boston 3 vs. Quebec 3)
72	(December 10, 1970 at Boston 8 vs. Buffalo 2)

MOST SHOTS ON GOAL — ONE PERIOD

33	(March 4, 1941 — 2nd period at Boston 3 vs. Chicago 2)

BOSTON BRUINS ALL-TIME LEADERS

MOST SEASONS

21	Johnny Bucyk
20	Dit Clapper
18	Ray Bourque

MOST GAMES

1436	Johnny Bucyk
1290	Ray Bourque
1027	Wayne Cashman

MOST POINTS

1363	Ray Bourque
1339	Johnny Bucyk
1012	Phil Esposito

MOST GOALS

545	Johnny Bucyk
459	Phil Esposito
402	Rick Middleton

MOST ASSISTS

1001	Ray Bourque
794	Johnny Bucyk
624	Bobby Orr

MOST PENALTY MINUTES

2095	Terry O'Reilly
1552	Mike Milbury
1261	Keith Crowder

GOALTENDERS

MOST SHUTOUTS

74	Tiny Thompson
35	Frank Brimsek
27	Ed Johnston

MOST WINS

252	Tiny Thompson
230	Frank Brimsek
229	Gerry Cheevers

MOST LOSSES

192	Ed Johnston
153	Tiny Thompson
144	Frank Brimsek

BEST GOALS AGAINST AVERAGE — MINIMUM 100 GAMES

1.99	Tiny Thompson	2.89	Gerry Cheevers
2.57	Terry Sawchuk	2.95	Gilles Gilbert
2.58	Frank Brimsek	2.95	Don Simmons
2.58	Jim Henry	2.99	Pete Peeters

BOSTON BRUINS LEADING THE LEAGUE

GOALS AGAINST AVERAGE

1982–83	Pete Peeters	2.36
1941–42	Frank Brimsek	2.35
1938–39	Frank Brimsek	1.56
1937–38	Tiny Thompson	1.80
1935–36	Tiny Thompson	1.68
1932–33	Tiny Thompson	1.76
1929–30	Tiny Thompson	2.19

POINTS

1974–75	Bobby Orr	135
1973–74	Phil Esposito	145
1972–73	Phil Esposito	130
1971–72	Phil Esposito	133
1970–71	Phil Esposito	152
1969–70	Bobby Orr	120
1968–69	Phil Esposito	126
1943–44	Herb Cain	82
1940–41	Bill Cowley	62
1939–40	Milt Schmidt	52
1929–30	Cooney Weiland	73

GOALS

1974–75	Phil Esposito	61
1973–74	Phil Esposito	68
1972–73	Phil Esposito	55
1971–72	Phil Esposito	66
1970–71	Phil Esposito	76
1969–70	Phil Esposito	43
1959–60	Bronco Horvath (tied with Bobby Hull)	39
1929–30	Cooney Weiland	43

ASSISTS

1992–93	Adam Oates	97
1973–74	Bobby Orr	90
1970–71	Bobby Orr	102
1969–70	Bobby Orr	87

PENALTY MINUTES

1954–55	Fern Flaman	150
1951–52	Gus Kyle	127
1944–45	Pat Egan	86
1927–28	Eddie Shore	165

LEAD LEAGUE IN GOALS SCORED — TEAM

1973–74	349		1940–41	168
1972–73	330		1939–40	170
1971–72	339		1938–39	156
1970–71	399		1930–31	143
1969–70	277		1929–30	179
1968–69	303		1928–29	89
1967–68	259		1925–26 (tied with Toronto)	92

LEAD LEAGUE IN GOALS AGAINST — TEAM

1982–83	228		1935–36	83
1941–42	118		1932–33	88
1938–39	76		1929–30	98
1937–38	89			

MOST GOALS AGAINST IN A SEASON — TEAM

1996–97	300
1966–67	253
1965–66	275
1964–65	253
1962–63	281
1961–62	306
1960–61	254
1924–25	119

FEWEST GOALS FOR IN A SEASON — TEAM

1966–67	182
1965–66	174
1964–65	166
1963–64	170
1961–62	177
1960–61	176
1955–56	147
1952–53	152

(tied with New York)

MISCELLANEOUS RECORDS

MOST POINT SCORING GAMES IN A ROW

22   Bronco Horvath (1959–60)
16 goals/17 assists

MOST GOAL SCORING GAMES IN A ROW

9   Phil Esposito (1970–71)
14 goals

MOST GAMES IN A ROW WITH AN ASSIST

18   Adam Oates (1992–93)
28 assists

MOST GOALS IN A SEASON

76   Phil Esposito (1970–71, 78 games)
68   Phil Esposito (1973–74, 78 games)
66   Phil Esposito (1971–72, 78 games)

MOST ASSISTS IN A SEASON

102   Bobby Orr (1970–71, 78 games)
97   Adam Oates (1992–93, 84 games)
90   Bobby Orr (1973–74, 78 games)

MOST PENALTY MINUTES IN A SEASON

302   Jay Miller (1987–88, 80 games)

MOST SHUTOUTS IN A SEASON

15   1927–28 (44 games)

MOST PENALTY MINUTES IN A SEASON

2,443   1987–88 (80 games)

MOST GOALS IN A GAME

14   January 21, 1945 (Boston 14 — New York Rangers 3)

LONGEST CONSECUTIVE GAMES STREAK

418   Johnny Bucyk (January 23, 1969 to March 2, 1975)

MOST GOALS — REGULAR SEASON GAME

4   Phil Esposito (4 times)
Herb Cain (2 times)
Bill Cowley (2 times)
Johnny Bucyk (2 times)
Cooney Weiland
Roy Conacher
Woody Dumart
Pit Martin
Chris Oddleifson
Wayne Cashman
Barry Pederson
Vladimir Ruzicka
Adam Oates

MOST ASSISTS — REGULAR SEASON GAME

6   Ken Hodge
Bobby Orr

MOST POINTS — REGULAR SEASON GAME

7   Bobby Orr
Phil Esposito
Barry Pederson
Cam Neely

MOST GOALS — PLAYOFF GAME

4   Phil Esposito

MOST ASSISTS — PLAYOFF GAME

5   Don McKenney

MOST POINTS — PLAYOFF GAME

6   Phil Esposito
Rick Middleton

ALL-TIME BOSTON BRUINS PLAYER REGISTER

STATISTICAL INFORMATION IS LISTED IN THE FOLLOWING ORDER:
games / goals / assists / points / penalty minutes.

Numbers after name indicate uniform number, if known.

RICK ADDUONO FORWARD *b.* Thunder Bay,
Ontario, January 25, 1955

1975–76	1	0	0	0	0

- Boston's third choice in the 1975 amateur draft

GARY ALDCORN FORWARD *b.* Shaunavon,
Saskatchewan, March 7, 1935

1960–61	21	2	3	5	12

- Traded from Detroit to Boston with Murray Oliver and Tom McCarthy for Leo Labine and Vic Stasiuk, January 1961

JASON ALLISON #41 FORWARD
b. North York, Ontario, May 29, 1975

1996–97	19	3	9	12	9

- Traded from Washington to Boston, along with Jim Carey and Anson Carter for Adam Oates, Rick Tocchet, and Bill Ranford, March 1, 1997

BILL ANDERSON DEFENSE *b.* Tillsonburg,
Ontario, December 13, 1912

1942–43	1	0	0	0	0

- Playoffs only

EARL ANDERSON #16 – 17 – 28 FORWARD
b. Roseau, Minnesota, February 24, 1951

1974–77	64	12	16	28	10
Playoffs	5	0	1	1	0

- Traded from Detroit to Boston with Hank Nowak for Walt McKechnie and a draft choice, February 18, 1975

JOHN ARBOUR #27 DEFENSE *b.* Niagara Falls, Ontario, September 28, 1945

1965–68	6	0	1	1	11

- Sold by Boston with Jean Pronovost to Pittsburgh, May 21, 1968

BOB ARMSTRONG #4 DEFENSE *b.* Toronto, Ontario, April 7, 1931

1950–62	542	13	86	99	671
Playoffs	42	1	7	8	28

SCOTT ARNIEL #29 FORWARD *b.* Cornwall, Ontario, September 12, 1962

1991–92	29	5	3	8	20

- Traded to Boston by Winnipeg for future considerations, November 22, 1991

BARRY ASHBEE #25 DEFENSE *b.* Weston, Ontario, July 28, 1939

1965–66	14	0	3	3	14

BRENT ASHTON #18 FORWARD *b.* Saskatoon, Saskatchewan, May 18, 1960

1991–93	87	19	24	43	58

- Traded to Boston by Winnipeg for Petri Skriko, October 29, 1991
- Traded by Boston to Calgary for C.J. Young, February 1, 1993

STEVE ATKINSON FORWARD *b.* Toronto, Ontario, October 16, 1948

1968–69	1	0	0	0	0

- Claimed on waivers from Boston by Buffalo, November 1, 1970

OSCAR AUBUCHON #15 FORWARD *b.* St. Hyacinthe, Quebec, January 1, 1917

1942–44	14	4	0	4	0

- Sold to the New York Rangers, November, 1943

DON AWREY #22 – 24 – 26 DEFENSE *b.* Kitchener, Ontario, July 18, 1943

1963–73	543	21	87	108	827
Playoffs	54	0	11	11	132

- Traded by Boston to St. Louis for Jake Rathwell and a draft pick, October 5, 1973
- Member of the 1970 and 1972 Stanley Cup Champions

PETE BABANDO #24 FORWARD *b.* Braeburn, Pennsylvania, May 10, 1925

1947–49	118	42	25	67	86
Playoffs	9	1	1	2	4

- Traded by Boston to Detroit with Clare Martin, Pete Dunham, and Jimmy Peters for Bill Quackenbush and Pete Horeck, August, 1949

Trivia Question #1
A former Bruins goaltender and an ex-Brooklyn Dodger manager have something in common. What is it?

GARNET BAILEY ("Ace") #14 FORWARD *b.* Lloydminster, Saskatchewan, June 13, 1948

1968–73	232	31	46	77	289
Playoffs	15	2	4	6	28

- Traded by Boston to Detroit for Gary Doak, March 1, 1973
- Member of the 1972 Stanley Cup Champions

MURRAY BALFOUR #12 FORWARD *b.* Regina, Saskatchewan, August 24, 1936

1964–65	15	0	2	2	26

- Traded to Boston by Chicago with Mike Draper for Jerry Toppazzini and Matt Ravlich, June 9, 1964

STAN BALUIK FORWARD *b.* Port Arthur, Ontario, October 5, 1935

1959–60	7	0	0	0	2

DARREN BANKS #56 FORWARD *b.* Toronto, Ontario, March 18, 1966

1992–93	20	2	2	4	73

- Signed as a free agent by Boston, July 16, 1992

Trivia Question #2
What two players wore #2, Eddie Shore's number, before it was retired on April 1, 1947?

RALPH BARAHONA #37 FORWARD *b.* Long Beach, California, November 16, 1965

1990–91	6	2	2	4	0

- Signed as a free agent by Boston, September 26, 1990

DAVE BARR #17 – 32 FORWARD *b.* Toronto, Ontario, November 30, 1960

1981–83	12	1	1	2	7
Playoffs	15	1	0	1	2

- Signed as a free agent by Boston, September 28, 1981
- Traded by Boston to the Rangers for Dave Silk, October 5, 1983

EDDIE BARRY #18 FORWARD *b.* Wellesley, Massachusetts, October 9, 1919

1946–47	19	1	3	4	2

MARTY BARRY #8 FORWARD *b.* St. Gabriel, Quebec, December 8, 1905

1929–35	279	130	88	218	141
Playoffs	20	6	6	12	26

- Hall of Fame elected 1965

RAY BARRY FORWARD *b.* Boston, Massachusetts, October 4, 1928

1951–52	18	1	2	3	6

JIMMY BARTLETT #24 FORWARD *b.* Verdun, Quebec, May 27, 1932

1960–61	63	15	9	24	95

- Drafted by Boston from the Rangers, June 8, 1960

BOBBY BAUER #17 FORWARD *b.* Waterloo, Ontario, February 16, 1935

1935–42, 1945–47, 1951–52				
Totals	328	123	137	260	36
Playoffs	48	11	8	19	6

- Second All-Star: 1939 – 1940 – 1941 – 1947
- Hall of Fame elected 1996
- Lady Byng Trophy: 1939–40, 1940–41, 1946–47
- Dufresne Trophy: 1941–42
- Member of the 1939 and 1941 Stanley Cup Champions

RED BEATTIE #11 FORWARD *b.* Ibstock, England, 1907

1930–38	288	58	79	137	127
Playoffs	16	2	0	2	4

BOB BECKETT #6 – 24 FORWARD *b.* Unionville, Ontario, April 8, 1936

1956–58, 1961–62, 1963–64				
Totals	66	7	6	13	18

CLAYTON BEDDOES #37 FORWARD *b.* Bentley, Alberta, November 10, 1970

1995–97	60	2	8	10	57

- Signed by Boston as a free agent, June 2, 1994

BOB BEERS #22 – 34 – 43 DEFENSE
b. Pittsburgh, Pennsylvania, May 20, 1967

1989–92, 1996–97					
Totals	77	3	11	14	53
Playoffs	21	1	1	2	22

- Traded by Boston to Tampa Bay for Stephane Richer, October 28, 1992
- Signed by Boston as a free agent, August 5, 1996

BILL BENNETT #7 FORWARD *b.* Warwick, Rhode Island, May 31, 1953

1978–79	7	1	4	5	2

- Claimed from Boston by Hartford in the expansion draft, June 13, 1979

BOBBY BENSON DEFENSE *b.* Buffalo, New York

1924–25	8	0	1	1	4

PAUL BERALDO #30 – 37 FORWARD
b. Hamilton, Ontario, October 5, 1967

1987–89	10	0	0	0	4

- Boston's 6th choice in the 1966 entry draft

FRED BERGDINON *b.* Quebec City, Quebec

1925–26	2	0	0	0	0

> **Trivia Question #3**
> April 12, April 13, & April 14
> of 1980 have what significance
> in Bruins history?

PHIL BESLER FORWARD *b.* Melville, Saskatchewan, 1911

1935–36	8	0	0	0	0

SAM BETTIO #9 FORWARD *b.* Copper Cliff, Ontario, December 1, 1928

1949–50	44	9	12	21	32

NICK BEVERLEY #6 – 27 DEFENSE
b. Toronto, Ontario, April 21, 1947

1966–67, 1969–70, 1971–74					
Totals	42	1	10	11	28
Playoffs	4	0	0	0	0

- Traded by Boston to Pittsburgh for Darryl Edestrand, October 25, 1973

JACK BIONDA #11 DEFENSE *b.* Huntsville, Ontario, September 18, 1933

1956–59	80	3	8	11	95
Playoffs	11	0	1	1	14

- Purchased from Toronto, 1956

DON BLACKBURN #7 FORWARD *b.* Kirkland Lake, Ontario, May 14, 1938

1962–63	6	0	5	5	4

MICKEY BLAKE DEFENSE *b.* Barriefield, Ontario, October 31, 1912

1935–36	7	0	0	0	2

> **Trivia Question #4**
> What former Bruin was the first
> living player to be inducted into
> the Hockey Hall of Fame?

JOHN BLUM #33 DEFENSE *b.* Detroit, Michigan, October 8, 1959

1983–86, 1987–88, 1989–90					
Totals	169	5	22	27	443
Playoffs	14	0	1	1	23

- Traded to Boston by Edmonton for Larry Melnyk, March 6, 1984

- Claimed from Boston by Washington in NHL waiver draft, October 6, 1986
- Traded to Boston by Washington for a future draft pick, June 1, 1987
- Signed by Boston as a free agent, July 6, 1989

GUS BODNAR #18 FORWARD *b.* Fort William, Ontario, August 24, 1925

1953–55	82	7	7	14	24
Playoffs	6	0	1	1	4

- Traded to Boston by Chicago for Jerry Toppazzini, February 16, 1954

LEO BOIVIN #20 DEFENSE *b.* Prescott, Ontario, August 2, 1932

1954–66	717	47	164	211	785
Playoffs	34	3	9	12	41

- Hall of Fame elected 1986
- Dufresne Trophy: 1960–61
- Traded to Toronto by Boston with Fernie Flaman, Ken Smith, and Phil Maloney for Bill Ezinicki and Vic Lynn, November 16, 1950
- Traded to Boston by Toronto for Joe Klukay, November, 1954
- Traded by Boston to Detroit with Dean Prentice for Gary Doak, Ron Murphy, and Bill Lesuk, February 18, 1966

IVAN BOLDIREV #21 – 23 FORWARD *b.* Zranjanin, Yugoslavia, August 15, 1949

1970–72	13	0	2	2	6

- Traded by Boston to California for Richie Leduc and Chris Oddliefson, November 17, 1971

FRANK BOLL ("Buzz") #14 FORWARD *b.* Filmore, Saskatchewan, March 6, 1911

1942–44	82	44	52	96	22

- Obtained by Boston along with Murph Chamberlain when the New York Americans went defunct, 1942

MARCEL BONIN #18 – 23 FORWARD *b.* Montreal, Quebec, September 12, 1932

1955–56	67	9	9	18	49

- Traded to Boston by Detroit with Vic Stasiuk, Lorne Davis, and Terry Sawchuk, for Eddie Sandford, Warren Godfrey, Real Chevrefils, Gilles Boisvert, and Norm Corcoran, June 3, 1955
- Drafted from Boston by Montreal, June, 1957

CARL BOONE ("Buddy") #6 FORWARD *b.* Kirkland Lake, Ontario, September 11, 1932

1956–58	34	5	3	8	28
Playoffs	22	2	1	3	25

BILLY BOUCHER FORWARD *b.* Ottawa, Ontario

1926–27	14	2	0	2	12
Playoffs	8	0	0	0	2

RAY BOURQUE #7 – 77 DEFENSE *b.* Montreal, Quebec, December 28, 1960

1979–97	1290	362	1001	1363	953
Playoffs	162	34	112	146	135

- First All-Star: 1980 – 1982 – 1984 – 1985 – 1987 – 1988 – 1990 – 1991 – 1992 – 1993 – 1994 – 1996
- Second All-Star: 1981 – 1983 – 1986 – 1989 – 1995
- James Norris Trophy: 1986–87, 1987–88, 1989–90, 1990–91, 1993–94
- Calder Memorial Trophy: 1979–80
- Dufresne Trophy: 1979–80, 1984–85, 1985–86, 1986–87, 1989–90, 1993–94, 1995–96
- Seventh Player Award: 1979–80

PAUL BOUTILIER #34 DEFENSE *b.* Sydney, Nova Scotia, May 3, 1962

1986–87	52	5	9	14	84

- Acquired by Boston as compensation for the Islanders signing of Brian Curran, August 6, 1987
- Traded by Boston to Minnesota for a future draft pick, March 10, 1987

IRWIN BOYD ("Yank") #19 FORWARD
b. Ardmore, Pennsylvania, November 13, 1908

1931–32, 1942–44					
Totals	55	16	16	32	37
Playoffs	5	0	1	1	4

Trivia Question #5
This former Bruin called the Conachers Roy, Charlie, and Lionel "uncle" Who is he?

JOHN "SPIDER" BRACKENBOROUGH
FORWARD

1925–26	7	0	0	0	0

BART BRADLEY FORWARD *b.* Fort William, Ontario, July 29, 1930

1949–50	1	0	0	0	0

TOM BRENNAN FORWARD *b.* Philadelphia, Pennsylvania, January 2, 1921

1943–45	22	2	2	4	2

ANDY BRICKLEY #25 FORWARD *b.* Melrose, Massachusetts, August 9, 1961

1988–92	177	37	76	113	38
Playoffs	12	0	2	2	0

- Claimed by Boston from New Jersey at the NHL waiver draft, October 3, 1988

ADAM BROWN #16 FORWARD *b.* Johnstone, Scotland, February 4, 1920

1951–52	33	8	9	17	6

- Traded to Boston from Chicago for Max Quackenbush, August 20, 1951

WAYNE BROWN #12 FORWARD *b.* Deloro, Ontario, November 16, 1930

1953–54	4	0	0	0	2

- Playoffs only

GORDIE BRUCE #12 – 20 FORWARD *b.* Ottawa, Ontario, May 9, 1919

1940–42, 1945–46					
Totals	28	4	9	13	13
Playoffs	7	2	3	5	4

RON BUCHANAN #27 FORWARD *b.* Montreal, Quebec, November 15, 1944

1966–67	3	0	0	0	0

- Drafted from Boston by Philadelphia, June 12, 1968

Trivia Question #6
During the six team era (1942–1967), one player and one goaltender played for five of the six NHL teams, the exception being Montreal.
What are the names of these two former Bruins, Leafs, Hawks, Wings, and Broadway Blueshirts?

JOHNNY BUCYK ("Chief") #9 FORWARD
b. Edmonton, Alberta, May 12, 1935

1957–78	1436	545	794	1339	436
Playoffs	109	40	60	100	34

- #9 is retired by the Bruins in his honor
- Played on the 1970 & 1972 Stanley Cup Champions
- First All-Star: 1971
- Second All-Star: 1968
- Hall of Fame elected 1981
- Lady Byng Trophy: 1970–71 & 1973–74
- Lester Patrick Trophy: 1977
- Dufresne Trophy: 1962–63 & 1965–66
- Traded to Boston by Detroit for Terry Sawchuk, July 24, 1957
- Member of the 1970 and 1972 Stanley Cup Champions

BILLY BURCH DEFENSE/FORWARD *b.* Yonkers, New York, November 20, 1900

1932–33	23	3	1	4	4

- Hall of Fame elected 1974
- Obtained by Boston from the New York Americans, 1932
- Sold by Boston to Chicago, 1933

BILL BUREGA DEFENSE *b.* Winnipeg, Manitoba, March 13, 1932

1955–56	4	0	1	1	4

EDDIE BURKE FORWARD *b.* Toronto, Ontario, June 3, 1907

1931–32	16	3	0	3	12

CHARLIE BURNS #10 FORWARD *b.* Detroit, Michigan, February 14, 1936

1959–63	262	48	70	118	118

- Drafted by Boston from Detroit, June 1959

RANDY BURRIDGE #12 FORWARD *b.* Fort Erie, Ontario, January 7, 1966

1985–91	359	108	115	223	275
Playoffs	78	12	30	42	89

- Dufresne Trophy: 1988–89
- Seventh Player Award: 1985–86, 1988–89
- Traded by Boston to Washington for Steve Leach, June 21, 1991

JOHN BYCE #42 FORWARD *b.* Madison, Wisconsin, August 9, 1967

1989–92	21	2	3	5	6
Playoffs	8	2	0	2	2

- Traded by Boston to Washington for Dennis Smith and Brent Hughes, February 24, 1992

GORDON BYERS DEFENSE *b.* Eganville, Ontario, March 11, 1930

1949–50	1	0	1	1	0

LYNDON BYERS #8 – 12 – 33 – 34 FORWARD *b.* Nipawin, Saskatchewan, February 29, 1964

1983–92	261	24	42	66	959
Playoffs	37	2	2	4	96

JACK CAFFERY #18 FORWARD *b.* Kingston, Ontario, June 30, 1934

1956–58	54	3	2	5	22
Playoffs	10	1	0	1	4

- Drafted by Boston from Toronto, June 5, 1956

CHARLES CAHILL #14 FORWARD

1925–27	32	0	1	1	4

HERB CAIN #4 FORWARD *b.* Newmarket, Ontario, December 24, 1913

1939–46	314	140	119	259	81
Playoffs	45	14	11	25	9

- Second All-Star: 1944
- Art Ross Trophy: 1943–44
- Traded to Boston by Montreal Canadiens for Ray Getliffe and Charlie Sands, 1939
- Member 1941 Stanley Cup Champions

NORM CALLADINE #7 FORWARD *b.* Peterborough, Ontario, 1916

1942–45	63	19	29	48	8

WADE CAMPBELL #27 – 28 – 38 DEFENSE *b.* Peace River, Alberta, January 2, 1961

1985–88	28	0	4	4	60
Playoffs	4	0	0	0	11

- Traded to Boston by Winnipeg for Bill Derlago, January 31, 1986

JACK CAPUANO #23 DEFENSE *b.* Cranston, Rhode Island, July 7, 1966

| 1991–92 | 2 | 0 | 0 | 0 | 0 |

- Signed by Boston as a free agent, August 1, 1991

WAYNE CARLETON ("Swoop") #11 FORWARD *b.* Sudbury, Ontario, August 4, 1946

| 1969–71 | 111 | 28 | 43 | 71 | 67 |
| Playoffs | 18 | 2 | 4 | 6 | 14 |

- Traded to Boston by Toronto for Jim Harrison, December 10, 1969
- Drafted from Boston by California in the intra-league draft, June 8, 1971
- Member of the 1970 Stanley Cup Champions

BOB CARPENTER #11 FORWARD *b.* Beverly, Massachusetts, July 13, 1963

| 1988–92 | 187 | 63 | 71 | 134 | 175 |
| Playoffs | 38 | 5 | 9 | 14 | 51 |

- Traded to Boston by Los Angeles for Steve Kasper, January 23, 1989

GEORGE CARROLL DEFENSE

| 1925–25 | 11 | 0 | 0 | 0 | 9 |

BILL CARSON #10 FORWARD *b.* Bracebridge, Ontario, November 25, 1900

| 1928–30 | 63 | 11 | 6 | 17 | 34 |
| Playoffs | 11 | 3 | 0 | 3 | 14 |

- Member, 1929 Stanley Cup Champions

ANSON CARTER #11 FORWARD *b.* Toronto, Ontario, June 6, 1974

| 1996–97 | 19 | 8 | 5 | 13 | 2 |

- Traded from Washington to Boston with Jason Allison and Jim Carey for Adam Oates, Rick Tocchet, and Bill Ranford, March 1, 1997

BILLY CARTER #12 FORWARD *b.* Cornwall, Ontario, December 2, 1937

| 1960–61 | 8 | 0 | 0 | 0 | 0 |

Trivia Question #7
Who is the only Bruin to play on 3 Stanley Cup championship teams?

JOHN CARTER #8 – 31 – 32 FORWARD *b.* Winchester, Massachusetts, May 3, 1963

| 1985–91 | 185 | 33 | 41 | 74 | 120 |
| Playoffs | 31 | 7 | 5 | 12 | 51 |

- Seventh Player Award: 1989–90
- Signed by Boston as a free agent, May 3, 1986

JOE CARVETH #9 FORWARD *b.* Regina, Saskatchewan, March 21, 1918

| 1946–48 | 73 | 29 | 24 | 53 | 12 |
| Playoffs | 5 | 2 | 1 | 3 | 0 |

- Traded to Boston from Detroit for Roy Conacher, 1946
- Traded by Boston to Montreal for John Quilty and Jimmy Peters, 1948

WAYNE CASHMAN #8 – 12 FORWARD *b.* Kingston, Ontario, June 24, 1945

1964–65, 1967–83					
Totals	1027	277	516	793	1041
Playoffs	145	31	57	88	250

- Second All-Star: 1974
- Member of the 1970 and 1972 Stanley Cup Champions

MURPH CHAMBERLAIN ("Old Hardrock") #19 FORWARD *b.* Shawville, Quebec, February 14, 1915

| 1942–43 | 45 | 9 | 24 | 33 | 67 |
| Playoffs | 6 | 1 | 1 | 2 | 12 |

- Obtained by Boston along with Buzz Boll when the New York Americans went defunct, 1942

Trivia Question #8
This former Bruins trainer was also the trainer for the Boston Red Sox. Can you name him?

ART CHAPMAN FORWARD *b.* Winnipeg, Manitoba, May 29, 1907

| 1930–34 | 159 | 24 | 29 | 53 | 65 |
| Playoffs | 10 | 0 | 1 | 1 | 9 |

- Sold to New York Americans, 1933

DICK CHERRY DEFENSE *b.* Kingston, Ontario, March 18, 1937

| 1956–57 | 6 | 0 | 0 | 0 | 4 |

- Drafted from Philadelphia by Boston in expansion draft, June 6, 1967. Drafted by Boston from Philadelphia in the intra-league draft, June 9, 1970

DON CHERRY ("Grapes") #24 DEFENSE *b.* Kingston, Ontario, February 5, 1934

| 1954–55 | 1 | 0 | 0 | 0 | 0 |

- Playoffs only
- Coach of the Boston Bruins (1974–75 to 1978–79)

DENIS CHERVYAKOV #43 DEFENSE *b.* Leningrad, USSR, April 20, 1970

| 1992–93 | 2 | 0 | 0 | 0 | 2 |

- Boston's ninth choice in the 1992 draft

REAL CHEVREFILS ("Chevy") #12 – 24 FORWARD *b.* Timmins, Ontario, May 2, 1932

| 1951–59 | 349 | 101 | 93 | 194 | 161 |
| Playoffs | 30 | 5 | 4 | 9 | 20 |

- Second All-Star: 1957

- Traded by Boston to Detroit along with Warren Godfrey, Gilles Boisvert, Eddie Sandford, and Norm Corcoran for Vic Stasiuk, Marcel Bonin, Lorne Davis and Terry Sawchuk, June 1955
- Traded from Detroit to Boston with Jerry Toppazzini for Lorne Ferguson and Murray Costello, January 17, 1956

ART CHISHOLM #12 FORWARD

| 1960–61 | 3 | 0 | 0 | 0 | 0 |

DAVE CHRISTIAN #27 FORWARD *b.* Warroad, Minnesota, May 12, 1959

| 1989–91 | 128 | 44 | 38 | 82 | 49 |
| Playoffs | 40 | 12 | 5 | 17 | 8 |

- Traded to Boston by Washington for Bobby Joyce, December 13, 1989

JACK CHURCH #18 DEFENSE *b.* Kamsack, Saskatchewan, May 24, 1915

| 1945–46 | 43 | 2 | 6 | 8 | 28 |
| Playoffs | 9 | 0 | 0 | 0 | 4 |

DEAN CHYNOWETH #28 DEFENSE *b.* Calgary, Alberta, October 30, 1968

| 1995–97 | 94 | 2 | 8 | 10 | 259 |
| Playoffs | 4 | 0 | 0 | 0 | 24 |

- Traded to Boston by the Islanders for a future draft pick, December 9, 1995

ROB CIMETTA #14 FORWARD *b.* Toronto, Ontario, February 15, 1970

| 1988–90 | 54 | 10 | 9 | 19 | 33 |
| Playoffs | 1 | 0 | 0 | 0 | 15 |

- Boston's first choice in the 1988 entry draft
- Traded by Boston to Toronto for Steve Bancroft, November 9, 1990

AUBREY CLAPPER ("Dit") #5 – 12
FORWARD/DEFENSE b. Newmarket, Ontario,
February 9, 1907

1927–47	833	228	246	474	462
Playoffs	86	13	17	30	50

- #5 is retired by the Bruins in his honor
- First All-Star: 1939 – 1940 – 1941
- Second All-Star: 1931 – 1935 – 1944
- Hall of Fame elected 1947
- Dufresne Trophy: 1939–40, 1940–41
- Member 1929, 1939, and 1941 Stanley Cup Champions
- Coach of the Boston Bruins, 1945–46 to 1948–49

ANDREW CLARK

1927–28	5	0	0	0	0

GORDIE CLARK FORWARD b. Glasgow,
Scotland, May 31, 1952

1974–76	8	0	1	1	0
Playoffs	1	0	0	0	0

- Boston's seventh choice in the 1972 amateur draft

SPRAGUE CLEGHORN ("Peg") #1 DEFENSE
b. Montreal, Quebec, March 11, 1890

1925–28	109	15	8	23	147
Playoffs	10	0	1	1	8

- Hall of Fame elected 1958

ROY CONACHER #9 FORWARD b. Toronto,
Ontario, October 5, 1916

1938–42, 1945–46					
Totals	166	94	51	145	40
Playoffs	37	11	11	22	12

- Traded by Boston to Detroit for Joe Carveth, 1946
- Member of the 1939 and 1941 Stanley Cup Champions

WAYNE CONNELLY #8 – 17 FORWARD
b. Rouyn, Quebec, December 16, 1939

1961–64, 1966–67					
Totals	169	25	38	63	60

- Sold to Boston by Montreal, June 10, 1961
- Drafted by Minnesota from Boston in the expansion draft, June 6, 1967

HARRY CONNOR #7 FORWARD b. Ottawa,
Ontario

1927–30	55	9	1	10	30
Playoffs	8	0	0	0	0

Trivia Question #9

Jimmy Bartlett, Jack Bionda, Marcel Bonin, Roger Jenkins, Al Pallazzari, Dave Pasin, Irvin Spencer, and Mats Thelin all have an unusual statistic that binds them together. What is it?

ALEX COOK ("Bud") b. Kingston, Ontario,
September 18, 1903

1931–32	28	4	4	8	14

FRED COOK ("Bun") #10 FORWARD
b. Kingston, Ontario, September 18, 1903

1936–37	40	4	5	9	8

- Sold by the Rangers to Boston, 1936

LLOYD COOK DEFENSE

1924–25	4	1	0	1	0

CARSON COOPER #7 FORWARD b. Cornwall,
Ontario

1924–27	58	33	6	39	14

- Traded by Boston to Montreal Canadiens for Billy Boucher, 1927

NORM CORCORAN FORWARD *b.* Toronto, Ontario, August 15, 1931

1949–50, 1952–53, 1954–55					
Totals	4	0	0	0	2
Playoffs	4	0	0	0	0

- Traded by Boston to Detroit along with Gilles Boisvert, Real Chevrefils, Warren Godfrey, and Eddie Sandford for Marcel Bonin, Lorne Davis, Vic Stasiuk, and Terry Sawchuk, June 1955

Trivia Question #10
This former Bruin, born in Helsinki, Finland, was a Calder Memorial Trophy winner with the Rangers. Who is he?

MARK CORNFORTH #40 DEFENSE *b.* Montreal, Quebec, November 13, 1972

1995–96	6	0	0	0	4

- Signed as a free agent by Boston, October 6, 1995

MURRAY COSTELLO #21 FORWARD *b.* South Porcupine, Ontario, February 24, 1934

1954–56	95	10	17	27	44
Playoffs	1	0	0	0	2

- Traded to Boston by Chicago for Frank Martin, October 4, 1954
- Traded by Boston to Detroit with Lorne Ferguson for Real Chevrefils, January 17, 1956

ALAIN CÔTÉ #26 – 37 – 40 DEFENSE *b.* Montmagny, Quebec, April 14, 1967

1985–89	68	2	9	11	65

- Boston's first choice in the 1985 entry draft
- Traded by Boston to Washington for Bobby Gould, September 28, 1989

GEOFF COURTNALL #14 – 32 – 34 FORWARD *b.* Duncan, British Columbia, August 18, 1962

1983–88	259	78	81	159	368
Playoffs	9	0	2	2	9

- Signed as a free agent by Boston, July 6, 1983
- Traded by Boston to Edmonton along with Bill Ranford for Andy Moog, March 8, 1988

BILLY COUTURE DEFENSE *b.* Sault Ste. Marie, Ontario

1926–27	41	1	1	2	25
Playoffs	7	1	0	1	4

BILL COWLEY #10 – 17 FORWARD *b.* Bristol, Quebec, June 12, 1912

1935–47	508	190	346	536	164
Playoffs	64	13	33	46	22

- First All-Star: 1938 – 1941 – 1943 – 1944
- Second All-Star: 1945
- Hall of Fame elected 1968
- Hart Trophy: 1940–41 & 1942–43
- Art Ross Trophy: 1940–41
- Dufresne Trophy: 1943–44
- Purchased along with Ted Graham when the St. Louis Eagles folded
- Member of the 1939 and 1941 Stanley Cup Champions

JOHN CRAWFORD ("Jack") #6 – 19 DEFENSE *b.* Dublin Ontario, October 26, 1916

1937–50	539	38	140	178	202
Playoffs	66	4	13	17	36

- First All-Star: 1946
- Second All-Star: 1943
- Dufresne Trophy: 1944–45, 1945–46
- Member of the 1939 and 1941 Stanley Cup Champions

LOU CRAWFORD #37 – 39 FORWARD *b.* Belleville, Ontario, November 5, 1962

1989–92	26	2	1	3	29
Playoffs	1	0	0	0	0

- Signed as a free agent by Boston, July 6, 1989

DAVE CREIGHTON #4 – 17 FORWARD b. Port Arthur, Ontario, June 24, 1930

| 1948–54 | 295 | 72 | 65 | 137 | 76 |
| Playoffs | 30 | 6 | 7 | 13 | 12 |

- Traded by Boston to Toronto for Fernie Flaman, 1954

TERRY CRISP #14 FORWARD b. Parry Sound, Ontario, May 28, 1934

| 1965–66 | 3 | 0 | 0 | 0 | 0 |

- Drafted from Boston by St. Louis in the expansion draft, June 6, 1967

BRUCE CROWDER #32 FORWARD b. Essex, Ontario, March 25, 1957

| 1981–84 | 217 | 43 | 44 | 87 | 133 |
| Playoffs | 31 | 8 | 4 | 12 | 43 |

- Signed as a free agent by Boston, September 29, 1981

KEITH CROWDER #18 FORWARD b. Windsor, Ontario, January 6, 1959

| 1980–89 | 607 | 219 | 258 | 477 | 1261 |
| Playoffs | 78 | 13 | 22 | 35 | 209 |

- Seventh Player Award: 1984–85

BILL CUPOLO #11 FORWARD b. Niagara Falls, Ontario, January 8, 1924

| 1944–45 | 47 | 11 | 13 | 24 | 10 |
| Playoffs | 7 | 1 | 2 | 3 | 0 |

BRIAN CURRAN #34 DEFENSE b. Toronto, Ontario, November 5, 1963

| 1983–86 | 115 | 3 | 7 | 10 | 407 |
| Playoffs | 5 | 0 | 0 | 0 | 11 |

- Boston's second pick in the 1982 entry draft

MARIUSZ CZERKAWSKI #19 FORWARD b. Radomsko, Poland, April 13, 1972

| 1993–96 | 84 | 19 | 21 | 40 | 41 |
| Playoffs | 18 | 4 | 3 | 7 | 4 |

- Traded by Boston to Edmonton along with Sean Brown and Boston's 1996 first-round draft pick for Bill Ranford, January 11, 1996

HAL DARRAGH ("Howl") FORWARD b. Ottawa, Ontario, September 13, 1902

| 1930–31 | 25 | 2 | 4 | 6 | 4 |
| Playoffs | 5 | 0 | 1 | 1 | 2 |

BOB DAVIE ("Pinkle") #10 – 16 FORWARD b. Beausejour, Manitoba, September 12, 1912

| 1933–36 | 41 | 0 | 1 | 1 | 25 |

LORNE DAVIS #24 FORWARD b. Regina, Saskatchewan, July 20, 1930

| 1955–60 | 25 | 1 | 2 | 3 | 10 |

- Traded to Boston by Detroit along with Marcel Bonin, Vic Stasiuk, and Terry Sawchuk for Gilles Boisvert, Real Chevrefils, Norm Corcoran, Warren Godfrey, and Eddie Sandford, June, 1955

MURRAY DAVISON DEFENSE b. Brantford, Ontario, June 10, 1938

| 1965–66 | 1 | 0 | 0 | 0 | 0 |

ARMAND DELMONTE ("Dutch") FORWARD b. Timmins, Ontario, June 3, 1927

| 1945–46 | 1 | 0 | 0 | 0 | 0 |

AB DEMARCO SR. #17 FORWARD b. North Bay, Ontario, May 10, 1916

| 1942–44 | 6 | 4 | 1 | 5 | 0 |
| Playoffs | 9 | 3 | 0 | 3 | 2 |

- Father of Ab DeMarco Jr., member of the Bruins in 1978–79

AB DEMARCO JR. #19 DEFENSE *b.* North Bay, Ontario, February 27, 1949

1978–79	3	0	0	0	0

- Signed as a free agent by Boston, October 23, 1978

CY DENNENY #16 FORWARD *b.* Cornwall, Ontario, 1897

1928–29	23	1	2	3	2
Playoffs	2	0	0	0	0

- Hall of Fame elected 1959
- Member 1929 Stanley Cup Champions
- Coach of the Boston Bruins, Stanley Cup Champions, 1928–29

BILL DERLAGO ("Billy D.") #14 FORWARD *b.* Birtle, Manitoba, August 25, 1958

1985–86	39	5	16	21	15

- Traded to Boston by Toronto for Tom Fergus, October 11, 1985
- Traded by Boston to Winnipeg for Wade Campbell, January 31, 1986

BOB DILLABOUGH #22 FORWARD *b.* Belleville, Ontario, April 14, 1941

1965–67	113	13	25	38	32

- Traded to Boston by Detroit along with Junior Langlois, Ron Harris, and Parker MacDonald for Ab McDonald, Bob McCord, and Ken Stephanson, May 31, 1965
- Drafted from Boston by Pittsburgh in the expansion draft, June 6, 1967

ROB DIMAIO #19 FORWARD *b.* Calgary, Alberta, February 19, 1968

1995–96	72	13	15	28	82

- Claimed on waivers from San Jose, September 30, 1996

GARY DOAK #25 DEFENSE *b.* Goderich, Ontario, February 26, 1946

1965–70, 1972–81					
Totals	609	20	80	100	656
Playoffs	66	2	4	6	75

- Traded to Boston from Detroit with Bill Lesuk and Ron Murphy for Leo Boivin and Dean Prentice, February 18, 1966
- Drafted from Boston by Vancouver in the expansion draft, June 10, 1970
- Traded to Boston by Detroit for Garnet Bailey, March 1, 1973
- Seventh Player Award: 1976–77
- Member of the 1970 Stanley Cup Champions

BRIAN DOBBIN #51 FORWARD *b.* Petrolia, Ontario, August 18, 1966

1991–92	7	1	0	1	22

- Traded to Boston by Philadelphia with Gord Murphy for Garry Galley and Wes Walz, January 2, 1992

> ### Trivia Question #11
> The Bruins' first Stanley Cup, won in 1928–29, was led by the "Dynamite Line." Name the 3 members of this line.

CLARK DONATELLI #50 FORWARD *b.* Providence, Rhode Island, November 22, 1967

1991–92	10	0	1	1	22
Playoffs	2	0	0	0	0

- Signed as a free agent by Boston, March 10, 1992

TED DONATO #21 – 46 FORWARD *b.* Boston, Massachusetts, April 28, 1969

1991–97	372	96	116	212	221
Playoffs	42	8	9	17	20

- Boston's sixth choice in the 1987 entry draft

DAVE DONNELLY #29 FORWARD
b. Edmonton, Alberta, February 2, 1962

1983–86	62	9	12	21	66
Playoffs	4	0	0	0	0

- Traded to Boston by Minnesota for Brad Palmer, June 9, 1982
- Traded by Boston to Detroit for Dwight Foster, March 11, 1986

GARY DORNHOEFER #8 – 27 FORWARD
b. Kitchener, Ontario, February 2, 1943

1963–66	62	12	12	24	35

- Drafted from Boston by Philadelphia in the expansion draft, June 6, 1967

PETER DOURIS #16 FORWARD b. Toronto, Ontario, February 19, 1966

1989–93	148	24	25	49	38
Playoffs	26	3	5	8	11

- Signed as a free agent by Boston, June 27, 1989

P.C. DROUIN #40 FORWARD b. St. Lambert, Quebec, April 22, 1974

1996–97	3	0	0	0	0

LUC DUFOUR #29 FORWARD b. Chicoutimi, Quebec, February 13, 1963

1982–84	114	20	15	35	154
Playoffs	17	1	0	1	30

- Traded by Boston to Quebec for Louis Sleigher, October 25, 1984

LORNE DUGUID #16 FORWARD b. Bolton, Ontario, April 4, 1910

1935–37	30	2	4	6	4

WOODY DUMART ("Porky") #14 FORWARD
b. Kitchener, Ontario, December 23, 1916

1935–42, 1945–54					
Totals	771	211	218	429	99
Playoffs	88	12	15	27	23

- Second All-Star: 1940 – 1941 – 1947
- Hall of Fame elected 1992
- Dufresne Trophy: 1941–42
- Member of the 1939 and 1941 Stanley Cup Champions

DALE DUNBAR #45 DEFENSE b. Winthrop, Massachusetts, October 14, 1961

1988–89	1	0	0	0	0

DARRYL EDESTRAND #6 DEFENSE
b. Strathroy, Ontario, November 6, 1945

1973–78	215	8	37	45	195
Playoffs	24	2	6	8	47

- Traded to Boston by Pittsburgh for Nick Beverley, October 25, 1973
- Sold by Boston to Los Angeles, March 13, 1978

MARTIN "PAT" EGAN #2 – 4 DEFENSE
b. Blackie, Alberta, April 25, 1918

1943–49	294	47	85	132	435
Playoffs	32	6	3	9	38

- Traded to Boston by Detroit for Flash Hollett, January 5, 1944
- Dufresne Trophy: 1948–49

GERRY "TEX" EHMAN FORWARD b. Cudworth, Saskatchewan, November 3, 1932

1957–58	1	1	0	1	0

- Drafted from Boston by Detroit, June 4, 1958

TODD ELIK #20 FORWARD b. Brampton, Ontario, April 15, 1966

1995–97	90	17	45	62	56
Playoffs	4	0	2	2	16

- Signed by Boston as a free agent, August 8, 1995

LEIGHTON EMMS ("Hap")
FORWARD/DEFENSE *b.* Barrie, Ontario,
January 16, 1905

1934–35	11	1	1	2	8

- Sold October 28, 1934 from Detroit

AUT ERICKSON #11 DEFENSE *b.* Lethbridge,
Alberta, January 25, 1938

1959–61	126	3	12	15	94

- Drafted by Boston from Chicago, June 1959
- Drafted by Chicago from Boston, June 1961

GRANT ERICKSON FORWARD *b.* Pierceland,
Saskatchewan, April 28, 1947

1968–69	2	1	0	1	0

Trivia Question #12
During the early 1970's, a popular movie had a title with an amazing resemblance to the top 4 Bruins defensemen of that era. Can you name the movie and the defensemen?

PHIL ESPOSITO #7 FORWARD *b.* Sault Ste.
Marie, Ontario, February 20, 1942

1967–76	625	459	553	1012	512
Playoffs	71	46	56	102	81

- #7 is retired by the Bruins in his honor
- First All-Star: 1969 – 1970 – 1971 – 1972 – 1973 – 1974
- Second All-Star: 1968 – 1975
- Hall of Fame elected 1984
- Hart Trophy: 1968–69 & 1973–74
- Art Ross Trophy: 1968–69, 1970–71, 1971–72, 1972–73, 1973–74
- Dufresne Trophy: 1967–68, 1968–69, 1970–71, 1972–73, 1973–74
- Traded to Boston by Chicago along with Fred Stanfield and Ken Hodge for Gilles Marotte, Pit Martin, and Jack Norris, May 15, 1967

- Traded by Boston to the Rangers along with Carol Vadnais for Brad Park, Jean Ratelle, and Joe Zanussi, November 7, 1975
- Member of the 1970 and 1972 Stanley Cup Champions

BILL EZINICKI #21 FORWARD *b.* Winnipeg,
Manitoba, March 11, 1924

1950–52	81	21	24	45	166
Playoffs	6	1	1	2	18

- Traded to Boston by Toronto along with Vic Lynn for Fernie Flaman, Ken Smith, and Phil Maloney, November 16, 1950
- Sold to Toronto by Boston, September 14, 1952

Trivia Question #13
This maskless netminder was the last goalie in the NHL to play in all of his teams' games. He was a former Bruin who accomplished this feat while tending the Boston nets. Can you name him?

GLEN FEATHERSTONE #6 DEFENSE
b. Toronto, Ontario, July 8, 1968

1991–94	99	7	13	20	274
Playoffs	1	0	0	0	0

- Signed by Boston as a free agent, July 25, 1991
- Traded by Boston to the Rangers for Daniel Lacroix, August 19, 1994

TOM FERGUS #28 FORWARD *b.* Chicago,
Illinois, June 16, 1962

1981–85	289	98	138	236	138
Playoffs	29	7	2	9	28

- Traded by Boston to Toronto for Bill Derlago, October 11, 1985
- Boston's second choice in the 1980 entry draft

LORNE FERGUSON #12 – 23 – 24 FORWARD
b. Palmerston, Ontario, May 26, 1930

1949–52, 1954–56					
Totals	201	47	41	88	87
Playoffs	10	2	0	2	4

- Traded by Boston to Detroit with Murray Costello, for Jerry Toppazzini and Real Chevrefils, 1955

GUYLE FIELDER #20 FORWARD *b.* Potlatch, Idaho, November 21, 1930

1953–54	2	0	0	0	2

- Playoffs only
- Sold to Boston by Detroit, September 24, 1953
- Purchased from Boston by Detroit, June 5, 1957

MARCEL FILION FORWARD *b.* Thetford Mines, Quebec, May 28, 1923

1944–45	1	0	0	0	0

TOM FILMORE FORWARD *b.* Thamesford, Ontario, 1906

1933–34	3	0	0	0	0

EDDIE FINNIGAN *b.* Shawville, Quebec

1935–36	3	0	0	0	0

DUNCAN FISHER #9 FORWARD *b.* Regina, Saskatchewan, August 30, 1927

1950–53	129	24	33	57	22
Playoffs	8	1	0	1	0

- Traded to Boston by the Rangers for Ed Harrison and Zelio Toppazzini, November 16, 1950

FERDINAND FLAMAN ("Fernie") #4 – 10 – 14 DEFENSE *b.* Dysart, Saskatchewan, January 25, 1927

1944–51, 1954–61					
Totals	682	30	147	177	1002
Playoffs	48	3	6	9	67

- Second All-Star: 1955 – 1957 – 1958
- Hall of Fame elected 1990
- Traded by Boston to Toronto with Ken Smith and Phil Maloney for Bill Ezinicki and Vic Lynn, November 16, 1950
- Traded to Boston by Toronto for Dave Creighton, July 20, 1954

Trivia Question #14
What do Cam Neely and
Al Iafrate have in common?

REGGIE FLEMING #19 FORWARD
b. Montreal, Quebec, April 21, 1936

1964–66	101	22	29	51	178

- Traded to Boston from Chicago with Ab McDonald for Doug Mohns, June 8, 1964
- Traded by Boston to the Rangers for John McKenzie, January 10, 1966

RON FLOCKHART #36 FORWARD *b.* Smithers, British Columbia, October 10, 1960

1988–89	4	0	0	0	0

- Traded to Boston by St. Louis for future considerations, February 13, 1989

DAVE FORBES #14 FORWARD *b.* Montreal, Quebec, November 16, 1948

1973–77	284	53	52	105	220
Playoffs	45	1	4	5	13

- Claimed from Boston by Washington in waiver draft, October 10, 1977

MIKE FORBES #6 DEFENSE *b.* Brampton, Ontario, September 20, 1957

1977–78	32	0	4	4	15

- Claimed from Boston by Edmonton in the expansion draft, June 13, 1979

DWIGHT FOSTER #20 – 27 FORWARD
b. Toronto, Ontario, April 2, 1957

1977–81, 1985–87					
Totals	252	51	82	133	165
Playoffs	29	5	11	16	4

- Boston's first choice in the 1977 amateur draft
- Traded to Boston by Detroit for Dave Donnelly, March 11, 1986

HARRY FOSTER ("Yip") DEFENSE b. Guelph, Ontario, November 25, 1907

1931–32	34	1	2	3	12

FRANK FREDERICKSON #5 FORWARD
b. Winnipeg, Manitoba

1926–29	84	27	12	39	140
Playoffs	10	2	5	7	26

- Hall of Fame elected 1958
- Traded to Boston from Detroit for Duke Keats, 1926
- Traded by Boston to Pittsburgh for Mickey Mackay, 1929
- Member of the 1929 Stanley Cup Champions

HARRY FROST #19 FORWARD b. Kerr Lake, Ontario, August 17, 1914

1938–39	3	0	0	0	0
Playoffs	1	0	0	0	0

ART GAGNE FORWARD

1929–30	6	0	1	1	6

PIERRE GAGNE FORWARD b. North Bay, Ontario, June 5, 1940

1959–60	2	0	0	0	0

JOHNNY GAGNON ("Black Cat") FORWARD
b. Chicoutimi, Quebec, June 8, 1905

1934–35	24	1	1	2	9

- Sold to the Montreal Canadiens, 1935

NORMAN GAINOR ("Dutch") #8 FORWARD
b. Calgary, Alberta, April 10, 1904

1927–31	155	48	43	91	118
Playoffs	18	2	1	3	12

- Sold to the Rangers, 1931
- Member of the 1929 Stanley Cup Champions

Trivia Question #15
The "BOW" line was named after what 3 Boston forwards of the early to mid-1960s?

PERCY GALBRAITH ("Perk") #6 FORWARD
b. Toronto, Ontario, 1899

1926–34	345	29	31	60	223
Playoffs	31	4	7	11	24

- Member 1929 Stanley Cup Champions

GARRY GALLEY #28 DEFENSE b. Montreal, Quebec, April 16, 1963

1988–92	257	24	82	106	322
Playoffs	46	4	9	13	84

- Signed by Boston as a free agent, July 8, 1988
- Traded by Boston to Philadelphia with Wes Walz for Gord Murphy and Brian Dobbin

DON GALLINGER #11 FORWARD b. Port Colborne, Ontario, April 10, 1925

1942–44, 1945–48					
Totals	222	65	88	153	89
Playoffs	23	5	5	10	19

- Suspended by the NHL for betting on games

CAL GARDNER ("Ginger"/"Red") #9 FORWARD b. Transcona, Manitoba, October 30, 1924

1953–57	280	57	83	140	225
Playoffs	19	3	2	5	6

- Claimed on waivers from Chicago, 1953

RAY GARIEPY ("Rockabye Ray") #24
DEFENSE b. Toronto, Ontario, September 4, 1928

1953–54	35	1	6	7	39

- Purchased from Boston by Toronto, September 23, 1955

ARMAND GAUDREAULT #14 FORWARD
b. Lake Saint John, Quebec, July 14, 1921

1944–45	44	15	9	24	27
Playoffs	7	0	2	2	8

JEAN GAUTHIER #27 DEFENSE b. Montreal, Quebec, April 29, 1937

1968–69	11	0	2	2	8

- Drafted by Boston from Philadelphia, June 12, 1968
- Claimed by Montreal from Boston in the reverse draft, June 12, 1969

JEAN-GUY GENDRON ("Smitty") #23
FORWARD b. Montreal, Quebec, August 30, 1934

1958–64	260	66	62	128	230
Playoffs	7	1	0	1	18

- Drafted by Boston with Gord Redahl from the Rangers, June 4, 1958
- Traded by Boston to Montreal for Andre Pronovost, November 27, 1960
- Drafted by Boston from the Rangers, June 1, 1962

GEORGE GERAN ("Jerry") FORWARD
b. Holyoke, Massachusetts, August 3, 1896

1925–26	33	5	1	6	6

RAY GETLIFFE #6 – 8 – 15 FORWARD b. Galt, Ontario, April 3, 1914

1935–39	128	37	40	77	57
Playoffs	19	3	3	6	6

- Traded by Boston along with Charlie Sands to the Montreal Canadiens for Herb Cain, 1940

- Member of the 1939 Stanley Cup Champions

BARRY GIBBS #24 DEFENSE b. Lloydminster, Saskatchewan, July 18, 1943

1967–69	24	0	0	0	4

- Traded by Boston along with Tommy Williams to Minnesota for Fred O'Donnell and Minnesota's first draft choice in the 1969 amateur draft, May 7, 1969

DOUG GIBSON #33 – 27 – 28 FORWARD
b. Peterborough, Ontario, September 28, 1953

1973–76	52	7	18	25	0
Playoffs	1	0	0	0	0

- Claimed on waivers by Washington from Boston, May 29, 1977

JEANNOT GILBERT #8 FORWARD b. Grande Baie, Quebec, December 29, 1940

1962–65	9	0	0	0	4

- Drafted from Boston by Pittsburgh in the expansion draft, June 6, 1967

MIKE GILLIS #14 – 22 – 34 FORWARD
b. Sudbury, Ontario, December 1, 1958

1980–84	125	17	24	41	104
Playoffs	27	2	5	7	10

- Traded to Boston from Colorado for Bob Miller, February 18, 1981

ART GIROUX FORWARD b. Strathmore, Alberta, June 6, 1907

1934–35	10	1	0	1	0

PAUL GLADU #19 FORWARD b. St. Hyacinthe, Quebec, June 20, 1922

1944–45	40	6	14	20	2
Playoffs	7	2	2	4	0

MATT GLENNON #39 FORWARD *b.* Hull, Massachusetts, September 20, 1968

1991–92	3	0	0	0	2

- Boston's seventh choice in the 1987 entry draft

WARREN GODFREY ("Rocky") #6 – 25 DEFENSE *b.* Toronto, Ontario, March 23, 1931

1952–55, 1962–63					
Totals	258	9	28	57	225
Playoffs	18	0	1	1	6

- Traded by Boston along with Gilles Boisvert, Real Chevrefils, Norm Corcoran, and Eddie Sandford to Detroit for Marcel Bonin, Lorne Davis, Terry Sawchuk, and Vic Stasiuk, June 1955
- Drafted by Boston from Detroit, June 1962
- Traded by Boston to Detroit for Gerry Odrowski, October 10, 1963

BILL GOLDSWORTHY #26 – 28 FORWARD *b.* Waterloo, Ontario, August 24, 1944

1964–67	33	6	6	12	27

- Drafted by Minnesota from Boston in the expansion draft, June 6, 1967

ROY GOLDSWORTHY #9 DEFENSE/FORWARD *b.* Two Harbors, Minnesota, October 18, 1908

1936–38	92	17	16	33	22
Playoffs	6	0	0	0	2

- Sold to the Americans, 1939

FRED GORDON #10 FORWARD

1927–28	41	3	2	5	40
Playoffs	1	0	0	0	0

BUTCH GORING #22 FORWARD *b.* St. Boniface, Manitoba, October 22, 1959

1984–85	39	13	21	34	6
Playoffs	5	1	1	2	0

- Claimed on waivers by Boston from the New York Islanders, January 8, 1985
- Coach of the Boston Bruins (1985–86 to 1986–87)

BOB GOULD #18 FORWARD *b.* Petrolia, Ontario, September 2, 1957

1989–90	77	8	17	25	92
Playoffs	17	0	0	0	4

- Traded to Boston by Washington for Alain Cote, September 28, 1989

BOB GRACIE #6 FORWARD *b.* North Bay, Ontario, November 8, 1910

1933–34	24	2	6	8	16

- Bought from Toronto, 1933
- Sold to the Americans, 1934

THOMAS GRADIN #10 FORWARD *b.* Solleftea, Sweden, February 18, 1956

1986–87	64	12	31	43	18
Playoffs	4	0	4	4	0

- Signed as a free agent, June 24, 1986

ROD GRAHAM #27 FORWARD *b.* London, Ontario, August 19, 1946

1974–75	14	2	1	3	7

EDWARD GRAHAM ("Ted") #4 DEFENSE *b.* Owen Sound, Ontario, June 30, 1906

1935–36	48	4	1	5	37
Playoffs	2	0	0	0	2

- Traded by Boston to the Americans for Walt Kalbfleisch, 1936

TERRY GRAY #12 FORWARD *b.* Montreal, Quebec, March 21, 1938

1961–62	42	8	7	15	15

- Traded to Boston from Montreal for Stan Maxwell and Willie O'Ree, 1961

REDVERS GREEN #7 FORWARD *b.* Sudbury, Ontario

1928–29	25	0	0	0	16

- Member of the 1929 Stanley Cup Champions

A SALUTE TO THE COURAGEOUS TED GREEN

TED GREEN #6 DEFENSE *b.* St. Boniface, Manitoba, March 23, 1940

1960–69, 1970–72					
Totals	620	48	206	254	1029
Playoffs	31	4	8	12	54

- Second All-Star: 1969
- Dufresne Trophy: 1964–65
- Member of the 1972 Stanley Cup Champions

LLOYD GRONSDAHL FORWARD *b.* Norquay, Saskatchewan, May 10, 1921

1941–42	10	1	2	3	0

LLOYD GROSS FORWARD *b.* Kitchener, Ontario, October 15, 1907

1933–34	6	1	0	1	6

DON GROSSO ("Count") #19 FORWARD *b.* Sault Ste. Marie, Ontario, April 12, 1915

1946–47	33	0	2	2	2

- Obtained from Chicago, 1946

JOHN GRUDEN #36 DEFENSE *b.* Hastings, Minnesota, April 6, 1970

1993–96	59	0	7	7	28
Playoffs	3	0	1	1	0

- Boston's seventh draft choice in the 1990 amateur draft

> ### *Trivia Question #16*
> Of all the Bruins' retired numbers, 2, 3, 4, 5, 7, 9, and 15, all but 2 of the numbers were worn after the player retired. What were the 2 numbers?

BOB GRYP #28 FORWARD *b.* Chatham, Ontario, May 6, 1950

1973–74	1	0	0	0	0

- Drafted by Washington from Boston in the expansion draft, June 12, 1974

PAUL GUAY #37 FORWARD *b.* Providence, Rhode Island, September 2, 1963

1988–89	5	0	2	2	0

- Traded to Boston by Los Angeles for the rights to Dave Pasin, November 3, 1988

ARMAND GUIDOLIN ("Bep") #12 FORWARD
b. Thorold, Ontario, December 9, 1925

1942–44, 1945–47					
Totals	195	49	70	119	236
Playoffs	22	5	7	12	31

- Traded by Boston to Detroit for Billy Taylor, 1947
- Coach of the Boston Bruins (1972–73 to 1973–74)

MATTI HAGMAN #28 FORWARD b. Helsinki, Finland, September 21, 1955

1976–78	90	15	18	33	2
Playoffs	8	0	1	1	0

- Boston's sixth choice in the 1975 draft

TAYLOR HALL #23 FORWARD b. Regina, Saskatchewan, February 20, 1964

1987–88	7	0	0	0	4

- Signed as a free agent by Boston, July 20, 1987

DOUG HALWARD #29 DEFENSE b. Toronto, Ontario, November 1, 1955

1975–78	65	3	9	12	14
Playoffs	7	0	0	0	4

- Traded by Boston to Los Angeles for future considerations, September 18, 1978

ROBERT HAMILL ("Red") #11 – 18 FORWARD
b. Toronto, Ontario, January 11, 1918

1937–42	58	16	14	30	20
Playoffs	16	0	1	1	13

- Member of the 1939 Stanley Cup Champions

KEN HAMMOND #55 DEFENSE b. Port Credit, Ontario, August 22, 1963

1990–91	1	1	0	1	2
Playoffs	8	0	0	0	10

- Traded to Boston by Toronto for cash, August 20, 1990

BRETT HARKINS #40 – 65 FORWARD
b. North Ridgeville, Ohio, July 2, 1970

1994–97	47	4	15	19	8

- Signed as a free agent by Boston, July 1, 1994

WALTER HARNOTT ("Happy") FORWARD
b. Montreal, Quebec, September 24, 1912

1933–34	6	0	0	0	6

LELAND HARRINGTON ("Hago") #14 FORWARD b. Melrose, Massachusetts,

1925–28	48	8	2	10	13
Playoffs	2	0	0	0	0

FRED HARRIS ("Smokey") FORWARD

1924–31	40	5	5	10	28
Playoffs	2	0	0	0	0

ED HARRISON #16 FORWARD b. Mimico, Ontario, July 25, 1927

1947–51	190	26	24	50	51
Playoffs	9	1	0	1	2

- Cousin of Bruin Eddie Sandford (1947–48 to 1954–55)
- Traded by Boston along with Zelio Toppazzini to the New York Rangers for Dunc Fisher, November 16, 1950

JIM HARRISON #21 FORWARD b. North Kamloops, British Columbia, June 2, 1947

1968–70	39	4	3	7	37

- Traded by Boston to Toronto for Wayne Carleton, December 10, 1969

GREG HAWGOOD #35 – 38 DEFENSE
b. Edmonton, Alberta, August 10, 1968

1987–90	134	27	51	78	160
Playoffs	28	2	5	7	14

- Traded by Boston to Edmonton for Vladimir Ruzicka, October 22, 1990

CHRIS HAYES #27 FORWARD *b.* Rouyn, Quebec, August 24, 1946

1971–72	1	0	0	0	0

- Playoffs only
- Member of the 1972 Stanley Cup Champions

PAUL HAYNES #17 FORWARD *b.* Montreal, Quebec, March 1, 1910

1934–35	37	4	3	7	8
Playoffs	4	0	0	0	0

- Purchased from the Montreal Maroons, 1934

FERN HEADLEY FORWARD *b.* Christie, North Dakota, March 2, 1901

1924–25	11	0	1	1	2

ANDY HEBENTON #12 FORWARD *b.* Winnipeg, Manitoba, October 3, 1929

1963–64	70	12	11	23	8

- Drafted by Boston from the Rangers, 1963
- Traded by Boston along with Orland Kurtenbach and Pat Stapleton to Toronto for Ron Stewart, June 8, 1965

LIONEL HEINRICH #6 DEFENSE/FORWARD *b.* Churchbridge, Saskatchewan, April 20, 1934

1955–56	35	1	1	2	33

STEVE HEINZE #23 – 45 FORWARD *b.* Lawrence, Massachusetts, January 30, 1970

1991–97	306	71	57	128	155
Playoffs	34	4	8	12	30

- Boston's 2nd pick in the 1988 draft

MURRAY HENDERSON ("Moe") #8 DEFENSE *b.* Toronto, Ontario, September 5, 1921

1944–52	405	24	62	86	305
Playoffs	41	2	3	5	23

> ## *Trivia Question #17*
> On February 23, 1972, Fred Stanfield scored 3 goals against the California Golden Seals. What is unusual about this feat?

JIMMY HERBERTS #4 FORWARD/DEFENSE *b.* Collingwood, Ontario, 1897

1924–27	101	58	17	75	148
Playoffs	8	3	0	3	33

- Sold to Toronto, 1927

PHIL HERGESHEIMER FORWARD *b.* Winnipeg, Manitoba, July 9, 1914

1941–42	3	0	0	0	2

MATT HERVEY #43 DEFENSE *b.* Whittier, California, May 16, 1966

1991–92	16	0	1	1	55
Playoffs	5	0	0	0	4

- Signed as a free agent, August 15, 1991
- Traded by Boston with Ken Hodge Jr. to Tampa Bay for Darin Kimble, September 4, 1992

ORVILLE HEXIMER ("Obs") FORWARD *b.* Niagara Falls, Ontario, February 16, 1910

1932–33	48	7	5	12	24
Playoffs	5	0	0	0	2

WAYNE HICKS #12 FORWARD *b.* Aberdeen, Washington, April 9, 1937

1962–63	65	7	9	16	14

MEL HILL ("Sudden Death") #11 – 16 – 18 FORWARD *b.* Glenboro, Manitoba, February 15, 1914

1937–41	130	26	25	51	41
Playoffs	24	7	4	11	12

- Member of the 1939 and 1941 Stanley Cup Champions

WILBERT HILLER ("Dutch") #12 FORWARD
b. Kitchener, Ontario, May 11, 1915

1941–42	43	7	10	17	19
Playoffs	5	0	1	1	0

- Traded November, 1941 to Boston

RANDY HILLIER #23 DEFENSE b. Toronto, Ontario, March 30, 1960

1981–84	164	3	30	33	253
Playoffs	11	0	1	1	20

- Traded by Boston to Pittsburgh for a future draft pick, October 15, 1984

FLOYD HILLMAN DEFENSE b. Ruthven, Ontario, November 19, 1933

1956–57	6	0	0	0	10

LARRY HILLMAN #22 DEFENSE b. Kirkland Lake, Ontario, February 5, 1937

1957–60	127	6	30	36	81
Playoffs	18	0	3	3	6

- Claimed on waivers by Boston from Chicago, October 1957
- Claimed on waivers from Boston by Toronto, June 1960

LIONEL HITCHMAN #3 DEFENSE b. Toronto, Ontario, 1903

1924–34	377	26	26	52	466
Playoffs	31	3	1	4	52

- #3 is retired by the Bruins in his honor
- Member of the 1929 Stanley Cup Champions

KEN HODGE JR. #10 FORWARD b. Windsor, Ontario, April 13, 1966

1990–92	112	36	40	76	30
Playoffs	15	4	6	10	6

- Traded to Boston by Minnesota for future considerations, August 21, 1990
- Traded by Boston along with Matt Hervey to Tampa Bay for Darin Kimble, September 4, 1992
- Son of former Bruin, Ken Hodge, 1967 to 1976

KEN HODGE SR. #8 FORWARD
b. Birmingham, England, June 25, 1944

1967–76	652	289	385	674	620
Playoffs	86	34	47	81	118

- First All-Star: 1971 – 1974
- Seventh Player Award: 1990–91
- Traded to Boston along with Phil Esposito and Fred Stanfield by Chicago for Jack Norris, Pit Martin, and Gilles Marotte, May 15, 1967
- Member of the 1970 and 1972 Stanley Cup Champions

TED HODGSON #24 FORWARD b. Hobbema, Alberta, June 30, 1945

1966–67	4	0	0	0	0

WILLIAM HOLLETT ("Flash") #2 – 3 – 12 DEFENSE/FORWARD b. North Sydney, Nova Scotia, April 13, 1912

1935–44	357	84	115	199	218
Playoffs	48	5	20	25	20

- Purchased from Toronto, 1936
- Traded by Boston to Detroit for Pat Egan, January 5, 1944
- Second All-Star: 1943
- Member of the 1939 and 1941 Stanley Cup Champions

RON HOOVER #44 FORWARD b. Oakville, Ontario, October 28, 1966

1989–91	17	4	0	4	31
Playoffs	8	0	0	0	18

- Signed as a free agent by Boston, September 1, 1989

PETE HORECK #24 FORWARD *b.* Massey, Ontario, June 15, 1923

1949–51	100	15	18	33	79
Playoffs	4	0	0	0	13

- Traded to Boston along with Bill Quackenbush from Detroit for Lloyd Dunham, Pete Babando, Clare Martin, and Jimmy Peters, August 6, 1949

JOSEPH HORVATH ("Bronco") #6 FORWARD *b.* Port Colborne, Ontario, March 12, 1930

1957–61	227	103	112	215	204
Playoffs	19	7	6	13	8

- Second All-Star: 1960
- Dufresne Trophy: 1959–60
- Drafted by Boston from Montreal, June 5, 1957
- Drafted by Chicago from Boston, June 1961

MARTY HOWE #27 DEFENSE *b.* Detroit, Michigan, February 18, 1954

1982–83	78	1	11	12	24
Playoffs	12	0	1	1	9

- Son of Hall of Famer, Gordie Howe
- Signed as a free agent by Boston, October 1, 1982
- Signed by Hartford, August 1983

BILL HUARD #61 FORWARD *b.* Welland, Ontario, June 24, 1967

1992–93	2	0	0	0	0

- Signed as a free agent by Boston, December 4, 1992

BRENT HUGHES #18 – 42 FORWARD *b.* New Westminster, British Columbia, April 5, 1966

1991–95	191	25	22	47	511
Playoffs	29	4	1	5	53

- Traded to Boston by Washington for John Byce and Dennis Smith, February 24, 1992

RYAN HUGHES #47 FORWARD *b.* Montreal, Quebec, January 17, 1972

1995–96	3	0	0	0	0

- Signed as a free agent by Boston, October 6, 1995

PAUL HURLEY #27 DEFENSE *b.* Melrose, Massachusetts, July 12, 1946

1968–69	1	0	1	1	0

JAMIE HUSCROFT #28 DEFENSE *b.* Creston, British Columbia, January 9, 1967

1993–95	70	0	7	7	247
Playoffs	9	0	0	0	20

- Signed as a free agent by Boston, July 23, 1992

BILL HUTTON #15 DEFENSE *b.* Calgary, Alberta, January 28, 1910

1929–31	25	2	0	2	4

DAVE HYNES #27 FORWARD *b.* Cambridge, Massachusetts, April 17, 1951

1973–75	22	4	0	4	2

- Boston's fifth choice in the 1971 amateur draft

GORD HYNES #47 DEFENSE *b.* Montreal, Quebec, July 22, 1966

1991–92	15	0	5	5	6
Playoffs	12	1	2	3	6

- Boston's 5th choice in the 1985 amateur draft

AL IAFRATE #43 DEFENSE *b.* Dearborn, Michigan, March 21, 1996

1993–94	12	5	8	13	20
Playoffs	12	5	8	13	6

- Traded to Boston from Washington for Joe Juneau, March 21, 1994
- Traded by Boston to San Jose for Jeff Odgers, June 21, 1966

JACK INGRAM FORWARD *b.* Graven, Saskatchewan, September 17, 1907

1924–25	I	O	O	O	O

TED IRVINE FORWARD *b.* Winnipeg, Manitoba, December 8, 1944

1963–64	I	O	O	O	O

- Drafted from Boston by Los Angeles in the expansion draft, June 6, 1967

Trivia Question #18
What former baseball Cy Young Award winner once appeared in a Bruins media guide?

ART JACKSON #16 – 18 FORWARD *b.* Toronto, Ontario, December 15, 1915

1937–38, 1939–45					
Totals	305	87	131	218	103
Playoffs	33	8	9	17	23

- Sold to Toronto, 1944
- Member of the 1941 Stanley Cup Champions

HARVEY JACKSON ("Busher") #16 – 18 FORWARD *b.* Toronto, Ontario, January 17, 1911

1941–44	113	35	43	78	81
Playoffs	14	I	3	4	10

- Hall of Fame elected 1971
- Purchased from the New York Americans, 1941

STAN JACKSON FORWARD *b.* Amherst, Nova Scotia, 1898

1924–26	52	8	3	II	66

CRAIG JANNEY #23 FORWARD *b.* Hartford, Connecticut, September 26, 1967

1987–92	262	85	198	283	44
Playoffs	69	17	56	73	45

- Boston's first round pick in the entry 1986 draft
- Traded by Boston along with Stephane Quintal to St. Louis for Adam Oates, February 7, 1992

ROGER JENKINS #8 DEFENSE *b.* Appleton, Wisconsin, November 18, 1911

1935–36	42	2	6	8	51
Playoffs	2	O	I	I	2

- Acquired from Montreal Canadiens, 1935

BILL JENNINGS #17 FORWARD *b.* Toronto, Ontario, June 28, 1917

1944–45	39	20	13	33	25
Playoffs	7	2	2	4	6

ED JEREMIAH DEFENSE/FORWARD *b.* Worcester, Massachusetts, November 4, 1905

1932–33	6	O	O	O	O

FRANK JERWA DEFENSE/FORWARD *b.* Bankhead, Alberta, February 28, 1910

1931–35	75	7	9	16	39

JOE JERWA #4 DEFENSE *b.* Bankhead, Alberta, January 20, 1908

1931–32, 1933–34, 1936–37					
Totals	35	3	5	8	46

- Purchased from Boston by the Americans 1934
- Traded to Boston by the Americans for Joe Jerwa, 1936

NORM JOHNSON #18 FORWARD *b.* Moose Jaw, Saskatchewan, November 27, 1932

1957–58	15	2	3	5	8
Playoffs	12	4	O	4	6

- Placed on waivers and claimed by Chicago, January 1959

TOM JOHNSON #10 DEFENSE b. Baldur, Manitoba, February 18, 1928

1963–65	121	4	30	34	63

- Hall of Fame elected 1970
- Claimed on waivers by Boston from Montreal, June 4, 1963
- Coach of the Boston Bruins, (1970–71 to 1972–73)
- Coach of the Boston Bruins, Stanley Cup Champions, 1971–72

GREG JOHNSTON #29 – 33 – 39 FORWARD b. Barrie, Ontario, January 14, 1965

1983–90	183	26	28	54	119
Playoffs	22	2	1	3	12

- Traded by Boston to the Rangers for Chris Nilan, June 28, 1990
- Boston's second pick in the 1983 entry draft

Trivia Question #19

Besides scoring the first goal in both venues, what do the scorers of the first goal at Boston Garden and the first goal at the FleetCenter have in common? What are their names?

STAN JONATHAN #17 FORWARD b. Ohsweken, Ontario, May 9, 1955

1975–83	391	91	107	198	738
Playoffs	63	8	4	12	137

- Seventh Player Award: 1977–78
- Boston's fifth choice in the 1975 draft
- Traded by Boston to Pittsburgh for future considerations, November 8, 1982

RON JONES DEFENSE b. Vermillion, Alberta, April 11, 1951

1971–73	8	0	0	0	2

- Boston's first choice in the 1971 amateur draft
- Drafted from Boston by Pittsburgh in the intraleague draft, June 12, 1973

BOBBY JOYCE #27 FORWARD b. Saint John, New Brunswick, July 11, 1966

1987–90	115	26	38	64	78
Playoffs	32	13	8	21	20

- Traded by Boston to Washington for Dave Christian, December 13, 1989

JOE JUNEAU #49 FORWARD b. Pont-Rouge, Quebec, January 5, 1968

1991–94	161	51	141	192	72
Playoffs	19	6	12	18	27

- Traded by Boston to Washington for Al Iafrate, March 21, 1994
- Boston's third pick in the 1988 entry draft

WALT KALBFLEISH ("Jeff") DEFENSE b. New Hamburg, Ontario, December 18, 1911

1937–38	1	0	0	0	0

- Traded to Boston from the New York Americans for Ted Graham, 1936

MAX KAMINSKY #15 FORWARD b. Niagara Falls, Ontario, April 19, 1913

1934–36	75	13	17	30	24
Playoffs	4	0	0	0	0

- Purchased from the St. Louis Eagles, 1935

ALEXEI KASATONOV #6 DEFENSE b. Leningrad, USSR, October 14, 1959

1994–96	63	3	14	17	45
Playoffs	5	0	0	0	2

- Signed as a free agent by Boston, June 22, 1994

STEVE KASPER #11 FORWARD b. Montreal, Quebec, September 28, 1961

1980–89	564	135	220	355	450
Playoffs	63	14	16	30	62

- Boston's third choice in the 1980 entry draft

- Traded by Boston to Los Angeles for Bobby Carpenter, January 23, 1989
- Franke J. Selke Trophy: 1981–82
- Seventh Player Award: 1980–81
- Coach of the Boston Bruins, (1995–96 to 1996–97)

Trivia Question #20

Name the persons and the numbers of the Hockey Hall of Fame members whose banners hang from the rafters of the FleetCenter.

JARMO KEKALAINEN #29 FORWARD
  b. Tampere, Finland, July 3, 1966

1989–91	27	4	3	7	14

- Signed by Boston as a free agent, May 3, 1989

FORBES KENNEDY #14 FORWARD
  b. Dorchester, New Brunswick, August 18, 1935

1962–66	221	30	45	75	237

- Traded to Boston by Detroit for Andre Pronovost, December 1962
- Drafted from Boston by Philadelphia in the expansion draft, June 6, 1967

SHELDON KENNEDY #33 FORWARD
  b. Elkhorn, Manitoba, June 15, 1969

1996–97	56	8	10	18	30

- Signed as a free agent, August 7, 1996

DARIN KIMBLE #29 FORWARD b. Lucky Lake, Saskatchewan, November 22, 1968

1992–93	55	7	3	10	177
Playoffs	4	0	0	0	2

- Traded to Boston by Tampa Bay for Ken Hodge and Matt Hervey, September 4, 1992

JIM KLEIN ("Dede") FORWARD b. Saskatoon, Saskatchewan, January 13, 1910

1928–29, 1931–32				
Totals	20	2	0	2	5

- Member of the 1929 Stanley Cup Champions

JOE KLUKAY #22 FORWARD b. Sault Ste. Marie, Ontario, November 6, 1922

1952–55	150	33	33	66	51
Playoffs	15	1	2	3	9

- Purchased from Toronto, September 16, 1952
- Traded by Boston to Toronto for Leo Boivin, November, 1954

GORD KLUZAK #6 DEFENSE b. Climax, Saskatchewan, March 4, 1964

1982–91	209	25	98	123	543
Playoffs	46	6	13	19	129

- Bill Masterton Memorial Trophy: 1989–90

BILLY KNIBBS #22 FORWARD b. Toronto, Ontario, January 24, 1942

1964–65	53	7	10	17	4

FRED KNIPSCHEER #48 FORWARD b. Fort Wayne, Indiana, September 3, 1969

1993–95	27	6	3	9	16
Playoffs	16	2	1	3	6

- Signed as a free agent by Boston, April 30, 1993
- Traded by Boston to St. Louis for Rick Zombo, October 2, 1995

RUSS KOPAK #19 FORWARD b. Edmonton, Alberta, April 26, 1924

1943–44	24	7	9	16	0

DOUG KOSTYNSKI #25 – 34 FORWARD
b. Castlegar, British Columbia, February 23, 1963

1983–85	15	3	I	4	4

- Boston's ninth choice in the 1982 entry draft

STEVE KRAFTCHECK DEFENSE b. Tinturn, Ontario, March 3, 1929

1950–51	22	O	O	O	8
Playoffs	6	O	O	O	7

- Sold by Boston with Ed Reigle to Rangers, May 14, 1951

Trivia Question #21

This is an "Original Six" era question. What do Pete Babando, Clare Martin, Johnny McKenzie, and Ron Murphy have in common?

PHIL KRAKE ("Skip") #21 FORWARD b. North Battleford, Saskatchewan, October 14, 1943

1963–64, 1965–68					
Totals	87	II	9	20	17

- Traded by Boston to Los Angeles, May 20, 1968

MIKE KRUSHELNYSKI #25 – 33 FORWARD
b. Montreal, Quebec, April 27, 1960

1981–84	162	51	65	116	100
Playoffs	20	8	6	14	14

- Traded by Boston to Edmonton for Ken Linseman, June 21, 1984
- Boston's seventh pick in the 1979 amateur draft

ED KRYZANOWSKI #22 DEFENSE b. Fort Francis, Ontario, November 14, 1925

1948–52	234	15	22	37	65
Playoffs	18	O	I	I	4

- Sold by Boston with Vic Lynn to Chicago, August 14, 1952

ARNIE KULLMAN #24 FORWARD
b. Winnipeg, Manitoba, October 9, 1927

1947–48, 1949–50 Totals	13	O	I	I	II

ORLAND KURTENBACH #7 – 14 FORWARD
b. Cudworth, Saskatchewan, September 7, 1936

1961–62, 1963–65 Totals	142	18	45	63	183

- Drafted by Boston from the Rangers, June 14, 1961
- Traded by Boston along with Pat Stapleton and Andy Hebenton to Toronto for Ron Stewart, June 8, 1965

DMITRI KVARTALNOV #10 FORWARD
b. Voskresensk, Soviet Union, March 25, 1966

1992–94	112	42	49	91	26
Playoffs	4	O	O	O	O

- Boston's first pick in the 1992 entry draft

GUS KYLE #6 DEFENSE b. Dysart, Saskatchewan, September 11, 1923

1951–52	69	I	12	13	127
Playoffs	2	O	O	O	4

- Traded to Boston along with Pentti Lund from the New York Rangers for Paul Ronty, 1951

LEO LABINE #16 FORWARD b. Haileybury, Ontario, January 22, 1931

1951–61	571	123	180	303	626
Playoffs	49	8	10	18	98

- Traded by Boston along with Vic Stasiuk to Detroit for Gary Aldcorn, Murray Oliver, and Tom McCarthy, January, 1961
- Dufresne Trophy: 1954–55

> **Trivia Question #22**
> Name the only Bruin who has won the Hart Trophy, (he did it twice), and whose number is not hanging from the FleetCenter?

GUY LABRIE #8 DEFENSE *b.* St. Charles Bellechase, Quebec, August 20, 1920

1943–44	15	2	7	9	2

DANIEL LACROIX #40 FORWARD *b.* Montreal, Quebec, March 11, 1969

1994–95	23	I	O	I	38

- Traded by Boston to the Rangers for Glen Featherstone, August 19, 1994
- Claimed on waivers by the Rangers from Boston, March 23, 1995

BOBBY LALONDE #19 FORWARD *b.* Montreal, Quebec, March 27, 1951

1979–81	133	14	37	51	59
Playoffs	7	2	2	4	4

- Traded to Boston by Atlanta for future considerations, October 23, 1979

JOE LAMB #10 FORWARD *b.* Sussex, New Brunswick, June 18, 1906

1932–34	90	21	23	44	115
Playoffs	5	O	I	I	6

- Purchased from the Americans, 1932
- Traded by Boston to St. Louis for Max Kaminsky, 1934

MYLES LANE #2 DEFENSE *b.* Melrose, Massachusetts, October 2, 1905

1928–30, 1933–34					
Totals	36	3	I	4	19
Playoffs	10	O	O	O	O

- Member of the 1929 Stanley Cup Champions

STEVE LANGDON #32 FORWARD *b.* Toronto, Ontario, December 23, 1953

1974–76, 1977–78					
Totals	7	O	I	I	2
Playoffs	4	O	O	O	O

AL LANGLOIS ("Junior") #4 DEFENSE *b.* Magog, Quebec, November 6, 1934

1965–66	65	4	10	14	54

- Traded to Boston along with Ron Harris, Parker MacDonald, and Bob Dillabough to Detroit for Ab McDonald, Bob McCord, and Ken Stephenson, May 31, 1965

GUY LAPOINTE #5 – 27 DEFENSE *b.* Montreal, Quebec, March 18, 1948

1983–84	25	2	16	18	34

- Hall of Fame elected 1993
- Signed as a free agent by Boston, August 15, 1983

CHARLES LAROSE FORWARD

1925–26	6	O	O	O	O

GUY LAROSE #41 FORWARD *b.* Hull, Quebec, August 31, 1967

1994–95	4	O	O	O	O

- Playoffs only
- Signed as a free agent by Boston, July 11, 1994
- Son of former NHLer Claude Larose

REED LARSON #28 DEFENSE *b.* Minneapolis, Minnesota, July 30, 1956

1985–88	141	25	52	77	196
Playoffs	15	I	3	4	14

- Traded to Boston by Detroit for Mike O'Connell, March 10, 1986.

MARTIN LAUDER #14

1927–28	3	0	0	0	2

DOMINIC LAVOIE #37 *b.* Montreal, Quebec, November 21, 1967

1992–93	2	0	0	0	2

- Claimed on waivers by Boston from Ottawa, November 20, 1992

BRIAN LAWTON #29 FORWARD *b.* New Brunswick, New Jersey, June 29, 1964

1989–90	8	0	0	0	14

- Signed as a free agent by Boston, February 7, 1990

HAL LAYCOE #10 DEFENSE *b.* Sutherland, Saskatchewan, June 23, 1922

1950–56	258	17	39	56	180
Playoffs	31	2	4	6	26

- Traded to Boston by Montreal for Ross Lowe, February 14, 1951

JEFF LAZARO #14 FORWARD *b.* Waltham, Massachusetts, March 21, 1968

1990–92	76	8	19	27	98
Playoffs	28	3	3	6	32

- Signed as a free agent by Boston, September 26, 1990
- Claimed from Boston by Ottawa in the expansion draft, June 18, 1992

LARRY LEACH #24 FORWARD *b.* Humboldt, Saskatchewan, June 18, 1936

1958–60, 1961–62					
Totals	126	13	29	42	91
Playoffs	7	1	1	2	8

REGGIE LEACH #27 FORWARD *b.* Riverton, Manitoba, April 23, 1950

1970–72	79	9	17	26	12
Playoffs	3	0	0	0	0

- Traded by Boston along with Rick Smith and Bob Stewart to California for Carol Vadnais and Don O'Donoghue, February 23, 1972

STEVE LEACH #27 FORWARD *b.* Cambridge, Massachusetts, January 16, 1966

1991–96	293	76	83	159	501
Playoffs	24	5	2	7	14

- Traded to Boston by Washington for Randy Burridge, June 21, 1991
- Traded by Boston to St. Louis for Kevin Sawyer and Steve Staios, March 8, 1996

Trivia Question #23
Why was January 18 unique to the Bruins in the 1980s?

RICHIE LEDUC #18 FORWARD *b.* Ile Perrot, Quebec, August 24, 1951

1972–74	33	4	4	8	14
Playoffs	5	0	0	0	9

- Traded to Boston by California along with Chris Oddliefson for Ivan Boldirev, November 17, 1971

TOMMY LEHMANN #20 FORWARD *b.* Slona, Sweden, February 3, 1964

1987–89	35	5	5	10	16

- Traded by Boston to Edmonton for a future draft pick, June 17, 1989

BOBBY LEITER #21 – 24 FORWARD *b.* Winnipeg, Manitoba, March 22, 1941

1962–66, 1968–69					
Totals	135	20	28	48	85

> **Trivia Question #24**
> When Bill Mosienko of the Chicago Blackhawks scored 3 goals in 21 seconds in 1952, the record stood until February 25, 1971, when the Bruins scored 3 goals in 20 seconds. Who scored the 3 goals for Boston?

MOE LEMAY #37 FORWARD b. Saskatoon, Saskatchewan, February 18, 1962

1987–89	14	0	0	0	23
Playoffs	15	4	2	6	32

- Traded to Boston by Edmonton for Alan May, March 8, 1988
- Traded by Boston to Winnipeg for Ray Neufeld, December 30, 1988

BILL LESUK #21 – 22 FORWARD b. Moose Jaw, Saskatchewan, November 1, 1946

1968–70	8	0	1	1	0
Playoffs	3	0	0	0	0

- Drafted from Boston by Philadelphia in the intra-league draft, June 9, 1970
- Member of the 1970 Stanley Cup Champions

PETE LESWICK FORWARD b. Saskatoon, Saskatchewan, July 12, 1917

1944–45	2	0	0	0	0

NORMAND LEVEILLE #19 FORWARD b. Montreal, Quebec, January 10, 1963

1981–83	75	17	25	42	49

- Boston's first choice in the 1981 entry draft

KEN LINSEMAN #13 FORWARD b. Kingston, Ontario, August 11, 1958

1984–90	389	125	247	372	744
Playoffs	35	16	22	38	103

- Traded to Boston by Edmonton for Mike Krushelnyski, June 21, 1984
- Traded by Boston to Philadelphia for Dave Poulin, January 16, 1990

ROSS LONSBERRY #29 FORWARD b. Humboldt, Saskatchewan, February 7, 1947

1966–69	33	2	2	4	16

- Traded by Boston along with Eddie Shack to Los Angeles for Ken Turlik, and Los Angeles' first pick in the amateur draft in 1971 & 1973

JIM LORENTZ #21 – 22 FORWARD b. Waterloo, Ontario, May 1, 1947

1968–70	79	8	19	27	36
Playoffs	11	1	0	1	4

- Traded by Boston to St. Louis for St. Louis's first draft choice in the 1970 amateur draft, 1979
- Member of the 1970 Stanley Cup Champions

ROSS LOWE DEFENSE b. Oshawa, Ontario, September 21, 1928

1949–51	43	5	3	8	34

- Traded by Boston to Montreal for Hal Laycoe, February 14, 1951

MORRIS LUKOWICH #12 FORWARD b. Speers, Saskatchewan, June 1, 1956

1984–86	36	6	12	18	31
Playoffs	1	0	0	0	0

- Traded to Boston by Winnipeg for Jim Nill, February 4, 1985
- Claimed on waivers from Boston by Los Angeles, November 15, 1985

PENTTI LUND ("Penny") #19 FORWARD b. Helsinki, Finland, December 6, 1925

1946–48, 1951–53 Totals	77	8	14	22	2
Playoffs	7	1	0	1	0

- Traded by Boston along with Billy Taylor to the Rangers for Grant Warwick, 1948
- Traded to Boston with Gus Kyle by the Rangers for Paul Ronty, September 20, 1951

VIC LYNN FORWARD *b.* Saskatoon, Saskatchewan, January 26, 1925

1950–52	68	16	8	24	73
Playoffs	5	0	0	0	2

- Traded to Boston along with Bill Ezinicki from Toronto for Fernie Flaman, Leo Boivin, Ken Smith, and Phil Maloney, November, 1950
- Sold by Boston with Ed Kryzanowski to Chicago, August 14, 1952

Trivia Question #25
The Art Ross Trophy is awarded annually to the leading scorer in the NHL. What was the trophy originally awarded for?

PEACHES LYONS FORWARD

1930–31	14	0	0	0	21
Playoffs	5	0	0	0	0

PARKER MACDONALD #21 FORWARD *b.* Sydney, Nova Scotia, June 14, 1933

1965–66	29	6	4	10	6

- Traded to Boston with Junior Langlois, Ron Harris, and Bob Dillabough from Detroit for Ab McDonald, Bob McCord, and Ken Stephanson, May 31, 1965
- Traded by Boston to Detroit for Pit Martin, December 30, 1965

MICKEY MACKAY FORWARD *b.* Chesley, Ontario, May 21, 1894

1928–30	70	12	7	19	31
Playoffs	9	0	0	0	6

- Hall of Fame elected 1952
- Member of the 1929 Stanley Cup Champions

FLEMING MACKELL #8 – 20 FORWARD *b.* Montreal, Quebec, April 30, 1929

1951–60	513	127	185	312	474
Playoffs	53	17	33	50	51

- Traded to Boston by Toronto for Jim Morrison, January 9, 1952
- First All-Star: 1953
- Dufresne Trophy: 1952–53

CRAIG MACTAVISH #14 – 27 – 32 FORWARD *b.* London, Ontario, August 15, 1958

1979–84	217	44	66	110	74
Playoffs	28	5	4	9	25

- Boston's ninth choice in the 1984 entry draft

MIKKO MAKELA #42 FORWARD *b.* Tampere, Finland, February 28, 1965

1994–95	11	1	2	3	0

- Signed by Boston as a free agent, July 18, 1994

DEAN MALKOC #44 DEFENSE *b.* Vancouver, British Columbia, January 26, 1970

1996–96	33	0	0	0	68

- Claimed on waivers from Vancouver, September 30, 1996

TROY MALLETTE #29 FORWARD *b.* Sudbury, Ontario, February 25, 1970

1996–97	68	6	8	14	155

- Signed as a free agent, July 24, 1996

PHIL MALONEY #21 FORWARD *b.* Ottawa, Ontario, October 6, 1927

1949–51	83	17	31	48	8

- Traded by Boston along with Fernie Flaman, Leo Boivin, and Ken Smith, to Toronto for Bill Ezinicki and Vic Lynn, November 16, 1950

RAY MALUTA #23 DEFENSE b. Flin Flon, Manitoba, July 24, 1954

1975–77	25	2	3	5	6
Playoffs	2	0	0	0	0

- Boston's eighth choice in the 1974 entry draft

RAY MANSON FORWARD b. St. Boniface, Manitoba, December 3, 1926

1947–48	1	0	0	0

SYLVIO MANTHA DEFENSE b. Montreal, Quebec, April 14, 1902

1936–37	4	0	0	0	2

- Purchased by Boston, 1936
- Hall of Fame elected 1960
- Scored the first goal in Boston Garden history as a member of the Montreal Canadiens

DON MARCOTTE #21 – 27 – 29 FORWARD b. Asbestos, Quebec, April 15, 1947

1965–66, 1968–82					
Totals	868	230	254	484	317
Playoffs	132	34	27	61	81

- Seventh Player Award: 1973–74
- Member of the 1970 and 1972 Stanley Cup Champions

FRANK MARIO #9 – 11 FORWARD b. Esterhazy, Saskatchewan, February 25, 1921

1941–45	53	9	19	28	24

NEVIN MARKWART #17 FORWARD b. Toronto, Ontario, December 9, 1964

1983–88, 1989–92					
Totals	299	39	67	106	769
Playoffs	19	1	0	1	33

- Boston's first choice in the 1983 entry draft

DANIEL MAROIS #33 FORWARD b. Montreal, Quebec, October 3, 1968

1993–94	22	7	3	10	18
Playoffs	11	0	1	1	16

- Traded to Boston by the New York Islanders for a future draft pick, March 18, 1993

GILLES MAROTTE #10 DEFENSE b. Montreal, Quebec, June 7, 1945

1965–67	118	10	25	35	117

- Traded by Boston along with Jack Norris and Pit Martin to Chicago for Phil Esposito, Ken Hodge, and Fred Stanfield, May 15, 1967

MARK MARQUESS #19 FORWARD b. Bassano, Alberta, March 26, 1925

1946–47	27	5	4	9	27
Playoffs	4	0	0	0	0

CLARE MARTIN #19 – 21 DEFENSE b. Waterloo, Ontario, February 25, 1922

1941–42, 1946–48					
Totals	78	8	14	22	38
Playoffs	15	0	1	1	6

- Traded by Boston along with Pete Babando, Lloyd Durham, and Jimmy Peters to Detroit for Bill Quackenbush and Pete Horeck, August 16, 1949

FRANK MARTIN #21 DEFENSE b. Cayuga, Ontario, May 1, 1933

1952–54	82	3	19	22	44
Playoffs	10	0	1	1	2

- Traded by Boston to Chicago for Murray Costello, October 4, 1954

HUBERT MARTIN ("Pit") #7 FORWARD b. Noranda, Quebec, December 9, 1943

1965–67	111	36	33	69	50

- Traded to Boston from Detroit for Parker Mac-Donald, December 30, 1965
- Traded by Boston along with Jack Norris and Gilles Marotte to Chicago for Phil Esposito, Fred Stanfield, and Ken Hodge, May 15, 1967

JOE MATTE DEFENSE *b.* Bourget, Ontario, 1893

1925–26	3	0	0	0	0

WAYNE MAXNER #12 – 23 FORWARD
b. Halifax, Nova Scotia, September 27, 1942

1964–66	62	8	9	17	48

ALAN MAY #40 FORWARD *b.* Swan Hills, Alberta, January 14, 1965

1987–88	3	0	0	0	15

- Signed as a free agent by Boston, October 30, 1987
- Traded by Boston to Edmonton for Moe Lemay, March 8, 1988

NORM McATEE #18 FORWARD *b.* Stratford, Ontario, June 28, 1921

1946–47	13	0	1	1	0

TOM McCARTHY FORWARD *b.* Toronto, Ontario, September 15, 1934

1960–61	24	4	5	9	0

- Traded to Boston along with Murray Oliver and Gary Aldcorn from Detroit for Leo Labine and Vic Stasiuk, January 1961

TOM McCARTHY #19 FORWARD *b.* Toronto, Ontario, July 31, 1960

1986–88	75	32	34	66	37
Playoffs	17	4	5	9	22

- Traded to Boston by Minnesota for a draft choice, May 16, 1986

TRENT McCLEARY #25 FORWARD *b.* Swift Current, Saskatchewan, October 10, 1972

1996–97	59	3	5	8	33

- Traded from Ottawa to Boston for Sean McEachern, June 22, 1996

BOB McCORD #4 DEFENSE *b.* Matheson, Ontario, March 30, 1934

1963–65	108	1	15	16	75

- Purchased by Boston from the Springfield Indians (AHL) for Bruce Gamble, Terry Gray, Dale Rolfe, and Randy Miller
- Traded by Boston along with Ab McDonald and Ken Stephanson to Detroit for Junior Langlois, Ron Harris, Parker MacDonald, and Bob Dillabough, May 31, 1965

PAT McCREAVY #12 FORWARD *b.* Owen Sound, Ontario, January 16, 1918

1938–42	21	0	2	2	4
Playoffs	20	3	3	6	9

- Member of the 1941 Stanley Cup Champions

BYRON McCRIMMON ("Brad") #29 DEFENSE
b. Dodsland, Saskatchewan, March 29, 1959

1979–82	228	17	37	54	325
Playoffs	15	1	2	3	32

- Boston's second choice in the 1979 entry draft
- Traded by Boston to Philadelphia for Pete Peeters, June 9, 1982

ALVIN McDONALD ("Ab") #21 FORWARD
b. Winnipeg, Manitoba, February 18, 1936

1964–65	60	9	9	18	6

- Traded to Boston with Reggie Fleming from Chicago for Doug Mohns, June 8, 1964
- Traded by Boston with Bob McCord and Ken Stephanson to Detroit for Parker MacDonald, Junior Langlois, Ron Harris, and Bob Dillabough, May 31, 1965

SHAWN McEACHERN #14 FORWARD
b. Waltham, Massachusetts, February 28, 1969

1995–96	82	24	29	53	34
Playoffs	5	1	2	3	8

- Traded to Boston with Kevin Stevens from Pittsburgh for Bryan Smolinski and Glen Murray, August 2, 1995
- Traded by Boston to Ottawa for Trent McCleary, June 22, 1996

Trivia Question #26
This question is related to Trivia Question #16. Identify the numbers and names of the players whose numbers are retired but were worn by other players. Who are the players that wore those previously retired numbers?

JACK McGILL ("Big Jack") #11 – 16 – 19
FORWARD b. Edmonton, Alberta, September 19, 1921

1941–42, 1944–47 Totals	97	23	36	59	42
Playoffs	27	7	4	11	17

BERT McINENLY #4 FORWARD/DEFENSE
b. Quebec City, Quebec, May 6, 1906

1933–36	43	2	1	3	28
Playoffs	4	0	0	0	2

JACK McINTYRE #18 FORWARD b. Brussels, Ontario, September 8, 1930

1949–53	123	19	35	54	49
Playoffs	19	5	4	9	4

- Traded by Boston to Chicago for Cal Gardner, January 20, 1954

WALT McKECHNIE #18 FORWARD b. London, Ontario, June 19, 1947

1974–75	53	3	3	6	8

- Traded to Boston from the Rangers for Derek Sanderson, June 12, 1974
- Traded by Boston to Detroit for Hank Nowak and Earl Anderson, February 18, 1975

DON McKENNEY #17 FORWARD b. Smiths Falls, Ontario, April 30, 1934

1954–63	592	195	267	462	226
Playoffs	34	13	20	33	8

- Traded by Boston to the Rangers for Dean Prentice, February 1963
- Lady Byng Trophy: 1959–60

Trivia Question #27
On November 10, 1977, this Bruin scored his only career hat trick. Since his retirement, no other Bruin has worn his number. Who is this player?

JOHN McKENZIE #19 FORWARD b. High River, Alberta, December 12, 1937

1965–72	453	169	227	396	700
Playoffs	50	15	30	45	119

- Second All-Star: 1970
- Seventh Player Award: 1969–70
- Traded to Boston from the Rangers for Reggie Fleming, January 10, 1966
- Sold by Boston to Philadelphia, August 3, 1972
- Member of the 1970 and 1972 Stanley Cup Champions

ANDREW McKIM #45 FORWARD b. Saint John, New Brunswick, July 6, 1970

1992–94	36	1	4	5	4

- Signed as a free agent by Boston, July 23, 1992

KYLE McLAREN   #18 – 46 DEFENSE
b. Humboldt, Saskatchewan, June 18, 1977

1995–97	132	10	21	31	127
Playoffs	5	0	0	0	14

- Boston's first choice in the 1995 entry draft
- NHL All–Rookie team, 1996
- Seventh Player Award: 1995–96

SCOTT McLELLAN   #33 FORWARD b. Toronto, Ontario, February 10, 1963

1982–83	2	0	0	0	0

- Boston's third choice in the 1981 entry draft

MIKE McMAHON DEFENSE b. Quebec City, Quebec, February 1, 1917

1945–46	2	0	0	0	2

SAMMY McMANUS b. Belfast, Northern Ireland, 1909

1936–37	1	0	0	0	0

PETER McNAB   #8 b. Vancouver, British Columbia, May 8, 1952

1976–84	595	263	324	587	111
Playoffs	79	38	36	74	16

- Signed as a free agent by Boston, June 11, 1976
- Traded by Boston to Vancouver for Jim Nill, February 3, 1984

HARRY MEEKING FORWARD b. Kitchener, Ontario, November 4, 1894

1926–27	23	1	0	1	2
Playoffs	8	0	0	0	0

- Traded January 1927 from Detroit

DICK MEISSNER   #22 FORWARD
b. Kindersley, Saskatchewan, January 6, 1940

1959–62	135	8	10	18	37

- Drafted from Boston by the Rangers, June 4, 1963

LARRY MELNYK   #29 – 33 DEFENSE b. New Westminster, British Columbia, February 21, 1960

1980–83	75	0	12	12	123
Playoffs	22	0	3	3	49

- Traded by Boston to Edmonton for John Blum, March 6, 1984

NICK MICKOSKI   #12 FORWARD b. Winnipeg, Manitoba, December 7, 1927

1959–60	18	1	0	1	2

- Traded by Boston to Detroit for Jim Morrison, August 25, 1959

RICK MIDDLETON   #16 – 17 FORWARD
b. Toronto, Ontario, December 4, 1953

1976–88	881	402	496	898	124
Playoffs	111	45	55	100	17

- Second All-Star: 1982
- Lady Byng Trophy: 1981–82
- Dufresne Trophy: 1978–79, 1980–81, 1981–82, 1983–84
- Seventh Player Award: 1978–79
- Traded to Boston from the Rangers for Ken Hodge, May 26, 1976

MIKE MILBURY   #26 DEFENSE b. Brighton, Massachusetts, June 17, 1952

1975–87	754	49	189	238	1552
Playoffs	86	4	24	28	219

- Coach of the Boston Bruins, (1989–90 to 1990–91)

MIKE MILLAR   #42 FORWARD b. St. Catharine's Ontario, April 28, 1965

1989–90	15	1	4	5	0

- Traded to Boston by Washington for Alfie Turcotte, October 2, 1989

BOB MILLER   #14 FORWARD *b.* Medford, Massachusetts, September 28, 1956

1977–81	263	55	82	137	143
Playoffs	34	4	6	10	27

- Boston's third choice in the 1976 entry draft
- Traded by Boston to Colorado for Mike Gillis, February 18, 1981

JAY MILLER   #29 FORWARD *b.* Wellesley, Massachusetts, July 16, 1960

1985–89	216	13	20	33	856
Playoffs	14	0	0	0	141

- Signed as a free agent by Boston, October 1, 1985
- Traded by Boston to Los Angeles for future considerations, January 22, 1989

HERB MITCHELL

1924–26	53	6	0	6	38

SANDY MOGER   #45 FORWARD *b.* 100 Mile House, British Columbia, March 21, 1969

1994–97	132	27	23	50	116
Playoffs	5	2	2	4	12

- Signed as a free agent by Boston, June 22, 1994

DOUG MOHNS   #19 FORWARD/DEFENSE *b.* Capreol, Ontario, December 13, 1933

1953–64	710	118	229	347	671
Playoffs	35	6	15	21	40

- Dufresne Trophy: 1961–62
- Traded by Boston to Chicago for Reggie Fleming and Ab McDonald, June 8, 1964

CARL MOKOSAK   #45 FORWARD *b.* Fort Saskatchewan, Alberta, September 22, 1962

1988–89	7	0	0	0	31
Playoffs	1	0	0	0	0

BERNIE MORRIS FORWARD

1924–25	6	2	0	2	0

JON MORRIS   #29 FORWARD *b.* Lowell, Massachusetts, May 6, 1966

1993–94	4	0	0	0	0

- Sold to Boston by San Jose, October 28, 1993

DOUG MORRISON   #11 – 23 – 38 FORWARD *b.* Vancouver, British Columbia, February 1, 1960

1979–82, 1984–85					
Totals	23	7	3	10	15

- Boston's third choice in the 1979 entry draft

JIM MORRISON   #10 – 20 DEFENSE *b.* Montreal, Quebec, October 11, 1931

1951–59	84	8	19	27	44
Playoffs	6	0	6	6	13

- Traded by Boston to Toronto for Fleming Mackell, January 9, 1952
- Traded to Boston by Toronto for Allan Stanley, October 8, 1958
- Traded by Boston to Detroit for Nick Mickoski, August 25, 1959

ALEX MOTTER   #10 FORWARD *b.* Melville, Saskatchewan, June 20, 1913

1934–36	28	1	4	5	4
Playoffs	6	0	0	0	0

- Sold by Boston to Detroit, December 22, 1957 for cash and Clarence Drouillard

JOE MULLEN   #11 FORWARD *b.* February 26, 1957, New York, New York

1995–96	37	8	7	15	0

- Signed as a free agent by Boston, September 13, 1995

GORD MURPHY #28 DEFENSE *b.* Willowdale, Ontario, March 23, 1967

1991–93	91	8	18	26	113
Playoffs	15	I	0	I	12

- Traded to Boston with Brian Dobbin by Philadelphia for Garry Galley and Wes Walz, January 2, 1992
- Traded by Boston to Dallas for future considerations, June 20, 1993

RON MURPHY #28 FORWARD *b.* Hamilton, Ontario, April 10, 1933

1965–70	133	29	61	90	44
Playoffs	14	4	4	8	12

- Traded to Boston by Detroit with Gary Doak and Bill Lesuk for Dean Prentice and Leo Boivin, February 18, 1966

GLEN MURRAY #44 FORWARD *b.* Halifax, Nova Scotia, November 1, 1972

1991–95	148	29	20	49	102
Playoffs	30	8	7	15	26

- Boston's first choice in the 1991 entry draft
- Traded by Boston along with Bryan Smolinski to Pittsburgh for Kevin Stevens and Sean McEachern, August 2, 1995

ANDERS MYRVOLD #14 – 41 DEFENSE *b.* Lorenskog, Norway, August 12, 1975

1996–97	9	0	2	2	4

- Traded from Colorado to Boston along with Landon Wilson for Boston's first round pick in the 1998 amateur draft, November 22, 1996

MATS NASLUND #26 FORWARD *b.* Timra, Sweden, October 31, 1959

1994–95	34	8	14	22	4
Playoffs	5	I	0	I	0

- Signed as a free agent by Boston, February 21, 1995

CAM NEELY #8 FORWARD *b.* Comox, British Columbia, June 6, 1965

1986–96	525	344	246	590	921
Playoffs	86	55	32	87	160

- Second All-Star: 1988 – 1990 – 1991 – 1994
- Bill Masterton Memorial Trophy: 1993–94
- Dufresne Trophy: 1987–88, 1990–91, 1994–95
- Seventh Player Award: 1986–87, 1993–94
- Traded to Boston by Vancouver along with Vancouver's first round pick for Barry Pederson, June 6, 1986

RAY NEUFELD #19 FORWARD *b.* St. Boniface, Manitoba, April 15, 1959

1988–90	15	I	3	4	28
Playoffs	10	2	3	5	9

- Traded to Boston by Winnipeg for Moe Lemay, December 30, 1988

Trivia Question #28
Their names were Larry, Floyd, and Wayne and they were brothers. Larry and Floyd played for the Bruins. What was their last name?

AL NICHOLSON #25 FORWARD *b.* Estevan, Saskatchewan, April 26, 1936

1955–57	19	0	I	I	4

GRAEME NICOLSON DEFENSE *b.* North Bay, Ontario, January 13, 1958

1978–79	I	0	0	0	0

KRAIG NIENHUIS #38 *b.* Sarnia, Ontario, May 9, 1961

1985–88	88	20	16	36	39
Playoffs	2	0	0	0	14

- Signed as a free agent by Boston, May 28, 1985

CHRIS NILAN #30 FORWARD *b*. Boston, Massachusetts, February 9, 1958

1990–92	80	11	14	25	463
Playoffs	19	0	2	2	62

- Traded to Boston by the Rangers for Greg Johnston, June 28, 1990
- Claimed on waivers from Boston by Montreal, February 12, 1992

JIM NILL #8 FORWARD *b*. Hanna, Alberta, April 11, 1958

1983–85	76	4	11	15	143
Playoffs	3	0	0	0	4

- Traded to Boston by Vancouver for Peter McNab, February 3, 1984
- Traded by Boston to Winnipeg for Morris Lukowich, February 14, 1985

HANK NOWAK #18 *b*. Oshawa, Ontario, November 24, 1950

1974–77	111	18	15	33	81
Playoffs	13	1	0	1	8

- Traded to Boston along with Earl Anderson from Detroit for Walt McKechnie and a future draft pick, February 18, 1975

ADAM OATES #12 FORWARD *b*. Weston, Ontario, August 27, 1962

1991–97	368	142	357	499	123
Playoffs	42	11	37	48	20

- Traded to Boston by St. Louis for Craig Janney and Stephane Quintal, February 7, 1992
- Traded by Boston along with Rick Tocchet and Bill Ranford to Washington for Jim Carey, Anson Carter, and Jason Allison, March 1, 1997
- Dufresne Trophy: 1992–93

DENNIS O'BRIEN #28 DEFENSE *b*. Port Hope, Ontario, June 10, 1949

1977–80	83	4	11	15	138
Playoffs	14	0	0	0	28

- Claimed on waivers by Boston from Cleveland, March 10, 1978.
- Played for four teams in the 1977–78 season (Minnesota, Colorado, Cleveland, and Boston)

Trivia Question #29
It was an unassisted goal at 4:13 of the third-period loss to the Montreal Canadiens at Boston Garden. The date was October 23, 1966, Bobby Orr's first goal. Who was the goaltender for the Habs?

ELLARD O'BRIEN ("Obie") DEFENSE/FORWARD *b*. St. Catharines, Ontario, May 27, 1930

1955–56	2	0	0	0	0

MIKE O'CONNELL #20 DEFENSE *b*. Chicago, Illinois, November 25, 1955

1980–86	424	70	198	268	312
Playoffs	38	7	15	22	34

- Traded to Boston by Chicago for Al Secord, December 18, 1980
- Traded by Boston to Detroit for Reed Larson, March 10, 1986
- Seventh Player Award: 1983–84

CHRIS ODDLEIFSON #18 – 22 FORWARD *b*. Brandon, Manitoba, September 7, 1950

1972–74	55	10	11	21	25

- Traded to Boston along with Richie Leduc by California for Ivan Boldirev, November 17, 1971
- Traded by Boston along with Fred O'Donnell to Vancouver for Bobby Schmautz, February 7, 1974

JEFF ODGERS #36 FORWARD *b*. Spy Hill, Saskatchewan, May 31, 1969

1996–97	80	7	8	15	197

- Traded by San Jose to Boston for Al Iafrate, June 21, 1996

FRED O'DONNELL #16 *b.* Kingston, Ontario, December 6, 1949

1972–74	115	15	11	26	98
Playoffs	5	0	1	1	5

- Traded by Boston along with Chris Oddleifson to Vancouver for Bobby Schmautz, February 7, 1974

BILLY O'DWYER #10 FORWARD *b.* South Boston, Massachusetts, June 25, 1960

1987–90	102	8	13	21	93
Playoffs	10	0	0	0	2

- Signed as a free agent by Boston, August 13, 1987

HARRY OLIVER #9 FORWARD *b.* Selkirk, Manitoba, 1899

1926–34	355	109	59	168	129
Playoffs	30	9	4	13	22

- Member of the 1929 Stanley Cup Champions
- Hall of Fame elected 1967
- Sold to the New York Americans, 1934

MURRAY OLIVER #16 FORWARD *b.* Hamilton, Ontario, November 14, 1937

1960–67	426	116	214	330	230

- Traded to Boston along with Tom McCarthy and Gary Aldcorn by Detroit for Leo Labine and Vic Stasiuk, January, 1961
- Traded by Boston to Toronto for Eddie Shack, May 15, 1967

JAMES O'NEIL ("Peggy") #14 – 15 FORWARD *b.* Semans, Saskatchewan, April 3, 1913

1933–37	141	6	26	32	105
Playoffs	5	1	1	2	13

PAUL O'NEIL FORWARD *b.* Boston, Massachusetts, August 24, 1953

1975–76	1	0	0	0	0

- Signed as a free agent by Boston, October 10, 1975

WILLIE O'REE #22 FORWARD *b.* Fredericton, New Brunswick, October 15, 1935

1957–61	45	4	10	14	26

- First black man to play in the NHL
- Traded from Boston with Stan Maxwell to Montreal for Cliff Pennington and Terry Gray, 1961

TERRY O'REILLY #23 – 24 FORWARD *b.* Niagara Falls, Ontario, June 7, 1951

1971–85	891	204	402	606	2095
Playoffs	108	25	42	67	335

- Dufresne Trophy: 1977–78
- Seventh Player Award: 1974–75
- Boston's second choice in the 1971 entry draft
- Coach of the Boston Bruins (1986–87 to 1988–89)

BOBBY ORR #4 DEFENSE *b.* Parry Sound, Ontario, March 20, 1948

1966–76	631	264	624	888	924
Playoffs	74	26	66	92	107

- First All-Star: 1968 – 1969 – 1970 – 1971 – 1972 – 1973 – 1974 – 1975
- Second All-Star: 1967
- Hall of Fame elected 1979
- Hart Trophy: 1969–70, 1970–71, & 1971–72
- Art Ross Trophy: 1969–70 & 1974–75
- James Norris Trophy: 1967–68, 1968–69, 1969–70, 1970–71, 1971–72, 1972–73, 1973–74, 1974–75
- Calder Memorial Trophy: 1966–67
- Conn Smythe Trophy: 1969–70 & 1971–72
- Dufresne Trophy: 1966–67, 1969–70, 1971–72, 1973–74, 1974–75
- Member of the 1970 and 1972 Stanley Cup Champions
- The number 4 was retired

GERRY OUELLETTE #12 FORWARD *b.* Grand Falls, New Brunswick, November 1, 1938

| 1960–61 | 39 | 5 | 4 | 9 | 0 |

GEORGE OWEN #4 DEFENSE *b.* Hamilton, Ontario

| 1928–33 | 192 | 44 | 33 | 77 | 151 |
| Playoffs | 21 | 2 | 5 | 7 | 25 |

- Member of the 1929 Stanley Cup Champions

CLAYTON PACHAL #6 – 28 *b.* Yorkton, Saskatchewan, April 21, 1956

| 1976–78 | 11 | 0 | 0 | 0 | 26 |

- Boston's first choice in the 1976 entry draft
- Traded by Boston to Colorado for Mark Suzor, October 11, 1978

AL PALLAZZARI #9 FORWARD *b.* Eveleth, Minnesota, July 25, 1918

| 1943–44 | 23 | 6 | 3 | 9 | 4 |

Trivia Question #30
The 4's were wild for the Bruins on May 10, 1970. How many incidents relating to the #4 can you recall?

BRAD PALMER #21 FORWARD *b.* Duncan, British Columbia, December 14, 1961

| 1982–83 | 73 | 6 | 11 | 17 | 18 |
| Playoffs | 7 | 1 | 0 | 1 | 0 |

- Traded to Boston by Minnesota for Dave Donnelly, June 9, 1982

ED PANAGABKO #22 FORWARD *b.* Norquay, Saskatchewan, May 17, 1934

| 1955–57 | 29 | 0 | 3 | 3 | 38 |

GRIGORI PANTELEEV #13 FORWARD *b.* Gastello, USSR, November 13, 1972

| 1992–95 | 50 | 8 | 6 | 14 | 12 |

- Boston's fifth choice in the 1992 entry draft

JEAN-PAUL PARISE #17 — 27 FORWARD *b.* Smooth Rock Falls, Ontario, December 11, 1941

| 1965–67 | 21 | 2 | 2 | 4 | 10 |

- Drafted by Oakland from Boston in the expansion draft, June 6, 1967

BRAD PARK #22 DEFENSE *b.* Toronto, Ontario, July 6, 1948

1975–83	501	100	317	417	553
Playoffs	91	23	55	78	77

- First All-Star: 1976 – 1978
- Hall of Fame elected 1988
- Dufresne Trophy: 1977–78
- Traded to Boston along with Jean Ratelle and Joe Zanussi by the Rangers for Phil Esposito and Carol Vadnais, November 7, 1975

DAVE PASIN #37 FORWARD *b.* Edmonton, Alberta, July 8, 1966

1985–86	71	18	19	37	50
Playoffs	3	0	1	1	0

- Boston's first choice in the 1984 entry draft

GEORGE PATTERSON FORWARD *b.* Kingston, Ontario, May 22, 1906

1933–34	10	0	1	1	2

- Purchased from the Americans, 1934

DAVIS PAYNE #17 – 44 FORWARD *b.* Port Alberni, British Columbia, September 24, 1970

1995–97	24	0	1	1	14

- Signed as a free agent by Boston, September 6, 1995

ALLEN PEDERSEN #41 DEFENSE *b.* Fort Saskatchewan, Alberta, January 13, 1965

1986–91	333	4	31	35	408
Playoffs	64	0	0	0	89

- Boston's fifth choice in the 1983 entry draft
- Claimed from Boston by Minnesota in the expansion draft, May 30, 1991

BARRY PEDERSON #10 – 12 – 18 FORWARD *b.* Big River, Saskatchewan, March 13, 1961

1980–86, 1991–92					
Totals	379	166	251	417	248
Playoffs	34	22	30	52	25

- Seventh Player Award: 1981–82
- Boston's first choice in the 1980 entry draft
- Traded by Boston to Vancouver for Cam Neely and Vancouver's first draft pick, June 6, 1986
- Traded to Boston by Hartford for future considerations, November 14, 1991

JOHN PEIRSON #23 FORWARD *b.* Winnipeg, Manitoba, July 21, 1925

1946–54, 1955–58					
Totals	545	153	173	326	315
Playoffs	48	9	17	26	26

CLIFF PENNINGTON #7 FORWARD *b.* Winnipeg, Manitoba, April 18, 1940

1961–63	97	16	42	58	6

- Traded to Boston from Montreal for Willie O'Ree & Stan Maxwell, 1961

GARRY PETERS #25 FORWARD *b.* Regina, Saskatchewan, October 9, 1942

1971–72	2	0	0	0	2
Playoffs	1	0	0	0	0

- Drafted by Boston from Philadelphia in the intraleague draft, June 8, 1971
- Drafted by the Islanders in the expansion draft, June 6, 1972
- Member of the 1972 Stanley Cup Champions

JIMMY PETERS #9 FORWARD *b.* Verdun, Quebec, October 2, 1922

1947–49	97	28	30	58	46
Playoffs	9	1	3	4	2

- Traded to Boston with John Quilty by Montreal for Joe Carveth, 1948

- Traded by Boston along with Pete Babando, Clare Martin, and Lloyd Durham to Detroit for Bill Quackenbush and Pete Horeck, August 16, 1949

ERIC PETTINGER ("Cowboy") #4 FORWARD b. Regina, Saskatchewan

| 1928–29 | 17 | 0 | 0 | 0 | 17 |

- Purchased from Toronto, 1929
- Member of the 1929 Stanley Cup Champions

GORDON PETTINGER #11 FORWARD b. Regina, Saskatchewan, November 17, 1911

| 1937–40 | 104 | 20 | 30 | 50 | 20 |
| Playoffs | 15 | 1 | 1 | 2 | 7 |

- Traded from Detroit December 19, 1937 for Red Beattie
- Member of the 1939 Stanley Cup Champions

HARRY PIDHIRNY FORWARD b. Toronto, Ontario, March 5, 1928

| 1957–58 | 2 | 0 | 0 | 0 | 0 |

WILLI PLETT #25 b. Paraguay, South America, June 7, 1955

| 1987–88 | 65 | 2 | 3 | 5 | 170 |
| Playoffs | 17 | 2 | 4 | 6 | 74 |

- Claimed by Boston in the NHL waiver draft, October 5, 1987

RAY PODLOSKI #43 FORWARD b. Edmonton, Alberta, January 5, 1966

| 1988–89 | 8 | 0 | 1 | 1 | 17 |

- Boston's second choice in the 1984 entry draft

NORMAN POILE ("Bud") #4 FORWARD b. Fort William, Ontario, February 10, 1924

| 1949–50 | 39 | 16 | 14 | 30 | 6 |

- Sold to Boston by the Rangers, December 4, 1949

DAN POLIZIANI FORWARD b. Sydney, Nova Scotia, January 8, 1935

| 1958–59 | 1 | 0 | 0 | 0 | 0 |
| Playoffs | 3 | 0 | 0 | 0 | 0 |

PAUL POPIEL #29 DEFENSE b. Sollested, Denmark, February 28, 1943

| 1965–66 | 3 | 0 | 1 | 1 | 2 |

- Drafted from Boston by Los Angeles in the expansion draft, June 6, 1967

JACK PORTLAND #8 DEFENSE b. Collingwood, Ontario, July 30, 1912

| 1934–40 | 187 | 7 | 20 | 27 | 148 |
| Playoffs | 18 | 0 | 0 | 0 | 19 |

- Purchased from Montreal, 1935
- Traded from Boston to Chicago for Des Smith, 1940
- Member of the 1939 Stanley Cup Champions

MARC POTVIN #29 FORWARD b. Ottawa, Ontario, January 29, 1967

| 1994–96 | 33 | 0 | 1 | 1 | 14 |
| Playoffs | 5 | 0 | 1 | 1 | 18 |

- Signed as a free agent by Boston, June 29, 1994

DAVE POULIN #19 FORWARD b. Timmins, Ontario, December 17, 1958

| 1989–93 | 165 | 34 | 68 | 102 | 117 |
| Playoffs | 53 | 12 | 18 | 30 | 60 |

- Traded to Boston by Philadelphia for Ken Linseman, January 16, 1990
- Signed as a free agent by Washington, August 3, 1993

PETR PRAJSLER #52 DEFENSE b. Hradec Kralove, Czechoslovakia, September 21, 1965

| 1991–92 | 3 | 0 | 0 | 0 | 2 |

- Signed as a free agent, August 1, 1991

JACK PRATT b. Edinburgh, Scotland

1930–32	37	2	0	2	42
Playoffs	4	0	0	0	0

WALTER PRATT ("Babe") #4 – 21 DEFENSE
b. Stony Mountain, Manitoba, January 7, 1916

1946–47	31	4	4	8	25

- Hall of Fame elected 1966
- Purchase Babe Pratt from Toronto, 1946

DEAN PRENTICE #17 FORWARD
b. Schumacher, Ontario, October 5, 1932

1962–66	170	50	56	106	63

- Traded to Boston by the Rangers for Don McKenney, February, 1963
- Traded by Boston with Leo Boivin to Detroit for Ron Murphy, Gary Doak, and Bill Lesuk, February 18, 1966

ANDRE PRONOVOST #14 – 23 FORWARD
b. Shawinigan Falls, Quebec, July 9, 1936

1960–63	138	26	21	47	104

- Traded to Boston by Montreal for Jean-Guy Gendron, November 1960
- Traded by Boston to Detroit for Forbes Kennedy, December 1962

BRIAN PROPP #36 FORWARD b. Lanigan, Saskatchewan, February 15, 1959

1989–90	14	3	9	12	10
Playoffs	20	4	9	13	2

- Traded to Boston by Philadelphia for a future draft pick, March 2, 1990

JEAN PUSIE DEFENSE b. Montreal, Quebec, October 15, 1910

1934–35	4	1	0	1	0
Playoffs	4	0	0	0	0

- Obtained from Rangers, 1935

HUBERT QUACKENBUSH ("Bill") #11
DEFENSE b. Toronto, Ontario, March 2, 1922

1949–56	461	22	133	155	46
Playoffs	33	0	13	13	4

- First All-Star: 1951
- Second All-Star: 1953
- Hall of Fame elected 1976
- Traded to Boston with Pete Horeck from Detroit for Pete Babando, Jimmy Peters, Lloyd Durham, and Clare Martin, 1949

MAX QUACKENBUSH DEFENSE b. Toronto, Ontario, August 29, 1928

1950–51	47	4	6	10	26
Playoffs	6	0	0	0	4

- Brother of Bill Quackenbush, Bruin 1949–50 to 1955–56

Trivia Question #31
Bruins goaltender Terry Sawchuk was victimized by this great player on November 5, 1955. This slick forward scored 3 power play goals in 44 seconds. Who was the player?

JOHN QUILTY #21 FORWARD b. Ottawa, Ontario, January 21, 1921

1947–48	6	3	2	5	2

- Traded to Boston with Jimmy Peters from Montreal for Joe Carveth

STEPHANE QUINTAL #21 DEFENSE
b. Boucherville, Quebec, October 22, 1968

1988–92	157	8	19	27	217
Playoffs	3	0	1	1	7

- Boston's second round pick in the 1987 entry draft
- Traded by Boston along with Craig Janney to St. Louis for Adam Oates, February 7, 1992

GEORGE RANIERI FORWARD *b.* Toronto, Ontario, January 14, 1936

1956–57	2	0	0	0	0

JEAN RATELLE #10 FORWARD *b.* Lac St. Jean, Quebec, October 3, 1940

1975–81	419	155	295	450	84
Playoffs	58	23	33	56	10

- Hall of Fame elected 1985
- Lady Byng Trophy: 1975–76
- Dufresne Trophy: 1976–77
- Traded to Boston along with Brad Park and Joe Zanussi from the Rangers for Phil Esposito and Carol Vadnais, November 7, 1975

JACK RATHWELL FORWARD *b.* Temiscaming, Quebec, August 12, 1947

1974–75	1	0	0	0	0

- Traded to Boston from St. Louis for Don Awrey, October 5, 1973

MATT RAVLICH #23 DEFENSE *b.* Sault Ste. Marie, Ontario, July 12, 1938

1962–63, 1971–73					
Totals	32	1	2	3	2

- Traded by Boston with Jerry Toppazzini to Chicago for Murray Balfour and Mike Draper, June 9, 1964

TERRY REARDON #7 – 19 DEFENSE/ FORWARD *b.* Winnipeg, Manitoba, April 6, 1919

1938–41, 1945–47					
Totals	147	24	30	54	57
Playoffs	27	6	8	14	10

- Traded by Boston to Montreal for Paul Gauthier, 1941
- Purchased by Boston from Montreal, 1946
- Member of the 1941 Stanley Cup Champions

GEORGE REDAHL #12 FORWARD *b.* Kinistino, Saskatchewan, August 8, 1935

1958–59	18	0	1	1	2

- Drafted by Boston with Jean-Guy Gendron from the Rangers, June 4, 1958

GEORGE REDDING DEFENSE

1924–26	35	3	2	5	10

DICK REDMOND #6 DEFENSE *b.* Kirkland Lake, Ontario, August 14, 1949

1978–82	235	36	79	115	124
Playoffs	26	1	7	8	13

- Traded to Boston by Atlanta for Greg Sheppard, September 6, 1978

Trivia Question #32

On October 19, 1966, in a Bruins 6–2 victory over Detroit, Gordie Howe broke what record shared by Bill Gadsby and a former Bruin? Who was the former Bruin?

LARRY REGAN #15 – 24 FORWARD *b.* North Bay, Ontario, August 9, 1930

1956–59	164	30	53	83	61
Playoffs	20	3	10	13	16

- Calder Memorial Trophy: 1956–57
- Claimed on waivers from Boston by Toronto, January 7, 1959

EARL REIBEL ("Dutch") #11 FORWARD *b.* Kitchener, Ontario, July 21, 1930

1958–59	63	6	8	14	16
Playoffs	4	0	0	0	0

- Drafted by Boston from Chicago, June 4, 1958

DAVE REID #17 – 34 – 36 FORWARD
b. Toronto, Ontario, May 15, 1964

1983–88, 1991–93, 1994–96				
Totals	387	89	92	181	115
Playoffs	45	5	8	13	8

- Boston's fourth pick in the 1982 entry draft
- Signed as a free agent by Boston, December 1, 1991

ED REIGLE ("Rags") DEFENSE *b.* Winnipeg, Manitoba, June 19, 1924

1950–51	17	0	2	2	25

- Sold by Boston with Steve Kraftcheck to the Rangers, May 14, 1951

STEPHANE RICHER #25 DEFENSE *b.* Hull, Quebec, April 28, 1966

1992–93	21	1	4	5	18
Playoffs	3	0	0	0	0

- Traded to Boston by Tampa Bay for Bob Beers, October 28, 1992
- Claimed by Florida from Boston in the expansion draft, June 24, 1993

BARRY RICHTER #46 DEFENSE *b.* Madison, Wisconsin, September 11, 1970

1996–97	50	5	13	18	32

- Signed as a free agent, July 19, 1996

JACK RILEY #9 FORWARD *b.* Berckenia, Ireland, December 29, 1910

1935–36	8	0	0	0	0

VIC RIPLEY #12 FORWARD *b.* Elgin, Ontario, May 30, 1906

1932–34	37	4	6	10	27
Playoffs	5	1	0	1	0

- Purchased from Chicago, 1933
- Traded by Boston with Roy Burmeister to the Rangers for Babe Siebert, 1934

ALAN RITTINGER #17 FORWARD *b.* Regina, Saskatchewan, January 28, 1925

1943–44	19	3	7	10	0

JOHN RIVERS ("Wayne") #21 – 25 – 27 FORWARD *b.* Hamilton, Ontario, February 1, 1942

1963–67	80	11	26	37	139

- Drafted by Boston from Detroit, June 1963
- Drafted from Boston by St. Louis in the expansion draft, June 6, 1967

DOUG ROBERTS #28 FORWARD/DEFENSE *b.* Detroit, Michigan, October 28, 1942

1971–74	55	5	8	13	9
Playoffs	5	2	0	2	6

- Brother of Gord Roberts, Bruin from 1992–93 to 1993–94
- Sold to Boston by California, September 4, 1971
- Sold by Boston to Detroit, November 23, 1973

GORD ROBERTS #14 DEFENSE *b.* Detroit, Michigan, October 2, 1957

1992–94	124	6	18	24	145
Playoffs	16	0	1	1	14

- Signed as a free agent by Boston, July 23, 1992

RANDY ROBITAILLE #48 FORWARD *b.* Ottawa, Ontario, October 12, 1975

1996–97	1	0	0	0	0

- Signed as a free agent, March 25, 1997

EARL ROCHE FORWARD *b.* Prescott, Ontario, February 22, 1910

1932–33	3	0	0	0	0

EDDIE RODDEN #10 FORWARD *b.* Toronto, Ontario, March 22, 1901

1928–29	20	0	0	0	10

- Member of the 1929 Stanley Cup Champions

JON ROHLOFF #38 DEFENSE *b.* Mankato, Minnesota, October 3, 1969

1994–97	149	7	25	32	129
Playoffs	10	1	2	3	8

- Boston's seventh pick in the 1988 entry draft

DALE ROLFE DEFENSE *b.* Timmins, Ontario, April 30, 1940

1959–60	3	0	0	0	0

- Traded by Boston along with Bruce Gamble, Terry Gray, and Randy Miller to the Springfield Indians of the AHL for Bob McCord

PAUL RONTY #20 FORWARD *b.* Toronto, Ontario, June 12, 1928

1947–51	224	56	98	154	39
Playoffs	16	1	7	8	4

- Traded by Boston to the Rangers for Gus Kyle and Pentti Lund, September 20, 1951

BOBBY ROWE DEFENSE

1924–25	4	1	0	1	0

ANDRE ROY #49 FORWARD *b.* Port Chester, New York, February 8, 1975

1995–97	13	0	2	2	12

- Boston's fifth pick in the 1994 entry draft

JEAN-YVES ROY #43 FORWARD *b.* Rosemere, Quebec, February 17, 1969

1996–97	52	10	15	25	22

- Signed as a free agent, July 15, 1996

GINO ROZZINI #9 – 12 FORWARD *b.* Shawinigan Falls, Quebec, October 24, 1918

1944–45	31	5	10	15	20
Playoffs	6	1	2	3	6

KENT RUHNKE FORWARD

1975–76	2	0	1	1	0

PAUL RUNGE #9 FORWARD *b.* Edmonton, Alberta, September 10, 1909

1930–32, 1935–36					
Totals	49	8	3	11	22
Playoffs	2	0	0	0	2

- Purchased from Montreal, 1936

VLADIMIR RUZICKA #38 FORWARD *b.* Most, Czechoslovakia, June 6, 1963

1990–93	166	66	66	132	105
Playoffs	30	4	14	18	2

- Dufresne Trophy: 1991–92
- Seventh Player Award: 1991–92
- Traded to Boston by Edmonton for Greg Hawgood, October 22, 1990

DEREK SANDERSON #16 – 17 – 23 – 27 FORWARD *b.* Niagara Falls, Ontario, June 16, 1946

1965–74	391	135	159	294	686
Playoffs	50	17	12	29	187

- Calder Memorial Trophy: 1967–68
- Seventh Player Award: 1971–72
- Signed by Boston after stint with WHA, February 1973
- Traded by Boston to the Rangers for Walt McKechnie, June 12, 1974
- Member of the 1970 and 1972 Stanley Cup Champions.

EDDIE SANDFORD ("Sandy") #7 FORWARD *b.* New Toronto, Ontario, August 20, 1928

1947–55	439	94	136	230	299
Playoffs	42	13	11	24	27

- Cousin of former Bruin, Ed Harrison, 1947–48 to 1950–51
- Second All-Star: 1954

- Traded by Boston along with Warren Godfrey, Gilles Boisvert, Real Chevrefils, and Norm Corcoran to Detroit for Vic Stasiuk, Marcel Bonin, Lorne Davis, and Terry Sawchuk, June 3, 1955

CHARLIE SANDS #4 – 6 FORWARD b. Fort William, Ontario, March 23, 1910

1935–39	215	64	38	101	36
Playoffs	24	2	3	5	0

- Traded by Boston with Ray Getliffe to Montreal Canadiens for Herb Cain, 1939
- Member of the 1939 Stanley Cup Champions.

CRAIG SARNER FORWARD b. St. Paul, Minnesota, June 20, 1949

1974–75	7	0	0	0	0

GLEN SATHER #14 FORWARD b. High River, Alberta, September 2, 1943

1966–69	146	12	23	35	101
Playoffs	13	0	0	0	18

- Drafted by Boston from Detroit, June 1965
- Drafted from Boston by Pittsburgh, June 11, 1969

GORDON SAVAGE ("Tony") DEFENSE b. Calgary, Alberta, July 18, 1906

1934–35	8	0	0	0	2

ANDRE SAVARD #11 FORWARD b. Temiscaming, Quebec, February 9, 1953

1973–76	228	52	62	114	144
Playoffs	31	5	7	12	35

- Boston's first choice in the 1973 entry draft
- Signed as a free agent by Buffalo from Boston, June 11, 1976

KEVIN SAWYER #14 – 19 FORWARD b. Christina Lake, British Columbia, February 21, 1974

1995–97	4	0	0	0	5

- Traded to Boston along with Steve Staios by St. Louis for Steve Leach, March 8, 1996

CHARLIE SCHERZA #9 FORWARD b. Brandon, Manitoba, February 15, 1923

1943–44	10	1	1	2	4

BOB SCHMAUTZ #11 – 16 – 17 FORWARD b. Saskatoon, Saskatchewan, March 28, 1945

1973–80	354	134	161	295	444
Playoffs	70	26	30	56	90

- Traded to Boston by Vancouver for Fred O'Donnell and Chris Oddleifson, February 7, 1974
- Traded by Boston to Edmonton for Dan Newman, December 10, 1979

CLARENCE SCHMIDT FORWARD b. Williams, Minnesota, 1923

1943–44	7	1	0	1	2

JOHN SCHMIDT #7 FORWARD b. Odessa, Saskatchewan, November 11, 1924

1942–43	45	6	7	13	6
Playoffs	5	0	0	0	0

JOSEPH SCHMIDT #7 FORWARD b. Odessa, Saskatchewan, November 5, 1926

1943–44	2	0	0	0	0

MILT SCHMIDT #15 FORWARD b. Kitchener, Ontario, March 5, 1918

1936–42, 1945–55					
Totals	778	229	346	575	466
Playoffs	86	24	25	49	60

- First All-Star: 1940 – 1947 – 1951
- Second All-Star: 1952
- Hall of Fame elected 1961
- Hart Trophy: 1950–51
- Art Ross Trophy: 1939–40
- Lester Patrick Trophy: 1996

- Dufresne Trophy: 1941–42, 1946–47, 1949–50, 1950–51
- Member of the 1939 and 1941 Stanley Cup Champions
- Coach of the Boston Bruins, (1954–55 to 1960–61 & 1962–63 to 1965–66)

WERNER SCHNARR FORWARD

1924–26	25	0	0	0	0

DANNY SCHOCK #23 – 25 FORWARD
b. Terrace Bay, Ontario, December 30, 1948

1969–71	6	0	0	0	0
Playoffs	1	0	0	0	0

- Brother of Ron Schock, Bruin from 1963–64 to 1966–67
- Traded by Boston with Rick MacLeish to Philadelphia for Mike Walton, February 1, 1971
- Member of the 1970 Stanley Cup Champions

> **Trivia Question #33**
> On December 18, 1951, and February 26, 1952, the Bruins drew crowds of 4,049 fans to both games against the Detroit Red Wings. What is so unusual about this?

RON SCHOCK #22 – 23 FORWARD
b. Chapleau, Ontario, December 19, 1943

1963–67	128	17	31	48	28

- Drafted from Boston by St. Louis in the expansion draft, June 6, 1967

JIM SCHOENFELD #13 DEFENSE b. Galt, Ontario, September 4, 1952

1983–84	39	0	2	2	20

- Signed as a free agent by Boston, August 19, 1983

AL SECORD #20 FORWARD b. Sudbury, Ontario, March 3, 1958

1978–81	166	39	26	65	337
Playoffs	14	0	3	3	69

- Traded by Boston to Chicago for Mike O'Connell, December 18, 1980

JEFF SEROWIK #49 DEFENSE b. Manchester, New Hampshire, January 10, 1967

1994–95	1	0	0	0	0

- Signed as a free agent by Boston, June 29, 1994

EDDIE SHACK #23 FORWARD b. Sudbury, Ontario, February 11, 1937

1967–69	120	34	30	64	181
Playoffs	13	0	3	3	29

- Traded to Boston by Toronto for Murray Oliver, may 15, 1967
- Traded by Boston with Ross Lonsberry to Los Angeles for Ken Turlik and Los Angeles' first pick in the 1971 and 1973 entry drafts, May 14, 1969

YEVGENY SHALDYBIN #62 DEFENSE
b. Novosibirsk, USSR, July 29, 1975

1996–97	3	1	0	1	0

- Boston's 6th choice in the 1995 amateur draft

SEAN SHANAHAN #7 b. Toronto, Ontario, February 8, 1951

1977–78	6	0	0	0	7

- Signed as a free agent by Boston, October 13, 1977

GERRY SHANNON #15 – 16 FORWARD
b. Campbellford, Ontario, October 25, 1910

1934–36	42	1	2	3	10
Playoffs	4	0	0	0	2

- Purchased from St. Louis, 1935

DAVID SHAW #34 DEFENSE b. St. Thomas, Ontario, May 25, 1964

1992–95	176	14	27	41	229
Playoffs	2	1	4	5	26

- Traded to Boston by Minnesota for future considerations, September 2, 1992
- Traded by Boston to Tampa Bay for a future draft pick, August 17, 1996

NORMIE SHAY FORWARD

1924–26	31	2	1	3	16

- Sold to Toronto January 13, 1926

JOHN SHEPHARD #15 FORWARD b. Montreal, Quebec, October 19, 1907

1933–34	4	0	0	0	0

GREG SHEPPARD #19 FORWARD b. North Battleford, Saskatchewan, April 23, 1949

1972–78	416	155	220	375	130
Playoffs	65	28	33	61	29

- Dufresne Trophy: 1975–76
- Seventh Player Award: 1975–76
- Traded by Boston to Atlanta for Dick Redmond, September 6, 1948

JACK SHEWCHUCK #8 – 12 – 18 – 19 – 21 DEFENSE b. Brantford, Ontario, June 19, 1917

1938–43, 1944–45 Totals	187	9	19	28	160
Playoffs	20	0	1	1	19

ALAN SHIELDS DEFENSE b. Ottawa, Ontario, May 10, 1907

1936–37	18	0	4	4	15
Playoffs	3	0	0	0	2

- Traded to Boston by the New York Americans for Joe Jerwa, 1936

BILL SHILL #9 FORWARD b. Toronto, Ontario, March 6, 1923

1942–43, 1945–47 Totals	79	21	13	34	18
Playoffs	7	1	2	3	2

JACK SHILL #16 – 18 FORWARD b. Toronto, Ontario, January 12, 1913

1934–35	45	4	4	8	22
Playoffs	4	0	0	0	0

- Purchased from Toronto, 1934

BRUCE SHOEBOTTOM #40 DEFENSE b. Windsor, Ontario, August 20, 1965

1987–91	35	1	4	5	53
Playoffs	14	1	2	3	77

- Signed as a free agent by Boston, July 20, 1987

Trivia Question #34
From the 1967–68 season to the 1972–73 season, the Bruins did not have one of these. What was it?

EDDIE SHORE #2 DEFENSE b. Fort Qu'Appelle-Cupar, Saskatchewan, November 25, 1902

1926–40	543	103	176	279	1038
Playoffs	52	6	11	17	185

- Member 1929 and 1939 Stanley Cup Champions
- First All-Star: 1931 – 1932 – 1933 – 1935 – 1936 – 1938 – 1939
- Second All-Star: 1934
- Hall of Fame elected 1945
- Hart Trophy: 1932–33, 1934–35, 1935–36, & 1937–38
- Lester Patrick Trophy: 1970
- Dufresne Trophy: 1936–37, 1937–38, 1938–39
- Traded by Boston to the New York Americans for Eddie Wiseman, January 25, 1940
- The number 2 was retired

ALBERT SIEBERT ("Babe") #12
DEFENSE/FORWARD b. Plattsville, Quebec,
January 14, 1904

1933–36	107	18	28	46	164
Playoffs	6	0	1	1	6

- First All-Star: 1936
- Hall of Fame elected 1964
- Traded to Boston from the Rangers for Vic Ripley and Roy Burmeister, 1933
- Traded by Boston to the Montreal Canadiens for Leroy Goldsworthy, 1936

DAVE SILK #21 FORWARD b. Scituate, Massachusetts, January 1, 1958

1983–85	64	20	22	42	86
Playoffs	3	0	0	0	7

- Traded to Boston by the Rangers for Dave Barr, October 5, 1983
- Claimed on waivers from Boston by Detroit, December 21, 1985

CHARLIE SIMMER #23 FORWARD b. Terrace Bay, Ontario, March 20, 1954

1984–87	198	98	94	192	136
Playoffs	9	2	2	4	8

- Traded to Boston by Los Angeles for Boston's first draft pick in the 1985 entry draft
- Claimed by Pittsburgh in the NHL waiver draft, October 5, 1987
- Bill Masterton Memorial Trophy: 1985–86

Trivia Question #35
This former Bruin had to buy his way out of the Royal Canadian Mounted Police so that he could get married. Who was he?

AL SIMMONS #29 DEFENSE b. Winnipeg, Manitoba, September 25, 1951

1973–76	10	0	1	1	21
Playoffs	1	0	0	0	0

- Sold to Boston by San Diego (WHL), February 7, 1974
- Sold by Boston to the Rangers, November 14, 1975

FRANK SIMONETTI #21 DEFENSE b. Melrose, Massachusetts, September 11, 1962

1984–88	115	5	8	13	76
Playoffs	12	0	1	1	8

- Signed as a free agent by Boston, October 4, 1984

AL SIMS #20 – 23 – 29 DEFENSE b. Toronto, Ontario, April 18, 1953

1973–79	311	22	48	70	172
Playoffs	37	0	2	2	12

- Boston's fourth choice in the 1973 entry draft
- Claimed from Boston by Hartford in the expansion draft, June 13, 1979

ALFIE SKINNER FORWARD b. Toronto, Ontario, April 23, 1961

1924–25	9	0	0	0	6

PETRI SKRIKO #18 FORWARD b. Laapeenrenta, Finland, March 12, 1962

1990–92	37	6	14	20	15
Playoffs	18	4	4	8	4

- Traded to Boston by Vancouver for Boston's second pick in the 1992 entry draft, January 16, 1991
- Traded by Boston to Winnipeg for Brent Ashton, October 29, 1991

LOUIS SLEIGHER #25 FORWARD b. Nouvelle, Quebec, October 23, 1958

1984–86	83	16	21	37	65
Playoffs	6	0	0	0	18

- Traded to Boston by Quebec for Luc Dufour, October 25, 1984

DON SMILLIE FORWARD

1933–34	12	2	2	4	4

ALEX SMITH #4 DEFENSE *b.* Liverpool, England, April 2, 1905

1932–34	63	9	10	19	62
Playoffs	5	0	2	2	6

BARRY SMITH #28 FORWARD *b.* Surrey, British Columbia, April 25, 1955

1975–76	19	1	0	1	2

- Boston's second choice in the 1975 entry draft

DALLAS SMITH #8 – 11 – 20 DEFENSE *b.* Hamiota, Manitoba, October 10, 1941

1959–62, 1965–77					
Totals	861	54	248	302	934
Playoffs	85	3	28	31	128

- Seventh Player Award: 1972–73
- Member of the 1970 and 1972 Stanley Cup Champions

DES SMITH #8 DEFENSE *b.* Ottawa, Ontario, February 22, 1914

1939–42	114	15	17	32	154
Playoffs	22	1	4	5	14

- Traded to Boston by Chicago for Des Smith, January 26, 1940
- Member of the 1941 Stanley Cup Champions

Trivia Question #36

This former Bruins star was known as the "Red Grange" of hockey. Who are we talking about?

FLOYD SMITH #22 FORWARD *b.* Perth, Ontario, May 16, 1935

1954–57	26	0	1	1	6

KEN SMITH #15 – 17 – 18 – 20 FORWARD *b.* Moose Jaw, Saskatchewan, May 8, 1924

1944–51	331	80	91	171	49
Playoffs	30	8	13	21	6

- Traded by Boston with Fernie Flaman, Leo Boivin, and Phil Maloney to Toronto for Bill Ezinicki and Vic Lynn, November 16, 1950

REGINALD SMITH ("Hooley") #6 DEFENSE/FORWARD *b.* Toronto, Ontario, January 7, 1905

1936–37	43	8	10	18	36
Playoffs	3	0	0	0	0

- Traded to Boston by Montreal Maroons for Chuck Shannon, 1936
- Hall of Fame elected 1972

RICK SMITH #10 – 23 DEFENSE *b.* Kingston, Ontario, June 29, 1948

1968–72, 1976–80					
Totals	512	36	125	161	391
Playoffs	75	3	22	25	69

- Traded by Boston with Reggie Leach to California and Bob Stewart for Carol Vadnais and Don O'Donoghue, February 23, 1972
- Traded to Boston by St. Louis for Joe Zanussi, December 20, 1976
- Member of the 1970 Stanley Cup Champions

BRYAN SMOLINSKI #20 FORWARD *b.* Toledo, Ohio, December 27, 1971

1992–95	136	50	36	86	113
Playoffs	22	6	5	11	10

- Boston's first choice in the 1990 entry draft
- Traded by Boston along with Glen Murray to Pittsburgh for Kevin Stevens and Sean McEachern, August 2, 1995

TOM SONGIN #19 – 28 FORWARD
b. Norwood, Massachusetts, December 20, 1953

1978–81	43	5	5	10	22

- Signed as a free agent by Boston, October 3, 1978

EMORY SPARROW FORWARD

1925–25	6	0	0	0	4

BILL SPEER #24 DEFENSE b. Lindsay, Ontario, March 20, 1942

1969–71	28	1	3	4	8
Playoffs	8	1	0	1	4

- Claimed by Boston from Pittsburgh at the intra-league draft, June 11, 1969
- Member of the 1970 Stanley Cup Champions

IRVIN SPENCER ("Spinner") #22 DEFENSE/FORWARD b. Sudbury, Ontario, December 4, 1937

1962–63	69	5	17	22	34

- Drafted by Boston from the Rangers, June 1962
- Drafted from Boston by Detroit, June 1963

FRANK SPRING #28 FORWARD b. Cranbrook, British Columbia, October 19, 1949

1969–70	1	0	0	0	0

- Boston's second choice in the 1969 entry draft
- Drafted from Boston by Philadelphia in the intra-league draft, June 8, 1971

STEVE STAIOS DEFENSE b. Hamilton, Ontario, July 28, 1973

1995–97	66	3	8	11	75
Playoffs	3	0	0	0	0

- Traded to Boston along with Kevin Sawyer by St. Louis for Steve Leach, March 8, 1996
- Placed on waivers by Boston, March 18, 1997. Signed by Vancouver

FRED STANFIELD #17 FORWARD b. Toronto, Ontario, May 4, 1944

1967–73	448	135	274	409	80
Playoffs	55	17	29	46	6

- Seventh Player Award: 1970–71
- Traded to Boston along with Ken Hodge and Phil Esposito from Chicago for Jack Norris, Gilles Marotte, and Pit Martin, May 15, 1967
- Traded by Boston to Minnesota for Gilles Gilbert, May 22, 1973
- Member of the 1970 and 1972 Stanley Cup Champions

ALLAN STANLEY #10 DEFENSE b. Timmins, Ontario, March 1, 1926

1956–58	129	12	50	62	82
Playoffs	12	1	3	4	6

- Sold to Boston by Chicago, October 1956
- Traded by Boston to Toronto for Jim Morrison, October 1958
- Hall of Fame elected 1981

PAUL STANTON #25 DEFENSE b. Boston, Massachusetts, June 22, 1967

1993–94	71	3	7	10	54

- Traded to Boston by Pittsburgh for a future draft pick, October 8, 1993
- Traded by Boston to the Islanders for a future draft pick, February 10, 1995

PAT STAPLETON ("Whitey") #4 – 11 DEFENSE b. Sarnia, Ontario, July 4, 1940

1961–63	90	2	8	10	50

- Drafted by Boston from Chicago, June 1961
- Traded by Boston along with Orland Kurtenbach and Andy Hebenton to Toronto for Ron Stewart, June 8, 1965

VIC STASIUK #7 FORWARD b. Lethbridge, Alberta, May 23, 1929

1955–61	378	125	166	291	442
Playoffs	29	6	8	14	26

- Dufresne Trophy: 1958–59
- Traded to Boston with Marcel Bonin, Lorne Davis, and Terry Sawchuk, by Detroit for Eddie Sandford, Gilles Boisvert, Real Chevrefils, Norm Corcoran, and Warren Godfrey, June 1955
- Traded by Boston with Leo Labine to Detroit for Gary Aldcorn, Tom McCarthy, and Murray Oliver, January 1961

KEVIN STEVENS #25 FORWARD b. Brockton, Massachusetts, April 15, 1965

1995–96	41	10	13	23	49

- Traded to Boston along with Sean McEachern by Pittsburgh for Bryan Smolinski and Glen Murray, August 2, 1995
- Traded by Boston to Los Angeles for Rick Tocchet, January 25, 1996

MIKE STEVENS #36 FORWARD b. Kitchener, Ontario, December 30, 1965

1987–88	7	0	1	1	9

- Traded to Boston by Vancouver for cash, October 6, 1987

PAUL STEVENS DEFENSE

1925–26	17	0	0	0	0

SHAYNE STEVENSON #49 FORWARD b. Newmarket, Ontario, October 26, 1970

1990–92	19	0	1	1	28

- Boston's first choice in the 1989 entry draft
- Claimed from Boston by Tampa Bay in the expansion draft, June 18, 1992

AL STEWART #31 FORWARD b. Grande Centre, Alberta, January 31, 1964

1991–92	4	0	0	0	17

- Traded to Boston by New Jersey for future considerations, October 16, 1991

BOB STEWART #24 – 28 DEFENSE b. Charlottetown, Prince Edward Island, November 10, 1950

1971–72	8	0	0	0	15

- Traded by Boston with Reggie Leach and Rick Smith to California for Carol Vadnais and Don O'Donoghue, February 23, 1972

CAM STEWART #16 – 26 FORWARD b. Kitchener, Ontario, September 18, 1971

1993–97	83	3	7	10	72
Playoffs	13	1	3	4	9

- Boston's second choice in the 1990 entry draft

NELS STEWART #7 FORWARD b. Montreal, Quebec, December 29, 1902

1932–35, 1936–37					
Totals	152	63	55	118	181
Playoffs	9	2	1	3	4

- Hall of Fame elected 1962
- Sold to Boston by the Montreal Maroons, 1933
- Sold to the Americans, 1937

RON STEWART #7 – 12 FORWARD/DEFENSE b. Calgary, Alberta, July 12, 1932

1965–67	126	34	26	60	48

- Traded to Boston by Toronto for Orland Kurtenbach, Andy Hebenton, and Pat Stapleton, June 8, 1965
- Drafted from Boston by St. Louis in the expansion draft, June 6, 1967

BILLY STUART ("Red") #12 DEFENSE b. Sackville, Nova Scotia

1924–27	100	14	4	18	93
Playoffs	8	0	0	0	6

- Sold to Boston December 14, 1924 from Toronto

JOZEF STUMPEL #16 – 22 FORWARD
b. Nitra, Czechoslovakia, June 20, 1972

1991–97	274	54	122	176	54
Playoffs	23	2	9	11	4

- Boston's second choice in the 1991 entry draft

GEORGE SULLIVAN ("Red") #12 FORWARD
b. Peterborough, Ontario, December 24, 1929

1949–53	102	15	21	36	32
Playoffs	12	0	0	0	2

- Purchased from Boston by Chicago, September 10, 1954.

RON SUTHERLAND DEFENSE b. Eston, Saskatchewan, February 8, 1913

1931–32	2	0	0	0	0

RON SUTTER #10 FORWARD b. Viking, Alberta, December 2, 1963

1995–96	18	5	7	12	24
Playoffs	5	0	0	0	8

- Signed as a free agent by Boston, March 9, 1996

BOB SWEENEY #20 – 42 FORWARD
b. Concord, Massachusetts, January 25, 1964

1986–92	382	81	112	193	509
Playoffs	87	13	16	29	185

- Boston's sixth choice in the 1982 entry draft
- Claimed on waivers from Boston by Buffalo, October 9, 1992

DON SWEENEY #32 DEFENSE b. St. Stephen, New Brunswick, August 17, 1966

1988–97	611	40	142	182	442
Playoffs	81	6	8	14	71

- Boston's eighth pick in the 1984 entry draft
- Seventh Player Award: 1992–93

TIM SWEENEY #41 – 42 FORWARD b. Boston, Massachusetts, April 12, 1967

1992–93, 1995–97					
Totals	91	19	26	45	34
Playoffs	4	0	0	0	2

- Signed as a free agent by Boston, September 16, 1992
- Claimed from Boston by Anaheim in the expansion draft, June 24, 1993
- Signed as a free agent by Boston, August 9, 1995

MIKHAIL TATARINOV #28 DEFENSE
b. Angarsk, USSR, July 16, 1966

1993–94	2	0	0	0	2

- Signed as a free agent by Boston, July 30, 1993

BILLY TAYLOR #12 FORWARD b. Winnipeg, Manitoba, May 3, 1919

1947–48	39	4	16	20	25

- Traded to Boston by Detroit for Bep Guidolin, October 1947

BOBBY TAYLOR FORWARD b. Newton, Massachusetts, August 12, 1904

1929–30	8	0	0	0	6

ALLEN TEAL ("Skip") FORWARD b. Ridgeway, Ontario, July 17, 1933

1954–55	1	0	0	0	0

ORVAL TESSIER #18 FORWARD b. Cornwall, Ontario, June 30, 1933

1955–56, 1960–61					
Totals	57	5	7	12	6

- Drafted by Boston from Montreal, May 31, 1955

MATS THELIN #27 DEFENSE b. Stockholm, Sweden, March 30, 1961

1984–87	163	8	19	27	176
Playoffs	5	0	0	0	6

- Boston's sixth choice in the 1981 entry draft

MICHAEL THELVEN #22 DEFENSE
b. Stockholm, Sweden, January 7, 1961

1985–90	207	20	80	100	217
Playoffs	34	4	10	14	32

- Boston's eighth choice in the 1980 entry draft

DAVE THOMLINSON #41 FORWARD
b. Edmonton, Alberta, October 22, 1966

1991–92	12	0	1	1	17

- Signed as a free agent by Boston, July 30, 1991

CLIFF THOMPSON #18 – 21 DEFENSE
b. Winchester, Massachusetts, December 9, 1918

1941–42, 1948–49					
Totals	13	0	1	1	2

BILL THOMS FORWARD *b.* Newmarket, Ontario, March 5, 1910

1944–45	17	4	2	6	0
Playoffs	1	0	0	0	2

MATTIAS TIMANDER #47 DEFENSE
b. Solleftea, Sweden, April 16, 1974

1996–97	41	1	8	9	14

- Boston's 7th choice in the 1992 amateur draft

RICK TOCCHET #22 FORWARD
b. Scarborough, Ontario, April 9, 1964

1995–97	67	32	22	54	131
Playoffs	5	4	0	4	21

- Traded to Boston by Los Angeles for Kevin Stevens, January 25, 1996
- Traded by Boston along with Adam Oates and Bill Ranford to Washington for Jim Carey, Anson Carter, and Jason Allison, March 1, 1997

JERRY TOPPAZZINI #20 – 21 FORWARD
b. Copper Cliff, Ontario, July 29, 1931

1952–54, 1955–64					
Totals	659	148	216	364	328
Playoffs	40	13	9	22	13

- Dufresne Trophy: 1956–57, 1957–58
- Brother of Zelio Toppazzini, Bruin from 1948–49 to 1950–51
- Traded by Boston to Chicago for Gus Bodnar, February, 1954
- Traded to Boston with Real Chevrefils by Detroit for Murray Costello and Lorne Ferguson, January 17, 1956
- Traded by Boston with Matt Ravlich to Chicago for Murray Balfour and Mike Draper, June 9, 1964

ZELIO TOPPAZZINI #19 FORWARD *b.* Copper Cliff, Ontario, January 5, 1930

1948–51	45	6	7	13	18
Playoffs	2	0	0	0	0

- Traded by Boston with Ed Harrison to the Rangers for Dunc Fisher, November 16, 1950

GRAEME TOWNSHEND #48 *b.* Kingston, Jamaica, October 2, 1965

1989–91	22	2	5	7	19

- Signed as a free agent by Boston, May 12, 1989

BILL TOUHEY FORWARD *b.* Ottawa, Ontario, March 23, 1906

1931–32	26	5	4	9	12

GORDON TURLIK FORWARD *b.* Mickel, British Columbia, September 17, 1939

1959–60	2	0	0	0	2

CAROL VADNAIS #10 FORWARD/DEFENSE
b. Montreal, Quebec, September 25, 1945

1971–76	263	47	134	181	433
Playoffs	39	2	19	21	93

- Seventh Player Award: 1973–74

- Traded to Boston with Don O'Donoghue by California for Reggie Leach, Rick Smith, and Bob Stewart, February 23, 1972
- Traded by Boston with Phil Esposito to the Rangers for Brad Park, Jean Ratelle, and Joe Zanussi
- Member of the 1972 Stanley Cup Champions

JIM VESEY #54 FORWARD *b.* Charlestown, Massachusetts, October 29, 1965

1991–92	4	0	0	0	0

- Traded to Boston by Winnipeg for future considerations, June 20, 1991

Trivia Question #37
On April 11, 1971, Bobby Orr accomplished a feat that had never been attained in the history of the NHL. What was that feat?

PHIL VON STEFENELLI #41 DEFENSE
b. Vancouver, British Columbia, April 10, 1969

1995–96	27	0	4	4	16

- Signed as a free agent by Boston, September 10, 1994

MIKE WALTON ("Shaky") #11 – 25 – 27 FORWARD *b.* Kirkland Lake, Ontario, January 3, 1945

1970–73, 1978–79					
Totals	168	60	57	117	92
Playoffs	25	9	7	16	34

- Traded to Boston by Philadelphia for Danny Schock and Rick MacLeish, February 1, 1971
- Traded by Boston with Chris Oddleifson and Fred O'Donnell to Vancouver for Bobby Schmautz, February 8, 1974
- Signed as a free agent by Boston, December 5, 1978
- Member of the 1972 Stanley Cup Champions

WES WALZ #13 FORWARD *b.* Calgary, Alberta, May 15, 1970

1989–91	73	9	12	21	44
Playoffs	2	0	0	0	0

- Boston's third choice in the 1989 entry draft
- Traded by Boston along with Garry Galley to Philadelphia for Gord Murphy and Brian Dobbin, January 2, 1992

DON WARD #12 DEFENSE *b.* Sarnia, Ontario, October 19, 1935

1959–60	31	0	1	1	160

- Drafted from Chicago, 1959

GRANT WARWICK ("Knobby") #12 FORWARD *b.* Regina, Saskatchewan, October 11, 1921

1947–49	76	28	20	48	22
Playoffs	10	2	3	5	4

- Traded to Boston from the New York Rangers for Pentti Lund and Billy Taylor, 1947
- Sold by Boston to Montreal, October 10, 1949

JOE WATSON #14 DEFENSE *b.* Smithers, British Columbia, July 6, 1943

1964–65, 1966–67					
Totals	73	2	14	16	38

- Drafted from Philadelphia by Boston in the expansion draft, June 6, 1967

TOM WEBSTER #11 – 21 – 22 FORWARD *b.* Kirkland Lake, Ontario, October 4, 1948

1968–70	11	0	4	4	11
Playoffs	1	0	0	0	0

- Drafted from Boston by Buffalo in the expansion draft, June 10, 1970

RALPH WEILAND ("Cooney") #7 – 14 FORWARD *b.* Egmondville, Ontario, November 5, 1904

1928–32, 1935–39					
Totals	266	131	105	236	123
Playoffs	36	10	8	18	8

- Sold to Ottawa, 1932
- Traded to Boston from Detroit for Marty Barry, 1935
- Hall of Fame elected 1971
- Art Ross Trophy: 1929–30

- Lester Patrick Trophy: 1972
- Member of the 1929 and 1939 Stanley Cup Champions
- Coach of the Boston Bruins, (1939–40 to 1940–41)
- Coach of the Boston Bruins, Stanley Cup Champions, 1940–41

JOHN WENSINK #18 FORWARD b. Cornwall, Ontario, April 1, 1953

1976–80	248	57	55	112	429
Playoffs	40	2	6	8	86

- Signed as a free agent by Boston, October 12, 1976
- Claimed from Boston by Quebec in the waiver draft, October 10, 1980

GLEN WESLEY #26 DEFENSE b. Red Deer, Alberta, October 2, 1968

1987–94	537	77	230	307	417
Playoffs	105	15	32	47	109

- Seventh Player Award: 1987–88
- Boston's first choice in the 1987 entry draft
- Traded by Boston to Hartford for Hartford's first draft choices in 1995, 1996, and 1997

ED WESTFALL #18 DEFENSE/FORWARD b. Oshawa, Ontario, September 19, 1940

1961–72	734	126	213	339	410
Playoffs	50	13	17	30	29

- Seventh Player Award: 1968–69
- Drafted from Boston by the Islanders in the expansion draft, June 6, 1972
- Member of the 1970 and 1972 Stanley Cup Champions

JIM WIEMER #30 – 36 DEFENSE b. Sudbury, Ontario, January 9, 1961

1989–94	201	11	47	58	259
Playoffs	40	2	7	9	36

- Signed as a free agent by Boston, July 6, 1989

ARCHIE WILCOX DEFENSE b. Montreal, Quebec, May 9, 1903

1933–34	16	0	1	1	2

BARRY WILKINS #27 DEFENSE b. Toronto, Ontario, February 28, 1947

1966–67, 1968–70					
Totals	8	1	0	1	2

- Drafted from Boston by Vancouver in the expansion draft, June 10, 1970

Trivia Question #38
This former Bruin, while a member of the New York Rangers, scored the first short-handed goal in All-Star game history on October 1, 1960. Name this player?

JACK WILKINSON #8 DEFENSE

1943–44	9	0	0	0	2

CARL WILLIAMS ("Burr") DEFENSE b. Okemah, Oklahoma, August 30, 1909

1934–35	7	0	0	0	6

TOM WILLIAMS #11 FORWARD b. Duluth, Minnesota, April 17, 1940

1961–69	390	96	136	232	115
Playoffs	4	1	0	1	2

- Traded by Boston with Barry Gibbs to Minnesota for Fred O'Donnell and Minnesota's first draft choice in the 1969 entry draft, May 7, 1969

GORDIE WILSON FORWARD b. Port Arthur, Ontario, August 13, 1932

1954–55	2	0	0	0	0

- Playoffs only

LANDON WILSON #27 FORWARD b. St. Louis, Missouri, March 13, 1975

1996–97	40	8	12	20	72

- Traded from Colorado to Boston along with Anders Myrvold, for Boston's 1st round pick in the 1998 amateur draft, November 22, 1996

> ### Trivia Question #39
> On April 24, 1983, the Bruins scored the 1,000th goal in their playoff history, an overtime winner against the Buffalo Sabres that eliminated the Sabres from the playoffs. Can you name the Bruin that scored this goal?

WALLY WILSON #22 FORWARD b. Berwick, Nova Scotia, May 25, 1921

1947–48	53	11	8	19	18
Playoffs	1	0	0	0	0

CHRIS WINNES #40 FORWARD b. Ridgefield, Connecticut, February 12, 1968

1990–93	29	1	4	5	6
Playoffs	1	0	0	0	0

- Boston's ninth choice in the 1987 entry draft

EDDIE WISEMAN #7 FORWARD b. Newcastle, New Brunswick, December 28, 1912

1939–42	110	30	52	82	18
Playoffs	22	8	4	12	2

- Traded to Boston from the New York Americans for Eddie Shore, January 25, 1940
- Member of the 1941 Stanley Cup Champions

BOB WOYTOWICH #8 DEFENSE b. Winnipeg, Manitoba, August 18, 1941

1964–67	153	6	34	40	134

- Drafted by Boston from the Rangers, June 10, 1964
- Drafted from Boston by Minnesota in the expansion draft, June 6, 1967

KEN YACKEL FORWARD b. St. Paul, Minnesota, March 5, 1932

1958–59	6	0	0	0	2
Playoffs	2	0	0	0	2

> ### Trivia Question #39
> This Bruin goaltender faced the first penalty shot in playoff history, March 25, 1937. He successfully stopped Lionel Conacher of the Montreal Maroons. Who was this Bruin netminder?

C.J. YOUNG #18 FORWARD b. Waban, Massachusetts, b. January 1, 1968

1992–93	15	4	5	9	12

- Traded to Boston by Calgary for Brent Ashton, February 1, 1993

JOE ZANUSSI #29 DEFENSE b. Rossland, British Columbia, September 25, 1947

1975–77	68	1	8	9	38
Playoffs	4	0	1	1	2

- Traded to Boston along with Jean Ratelle and Brad Park by the Rangers for Phil Esposito and Carol Vadnais, November 7, 1975
- Traded by Boston to St. Louis for Rick Smith, December 20, 1976

SERGEI ZHOLTOK #11 FORWARD b. Riga, Latvia, December 2, 1972

1992–94	25	2	2	4	2

- Boston's second choice in the 1992 entry draft

RICK ZOMBO #34 DEFENSE b. Des Plaines, Illinois, May 8, 1963

1995–96	67	4	10	14	53

- Traded to Boston by St. Louis for Fred Knipscheer, October 2, 1995

GOALIES
1924–25 to 1996–97

INFORMATION ON GOALIES IS LISTED IN THE FOLLOWING ORDER:
games played / won-lost-tied record / shutouts / goals against / goals against average / minutes played

GEORGE ABBOTT #1

1943–44	I	0–1–0	0	7	7.00	60

- Ordained minister
- Played 11/27/43 in game at Toronto.
- Was Maple Leaf practice goalie.
- Played for Boston when Bruins were short a netminder for game. During war year, teams were only required to carry one goaltender

JOHN ADAMS #31 *b.* Port Arthur, Ontario, July 27, 1946

1972–73	14	9–3–1	I	39	3.00	780

- Last club: Dayton Gems (IHL)
- Sold to San Diego Gulls (part of deal bringing Ken Broderick to Boston), June 1773

SCOTT BAILEY ("Bailes") #39 *b.* Calgary, Alberta, May 2, 1972

1995–97	19	6–5–2	0	55	3.43	965

- Last junior club: Spokane (WHL)
- Drafted as Boston's fourth pick (112th overall), 1992 draft

MIKE BALES #30 *b.* Prince Albert, Saskatchewan, August 6, 1971

1992–93	I	0–0–0	0	I	2.40	25

- Last amateur club: Ohio State University
- Drafted as Boston's fourth pick (105th overall), 1990 draft

- Signed as a free agent by Ottawa Senators on July 4, 1994.

MARCO BARON #31 *b.* Montreal, Quebec, April 8, 1959

1979–83	64	31–2–5	I	203	3.40	3578
Playoffs	I	0–1–0	0	3	9.00	20

- Last amateur club: Montreal Juniors
- Drafted as Boston's sixth pick (99th overall) 1979 draft
- Traded to the Kings for Bob LaForest on January 3, 1984

YVES BELANGER #31 *b.* Baie Comeau, Quebec, September 30, 1952

1979–80	8	2–0–3	0	19	3.48	328

- Last club: Syracuse Blazers (EHL)
- Signed as a free agent by Boston, October 8, 1979

HARVEY BENNETT #1 *b.* Edington, Saskatchewan, July 23, 1925

1944–45	24	10–1–2	0	106	4.33	1470

- Father of future NHLers Bill (Boston, Hartford) and Curt (St. Louis, Rangers, and Atlanta)

DANIEL BERTHIAUME #31 *b.* Longueuil, Quebec, January 26, 1966

1991–92	8	1–4–2	0	21	3.14	401

- Last amateur club: Chicoutimi (QMJHL)

- Traded to Boston from Winnipeg for Doug Evans, June 10, 1992
- Signed as a free agent by Ottawa, December 15, 1992

Trivia Question #41

Former NHLer Phil Goyette holds a playoff distinction in Bruins history. Can you name what it might be?

PAUL BIBEAULT #1 b. Montreal, Quebec, April 13, 1919

1944–46	42	2–6–2	1	58	3.81	2490
Playoffs	7	3	4–0–0	22	3.02	437

- Signed on loan from Montreal, 1944
- Returned to Montreal after injury to goaltender Bill Durnan, 1946

CRAIG BILLINGTON #1 b. London, Ontario, September 11, 1966

1994–96	35	15	14–3–1	98	3.35	1753
Playoffs	2	0	1–0–0	7	4.94	85

- Last amateur club: Belleville (OHL)
- Traded to Boston by Ottawa for Islanders draft pick (previously acquired by the Bruins) April 7, 1995
- Signed as a free agent by Florida, August 1996

DICK BITTNER #1 b. New, January 12, 1922 Haven, Connecticut

1949–50	1	0–0–1	0	3	3.00	60

JOHN BLUE #39 b. Huntington Beach, California, February 19, 1966

1992–94	41	14	16–7–1	111	2.94	2266
Playoffs	2	0	1–0–0	5	3.13	96

- Last amateur club: University of Minnesota
- Signed as a free agent by Boston, August 1, 1991
- Signed as a free agent by Buffalo, December 28, 1995

FRANK BRIMSEK ("Mr. Zero") #1 b. Eveleth, Minnesota, September 26, 1915

1938–43, 1946–49						
Totals	444	230	144–70–3	1160	2.58	27010
Playoffs	68	32	36–0–2	186	2.56	4365

- Served in the U.S. Coast Guard from 1943 to 1945
- Sold to Chicago, September 8, 1949
- Hockey Hall of Fame – elected 1966
- Vezina Trophy (best goalkeeper): 1938–39 & 1941–42
- 1st Team All-Star – 1938–39, 1941–42
- 2nd Team All-Star – 1939–40, 1940–41, 1942–43, 1945–46, 1946–47, 1947–48
- Member of the 1939 and 1941 Stanley Cup Champions
- Dufresne Trophy: 1942–43, 1947–48
- Calder Memorial Trophy: 1938–39

KEN BRODERICK #31 b. Toronto, Ontario, February 16, 1942

1973–75	20	9	8–1–1	48	2.61	1104

- Last amateur club: Canadian National Team
- Purchased from the San Diego Gulls, March 1973

ROSS BROOKS #30 b. Toronto, Ontario, October 17, 1937

1972–75	54	37	7–6–4	134	2.64	3047
Playoffs	1	0	0–0–0	3	9.00	20

- Last club: Johnstown Jets (EHL)

JIM CAREY #30 b. Dorchester, Massachusetts, May 31, 1974

1996–97	19	5	13–0–0	64	3.82	1005

- Traded to Boston from Washington along with Anson Carter and Jason Allison for Bill Ranford, Adam Oates, and Rick Tocchet, March 1, 1997
- NHL first All-Star team, 1996 (with Washington)
- Vezina Trophy winner, 1996 (with Washington)

JON CASEY #30 b. Grand Rapids, Minnesota, March 29, 1962

1993–94	57	30	15–9–4	153	2.87	3196
Playoffs	11	5	6–0–0	34	2.92	698

- Last amateur club: North Dakota (WCHA)

- Traded to Boston by Dallas for Andy Moog, June 20, 1993
- Signed as a free agent by St. Louis, June 29, 1994

ED CHADWICK #1 b. Fergus, Ontario, May 8, 1933

1961–62	4	0	3–1–0	22	5.50	240

- Last amateur club: Sault Ste. Marie Greyhounds (OHA)
- Traded to Boston by Toronto for Don Simmons, January 31, 1961

GERRY CHEEVERS #30 – 31 b. St. Catharine's, Ontario, December 2, 1940

1965–72, 1975–80						
Totals	416	229	102–7–26	1168	2.89	24274
Playoffs	88	53	34–0–7	242	2.69	5396

- Last amateur club: St. Michael's (OHA)
- Claimed by Boston at the Intra-league draft, June 9, 1965
- Signed with Cleveland (WHA) 1972
- Returned to Boston, 1976
- Elected Hockey Hall of Fame – 1985
- Member of the 1970 and 1972 Stanley Cup Champions

TIM CHEVELDAE #31 b. Melville, Saskatchewan, February 15, 1968

1996–97	2	0	1–0–0	5	3.23	93

- Signed as a free agent, August 27, 1996

LES COLVIN #1 b. Oshawa, Ontario, February 8, 1921

1948–49	1	0	1–0–0	4	4.00	60

MAURICE COURTEAU #1 b. Quebec City, Quebec, February 18, 1918

1943–44	6	2	4–0–0	33	5.50	360

JIM CRAIG #30 b. North Easton, Massachusetts, May 31, 1957

1980–81	23	9	7–6–0	78	3.68	1272

- Last amateur club: U.S. Olympic Team
- Traded to Boton to Boston from Atlanta for Boston's second pick in the 1980 draft (Steve Konroyd) and Boston's third pick in the 1981 draft (Mike Vernon), June 2, 1980

Trivia Question #42
On February 28, 1963, in a game against the Detroit Red Wings at Boston Garden, an unusual event happened between the first and the second period. Can you recall what it was?

WILF CUDE b. Barry, Wales, July 4, 1910

1931–32	2	1	1–0–1	6	3.00	120

NICK DAMORE #19 b. Niagara Falls, Ontario, July 17, 1916

1941–42	1	0	1–0–0	3	3.00	60

CLEON DASKALAKIS #35 b. Boston, Massachusetts, December 29, 1962

1984–87	12	3	4–1–0	41	4.86	506

- Last amateur club: Boston University (HE)
- Signed as a free agent by Boston, June 1, 1984

NORM DEFELICE #1 b. Schumacher, Ontario, January 19, 1933

1956–57	10	3	5–2–0	30	3.00	600

MATT DELGIUDICE #33 b. West Haven, Connecticut, March 5, 1967

1990–92	11	2	5–1–0	28	3.87	434

- Boston's fifth pick (77th overall) in the 1987 draft
- Last amateur club: U. of Maine (HE)

CLAUDE EVANS #1 *b.* Longueuil, Quebec, April 28, 1933

| 1957–58 | 1 | 0 | 0–1–0 | 4 | 4.00 | 60 |

- Last amateur club: Cincinnati Mohawks

NORM FOSTER #39 *b.* Vancouver, British Columbia, February 10, 1965

| 1990–91 | 3 | 2 | 1–0–0 | 14 | 4.57 | 184 |

- Last amateur club: Michigan State (CCHA)
- Boston's 11th choice (222nd overall), 1983 draft
- Traded to Edmonton by Boston for Edmonton's 6th choice in the 1992 draft, September 11, 1991

NORMAN FOWLER ("Hec")

| 1924–25 | 7 | 1 | 6–0–0 | 43 | 6.14 | 420 |

JIM FRANKS #1 *b.* Melville, Saskatchewan, November 8, 1914

| 1943–44 | 1 | 0 | 1–0–0 | 6 | 6.00 | 60 |

BRUCE GAMBLE #1 *b.* Port Arthur, Ontario, May 24, 1938

| 1960–62 | 80 | 18 | 41–1–1 | 318 | 3.98 | 4800 |

- Drafted by Boston from the Rangers, June 1959
- Traded to Springfield (AHL) by Boston with Terry Gray, Randy Miller, and Dale Rolfe for Bob McCord, June 1963

BERT GARDNER #1 *b.* Saskatoon, Saskatchewan, March 25, 1913

| 1943–44 | 41 | 17 | 19–5–1 | 212 | 5.17 | 2460 |

JACK GELINEAU #1 *b.* Toronto, Ontario, November 11, 1924

| 1948–51 | 141 | 46 | 62–3–7 | 429 | 3.04 | 8460 |
| Playoffs | 4 | 2 | 2–0–1 | 7 | 1.62 | 260 |

- Winner of the Calder Trophy, 1950–51
- Purchased from Boston by Chicago, November 28, 1953

GILLES GILBERT #1 *b.* St. Esprit, Quebec, March 31, 1949

| 1973–80 | 277 | 155 | 73–3–16 | 782 | 2.95 | 15915 |
| Playoffs | 21 | 7 | 14–0–1 | 93 | 3.00 | 1859 |

- Last amateur club: London Knights (OHA)
- Traded to Boston from Minnesota for Fred Stanfield, May 22, 1973
- Traded to Detroit from Boston for Rogie Vachon, July 15, 1980

ANDRE GILL #30 *b.* Sorel, Quebec, September 19, 1941

| 1967–68 | 5 | 3 | 2–0–1 | 13 | 2.89 | 270 |

- Last amateur club: Sorel, Quebec

RON GRAHAME #31 *b.* Victoria, British Columbia, June 7, 1950

| 1977–78 | 40 | 26 | 6–7–3 | 107 | 2.76 | 2328 |
| Playoffs | 4 | 2 | 1–0–0 | 7 | 2.08 | 202 |

- Last amateur club: Denver University (WCHA)
- Signed as a free agent by Boston, October 13, 1977
- Traded to Los Angeles for the Kings first draft pick in the 1979 draft (Ray Bourque), October 9, 1978

BENNY GRANT #1 *b.* Owen Sound, Ontario, July 14, 1908

| 1943–44 | 1 | 0 | 1–0–0 | 10 | 10.00 | 60 |

DON HEAD #1 *b.* Mount Dennis, Ontario, June 30, 1933

| 1961–62 | 38 | 9 | 26–3–2 | 161 | 4.24 | 2280 |

- Last amateur club: Windsor Bulldogs

JOHN HENDERSON ("Long John") #1 *b.* Toronto, Ontario, March 25, 1933

| 1954–56 | 45 | 15 | 5–15–5 | 113 | 2.52 | 2688 |
| Playoffs | 2 | 0 | 2–0–0 | 8 | 4.00 | 120 |

- Last amateur club: Toronto Marlboros (OHA)

GORDON HENRY ("Red") #1 *b.* Owen Sound, Ontario, August 17, 1926

1948–51, 1952–53						
Totals	3	1	2–0–1	5	1.67	180
Playoffs	5	0	4–0–0	21	4.45	283

- Last amateur club: Boston Olympics

JIM HENRY ("Sugar Jim") #1 *b.* Winnipeg, Manitoba, October 23, 1920

1951–55	236	91	103–4–23	608	2.58	14132
Playoffs	23	9	14–0–1	68	2.95	1381

- Obtained from the Chicago Blackhawks, 1951
- Second Team All-Star – 1951–52
- Dufresne Trophy: 1951–52, 1953–54
- Sold to Boston by Detroit, August 20, 1951

PERCY JACKSON *b.* Canmore, Alberta, July 21, 1907

1931–32	4	1	1–1–0	8	2.07	232

ED JOHNSTON #1 *b.* Montreal, Quebec, November 23, 1935

1962–73	443	182	192–5–27	1383	3.23	25713
Playoffs	13	7	6–0–1	37	2.90	765

- Last club: Johnstown Jets (EHL)
- Traded to Toronto by Boston, May 22, 1973, to complete earlier deal in which the Bruins received Jacques Plante
- Member of the 1970 & 1972 Stanley Cup Champions
- Dufresne Trophy: 1963–64

JOE JUNKIN #1 *b.* Belleville, Ontario, September 8, 1946

1968–69	1	0	0–0–0	0	0.00	8

- Last amateur club: Belleville Mohawks

DOUG KEANS #31 *b.* Pembroke, Ontario, January 7, 1958

1983–88	154	83	46–13–4	479	3.33	8635
Playoffs	6	2	4–0–0	26	4.33	360

- Last amateur club: Oshawa (OHA)
- Claimed on waivers from Los Angeles, May 24, 1983

DON KEENAN #1

1958–59	1	0	1–0–0	4	4.00	60

- Last amateur club: St. Michael's (OHA)

BLAINE LACHER #31 *b.* Medicine Hat, Alberta, September 5, 1970

1994–96	47	22	16–4–4	123	2.80	2636
Playoffs	5	1	4–0–0	12	2.54	283

- Last amateur club: Lake Superior State (CCHA)
- Signed as a free agent by Boston, June 2, 1994
- Seventh Player Award: 1994–95

REGGIE LEMELIN #1 *b.* Quebec City, Quebec, November 19, 1954

1987–93	183	92	62–1–6	531	3.09	10322
Playoffs	28	12	10–0–1	77	3.08	1501

- Last amateur club: Sherbrooke
- Signed as a free agent, August 13, 1987
- Jennings Trophy (fewest goals against) with Andy Moog – 1989–90

HOWARD LOCKHART

1924–25	2	0	2–0–0	11	5.50	120

HARRY LUMLEY ("Apple Cheeks") #1
b. Owen Sound, Ontario, November 11, 1926

1957–60	78	37	31–1–6	245	3.14	4680
Playoffs	8	3	5–0–0	25	3.02	496

- Last amateur club: Barrie Colts
- Hockey Hall of Fame – elected 1980

AL MILLAR #1 *b.* Winnipeg, Manitoba,
September 18, 1929

1957–58	6	1	3–2–0	25	4.17	360

- Last amateur club: Sault Ste. Marie Indians

MIKE MOFFAT #30 *b.* Galt, Ontario,
February 4, 1962

1981–84	19	7	7–2–0	70	4.29	979
Playoffs	11	6	5–0–0	38	3.44	663

- Drafted seventh (165th overall), 1980 draft

ANDY MOOG #35 *b.* Penticton, British
Columbia, February 18, 1960

1987–93	261	136	75–3–13	772	3.07	15067
Playoffs	70	36	32–0–2	203	2.99	4071

- Last amateur club: Billings (WHL)
- Traded from Edmonton to Boston for Bill Ranford, Geoff Courtnall, and Boston's second pick in the 1988 draft, March 8, 1988
- Traded to Dallas for Jon Casey, June 20, 1993
- Jennings Trophy (fewest goals against) with Reggie Lemelin – 1989–90

JACK NORRIS #17 *b.* Saskatoon,
Saskatchewan, August 5, 1942

1964–65	23	9	12–2–1	86	3.74	1380

- Last amateur club: Estevan Bruins (WCJHL)
- Traded to the Blackhawks along with Gilles Marotte and Pit Martin for Phil Esposito, Ken Hodge, and Fred Stanfield, May 15, 1967

BERNIE PARENT #30 *b.* Montreal, Quebec,
April 3, 1945

1965–67	57	14	31–5–1	496	3.67	3105

- Last amateur club: Niagara Falls Flyers (OHA)
- Drafted by the Philadelphia Flyers in the expansion draft, June 6, 1967
- Hockey Hall of Fame – elected 1984

PETE PEETERS #1 – 33 *b.* Edmonton,
Alberta, August 17, 1957

1982–86	171	91	57–1–9	496	2.99	9939
Playoffs	21	9	12–0–1	75	3.56	1264

- Last amateur club: Medicine Hat (WHL)
- Traded to Boston from Philadelphia for Brad McCrimmon, June 9, 1982
- Traded to Washington for Pat Riggin, November 14, 1985
- Vezina Trophy (best goalkeeper), 1982–83
- First Team All-Star – 1982–83

- Seventh Player Award: 1982–83
- Dufresne Trophy: 1982–83

BOB PERRAULT ("Miche") #1 b. Three Rivers, Quebec, January 28, 1931

1962–63	22	3	12–6–1	85	3.86	1320

- Last amateur club: Three Rivers Reds

JIM PETTIE ("Seaweed") #31 b. Toronto, Ontario, October 24, 1953

1976–79	21	9	7–2–1	71	3.68	1157

- Last club: Dayton Gems (IHL)
- Boston's 10th choice (142nd overall), 1973 draft

JACQUES PLANTE ("Jake the Snake") #31 b. Mont Carmel, Quebec, January 17, 1929

1972–73	8	7	1–0–2	16	2.00	480
Playoffs	2	0	2–0–0	10	5.00	120

- Obtained from the Toronto Maple Leafs, March 3, 1973 for future considerations (Eddie Johnston) and first-round draft choice
- Hockey Hall of Fame – elected 1978

CLAUDE PRONOVOST #1 b. Shawinigan Falls, Quebec, July 22, 1935

1955–56	11–0–0		1	0	0.00	60

BILL RANFORD #30 b. Brandon, Manitoba, December 14, 1966

1985–87, 1995–97						
Totals	122	52	49–1–6	368	3.01	4782
Playoffs	8	1	7–0–0	31	3.85	483

- Last amateur club: New Westminster (WHL)
- Traded to Edmonton for Andy Moog, Geoff Courtnall and future considerations, March 8, 1988
- Traded to Boston for Mariusz Czerkawski, Sean Brown, and Boston's first choice in the 1996 draft
- Traded by Boston along with Adam Oates and Rick Tocchet to Washington for Jim Carey, Jason Allison, and Anson Carter, March 1, 1997

DAVE REECE #30 b. Troy, New York, December 13, 1948

1975–76	14	7	5–2–2	43	3.32	777

- Last club: Dayton Gems (IHL)

VINCENT RIENDEAU #37 b. St. Hyacinthe, Quebec, April 20, 1966

1993–95	29	10	12–2–1	77	3.00	1541
Playoffs	2	1	1–0–0	8	4.00	120

- Last amateur club: Drummondville (QMJHL)
- Traded to Boston by Detroit for Boston's fifth-round choice in the 1995 amateur draft, January 17, 1994

PAT RIGGIN #1 b. Kincardine, Ontario, May 26, 1959

1985–87	49	20	16–9–1	156	3.36	2785
Playoffs	1	0	1–0–0	3	3.00	60

- Traded to Boston by Washington for Pete Peeters, November 14, 1985
- Son of former Detroit Red Wings goaltender Dennis Riggin

BOBBY RING #29

1965–66	10–0–0		0	4	7.06	34

MAURICE ROBERTS ("Moe") b. Waterbury, Connecticut, December 13, 1907

1925–26	2	0	1–0–0	5	3.33	90

ROBERTO ROMANO #35 b. Montreal, Quebec, October 10, 1962

1986–87	1	0	1–0–0	6	6.00	60

- Last amateur club: Hull Olympiques (QMJHL)
- Traded to Boston from Pittsburgh for Pat Riggin. February 6, 1987

TERRY SAWCHUK #1 *b.* Winnipeg, Manitoba, December 28, 1929

1955–57	102	40	43–1–11	262	2.57	6120

- Last amateur club: Windsor Spitfires (OHA)
- Traded to Boston by Detroit with Marcel Bonin, Lorne Davis, and Vic Stasiuk for Gilles Boisvert, Norm Corcoran, Warren Godfrey, and Eddie Sandford, June 1955
- Traded to Detroit by Boston for Johnny Bucyk, July 1957
- Hockey Hall of Fame – elected 1971
- Dufresne Trophy: 1955–56

PAXTON SCHAFER #1 *b.* Medicine Hat, Alberta, February 26, 1979

1996–97	3	0	0–0–0	6	4.68	77

DON SIMMONS #1 *b.* Port Colborne, Ontario, September 13, 1931

1956–61	168	65	74–2–15	493	2.95	10028
Playoffs	21	11	10–0–3	56	2.64	1271

- Last club: Johnstown Jets (EHL)
- Traded to Toronto by Boston for Eddie Chadwick, January 31, 1961

CHARLES STEWART ("Doc") #11

1924–27	77	31	31–5–10	194	2.46	4737

JIM STEWART #33

1979–80	1	0	1–0–0	5	15.00	20

DON SYLVESTRI #30 *b.* Sudbury, Ontario, June 2, 1961

1984–85	3	0	0–2–0	6	3.53	102

- Last amateur club: Clarkson (ECAC)
- Boston's eighth pick (182nd overall) in the 1981 draft

ROB TALLAS #35 *b.* Edmonton, Alberta, March 20, 1973

1995–97	29	9	12–1–1	72	3.31	1304

- Last amateur club: Seattle (WHL)
- Attended 1994 Bruins camp on a tryout basis

CECIL THOMPSON #1 *b.* Sandon, British Columbia, May 31, 1905

1928–39	468	252	153–6–74	962	1.99	28948
Playoffs	33	15	16–0–6	66	1.72	2296

- Sold to the Chicago Blackhawks, 1938
- Hockey Hall of Fame – elected 1959
- Vezina Trophy (best goalkeeper) 1929–30, 1932–33, 1935–36, 1937–38
- 1st Team All-Star – 1935–36, 1937–38
- 2nd Team All-Star – 1930–31, 1934–35
- Member of the 1929 Stanley Cup Champions

ROGIE VACHON #1 *b.* Palmarolle, Quebec, September 8, 1945

1980–82	91	44	30–1–2	300	3.47	5186
Playoffs	4	0	2–0–0	17	5.54	184

- Traded to Boston by Detroit for Gilles Gilbert, July 15, 1980

ROSS WILSON ("Lefty") #1 *b.* Toronto, Ontario, October 15, 1919

1957–58	1	0	0–1–0	1	1.15	52

- Trainer, Detroit Red Wings
- Played in game on December 29, 1957, at Detroit. Bruins' goaltender Don Simmons suffered a dislocated shoulder in the first period

HAL WINKLER #11 *b.* Gretna, Manitoba, March 20, 1892

1926–28	67	32	22–1–19	110	1.56	4225
Playoffs	10	2	3–5–2	18	1.69	640

- Obtained from the Rangers

GOALIES SCORING

No Boston Bruins goaltender has ever scored a goal in a league or Stanley Cup playoff game.

	ASSISTS	POINTS		ASSISTS	POINTS
Eddie Johnston	10	10	Reggie Lemelin	2	2
Andy Moog	10	10	Jacques Plante	2	2
Gerry Cheevers	9	9	Rogie Vachon	2	2
Gilles Gilbert	5	5	Ken Broderick	1	1
Doug Keans	5	5	Ross Brooks	1	1
Pete Peeters	4	4	Jim Craig	1	1
Bill Ranford	3	3	Bert Gardiner	1	1
Marco Baron	2	2	Ron Grahame	1	1
John Blue	2	2	Blaine Lacher	1	1
Jon Casey	2	2	Vincent Riendeau	1	1

PLAYOFF SCORING

	ASSISTS	POINTS		ASSISTS	POINTS
Gilles Gilbert	4	4	Reggie Lemelin	1	1
Andy Moog	2	2	Mike Moffat	1	1
Gerry Cheevers	1	1			

PENALTY MINUTES

Gerry Cheevers	206	Jim Craig	11
Andy Moog	110	Blaine Lacher	8
Pete Peeters	93	Bill Ranford	8
Gilles Gilbert	86	Rogie Vachon	6
Reggie Lemelin	56	Craig Billington	4
Marco Baron	46	Frank Brimsek	4
Doug Keans	46	Jack Gelineau	4
Terry Sawchuk	34	Pat Riggin	4
Eddie Johnston	24	Ross Brooks	2
Jim Pettie	23	Mike Moffat	2
Bruce Gamble	18	Bernie Parent	2
Jon Casey	14	Jacques Plante	2
Don Head	14	Claude Pronovost	2
Don Simmons	14	Vincent Riendeau	2
Harry Lumley	14	Don Sylvestri	2
John Blue	13		

PLAYOFF PENALTY MINUTES

Andy Moog	27	Doug Keans	4
Gerry Cheevers	16	Reggie Lemelin	4
Gilles Gilbert	10	Craig Billington	2
Pete Peeters	10	Eddie Johnston	2
Mike Moffat	8	Pat Riggin	2

Leighton "Hap" Emms

Art Ross

Lynn Patrick

Harry Sinden

GENERAL MANAGERS

ART ROSS General Manager from November 1, 1924 to 1953–54, *b.* Naughton, Ontario, January 13, 1886 *d.* August 5, 1964

- Elected Hockey Hall of Fame, 1945
- Presented the National Hockey League with a trophy to honor the outstanding player in the league, later changed to the leading scorer, 1941
- Inventor of the Ross puck and Ross goal net
- General Manager of 3 Stanley Cup teams, 1929, 1939, 1941
- Coach of Stanley Cup winners, 1939
- Coach: 1924–25 to 1927–28, 1929–30 to 1933–34, 1936–37 to 1938–39, 1941–42 to 1944–45

LYNN PATRICK General Manager from 1953–54 to 1963–64 *b.* Victoria, British Columbia, February 3, 1912

- Elected Hockey Hall of Fame, 1980
- Son of Lester Patrick, former General Manager of the Rangers
- Brother of Murray "Muzz" Patrick, defenseman, Rangers
- Father of Craig Patrick, General Manager of the Penguins
- Coach: 1950–51 to 1954–55

LEIGHTON "HAP" EMMS General Manager from 1965–66 to 1966–67 *b.* Barrie, Ontario, January 12, 1905

- Former owner of Bruins farm club, the Niagara Falls Flyers

MILT SCHMIDT General Manager from 1967–68 to 1971–72 *b.* Kitchener, Ontario, March 5, 1918

- Elected Hockey Hall of Fame, 1961
- General Manager of 2 Stanley Cup teams, 1970, 1972
- Coach: 1954–55 to 1960–61, 1962–63 to 1965–66

HARRY SINDEN General Manager from October 5, 1972 to present, *b.* Collins Bay, Ontario, September 14, 1932

- Elected Hockey Hall of Fame, 1983
- Coach of Stanley Cup winners, 1970
- Coach: 1966–67 to 1969–70, 1979–80, 1984–85

COACHES

Records are as coach of the Bruins:

GEORGE "BUCK" BOUCHER Coach 1949–50,
b. Ottawa, Ontario, 1896 d. October 17, 1960

Regular Season	22	32	16
Playoffs	–	–	–

- Elected Hockey Hall of Fame, 1960
- Played in the National Hockey League:
- Ottawa Senators – 1916 to 1929
- Montreal Maroons – 1929 to 1931
- Chicago Blackhawks – 1932
- Brother of George, Billy, and Bobby Boucher, former National Hockey League players

RICK BOWNESS Coach 1991–92, b. Moncton,
New Brunswick, January 25, 1955

Regular season	36	32	12
Playoffs	8	7	–

- Played in the National Hockey League: Flames – 1975–76 to 1976–77; Red Wings – 1977–78; Blues – 1978–79 to 1979–80; Jets – 1980–81 to 1981–82

PAT BURNS Coach 1997– , b. St. Henri,
Quebec, April 4, 1952

- Appointed Bruins coach, May 21, 1997

GERRY CHEEVERS Coach 1980–81 to
1984–85 b. St. Catharines, Ontario,
December 7, 1940

Regular season	204	126	64
Playoffs	15	19	0

- Played in the National Hockey League: Bruins – 1965–66 to 1971–72, 1975–76 to 1979–80
- Elected Hockey Hall of Fame, 1985

- Member of the 1970 & 1972 Stanley Cup champion Bruins

DON CHERRY Coach 1974–75 to 1978–79
b. Kingston, Ontario, February 5, 1934

Regular season	231	105	64
Playoffs	31	24	0

- Played in one playoff game in the National Hockey League: Bruins – 1954–55
- Jack Adams Trophy winner, "Coach of the Year," 1975–76

AUBREY "DIT" CLAPPER Coach 1945–46 to
1948–49 b. Newmarket, Ontario, February
9, 1907

Regular season	102	88	40
Playoffs	8	17	0

- Played in the National Hockey League: Bruins – 1928–29 to 1946–47
- Elected Hockey Hall of Fame, 1947
- Member of the 1929, 1939, & 1941 Stanley Cup Champion Bruins
- First team All-Star, 1939, 1940, 1941
- Second team All-Star, 1931, 1935, 1944

FRED CREIGHTON Coach 1979–80
b. Hamiota, Manitoba, July 14, 1933

Regular season	40	20	13
Playoffs	–	–	–

- Coached in the National Hockey League: Flames – 1974–75 to 1978–79

Terry O'Reilly fights off Borje Salming.

CY DENNENY Coach 1928–29 *b.* Farrans
Point, Ontario, 1897 *d.* 1970

Regular season	26	13	5
Playoffs	5	0	0

- Member and coach of the 1929 Stanley Cup champion Bruins
- Played in the National Hockey League: Senators – 1917 to 1928; Bruins – 1929
- Elected Hockey Hall of Fame, 1959

BUTCH GORING Coach 1985–86 to 1986–87
b. St. Boniface, Manitoba, October 22, 1949

Regular season	42	38	13
Playoffs	0	3	0

- Played in the National Hockey League: Kings – 1969–70 to 1979–80; Islanders – 1979–80 to 1984–85; Bruins – 1984–85
- Bill Masterton Trophy with Kings, 1978
- Lady Byng Trophy with Kings, 1978
- Conn Smythe Trophy with Islanders, 1981

ARMAND "BEP" GUIDOLIN Coach 1972–73 to
1973–74 *b.* Thorold, Ontario, December 9,
1925

Regular season	72	23	9
Playoffs	11	10	0

- Played in the National Hockey League: Bruins – 1942–43 to 1943–44, 1945–46 to 1946–47; Red Wings – 1947–48 to 1948–49; Blackhawks – 1948–49 to 1951–52
- Youngest player to ever play for the Bruins at age 16

TOM JOHNSON Coach 1970–71 to 1972–73
b. Baldur, Manitoba, February 18, 1928

Regular season	142	43	23
Playoffs	15	7	0

- Played in the National Hockey League: Canadiens – 1947–48, 1949–50 to 1962–63; Bruins – 1963–64 to 1964–65
- Elected Hockey Hall of Fame – 1970
- Coach of the 1972 Stanley Cup champion Bruins
- Played on six Stanley Cup teams with the Canadiens

- Awarded the Norris Trophy as the NHL's best defenseman, 1959
- First All-Star team with Montreal, 1959
- Second All-Star team with Montreal, 1956

STEVE KASPER Coach 1995–96 to 1996–97
b. Montreal, Quebec, September 28, 1961

Regular season	66	78	20
Playoffs	1	4	0

- Played in the National Hockey League: Bruins – 1980–81 to 1988–89; Kings – 1988–89 to 1990–91; Flyers – 1991–92 to 1992–93; Lightning – 1992–93
- Winner of the Selke Trophy as the top defensive forward, 1981–82

MIKE MILBURY Coach 1989–90 to 1990–91
b. Brighton, Massachusetts, June 17, 1952

Regular season	90	49	21
Playoffs	23	17	0

- Played in the National Hockey League: Bruins – 1975–76 to 1986–87

TERRY O'REILLY Coach 1986–87 to 1988–89
b. Niagara Falls, Ontario, June 7, 1951

Regular season	115	86	26
Playoffs	17	19	0

- Played in the National Hockey League: Bruins – 1971–72 to 1984–85
- Bruins career penalty leader with 2,095 minutes

FRANK PATRICK Coach 1934–35 to 1935–36
b. Ottawa, Ontario, 1886 *d.* June 29, 1960

Regular season	48	36	12
Playoffs	2	4	0

- Member of the 1915 Stanley Cup champion Vancouver Millionaires

LYNN PATRICK Coach 1950–51 to 1954–55
b. Victoria, British Columbia, February 3,
1912

Regular season	117	130	63
Playoffs	9	18	1

- Member of the 1940 Stanley Cup champion New York Rangers
- General Manager of the Bruins, 1953–54 to 1964–65
- Elected Hockey Hall of Fame, 1980
- Played in the National Hockey League: New York Rangers – 1934–35 to 1942–43, 1945–46

ART ROSS Coach 1924–25 to 1927–28, 1929–30 to 1933–34, 1936–37 to 1938–39, 1941–42 to 1944–45 *b.* Naughton, Ontario, January 13, 1886 *d.* August 5, 1964

Regular season	361	277	90
Playoffs	27	33	5

- Member of the January 1907 Kenora Thistles, Stanley Cup champions
- Member of the Montreal Wanderers, 1908 Stanley Cup champions
- Coach of the 1939 Stanley Cup champion Bruins
- General Manager of the Bruins, November 1, 1924 to 1953–54
- Played in the National Hockey League: Montreal Wanderers – 1918
- Elected to the Hockey Hall of Fame – 1945

MILT SCHMIDT Coach 1954–55 to 1960–61, 1962–63 to 1965–66 *b.* Kitchener, Ontario, March 5, 1918

Regular season	245	360	121
Playoffs	15	19	0

- General Manager of the Bruins, 1967–68 to 1971–72
- Member of the 1939 and 1941 Stanley Cup champion Bruins
- Played in the National Hockey League: Boston Bruins – 1936–37 to 1941–42, 1945–46 to 1954–55
- First team All-Star, 1940, 1947, 1951
- Second team All-Star, 1952
- Winner of the Hart Trophy, 1950–51
- Winner of the Art Ross Trophy, 1939–40
- Winner of the Lester Patrick Trophy, 1996
- Elected to the Hockey Hall of Fame, 1961
- Replaced Phil Watson as head coach, 1962–63

HARRY SINDEN Coach 1966–67 to 1969–70, 1979–80, 1984–85 *b.* Collins Bay, Ontario, September 14, 1932

Regular season	153	116	58
Playoffs	24	19	0

- General Manager of the Bruins, October 5, 1972 to present
- Elected to the Hockey Hall of Fame, 1983
- Replaced Fred Creighton as coach during the 1979–80 season
- Replaced Gerry Cheevers as coach during the 1984–85 season
- Coach of the 1970 Stanley Cup champion Bruins

BRIAN SUTTER Coach 1992–93 to 1994–95 *b.* Viking, Alberta, October 7, 1956

Regular season	120	73	23
Playoffs	7	15	0

- Played in the National Hockey League: St. Louis Blues – 1976–77 to 1987–88

PHIL WATSON Coach 1961–62 to 1962–63 *b.* Montreal, Quebec, April 24, 1914

Regular season	16	55	13
Playoffs	0	0	0

- Played in the National Hockey League: Rangers– 1935–36 to 1942–43, 1944–45 to 1947–48; Canadiens – 1943–44
- Member of the 1940 Stanley Cup champion Rangers
- Member of the 1944 Stanley Cup champion Canadiens

RALPH "COONEY" WEILAND Coach 1939–40 to 1940–41 *b.* Seaforth, Ontario, November 5, 1904

Regular season	58	20	18
Playoffs	10	7	0

- Played in the National Hockey League: Bruins – 1928–29 to 1931–32, 1935–36 to 1938–39; Senators – 1932–33 to 1933–34; Red Wings – 1933–34 to 1934–35
- Member of the 1929 and 1939 Stanley Cup champion Bruins
- Coach of the 1941 Stanley Cup champion Bruins
- Elected Hockey Hall of Fame, 1971

ASSISTANT COACHES

1981–85   HEAD COACH: Gerry Cheevers
          ASSISTANT COACHES: Gary Doak & Jean Ratelle

1985–86   HEAD COACHES: Butch Goring & Terry O'Reilly
          ASSISTANT COACH: Mike Milbury

1987–89   HEAD COACH: Terry O'Reilly
          ASSISTANT COACH: John Cunniff
          GOALTENDER COACH: Joe Bertagna

1989–91   HEAD COACH: Mike Milbury
          ASSISTANT COACHES: Gordie Clark & Ted Sator
          GOALTENDER COACH: Joe Bertagna

1991–92   HEAD COACH: Rick Bowness
          ASSISTANT COACHES: Gordie Clark & Mike O'Connell

1992–95   HEAD COACH: Brian Sutter
          ASSISTANT COACH: Tom McVie

1995–96   HEAD COACH: Steve Kasper
          ASSISTANT COACH: Cap Raeder & Tim Watters

1996–97   HEAD COACH: Steve Kasper
          ASSISTANT COACH: Cap Raeder

1997–98   HEAD COACH: Pat Burns
          ASSISTANT COACH: Jacques Laperriere & Bobby Francis

Milt Schmidt

*Don Cherry in his only NHL
appearance as a player.*

CAPTAINS

1924–27	No Captain
1927–31	Lionel Hitchman
1931–32	George Owen
1932–38	Dit Clapper
1938–39	Cooney Weiland
1939–47	Dit Clapper
1946–50	Johnny Crawford
1950–54	Milt Schmidt
1954–55	Eddie Sandford
1955–61	Fern Flaman
1961–63	Don McKenney
1963–66	Leo Boivin
1966–67	Johnny Bucyk
1967–73	No Captain
1973–77	Johnny Bucyk
1977–83	Wayne Cashman
1983–85	Terry O'Reilly
1985–87	Rick Middleton & Ray Bourque
1987–97	Ray Bourque

Lionel Hitchman

Ralph "Cooney" Weiland

George Owen

Dit Clapper

Eddie Sandford

Wayne Cashman

Johnny Bucyk

Leo Boivin

Fern Flaman

Don McKenney

TRAINERS & THERAPISTS

Tommy Murray and Win Green . . . . 1926–27 & 1927–28
Win Green 1928–36
Win Green and Hammy Moore 1935–6
Hammy Moore and Dan Canney 1963–64
Dan Canney and Dave Johnson 1964–65
Dan Canney and John Forristall 1965–76
Dan Canney, John Forristall, and Jim Kausek . . . 1976–84
Dan Canney, Jim Kausek, and Bud Carpenter . . . 1984–85
Jim Narrigan and Larry Ness 1985–86
Jim Narrigan, Larry Ness, and Don Worden 1986–88
Jim Narrigan and Don Worden 1988–92
Jim Narrigan and Scott Waugh 1992–93
Don Del Negro and Mike Murphy 1993–94
Don Del Negro and Tim Trahant 1994–97

STANLEY CUP CLINCHING GAMES

The Boston Bruins have won the Stanley Cup 5 times. The following game summaries are the recaps of the Stanley Cup clinching games:

Stanley Cup #1
At Madison Square Garden, New York
Friday – March 29, 1929
Boston Bruins 2 – New York Rangers 1

Boston Bruins	*New York Rangers*
Tiny Thompson	John Roach
Eddie Shore	Taffy Abel
Lionel Hitchman	Ching Johnson
Bill Carson	Frank Boucher
Harry Oliver	Bill Cook
Percy Galbraith	Butch Keeling
Cooney Weiland	Bun Cook
Dit Clapper	Murray Murdoch
Mickey Mackay	Paul Thompson
Dutch Gainor	Melville Vail
George Owen	Leo Bourgeault
Myles Lane	

FIRST PERIOD

no scoring

penalty: Boston, Carson (interference)
penalty: Boston, Hitchman (holding)
penalty: New York, Abel (tripping)
penalty: Boston, Hitchman (tripping)

SECOND PERIOD

Boston HARRY OLIVER 14:01

penalty: Boston, Oliver (board check)
penalty: New York, Bill Cook (cross check)
penalty: Boston, Shore (high sticking)
penalty: New York, Bun Cook (high sticking)

THIRD PERIOD

New York BUTCH KEELING 6:48

Boston BILL CARSON 18:02

penalty: Boston, Shore (interference)

Shots against by period/total saves:

Boston (Thompson)	7	11	14	32
New York (Roach)	10	15	12	37

REFEREES: Bobby Hewitson & George Mallinson

ATTENDANCE: 14,000 (estimated)

Stanley Cup #2
At Boston Garden
Sunday – April 16, 1939
Boston Bruins 3 – Toronto Maple Leafs 1

Boston Bruins	*Toronto Maple Leafs*
Frank Brimsek	Turk Broda
Eddie Shore	Bingo Kampman
Jack Portland	Red Horner
Gordon Pettinger	Gus Marker
Flash Hollett	Murph Chamberlain
Ray Getliffe	Bob Davidson
Dit Clapper	Reg Hamilton
Cooney Weiland	Pete Langelle
Roy Conacher	Syl Apps
Bill Cowley	Gordie Drillon
Woody Dumart	Nick Metz
Milt Schmidt	Bucko McDonald
Red Hamill	Bob Heron
Bobby Bauer	Don Metz
Mel Hill	Jack Church
Jack Crawford	Doc Romnes
Charlie Sands	

FIRST PERIOD

Boston HILL (Cowley, Conacher) 14:10

Toronto KAMPMAN (Romnes) 18:40

penalty: Boston, Shore (tripping)
penalty: Toronto, Drillon (tripping)
penalty: Boston, Hill (hooking)

SECOND PERIOD

Boston CONACHER (Cowley, Shore) 17:54

no penalties

THIRD PERIOD

Boston HOLLETT (Schmidt, Crawford) 19:23

penalty: Toronto, Hamilton (tripping)
penalty: Toronto, Kampman (tripping)
penalty: Boston, Shore (board check)
penalty: Toronto, Nick Metz (roughing)

Shots against by period/total saves:

Boston (Brimsek)	10	5	8	23
Toronto (Broda)	3	9	5	17

REFEREE: Mickey Ion

LINESMAN: Rabbit McVeigh

ATTENDANCE: 16,695

Stanley Cup #3
At the Detroit Olympia
Saturday – April 12, 1941
Boston Bruins 3 – Detroit Red Wings 1

Boston Bruins	Detroit Red Wings
Frank Brimsek	Johnny Mowers
Dit Clapper	Jimmy Orlando
Des Smith	Jack Stewart
Milt Schmidt	Don Grosso
Woody Dumart	Eddie Wares
Bobby Bauer	Sid Abel
Mel Hill	Mud Bruneteau
Roy Conacher	Syd Howe
Eddie Wiseman	Gus Giesebrecht
Pat McReavy	Bob Whitelaw
Jack Crawford	Hal Jackson
Flash Hollett	Connie Brown
Herb Cain	Bill Jennings
Art Jackson	Carl Liscombe
Terry Reardon	Alex Motter

FIRST PERIOD

Detroit LISCOMBE (Howe, Giesebrecht) 10:14

penalty: Boston, Reardon (high sticking)
penalty: Detroit, Orlando (tripping)

SECOND PERIOD

Boston HOLLETT (Schmidt). 7:42

Boston BAUER (Schmidt). 8:43

Boston WISEMAN (McReavy, Conacher) 19:32

no penalties

THIRD PERIOD

no goals

penalty: Boston, Smith (holding)
penalty: Boston, McReavy (fighting)
penalty: Detroit, Liscombe

REFEREE: King Clancy

LINESMAN: Bill Chadwick

ATTENDANCE: 8,125

Stanley Cup #4
At Boston Garden
Sunday – May 10, 1970
Boston Bruins 4 – St. Louis Blues 3

Boston Bruins	St. Louis Blues
Gerry Cheevers	Glenn Hall
Bobby Orr	Bob Plager
Don Awrey	Noel Picard
Derek Sanderson	Red Berenson
Eddie Westfall	Jimmy Roberts
Wayne Carleton	Keith McCreary
Rick Smith	Ray Fortin
Dallas Smith	Jean Guy Talbot
Gary Doak	Bill Plager
Billy Speer	Frank St. Marseille
Phil Esposito	Phil Goyette
Ken Hodge	Gary Sabourin
Wayne Cashman	Terry Crisp
Fred Stanfield	Tim Ecclestone
John McKenzie	Larry Keenan
Johnny Bucyk	Ab McDonald
Jim Lorentz	Andre Boudrias
Don Marcotte	Terry Gray
Eddie Johnston	Ernie Wakely

FIRST PERIOD

Boston RICK SMITH (Sanderson) 5:28

St. Louis BERENSON (Bob Plager,
   Ecclestone) 19:17

penalty: Boston, Sanderson (butt ending) 00:40
penalty: St. Louis, Fortin (holding) 4:41
penalty: Boston, McKenzie, Orr (roughing) . . . 4:41
penalty: St. Louis, Picard, Ecclestone (roughing) 4:41
penalty: Boston, McKenzie (slashing) 7:13
penalty: St. Louis, Picard (interference). 8:07
penalty: Boston, Stanfield (high sticking) 12:58
penalty: Boston, Awrey (charging) 16:04
penalty: Boston, Stanfield (roughing) 18:36
penalty: St. Louis, Boudrias (roughing) 18:36

SECOND PERIOD

St. Louis SABOURIN (St. Marseille) 3:22

Boston ESPOSITO (Hodge) 14:22

penalty: Boston, Sanderson (elbowing) 4:21
penalty: St. Louis, Berenson (hooking) 6:32
penalty: Boston, McKenzie (slashing) 11:55
penalty: Boston, Dallas Smith (interfenece). . . . 18:53

THIRD PERIOD

St. Louis KEENAN (Goyette, Roberts) 00:19

Boston BUCYK (McKenzie, Rick Smith) 13:28

penalty: St. Louis, Fortin (holding) 6:15
penalty: Boston, Esposito (roughing) 6:15

penalty: St. Louis, Bob Plager (tripping) 8:25

FIRST OVERTIME:

Boston ORR (Sanderson) 00:40

Shots against by period/total saves:
Boston (Cheevers)   14   7   10   0   31
St. Louis (Hall)   10   8   13   1   32

REFEREE: Bruce Hood

LINESMEN: Matt Pavelich, Ron Ego

ATTENDANCE: 14,835

Stanley Cup #5
At Madison Square Garden, New York
Thursday – May 11, 1972
Boston Bruins 3 – New York Rangers 0

Boston Bruins	New York Rangers
Gerry Cheevers	Gilles Villemure
Bobby Orr	Gary Doak
Dallas Smith	Brad Park
Phil Esposito	Walter Tkaczuk
Ken Hodge	Bill Fairbairn
Wayne Cashman	Peter Stemkowski
Don Awrey	Noel Picard
Carol Vadnais	Dale Rolfe
Ted Green	Rod Seiling
Fred Stanfield	Jim Dorey
John McKenzie	Jean Ratelle
Johnny Bucyk	Rod Gilbert
Garnet Bailey	Vic Hadfield
Eddie Westfall	Bobby Rousseau
Mike Walton	Bruce MacGregor
Derek Sanderson	Ted Irvine
Don Marcotte	Glen Sather
Doug Roberts	Phil Goyette
Eddie Johnston	Gene Carr
	Eddie Giacomin

FIRST PERIOD

Boston ORR (Hodge, Bucyk) 11:18

penalty: Boston, McKenzie (slashing) 2:32
penalty: New York, Irvine (slashing) 5:44
penalty: Boston, Hodge (tripping) 7:07
penalty: New York, Tkaczuk (hooking) 10:25
penalty: Boston, Hodge (high sticking, fighting) 13:06
penalty: New York, Hadfield (high sticking,
    fighting) 13:06
penalty: Boston, Cashman (charging) 14:46
penalty: Boston, Orr (misconduct) 14:46
penalty: New York, Doak (high sticking) 14:46

SECOND PERIOD

no goals

penalty: Boston, Vadnais (holding) 3:45
penalty: New York, Hadfield (roughing) 3:45
penalty: Boston, Marcotte (boarding) 4:33
penalty: Boston, Sanderson (kneeing, fighting) . 4:33
penalty: New York, Gilbert (fighting) 4:33
penalty: New York, Carr (tripping) 9:16
penalty: New York, Doak (high sticking) 12:05
penalty: Boston, Cashman (high sticking) 12:05
penalty: Boston, Cashman (fighting) 16:01
penalty: New York, Hadfield (fighting) 16:01

THIRD PERIOD

Boston CASHMAN (Orr, Esposito) 5:10

Boston CASHMAN (Esposito, Hodge) 18:11

penalty: New York, Rolfe (holding) 3:20
penalty: Boston, Dallas Smith (tripping) 10:35

Shots against by period/total saves:
Boston (Cheevers)   9   11   13   33
New York (Villemure) 8   9   10   27

REFEREE: Art Skov

LINESMAN: Neil Armstrong, Matt Pavelich

ATTENDANCE: 17,250

ALL-STAR GAMES IN BOSTON

The Boston Bruins have hosted 2 All-Star games. The following is a recap of both games.

First Game
January 19, 1971
Boston Garden
West Division 2 – East Division 1

REFEREE: Bill Friday

LINESMEN: Neil Armstrong and John D'Amico

FIRST PERIOD

West CHICO MAKI (unassisted) . . . . :36

West BOBBY HULL (Flett) . . . . 4:38 (pp)

East YVAN COURNOYER (D. Smith, Balon) . . 6:19

penalty: (W) Harris (tripping). 2:17

penalty: (E) F. Mahovlich (interference). 3:09

penalty: (W) B. Hull (hooking) 11:14

SECOND PERIOD

no scoring

penalty: (E) Bucyk (interference) 1:22

THIRD PERIOD

no scoring

penalty: (W) Stapleton (interference) 2:48

penalty: (W) Magnuson (tripping) 8:34

IN GOAL

East: Giacomin, 31 minutes, 2 goals against
        Villemure, 29 minutes, 0 goals against

West: Esposito, 31 minutes, 1 goal against
        Wakely, 29 minutes, 0 goals against

SHOTS ON GOAL

East	13	8	7	28
West	13	12	2	27

ATTENDANCE: 14,790

GOAL

West Division	East Division
Tony Esposito (Chicago)	Ed Giacomin (New York)
Ernie Wakely (St. Louis)	Gilles Villemure (New York)

DEFENSE

Bill White (Chicago)	Brad Park (New York)
Keith Magnuson (Chicago)	Jim Neilson (New York)
Pat Stapleton (Chicago)	Bobby Orr (Boston)
Jim Roberts (St. Louis)	Dallas Smith (Boston)
Barclay Plager (St. Louis)	Dale Tallon (Vancouver)

Ted Harris (Minnesota)	J.C. Tremblay (Montreal)

FORWARDS

Pit Martin (Chicago)	Johnny Bucyk (Boston)
Bobby Hull (Chicago)	Phil Esposito (Boston)
Dennis Hull (Chicago)	Ken Hodge (Boston)
Chico Maki (Chicago)	Ed Westfall (Boston)
Stan Mikita (Chicago)	Gordie Howe (Detroit)
Tim Ecclestone (St. Louis)	Gilbert Perreault (Buffalo)
Gary Sabourin (St. Louis)	Dave Keon (Toronto)
Red Berenson (St. Louis)	Dave Balon (New York)
Bobby Clarke (Philadelphia)	Jean Ratelle (New York)
Danny Grant (Minnesota)	Yvan Cournoyer (Montreal)
Greg Polis (Pittsburgh)	Pete Mahovlich (Montreal)
Bill Flett (Los Angeles)	Frank Mahovlich (Montreal)

COACHES

Scotty Bowman (St. Louis)	Harry Sinden (Boston)

Second Game
January 20, 1966
FleetCenter
Eastern Conference 5 – Western Conference 4

REFEREE: Mark Faucette

LINESMEN: Ron Asselstine & Brad Lazarowich

FIRST PERIOD

Eastern LINDROS (Leetch, LeClair) 11:05

Eastern VERBEEK (Lemieux, Schneider) 13:49

penalty: (W) too many men on ice. 4:35

SECOND PERIOD

Eastern JAGR (Lemieux, Francis) 2:07

Western HULL (Kariya, Coffey) 5:33

Eastern SHANAHAN (Turgeon, Neely) 8:57

Western COFFEY (Federov, Mogilny) 11:42

Western KARIYA (Sundin) 17:47

penalty: (E) too many men on ice

THIRD PERIOD

Western SELANNE 16:31

Eastern BOURQUE (Messier, Verbeek) 19:22

IN GOAL

East: Brodeur, 20 minutes, 0 goals against
Vanbiesbrouck, 20 minutes, 3 goals against
Hasek, 20 minutes, 1 goal against

West: Belfour, 20 minutes, 2 goals against
Osgood, 20 minutes, 2 goals against
Potvin, 20 minutes, 1 goal against

SHOTS ON GOAL

East	18	15	8	41
West	12	7	13	32

ATTENDANCE: 17,565

GOAL

West Division

Martin Brodeur (New Jersey)
John Vanbiesbrouck (Florida)
Dominik Hasek (Buffalo)

East Division

Ed Belfour (Chicago)
Chris Osgood (Detroit)
Felix Potvin (Toronto)

DEFENSE

Brian Leetch (Rangers)
Scott Stevens (New Jersey)

Al MacInnis (St. Louis)
Kevin Hatcher (Dallas)

Eric DesJardins (Philadelphia)
Roman Hamrlik (Tampa Bay)
Mathieu Schneider (Islanders)
Ray Bourque (Boston)

Nicklas Lidstrom (Detroit)
Chris Chelios (Chicago)
Larry Murphy (Toronto)
Paul Coffey (Detroit)

FORWARDS

Cam Neely (Boston)
Pierre Turgeon (Montreal)
Ron Francis (Pittsburgh)
Mario Lemieux (Pittsburgh)
Jaromir Jagr (Pittsburgh)
Mark Messier (Rangers)
Pat Verbeek (Rangers)
Eric Lindros (Philadelphia)
John LeClair (Philadelphia)
Craig MacTavish (Philadelphia)
Scott Mellanby (Florida)
Brendan Shanahan (Hartford)
Peter Bondra (Washington)
Daniel Alfredsson (Ottawa)

Teemu Selanne (Winnipeg)
Wayne Gretzky (Los Angeles)
Alex Mogilny (Vancouver)
Joe Sakic (Colorado)
P. Forsberg (Colorado)
Theoren Fleury (Calgary)
Brett Hull (St. Louis)
Denis Savard (Chicago)
Mats Sundin (Toronto)
Mike Gartner (Toronto)
Paul Kariya (Anaheim)
Owen Nolan (San Jose)
Doug Weight (Edmonton)
Sergei Federov (Detroit)

COACHES

Doug MacLean (Florida)

Scotty Bowman (Detroit)

PLAYERS WHO HAVE APPEARED
IN ALL-STAR GAMES

The following is a recap of the Boston Bruins players
who have appeared and scored in All-Star games.

2/14/34　　"Ace" Bailey benefit game at Maple Leaf Gardens, Toronto
　　　　　　Eddie Shore – Nels Stewart

11/2/37　　Howie Morenz benefit game at Montreal Forum
　　　　　　Dit Clapper, Eddie Shore, Tiny Thompson

10/29/39　　"Babe" Siebert benefit at Montreal Forum
　　　　　　Frank Brimsek, Eddie Shore, Dit Clapper, Bobby Bauer
　　　　　　Bobby Bauer (1 goal, 1 assist)
　　　　　　Eddie Shore (1 goal)

10/13/47　　At Maple Leaf Gardens, Toronto
　　　　　　Frank Brimsek, Milt Schmidt, Woody Dumart, Bobby Bauer
　　　　　　Milt Schmidt (1 assist)

11/3/48　　At Chicago Stadium
　　　　　　Frank Brimsek, Woody Dumart, Milt Schmidt
　　　　　　Woody Dumart (1 goal)

10/10/49　　At Maple Leaf Gardens, Toronto
　　　　　　Bill Quackenbush, Paul Ronty
　　　　　　Paul Ronty (1 goal) – Bill Quackenbush (1 assist)

10/8/50　　At Detroit Olympia
　　　　　　Lynn Patrick (coach)
　　　　　　Bill Quackenbush, Paul Ronty, John Peirson
　　　　　　John Peirson (1 assist)

10/9/51　　At Maple Leaf Gardens, Toronto
　　　　　　1st All-Star team: Bill Quackenbush, Milt Schmidt, Johnny Pierson, Eddie Sandford
　　　　　　John Peirson (1 goal) – Milt Schmidt (1 assist)

10/5/52　　At Detroit Olympia
　　　　　　1st All-Star team: Bill Quackenbush, Dave Creighton, Eddie Sandford
　　　　　　2nd All-Star team: Milt Schmidt, Jim Henry
　　　　　　Dave Creighton (1 assist)

10/3/53　　At Montreal Forum
　　　　　　Lynn Patrick (coach)
　　　　　　Bill Quackenbush, Eddie Sandford

10/2/54　　At Detroit Olympia
　　　　　　Bill Quackenbush, Fleming Mackell, Eddie Sandford, Doug Mohns
　　　　　　Doug Mohns (1 goal)

10/2/55　　At Detroit Olympia
　　　　　　Terry Sawchuk, Fernie Flaman, Leo LaBine

10/9/56　　At Montreal Forum
　　　　　　Terry Sawchuk, Fernie Flaman, Leo Labine

10/5/57　　At Montreal Forum
　　　　　　Milt Schmidt (coach)
　　　　　　Fernie Flaman, Real Chevrefils, Allan Stanley, Don McKenney
　　　　　　Allan Stanley (1 goal)

10/4/58　　At Montreal Forum
　　　　　　Milt Schmidt (coach)

The Kraut Line: Bobby Bauer, Milt Schmidt, and Woody Dumart.

	Fernie Flaman, Doug Mohns, Jerry Toppazzini, Don McKenney
	Jerry Toppazzini (1 assist)
10/3/59	At Montreal Forum
	Fernie Flaman, Doug Mohns, Jerry Toppazzini, Don McKenney
	Don McKenney (1 goal)
10/1/60	At Montreal Forum
	Bob Armstrong, Bronco Horvath, Vic Stasiuk, Don McKenney
10/7/61	At Chicago Stadium
	Don McKenney, Leo Boivin, Doug Mohns
	Don McKenney (1 goal)
10/6/62	At Maple Leaf Gardens, Toronto
	Doug Mohns, Leo Boivin, Don McKenney
10/5/63	At Maple Leaf Gardens, Toronto
	Tom Johnson, Murray Oliver, Johnny Bucyk, Dean Prentice
	Johnny Bucyk (1 assist) – Murray Oliver (1 assist)
10/10/64	At Maple Leaf Gardens, Toronto
	Leo Boivin, Murray Oliver, Johnny Bucyk
	Murray Oliver (1 goal, 1 assist) – Leo Boivin (1 goal)
	Johnny Bucyk (1 assist)

10/20/65	At Montreal Forum
	Ted Green, Murray Oliver, Johnny Bucyk
	Johnny Bucyk (1 goal) – Murray Oliver (2 assists)
1966	No game in calendar year

Beginning in 1967, the NHL game was moved to the mid-season.

1/18/67	At Montreal Forum
	Murray Oliver
1/16/68	At Maple Leaf Gardens, Toronto
	Bobby Orr, Johnny Bucyk
	Bobby Orr (1 assist)
1/21/69	At Montreal Forum
	Gerry Cheevers, Bobby Orr, Ted Green, Phil Esposito
1/20/70	At St. Louis Arena
	Bobby Orr, Phil Esposito, Johnny Bucyk, John McKenzie
	Johnny Bucyk (1 assist) – John McKenzie (1 assist)
1/19/71	At Boston Garden
	Harry Sinden (coach)
	Bobby Orr, Dallas Smith, Johnny Bucyk, Phil Esposito, Ken Hodge, Eddie Westfall
	Dallas Smith (1 assist)
1/25/72	At Metropolitan Sports Center, Bloomington, Minnesota
	Bobby Orr, Dallas Smith, Phil Esposito, John McKenzie
	John McKenzie (1 goal) – Phil Esposito (1 goal)
	Bobby Orr (1 assist) – Dallas Smith (1 assist)
1/30/73	At Madison Square Garden, New York
	Tom Johnson (coach)
	Bobby Orr, Dallas Smith, Phil Esposito, Ken Hodge
	Phil Esposito (1 assist) – Ken Hodge (1 assist)
1/29/74	At Chicago Stadium
	Gilles Gilbert, Dallas Smith, Phil Esposito, Ken Hodge, Wayne Cashman
1/21/75	At Montreal Forum
	Bep Guidolin (coach)
	Bobby Orr, Carol Vadnais, Phil Esposito, Terry O'Reilly
	Terry O'Reilly (1 goal, 1 assist) – Phil Esposito (1 goal) – Bobby Orr (1 goal) – Carol Vadnais (1 assist)
1/20/76	At Philadelphia Spectrum
	Brad Park, Greg Sheppard
	Brad Park (1 goal)
1/25/77	At Pacific Coliseum, Vancouver
	Brad Park, Peter McNab
	Peter McNab (1 assist)
1/24/78	At Memorial Auditorium, Buffalo
	Brad Park, Terry O'Reilly
	Brad Park (1 assist) – Terry O'Reilly (1 assist)
1979	Challenge Cup At Madison Square Garden, New York
	2/8/79, 2/10/79, 2/11/79
	Gerry Cheevers, Don Marcotte
2/5/80	At Joe Louis Arena, Detroit
	Jean Ratelle
	Jean Ratelle (1 assist)
2/10/81	At The Forum, Los Angeles
	Ray Bourque, Rick Middleton

Phil Esposito

2/9/82	At The Capital Center, Landover, Maryland
	Ray Bourque, Rick Middleton
	Ray Bourque (1 goal) – Rick Middleton (1 assist)
2/8/83	At Nassau Coliseum, Uniondale, Long Island, New York
	Ray Bourque, Pete Peeters, Barry Pederson
	Ray Bourque (1 assist)
1/31/84	At Meadowlands Arena, East Rutherford, New Jersey
	Pete Peeters, Rick Middleton, Mike O'Connell, Ray Bourque, Barry Pederson
	Rick Middleton (1 goal) – Barry Pederson (1 assist)
2/12/85	At Olympic Saddledome, Calgary
	Ray Bourque
	Ray Bourque (4 assists)
2/4/86	At Hartford Civic Center
	Ray Bourque
	Ray Bourque (1 assist)
1987	Rendez–vous '87 At Quebec City
	2/11/87, 2/13/87
	Ray Bourque
2/9/88	At St. Louis Arena
	Cam Neely, Ray Bourque
2/7/89	At Northlands Coliseum, Edmonton
	Terry O'Reilly (coach)
	Reggie Lemelin, Glen Wesley, Ray Bourque, Cam Neely, Cam Neely (1 goal) –
	Glen Wesley (1 goal) – Ray Bourque (1 assist)
1/21/90	At Pittsburgh Civic Center
	Ray Bourque, Cam Neely
	Cam Neely (1 goal, 2 assists) – Ray Bourque (1 assist)
1/19/91	At Chicago Stadium
	Mike Milbury (coach)
	Andy Moog, Garry Galley, Ray Bourque, Cam Neely, Dave Christian
	Ray Bourque (1 assist)
1/18/92	At Philadelphia Spectrum
	Ray Bourque
	Ray Bourque (1 assist)
2/6/93	At Montreal Forum
	Ray Bourque, Adam Oates
	Adam Oates (4 assists) – Ray Bourque (1 assist)
1/22/94	At Madison Square Garden, New York
	Ray Bourque, Adam Oates
	Ray Bourque (1 assist) – Adam Oates (1 assist)
1995	NO GAME
1/20/96	At FleetCenter, Boston
	Ray Bourque, Cam Neely
	(Ray Bourque (1 goal) – Cam Neely (1 assist)
1/18/97	At San Jose Arena
	Ray Bourque, Adam Oates
	Adam Oates (2 assists)

Bill Quackenbush

BOSTON BRUINS ALL-STAR GAME SCORING

	G	G	A	P			G	G	A	P
Ray Bourque	16	3	11	14	Dave Creighton	1	0	1	1
Adam Oates	3	0	7	7	Peter McNab	1	0	1	1
Cam Neely	5	2	3	5	Jean Ratelle	1	0	1	1
Murray Oliver	4	1	4	5	Carol Vadnais	1	0	1	1
Johnny Bucyk	6	1	3	4	Fernie Flaman	5	0	0	0
Phil Esposito	7	2	1	3	Eddie Sandford	4	0	0	0
Bobby Orr	7	1	2	3	Ted Green	2	0	0	0
Terry O'Reilly	2	1	2	3	Leo Labine	2	0	0	0
Don McKenney	6	2	0	2	Eddie Shore	2	0	0	0
Milt Schmidt	4	1	1	2	Bob Armstrong	1	0	0	0
Rick Middleton	3	1	1	2	Bobby Bauer	1	0	0	0
Brad Park	3	1	1	2	Wayne Cashman	1	0	0	0
John Peirson	2	1	1	2	Real Chevrefils	1	0	0	0
John McKenzie	2	1	1	2	Dave Christian	1	0	0	0
Dallas Smith	4	0	2	2	Dit Clapper	1	0	0	0
Doug Mohns	5	1	0	1	Garry Galley	1	0	0	0
Leo Boivin	3	1	0	1	Bronco Horvath	1	0	0	0
Woody Dumart	2	1	0	1	Tom Johnson	1	0	0	0
Paul Ronty	2	1	0	1	Fleming Mackell	1	0	0	0
Allan Stanley	1	1	0	1	Don Marcotte	1	0	0	0
Glen Wesley	1	1	0	1	Mike O'Connell	1	0	0	0
Bill Quackenbush	6	0	1	1	Dean Prentice	1	0	0	0
Ken Hodge	3	0	1	1	Greg Sheppard	1	0	0	0
Barry Pederson	2	0	1	1	Vic Stasiuk	1	0	0	0
Jerry Toppazzini	2	0	1	1	Nels Stewart	1	0	0	0
					Eddie Westfall	1	0	0	0

BOSTON BRUINS GOALTENDERS' APPEARANCES IN ALL-STAR GAMES

Frank Brimsek	2	Jim Henry	1
Gerry Cheevers	2	Reggie Lemelin	1
Pete Peeters	2	Andy Moog	1
Terry Sawchuk	2	Tiny Thompson	1
Gilles Gilbert	1		

BOSTON BRUINS ALL-STAR GAMES COACHED

Lynn Patrick	2	Mike Milbury	1
Milt Schmidt	2	Terry O'Reilly	1
Bep Guidolin	1	Harry Sinden	1
Tom Johnson	1		

BOSTON BRUINS NHL
AMATEUR DRAFT SELECTIONS

(number in parenthesis represents overall pick)

1963
(picking 3rd overall)
1. Orest Romashyma (3rd)
2. Terrance Lane (9th)
3. Roger Bamburak (14th)
4. Jim Blair (19th)

1964
(picking 2nd overall)
1. Alec Campbell (2nd)
2. Jim Booth (8th)
3. Ken Dryden (14th)
4. Allister Blair (20th)

1965
(picking 4th overall)
1. Joe Bailey (4th)
9. Bill Ramsay (9th)

1966
(picking 1st overall)
1. Barry Gibbs . . . . Estevan Bruins (1st)
2. Rick Smith . . . . Hamilton Red Wings (7th)
3. Garnet Bailey . . . . . Edmonton Oil Kings (13th)
4. Tom Webster . . . . . . Niagara Falls Flyers (19th)

1969
1. Don Tannahill . . . . . . Niagara Falls Flyers (3rd)
2. Frank Spring . . . . . . Edmonton Oil Kings (4th)
3. Ivan Boldirev . . . . Oshawa Generals (11th)
4. Art Quoquochi
. . . . Montreal Junior Canadiens (22nd)

1970
1. Reg Leach . . . . Flin Flon Bombers (3rd)
2. Rick MacLeish . . . . . Peterborough Petes (4th)
3. Ron Plumb . . . . Peterborough Petes (9th)
4. Bob Stewart . . . . Oshawa Generals (13th)
5. Dan Bouchard . . . . London Knights (27th)
6. Ray Brownlee . . . . . Brandon University (41st)
7. Gordon Davies . . . . . Toronto Marlboros (55th)
8. Robert Roselle . . . . Sorel (69th)
9. Murray Wing . . . . . . U. of North Dakota (83rd)
10. Glen Siddell . . . . Kitchener Rangers (96th)

1971
1. Ron Jones . . . . Edmonton Oil Kings (6th)
2. Terry O'Reilly . . . . . . Oshawa Generals (14th)
3. Curt Ridley . . . . Portage Terriers (28th)

4. Dave Bonter . . . . Estevan Bruins (42nd)
5. Dave Hynes . . . . Harvard University (56th)
6. Bert Scott . . . . Edmonton Oil Kings (70th)
7. Bob McMahon . . . . St. Catharines (84th)

1972
1. Mike Bloom
. . . . St. Catharines Black Hawks (16th)
2. Wayne Elder . . . . London Knights (32nd)
3. Michel Boudreau . . . . Laval Saints (48th)
4. Les Jackson . . . . New Westminster Royals (64th)
5. Brian Coates . . . . . Brandon Wheat Kings (80th)
6. Peter Gaw . . . . Ottawa 67's (96th)
7. Gordie Clark . . . . U. of New Hampshire (112th)
8. Roy Carmichael
. . . . New Westminster Royals (128th)

1973
1. Andre Savard . . . . Quebec Remparts (6th)
2. Jim Jones . . . . Peterborough Petes (31st)
3. Doug Gibson . . . . . . Peterborough Petes (36th)
4. Al Sims . . . . Cornwall Royals (47th)
5. Steve Langdon . . . . London Knights (62nd)
6. Peter Crosbie . . . . London Knights (78th)
7. J. P. Bourgouyne
. . . . Shawinigan Falls Bruins (94th)
8. Walter Johnson . . . . . . Oshawa Generals (110th)
9. Virgil Gates . . . . Swift Current Broncos (126th)
10. Jim Pettie . . St. Catharines Black Hawks (141st)
11. Yvon Bouillon . . . . . . Cornwall Royals (156th)

1974
1. Don Larway . . . . Swift Current Broncos (18th)
2. Mark Howe . . . . Toronto Marlboros (25th)
3. Peter Sturgeon . . . . Kitchener Rangers (36th)
4. Tom Edur . . . . Toronto Marlboros (54th)
5. Bill Reed
. . . . . . Sault Ste. Marie Greyhounds (72nd)
6. Jim Bateman . . . . Quebec Remparts (90th)
7. Bill Best . . . . Sudbury Wolves (108th)
8. Ray Maluta . . . . Flin Flon Bombers (126th)
9. Darryl Drader . . . . . U. of North Dakota (143rd)
10. Peter Roberts . . . . St. Cloud State (160th)
11. Peter Waselovich . . . U. of North Dakota (175th)

1975
1. Doug Halward . . . . . . Peterborough Petes (14th)
2. Barry Smith . . . New Westminster Bruins (32nd)

3. Rick Adduono
.... St. Catharines Black Hawks (60th)
4. Denis Daigle .... Montreal B–B–R (68th)
5. Stan Jonathan...... Peterborough Petes (86th)
6. Matti Hagman .... Helsinki IFK (104th)
7. Gary Carr....... Toronto Marlboros (122nd)
8. Bo Berglund.............. Sweden (140th)
9. Joe Rando...... U. of New Hampshire (156th)
10. Kevin Nugent....... U. of Notre Dame (171st)

1976

1. Clayton Pachal
.... New Westminster Bruins (16th)
2. Larry Gloeckner...... Victoria Cougars (34th)
3. Bob Miller .... Ottawa 67's (70th)
4. Peter Vandemark ..... Oshawa Generals (88th)
5. Ted Olson........ Calgary Centennials (106th)

1977

1. Dwight Foster ...... Kitchener Rangers (16th)
2. Dave Parro......... Saskatoon Blades (34th)
3. Mike Forbes.... St. Catharines Fincups (52nd)
4. Brian McGregor........... Saskatoon (70th)
5. Doug Butler....... St. Louis University (88th)
6. Keith Johnson ...... Saskatoon Blades (106th)
7. Ralph Cox ..... U. of New Hampshire (122nd)
8. Mario Claude..... Sherbrooke Castors (138th)

1978

1. Al Secord .... Hamilton Fincups (16th)
2. Graeme Nicolson...... Cornwall Royals (35th)
3. Brad Knelson..... Lethbridge Broncos (52nd)
4. George Buat......... Seattle Breakers (68th)
5. Darryl MacLeod .... Boston University (85th)
6. Jeff Brubaker ..... Peterborough Petes (102nd)
7. Murray Skinner ... Lake Superior State (119th)
8. Robert Hehir .... Boston College (136th)
9. Craig MacTavish .... Lowell University (153rd)

1979

1. Ray Bourque ...... Verdun Black Hawks (8th)
2. Brad McCrimmon
.... Brandon Wheat Kings (15th)
3. Doug Morrison .... Lethbridge Broncos (36th)
4. Keith Crowder..... Peterborough Petes (57th)
5. Larry Melnyk.. New Westminster Bruins (78th)
6. Marco Baron .... Montreal Juniors (99th)
7. Mike Krushelnyski... Montreal Juniors (120th)

1980

1. Barry Pederson ...... Victoria Cougars (18th)
2. Tom Fergus .... Peterborough Petes (60th)
3. Steve Kasper ..... Verdun Black Hawks (81st)
4. Randy Hillier .... Sudbury Wolves (102nd)
5. Steve Lyons ... Matignon High School (123rd)
6. Tony McMurchy
.... New Westminster Bruins (144th)

7. Mike Moffat ..... Kingston Canadians (165th)
8. Michael Thelven . Djurgardens, Sweden (186th)
9. Jens Ohling ..... Djurgardens, Sweden (207th)

1981

1. Normand Leveille
.... Chicoutimi Sagueneens (14th)
2. Luc Dufour .... Chicoutimi Sagueneens (35th)
3. Scott McLellan .... Niagara Falls Flyers (77th)
4. Joe Mantione........ Cornwall Royals (98th)
5. Bruce Milton...... Boston University (119th)
6. Mats Thelin........... AIK Sweden (140th)
7. Armel Parisee .. Chicoutimi Sagueneens (161st)
8. Don Sylvestri........ Clarkson College (182nd)
9. Richard Bourque.. Sherbrooke Beavers (203rd)

1982

1. Gord Kluzak .... Billings Bighorns (1st)
2. Brian Curran... Portland Winter Hawks (22nd)
3. Lyndon Byers .... Regina Pats (39th)
4. Dave Reid .... Peterborough Petes (60th)
5. Bob Nicholson ...... London Knights (102nd)
6. Bob Sweeney...... Acton High School (123rd)
7. John Meulenbroeks
.... Brantford Alexanders (144th)
8. Tony Fiore........ Montreal Jrs. (165th)
9. Doug Kostynski ..... Kamloops Oilers (186th)
10. Tony Gilliard.... Niagara Falls Flyers (207th)
11. Tommy Lehmann .. Stocksund, Sweden (228th)
12. Bruno Campese
.... University of Northern Michigan (249th)

1983

1. Nevin Markwart .... Regina Pats (21st)
2. Greg Johnston..... Toronto Marlboros (42nd)
3. Greg Puhalski ...... Kitchener Rangers (62nd)
4. Allan Larochelle ..... Saskatoon Blades (82nd)
5. Terry Tallifer .... St. Albert Saints (122nd)
6. Ian Armstrong.... Peterborough Petes (142nd)
7. Francois Olivier ...... St. Jean Castors(162nd)
8. Hatti Laurilla .... Reipas, Finland(182nd)
9. Paul Fitzsimmons
.... Northeastern University (202nd)
10. Norm Foster ...... Penticton Knights (222nd)
11. Greg Murphy .... (242nd)

1984

1. Dave Pasin....... Prince Albert Raiders (19th)
2. Ray Podloski .... Portland Winter Hawks(40th)
3. Jeff Cornelius ...... Toronto Marlboros (61st)
4. Bobby Joyce
.... Notre Dame High School (82nd)
5. Mike Bishop .... London Knights (103rd)
6. Randy Oswald........ Michigan Tech (124th)
7. Mark Thietke....... Saskatoon Blades (145th)
8. Don Sweeney .. St. Paul's High School (166th)

9. Kevin Heffernan
. . . . Weymouth High School (186th)
10. J.D. Urbanic. . . . . . . Windsor Spitfires (207th)
11. Bill Kopecky. . Austin Prep High School (227th)
12. Jim Newhouse   Matignon High School (248th)

1985

1. Alain Cote . . . . Quebec (31st)
2. Bill Ranford . . . . New Westminster (52nd)
3. Jaime Kelly. . . . . . . Scituate High School (73rd)
4. Steve Moore. . . . . London Jr. B (94th)
5. Gork Hynes . . . . Medicine Hat (115th)
6. Per Martinelle . . . . Aik, Stockholm (136th)
7. Randy Burridge . . . . Peterborough (157th)
8. Gord Cruickshank . Providence College (178th)
9. Dave Buda . . . . Streetsville Jr. B (199th)
10. Bob Beers. . . . . Buffalo Jr. Sabres (210th)
11. John Byce
. . . . Madison Memorial High School (220th)
12. Marc West. . . . . Burlington Jr. B (241st)

1986

1. Craig Janney. . . . . Boston College (13th)
2. Pekka Tirkkonen . . . . Sapko, Finland (34th)
3. Dean Hall. . . . . St. James (76th)
4. Matt Pesklewis . . . . St. Albert (97th)
5. Garth Premak . . . . . . New Westminster (118th)
6. Paul Beraldo. . . . . Sault Ste. Marie (139th)
7. Brian Ferreira. . Falmouth High School (160th)
8. Jeff Flaherty . . . Weymouth High School (181st)
9. Greg Hawgood. . . . . Kamloops (202nd)
10. Staffan Malmquist . . . . Leksand (223rd)
11. Joel Gardner. . . . . Sarnia (244th)

1987

1. Glen Wesley . . . . Portland (3rd)
pick from Vancouver
2. Stephane Quintal . . . . Granby (14th)
3. Todd Lalonde. . . . . Sudbury (56th)
4. Darwin McPherson . . . New Westminster (67th)
pick from Minnesota
5. Matt Delguidice. . . . . St. Anselm (77th)
6. Ted Donato . . . . Catholic Memorial (98th)
7. Matt Glennon
. . . Archbishop Williams High School (119th)
8. Rob Cheevers. . . . . Boston College (140th)
9. Chris Winnes . Northwood High School (161st)
10. Paul Ohman . . Saint John High School (182nd)
11. Casey Jones . . . . Cornell University (203rd)
12. Eric Lemarque
. . . . Northern Michigan University (224th)
13. Sean Gorman . . Matignon High School (245th)

1988

1. Rob Cimetta. . . . . . Toronto Marlboros (18th)
2. Steve Heinze . . . . . Lawrence Academy (60th)

3. Joe Juneau . . . . R.P.I. (81st)
4. Daniel Murphy . . . . Gunnery (102nd)
5. Derek Geary . . . . Gloucester (123rd)
6. Mark Krys. . . . . Boston University (165th)
7. Jon Rohloff . . . . Grand Rapids (186th)
8. Eric Reisman. . . . . Ohio State (228th)
9. Doug Jones . . . . Kitchener (249th)

1989

1. Shayne Stevenson . . . . Kitchener (17th)
2. Mike Parson . . . . Guelph (38th)
3. Wes Walz . . . . Lethbridge (57th)
(from Edmonton)
4. Jackson Penney . . . . Victoria (80th)
5. Mark Montanari . . . . Kitchener (101st)
6. Stephen Foster . . . . Catholic Memorial (122nd)
7. Otto Hascak . . . . Dukla Trencin (143rd)
8. Rick Allain. . . . . Kitchener (164th)
9. James Lavish . . . . . Deerfield Academy (185th)
10. Geoff Simpson . . . . Estevan T-II Jr. A (206th)
11. David Franzosa . . . . Boston College (227th)

1990

1. Bryan Smolinski . . . . Michigan State (21st)
2. Cam Stewart. . . . . Elmira Jr. B (63rd)
3. Jerome Buckley . . . . . Northwood Prep (84th)
4. Mike Bales . . . . Ohio State (105th)
5. Mark Wolff. . . . . Spokane (126th)
6. Jim Mackey . . . . Hotchkiss (147th)
7. John Gruden . . . . Waterloo Jr. B (168th)
8. Darren Wetherill . . . . . Minot T-II Jr. A (189th)
9. Dean Capuano . . . . Mount St. Charles (210th)
10. Andy Bezeau . . . . Niagara Falls (231st)
11. Ted Miskolczi . . . . Belleville (252nd)

1991

1. Glen Murray . . . . Sudbury (18th)
2. Jozef Stumpel . . . . Nitra (40th)
3. Marcel Cousineau . . . . Beauport (62nd)
4. Brad Tiley . . . . Sault Ste. Marie (84th)
5. Mariusz Czerkawski . . . . . . GKS Tychy (106th)
6. Gary Golczewski
. . . . Trinity-Pawling High School (150th)
7. John Moser . . . . Park High School (172nd)
8. Dan Hodge . . . . . . Merrimack College (194th)
9. Steve Norton. . . . . Michigan State (216th)
10. Steve Lombardi   Deerfield High School (238th)
11. Torsten Kienass. . . . . . Dynamo Berlin (260th)

1992

1. Dmitri Kvartalnov. . . . . San Diego (16th)
2. Sergei Zholtok. . . . . HC Riga (55th)
from Philadelphia
3. Scott Bailey . . . . Spokane (112th)
4. Jiri Dopita . . . . DS Olomouc (133rd)
from Edmonton

5. Grigori Panteleev . . . . HC Riga (136th)
6. Kurt Seher . . . . Seattle (184th)
7. Mattias Timander. . . . . MoDo (208th)
8. Chris Crombie . . . . London (232nd)
9. Denis Chervyakov . . . . HC Riga (256th)
10. Evgeny Pavlov . . . . SKA Leningrad (257th)
    from Chicago

1993

1. Kevyn Adams . . . . Miami–Ohio (25th)
2. Matt Alvey . . . . Springfield Jr. B (51st)
3. Charles Paquette . . . . Sherbrooke (88th)
    from Philadelphia
4. Shawn Bates . . . . Medford High School (103rd)
5. Andrei Sapozhnikov
    . . . . Traktor Chelyabinsk (129th)
6. Milt Mastad . . . . Seattle (155th)
7. Ryan Golden . . . . Reading High School (181st)
8. Hal Gill . . . . Nashoba (207th)
9. Joel Prpic . . . . Waterloo Jr. B (233rd)
10. Joakim Persson
    . . . . Hammarby Stockholm (259th)

1994

1. Evgeni Ryabchikov . . . . Molot Perm (21st)
2. Daniel Goneau . . . . Laval (47th)
3. Eric Nickulas . . . . Cushing Academy (99th)
4. Darren Wright . . . . Prince Albert (125th)
5. Andre Roy . . . . Chicoutimi (151st)
6. Jeremy Schafer . . . . Medicine Hat (177th)
7. John Grahame . . . . . Sioux City Jr. A (229th)
8. Neil Savary . . . . Hull (255th)
9. Andrei Yakhanov . . . Salavat Yulayev UFA (281st)

1995

1. Kyle McLaren . . . . Tacoma (9th)
    from Hartford
2. Sean Brown . . . . Belleville (21st)
3. Paxton Schafer . . . . Medicine Hat (47th)

4. Bill McCauley . . . . Detroit Jr. Red Wings (73rd)
5. Cameron Mann . . . . Peterborough (99th)
6. Yevgeny Shaldybin . . . Torpedo Yaroslavl (151st)
7. Per Johan Axelsson
    . . . . V. Frolunda Jr. Goteborg (177th)
8. Sergei Zhukov . . . . . . Torpedo Yaroslavl (203rd)
9. Jonathan Murphy . . . . . . Peterborough (229th)

1996

1. Jonathan Aitken . . . . Medicine Hat (8th)
    pick from Hartford
2. Henry Kuster . . . . Medicine Hat (45th)
3. Eric Naud . . . . St.-Hyacinthe (53rd)
    pick from Ottawa
4. Jason Doyle . . . . Sault Ste. Marie (80th)
    pick from Tampa Bay
5. Trent Whitfield . . . . Spokane (100th)
6. Elias Abrahamsson . . . . Halifax (132nd)
    pick from San Jose
7. Chris Lane . . . . Spokane (155th)
8. Thomas Brown . . . . Sarnia (182nd)
9. Bob Prier . . . . . St. Lawrence University (208th)
10. Anders Soderberg
    . . . . MoDo Ornskoldsvik (234th)

1997

1. Joe Thornton . . . . Sault Ste. Marie (1st)
2. Sergei Samsonov . . . . Detroit, IHL (8th)
3. Ben Clymer . . . . University of Minnesota (27th)
4. Mattias Karlin . . . . Mo Do Sweden (54th)
5. Lee Goren . . University of North Dakota (63rd)
6. Karol Bartanus . . . . Drummondville (81st)
7. Denis Timofeev . . . . CSKA Moscow (135th)
8. Joel Trottier . . . . Ottawa (162nd)
9. Jim Baxter . . . . Oshawa (180th)
10. Antti Laaksonen . . University of Denver (191st)
11. Eric Van Acker . . . . Chicoutimi (218th)
12. Jay Henderson . . . . Edmonton (246th)

JANUARY 1 GAMES

The Boston Bruins have played 40 times on New Year's Day, January 1.
The following is a recap of Bruins games on the first day of the year.

GAMES PLAYED: 40
    (21 wins, 16 losses, 3 ties)
AT BOSTON: 28
    (18 wins, 8 losses, 2 ties)
vs. New York Rangers: 14
    (9 wins, 5 losses)
vs. Montreal: 4
    (1 win, 2 losses, 1 tie)
vs. Toronto: 4
    (3 wins, 1 tie)
vs. Detroit: 3
    (2 wins, 0 losses, 1 tie)
vs. Ottawa: 1
    (1 win, 0 losses)
vs. New York Americans: 2
    (2 wins, 0 losses)

ON THE ROAD: 12
    (3 wins, 8 losses, 1 tie)
At New York Rangers: 1
    (1 win, 0 losses)
At Toronto: 1
    (0 wins, 1 loss)
At Vancouver: 2
    (1 win, 0 losses, 1 tie)
At Chicago: 1
    (0 wins, 1 loss)
At Buffalo: 1
    (0 wins, 1 loss)
At Los Angeles: 1
    (0 wins, 1 loss)
At Washington: 1
    (0 wins, 1 loss)
At Ottawa: 2
    (0 wins, 2 losses)
At New York Americans: 2
    (1 win, 1 loss)

MOST CONSECUTIVE GAMES ON JANUARY 1

22 (1946–1967)

MOST CONSECUTIVE APPEARANCES AT BOSTON ON JANUARY 1

6 New York Rangers 1947–1952

LAST HOME GAMES ON JANUARY 1

(L) 1962 vs. New York 4–2
(T) 1964 vs. Montreal 3–3
(W) 1965 vs. Toronto 3–0

LAST ROAD GAMES ON JANUARY 1

(W) 1973 at Vancouver 8–2
(T) 1974 at Vancouver 2–2
(L) 1997 at Ottawa 3–2

Season's Greetings

GAMES PLAYED CHRISTMAS DAY

The Boston Bruins have played 37 times on Christmas Day.
The following is a recap of Christmas Day action.

Games played: . . . . 37 (18 wins, 17 losses, 2 ties)

AT BOSTON: . . . . 34 (17 wins, 15 losses, 2 ties)
vs. Chicago: . . . . 14 (6 wins, 6 losses, 2 ties)
vs. New York Rangers: . . . . . 6 (2 wins, 4 losses)
vs. Toronto: . . . . 4 (2 wins, 2 losses)
vs. Montreal: . . . . 1 (0 wins, 1 loss)
vs. Detroit: . . . . 1 (1 win, 0 losses)
vs. Philadelphia: . . . . 1 (1 win, 0 losses)
vs. Los Angeles: . . . . 1 (1 win, 0 losses)
vs. Pittsburgh: . . . . 1 (1 win, 0 losses)
vs. Oakland: . . . . 2 (1 win, 1 losses)
vs. Montreal Maroons: . . . . . 1 (0 wins, 1 loss)
vs. New York Americans: . . . . 1 (1 win, 0 losses)

ON THE ROAD: . . . . 3 (0 wins, 3 losses)
At Montreal: . . . . 1 (0 wins, 1 loss)
At Toronto: . . . . 1 (0 wins, 1 loss)
At New York Americans: . . . . 1 (0 wins, 1 loss)

LAST GAMES ON CHRISTMAS DAY

(W) 1971 vs. Philadelphia 5–1
(L) 1968 vs. Oakland 3–1
(T) 1954 vs. Chicago 3–3

MOST CONSECUTIVE YEARS PLAYING ON CHRISTMAS

26   (1946–1971)

FEBRUARY 29 GAMES

The Boston Bruins have played 8 games on February 29 in their history.
The following is a recap of those games.

1940	Boston 4 at Montreal 2
1944	Toronto 7 at Boston 3
1948	Boston 1 at Chicago 5
1956	Boston 2 at New York Rangers 4
1964	Boston 2 at Detroit 1
1968	Boston 4 at Toronto 1
1976	Boston 5 at Vancouver 3
1992	Boston 5 at Washington 5

Games played: . . . . 8 (4 wins, 3 losses, 1 tie)
At Boston: . . . . (3 wins, 1 loss, 1 tie)
At Montreal: . . . . (1 win)
At Chicago: . . . . (1 loss)
At New York: . . . . (1 loss)

BOSTON BRUINS BIRTHPLACES

The following is a recap of player's birthplaces by provinces, states, and countries.

CANADA
Ontario	269
Quebec	86
Saskatchewan	68
Alberta	41
Manitoba	39
British Columbia	25
New Brunswick	8
Nova Scotia	8
Prince Edward Island	1
Newfoundland	0

UNITED STATES
Massachusetts	39
Minnesota	14
Connecticut	5
Michigan	5
New York	5
Pennsylvania	4
Rhode Island	4
California	3
Illinois	3
Ohio	3
Wisconsin	3
Idaho	1
Indiana	1
Missouri	1
New Hampshire	1
New Jersey	1
North Dakota	1
Oklahoma	1
Washington	1

EUROPE / U S S R
Sweden	6
USSR	6
Finland	5
Czechoslovakia	3
England	3
Scotland	3
Denmark	1
Ireland	1
Northern Ireland	1
Norway	1
Poland	1
Wales	1
Yugoslavia	1

CARRIBBEAN / SOUTH AMERICA
Jamaica	1
Paraguay	1

Unknown	31

LONGEST ROAD TRIPS

The longest road trip in Bruins history consisted of 8 games and occurred in the 1994–95, lockout shortened season. The trip went as follows:

February 12	At Buffalo	Win	2–1
February 14	At Pittsburgh	Loss	5–3
February 17	At Florida	Win	5–4
February 18	At Tampa Bay	Loss	3–1
February 22	At Hartford	Loss	3–2
February 23	At New Jersey	Win	3–2
February 25	At Quebec	Tie	1–1
February 27	At Ottawa	Win	2–0
Games played:	8 (4 wins–3 losses–1 tie)		

The Bruins have made sixteen 7-game road trips in their history.

1952–53	1983–84
1954–55	1985–86
1955–56	1990–91
1967–68	1992–93
1971–72	1993–94
1981–82 (twice)	1995–96
1982–82 (twice)	1996–97

During the 1952–53, 7-game road trip, the Bruins visited Chicago 3 times, the only time in their history that they have visited the same city 3 times in 1 road trip. The trip was as follows:

February 18	At New York	Loss	4–2
February 21	At Toronto	Tie	2–2
February 22	At Chicago	Loss	2–0
February 25	At New York	Loss	2–1
February 27	At Chicago	Loss	3–0
March 1	At Chicago	Tie	2–2
March 2	At Detroit	Loss	10–2

LONGEST HOME STANDS

The Bruins have had five 7-game homestands in their history.

1946–47
1947–48
1949–50
1952–53
1980–81

The Boston Bruins once played a stretch of 12 out of 13 games at home. This occurred in the 1952–53 season and went as follows:

January 11	Chicago	February 1	Montreal
January 15	Detroit	February 5	Chicago
January 18	Toronto	February 8	Detroit
January 24	New York	February 12	Detroit
January 25	New York	February 14	New York
January 29	Toronto	February 15	Montreal
January 31	(At Montreal)		

The New York Rangers and Detroit Red Wings both visited the Boston Garden 3 times during this homestand with both teams making back to back games at the Garden.

Brothers Thompson — Tiny of the Bruins, and
Paul of the Blackhawks — in the 1930s.

0 – 0 GAMES

The Boston Bruins have been involved in 33 regular season and 2 playoff, scoreless games in their history. The following is a recap of those games. The goaltenders for each team are under their clubs.

REGULAR SEASON GAMES

1. December 1, 1927 — Boston Bruins at Pittsburgh Pirates
   (Hal Winkler) (Roy Worters)

2. January 3, 1928 — Pittsburgh Pirates at Boston Bruins
   (Roy Worters) (Hal Winkler)

3. January 24, 1928 — Pittsburgh Pirates at Boston Bruins
   (Roy Worters) (Hal Winkler)

4. March 3, 1928 — Boston Bruins at Toronto Maple Leafs
   (Hal Winkler) (Joe Ironstone)

5. January 22, 1929 — Montreal Canadiens at Boston Bruins
   (George Hainsworth) (Tiny Thompson)

6. January 3, 1932 — Boston Bruins at New York Americans
   (Tiny Thompson) (Roy Worters)

7. January 7, 1932 — Boston Bruins at Detroit Falcons
   (Tiny Thompson) (Alex Connell)

8. February 18, 1932 — Boston Bruins at Detroit Falcons
   (Tiny Thompson) (Alex Connell)

9. January 3, 1933 — New York Americans at Boston Bruins
   (Roy Worters) (Tiny Thompson)

10. January 5, 1933 — Boston Bruins at Chicago Blackhawks
    (Tiny Thompson) (Charlie Gardiner)

11. February 28, 1993 — Ottawa Senators at Boston Bruins
    (Bill Beveridge) (Tiny Thompson)

12. March 18, 1933 — Boston Bruins at Montreal Canadiens
    (Tiny Thompson) (George Hainsworth)

13. January 11, 1934 — Boston Bruins at Chicago Blackhawks
    (Tiny Thompson) (Charlie Gardiner)

14. December 30, 1934 — Boston Bruins at New York Rangers
    (Tiny Thompson) (Dave Kerr)

15. February 24, 1935 — Boston Bruins at New York Rangers
    (Tiny Thompson) (Dave Kerr)

16. December 19, 1935 — Boston Bruins at Toronto Maple Leafs
    (Tiny Thompson) (George Hainsworth)

17. March 14, 1940 — Boston Bruins at New York Rangers
    (Frank Brimsek) (Dave Kerr)

18. March 1, 1941 — Boston Bruins at Toronto Maple Leafs
    (Frank Brimsek) (Turk Broda)

19.	January 27, 1942	Toronto Maple Leafs at Boston Bruins (Turk Broda) (Frank Brimsek)
20.	November 30, 1947	Toronto Maple Leafs at Boston Bruins (Turk Broda) (Frank Brimsek)
21.	March 17, 1948	Detroit Red Wings at Boston Bruins (Harry Lumley) (Frank Brimsek)
22.	October 23, 1949	Montreal Canadiens at Boston Bruins (Bill Durnan) (Jack Gelineau)
23.	October 22, 1950	New York Rangers at Boston Bruins (Chuck Rayner) (Jack Gelineau)
24.	November 6, 1951	Detroit Red Wings at Boston Bruins (Terry Sawchuk) (Jim Henry)
25.	January 31, 1952	Boston Bruins at Chicago Blackhawks (Jim Henry) (Harry Lumley)
26.	January 31, 1953	Boston Bruins at Montreal Canadiens (Jim Henry) (Gerry McNeil)
27.	November 1, 1953	Boston Bruins at Chicago Blackhawks (Jim Henry) (Al Rollins)
28.	October 22, 1955	Boston Bruins at Detroit Red Wings (Terry Sawchuk) (Glenn Hall)
29.	November 13, 1955	Detroit Red Wings at Boston Bruins (Glenn Hall) (Terry Sawchuk)
30.	December 28, 1957	Boston Bruins at Chicago Blackhawks (Don Simmons) (Glenn Hall)
31.	November 30, 1963	Boston Bruins at Montreal Canadiens (Ed Johnston) (Charlie Hodge)
32.	December 21, 1968	Boston Bruins at Montreal Canadiens (Gerry Cheevers) (Tony Esposito)
33.	March 11, 1970	Boston Bruins at Chicago Blackhawks (Gerry Cheevers) (Tony Esposito)

0 – 0 GAMES RECAP

At Boston	12
Away	21

At Boston	12
vs. Detroit Red Wings	3
vs. Pittsburgh Pirates	2
vs. Montreal Canadiens	2
vs. Toronto Maple Leafs	2
vs. New York Americans	1
vs. Ottawa Senators	1
vs. New York Rangers	1

Last 0–0 game at Boston, November 13, 1955

At Chicago   6
Last 0–0 game at Chicago, March 11, 1970

At Montreal Canadiens   4
Last 0–0 game at Montreal, December 21, 1968

At Detroit   3
Last 0–0 game at Detroit, October 22, 1955

At Toronto   3
Last 0–0 game at Toronto, March 1, 1941

At New York Rangers   3
Last 0–0 game at New York Rangers, March 14, 1940

At Pittsburgh   1
Last 0–0 game at Pittsburgh, December 1, 1927

At New York Americans   1
Last 0–0 game at New York Americans, January 3, 1931

BOSTON BRUINS GOALTENDERS INVOLVED IN 0 – 0 GAMES

Tiny Thompson	12	Jack Gelineau	2
Frank Brimsek	5	Gerry Cheevers	2
Hal Winkler	4	Ed Johnston	1
Jim Henry	4	Don Simmons	1
Terry Sawchuk	2		

OPPOSITION GOALTENDERS INVOLVED IN 0 – 0 GAMES

5 shutouts
- Roy Worters (Pittsburgh) 3
- Roy Worters (New York Americans) 2

3 shutouts
- George Hainsworth (Montreal) 2
- George Hainsworth (Toronto) 1
- Glenn Hall (Detroit) 2
- Glenn Hall (Chicago) 1
- Turk Broda (Toronto)
- Dave Kerr (New York Rangers)

2 shutouts
- Harry Lumley (Detroit) 1
- Harry Lumley (Chicago) 1
- Tony Esposito (Chicago) 1
- Tony Esposito (Montreal) 1
- Charlie Gardiner (Chicago)
- Alex Connell (Detroit)

1 shutout
- Joe Ironstone (Toronto)
- Bill Beveridge (Ottawa)
- Bill Durnan (Montreal)
- Terry Sawchuk (Detroit)
- Gerry McNeil (Montreal)
- Al Rollins (Chicago)
- Charlie Hodge (Montreal)
- Chuck Rayner (New York Rangers)

Gerry Cheevers with the stitched mask.

MOST TO LEAST 0 – 0 GAME MATCHUPS

Hal Winkler vs. Roy Worters (Pittsburgh Pirates). 3

Frank Brimsek vs. Turk Broda (Toronto Maple Leafs) 3

Tiny Thompson vs. George Hainsworth (Montreal Canadiens) 2

Tiny Thompson vs. George Hainsworth (Toronto Maple Leafs). 1

Tiny Thompson vs. Roy Worters (New York Americans) 2

Tiny Thompson vs. Alex Connell (Detroit Falcons) 2

Tiny Thompson vs. Charlie Gardiner (Chicago Blackhawks) 2

Tiny Thompson vs. Dave Kerr (New York Rangers) 2

Terry Sawchuk vs. Glenn Hall (Detroit Red Wings) 2

Gerry Cheevers vs. Tony Esposito (Montreal Canadiens) 1

Gerry Cheevers vs. Tony Esposito (Chicago Blackhawks) 1

Hal Winkler vs. Joe Ironstone (Toronto Maple Leafs) 1

Tiny Thompson vs. Bill Beveridge (Ottawa Senators) 1

Frank Brimsek vs. Dave Kerr (New York Rangers) 1

Frank Brimsek vs. Harry Lumley (Detroit Red Wings) 1

Jack Gelineau vs. Bill Durnan (Montreal Canadiens) 1

Jack Gelineau vs. Chuck Rayner (New York Rangers) 1

Jim Henry vs. Terry Sawchuk (Detroit Red Wings) 1

Jim Henry vs. Harry Lumley (Chicago Blackhawks) 1

Jim Henry vs. Gerry McNeil (Montreal Canadiens) 1

Jim Henry vs. Al Rollins (Chicago Blackhawks) 1

Don Simmons vs. Glenn Hall (Chicago Blackhawks) 1

Ed Johnston vs. Charlie Hodge (Montreal Canadiens) 1

PLAYOFF 0 – 0 GAMES RECAP

At Boston 2

Away 0

1.   April 2, 1927   New York Rangers at Boston Bruins
(Lorne Chabot)   (Hal Winkler)

2.   April 7, 1927   Ottawa Senators at Boston Bruins
(Alex Connell)   (Hal Winkler)

UNITED STATES PRESIDENTS
AND CANADIAN PRIME MINISTERS

BOSTON BRUINS STANLEY CUP YEARS

1929	President Franklin Roosevelt Prime Minister W.L. Mackenzie King
1939	President Franklin Roosevelt Prime Minister W.L. Mackenzie King
1941	President Franklin Roosevelt Prime Minister W.L. Mackenzie King
1970	President Richard Nixon Prime Minister Pierre Trudeau
1972	President Richard Nixon Prime Minister Pierre Trudeau

The following Boston Bruins have famous surnames. The name in parentheses is the actual name of the President of the United States or the Prime Minister of Canada.

PRESIDENT BRUIN

John (John, John Quincy) Adams
Ron (James) Buchanan
Billy, John, Anson (Jimmy) Carter
Benny (Ulysses) Grant
Ed, Jim (Benjamin, William) Harrison
Chris (Rutherford) Hayes
Ron (Herbert) Hoover
Art, Harvey, Percy, Stan (Andrew) Jackson
Norm, Tom (Lyndon, Andrew) Johnson
Forbes, Sheldon (John) Kennedy
Larry (*Ronald Reagan) Regan
Billy, Bobby (Zachary) Taylor
Gordon, Ross, Wally, Landon (Woodrow) Wilson

PRIME MINISTER BRUIN

John (Lester Pearson)* Peirson
* poetic license

BOSTON BRUINS FACTOIDS

- The Bruins toured Europe in the Spring of 1959.
- The Bruins have played more games on January 1 (40) than any other date, followed by December 5 (37) and March 5 (37).
- The Bruins' earliest opening date is October 3, having played once on that date. The Bruins' latest regular season game was played on May 3, 1995, at Montreal. The Bruins' latest playoff game was played on May 26, 1988, at Edmonton. The Bruins have never played on October 1 and 2.
- The Bruins and Celtics played back-to-back exhibition games as a double header on October 4, 1959. The Celtics played the Minneapolis Lakers and the Bruins played their farm team, the Providence Reds. Prices for tickets were $1.50 and were sold on a first come, first serve basis.
- The final scores: Celtics 107 – Minneapolis 84; Bruins 6 – Providence 6
- The Bruins have won more games (22) on March 13 than on any other date.
- The Bruins have lost 18 games on January 5 and February 18.
- If a tie game is as pleasant as kissing your sister, avoid Bruins games on October 23, October 30, March 10, and March 16. The Bruins have played 8 tie games on each of those dates.
- Weston Adams Sr. was once the traveling secretary of the Boston Braves baseball team.
- Jason Allison was the 1994 Canadian Major Junior Player of the Year.
- Earl Anderson played one season in the Detroit Red Wings minor league system in London, England.
- Murray Balfour was a member of Chicago's Million Dollar Line with Red Hay and Bobby Hull.
- Marco Baron speaks three languages: French, English, and Italian.
- John Blum is the brother-in-law of Mark Messier.
- Leo Boivin once scouted for the Hartford Whalers.
- Ray Bourque was the first non-goaltender to win the Calder Trophy and be named to the first All-Star team in the same season.
- Paul Boutilier was named best defenseman in the 1982 Memorial Cup playoffs.
- John Brackenborough's nickname was "Spider."
- Andy Brickley was a 1982 NCAA All-American at the University of New Hampshire. His brother is a scout with the Kansas City Royals baseball team.
- Archie Briden's nickname was "Bones."
- Ken Broderick has a degree in physical education from the University of British Columbia.
- Ross Brooks was the 1973 Rhode Island Jewish Athlete of the Year.
- Adam Brown's father, Andy, was the chief Ontario scout for the New York Rangers.
- Johnny Bucyk won the Lady Byng Memorial Trophy at the age of 39.
- Charlie Burns played with a silver plate in his head, which required him to wear a helmet.
- Randy Burridge was known as "Stump."
- Lyndon Byers is a leap-year baby.
- Charlie Cahill's nickname was "Moose."
- Jim Carey was the 1996 Vezina Trophy winner with the Washington Capitals.
- Wayne Carleton trained and raced horses.
- Bobby Carpenter was the first American to go from high school (Saint John's Prep, Danvers, Massachusetts) directly to the NHL.
- Anson Carter was a CCHA first team All-Star in 1994 and 1995.
- John Carter was an All-American in 1984–85 at RPI.
- Joe Carveth was a milkman.

- Wayne Cashman was the last player to have played when there were only 6 teams in the league (1966–67). Wayne retired after the 1982–83 season.
- Punch Imlach, General Manager of the Toronto Maple Leafs, tried to protect Gerry Cheevers as a forward. The Bruins drafted him anyway.
- Don Cherry won the Louis Pieri Award for being the outstanding coach in the American Hockey League.
- Dave Christian's family manufactures Christian Brothers hockey sticks.
- Dean Chynoweth was a 1987 first-round draft pick of the New York Islanders.
- Although he did not drink beer, Wayne Connelly worked in a brewhouse in San Francisco during the summer of 1966.
- Carson Cooper, nicknamed "Bullet," became the chief scout for the Detroit Red Wings.
- Harold "Baldy" Cotton was the Bruins' first scout.
- Geoff Courtnall is the brother of Russ Courtnall.
- Jim Craig was a member of the 1980 U.S. Olympic Gold medal-winning team.
- Johnny Crawford was a grocery salesman on Cape Cod.
- Bruce Crowder was the coach of the University of Lowell and Northeastern University, thus becoming the second Bruin after Fernie Flaman to coach Northeastern University.
- Keith Crowder set the Bruins' penalty record for 1 game with 43 minutes on February 26, 1981, against Minnesota.
- Billy Coutu's nickname was "Beaver."
- Gary Doak is the Director of Recreational Services for the Metropolitan District Commission in Boston.
- Ted Donato appeared in the 1987–88 Bruins media guide as the winner of the John Carlton Memorial Trophy, the award for the outstanding student athlete. John Carlton was a former scout for the Bruins.
- Dave Donnelly was a member of the 1982 University of North Dakota, NCAA championship team.
- Gary Dornhoefer was once Ontario junior golf champion.
- Peter Douris was Winnipeg's first pick in the 1984 entry draft.
- Luc Dufour is a brother-in-law of former Quebec Nordiques Alain Cote.
- Woody Dumart owned a sporting goods store in Needham Heights, Massachusetts.
- Pat Egan wore pennies under his shoelaces for good luck.
- General Manager "Hap" Emms owned the Niagara Falls Flyers.
- Autrey Erickson was named after the cowboy Gene Autry.
- Phil Esposito had a nightly sports program in Sault Ste. Marie, Ontario.
- Phil is general manager of the Tampa Bay Lightning.
- Bill Ezinicki was the professional at both the Colonial Country Club in Lynnfield and the Idle Hour course in Saugus.
- Dunc Fisher was a swimming instructor in Regina, Saskatchewan.
- Fernie Flaman poured the concrete for many of the sidewalks in Regina, Saskatchewan.
- He was also involved in a bowling alley in Beverly, Massachusetts, with former Red Sox catcher Pete Daley.
- He also coached the Northeastern University hockey team and was a scout for the New Jersey Devils.
- Reggie Fleming's roommate in Chicago was Cubs catcher Dick Bertell.
- Dave Forbes graduated from the American International College in Springfield, Massachusetts.
- Dwight Foster led the Ontario Hockey Association in scoring in 1976–77.
- Frank Frederickson sold life insurance.
- Dutch Gainor's played hockey with the Crow's Nest Pass Club.
- Garry Galley was an All-American at Bowling Green University in 1983–84.
- Because of his constant chatter, Don Gallinger was known as "Gabby."
- Bruce Gamble was a member of the Hull-Ottawa Junior Canadiens Memorial Cup winning team.

- Cal Gardner's sons Dave and Paul played in the National Hockey League. Cal also did color commentary on Bruins radio broadcasts.
- Jean Gauthier and Harry Sinden were once tied for the honor of top defenseman of the Eastern Pro Hockey League.
- Jack Gelineau was the first player to go from college directly to the NHL.
- Jean-Guy Gendron was an assistant pro at a Montreal golf course.
- Doug Gibson was the Minor League Player of the Year for 1974–75 playing with the Rochester Americans.
- Mike Gillis became a lawyer and player agent.
- Thomas Gradin was the captain of Team Sweden in the 1984 Canada Cup.
- Ron Grahame was a graduate of Denver University where he won the MVP of the Western Collegiate Hockey Association.
- Ted Green once trained his dog to find lost golf balls near his Winnipeg home.
- Trainer Win Green was the Director of the Boston Arena band, the Ironworker.
- Bep Guidolin, at the age of 16, became the youngest player in the history of the NHL.
- Ed Harrison, a cousin to Eddie Sandford, claimed that milk was his favorite drink.
- Greg Hawgood was named the WHL's best defenseman in 1987–88.
- Chris Hayes was a junior teammate of Bobby Orr, Wayne Cashman, and Nick Beverley.
- Murray Henderson was a nephew to Lionel and Roy Conacher.
- "Sugar Jim" Henry ran a hockey school with New York Rangers goalie Chuck Rayner.
- "Sailor" Jimmy Herberts was a mariner on the Great Lakes.
- Herberts is the only player in Bruins history to lead the team in goals (17), assists (5), points (22), and penalty minutes (50) in the same season, 1924–25.
- Lionel Hitchman was a hotel clerk in Berlin, New Hampshire.
- Ken Hodge Sr. is actively involved in Special Olympics.
- Ken Hodge Jr. was a 1984 second-round draft pick of the Minnesota North Stars.
- Ted Hodgson played with the 1966 Memorial Cup-winning Edmonton Oil Kings.
- Flash Hollett, while playing with Detroit, became the first defenseman to score 20 goals in a season.
- Craig Janney was a member of the 1987 Hockey East champions at Boston College.
- Norm Johnson was in the lumber business.
- During the off-season of 1966, Eddie Johnston, the last goaltender to play all of his team's games (1963–64), ran a hockey school with Forbes Kennedy in Saint John, New Brunswick.
- Stan Jonathan was a member of the Tuscarora Indian Tribe.
- Bobby Joyce played on the 1988 Canadian Olympic hockey team.
- Steve Kasper scored the 11,000th goal in Bruins history.
- Doug Keans played on the Canadian National Midget championship team at age 15.
- Gord Kluzak played on the 1982 Canada World Junior championship team.
- Ed Kryzanowski scored a goal on his first shot in an NHL game against "Sugar Jim" Henry, then goaltender for Chicago.
- When word got out to the Gallery Gods that Orland Kurtenbach claimed he had trouble finding his legs before Christmas, at the next home game, they sang him a rendition of "Jingle Bells."
- Gus Kyle was a member of the Royal Canadian Mounted Police.
- Bobby Lalonde scored 2 short-handed goals in 1 period during a 1981 playoff game against Minnesota.
- Myles Lane was a federal judge in New York.
- Junior Langlois was the last player to wear #4 before Bobby Orr.
- Guy Lapointe was the last Bruin to wear #5.
- Guy Larose is the son of former Montreal Canadien Claude Larose.
- Reed Larson was a first team WCHA All-Star in 1975–76.
- Martin Lauder sold automobiles.

- Brian Lawton was the first player taken in the 1983 amateur draft. Lawton was drafted #1 by the Minnesota North Stars.
- Hal Laycoe wore unbreakable glasses during games.
- Because he was part Indian, Reggie Leach was known as "Little Beaver."
- Bobby Leiter worked for the Manitoba Liquor Commission.
- Reggie Lemelin played for Team Canada in 1984.
- Normand Leveille was the Bruins' leading scorer at the time of his October 23, 1982, brain hemorrhage.
- Ken Linseman scored the Stanley Cup winning goal for the 1984 Edmonton Oilers.
- Morris Lukowich began his pro career with the Houston Aeros of the WHA.
- Harry Lumley raced harness horses in the off-season.
- Fleming Mackell worked for a Quincy, Massachusetts, Chevrolet dealership.
- Craig MacTavish was the last player in the NHL to play without a helmet.
- Troy Mallette was the 1988 first-round draft pick of the New York Rangers.
- Don Marcotte was the only Bruin chosen in the 1979 Challenge Cup in New York.
- Nevin Markwart was named after former Toronto Maple Leaf Bob Nevin.
- Daniel Marois was a 1987 second-round pick of the Toronto Maple Leafs.
- Hubert "Pit" Martin was named after a French cartoon character.
- Tom McCarthy (1960–61) and Tom McCarthy (1986–87 to 1987–88) were not related.
- Bob McCord worked for the Ontario Forestry Commission.
- Brad McCrimmon's best man at his wedding was Ray Bourque.
- Don McKenney was a neighbor of former Bruins great Bill Cowley in Smith Falls, Ontario.
- John McKenzie was a calf roper in Calgary, Alberta.
- Peter McNab won the American Hockey League Rookie of the Year Award with the Cincinnati Swords.
- Peter McNab's father Max was the General Manager of the Washington Capitals.
- Rick Middleton was the first draft choice for the New York Rangers in 1973.
- Mike Milbury became the Coach and General Manager of the New York Islanders.
- Bobby Miller was a member of the 1976 U.S. Olympic team.
- Jay Miller has a business degree from the University of New Hampshire.
- The first player signed to a Bruins contract, Herb Mitchell, was a druggist in Toronto.
- Mike Moffat won the 1981 Hap Holmes Trophy as the outstanding goalie in the OHA.
- Doug Mohns and Ferny Flaman ran Sportsmens's Park in Hanover, Massachusetts.
- Andy Moog's first NHL win, as a member of the Edmonton Oilers, came against Boston on January 1, 1981.
- Trainer Hammy Moore ran a driving range and dance hall in Lynnfield.
- Jim Morrison was a runner-up in the Canadian tandem canoeing championships in 1949.
- Ron Murphy was a member of the Memorial Cup champion Guelph Biltmores.
- Cam Neely, the 1983 first-round draft pick of the Vancouver Canucks, played with the 1983 Memorial Cup champion Portland Winter Hawks. Cam also appeared in the movie Dumb and Dumber.
- Kraig Nienhuis was a member of the 1985 NCAA championship team at RPI.
- Chris Nilan led the American Hockey league in penalty minutes in 1979–80 with Nova Scotia.
- Jim Nill was a member of the 1980 Canadian Olympic hockey team.
- On January 30, 1965, Jack Norris was supposed to play his first game as a Bruin because Eddie Johnston was ill. Instead, Norris could not play because his goaltending equipment was stolen from the Royal York Hotel in Toronto.
- Hank Nowak was a junior teammate of Terry O'Reilly.
- Dennis O'Brien played for 4 teams, Minnesota, Cleveland, Colorado, and Boston in 1977–78.
- Mike O'Connell's father, Tommy, played quarterback for the Cleveland Browns.

- Fred O'Donnell was married on September 8, 1973, the same day that Bobby Orr was married.
- Harry "Pee Wee" Oliver was an electrician.
- Terry O'Reilly, an ardent chess player, is actively involved in the American Liver Foundation.
- Brad Palmer was the 1980 first-round pick of the Minnesota North Stars.
- Bernie Parent, the youngest rookie goalie to play for the Bruins, was a member of the Niagara Falls Flyers, the 1965 Memorial Cup Champions.
- Brad Park works on behalf of Cerebral Palsy.
- Former general manager Lynn Patrick is the father of long-time Pittsburgh Penguins general manager, Craig Patrick.
- Allen Pedersen scored his first NHL game in Terry O'Reilly's coaching debut, November 8, 1986.
- Barry Pederson was selected to the 1981 first All-Star team in the Western Hockey League.
- Johnny Peirson's father sold all insurance for the Montreal Forum.
- Cliff Pennington was a timer and identification chief at the Assiniboia Downs race track in Winnipeg, Manitoba.
- Bob Perreault blanked the Montreal Canadiens 5-0 in his first game with the Bruins.
- Dave Poulin coaches hockey at Notre Dame University.
- Dean Prentice worked for Canadian Gypsum in Guelph, Ontario.
- Jean Pusie was a professional wrestler.
- Bill Quackenbush won the Lady Byng Memorial Trophy as a member of the Detroit Red Wings, thus becoming the first defenseman to ever win that award.
- Dick Redmond, the 1969 first-round draft pick of the Minnesota North Stars, was the brother of Mickey Redmond, former member of the Montreal Canadiens and Detroit Red Wings. Dick appeared on the cover of the 1975–76 Bruins media guide as a member of the Chicago Blackhawks.
- Larry Regan was the first general manager of the Los Angeles Kings.
- Pat Riggin is the son of former Detroit goaltender Dennis Riggin.
- Doug Roberts was an All-American at Michigan State.
- Moe Roberts, who was born in Connecticut but grew up in Somerville, Massachusetts, was the first Jewish goalie to play for the Bruins.
- Art Ross designed the puck, goal nets, and tendon guards on hockey skates.
- Derek Sanderson owned Bachelors Three nightclub in Boston's Back Bay.
- Eddie Sandford's father was president of the Ontario Lacrosse Association.
- Andre Savard used his signing bonus to help pay for his father's heart operation.
- Glen Sather had a clause in his contract with the Detroit Red Wings that they pay for his college tuition.
- Terry Sawchuk won the rookie award in 3 different leagues — the United States, the American, and the NHL — in 3 successive years.
- In the 1976–77 playoffs against the Los Angeles Kings, Bobby Schmautz scored 5 goals on his first 5 shots. All in all, Schmautz scored 8 goals on 12 shots in the 6 games against the Kings.
- Milt Schmidt graced the cover of the 1947–48 Bruins yearbook.
- Milt, who was the first coach to pull the goaltender for an extra attacker, was also the first General manager of the Washington Capitals.
- Ron Schock scored his first goal in his first game against Detroit at the Boston Garden.
- Jim Schoenfeld was a 1972 first-round draft choice of the Buffalo Sabres.
- David Shaw was the 1982 first-round draft pick of the Quebec Nordiques.
- Greg Sheppard was a neighbor of Johnny Bucyk in Boxford, Massachusetts.
- Bruce Shoebottom was a 1983 first-round draft pick of the Los Angeles Kings.
- Eddie Shore sold automobiles and shovelled coal for the railroad. He also was owner of the Springfield Indians of the American Hockey League.
- Dave Silk is a cousin of Mike Milbury.

- Charlie Simmer scored his first NHL goal against the Bruins on December 27, 1974, as a member of the California Seals.
- Don Simmons made his debut for the Bruins on January 26, 1957, in a CBS Saturday afternoon contest. He also owns a goalie equipment store in Fort Erie, Ontario.
- Frank Simonetti was a Division II All-American at Norwich.
- Harry Sinden sold real estate in Collins Bay, Ontario.
- Dallas Smith owns a farm in Manitoba.
- Des Smith was a referee in the American Hockey League. He was also the father of future NHLers Brian, and Gary (Suitcase) Smith.
- Hooley Smith operated a billiard parlor in Montreal.
- Billy Speer ran a barber shop in his hometown of Lindsay, Ontario.
- Steve Staios was the 1991 first-round draft pick of the St. Louis Blues.
- Allan Stanley was known as "Big Sam" to his teammates.
- Vic Stasiuk ran a soft-drink vending-machine business.
- Ron Stewart worked as an automobile dealer in Barrie, Ontario.
- Red Sullivan coached the New York Rangers.
- Ron Sutter was a 1982 first-round draft pick of the Philadelphia Flyers.
- Bob Sweeney was the MVP of the 1983 Beanpot hockey tournament.
- Don Sweeney was named 1988 NCAA East All-American at Harvard University.
- Orval Tessier coached the Chicago Blackhawks.
- Tiny Thompson, in addition to being the first goalie to record an assist in 1936 and the first goalie to earn 4 Vezina Trophies, was the chief scout for the Chicago Blackhawks.
- Jerry Toppazzini owned a men's clothing business in Sudbury, Ontario.
- Rogie Vachon became the general manager of the Los Angeles Kings.
- Mike Walton and Bobby Orr ran a hockey camp in Orillia, Ontario.
- Cooney Weiland was the coach of the Harvard University hockey team.
- John Wensink is a carpenter.
- Glen Wesley was voted the WHL's best defenseman with the Portland Winter Hawks in 1985–86 & 1986–87.
- Eddie Westfall became a color commentator for the New York Islanders. Eddie was also the first winner of the Channel 38, 7th-player award.
- Tommy Williams was a member of the 1960 U.S. Olympic hockey team.
- Wally Wilson was a Flight Instructor in the Royal Canadian Air Force.
- Hal Winkler, the first goalie that the Bruins acquired in a trade, sold life insurance. By the way, he was acquired from the New York Rangers.
- Ken Yackel was a member of the 1952 United States Olympic hockey team.
- On April 7, 1932, a Stanley Cup playoff game was played at Boston Garden, but it did not involve the Bruins. Because of the circus in New York, a game between Toronto and New York was moved to Boston where the Maple Leafs defeated the Rangers 6–2. 12,000 fans attended the game as King Clancy and Charlie Conacher scored 2 goals each for Toronto.
- Tim Sweeney's uncle, Major General Charles Sweeney, was the Commander on the plane that dropped the atomic bomb on Nagasaki.

MILESTONE GOALS

REGULAR SEASON

GOAL NO.	DATE	SCORED BY	VENUE	OPPONENT
1	12/1/24	Fred Harris	Boston	Montreal Maroons
100	2/4/26	Lionel Hitchman	Ottawa	Senators
500	1/14/30	Perk Galbraith	Boston	Ottawa
1000	12/12/33	Vic Ripley	Boston	Toronto
2000	2/4/41	Bill Cowley	Boston	Montreal Canadiens
3000	11/2/46	Bill Cowley	Toronto	Maple Leafs
4000	2/5/52	Milt Schmidt	Boston	Chicago
5000	1/5/58	Fleming Mackell	Chicago	Blackhawks
6000	1/20/63	Johnny Bucyk	Boston	Montreal Canadiens
7000	3/10/68	Glen Sather	Boston	Detroit
8000	4/4/71	Phil Esposito	Boston	Montreal Canadiens
9000	3/31/74	Johnny Bucyk	Boston	Detroit
10000	10/25/77	Rick Smith	Colorado	Rockies
11000	11/22/80	Steve Kasper	Washington	Capitals
12000	11/19/83	Keith Crowder	Boston	New York Rangers
13000	1/12/87	Charlie Simmer	Boston	New York Rangers
14000	3/10/90	John Carter	New York	Islanders
15000	11/20/93	Adam Oates	Boston	Philadelphia

PLAYOFFS

GOAL NO.	DATE	SCORED BY	VENUE	OPPONENT
1	3/29/27	Frank Fredrickson	New York	Chicago Blackhawks
100	4/13/39	Roy Conacher	Toronto	Maple Leafs
200	3/24/46	Woody Dumart	Detroit	Red Wings
300	4/11/53	Eddie Sandford	Montreal	Canadiens
400	4/7/59	Vic Stasiuk	Boston	Toronto
500	5/3/70	Phil Esposito	St. Louis	Blues
600	5/9/72	Wayne Cashman	Boston	New York Rangers
700	4/17/76	Jean Ratelle	Los Angeles	Kings
800	5/4/78	Rick Middleton	Boston	Philadelphia
900	4/22/80	Peter McNab	Boston	New York Islanders
1000	4/24/83	Brad Park	Boston	Buffalo
1100	4/26/88	Cam Neely	Montreal	Canadiens
1200	4/21/90	Garry Galley	Boston	Montreal
1300	4/23/92	Ray Bourque	Buffalo	Sabres
1400	4/25/96	Cam Stewart	Boston	Florida

STANLEY CUP CLINCHING GOALS

	DATE	SCORED BY	VENUE	OPPONENT
1	3/29/29	Bill Carson	New York	Rangers
2	4/16/39	Roy Conacher	Boston	Toronto
3	4/12/41	Bobby Bauer	Detroit	Red Wings
4	5/10/70	Bobby Orr	Boston	St. Louis
5	5/11/72	Bobby Orr	New York	Rangers

GAMES PLAYED — REGULAR SEASON AND PLAYOFFS

Total . . . 5,288 (1 playoff game suspended)

	OCT	NOV	DEC	JAN	FEB	MAR	APR	MAY
1		20	31	40	32	31	26	6
2		24	24	29	36	31	18	4
3	1	20	32	27	28	36	26	8
4	1	22	28	25	33	29	18	4
5	5	25	37	33	32	37	17	7
6	3	18	24	18	32	25	17	2
7	8	26	30	35	30	34	17	11
8	10	19	33	29	28	29	20	3
9	15	19	28	26	31	32	19	7
10	11	25	32	29	27	30	16	5
11	23	29	29	32	33	32	22	4
12	20	22	34	35	24	34	9	4
13	17	22	29	28	31	36	16	1
14	20	31	27	31	33	28	12	4
15	19	28	34	32	25	35	9	1
16	20	27	26	33	31	33	9	2
17	21	29	31	31	26	25	11	1
18	19	29	30	24	30	29	9	3
19	22	28	31	33	24	33	10	2
20	18	29	29	27	32	21	8	2
21	13	31	30	30	35	29	12	2
22	25	23	30	36	21	33	8	2
23	15	36	29	32	32	26	11	2
24	21	33	4	25	25	32	7	1*
25	19	29	37	32	30	23	10	1
26	19	35	25	32	19	28	6	1
27	16	31	29	31	30	27	6	
28	15	26	28	29	23	28	5	
29	24	26	32	31	8	23	4	
30	22	29	20	27		26	4	
31	19		30	30		22		
Tot.	*461*	*792*	*893*	*932*	*821*	*917*	*382*	*90*

MOST GAMES: January 1 (40)

LEAST GAMES: (1) October 3 & 4

NO GAMES: October 1 & 2, May 27, 28, 29, 30, 31

* Suspended due to blackout

GAMES PLAYED — REGULAR SEASON

Total . . . 4,812

	OCT	NOV	DEC	JAN	FEB	MAR	APR	MAY
1		20	31	40	32	31	14	
2		24	24	29	36	31	11	
3	1	20	32	27	28	36	15	1
4	1	22	28	25	33	29	10	
5	5	25	37	33	32	37	7	
6	3	18	24	18	32	25	8	
7	8	26	30	35	30	34	4	
8	10	19	33	29	28	29	5	
9	15	19	28	26	31	32	3	
10	11	25	32	29	27	30	3	
11	23	29	29	32	33	32	3	
12	20	22	34	35	24	34	2	
13	17	22	29	28	31	36	4	
14	20	31	27	31	33	28	4	
15	19	28	34	32	25	35	2	
16	20	27	26	33	31	33		
17	21	29	31	31	26	25		
18	19	29	30	24	30	29		
19	22	28	31	33	24	30	1	
20	18	29	29	27	32	18	1	
21	13	31	30	30	35	24		
22	25	23	30	36	21	27		
23	15	36	29	32	32	20	1	
24	21	33	4	25	25	21	1	
25	19	29	37	32	30	13		
26	19	35	25	32	19	16	1	
27	16	31	29	31	30	18		
28	15	26	28	29	23	16	1	
29	24	26	32	31	8	12		
30	22	29	20	27		15	1	
31	19		30	30		14		
Tot.	*461*	*792*	*893*	*932*	*821*	*810*	*101*	*1*

MOST GAMES: January 1 (40)

LEAST GAMES: (1) October 3 & 4

GAMES PLAYED — PLAYOFFS

Total ... 476 (1 game suspended)

	MAR	APR	MAY
1		12	5
2		7	4
3		12	7
4		8	4
5		10	7
6		9	2
7		13	11
8		15	3
9		16	7
10		13	5
11		19	4
12		7	4
13		12	1
14		8	4
15		7	1
16		9	2
17		11	1
18		9	3
19	3	9	2
20	3	7	2
21	4	12	2
22	6	8	2
23	6	10	2
24	11	6	1*
25	10	10	1
26	12	5	1
27	9	6	
28	12	4	
29	11	4	
30	11	3	
31	8		
Tot.	107	281	88

MOST PLAYOFF GAMES: April 11 (19)
EARLIEST GAME: March 19, 1929; March 19, 1940; March 19, 1946
LATEST GAME: May 26, 1988

* Suspended due to blackout

REGULAR SEASON WINS

Total ... 2,306

	OCT	NOV	DEC	JAN	FEB	MAR	APR	MAY
1		10	14	22	13	17	2	1
2		9	12	12	18	14	5	
3	1	8	14	15	15	15	9	1
4	1	10	15	15	17	17	6	
5	2	9	17	11	19	17	2	
6	3	11	13	8	11	13	2	
7	2	11	10	16	17	19	4	
8	3	10	13	10	15	14	4	
9	7	9	10	12	15	17	1	
10	6	16	15	16	13	13	2	
11	9	14	14	19	15	18	2	
12	10	9	10	15	14	19	0	
13	9	11	14	9	17	22	3	
14	12	16	16	18	16	18	2	
15	8	15	15	15	12	21	1	
16	9	14	12	18	13	17		
17	6	12	14	14	11	12		
18	8	20	16	16	11	15		
19	13	16	13	13	9	11	1	
20	10	12	16	12	10	11	1	
21	4	18	15	20	14	15		
22	10	11	13	17	11	11		
23	2	19	16	13	15	11	1	
24	7	15	2	15	9	10	0	
25	8	13	17	16	12	7		
26	8	18	13	19	9	8	1	
27	11	16	8	14	17	8		
28	8	11	14	12	14	7	0	
29	10	14	13	17	4	6		
30	5	12	7	13		8	1	
31	6		11	17		9		
Tot.	198	389	402	459	386	420	50	2

MOST WINS: January 1 & March 13 (22)

REGULAR SEASON LOSSES

Total ... 1,800

	OCT	NOV	DEC	JAN	FEB	MAR	APR	MAY
1		8	15	15	12	8	9	0
2		12	8	13	12	12	6	
3	0	8	12	6	9	14	4	0
4	0	9	7	7	11	6	1	
5	2	10	13	18	11	14	4	
6	0	3	9	6	17	10	3	
7	5	11	13	14	6	12	0	
8	5	7	15	15	11	14	1	
9	6	9	13	13	11	11	2	
10	3	3	14	11	10	9	1	
11	7	10	12	9	15	8	1	
12	6	11	17	16	7	12	1	
13	4	8	8	13	9	11	1	
14	5	13	6	11	10	7	2	
15	6	7	15	15	9	8	0	
16	6	7	12	11	16	8		
17	12	10	14	12	13	11		
18	9	8	11	5	14	7		
19	7	6	14	15	9	15		0
20	5	12	7	13	18	5		0
21	7	9	11	9	15	6		
22	9	10	16	14	10	14		
23	5	11	8	14	13	8		0
24	13	11	1	8	12	9	1	
25	5	9	18	11	14	5		
26	9	14	7	10	9	6		0
27	4	9	16	12	10	7		
28	6	10	10	14	3	6	1	
29	9	8	13	9	3	4		
30	9	14	10	13		4		0
31	10		14	7		3		
Tot.	*174*	*277*	*359*	*359*	*319*	*274*	*38*	*0*

MOST LOSSES: January 5 (18); February 20 (18); January 25 (18)

REGULAR SEASON TIES

Total ... 706

	OCT	NOV	DEC	JAN	FEB	MAR	APR	MAY
1		2	2	3	7	6	3	0
2		3	4	4	6	5	0	
3	0	4	6	6	4	7	1	0
4	0	3	6	3	5	6	3	
5	1	6	7	4	2	6	1	
6	0	4	2	4	4	2	3	
7	1	4	7	5	7	3	0	
8	2	2	5	4	2	1	0	
9	2	1	5	1	5	4	0	
10	2	6	3	2	4	8	0	
11	7	6	3	4	3	6	0	
12	4	2	7	4	3	3	1	
13	4	3	7	6	5	3	0	
14	3	2	5	2	7	3	0	
15	5	6	4	2	4	6	1	
16	5	6	2	4	2	8		
17	3	7	3	5	2	2		
18	2	1	3	3	5	7		
19	2	6	4	5	6	4		0
20	3	5	6	2	4	2		0
21	2	4	4	1	6	3		
22	6	2	1	5	0	2		
23	8	6	5	5	4	1		0
24	1	7	1	2	4	2		0
25	6	7	2	5	4	1		
26	2	3	5	3	1	2		0
27	1	6	5	5	3	3		
28	1	5	4	3	6	3		0
29	5	4	6	5	1	2		
30	8	3	3	1		3		0
31	3		5	6		2		
Tot.	*89*	*126*	*132*	*114*	*116*	*116*	*13*	*0*

MOST TIES: October 23 (8); October 30 (8); March 10 (8); March 16 (8)

PLAYOFF WINS

Total ... 228

Day	MAR	APR	MAY	Day	MAR	APR	MAY
1		4	5	18		3	1
2		3	3	19	3	3	0
3		4	6	20	2	5	1
4		3	2	21	4	10	1
5		6	4	22	3	2	0
6		5	1	23	4	7	0
7		8	5	24	5	3	0
8		6	1	25	3	6	0
9		3	3	26	7	3	0
10		6	3	27	4	3	
11		11	2	28	3	3	
12		2	0	29	5	2	
13		7	0	30	4	1	
14		6	1	31	2		
15		4	0				
16		5	1	Tot.	49	140	39
17		5	0	MOST WINS: April 11 (11)			

PLAYOFF LOSSES

Total ... 242

Day	MAR	APR	MAY	Day	MAR	APR	MAY
1		8	0	18		6	2
2		3	1	19	1	6	2
3		8	1	20	0	2	1
4		5	2	21	1	2	1
5		4	3	22	3	6	2
6		4	1	23	2	3	2
7		4	6	24	6	3	1
8		9	2	25	7	4	1
9		13	4	26	5	2	1
10		7	2	27	5	3	
11		7	2	28	9	1	
12		5	4	29	6	2	
13		5	1	30	7	2	
14		2	3	31	3		
15		3	1				
16		4	1	Tot.	55	138	49
17		6	1	MOST LOSSES: April 9 (13)			

PLAYOFF TIES

Total ... 6

Day	MAR	APR	MAY
1		o	o
2		I	o
3		o	o
4		o	o
5		o	o
6		o	o
7		I	o
8		o	o
9		o	o
10		o	o
11		I	o
12		o	o
13		o	o
14		o	o
15		o	o
16		o	o
17		o	o
18		o	o
19	o	o	o
20	o	o	o
21	o	o	o
22	o	o	o
23	o	o	o
24	o	o	I
25	o	o	o
26	o	o	o
27	o	o	
28	o	o	
29	o	o	
30	o	o	
31	3		
Tot.	*3*	*3*	*I*

MOST TIES: March 31 (3)
* Suspended game (Boston 3–Edmonton 3)

ALL-TIME MONTHLY RECORDS REGULAR SEASON

	W	L	T
October	198	174	89
November	389	277	126
December	402	359	132
January	459	359	114
February	386	319	116
March	420	274	116
April	50	38	13
May	2	0	0
Total	2306	1800	706

ALL-TIME MONTHLY RECORDS PLAYOFFS

	W	L	T
March	49	55	3
April	140	138	3
May	39	49	0
Total	228	242	6

DAILY ALL-TIME RECORDS AND EVENTS

January 1
Games played: 40
22–15–3

1917   Oscar Aubuchon is born in St. Hyacinthe, Quebec.

1925   Lose at Ottawa, 5–2.

1946   Defeat Detroit at Boston, 4–0. First regular season win over Detroit since 1943. Paul Bibeault records shutout.

1951   Defeat Rangers at Boston, 3–2. Bill Quackenbush sets up goals by brother Max, and Milt Schmidt.

1953   Defeat Toronto at Boston, 5–1. Ted Kennedy of the Leafs breaks his collarbone in a fight with Milt Schmidt. Dave Creighton scores two goals for Boston but is taken out of game after breaking his leg.

1963   Defeat Toronto at Boston, 3–0. Eddie Johnston records shutout.
Former Bruin Art Chapman dies.

1973   Win at Vancouver, 8–2. Phil Esposito scores 3 goals while Bobby Orr has six assists.

1997   Despite a short-handed goal by Adam Oates, the Bruins lose to the Senators at Ottawa, 3–2. This is the first loss to Ottawa since the Senators returned to the National Hockey League in 1992.

January 2
Games played: 29
12–13–4

1982   Tie at Edmonton, 4–4. Wayne Cashman scores 250th goal. Peter McNab plays in 500th game.

1992   Lose to Winnipeg at Boston, 3–1.
Acquire Gord Murphy from Philadelphia with Brian Dobbin for Garry Galley and Wes Walz.

1994   Bruins defeat Washington at Boston, 8–2. Cam Neely scores the hat trick. Three Capitals and two Bruins ejected for fighting.

1995   Game against Tampa Bay at Boston is postponed, then canceled due to NHL lockout.

January 3
Games played: 27
15–6–6

1929   Defeat Maroons at Montreal, 1–0. Eddie Shore scores lone goal and is fined by Art Ross for missing train to Montreal.

1931   Lose to Maroons at Montreal, 5–3. Nels Stewart of the Maroons scores 2 goals in 4 seconds.

1937   Defeat Rangers at Boston, 3–2. Eddie Shore scores tying and winning goal.

1971   Win at Philadelphia, 5–1. Johnny Bucyk gets hat trick.
Former Bruins farmhand Doug Favell in goal for Philadelphia.

1996   Tie Maple Leafs at Toronto, 4–4, in a game marked with controversy as Coach Steve Kasper benches Cam Neely and Kevin Stevens.

January 4
Games played: 25
15–7–3

1930   Defeat Maroons at Montreal, 4–2 for their 14th consecutive victory.

1934   Lose at Ottawa, 9–2. Bruins players all wear leather helmets.

1958   Defeat Rangers at New York, 7–4. Johnny Bucyk scores hat trick. Gump Worsley in goal for the Rangers.

1964   Lose at Montreal, 5–1. Leo Boivin scores on penalty shot.
Charlie Hodge in goal for Montreal.

1975   Win at Minnesota, 8–0. Dave Forbes–Henry Boucha stick incident. Johnny Bucyk scores game winner.

1986   Win at Buffalo, 4–0. Pat Riggin records his first Bruins shutout.

January 5
Games played: 33
11–18–4

1926   Defeat Pittsburgh at Boston, 3–0.
Jimmy Herberts becomes first Bruin to score hat trick.

1944 Trade Flash Hollett to Detroit for Pat Egan.

1950 Lose at Montreal, 5–3. 40th anniversary of Montreal franchise.

1958 Lose at Chicago, 4–3.
Fleming Mackell scores the 5,000th goal in Bruins history.

1983 Win at Chicago, 4–1. Rick Middleton nets hat trick. Tony Esposito in goal for the Blackhawks.

1995 Game against Philadelphia at Boston is postponed, then canceled due to NHL lockout.

January 6
Games played: 18
8–6–4

1940 Dick Meissner is born in Kindersley, Saskatchewan.

1994 Defeat Winnipeg at Boston, 5–4. Don Sweeney scores short-handed goal.

January 7
Games played: 35
16–14–5

1945 Lose at Detroit, 8–4. Red Wings score 3 goals in 46 seconds.

1959 Former Calder winner Larry Regan is placed on waivers and claimed by the Toronto Maple Leafs.

1964 Lose to Detroit at Boston, 5–0. 7,246 fans chant "we shall overcome." This is a game that was rescheduled from November 24, 1963 due to President Kennedy's assassination.

1965 Defeat Detroit at Boston, 5–2. Gordie Howe receives major penalty after slamming Billy Knibbs into the boards.

1983 Tie at New Jersey, 2–2. Bruins record no shots on goal in the third period.

1985 Defeat Los Angeles at Boston in overtime, 5–4. Ray Bourque collects 300th NHL point. Charlie Simmer scores winner in overtime.

1995 Game against Detroit at Boston is postponed, then canceled due to NHL lockout.

January 8
Games played: 29
10–15–4

1935 Defeat Toronto at Boston, 3–1. Eddie Shore misses penalty shot. George Hainsworth in goal for Toronto.
Dan Poliziani is born in Sydney, Nova Scotia.

1944 Lose at Toronto, 12–3. Babe Pratt, Toronto defenseman, registers 6 assists for the Maple Leafs. George Boothman scores 3 goals for Toronto.

1953 Lose at Detroit, 4–0. Glenn Hall, subbing for Terry Sawchuk, records shutout.

1985 Obtain Butch Goring on waivers from Islanders.

1996 Due to a snowstorm in Boston, the game with the Colorado Avalanche is postponed to the following evening, January 9 at 7:00 p.m.

January 9
Games played: 26
12–13–1

1952 Trade Jim Morrison to Toronto for Fleming MacKell.

1975 Defeat Vancouver at Boston, 5–1. For the third time in three weeks, Phil Esposito records the hat trick. Greg Sheppard scores game winner.

1979 Bobby Orr Night at the Garden as Orr's #4 is retired before an exhibition game between the Bruins and the Soviet Wings.

1985 Win at Toronto, 5–3. Steve Kasper scores two short-handed goals 50 seconds apart.

1992 Defeat Quebec at Boston, 5–4. Craig Janney misses penalty shot attempt.

January 10
Games played: 29
16–11–2

1925 Defeat Canadiens at Montreal, 3–2. 1st overtime win in team history as Bruins break 11-game losing streak.

1960 Defeat Toronto at Boston, 4–0. Don Simmons, wearing mask, records shutout.

1966 Trade Reggie Fleming to New York for John McKenzie.

1976 Defeat California at Boston, 3–2. Johnny Bucyk scores game winner. Wayne King of California misses penalty shot attempt against Gilles Gilbert.

Sunday, January 14, 1968

BOSTON BRUINS

1.	ED JOHNSTON	G
30.	GERRY CHEEVERS	G
4.	BOBBY ORR	D
6.	TED GREEN (A)	D
7.	PHIL ESPOSITO (A)	C
8.	KEN HODGE	L.W.
9.	JOHN BUCYK (A)	L.W.
11.	TOM WILLIAMS	R.W.
14.	GLEN SATHER	L.W.
16.	DEREK SANDERSON	C
17.	FRED STANFIELD	C
18.	ED WESTFALL	D
19.	JOHN McKENZIE	R.W.
20.	DALLAS SMITH	D
21.	PHIL "SKIP" KRAKE	C
23.	EDDIE SHACK	R.W.
25.	GARY DOAK	D
26.	DON AWREY	D
28.	RON MURPHY	L.W.
29.	ROSS LONSBERRY	L.W.

Coach—Harry Sinden
General Manager—Milt Schmidt
Trainers—Don Canney and John Forristall

MINNESOTA NORTH STARS

1.	GARRY BAUMAN	G
30.	CESARE MANIAGO	G
2.	BOB WOYTOWICH (C)	D
3.	BOB McCORD	D
4.	ELMER VASKO (A)	D
5.	PETE GOEGAN	D
6.	MIKE McMAHON (A)	D
8.	BILL GOLDSWORTHY	R.W.
9.	MILAN MARCETTA	C
10.	RAY CULLEN	C
11.	JEAN PAUL PARISE	L.W.
12.	WAYNE CONNELLY	R.W.
14.	PARKER MacDONALD	L.W.
15.	ANDRE BOUDRIAS	C
17.	DAVE BALON	L.W.
18.	BILL COLLINS	R.W.
19.	BILL MASTERTON	C

Manager-Coach—Wren Blair
Trainers—Stan Waylett and Al Schuenman

1994 — Lose to Toronto at Boston, 3–0. First Toronto shutout in 33 years at Boston. Felix Potvin in goal for Maple Leafs.

January 11
Games played: 32

19–9–4

1927 — Defeat Chicago at Boston, 6–3. Harry Oliver scores four goals for the Bruins.

1940 — Win at Toronto, 5–2. Herb Cain scores 4 goals for the Bruins.

1948 — Lose at Chicago, 4–1. John Quilty's career ends when he suffers broken leg.

1995 — Game at Ottawa is postponed, then canceled due to NHL lockout.

1996 — Defeat Anaheim at Boston, 7–2. Trade Marius Czerkawski, their second pick in the first round of the 1995 draft, Sean Brown, and their 1996 first-round pick to Edmonton for Bill Ranford.

January 12
Games played: 35

15–16–4

1946 — Defeat Chicago at Boston, 4–3. John Mariucci, Joe Cooper, and Reg Hamilton along with trainer Ed Froelich of the Blackhawks are charged with assault and battery.

1949 — Lose to Canadiens at Boston, 5–3. Ken Reardon scores on penalty shot against Frank Brimsek.

1978 — Defeat Los Angeles at Boston, 6–1. Greg Sheppard nets 3 goals.

1987 — Defeat Rangers at Boston, 4–1. Charlie Simmer scores Bruins 13,000th goal.

1993 — Defeat Buffalo at Boston, 5–2. Joe Juneau records the hat trick for the Bruins.

January 13
Games played: 28

9–13–6

1974 — Win at Pittsburgh, 5–3. Don Marcotte nets game winner.

1980 — Defeat Colorado at Boston, 6–2. Stan Jonathan scores hat trick.

January 14
Games played: 31

18–11–2

1930 — Defeat Ottawa at Boston, 5–1. Perk Galbraith scores the 500th goal in Bruins history.

1936 — Beat Toronto at Boston, 4–1. Tiny Thompson becomes first goaltender in NHL history to receive an assist.

1956   Defeat Canadiens at Montreal, 2–0. Claude Pronovost, brother of Detroit's Marcel, records shutout.

1971   Defeat Los Angeles at Boston, 9–5. Phil Esposito records his 5th hat trick of the season.

1973   Defeat Buffalo at Boston, 6–0. Phil Esposito scores 4 goals against Dave Dryden, in net for the Sabres.

1993   Defeat Pittsburgh at Boston, 7–0. Steve Heinze nets 3 goals. John Blue records shutout.

January 15
Games played: 32

15–15–2

1935   Beat St. Louis Eagles at Boston, 5–3. Due to an ice making problem, a patch of no ice was created at the east end of the Garden. The President of the NHL, Frank Calder, ordered that a rubber mat be placed over the area of no ice. Rather than the teams switching ends every 20 minutes, the teams swapped ends every 10 minutes for the game.

1962   Bruce Gamble called up to replace Don Head who is sent to Portland of the WHL.

1976   Defeat Los Angeles at Boston, 4–0. Wayne Cashman scores game winner.

1987   Defeat Hartford at Boston, 6–4. Reed Larson scores 200th career goal.

January 16
Games played: 33

18–11–4

1932   Tie Canadiens at Montreal, 2–2. Percy Jackson replaces the injured Tiny Thompson in goal.

1945   Defeat Toronto at Boston, 5–3. Herb Cain has four goal game for second time in his career.

1963   Win at Chicago, 5–4. Murray Oliver misses penalty shot against Glenn Hall.

1972   Defeat Detroit at Boston, 9–2. Derek Sanderson nets 3 goals for the Bruins.

1990   Ken Linseman traded to Philadelphia for Dave Poulin.

January 17
Games played: 31

14–12–5

1991   Defeat Los Angeles at Boston, 5–3. Cam Neely scores the hat trick for Boston.

January 18
Games played: 24

16–5–3

1927   Defeat Rangers in Boston, 7–3. Frank Fredrickson scores four goals for the Bruins.

1936   Lose at Toronto, 5–2. Babe Siebert scores on penalty shot against George Hainsworth.

1941   Win at Toronto, 1–0. Dit Clapper scores 200th goal of career. Frank Brimsek in the net for Boston.

1942   Win at Chicago, 4–3. Woody Dumart gets called to report to the Army for World War II becoming first NHL player to be drafted.

1948   Tie Canadiens at Boston, 1–1. Maurice Richard thrown out of game after breaking stick on Milt Schmidt's arm.

1958   Win at Montreal, 3–0. Willie O'Ree, NHL's first black player, makes debut for Boston.

1964   Win at Toronto, 11–0, in biggest shutout victory in team history. Eddie Johnston records shutout for the Bruins.

1973   Lose to Islanders at Boston, 9–7, despite Johnny Bucyk scoring 4 goals against Billy Smith.

January 19
Games played: 33

13–15–5

1926   Tie Montreal Maroons at Boston, 3–3. Carson Cooper scores last-second goal.

1937   Lose to Toronto at Boston, 6–2. As a publicity stunt, Conn Smythe of Toronto and Weston Adams of Boston wear top hat and tails to game. Gord Drillon nets 3 goals for Toronto.

1967   Lose to Chicago at Boston, 4–2. For the second time in a little over a month, former Bruin Doug Mohns scores a hat trick against his former team.

1971   NHL All-Star game played in Boston for the first time (West 2, East 1).

COCA-COLA NHL
ALL★STAR FRIDAY

AT THE FLEETCENTER, JANUARY 19, 1996 - 7:15 PM

PRICE $32.50

SECTION	ROW	SEAT
BAL310	11	5

Topps SUPER SKILLS

HEROES OF HOCKEY NHL

1954   Lose to Rangers at New York, 8–3. Muzz Patrick coaches New York, brother Lynn Patrick coaches Boston.

1962   Win at Toronto, 5–4. Wayne Connelly scores on penalty shot against Johnny Bower.

1963   Tie Canadiens at Boston, 3–3. Johnny Bucyk scores the 6,000th goal in Bruins history.

1996   In the 46th annual All-Star game played at the FleetCenter in Boston, the Eastern Conference defeats the Western Conference 5–4 on a goal by Ray Bourque of the Bruins with 37 seconds left in the game. Bourque was named the MVP of the game. This is the first All-Star game in Boston since 1971.

January 21
Games played: 30
20–9–1

1945   Defeat Rangers at Boston, 14–3. Bill Cowley nets 4 goals, Ken Smith nets 3 goals and Frank Mario scores 2 for Bruins. Bruins score four goals in 1:20.

1973   Defeat California at Boston, 5–2. Wayne Cashman scores three goals against Gilles Meloche.

1977   Win at Cleveland, 5–2. Greg Sheppard scores three goals against Gilles Meloche.

1978   Defeat Detroit at Boston, 7–1. 8,463 fans attend game on the day after a blizzard.

January 22
Games played: 36
17–14–5

1929   Scoreless tie at Boston versus Montreal. First tie game at Boston Garden.

1935   Defeat Montreal Maroons at Boston, 4–3. Tiny Thompson makes saves on two penalty shots. Shots were taken by Russ Blinco and Earl Robinson.

1938   Win at Toronto, 9–1. Milt Schmidt wears special face mask to protect broken jaw.

1942   Lose at Detroit, 4–3. Bill Cowley's jaw is broken in a mishap with Syd Howe of Detroit.

1949   Lose at Montreal, 4–2. Les Colvin replaces Frank Brimsek in goal as Brimsek returns to Minnesota to be with ill son.

1992   Win at Toronto, 5–2. Ray Bourque passes Bobby Orr to become leading goal scorer among Boston defensemen.

January 20
Games played: 27
12–13–2

1946   Defeat Canadiens at Boston, 3–0. Frank Brimsek records first shutout since return from service in World War II.

1995   Bruins open the 1995 season after the 103 day lockout with a 4–1 victory over the Philadelphia Flyers at Boston Garden. Cam Neely scores 3 goals and Blaine Lacher makes his debut in goal for the Bruins. This will be the last opening game for the old Boston Garden.

1996   Bruins fall in overtime at Pittsburgh, 7–6, as Mario Lemieux scores the winning goal short-handed. The Bruins had led the game 6–4 with less than a minute to play but still managed to lose. Ray Bourque scores short-handed goal for Boston.

January 23
Games played: 32

13–14–5

1937   Tie Americans at Boston, 6–6. Bruins rebound from 4 goal deficit.

1989   Bruins acquire Bob Carpenter from Los Angeles for Steve Kasper.

January 24
Games played: 25

15–8–2

1933   Defeat Canadiens at Boston, 3–2. Lionel Hitchman replaces Art Ross as coach. Eddie Shore of the Bruins and Sylvio Mantha engage in a brawl in which Referee Cooper Smeaton, attempting to stop the fight, takes three punches from Shore and suffers two broken ribs.

1953   Defeat Rangers at Boston, 9–0. Jerry Toppazzini scores three goals.

January 25
Games played: 32

16–11–5

1951   Tie at Detroit, 3–3. Bill Ezinicki of Boston and Ted Lindsay of Detroit receive match penalties after bloody battle.

1958   Defeat Detroit at Boston, 5–3. Gordie Howe of Detroit fractures ribs when checked by Leo Boivin and Real Chevrefils. Jack Adams of Detroit accuses Bruins of deliberate attack but later modifies charges.

1964   Win at Montreal, 6–0. Andy Hebenton and Gary Dornhoefer score two goals each. Ed Johnston records shutout.
Bob Sweeney is born in Concord, Massachusetts.

1976   Defeat Philadelphia at Boston, 5–3. Don Marcotte has goal and three assists.

1993   Lose at Montreal, 3–2. John Blue stops Denis Savard on a penalty shot attempt.

1996   Defeat Tampa Bay at Boston, 4–3, on Sandy Moger's 4th game winning goal of the season.

January 26
Games played: 32

19–10–3

1949   Lose to Toronto at Boston, 3–1. Jack Gelineau, a goalie from McGill University, replaces Frank Brimsek in goal when Brimsek's son passes away.

1957   Lose to Rangers at Boston, 5–3. Bruins appear on national television for first time. Don Simmons plays first game in goal for Boston replacing Terry Sawchuk.

1958   Tie Toronto at Boston, 3–3. Leo Labine scores a goal at 19:59 of the third period with the Bruins' net empty.

1987   Defeat Buffalo at Boston, 6–2. Bob Sweeney scores first career goal.

1995   Defeat New Jersey in overtime at Boston, 1–0.

January 27
Games played: 31

14–12–5

1931   Tie Philadelphia Quakers at Boston, 3–3.

1942   Scoreless tie versus Toronto at Boston. Turk Broda of Toronto and Frank Brimsek of the Bruins record shutouts.

1957   Defeat Canadiens at Boston, 5–2. Don Simmons replaces Norm DeFelice in Boston goal.

1962   Defeat Chicago at Boston, 5–3. Rudy Pilous, Chicago coach is fined $50.00 for going on the ice to argue a last-second first period goal by Jerry Toppazzini.

1977   Lose to Colorado at Boston, 6–4. Bob Schmautz scores hat trick against Doug Favell.

January 28
Games played: 29

12–14–3

1929   Bruins sign George Owen, Harvard football and hockey star.

1937   Tie Rangers at New York, 1–1. Eddie Shore suffers a cracked vertebra while crashing into the boards.

1996   In the Bruins last-ever game at the Montreal Forum, they lose to the Canadiens 5–4. Adam Oates scores the last Bruins goal in the old Forum.

January 29
Games played: 31

17–9–5

1970   Defeat Minnesota at Boston, 6–5. Ray Cullen of the North Stars scores 3 goals.

1983   Defeat Detroit at Boston, 7–3, on Luc Dufour's 3 goals.

January 30
Games played: 27

13–13–1

1965   Lose at Toronto, 6–1. Jack Norris is supposed to play goal for Boston but his equipment is stolen from the Royal York Hotel, so a sick Ed Johnston must play.

1966   Lose to Canadiens at Boston, 3–1. No penalties are called.

1976   Win at Atlanta, 4–2. Gary Doak scores first goal in 5 seasons, the game winner.

1988   Lose to Rangers at Boston, 4–2. Ken Linseman scores 200th career goal.

1997   Despite Ray Bourque's short-handed goal, Bruins lose to the Panthers in Miami, 3–1. This goal ties Bourque with Johnny Bucyk for the all-time lead in points scored, 1339, with the Bruins.

January 31
Games played: 30

17–7–6

1925   Lose at Hamilton, 8–3.

1928   Defeat New York Americans at Boston, 2–1.

1942   Win at Toronto, 3–2. Milt Schmidt scores winner in overtime. Dit Clapper is injured and out for the year after rupturing his Achilles tendon in collision with Bingo Kampman. Herb Cain's cheekbone is broken when boarded by Bucko MacDonald.

1960   Defeat Canadiens at Boston, 6–5, on Fern Flaman night. Vic Stasiuk scores hat trick.

1961   Trade Don Simmons to Toronto for Ed Chadwick.

1965   Lose to Toronto at Boston, 4–2. Jack Norris, wearing #17, makes debut in goal.

1971   Defeat St. Louis at Boston, 6–0. In a three-team swap, Rick MacLeish and Dan Schock traded to Philadelphia. Bernie Parent traded from Philadelphia to Toronto. Mike Walton traded from Toronto to Boston.

1985   Defeat Quebec at Boston, 6–5. Butch Goring collects 500th career assist.

1996   Defeat the Senators at Ottawa, 3–1. This is the first ever Bruins game at the new Ottawa Palladium.

February 1
Games played: 32

13–12–7

1948   Lose to Montreal at Boston, 3–0. Elmer Lach scores all 3 Canadien goals.

1973   Defeat Toronto at Boston, 5–2. Phil Esposito puts 3 past Jacques Plante in goal for Toronto.

1997   Bruins defeat the Lightning at Tampa Bay, 3–0. Rob Tallas records the shutout for the Bruins. Ray Bourque scores the first goal of the game, thus becoming the all-time leading scorer in Boston Bruins history with 1340 points. This is the first Bruins game in the new Tampa Bay Ice Palace.

February 2
Games played: 36

18–12–6

1937   Lose to Montreal Canadiens at Boston, 1–0. Milt Schmidt and Woody Dumart play first game as Bruins.

February 3
Games played: 28

15–9–4

1951   Lose at Montreal, 4–1. Rocket Richard scores three goals.

1976   Gerry Cheevers returns from WHA.

1989   Win at Winnipeg, 4–2. Phil DeGaetano traded to St. Louis for Scott Harlow.

1996   Defeat Buffalo at Boston, 4–2. Bill Ranford stops a penalty shot attempt by Randy Burridge of the Sabres. Rick Tocchet suffers a head injury.

This photo taken on February 1, 1970, depicts a bench-clearing brawl between members of the Bruins in the dark uniforms and the Toronto Maple Leafs in the light uniforms.

February 4
Games played: 33

17–11–5

1926	Win at Ottawa, 3–2. Lionel Hitchman scores the 100th goal in Bruins history.
1941	Defeat Montreal at Boston, 5–3. Bill Cowley scores the 2,000th goal in Bruins history.
1961	Lose to Rangers at Boston, 2–1. Game delayed for two hours due to late arrival of the Rangers who were held up in a snowstorm.
1965	Defeat Detroit at Boston, 3–1. Bill Gadsby of Detroit and Reggie Fleming of Boston engage in stick fight.
1967	Lose to Rangers at Boston, 4–3. Johnny Bucyk scores on a penalty shot.
1968	Defeat Detroit at Boston, 5–4. John McKenzie scores his 2nd hat trick against the Wings in this season.

February 5
Games played: 32

19–11–2

1952	Defeat Chicago at Boston, 5–0. Woody Dumart scores 200th goal of his career with only 4,869 in attendance. Milt Schmidt scores the 4,000th goal in Bruins history.
1973	Bep Guidolin replaces Tom Johnson as coach of the Bruins.

February 6
Games played: 32

11–17–4

1932	Lose at Toronto, 6–0. Charlie Conacher scores 7 seconds into the game.
1942	An All-Star game pitting the Bruins against retired NHL stars was played with proceeds going to the Army Relief Fund.
1943	Lose at Montreal, 8–3. Ray Getliffe scores 5 goals for Montreal.

1986   Lose to Buffalo at Boston, 8–6. Dave Andreychuk scores 5 goals for Buffalo.

1987   Trade Pat Riggin to Pittsburgh for Roberto Romano.

February 7
Games played: 30
17–6–7

1925   Defeat Maroons at Montreal, 1–0.

1943   Defeat Montreal at Boston, 7–1. Harvey Jackson scores three goals.

1960   Defeat Toronto at Boston, 3–0. Harry Lumley in goal for Boston.

1962   Tie at Toronto, 2–2. Bruce Gamble of the Bruins stops Ron Stewart on a penalty shot attempt.

1971   Tie Minnesota at Boston, 4–4. Bruins take 67 shots on goal.

1976   Lose at Toronto, 11–4. Darryl Sittler of the Maple Leafs scores 6 goals and 4 assists. Dave Reece was the victim in the Boston net.

1987   Defeat Toronto at Boston, 8–5. Cam Neely scores first career hat trick.

February 8
Games played: 28
15–11–2

1959   Defeat Rangers at Boston, 4–1. Bronco Horvath scores hat trick for Boston.

1967   Defeat Rangers at New York, 2–1. Bernie Geoffrion of the Rangers is suspended for elbowing linesman Walt Atanas.

1976   Defeat Detroit at Boston, 7–0. Gerry Cheevers, in his first game back with the Bruins after 2 years in the WHA, records the shutout.

1993   In a neutral site game played in Atlanta, Georgia, Bruins lose to Pittsburgh, 4–0.

February 9
Games played: 31
15–11–5

1907   Bruin great Dit Clapper is born in Newmarket, Ontario.

1947   Lose at Chicago, 6–4. 20,000 fans in attendance as Emile "The Cat" Francis debuts for Chicago.

1964   Tie Montreal at Boston, 4–4. Bill Hicke of Montreal and Leo Boivin of the Bruins stage a fight in the penalty box that is broken up by the police.

1966   NHL announces that six conditional franchises were to be awarded to Los Angeles, San Francisco, St. Paul-Minneapolis, St. Louis, Pittsburgh, and Philadelphia. Vancouver was rejected.

1992   Defeat Pittsburgh at Boston, 6–3. Vladimir Ruzicka nets 4 goals.

1995   Lose to Quebec at Boston, 4–3. Wendel Clark scores 3 goals for the Nordiques.

February 10
Games played: 27
13–10–4

1924   Directors of the National Hockey voted to admit Boston in the league.

1925   Lose to Toronto at Boston, 5–1. Babe Dye of the Leafs is awarded a goal after goaltender threw his stick.

1942   Defeat Montreal at Boston, 8–1. Kraut line of Milt Schmidt, Bobby Bauer and Woody Dumart play last game before going off to World War II.

1973   Defeat Pittsburgh at Boston, 6–3. Mike Walton scores 3 goals for Boston.

1994   Tie Buffalo at Boston, 3–3. Wayne Presley of Buffalo becomes first player in Bruins history to take a second penalty shot against Boston. Vincent Riendeau stops the penalty shot.

February 11
Games played: 33
15–15–3

1933   Lose to Maroons at Montreal, 4–2. Charles Adams resigns as Bruins governor to the NHL because of the NHL gag rule which provides for $1,000 fine for publicly criticizing officials.

1940   Defeat Americans at New York, 4–2. Roy Conacher scores 2 goals for Bruins.

1950   Lose to Detroit at Boston, 9–4. Gerry Couture scores 4 goals in a span of 9 minutes in the third period for Detroit against Jack Gelineau.

1986   Lose at Chicago, 5–4. Mike Milbury returns to ice as active player.

February 12
Games played: 24

14–7–3

1947	Defeat Rangers at Boston, 10–1. Dit Clapper night at Boston Garden. The Hockey Hall of Fame honors Clapper as the first living player to be inducted into the Hall. Boston management announces that Clapper's number 5 will be permanently retired, although Guy Lapointe wore it briefly in 1983–84.
1950	Tie Montreal at Boston, 3–3. Dick Bittner replaces Jack Gelineau in goal for Boston.
1961	Defeat Rangers at Boston, 8–3. Don McKenney scores three goals for Bruins.
1983	Game against Toronto at Boston is snowed out and rescheduled for February 28.
1994	Defeat New Jersey at Boston, 5–3. Cam Neely gets hat trick on first three shots taken on first three shifts.

February 13
Games played: 31

17–9–5

1941	Defeat Rangers at New York, 5–3. Art Ross calls this his "greatest team ever."
1960	Defeat Montreal at Boston, 7–6. Ab McDonald scores three goals for Montreal, Bronco Horvath scores two goals for the Bruins.

February 14
Games played: 33

16–10–7

1996	Defeat Whalers at Hartford, 3–0. Bill Ranford gets his first shutout since being traded back to the Bruins.

February 15
Games played: 25

12–9–4

1972	Defeat California at Boston, 6–3. Bobby Orr records four assists in the first period.
1976	Win at Chicago, 4–1. Jean Ratelle nets 3 goals for the Bruins.
1996	Lose at Chicago, 3–0, in the Bruins first ever game at the United Center.

February 16
Games played: 31

13–16–2

1961	Lose at Montreal, 9–1. Don Marshall scores three goals for Montreal.
1991	Win at Los Angeles in overtime, 5–4. Don Sweeney scores the game winner in overtime.

February 17
Games played: 26

11–13–2

1963	Lose at Chicago, 3–1. Bobby Hull scores three goals for the Blackhawks.
1972	Win at Philadelphia, 4–1. For the second time in less than a month, Phil Esposito gets the hat trick against the Flyers.
1996	Defeat Canucks at Vancouver, 4–1. This is the Bruins' first game at the GM Place in Vancouver.

February 18
Games played: 30

11–14–5

1966	Leo Boivin and Dean Prentice traded to Detroit for Bill Lesuk and Gary Doak.
1967	Lose at Toronto, 5–3. King Clancy replaces Punch Imlach behind the Leafs bench.
1975	Acquire Earl Anderson and Hank Nowak from Detroit for Walt McKechnie.
1997	Bruins lose to the Avalanche at Denver, 4–3 as Claude Lemieux scores the overtime winner with 3 seconds left in the game. After the game, Bruins center Adam Oates blasts Bruins' management, arguing his belief that the Bruins are not bringing in quality players. The Bruins subsequently strip Oates of his position as assistant captain.

February 19
Games played: 24

9–9–6

1929	Defeat Pittsburgh at Boston, 1–0.
1944	Lose at Toronto, 10–4. Bud Poile and Jack Hamilton net 3 goals for the Maple Leafs. One of Hamilton's 3 goals was scored on a penalty shot.

February 20
Games played: 32

10–18–4

1932   Lose at Chicago, 2–1. Eddie Shore receives match penalty for striking referee Cooper Smeaton. Bruins protest game on the grounds that Referee Smeaton had erred in not permitting a substitute for penalized player in last three minutes of game. President Calder of the NHL rules that the official had erred but that the Chicago club was innocent and so rejected the protest. Shore is suspended for one game and fined $100.

1942   Phil Esposito is born in Sault Ste. Marie, Ontario.

1971   Lose at Los Angeles, 5–4. Phil Esposito scores his 50th goal of the season.

1972   Win at Chicago, 3–1. Phil Esposito again scores his 50th goal of the season.

1974   Tie at Minnesota, 5–5, as Phil Esposito scores 3 goals including his 50th of the season. This is the third time Esposito has scored his 50th goal on his birthday.

1997   Bruins lose to the Blackhawks at Chicago, 5–3. Adam Oates scores in his 20th straight game.

February 21
Games played: 35

14–15–6

1939   Defeat Chicago at Boston, 8–2. Roy Conacher scores 4 goals.

1965   Lose at Chicago, 7–0. Wild brawl erupts with ten minutes left in game. Main combatants were Kurtenbach, Green, and Fleming for Boston and Mikita, MacNeil, and Mohns for Chicago.

1978   Win at Colorado, 3–2. No penalties called.

1982   Win at Philadelphia, 1–0. Marco Baron records his 1st career shutout.

1996   Lose in overtime at Anaheim, 4–3, on Alex Hicks' second goal of the game. Hicks is the son of former Bruin Wayne Hicks.

February 22
Games played: 21

11–10–0

1986   Win at Edmonton in overtime, 6–5. Keith Crowder scores hat trick. Ray Bourque records his 500th point.

February 23
Games played: 32

15–13–4

1955   Tie Chicago, 3–3 in a game played at St. Paul, Minnesota before 6,680 fans.

1972   Win at California, 8–6. Although Fred Stanfield is unsuccessful in penalty shot attempt against Gilles Meloche, he still manages to get the hat trick. Trade Reggie Leach, Rick Smith, and Bob Stewart to California for Carol Vadnais and Don O'Donoghue.

1997   Bruins lose to the Sabres at Buffalo, 5–1. Adam Oates's 20-game goal scoring streak is snapped.

February 24
Games played: 25

9–12–4

1925   Defeat Maroons at Boston, 2–1.

1929   Tie Americans at New York, 2–2.

1931   Win at Philadelphia, 5–1.

1934   Lose at Ottawa, 9–4.

1992   Trade John Byce and Dennis Smith to Washington for Brent Hughes.

February 25
Games played: 30

12–14–4

1930   Defeat Pittsburgh at Boston, 7–0 as Cooney Weiland scores 4 goals.

1941   Lose to Rangers at Boston, 2–0. Bruins streak of 23 unbeaten games is broken.

1967   Lose at Chicago, 6–3. Bruin Bob Dillabough is unsuccessful in a penalty shot attempt against Glenn Hall.

1971   Defeat Vancouver at Boston, 8–3. Johnny Bucyk scores his second hat trick on the season.

February 26
Games played: 19

9–9–1

1952   Lose to Detroit at Boston, 4–3. A section of roof over North Station track collapses. Brine pipes under ice snap forcing game to be transferred from Boston Garden to Boston Arena. 4,049 fans attend. Red Sullivan scores the last goal ever at the Boston Arena for the Bruins. Gordie Howe of Detroit nets the last ever NHL goal at the Boston Arena.

1966   Lose at Toronto, 3–2. Johnny Bucyk scores 200th career goal.

1981   Defeat Minnesota at Boston, 5–1. Rick Middleton scores 2 short-handed goals 1:16 apart. 406 penalty minutes called. Keith Crowder records 43 penalty minutes. Jean Ratelle scores his 491st, and last, career goal in the NHL.

February 27
Games played: 30
17–10–3

1946   Defeat Canadiens at Montreal, 5–3. Game is marred by bottle-throwing Canadiens' fans.

1980   Win at Hartford, 6–3. Peter McNab scores 3 goals.

1994   Shutout Blackhawks at Chicago, 4–0. Last Bruins regular season game at Chicago Stadium.

February 28
Games played: 23
14–3–6

1963   Defeat Detroit at Boston, 5–3. Because of a mix-up, the Bruins have to change uniforms between the first and second period. Both teams wore white jerseys for the first period. The Bruins changed to gold jerseys for the second and third period.

1965   Win at Chicago, 5–4. Tom Johnson plays final game for Bruins as he severs the peroneal muscle in his leg.

1974   Defeat Detroit at Boston, 8–1. Ross Brooks wins 14th consecutive game in goal.

1983   Defeat Toronto at Boston, 6–3. Game was originally scheduled for February 12 but was snowed out.

February 29
Games played: 8
4–3–1

1940   Defeat Canadiens at Montreal, 4–2.

1944   Lose to Toronto at Boston, 7–3. Bruin goalie Bert Gardiner records assist on goal by Bill Cowley, thus becoming first goaltender to record an assist.

1948   Lose at Chicago, 5–1

1956   Lose to Rangers at New York, 4–2.

1964   Defeat Red Wings at Boston, 2–1.

1968   Defeat Toronto at Boston, 4–1.

1976   Defeat Vancouver at Boston, 5–3.

1992   Tie Washington at Boston, 5–5.

March 1
Games played: 31
17–8–6

1941   Scoreless tie at Toronto. Frank Brimsek in goal for Boston and Turk Broda in the goal for the Maple Leafs.

1947   Defeat Canadiens at Montreal, 2–1. Dit Clapper is honored by the Canadiens and the NHL for his 20 years in the NHL.

1950   Defeat Toronto at Boston, 5–2. Bill Barilko of Toronto scores against Jack Gelineau on a penalty shot.

1977   Defeat Detroit at Boston, 8–3. Greg Sheppard nets his third hat trick on the season. Mike Milbury notches four assists.

1984   Defeat Los Angeles at Boston, in overtime, 4–3 on a goal by Rick Middleton. This is the first overtime regular season goal since 1942.

1986   Defeat New Jersey at Boston, 8–3. Steve Kasper, taking his 2nd penalty shot this season, fails to score against Alain Chevrier. Charlie Simmer notches his third hat trick on the season.

1997   In a day of dramatic events, the Bruins come back from 3–0 and 5–3 deficits to tie the Philadelphia Flyers, 5–5, at the FleetCenter. Trent Klatt of Philadelphia scores 3 goals for the Flyers. Sheldon Kennedy notches a short-handed goal for Boston as the Bruins score 2 goals in the final one minute and eighteen second to tie the game.

      After the game, the Bruins are involved in a blockbuster trade with the Washington Capitals. The Bruins trade Bill Ranford, Rick Tocchet, and Adam Oates to Washington for Jim Carey, Jason Allison, Anson Carter, and a 1997 third-round pick and a 1998 conditional second-round pick.

March 2
Games played: 31
14–12–5

1922   Bill Quackenbush is born in Toronto, Ontario.

1969   Defeat Pittsburgh at Boston, 4–0. Phil Esposito becomes first player in NHL history to score 100 points in a season.

1972 Defeat Vancouver at Boston, 7–3. Phil Esposito collects his third hat trick of the season.

March 3
Games played: 36
15–14–7

1928 In a 0–0 tie at Toronto, Hal Winkler records the shutout in the net for Boston. In his first and only NHL game, Joe Ironstone minds the Toronto net.

1968 Defeat St. Louis at Boston, 9–3. Eddie Shack nets 3 goals for the Bruins, his first NHL hat trick.

1973 Lose at Montreal, 5–1.
Obtain Jacques Plante from Toronto for Boston's first pick in the upcoming draft and a player to be named later (Eddie Johnston).

1983 Lose to Buffalo at Boston, 3–2. Paul Cyr of Buffalo scores a pure hat trick in recording all of the Sabres goals.

1997 In Jim Carey's first game as a Bruin since the trade with Washington, he allows 4 goals and is yanked after the first period in the Bruins 4–2 loss to the Maple Leafs at Toronto.

March 4
Games played: 29
17–6–6

1941 Defeat Chicago at Boston, 3–2, as Bruins fire 83 shots at Chicago goaltender, Sam LoPresti.

1944 Defeat Rangers at Boston, 10–9. Bill Cowley nets 4 goals.

1951 Defeat Chicago at Boston, 10–2. Woody Dumart scores 4 goals.

1971 Defeat California at Boston, 7–0. Johnny Bucyk registers his third hat trick on the season.

1989 Defeat Vancouver at Boston, 6–4. Randy Burridge scores 3 goals.

March 5
Games played: 37
17–14–6

1918 Milt Schmidt is born in Kitchener, Ontario.

1947 Defeat Toronto at Boston, 5–4. Bobby Bauer scores 3 goals.

March 6
Games played: 25
13–10–2

1926 Defeat Ottawa at Boston, 1–0.

1928 Defeat Ottawa at Boston, 1–0.

1971 Win at Pittsburgh, 6–3. Phil Esposito registers his sixth hat trick of the season.

1974 Win at St. Louis, 8–0, as Wayne Cashman scores 3 goals.

March 7
Games played: 34
19–12–3

1968 Defeat Philadelphia, 2–1, in a game played in Toronto. The Philadelphia Spectrum was not available due to the roof being damaged by a wind storm. Eddie Shack of the Bruins and Larry Zeidel of the Flyers engage in a vicious stick fight.

1994 Defeat Washington at Boston, 6–3. Cam Neely, playing in only his 44th game, scores two goals, his 49th and 50th of the season.

March 8
Games played: 29
14–14–1

1979 Lose at Atlanta, 7–5. Rick Middleton scores 3 goals.

1988 Lose at Detroit, 2–0.
Trade Bill Ranford and Geoff Courtnall to Edmonton for Andy Moog.

1997 Despite being down 4–1, the Bruins storm back and defeat the Lightning at Tampa Bay, 6–4. Anson Carter notches 2 goals, with one of the goals coming while the Bruins were short-handed.

March 9
Games played: 32
17–11–4

1966 Win at Montreal, 3–1. Johnny Bucyk scores his 200th career goal.

1975 Defeat Atlanta at Boston, 5–2. Greg Sheppard scores 2 short-handed goals in 21 seconds.

March 10
Games played: 30
13–9–8

1955	Lose to Chicago at Boston, 3–2. In a game at Toronto between the Leafs and Canadiens, the Zamboni ice resurfacing machine is introduced.
1968	Lose to Detroit at Boston, 7–5. Glen Sather scores the 7,000th goal in Bruins history.
1974	Lose at California, 6–2, as former Bruin Reggie Leach nets 3 goals.
1978	Acquire Dennis O'Brien from the Cleveland Barons.
1990	Tie Islanders at New York, 3–3. John Carter scores the 14,000th goal in Bruins history.

March 11
Games played: 32
18–8–6

1972	Lose at Pittsburgh, 6–4. Bobby Orr scores 500th career point.
1976	Defeat Toronto at Boston, 6–2. Ken Hodge scores 3 goals.
1982	Defeat Winnipeg at Boston, 7–4. Rick Middleton scores the hat trick.

March 12
Games played: 34
19–12–3

1975	Lose at Pittsburgh, 5–3, as Pierre Larouche scores 3 goals for the Penguins.
1988	Win at Quebec, 4–3. Craig Janney scores 3 goals for the Bruins.

March 13
Games played: 36
22–11–3

1958	Defeat Montreal at Boston, 7–3. Canadiens goaltender Jacques Plante suffers a concussion and is replaced by Bruins practice goalie John Aiken. Aiken allows six more goals in the game.
1961	Barry Pederson is born in Big River, Saskatchewan.
1980	Defeat Detroit at Boston, 4–2, on Johnny Bucyk Night as the #9 is retired.

March 14
Games played: 28
18–7–3

1933	Defeat Chicago at Boston, 3–2, in a forfeited game. Tommy Gorman, Blackhawks coach removed his team from the ice after a disputed goal by Marty Barry in overtime. Gorman punched referee Bill Stewart.
1954	Defeat Toronto at Boston, 3–0. Jim Henry records the shutout for Boston.
1971	Win at Detroit, 11–4. Gordie Howe of the Red Wings scores his last power play goal before his first retirement.
1989	Win at Pittsburgh, 8–2. Ken Linseman tallies 3 goals for the Bruins.
1996	Defeat Pittsburgh at Boston, 4–2, as Rick Tocchet scores three goals for Boston.

March 15
Games played: 35
21–8–6

1932	Defeat Toronto at Boston, 6–2. A 3-minute penalty to Maple Leaf goalie Lorne Chabot resulted in 3 Toronto defensemen tending the net while Chabot served the penalty. Marty Barry scored a goal on Red Horner and Alex Levinsky. George Owen netted a goal against King Clancy.
1962	Win at Detroit, 4–0, as Bruins end 20-game winless streak.
1970	Tie Detroit at Boston, 5–5. Bobby Orr becomes first defenseman to score 100 points in a season.
1979	Lose to the Rangers at Boston, 7–4. Phil Esposito scores 3 goals for the Rangers. Jim "Seaweed" Pettie is in goal for Boston.

March 16
Games played: 33
17–8–8

1911	Buzz Boll is born in Filmore, Saskatchewan.
1969	Defeat Toronto at Boston, 11–3. Derek Sanderson records his second hat trick of the season.
1993	Defeat New Jersey, 3–1 in a neutral-site game played at Providence, Rhode Island.

March 17
Games played: 25

12–11–2

1940   Defeat Montreal at Boston, 7–2. Bruins finish in first place. Top three scorers in the individual scoring race are Bruins: Milt Schmidt, Woody Dumart, and Bobby Bauer.

1942   Defeat Brooklyn Americans at Boston, 8–3.

1968   Defeat Montreal at Boston, 3–1. Clinch playoff spot for the first time in 8 years.

1984   Lose to New Jersey at Boston, 5–3. Tom Glavine of Billerica High School and later the Atlanta Braves wins the second annual John Carlton Memorial Trophy.

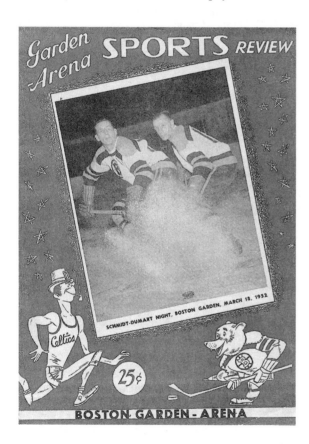

March 18
Games played: 29

15–7–7

1944   Lose at Toronto, 10–2. Bob Davidson scores 3 goals for Toronto. Boston is forced to use spare goaltender Benny Grant.

1952   Defeat Chicago at Boston, 4–0. Kraut Line is reunited and Milt Schmidt scores 200th career goal.

March 19
Games played: 33

14–15–4

Regular season 11–15–4

Playoffs 3–0–0

1929   The Bruins, winners of the American Division meet the Canadiens, winners of the Canadian Division. Game 1 of the semi-finals takes place at Boston Garden with Boston winning 1–0. Tiny Thompson records shutout with the goal being scored by Cooney Weiland.

1972   Defeat Minnesota at Boston, 7–3. Phil Esposito records his fourth hat trick of the season.

March 20
Games played: 21

14–5–2

Regular season 12–5–2

Playoffs 2–0–0

1948   Bobby Orr is born in Parry Sound, Ontario.

1969   Tie Chicago at Boston, 5–5, as Bobby Orr scores 21st goal and breaks record for goals by a defenseman.

March 21
Games played: 29

18–8–3

Regular season 15–7–3

Playoffs 3–1–0

1939   Bruins defeat Rangers at New York, 2–1 in game 1 of Stanley Cup opening round series. Mel "Sudden Death" Hill scored the winner in overtime for Boston.

1940   Game 2 of Stanley Cup opening round series at Boston is won by the Bruins 4–2. Mel Hill breaks ankle in tough contest.

1971   Lose to Buffalo at Boston, 7–5, as Eddie Shack scores 3 times for Buffalo.

1974   Defeat St. Louis at Boston, 7–0. Bobby Orr scores the hat trick.

1977   Lose to Montreal at Boston, 5–1. Jean Ratelle plays in his 1000th career game.

March 22

Games played: 33

14–17–2

Regular season 11–14–2
Playoffs 3–3–0

1955 Game 1 of the opening round of the Stanley Cup playoffs at Montreal is won by the Canadiens, 2–0. Jacques Plante records the shutout.

1975 Defeat Washington at Boston, 8–2. Bobby Orr scores 3 goals for Boston. This is Orr's 9th and final career hat trick.

1980 Win at Atlanta, 5–2.
Harry Sinden replaces Fred Creighton as coach of the Bruins.

March 23

Games played: 26

15–10–1

Regular season 11–8–1
Playoffs 4–2–0

1935 Game 1 of NHL championship series at Boston goes to the Bruins over Toronto in overtime, 1–0. 16,000 fans attend game as Tiny Thompson records shutout. Dit Clapper scores at 33 minutes and 26 seconds of overtime.

1937 Bruins lose game 1 of playoffs at Montreal to Maroons, 4–1. Dit Clapper aroused the passion of Montreal fans by slugging both officials, Dave Trottier and Clarence Campbell.

1939 Almost 17,000 fans attend game 2 of opening round series at Boston. Bruins defeat Rangers 3–2 on Mel "Sudden Death" Hill's goal in overtime, his second overtime goal in two games.

1940 Ted Green is born in St. Boniface, Manitoba.

1954 Game 1 of the opening round of the Stanley Cup playoffs at Montreal is won by the Canadiens, 2–0. Jacques Plante records the shutout.

1967 Lose to Toronto at Boston, 5–3. Peter Stemkowski scores 3 goals for the Maple Leafs.

March 24

Games played: 32

15–15–2

Regular season 10–9–2
Playoffs 5–6–0

1946 Bruins win game 3 of the opening round of the playoffs at Detroit, 5–2. Woody Dumart and Milt Schmidt score 2 goals each for Boston.
Woody Dumart scores the 200th goal in Bruins playoff history.

March 25

Games played: 23

10–12–1

Regular season 7–5–1
Playoffs 3–7–0

1933 Boston defeats Toronto in overtime, 2–1, at Boston in game 1 of the NHL championship series. Marty Barry scored the winning goal at 14 minutes and 14 seconds of overtime. Toronto's Ace Bailey is attacked by a fan while on his way to the dressing room.

1943 Boston wins third straight game of opening round series for the Stanley Cup by winning at Montreal over the Canadiens in overtime, 3–2. Busher Jackson scores the winner for Boston at 3 minutes and 20 seconds of overtime.

1951 Lose to Toronto at Boston, 1–0. For the second year in a row on this date, Al Rollins records the shutout for Toronto.

1954 Game 2 of the opening round of the Stanley Cup playoffs at Montreal is won by the Canadiens, 8–1. Jean Beliveau, Dickie Moore, and Bernie Geoffrion score 2 goals each for the Habs.

March 26

Games played: 28

15–11–2

Regular season 8–6–2
Playoffs 7–5–0

1938 A then record crowd of 15,341 fans at Toronto attended game 2 of NHL championship series. Toronto wins 2–1. Charlie Sands scores the lone Boston goal.

1939   Game 3 of opening round series attracts 16,981 fans, at the time, the largest crowd in Boston Garden history as Boston defeats the Rangers, 4–1. Milt Schmidt scores two goals for Boston.

1940   Game 4 of the Stanley Cup opening round series at New York is won by the Rangers, 1–0 before 16,504 fans at Madison Square Garden. Murray Patrick of the Rangers scores the lone goal of the game.

March 27
Games played: 27

12–12–3

Regular season 8–7–3
Playoffs 4–5–0

1930   Bruins defeat Montreal Maroons at Boston, 5–1, to win the championship of the NHL. Bill Carson, Dit Clapper, Lionel Hitchman, and Marty Barry (2), scored for Boston. Between 1929 and 1939, the first-place team in each section played in the first round of the playoffs to determine the championship of the NHL.

1947   Bruins lose game 2 of the opening round of the Stanley Cup playoffs at Montreal in overtime, 2–1. Ken Mosdell scores the overtime winner at 5 minutes and 38 seconds of overtime.

1993   Lose to Pittsburgh at Boston, 5–3. Bryan Smolinski scores 2 short-handed goals.

1997   Despite Ray Bourque recording his 1,000th career assist, the Bruins lose to the Islanders at Boston, 6–3. Bourque's assist helped him become the first player in NHL history to record 1,000 assists with the same team.

March 28
Games played: 28

10–15–3

Regular season 7–6–3
Playoffs 3–9–0

1929   For the first time in history, the Stanley Cup is contested for by two American teams, the Boston Bruins and Rangers. Game one at Boston goes to the Bruins 2–0. Clapper and Gainor score for Boston while Tiny Thompson records shutout win.

1973   Defeat Rangers at New York, 6–3. Phil Esposito scores 4 goals for the second time this season.

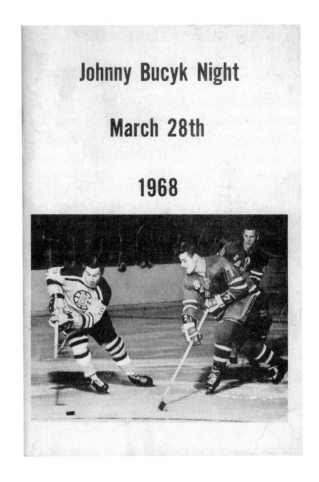

Johnny Bucyk Night

March 28th

1968

1979   Lose at Buffalo, 9–2. Rick Martin scores 3 goals for the Sabres.

March 29
Games played: 23

11–10–2

Regular season 6–4–2
Playoffs 5–6–0

1927   First ever Boston Bruins playoff game. Quarter-final series of the 1927 Stanley Cup playoffs against Chicago game was scheduled to be played at Chicago but was transferred to New York and played before a crowd of 7500 fans. Bruins win 6–1 behind two goals by Frank Fredrickson, who also scored the first goal in Bruins playoff history.

1929   Bruins win first Stanley Cup in their history with a 2–1 decision over the Rangers at New York. Bill Carson scores

Boston Garden, Thursday Evening, March 28, 1968

BOSTON BRUINS

1.	ED JOHNSTON	G
30.	GERRY CHEEVERS	G
4.	BOBBY ORR	D
6.	TED GREEN (A)	D
7.	PHIL ESPOSITO (A)	C
8.	KEN HODGE	R.W.
9.	JOHN BUCYK (A)	L.W.
11.	TOM WILLIAMS	R.W.
12.	WAYNE CASHMAN	W
14.	GLEN SATHER	L.W.
16.	DEREK SANDERSON	C
17.	FRED STANFIELD	C
18.	ED WESTFALL	R.W.
19.	JOHN McKENZIE	R.W.
20.	DALLAS SMITH	D
21.	PHIL "SKIP" KRAKE	C
23.	EDDIE SHACK	L.W.
25.	GARY DOAK	D
26.	DON AWREY	D
28.	RON MURPHY	L.W.

Coach—Harry Sinden
General Manager—Milt Schmidt
Trainers—Don Canney and John Forristall

NEW YORK RANGERS

1.	ED GIACOMIN	G
30.	DON SIMMONS	G
2.	WAYNE HILLMAN	D
3.	HARRY HOWELL (A)	D
4.	ARNIE BROWN	D
5.	BERNIE GEOFFRION	R.W.
7.	ROD GILBERT (A)	R.W.
8.	BOB NEVIN (C)	R.W.
9.	REG FLEMING	L.W.
10.	LARRY JEFFREY	L.W.
11.	VIC HADFIELD	L.W.
12.	RON STEWART	R.W.
15.	JIM NEILSON	D
16.	ROD SEILING	D
19.	JEAN RATELLE	C
20.	PHIL GOYETTE	C
21.	CAMILLE HENRY	L.W.
22.	DON MARSHALL (A)	L.W.
25.	ORLAND KURTENBACH	C

Manager-Coach — Emile Francis.
Trainers — Frank Paice and Jim Young.

the winning goal on a pass from Harry Oliver, who scored Boston's first goal. Tiny Thompson was in the net for the Bruins.

1938   Game 3 of NHL championship series was played before 16,523 fans at Boston Garden. Boston outshot Toronto 42 to 17 during regulation and despite 2 Bill Cowley goals, could only manage a 2-2 tie. Gordie Drillon of Toronto scores at 10 minutes and 4 seconds to win the game and wrap up the NHL championship series, 3 games to 0.

1941   Game 5 of the Stanley Cup opening round series at Boston is won by Toronto, 2-1, in overtime. 16,200 fans watched as Pete Langelle scored the winner for the Maple Leafs at 17 minutes and 31 seconds of overtime. This is the second consecutive game of this series to finish with a 2-1 score.

1942   Game 1 of the Stanley Cup semi-finals at Boston goes to the Red Wings, 6-4. Jack McGill scores 3 goals for Boston. It was the first Detroit victory in Boston since December 8, 1937.

March 30
Games played: 26

12-11-3

Regular season 8-4-3
Playoffs 4-7-0

1933   Game 3 of NHL championship series goes to Boston at Toronto, 2-1, on a goal by Eddie Shore at 4 minutes and 23 seconds of overtime. This is the third straight overtime game in this series.

1943   Bruins win game 5 of opening round of Stanley Cup playoffs at Boston over Canadiens 5-4 in overtime before 14,393 fans. This game eliminates Montreal, 4 games to 1. Ab DeMarco scores the game winner for Boston at 3 minutes and 41 seconds. This is the last playoff series win for Boston over Montreal until 1988.

1946   Game 1 of the 1946 Stanley Cup finals is won by the Canadiens in overtime, 4-3. Rocket Richard scores the winner in overtime at 9 minutes and 8 seconds.

1954   Game 4 of the opening round of the Stanley Cup playoffs at Boston is won by the Canadiens 2-0. Jacques Plante records the shutout. Montreal wins the series 4 games to 0. This is the last game of Woody Dumart's career.

Art Ross, long time General Manager of the Bruins announces his retirement and is replaced by Lynn Patrick.

March 31
Games played: 22

11-6-5

Regular season 9-3-2
Playoffs 2-3-3

1951   Game 2 of the opening round of the Stanley Cup playoffs at Toronto ends in a tie, 1-1. The game was called after 20 minutes of overtime at 11:45 p.m. because of the Sunday curfew laws.

1959   Game 4 of the opening round of the Stanley Cup series at Toronto is won by the Maple Leafs in overtime, 3-2. Frank Mahovlich scores the winner at 11 minutes and 21 seconds of overtime.

1973   Lose at Toronto, 7-3. Bobby Orr scores all of Boston's goals.

1974   Defeat Detroit at Boston, 6-1. Johnny Bucyk scores the 9,000th goal in Bruins history.

1996   In their last appearance at the Buffalo Memorial Auditorium, the Bruins defeat the Sabres, 6-5. Dave Reid's short-handed goal proves to be the game winner.

April 1
Games played: 26

6-17-3

Regular season 2-9-3
Playoffs 4-8-0

1941   Game 6 of the Stanley Cup opening round series at Toronto is won by Boston, 2-1. This is the third consecutive game of this series to finish with a 2-1 score.

1947   Game 4 of the opening round of the Stanley Cup playoffs at Boston Garden is won by the Canadiens, 5-1. Billy Reay of the Habs scores 4 goals. In a pre-game ceremony, Eddie Shore's #2, which had also been worn by Flash Hollett and Pat Egan, is retired.

1984   Win at New Jersey, 3-1. Bruins win last Adams Division championship on John Blum's first NHL goal.

April 2
Games played: 18
8–9–1
Regular season 5–6–0
Playoffs 3–3–1

1939   Game 7 of opening round series of the Stanley Cup playoffs is played at Boston Garden. Mel "Sudden Death" Hill scores at 48 minutes of overtime to defeat New York, 2–1, and win the series, 4 games to 3. This was the third game of this series that Mel Hill scored the overtime winner.

1969   Bruins shut out Toronto, 10–0, in the first game of the opening round of the Stanley Cup playoffs at Boston Garden as Phil Esposito scores 4 goals. Bruins score 6 power play goals. Forbes Kennedy of the Maple Leafs receives 38 minutes in penalties.
Gerry Cheevers records the shutout for Boston.

April 3
Games played: 26
13–12–1

Regular season 9–4–1
Playoffs 4–8–0

1928   Stanley Cup semi-final series game two at Boston. Rangers win 4–1. Rangers win semi-final series 5 goals to 2. This is the Bruins' last game at the Boston Arena until 1952. Game is played before 8500 fans.

1930   For the first time during the 1929–30 season, the Bruins lose for the second time in a row. This game however turned out to be the final game of the Stanley Cup series. The game was played at Montreal. Final score was Montreal 4, Boston 3.

1933   Game 5 of NHL championship series goes to Toronto, 1–0. Ken Doraty scores in 6th overtime period for Toronto win with 14,500 in attendance. The game finishes at 1:50 a.m.

1996   In the Bruins' first game at the Molson Centre, they defeat the Canadiens, 4–1. Dave Reid scores a short-handed goal for Boston.

April 4
Games played: 18
9–6–3
Regular season 6–1–3
Playoffs 3–5–0

1968   In their first playoff game in 8 seasons, the Bruins lose game 1 of the opening round of the Stanley Cup playoffs at Montreal.

1971   Defeat Montreal at Boston, 7–2. Phil Esposito records his 7th hat trick of the season, and 8,000th goal in Bruins history. This was Montreal star Jean Beliveau's last regular season game.

1982   Defeat Hartford at Boston, 7–2. Barry Pederson records 7 points on 3 goals and 4 assists.

April 5
Games played: 17
8–8–1

Regular season 2–4–1
Playoffs 6–4–0

1973   Lose game 2 of the opening round of the Stanley Cup playoffs at Boston to the Rangers, 4–2. Phil Esposito is injured and misses the rest of the playoffs.

April 6
Games played: 17
7–7–3

Regular season 2–3–3
Playoffs 5–4–0

1957   Rocket Richard scores 4 goals in game 1 of the Stanley Cup finals, a 5–1 Montreal victory in a game played at the Montreal Forum.

1968   Bruins lose game 2 of the opening round of the Stanley Cup playoffs at Montreal, 5–2. Bobby Orr scores 1st playoff point.

April 7
Games played: 17
12–4–1

Regular season 4–0–0
Playoffs 8–4–1

1932   A Stanley Cup final game is played at the Boston Garden but it does not involve the Bruins. Because of the unavailability of Madison Square Garden in New York, game 2 of the series between Toronto and the Rangers is played in Boston with the Maple Leafs winning, 6–2. 12,000 fans were in attendance.

1974   Defeat Toronto at Boston, 6–4. Wayne Cashman scores 3 goals for the Bruins. Toronto's Dave Keon records his only 5-minute major penalty in his career after a fight with Boston's Greg Sheppard.

April 8
Games played: 20
10–10–0

Regular season 4–1–0
Playoffs 6–9–0

1975   Bruins defeat Chicago, 8–2, at Boston in game 1 of the preliminary round of the Stanley Cup playoffs. Phil Esposito scores 3 goals for Boston.

1997   In Mario Lemieux's last regular season game at Pittsburgh and the night being dubbed Mario Lemieux night, the Penguins defeat the Bruins 3–1.

April 9
Games played: 19
4–15–0

Regular season 1–2–0
Playoffs 3–13–0

1927   Game two of the 1927 Stanley Cup finals is played in Boston. Ottawa wins 3–1. Eddie Shore is assessed five penalties.

1946   Game 5 of the Stanley Cup finals at Montreal is won by the Canadiens 6–3. The Canadiens win the series, 4 games to 1, while capturing their 6th Stanley Cup. This is Herb Cain's last game.

April 10
Games played: 16
8–8–0

Regular season 2–1–0
Playoffs 6–7–0

1988   Lose at Buffalo in overtime, 6–5, on John Tucker's goal at 5 minutes and 32 seconds of overtime in game 4 of the Stanley Cup division semi-finals.

1997   Bruins lose to the Buffalo Sabres at Boston, 5–1. Jason Allison of the Bruins misses on a penalty shot attempt against Dominik Hasek.

April 11
Games played: 22
13–8–1

Regular season 2–1–0
Playoffs 11–7–1

1971   Game 4 of the opening round of the Stanley Cup playoffs at Montreal is won by the Bruins, 5–2. Bobby Orr scores 3 goals for the Bruins. This is the only game in Orr's playoff career that he scored 3 goals.

April 12
Games played: 9
2–6–1

Regular season 0–1–1
Playoffs 2–5–0

1941   Game 4 of the Stanley Cup finals at Detroit before 8,125 fans is won by the Bruins, 3–1, as Boston captures their 3rd Stanley Cup in history. This was a 4-game sweep for Boston and the first time in NHL history in which a seven-game series ends in a four-game sweep.

April 13
Games played: 16
10–6–0

Regular season 3–1–0
Playoffs 7–5–0

1912   Flash Hollett is born in North Sydney, Nova Scotia.

1927   Game four of the 1927 Stanley Cup finals played at Ottawa with the Senators winning 3–1 to capture their ninth Stanley Cup. The game ended in a free-for-all with various participants being fined and the proceeds of said fines distributed to charities in Boston and Ottawa.

1939   Game 4 of the Stanley Cup finals at Toronto. Boston shuts out Toronto, 2–0. Roy Conacher scores both Boston goals, including the 100th in Bruins playoff history. Frank Brimsek records shutout.

1997   In Mario Lemieux's last regular season game, the Bruins defeat the Penguins at Boston, 7–3. Mario receives a 5-minute standing ovation from the Boston fans.

April 14
Games played: 12
8–4–0

Regular season 2–2–0
Playoffs 6–2–0

1980   Bruins defeat Pittsburgh at Boston, 6–2, in game 5 of the preliminary round of the Stanley Cup playoffs. Bruins win the preliminary round series over Pittsburgh, 3 games to 2. This is the last instance that the Bruins played on three consecutive days, having played April 12, April 13, and April 14.

April 15
Games played: 9
5–3–1

Regular season 1–0–1
Playoffs 4–3–0

1976   Game 3 of the quarter-final round of the Stanley Cup playoffs at Los Angeles is won by the Kings over the Bruins, 6–4. Marcel Dionne scores 3 goals for Los Angeles. Gilles Gilbert tends goal for the Bruins.

April 16
Games played: 9
5–4–0

Regular season 0–0–0
Playoffs 5–4–0

1939   Game 5 of the Stanley Cup finals at Boston Garden. Bruins defeat Toronto Maple Leafs, 3–1, to win their second Stanley Cup. Roy Conacher scored the Stanley Cup winning goal before 16,891 fans.

1953   Game 5 of the Stanley Cup finals at Montreal is won by the Canadiens, 1–0, in overtime. Elmer Lach's goal at 1 minute and 22 seconds of overtime helps to eliminate the Bruins in 5 games as Montreal wins the Stanley Cup.

1957   Montreal captures their second straight Stanley Cup by defeating the Bruins, 5–1, in game 5 of the Stanley Cup finals.

April 17
Games played: 11
5–6–0

Regular season 0–0–0
Playoffs 5–6–0

1958   Game 5 of the Stanley Cup finals at Montreal is won by the Canadiens in overtime, 3–2. Rocket Richard scores the game winner at 5 minutes and 45 seconds.

1976   Bruins win game 4 of the quarter-final round of the Stanley Cup playoffs at Los Angeles, 3–0.
Jean Ratelle scores the 700th goal in Bruins playoff history.

April 18
Games played: 9
3–6–0

Regular season 0–0–0
Playoffs 3–6–0

1972   Bruins win game 1 of the semi-finals of the Stanley Cup playoffs at Boston, defeating the St. Louis Blues, 6–1. Fred Stanfield scores 3 goals for Boston.

April 19
Games played: 10
4–6–0

Regular season 1–0–0
Playoffs 3–6–0

1970   Bruins defeat the Blackhawks, 6–3, at Chicago in game 1 of the semi-final round of the Stanley Cup playoffs. Phil Esposito scores 3 goals against brother Tony Esposito, in goal for the Blackhawks.

April 20
Games played: 8
6–2–0

Regular season 1–0–0
Playoffs 5–2–0

1958   Game 6 of the Stanley Cup finals at Boston is won by Montreal, 5–3, eliminating the Bruins in 6 games to capture their third straight Stanley Cup.

April 21
Games played: 12
10–2–0
Regular Season 0–0–0
Playoffs 10–2–0

1980   Bruins defeat the Islanders in game 4 of the quarter-final round for the Stanley Cup at New York in overtime, 4–3, on Terry O'Reilly's goal at 17 minutes and 13 seconds.

1990   Bruins defeat Montreal at Boston in overtime, 5–4, on Garry Galley's goal at 3 minutes and 42 seconds of overtime in game 2 of the Stanley Cup division finals. This goal was also the 1,200th goal in Bruins playoff history.

April 22
Games played: 8
2–6–0

Regular season 0–0–0
Playoffs 2–6–0

1980   Bruins lose to the Islanders at Boston, 4–2, in game 5 of the Stanley Cup quarter-final round. Islanders win quarter-final series, 4 games to 1.
Peter McNab's goal is the 900th in Bruins playoff history.

April 23
Games played: 11
8–3–0

Regular season 1–0–0
Playoffs 7–3–0

1978   Bruins win at Chicago, 5–2, in game 4 of the quarter-final Stanley Cup playoff series. Bruins sweep Chicago, 4 games to 0.

1982   Win at Quebec in overtime, 6–5, on Peter McNab's goal in game 6 of the Stanley Cup quarter-final round.

1992   Win at Buffalo, 3–2, in game 3 of the Stanley Cup division semi-finals. Ray Bourque scores the 1,300th goal in Bruins playoff history.

April 24
Games played: 7
3–4–0
Regular season 0–1–0
Playoffs 3–3–0

1969   Bruins lose game 6 of the Stanley Cup semi-finals at Boston Garden to Montreal in double overtime, 2–1, on Jean Beliveau's goal at 11 minutes and 28 seconds of double overtime. The Bruins are eliminated by Montreal in the playoffs, 4–2.

1983   Defeat Buffalo in game 7 in overtime at Boston, 3–2, on Brad Park's overtime goal. Bruins win division finals, 4 games to 3. Park's goal is the Bruins 1,000 goal in their playoff history

April 25
Games played: 10
6–4–0

Regular season 0–0–0
Playoffs 6–4–0

1991   Bruins defeat Montreal at Boston, 4–1, in game 5 of the Stanley Cup division finals. Cam Neely scores 3 goals for Boston.

1992   Win at Buffalo in overtime, 5–4, on Ted Donato's goal at 2 minutes and 8 seconds of overtime in game 4 of the Stanley Cup division semi-finals.

1996   Bruins win game 4 of the Eastern Conference quarter-final at Boston, 6–2, over the Florida Panthers. Cam Stewart's goal is the 1,400th goal in Bruins playoff history.

April 26
Games played: 6
4–2–0

Regular season 1–0–0
Playoffs 3–2–0

1977   Bruins win at Philadelphia in overtime, 5–4, on Terry O'Reilly's goal at 10 minutes and 7 seconds of the first overtime to take game 2 of the Stanley Cup semi-finals.

1988   Win at Montreal, 4–1, in game 5 of the Stanley Cup division finals. Bruins eliminate Montreal, 4 games to 1. Bruins defeat Montreal in the playoffs for the first time since 1943.
Cam Neely scores the 1,100th goal in Bruins playoff history.

April 27

Games played: 6

3–3–0

Regular season 0–0–0
Playoffs 3–3–0

1991   Bruins lose at Montreal in overtime, 3–2, on Shayne Corson's goal at 17 minutes and 47 seconds of overtime in game 6 of the Stanley Cup division finals.

April 28

Games played: 5

3–2–0

Regular season 0–1–0
Playoffs 3–1–0

1966   Stephane Richer is born in Hull, Quebec.
1977   Bruins defeat Philadelphia, 2–1, at Boston in game 3 of the Stanley Cup semi-finals.

April 29

Games played: 4

2–2–0

Regular season 0–0–0
Playoffs 2–2–0

1976   Bruins lose at Philadelphia in overtime, 2–1, on Reggie Leach's goal at 13 minutes and 38 seconds of the first overtime period. This is game 2 of the Stanley Cup semi-finals.

April 30

Games played: 4

2–2–0

Regular season 1–0–0
Playoffs 2–1–0

1972   Bruins win game 1 of the Stanley Cup finals over the Rangers at Boston, 6–5. Ken Hodge nets 3 goals for the Bruins.

May 1

Games played: 6

6–0–0

Regular season 1–0–0
Playoffs 5–0–0

1977   Bruins win game 4 and sweep the Stanley Cup semi-final round 4 games to 0 by defeating the Philadelphia Flyers, 3–0, at Boston.
1995   In the last regular season game at Boston Garden, Bruins defeat Ottawa, 5–4.

May 2

Games played: 4

3–1–0

Regular season 0–0–0
Playoffs 3–1–0

1972   Bruins win game 2 of the Stanley Cup finals at Boston over New York, 2–1.
1978   Bruins defeat Philadelphia in overtime, 3–2, at Boston on Rick Middleton's goal at 1 minute and 43 seconds of the first overtime period of game 1 of the Stanley Cup semi-finals.

May 3

Games played: 8

7–1–0

Regular season 1–0–0
Playoffs 6–1–0

1970   Bruins open up Stanley Cup final series at St. Louis by defeating the Blues in game 1, 6–1. Johnny Bucyk registers 3 goals for the Bruins.
Phil Esposito scores the 500th goal in Bruins playoff history.
1979   Bruins win game 4 of the Stanley Cup semi-finals over Montreal at Boston, 4–3, in overtime on Jean Ratelle's goal at 3 minutes and 46 seconds of the first overtime. It was Ratelle's third goal of the game.
1990   Bruins defeat Washington at Boston, 5–3, in game 1 of the Stanley Cup conference championships. Kelly Miller of Washington attempts a penalty shot but is thwarted by Andy Moog.

461

May 4
Games played: 4
2–2–0

Regular season 0–0–0
Playoffs 1–3–0

1978   Bruins defeat Philadelphia, 7–5, at Boston in game 2 of the Stanley Cup semi-finals. Rick Middleton scores the 800th goal in Bruins playoff history.

May 5
Games played: 7
4–3–0

Regular season 0–0–0
Playoffs 4–3–0

1992   Win at Montreal in overtime, 3–2, on Peter Douris' goal at 3 minutes and 12 seconds of overtime in game 2 of the Stanley Cup division finals.

May 6
Games played: 2
1–1–0

Regular season 0–0–0
Playoffs 1–1–0

1976   Bruins lose game 5 of the Stanley Cup quarter-final series to the Flyers at Philadelphia, 6–3. Philadelphia eliminates the Bruins, 4 games to 1. Reggie Leach scores 5 goals for the Flyers.

1985   Butch Goring named coach of the Bruins with Mike Milbury as the assistant coach.

May 7
Games played: 11
5–6–0

Regular season 0–0–0
Playoffs 5–6–0

1974   Bruins defeat Philadelphia, 3–2, in game 1 of the Stanley Cup finals as Bobby Orr scores with 22 seconds left in the game.

1983   Lose to the Islanders at New York, 8–4, in game 6 of the Stanley Cup semi-finals. Mike Bossy scores 4 goals for the Islanders. Islanders win semi-final series, 4 games to 2.

May 8
Games played: 3
1–2–0

Regular season 0–0–0
Playoffs 1–2–0

1979   Bruins defeat Montreal at Boston, 5–2, in game 6 of the Stanley Cup semi-finals. Stan Jonathan scores three goals for the Bruins.

May 9
Games played: 7
3–4–0

Regular season 0–0–0
Playoffs 3–4–0

1972   Game 5 of the Stanley Cup finals at Boston is won by the Rangers, 3–2. Wayne Cashman scores the 600th goal in Bruins playoff history.

1974   Bruins lose game 2 of the Stanley Cup finals, 3–2, in overtime to the Philadelphia Flyers at Boston on Bobby Clarke's goal at 12 minutes and 1 second of the first overtime.

1992   Defeat Montreal at Boston, 2–0, in game 4 of the Stanley Cup division finals. Bruins sweep Montreal in the division finals, 4 games to 0.

May 10
Games played: 5
3–2–0

Regular season 0–0–0
Playoffs 3–2–0

1970   Bruins win game 4 of the Stanley Cup finals over the St. Louis Blues at Boston Garden in overtime, 4–3, on Bobby Orr's goal at 40 seconds of the first overtime period. Bruins eliminate the Blues, 4 games to 0, to win their first Stanley Cup since 1941.

1979   Bruins lose game 7 of the semi-finals at Montreal in overtime, 5–4, on Yvon Lambert's goal at 9 minutes and 33 seconds of the first overtime period. Montreal had tied the game in the third period on a too-many-men-on-the-ice penalty. Montreal wins the series, 4 games to 3.

May 11
Games played: 4

2–2–0

Regular season 0–0–0
Playoffs 2–2–0

1972   Bruins win game 6 of the Stanley Cup finals at New York to eliminate the Rangers 4 games to 2. Final score is 3–0 as Boston wins its 5th Stanley Cup.

1997   The Bruins, in their first crack at the NHL lottery, win the drawing and will pick first in the 1997 amateur draft

May 12
Games played: 4

0–4–0

Regular season 0–0–0
Playoffs 0–4–0

1935   Johnny Bucyk is born in Edmonton, Alberta.

May 13
Games played: 1

0–1–0

Regular season 0–0–0
Playoffs 0–1–0

1978   Bruins lose game 1 of the Stanley Cup finals at Montreal, 4–1.

May 14
Games played: 4

1–3–0

Regular season 0–0–0
Playoffs 1–3–0

1970   Harry Sinden retires as Bruins coach to go into private business.

1995   In the last meaningful game ever played at Boston Garden, Bruins lose to New Jersey, 3–2, and get eliminated from the Stanley Cup playoffs, 4 games to 1.

May 15
Games played: 1

0–1–0

Regular season 0–1–0
Playoffs 0–1–0

1967   Trade Pit Martin, Jack Norris, and Gilles Marotte to Chicago for Phil Esposito, Ken Hodge, and Fred Stanfield. Trade Murray Oliver to Toronto for Eddie Shack.

1990   In the longest game ever played at Boston Garden, Bruins lose to Edmonton in overtime, 3–2, on Petr Klima's goal at 15 minutes and 13 seconds of the 3rd overtime in game 1 of the Stanley Cup finals.

May 16
Games played: 2

1–1–0

Regular season 0–0–0
Playoffs 1–1–0

1974   Bruins win game 5 of the Stanley Cup finals at Boston over the Flyers, 5–1.

1978   Bruins lose game 2 of the Stanley Cup finals at Montreal in overtime, 3–2, on Guy Lafleur's goal at 13 minutes and 9 seconds of the first overtime.

May 17
Games played: 1

0–1–0

Regular season 0–0–0
Playoffs 0–1–0

1992   Lose at Pittsburgh in overtime, 4–3, on Jaromir Jagr's goal at 9 minutes and 44 seconds of overtime in game 1 of the Stanley Cup conference championships. Bob Sweeney scores a short-handed goal for the Bruins.

1995   Bruins fire Brian Sutter as coach.

May 18
Games played: 3

1–2–0

Regular season 0–0–0
Playoffs 1–2–0

1990   Bruins lose to Edmonton at Boston, 7–2, in game 2 of the Stanley Cup finals. Peter Klima's penalty shot attempt is blocked by Reggie Lemelin. Jari Kurri scores 3 goals for the Oilers.

May 19

Games played: 2

0–2–0

Regular season 0–0–0
Playoffs 0–2–0

1974   Philadelphia defeats Boston, 1–0, in game 6 of the Stanley Cup finals at Philadelphia and take the playoff series, 4 games to 2, for their first Stanley Cup.

May 20

Games played: 2

1–1–0

Regular season 0–0–0
Playoffs 1–1–0

1985   Terry O'Reilly announces his retirement after 13 seasons with the Bruins.
1988   Bruins lose at Edmonton, 4–2, in game 2 of the Stanley Cup finals.
1990   Bruins win at Edmonton, 2–1, in game 3 of the Stanley Cup finals.

May 21

Games played: 2

1–1–0

Regular season 0–0–0
Playoffs 1–1–0

1978   Bruins defeat Montreal at Boston in overtime, 4–3, in game 4 of the Stanley Cup finals on Bobby Schmautz's goal at 6 minutes and 22 seconds of overtime.
1997   Bruins sign Pat Burns to succeed Steve Kasper as coach of the Bruins. Burns is the former coach of the Montreal Canadiens and Toronto Maple Leafs.

May 22

Games played: 2

0–2–0

Regular season 0–0–0
Playoffs 0–2–0

1973   Fred Stanfield traded to Minnesota for Gilles Gilbert.
Eddie Johnston sent to Toronto to complete the deal for Jacques Plante.
1988   Lose to Edmonton at Boston, 6–3, in game 3 of the Stanley Cup finals. Esa Tikkanen scores 3 goals for the Oilers.

1990   Bruins lose at Edmonton, 5–1, in game 4 of the Stanley Cup finals.

May 23

Games played: 2

0–2–0

Regular season 0–0–0
Playoffs 0–2–0

1992   Lose to Pittsburgh at Boston, 5–1, in game 4 of the Stanley Cup conference championships. Pittsburgh sweeps the Bruins 4 games to 0.

May 24

Games played: 2

0–1 (1 suspended)

Regular season 0–0–0
Playoffs 0–1

1988   Edmonton at Boston game is tied 3–3 when it is suspended at 16 minutes and 37 seconds of the second period because of a power outage. This was game 4 of the Stanley Cup finals.
1990   Bruins lose to Edmonton at Boston, 4–1, in game 5 of the Stanley Cup finals. Edmonton wins the finals series, 4 games to 1 to win the Stanley Cup.

May 25

Games played: 1

0–1–0

Regular season 0–0–0
Playoffs 0–1–0

1978   Montreal defeats Boston 4–1 in game 6 of the Stanley Cup finals at Boston Garden and wins the series, 4 games to 2, and the Stanley Cup.

May 26

Games played: 1

0–1–0

Regular season 0–0–0
Playoffs 0–1–0

1976   Trade Ken Hodge to the Rangers for Rick Middleton.
1988   Lose at Edmonton, 6–3, in game 5 of the Stanley Cup finals. Edmonton sweeps the Stanley Cup finals, 4 games to 0, with 1 game suspended.

May 27

1930   Obie O'Brien is born in St. Catharines, Ontario.

May 28

1981   Jean Ratelle announces his retirement and accepts a position as assistant coach of the Bruins.

May 29

1906   Art Chapman is born in Winnipeg, Manitoba.

May 30

1906   Vic Ripley is born in Elgin, Ontario.

May 31

1970   Former Bruin Terry Sawchuk dies of internal injuries suffered in a fight with teammate Ron Stewart.

June 1

1987   Trade a future draft pick to Washington for John Blum.

June 2

1980   Acquire Jim Craig from the Calgary Flames for 2 future draft picks.

June 3

1927   Dutch Delmonte is born in Timmins, Ontario.

June 4

1963   Claim Tom Johnson on waivers from Montreal.

June 5

1923   Pete Horeck is born in Massey, Ontario.

June 6

1961   Phil Watson named coach of the Bruins.

1963   Vladimir Ruzicka is born in Most, Czechoslovakia.

1986   Trade Barry Pederson to Vancouver for Cam Neely and Vancouver's first-round draft pick which turns out to be Glen Wesley.

June 7

1951   Terry O'Reilly is born in Niagara Falls, Ontario.

June 8

1965   Orland Kurtenbach, Pat Stapleton, and Andy Hebenton traded to Toronto for Ron Stewart.

June 9

1964   Jerry Toppazzini and Matt Ravlich traded to Chicago for Murray Balfour and Mike Draper.

1965   Draft Gerry Cheevers from Toronto and Paul Popiel from Chicago.

1982   Brad McCrimmon traded to Philadelphia for Pete Peeters.

1992   Name Brian Sutter head coach.

June 10

1992   Trade Daniel Berthiaume to Winnipeg for Doug Evans.

June 11

1969   Lose Glen Sather in the intra-league draft to Pittsburgh. Claim Billy Speer as a fill.

1976   Bruins trade free agent rights of Andre Savard to Buffalo for free agent rights to Peter McNab.

June 12

1974   Trade Derek Sanderson to the Rangers for Walt McKechnie.

June 13

1961   Former Bruin Joe Matte dies.

1974   Don Cherry signs a contract to coach the Bruins.

June 14

1933   Parker MacDonald is born in Sydney, Nova Scotia.

June 16

1946   Derek Sanderson is born in Niagara Falls, Ontario.

1962   Tom Fergus is born in Chicago, Illinois.

June 17

1952   Mike Milbury is born in Brighton, Massachusetts.

June 18

1936   Larry Leach is born in Lloydminster, Saskatchewan.

June 19

1947   Walt McKechnie is born in London, Ontario.

June 20

1972   Josef Stumpel is born in Nitra, Czechoslovakia.

June 21

1984   Trade Mike Krushelnyski to Edmonton for Ken Linseman.

1991   Trade Randy Burridge to Washington for Steve Leach.

1996   Trade Al Iafrate to San Jose for Jeff Odgers.

June 22

1994   Sign Alexei Kasatonov as a free agent.

June 23

1922   Hal Laycoe is born in Sutherland, Saskatchewan.

June 24

1976   Bobby Orr signs as a free agent with the Chicago Blackhawks.

June 25

1944   Ken Hodge is born in Birmingham, England.

1960   Billy O'Dwyer is born in South Boston, Massachusetts.

1966   Former Bruin Harvey "Busher" Jackson dies.

1993   Trade Andy Moog to Dallas for Jon Casey.

June 28

1990   Greg Johnston traded to the Rangers for Chris Nilan.

June 29

1965   Brian Lawton is born in New Brunswick, New Jersey.

June 30

1933   Orval Tessier is born in Cornwall, Ontario.

July 1

1988   Sign free agent Dave Jensen.

July 2

1970   Brett Harkins is born in North Ridgeville, Ohio.

July 3

1966   Jarmo Kekalainen is born in Tampere, Finland.

July 4

1940   Pat Stapleton is born in Sarnia, Ontario.

July 5

1979   Fred Creighton named coach of the Bruins.

July 6

1948   Brad Park is born in Toronto, Ontario.

July 7

1980   Name Gerry Cheevers coach.

July 8

1981   Bruins announce that their top farm club for 1981–82 will be the Erie Blades of the AHL.

July 9

1914   Phil Hergesheimer is born in Winnipeg, Manitoba.

July 10

1916   Nick Damore is born in Niagara Falls, Ontario.

July 11

1956   Former Bruin Sprague Cleghorn dies.

July 12

1912   Peter Leswick is born in Saskatoon, Saskatchewan.

July 13

1963 Bobby Carpenter is born in Beverly, Massachusetts.

July 14

1933 Fred Creighton is born in Hamiota, Manitoba.

July 15

1980 Trade Gilles Gilbert to Detroit for Rogatien Vachon.

July 16

1960 Jay Miller is born in Wellesley, Massachusetts.

1966 Mikhail Tatarinov is born in Irkutsk, Russia.

July 17

1933 Alan Teal is born in Ridgeway, Ontario.

July 18

1943 Don Awrey is born in Kitchener, Ontario.

1994 Sign free agent Mikko Makela.

July 20

1954 Acquire Fernie Flaman from the Toronto Maple Leafs for Dave Creighton.

July 21

1981 Trade Dwight Foster to Colorado for 1982 first-round draft pick Gord Kluzak and second-round pick Brian Curran.

July 22

1931 Leo Labine is born in Haileybury, Ontario.

1935 Claude Pronovost is born in Shawinigan Falls, Quebec.

July 23

1980 Trade Gilles Gilbert to the Detroit Red Wings for Rogie Vachon.

July 24

1957 Bruins trade Terry Sawchuk to Detroit for Johnny Bucyk.

July 25

1927 Ed Harrison, former Bruin and cousin of Ed Sandford, is born in Mimico, Ontario.

July 27

1987 Sign free agents Billy O'Dwyer and Bruce Shoebottom.

July 28

1939 Barry Ashbee is born in Weston, Ontario.

July 29

1931 Jerry Toppazzini is born in Copper Cliff, Ontario.

July 30

1956 Reed Larson is born in Minneapolis, Minnesota.

July 31

1973 Storer Broadcasting takes over control of the Bruins.

August 1

1957 Pete Peeters is born in Edmonton, Alberta.

August 2

1995 Trade Bryan Smolinski and Glen Murray to Pittsburgh for Kevin Stevens and Shawn McEachern.

August 3

1957 Nels Stewart dies.

August 4

1946 Wayne Carleton is born in Sudbury, Ontario.

August 5

1964 Art Ross, the Bruins' first general manager and coach, dies in West Medford, Massachusetts.

August 6

1971 Mike Bales is born in Prince Albert, Saskatchewan.

August 9

1930 1957 Calder Trophy winner Larry Regan is born in North Bay, Ontario.

August 10

1968   Greg Hawgood is born in Edmonton, Alberta.

August 11

1958   Ken Linseman is born in Kingston, Ontario.

August 12

1904   Bobby Taylor is born in Newton, Massachusetts.

August 13

1987   Sign free agent Reggie Lemelin.

August 14

1902   Sylvio Mantha, who scored the first goal in the Boston Garden in 1928 for Canadiens and later played for the Bruins, was born in Montreal, Quebec.

August 15

1983   Guy Lapointe signed as a free agent.

August 17

1995   Trade David Shaw to Tampa Bay for a future draft pick.

August 18

1935   Forbes Kennedy is born in Dorchester, New Brunswick.

August 19

1980   Announce that the Springfield Indians of the AHL will be their top farm team for 1980–81.

1983   Jim Schoenfeld signed as a free agent.

August 20

1965   Bruce Shoebottom is born in Windsor, Ontario.

August 21

1990   Obtain Ken Hodge Jr. from Minnesota for future considerations.

1996   Sign free agent goaltender Tim Cheveldae.

August 22

1963   Ken Hammond is born in Port Credit, Ontario.

1990   Sign Ken Hammond as a free agent.

August 24

1936   Murray Balfour is born in Regina, Saskatchewan.

August 25

1939   Babe Siebert dies in a drowning accident.

August 26

1994   Trade Glen Wesley to Hartford for Hartford's first-round picks in 1995, 1996, and 1997.

August 27

1962   Adam Oates is born in Weston, Ontario.

August 28

1935   Gordon Redahl is born in Kinistino, Saskatchewan.

August 29

1928   Max Quackenbush is born in Toronto, Ontario.

1997   Trade Jozef Stumpel, Sandy Moger, and a fourth-round pick for Dimitri Khristich and Byron Dafoe.

August 30

1909   Burr Williams is born in Okemah, Oklahoma.

August 31

1967   Guy Larose is born in Hull, Quebec.

September 2

1943   Glen Sather is born in High River, Alberta.

September 3

1969   Fred Knipscheer is born in Fort Wayne, Indiana.

September 4

1992   Trade Ken Hodge and Matt Hervey to Tampa Bay for Darin Kimble.

September 5

1996   Due to injuries, Bruin forward Cam Neely retires from hockey.

September 6

1978   Greg Sheppard traded to Pittsburgh in a 3-player swap that sees Dick Redmond come to Boston from Atlanta. Jean Pronovost goes to Atlanta from Pittsburgh.

September 7

1964   Walter Brown, former co-owner and President of the Boston Bruins, dies.

September 8

1945   Rogatien Vachon is born in Palmarolle, Quebec.

September 10

1908   Paul Runge is born in Edmonton, Alberta.

September 11

1923   Gus Kyle is born in Dysart, Saskatchewan.

September 12

1932   Marcel Bonin is born in Montreal, Quebec.

September 13

1931   Don Simmons is born in Port Colborne, Ontario.

1948   Dave Reece is born in Troy, New York.

September 14

1932   Harry Sinden is born in Collins Bay, Ontario.

September 15

1954   Art Ross retires and is replaced by Lynn Patrick.

September 16

1964   Bruin great Bobby Bauer dies.

September 17

1939   Gord Turlik is born in Mickel, British Columbia.

September 18

1903   Bun Cook is born in Kingston, Ontario.

September 19

1940   Eddie Westfall is born in Belleville, Ontario.

September 20

1968   Matt Glennon is born in Hull, Massachusetts.

September 21

1955   Matti Hagman is born in Helsinki, Finland.

1969   Infamous Ted Green–Wayne Maki stick fight during an exhibition game at Ottawa, Ontario. Green would miss the entire 1969–70 season due to the head injury incurred in the fight.

September 24

1912   Happy Harnott is born in Montreal, Quebec.

September 25

1945   Carol Vadnais is born in Montreal, Quebec.

September 26

1967   Craig Janney is born in Hartford, Connecticut.

1995   "The Last Hurrah," the nickname for the last ever hockey game at the Boston Garden, is played with the Bruins hosting the Montreal Canadiens in an exhibition game. The final score of the game is Boston 3 and Montreal 0. The game is played in two 25-minute periods. During the halftime, old opponents are honored. They include Stan Mikita, Jean Beliveau, Rocket Richard, Frank Mahovlich, Emile Francis, and John Ferguson. At the conclusion of the game, past Bruins are honored. Bruins goals are scored by Joe Mullen, Ray Bourque, and the last Garden goal is scored by Don Sweeney.

September 27

1942   Wayne Maxner is born in Halifax, Nova Scotia.

September 28

1961   Steve Kasper is born in Montreal, Quebec.

September 29

1962   Cleon Daskalakis is born in Boston, Massachusetts.

1965   Jim Vesey is born in Boston, Massachusetts.

September 30

1996   Obtain Rob DiMaio in the waiver draft from San Jose. Obtain Dean Malkoc from the Vancouver Canucks for future considerations.

October 1

1972   Harry Sinden is named Bruins Managing Director.

1985   Sign Jay Miller as a free agent.

1995   Opening game at Montreal is postponed, then canceled due to the lockout by the NHL.

October 2

1968   Glen Wesley is born in Red Deer, Alberta.

October 3
Games played: 1

1–0–0

1994   Game at Ottawa postponed, then canceled due to NHL lockout.

October 4
Games played: 1

1–0–0

1948   Tom Webster is born in Kirkland Lake, Ontario.

October 5
Games played: 5

2–2–1

1972   Harry Sinden is appointed Managing Director.

1983   Trade Dave Barr to the Rangers for Dave Silk.

1993   Defeat Rangers at New York, 4–3. Cam Neely scores game winner. Jon Casey stops a penalty shot attempt by Alexei Kovalev.

1996   In the season opener at Boston, Steve Heinze nets 2 goals, one a short-handed goal, in a 4–4 tie with the Rangers. This is Wayne Gretzky's first game as a member of the Rangers.

October 6
Games played: 3

3–0–0

1983   Defeat Quebec at Boston, 9–3. Mike O'Connell's consecutive game streaks ends at 309.

1994   Last opening night game at Boston Garden, against Quebec, postponed, then canceled due to NHL lockout.

October 7
Games played: 8

2–5–1

1956   Brian Sutter is born in Viking, Alberta.

1976   Defeat Minnesota at Boston, 6–2 as Rick Middleton scores 3 goals in his first game as a Bruin.

1995   The Bruins open up the new FleetCenter with a 4–4 tie against the Islanders before a crowd of 17,565 fans. Sandy Moger of the Bruins scored the first goal of the game and the first goal in the FleetCenter. Moger's initials, SM, are the same as the person to score the first goal in the Boston Garden, Sylvio Mantha of the Canadiens. Cam Neely scored the hat trick for the Bruins.
The Bruins also introduced new uniforms. Don Sweeney receives the first penalty in the new FleetCenter.

1996   The Phoenix Coyotes, formerly the Winnipeg Jets, play their first game in Boston and defeat the Bruins, 5–2.

October 8
Games played: 10

3–5–2

1993   Acquire Paul Stanton from Pittsburgh for a future draft pick.

October 9
Games played: 15

7–6–2

1978   Trade Ron Grahame to Los Angeles for the Kings' 1979 first round pick that the Bruins use to draft Ray Bourque.

1980   Defeat Rangers at Boston, 7–2 in Rogie Vachon's first game as a Bruin.

1982   Win at Hartford, 5–4 on Luc Dufour's game-winning first NHL goal.

1995 Defeat Buffalo at Boston, 5–3. Steve Leach receives the first major penalty, for fighting, in the new FleetCenter.

October 10
Games played: 11

6–3–2

1974 Lose at Buffalo, 9–5. Gil Perrault nets 3 goals for the Sabres. This is Don Cherry's first game as coach of the Bruins.

1985 Defeat Toronto at Boston, 3–1. This is Butch Goring's first game as Bruin's coach.

October 11
Games played: 23

9–7–7

1979 Defeat Winnipeg at Boston, 4–0. Ray Bourque collects a goal and an assist in his first game with the Bruins.

1985 Trade Tom Fergus to Toronto for Bill Derlago.

1995 Lose to the Colorado Avalanche at Denver, 3–1. This is the first Bruins' game in Denver since October 16, 1981, when the Bruins faced the Colorado Rockies. Sean McEachern scores a short-handed goal for Boston.

October 12
Games played: 20

10–6–4

1924 The Boston Bruins and the Montreal Maroons are admitted into the National Hockey League. The price of the franchise is $15,000.

1985 Win at Detroit, 9–2. Charlie Simmer nets 3 goals for Boston.

1996 After being down 3–0, the Bruins rally for 5 straight goals and defeat the Sharks at San Jose, 5–3.

October 13
Games played: 17

9–4–4

1976 Defeat Rangers at New York, 5–1, as Greg Sheppard gets 3 goals.

October 14
Games played: 20

12–5–3

1982 Defeat Vancouver at Boston, 2–1 on two goals by Normand Leveille. This would be Leveille's last two career goals.

1984 Defeat Hartford at Boston, 4–2. Cleon Daskalakis makes his debut in the third period and shuts out the Whalers.

1995 Lose at Dallas, 6–5. The Stars score 3 goals in the final 49 seconds. The Dallas goals were scored at 19:11, 19:44, and 19:55. Steve Heinze scores a short-handed goal in the losing cause for the Bruins.

October 15
Games played: 19

8–6–5

1919 Longtime Detroit Red Wings trainer, Ross "Lefty" Wilson, who played 1 game in goal for the Bruins as an emergency substitute, is born in Toronto, Ontario.

1935 Willie O'Ree is born in Fredericton, New Brunswick.

1967 Defeat Montreal at Boston, 6–2. Phil Esposito nets 4 goals.

October 16
Games played: 20

9–6–5

1949 Tie Rangers at Boston, 2–2. This was the first game in which the ice was painted white so that the puck could be more easily seen.

1955 Defeat Rangers at Boston, 4–1 as Leo Labine scores three goals.

1993 Tie at San Jose, 1–1. Bruins first game at new San Jose Arena.

October 17
Games played: 21

6–12–3

1954 Tie Toronto at Boston, 1–1. Joe Klukay of the Bruins is stopped on a penalty shot attempt by Harry Lumley.

1995 The Bruins play their first game in the St. Louis' Kiel Center and defeat the Blues, 7–4. Sean McEachern and Kevin Stevens score 2 goals each for the Bruins with one of McEachern's goals short-handed.

October 18
Games played: 19
8-9-2

1876	Charles F. Adams, founder of the Boston Bruins is born in Newport, Vermont.
1960	Former Coach George Boucher passes away.

October 19
Games played: 22
13-7-2

1947	Opening game at Boston was played in 80 degree heat as Bruins defeat Rangers, 3-1.
1957	Lose at Toronto, 7-0, as Billy Harris and Brian Cullen net hat tricks for the Maple Leafs. Eddie Chadwick records the shutout for Toronto.
1966	Defeat Detroit at Boston, 6-2. Gordie Howe of Detroit starts his 21st season in the NHL, breaking the record of Bruins great Dit Clapper. Bobby Orr collects first career assist in his first NHL game.
1985	Win at Calgary, 6-3. For the second time in a week, Charlie Simmer has the hat trick.

October 20
Games played: 18
10-5-3

1946	Tie Chicago at Boston, 2-2.
1948	Defeat Chicago at Boston, 8-3.

October 21
Games played: 13
4-7-2

1994	Game at Edmonton postponed, then canceled due to NHL lockout.

October 22
Games played: 25
10-9-6

1950	Scoreless tie against New York at Boston.
1966	Lose at Montreal, 3-1. Bobby Orr is assessed his first minor penalty.
1990	Trade Greg Hawgood to Edmonton for Vladimir Ruzicka.

October 23
Games played: 15
2-5-8

1946	With the Toronto goaltender pulled, Gaye Stewart of the Leafs scores to tie the game at 19:43 of the third period at Boston, final, 3-3.
1974	Tie at Pittsburgh, 5-5. Bobby Orr scores 3 goals for the Bruins.
1982	Lose at Vancouver 3-2. Normand Leveille stricken with a cerebral hemorrhage between the first and second period.
1984	Obtain Charlie Simmer from Los Angeles for the 1985 Bruins first round pick.
1993	Tie at Calgary, 3-3. Glen Wesley and Steve Heinze score short-handed for the Bruins.

October 24
Games played: 21
7-13-1

1953	Win at Toronto, 3-2. Ted Kennedy of the Maple Leafs scores 8 seconds into the game.
1982	Lose at Los Angeles, 5-4, as Gordie Kluzak scores his first NHL goal.

October 25
Games played: 19
8-5-6

1977	Tie at Colorado, 4-4. Rick Smith scores the 10,000th goal in Bruins history.

October 26
Games played: 19
8-9-2

1975	Defeat Detroit at Boston, 7-3. Bobby Schmautz records hat trick for the Bruins.
1980	Tie at Winnipeg, 7-7, in the Bruins highest scoring tie game in history.

October 27
Games played: 16
11-4-1

1974	Defeat Kansas City at Boston, 8-2.

October 28
Games played: 15
8–6–1

1978   Win at Toronto, 5–3. Lanny McDonald of the Maple Leafs scores on a penalty shot against Gilles Gilbert.

1993   Defeat Ottawa at Boston, 6–2. Cam Neely scores two goals. Obtain Jon Morris from San Jose for cash.

1995   Shutout Hartford at Boston, 3–0. Craig Billington records the shutout win for the Bruins.

October 29
Games played: 24
10–9–5

1949   Lose at Toronto, 8–1, as Harry Watson nets 3 goals and Cal Gardner collects 4 assists for Toronto.

1955   Defeat Rangers at New York, 1–0 as Terry Sawchuk records his first of nine shutouts.

1972   Defeat Islanders at Boston, 9–1. Greg Sheppard scores 3 goals for the Bruins.

October 30
Games played: 22
5–9–8

1965   Lose to Rangers at Boston, 8–2. Injured Eddie Johnston is replaced by Bobby Ring at 6:15 of period number 2.

1975   Defeat St. Louis at Boston, 3–2. Johnny Bucyk scores his 500th career goal against Yves Belanger.

1982   Tie at Montreal, 4–4. Pierre Mondou of the Habs scores a goal at 19:59 of the third period to tie the game.

October 31
Games played: 19
6–10–3

1968   Lose at Detroit, 7–5. Frank Mahovlich scores 3 goals for the Red Wings.

November 1
Games played: 20
10–8–2

1924   Charles Adams pays $15,000 for the first NHL franchise in the United States.

1952   Lose at Toronto, 3–2. This game was the first game televised coast to coast by the Canadian Broadcasting Corporation.

1970   Defeat Minnesota at Boston, 5–0 as the Bruins pepper 59 shots on goal.

November 2
Games played: 24
9–12–3

1946   Win at Toronto, 5–0. Milt Schmidt awarded a goal when Leaf goaler Turk Broda tosses his stick at Schmidt.
Bill Cowley scores the 3,000th goal in Bruins history.

1975   Defeat California at Boston, 5–0. Bobby Schmautz's penalty shot attempt is unsuccessful. Dave Reece records his first NHL shutout.

1993   Lose at Detroit, 6–1. On a delayed penalty, Josef Stumpel of the Bruins accidentally shoots the puck in his own net.

1995   Lose to Detroit in overtime at Boston, 6–5 on Steve Yzerman's second goal of the game. Bruins blow a three-goal lead.
Blaine Lacher stops Yzerman on a penalty shot attempt. This is the first penalty shot attempt at the FleetCenter. Dave Reid scores a short-handed goal.

November 3
Games played: 20
8–8–4

1938   Win at Toronto, 3–2. Frank Brimsek plays in his first game for the Bruins.

1948   In the NHL All-Star game at Chicago, Bruins goaltender Frank Brimsek wore number "0."

1972   Tie at California, 6–6. Joey Johnston gets the hat trick for the Seals against Ross Brooks, goaltender for Boston.

November 4
Games played: 22
10–9–3

1976   Defeat Chicago at Boston, 7–5. Peter McNab nets 3 goals for the Bruins.

1996   Tie the Los Angeles Kings at Boston, 4–4, on rookie Mattias Timander's first NHL goal with 64 seconds left in regulation.

November 5
Games played: 25
9–10–6

1955   Lose at Montreal, 4–2. Jean Beliveau scores all four goals for Montreal, scoring 3 of the goals in a 44 second span on the same power play. Terry Sawchuk was in goal for Boston.

1967   Tie Toronto at Boston, 2–2, in a game which featured a bench clearing brawl that started when Brian Conacher of Toronto accidentally struck Bobby Orr in the face. Bob Pulford of the Leafs was also unsuccessful in a penalty shot against Gerry Cheevers.

1975   Lose at Buffalo, 4–0. This proves to be Phil Esposito and Carol Vadnais's last game for the Bruins.

1983   Win at Montreal, 10–4. Tom Fergus scores 3 goals for Boston.

1991   Tie at Pittsburgh, 5–5. Vladimir Ruzicka nets 3 goals for the Bruins.

November 6
Games played: 18
11–3–4

1937   Defeat Maroons at Montreal, 4–2. Ray Getliffe nets 3 for the Bruins.

1946   Tie at Detroit, 3–3, in the Bruins first-ever penalty-free game.

1971   Win at Detroit, 2–1. Purchase Matt Ravlich from the Los Angeles Kings.

November 7
Games played: 26
11–11–4

1903   Hooley Smith is born in Toronto, Ontario.

1962   Tie at Chicago, 3–3, on Johnny Bucyk's goal with 7 seconds left in the game.

1974   Defeat Washington at Boston, 10–4. Bobby Orr nets his second hat trick of the season.

1975   Trade Phil Esposito and Carol Vadnais to the Rangers for Brad Park, Jean Ratelle, and Joe Zanussi.

1996   Shut out by the Edmonton Oilers at Boston, 6–0. Former Bruin Marius Czerkawski scores 3 goals for the Oilers.

November 8
Games played: 19
10–7–2

1975   Lose at Vancouver, 4–2. Rod Sedlbauer scores 3 goals for the Canucks. Bobby Orr returns from injury and is paired with Brad Park in Park's first game as a Bruin.

1984   Defeat Detroit at Boston, 5–2. Charlie Simmer scores 500th career point.

November 9
Games played: 19
9–9–1

1985   Lose at Philadelphia, 5–3. Tim Kerr has three goals for the Flyers.

1987   Lose at Quebec, 6–4. Mike Eagles scores on a penalty shot for the Nordiques with Doug Keans in the Boston net.

November 10
Games played: 25
16–3–6

1948   Game at Boston Garden against Detroit is postponed until November 11, the next day, because of fog in the Garden.

1960   Lose to Detroit at Boston, 4–1. Jerry Toppazzini becomes the last regular position player to play goal as he replaced the injured Don Simmons in goal for the last minute of play.

1966   Defeat Toronto at Boston, 4–0, in Gerry Cheevers first NHL shutout.

1977   Defeat Los Angeles at Boston, 5–2. Terry O'Reilly's 3 goals pace the win. This is O'Reilly's only career hat trick.

November 11
Games played: 30
14–10–6

1924   1950 Calder Trophy winner Jack Gelineau is born in Toronto, Ontario.

1948   Defeat Detroit at Boston, 4–1, in a make-up game from November 10 that had been postponed because of fog.

1952   Defeat Toronto at Boston, 4–0. Jim Henry, in goal for Boston, records the shutout.

November 12
Games played: 22
9–11–2

1947   Defeat Rangers at New York, 8–2, as Bruins score three third-period goals in 57 seconds. The goals are scored by Billy Taylor, Pete Babando, and Wally Wilson.

November 13
Games played: 22
11–8–3

1938   Lose to Americans at New York, 2–1.

1955   Scoreless tie at Boston against Detroit. This game was played one week after a scoreless tie in Detroit and was the last scoreless tie played at the Boston Garden.

November 14
Games played: 31
16–13–2

1965   Behind the goaltending of Bernie Parent, defeat Toronto at Boston, 2–0.

1971   Defeat Los Angeles at Boston, 11–2. Bobby Orr scores 3 goals and 3 assists for the Bruins.

1985   Tie at Toronto, 6–6. Rick Vaive scores three goals for the Maple Leafs.
Trade Pete Peeters to Washington for Pat Riggin.

1996   Defeat the Pittsburgh Penguins at Boston, 2–1, on Adam Oates' overtime goal.

November 15
Games played: 28
15–7–6

1924   The Bruins hold their first-ever practice at the Boston Arena where they will play their home games.

1927   Tie Chicago at Boston, 1–1, in a game witnessed by Babe Ruth, who sat next to the Blackhawks' bench.

1967   Lose at Toronto, 4–2. Mike Walton scores 3 goals for the Maple Leafs.

1973   Defeat Rangers at Boston, 10–2. Bobby Orr scores 3 goals and 4 assists to record the most points by a defenseman in a game.

November 16
Games played: 27
14–7–6

1926   Defeat Montreal Canadiens at Boston Arena, 4–1. Eddie Shore plays his first game for the Bruins.
Two live bears are presented to Bruins owner Charles Adams before the game.

1952   Lose to Detroit at Boston, 5–2.
Bruins celebrate 25th anniversary of the first game at Boston Garden. On hand for the occasion were former Bruins Eddie Shore, Lionel Hitchman, Dit Clapper, George Owen, Harry Oliver, Perk Galbraith, Cooney Weiland, Cy Denneny, and Myles Lane.

1996   Scheduled game at Buffalo against the Sabres is postponed due to the Jumbotron scoreboard crashing to the ice. The game is re-scheduled for March 17, 1997.

November 17
Games played: 29
12–10–7

1931   Defeat Detroit at Boston, 1–0, on Dit Clapper's overtime goal.

1951   With the Boston goaltender pulled, Milt Schmidt scores a goal at 19:35 of the third period in a 1–1 game at Toronto.

1973   Defeat Detroit at Boston, 8–0, as Bobby Orr becomes top assist leader for defensemen with 456.

November 18
Games played: 29
20–8–1

1962   Lose to Detroit at Boston, 3–1. Phil Watson is fired as Bruins coach and is replaced by Milt Schmidt.

1989   Defeat New Jersey at Boston, 6–4. Andy Brickley scores 3 goals for the Bruins.

November 19
Games played: 28
16–6–6

1960   Defeat Detroit at Boston, 6–4. Don McKenney scores 3 goals. Willie O'Ree called up from Hull–Ottawa.

1966   Tie Rangers at Boston, 3–3. Bobby Orr is assessed with his first major after a fight with Vic Hadfield.

1981   Defeat Hartford at Boston, 6–1. Wayne Cashman ties a league record with 4 assists in one period.

1983   Tie Rangers at Boston, 6–6. Keith Crowder scores the 12,000th goal in Bruins history.

November 20
Games played: 29
12–12–5

1928   In the first game ever played at the new Boston Garden, the Bruins lose to Montreal Canadiens, 1–0, on a goal by Sylvio Mantha. Due to the size of the crowd, Charles Adams ordered that all the doors to the Garden be opened to prevent a disaster as 17,000 fans rushed the doors. The Bruins first shot on goal is taken by Frank Fredrickson. The first shot on goal by Montreal was taken by Aurel Joliat with Tiny Thompson making the save.

1934   Defeat Detroit at Boston, 1–0. Tiny Thompson records his second straight 1–0 victory.

1946   Defeat Toronto at Boston, 4–1, as Bobby Bauer nets three goals against Turk Broda.

1954   Win at Toronto, 1–0. John Henderson records the shutout for Boston.

1993   Tie Philadelphia at Boston, 5–5. Adam Oates scores the 15,000th goal in Bruins history.

November 21
Games played: 31
18–9–4

1942   President Calder of the NHL announces that overtime play during regular season games would be discontinued because of the war.

1995   Defeat Winnipeg at Boston, 5–4, as Josef Stumpel registers the hat trick for the Bruins.

November 22
Games played: 23
11–10–2

1979   Defeat Quebec at Boston, 7–4. Jean Ratelle notches the hat trick.

1980   Tie at Washington, 2–2. Steve Kasper's goal is the 11,000 goal in Bruin history.

1996   Trade their 1998 first-round draft pick to the Colorado Avalanche for Landon Wilson and Anders Myrvold.

November 23
Games played: 36
19–11–6

1929   Defeat Maroons at Montreal, 4–3. Eddie Shore is attacked by Hooley Smith, Dave Trottier, and Babe Siebert of the Maroons. No penalty is called.

1933   Win at Detroit, 6–0. Eddie Barry and Joe Lamb score 3 goals each for the Bruins.

1989   Defeat Toronto at Boston, 6–0. Andy Moog records shutout for Boston.

November 24
Games played: 33
15–11–7

1942   Tie Chicago at Boston, 5–5. This was the first non-overtime game to end up in a tie since the NHL instituted an overtime ban because of wartime travel restrictions.

1963   Game against Detroit is postponed due to President Kennedy's assassination and is rescheduled to January 7, 1964.

1972   Win at Atlanta, 4–0, as John Adams records his only NHL shutout.

1995   Defeat the Los Angeles Kings at Boston, 2–1. The game started at 12:05 p.m. because of the need to change the ice surface over to a basketball court after the game. This is the earliest starting time in Bruins history.

November 25
Games played: 29
13–9–7

1902   Eddie Shore is born in Fort Qu'appelle, Saskatchewan.

1984   Defeat Montreal at Boston, 7–4. Steve Kasper scores the hat trick.

November 26
Games played: 35
18–14–3

1967   Defeat Detroit at Boston, 7–5. John McKenzie nets 3 goals for the Bruins.

1975   Defeat Rangers at New York, 6–4. This turned out to be Bobby Orr's last game as a Bruin. He had a goal and an assist. They were scored on by John Davidson, in goal for the Rangers.

1977   Defeat Rangers at Boston, 3–2. The Bruins scoreless string of 223:45 is broken by Eddie Johnstone of the Rangers. This goal was the first goal scored against the Bruins in eleven-and-a-half periods.

1996   With star player Rick Tocchet being benched, the Bruins still manage to shutout the Philadelphia Flyers at Boston, 2–0. Bill Ranford records the shutout.

November 27
Games played: 31
16–9–6

1943   Lose at Toronto, 7–4. Bruins goalie Bert Gardiner was ill and could not play. Bruins use Reverend George Abbott, an ordained minister and Toronto practice goalie, in the loss to the Maple Leafs. Bob Davidson scores 3 goals for the Maple Leafs. Don Gallinger scores 3 goals for the Bruins.

1947   Lose at Detroit, 4–1. Because of injury to Jack Crawford, Dit Clapper comes out of retirement to play defense.

November 28
Games played: 26
11–10–5

1938   Tiny Thompson is traded to the Detroit Red Wings for $15,000 and goaltender Norm Smith, who never reported to Boston.

1954   Defeat Detroit at Boston, 6–2 as Leo Labine scores 5 points in one period.

1985   Lose to Quebec at Boston, 3–0. Peter Stastny scores all the goals for the Nordiques.

November 29
Games played: 26
14–8–4

1991   Defeat Montreal at Boston in overtime, 5–4. Kirk Muller scores 3 goals for Montreal.

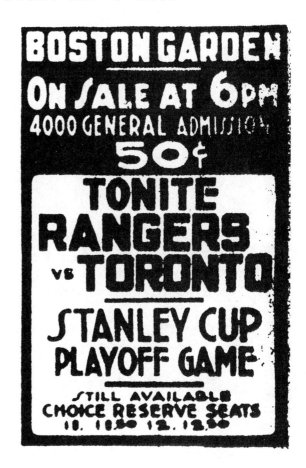

November 30
Games played: 29
12–14–3

1947   Scoreless tie against Toronto at Boston. Frank Brimsek of the Bruins and Turk Broda of the Leafs record the shutouts.

1995   Lose to Pittsburgh at Boston, 9–6, as Mario Lemieux scores 4 goals.

1996   Jaromir Jagr's 3 goals pace the Penguins past the Bruins at Pittsburgh, 6–2.

December 1
Games played: 31
14–15–2

1924   Defeat Montreal Maroons at Boston, 2–1, in their first National Hockey League game. Charley Dinsmore of the Montreal Maroons scores the first goal of the game. Fred Harris and Carson Cooper score for Boston with Harris scoring the first goal in Bruins history.

December 2
Games played: 24
12–8–4

1940   Gerry Cheevers is born in St. Catharines, Ontario.

1941   Defeat Toronto at Boston, 3–1. Bob Hamill and Eddie Wiseman score for the Bruins in overtime.

1970   Lose at Chicago, 4–3. Phil Esposito scores all of Boston's goals.

December 3
Games played: 32
14–12–6

1924   Lose at Toronto, 5–3, in first-ever road game.

1976   Lose at Atlanta, 3–1.

1977   Tie at Cleveland, 4–4. Peter McNab nets 3.

December 4
Games played: 28
15–7–6

1953   Rick Middleton is born in Toronto, Ontario.

1982   Win at Montreal, 6–4. Barry Pederson scores 3 goals. This is the first Bruin hat trick in Montreal since 1959.

1996   "Red in December" night at Montreal where the Canadiens wear their red sweaters while the Bruins wear the home whites. Even with Bill Ranford being hurt during the game and replaced by Scott Bailey, the Bruins manage to defeat Montreal, 4–3.

December 5
Games played: 37
17–13–7

1939   Defeat New York Americans at Boston, 2–1. Eddie Shore scores a goal in his last game with the Bruins.

1974   Lose to Detroit at Boston, 6–4. Marcel Dionne has 3 goals for the Red Wings.

1982   Defeat Philadelphia at Boston, 6–4. Barry Pederson scores the hat trick for the second game in a row.

December 6
Games played: 24
13–9–2

1970   Defeat Pittsburgh at Boston, 6–3. Phil Esposito nets his third hat trick of the season.

1981   Game against Toronto postponed until January 21, 1982, due to a snowstorm.

1983   Win at Pittsburgh, 5–3. Barry Pederson scores 3 goals for Boston.

December 7
Games played: 30
10–13–7

1941   Bruins lose to Rangers at New York, 5–4, on Pearl Harbor Day.

December 8
Games played: 33
13–15–5

1931   Lose to New York Americans at Boston, 3–2, as Eddie Shore accidentally scores against his own team.

1960   Defeat Chicago at Boston, 5–1. Charlie Burns scores 2 short-handed goals for the Bruins.

December 9
Games played: 28
10–13–5

1941   Tie Chicago at Boston, 2–2. The start of the game was delayed as President Roosevelt announces that war has been declared.

1961   Lose at Toronto, 9–2, as Frank Mahovlich registers 4 assists.

December 10
Games played: 32
15–14–3

1953   Defeat Detroit at Boston, 6–3. Eddie Sandford scores 3 goals for the Bruins.

1970   Defeat Buffalo at Boston, 8–2, as they pepper the Sabres with 72 shots on goal.

December 11

Games played: 29

14–12–3

1928	Lose to New York Americans at Boston, 3–0. Rangers offer Myles Lane in a trade for Eddie Shore. Bruins turn down offer with this retort: "You are so far from Shore, you need a life preserver."
1980	Lose to Quebec at Boston, 5–3, as Brad Park becomes 2nd defenseman to record 500 assists.

December 12

Games played: 34

10–17–7

1933	Lose to Toronto at Boston, 4–1. Infamous Eddie Shore–Ace Bailey incident occurs. Ace Bailey is taken to Audobon Hospital and then City Hospital with severe head injuries. Vic Ripley scores the 1,000th goal in Bruins history.
1964	Lose at Toronto, 6–3. Johnny Bucyk scores a goal on a penalty shot against Terry Sawchuk.
1978	Defeat Vancouver at Boston, 7–3. John Wensink scores 3 goals for the Bruins.

December 13

Games played: 29

14–8–7

1936	Defeat Americans at New York, 4–3. Milt Schmidt make his debut for the Bruins.
1970	Defeat Detroit at Boston, 6–2. Phil Esposito registers his 4th hat trick of the season.

December 14

Games played: 27

16–6–5

1968	Defeat Chicago at Boston, 10–5. Joe Junkin, spare goaltender, plays the final 8 minutes of the game in his only appearance in a Bruins uniform. Bobby Orr scores 3 goals for his first career hat trick.
1980	Defeat Los Angeles at Boston, 7–1. Doug Morrison of the Bruins scores a pure hat trick.
1995	Bruins defeat Florida at Boston, 6–4. Adam Oates scores 4 goals for the Bruins.

December 15

Games played: 34

15–15–4

1962	Lose at Toronto, 8–2. Eddie Johnston makes his debut in goal and plays the next 160 consecutive games.
1996	For the second game in a row, the Bruins are shutout, this time at Philadelphia by Ron Hextall, 6–0. This is the first Bruins game at the new CoreStates Center in Philadelphia.

December 16

Games played: 26

12–12–2

1995	Dave Reid's first career hat trick propels Bruins to 6–3 win over the Calgary Flames at Boston. Reid's third goal was an empty net short-handed goal.

December 17

Games played: 31

14–14–3

1996	Bruins defeat the Penguins at Pittsburgh for the first time since 1990, 7–4.

December 18

Games played: 30

16–11–3

1980	Lose to St. Louis at Boston, 7–3. Trade Al Secord to Chicago for Mike O'Connell.
1986	Lose to Hartford at Boston, 6–5. Charlie Simmer has three goals for the Bruins in a losing cause.

December 19

Games played: 31

13–14–4

1933	Defeat Montreal Maroons at Boston in overtime, 1–0. A crowd of 6,500 fans paid over $6,500 in gate receipts that are donated to the family of stricken Toronto star Ace Bailey.
1935	Scoreless tie at Toronto features Tiny Thompson in goal for Boston and George Hainsworth in goal for the Maple Leafs.
1939	Defeat Toronto at Boston in overtime, 3–2. Woody Dumart and Bobby Bauer score in overtime for the Bruins.

ATTENTION, HOCKEY FANS!

If you're tired of seeing the kind of hockey the Boston Bruins are playing

COME TO THE GARDEN TONIGHT

and see a real hockey club,

The TORONTO MAPLE LEAFS

CONN SMYTHE
General Manager, Toronto Maple Leafs.

1974	Defeat Rangers at Boston, 11–3. Phil Esposito's 3 goals and 4 assists paces the Boston win.
1984	Lose at Hartford, 6–5. Rick Middleton scores 800th career point.
1987	Lose to St. Louis at Boston, 7–5. An NHL record for the two fastest goals in a game are scored. Ken Linseman of the Bruins scored a goal at 19:50 of the third period. At 19:52, Doug Gilmour of the Blues scored a goal.

December 20

Games played: 29

16–7–6

1970	Defeat Minnesota at Boston, 7–2. John McKenzie scores 3 goals for the Bruins.
1976	Trade Joe Zanussi to St. Louis for Rick Smith.
1979	Defeat Toronto at Boston, 10–0. Gerry Cheevers in goal for Boston.

December 21

Games played: 30

15–11–4

1949	Win at Chicago, 4–1. Ken Smith's consecutive game streak ends at 247.
1972	Defeat Detroit at Boston, 8–1. Bobby Orr scores the 541st point of his career breaking Doug Harvey's total of 540. Orr broke the record in 423 regular season games.

December 22

Games played: 30

13–16–1

1951	Lose at Toronto, 3–2, on Turk Broda Night.
1974	Defeat Detroit at Boston, 5–4. Phil Esposito scores his 500th career goal off Jim Rutherford.

December 23

Games played: 29

16–8–5

1916	Woody Dumart is born in Kitchener, Ontario.
1975	Lose to Los Angeles at Boston, 4–3, as Marcel Dionne scores 3 goals for the Kings.

December 24

Games played: 4

2–1–1

1912	Herb Cain is born in Newmarket, Ontario.
1949	Win at Toronto, 8–4. Al Rollins of the Maple Leafs replaces Turk Broda in goal at the start of the second period.
1966	With Johnny Bower in goal for the Maple Leafs, lose at Toronto, 3–0.

December 25

Games played: 37

17–18–2

1930	Defeat Philadelphia at Boston, 8–0, as

game ends with a riot between the Bruins and Quakers.

1967   Defeat Oakland at Boston, 6–3. Game is marred by a riot between the Seals and the Bruins. Bert Olmstead, coach of the Seals, also participates. Andre Gill tends goal for Boston as both Gerry Cheevers and Eddie Johnston are injured.

1971   Defeat Philadelphia at Boston, 5–1. This is the last Christmas Day game played by the Bruins.

December 26
Games played: 25
13–7–5

1976   Defeat Cleveland at Boston, 6–3. Johnny Bucyk scores 545th career surpassing Maurice Richard on the all-time goals list.

1995   Tie Islanders at New York, 3–3, as Bruins overcome a three-goal deficit with three goals in the third period.

December 27
Games played: 29
8–16–5

1959   Lose at Chicago, 6–1. Bobby Hull of the Blackhawks scores his first career hat trick.

1964   Lose at Chicago, 6–2. Dean Prentice scores on a penalty shot.

December 28
Games played: 28
14–10–4

1912   Eddie Wiseman is born in Newcastle, New Brunswick.

1929   Defeat Canadiens at Montreal, 3–2. Terry Sawchuk is born in Winnipeg, Manitoba.

1960   Lose to the Hawks at Chicago, 4–3. Ray Bourque is born in Montreal, Quebec.

1965   Lose to Detroit at Boston, 1–0. For the first time in NHL history, two goaltenders share a shutout. Roger Crozier of Detroit was replaced by Hank Bassen of Detroit when Crozier was injured at 12:04 of the first period. Crozier returned to the nets at the beginning of the second period and played the rest of the game.

December 29
Games played: 32
13–13–6

1945   In a penalty-free game, the Bruins win at Toronto, 4–3.

1976   Win at Vancouver, 8–1 with Peter McNab netting 3 goals.

December 30
Games played: 20
7–10–3

1926   Lose at Toronto, 4–1. Art Ross protests this game because he feels that Toronto is using an ineligible player, Al Pudas.

1965   Trade Parker MacDonald to Detroit for Pit Martin.
Mike Stevens is born in Kitchener, Ontario.

1988   Trade Moe Lemay to Winnipeg for Ray Neufeld.

December 31
Games played: 30
11–14–5

1931   Defeat Montreal Canadiens at Boston, 5–0.

1936   Tie Rangers at New York, 2–2.

1937   Lose to Rangers at New York, 5–3.

1938   Lose to Rangers at New York, 2–1.

1939   Defeat Montreal at Boston, 6–1.

1940   Tie Rangers at Boston, 2–2.

1944   Lose to Rangers at New York, 3–2.

1947   Lose to Rangers at New York, 7–3.

1948   Tie Rangers at New York, 2–2.

1949   Lose to Rangers at New York, 4–1.

1950   Lose to Rangers at New York, 3–0.

1955   Lose to Rangers at New York, 6–2.

1958   Lose to Rangers at New York, 4–3.

1960   Lose at Montreal, 3–1.

1961   Defeat Rangers at New York, 7–4.

1966   Lose at Detroit, 3–1.

1967   Lose at Detroit, 6–4.

1969   Lose at Detroit, 5–1.

1993   Lose to Philadelphia, 4–3 in a game played at Minneapolis, Minnesota.

1995   Bruins win at Winnipeg, 5–3 in the last game for the Bruins at Winnipeg before the Jets move to Phoenix.

Dit Capper #5 and Pat Egan #2. Egan was the last player to wear the number 2 jersey before it was retired in honor of Eddie Shore.

TRIVIA ANSWERS

1. They are both named Harry Lumley.

2. Pat Egan & Flash Hollett

3. This is the only time in Bruins history that they played on three consecutive dates.

4. "Dit" Clapper

5. Murray Henderson

6. Dave Creighton and "Sugar" Jim Henry

7. "Dit" Clapper

8. Win Green

9. When these players left the Bruins, they had accumulated the same number of points as the number on the jersey they had worn:

Jimmy Bartlett	24	Al Pallazzari	9
Jack Bionda	11	Dave Pasin	37
Marcel Bonin	18	Irvin Spencer	22
Roger Jenkins	8	Mats Thelin	27

10. Pentti Lund

11. "Dutch" Gainor, "Cooney" Weiland, "Dit" Clapper

12. The movie "Bob, Ted, Carol & Alice." The defensemen: Bob Orr, Ted Green, Carol Vadnais, Dallas Smith.*
    * Dallas rhymes with Alice

13. Eddie Johnston

14. They were both traded to the Bruins on their birthdays.

15. Johnny Bucyk, Murray Oliver, Tommy Williams

16. #4 Bobby Orr & #9 Johnny Bucyk

17. Stanfield also had a penalty shot attempt during the game. He missed on the attempt.

18. Tommy Glavine appeared in the 1984–85 edition of the Bruins media guide as the winner of the John Carlton Memorial Trophy. This trophy is awarded annually to the outstanding student athlete in the Greater Boston area.

19. Sylvio Mantha scored the first goal at the Boston Garden. Sandy Moger scored the first goal at the FleetCenter. Both players have the initials "S.M."

20.
#2 Eddie Shore	#7 Phil Esposito
#3 Lionel Hitchman	#15 Milt Schmidt
#4 Bobby Orr	#1 Walter Brown – Celtics banner #1
#5 Dit Clapper	

21. During the six team era, there were four American teams. They were the only players during that era to play for just the four American teams.

22. Bill Cowley, 1941 & 1943

23. There were no games played by the Bruins on January 18th in the 1980s.

24. Johnny Bucyk, Ed Westfall, Ted Green

25. Beginning in 1948, the Art Ross Trophy, accepted by the NHL in 1941 as the annual award to the outstanding player, was awarded to the leading scorer.

26. #2   Flash Hollett & Pat Egan
    #3   Flash Hollett
    #5   Guy Lapointe
    #7   Sean Shanahan, Bill Bennett, and Ray Bourque
    #15   Larry Regan

27. #24 Terry O'Reilly

28. The Hillman Brothers

29. Lorne "Gump" Worsley

30. Bobby Orr, #4, scored the 4th goal in the 4th period of game #4 to help the Bruins capture their 4th Stanley Cup. Orr was tripped by #4, Noel Picard of the St. Louis Blues.

31. Jean Beliveau of the Montreal Canadiens

32. Gordie Howe began his 21st season of play breaking the record of Bill Gadsby and Dit Clapper of the Bruins.

33. The game of December 18, 1951 was played at Boston Garden. The game of February 26, 1951 was played at the Boston Arena because of damage to the ice plant at the Boston Garden.

34. The Bruins did not have a captain.

35. Gus Kyle, 1951–52

36. Eddie Shore

37. Bobby Orr became the first defenseman to score a hat trick in a playoff game.

38. Andy Hebenton

39. Brad Park

40. Tiny Thompson

41. Phil Goyette is the only opposing player in Bruins history to have faced the Bruins twice in losing efforts in Stanley Cup clinching games. Goyette was a member of the 1970 St. Louis Blues and the 1972 Rangers.

42. Because of some mix-up between the Bruins and Detroit, both teams showed up for the opening face-off wearing white jerseys. After the first period, the Bruins changed into the gold jerseys.

Harry Lumley

ACKNOWLEDGEMENTS

I would like to thank and acknowledge the following people for helping me in this labor of love: Charles L. Coleman and his three-volume "Trail of the Stanley Cup," which was the inspiration for writing this book; publisher Jack David for giving me the chance to put it all together; to Andrew Podnieks for showing me how to do it; to Craig Campbell at the Hockey Hall of Fame for referring me to Jack David; to Dennis and Daryl Vautour, my sons, for sharing their time so that I could spend time at the library and computer doing research; Harvey McKenney, by far and away the most knowledgeable Boston Bruin historian, for spending so much time with me, explaining some of the nuances of Bruins history; my neighbor Mark Darling for making sure the I's are dotted and the T's are crossed; to the people at the Boston Public Library's microtext room for their kindness and understanding over the many weeks I spent there; to Phil Castignetti and all the guys, Bobby, Danny et al. at Sportsworld in Everett, Massachusetts; Aaron Schmidt at the Boston Public Library Print Room; Marci Brennan at Corbis-Bettman in New York for helping me find the Richard Nixon picture; Nat Andriani from AP/Wide World Photos for being a real gentleman; the boys in my hockey pool, Paul, Paul M., and Michael Joyce, Rick Paone, Rich Losi, Sean Mullen, Bill Daley (Brass Ring), and the aforementioned Dennis and Daryl. See you at draft day in October to Carl DeFlumeri and Walter Bowen; to those purveyors of Bob Wills and western swing music, "Asleep at the Wheel," for helping to keep my toes tapping when my fingers weren't (I do have one bone to pick with them. On your salute to Bob Wills tape, the instrumental on side "A" could just as easily been called *Bruins* rather than what Bob Wills named it, *Red Wing*); to Lorraine and Joe Kelly for their support and great photography; to Paul Joyce and Phil Capone for your encouragement, "GO B's"; George Riley for taking me into the Boston Garden to help you when I was a mere child, filled with pimply hyperbole; to my special brother, Wayne, who makes me realize that the Boston Bruins are not the most important entity in my life; to Beverly, Billy, Ron, Don, Donna, Pat, Dennis, my late sisters Carol and Corrine; to my parents, Willard and Peg, for giving me Beverly, Billy, Ron, Don, Donna, Pat, Dennis, Wayne, Carol, and Corrine; and finally, to my wife Chris, whose patience, understanding, encouragement, love, and accounting ability made this project possible. To all, I am grateful and I thank you.

PHOTO CREDITS

6 – Kevin Vautour

10 – Courtesy Kevin Vautour

11 – Bradley H. Clarke

12 – Kevin Vautour

14 – Sports Action Archives

15 – Kevin Vautour

16 – Kevin Vautour

17 – Brian Babineau

18 – Steve Babineau

21 – Kevin Vautour

24 – Sports Action Archives

25 – Courtesy Kevin Vautour

36 – Courtesy Kevin Vautour

37 – (clockwise from top right) Boston Globe 2/11/24, 2/28/24, no date [probably 10/12/24]

40 – Courtesy Kevin Vautour

44 – Courtesy Kevin Vautour

45 – Courtesy Kevin Vautour

49 – Courtesy Kevin Vautour

50 – Boston Globe 3/28/29, Boston Globe 3/30/29

51 – Courtesy Kevin Vautour

57 – Courtesy Kevin Vautour

63 – Courtesy Kevin Vautour

65 – Courtesy Kevin Vautour

76 – Courtesy Kevin Vautour

78 – Courtesy Kevin Vautour

83 – Courtesy Kevin Vautour

88 – Courtesy Kevin Vautour

98 – Courtesy Kevin Vautour

99 – Courtesy Kevin Vautour

104 – Courtesy Kevin Vautour

108 – Courtesy Kevin Vautour

114 – Courtesy Kevin Vautour

129 – Imperial Oil–Turofsky/Hockey Hall of Fame

138 – Imperial Oil–Turofsky/Hockey Hall of Fame

141 – Courtesy Kevin Vautour

156 – Courtesy Kevin Vautour

159 – Courtesy Kevin Vautour

160 – Courtesy Kevin Vautour

162 – Courtesy Kevin Vautour

166 – Courtesy Kevin Vautour

167 – Courtesy Kevin Vautour

169 – Courtesy Kevin Vautour

170 – Courtesy Kevin Vautour

172 – Courtesy Kevin Vautour

175 – Courtesy Kevin Vautour

183 – Steve Babineau

185 – Kevin Vautour

193 – Boston Globe, no date [probably May 20, 1974]

199 – Courtesy Kevin Vautour

266 – Steve Babineau

286 – Steve Babineau

292 – Kevin Vautour

297 – Steve Babineau

303 – Sports Action Archives

336 – Courtesy Kevin Vautour

356 – Hockey Hall of Fame

357 – Boston Globe [no date]

380 – Graphic Artists/Hockey Hall of Fame

381 – Courtesy Kevin Vautour

385 – Kevin Vautour

386 – (clockwise from top right) Hockey Hall of Fame, Graphic Artists/Hockey Hall of Fame, Imperial Oil–Turofsky/Hockey Hall of Fame, courtesy Kevin Vautour

389 – Graphic Artists/Hockey Hall of Fame

392 – Courtesy Kevin Vautour, Sports Action Archives

393 – Hockey Hall of Fame, Hockey Hall of Fame

394 – (clockwise from top right) Imperial Oil–Turofsky/Hockey Hall of Fame, Graphic Artists/Hockey Hall of Fame, Hockey Hall of Fame, Hockey Hall of Fame

395 – (clockwise from top right): Imperial Oil/Hockey Hall of Fame, courtesy Kevin Vautour, Imperial Oil–Turofsky/Hockey Hall of Fame, Graphic Artists/Hockey Hall of Fame

401 – Courtesy Kevin Vautour

403 – Sports Action Archives

405 – Courtesy Kevin Vautour

407 – Imperial Oil–Turofsky/Hockey Hall of Fame

412 – Courtesy Kevin Vautour

414 – Courtesy Kevin Vautour

417 – Boston Globe [no date]

419 – Courtesy Kevin Vautour

423 – Courtesy Kevin Vautour

440 – Courtesy Kevin Vautour

442 – Courtesy Kevin Vautour

445 – UPI/Corbis–Bettmann

452 – Courtesy Kevin Vautour

454 – Courtesy Kevin Vautour

455 – Courtesy Kevin Vautour

477 – Courtesy Kevin Vautour

480 – Boston Globe December 19, 1939

482 – Sports Action Archives

485 – Courtesy Kevin Vautour

488 – AP/Wide World Press